# The Student's Guide to Cognitive Neuroscience

Reflecting recent changes in the way cognition and the brain are studied, this thoroughly updated third edition of the best-selling textbook provides a comprehensive and student-friendly guide to cognitive neuroscience. Jamie Ward provides an easy-to-follow introduction to neural structure and function, as well as all the key methods and procedures of cognitive neuroscience, with a view to helping students understand how they can be used to shed light on the neural basis of cognition.

The book presents an up-to-date overview of the latest theories and findings in all the key topics in cognitive neuroscience, including vision, memory, speech and language, hearing, numeracy, executive function, social and emotional behavior and developmental neuroscience, as well as a new chapter on attention. Throughout, case studies, newspaper reports and everyday examples are used to help students understand the more challenging ideas that underpin the subject.

In addition each chapter includes:

- Summaries of key terms and points
- Example essay questions
- Recommended further reading
- Feature boxes exploring interesting and popular questions and their implications for the subject.

Written in an engaging style by a leading researcher in the field, and presented in full-color including numerous illustrative materials, this book will be invaluable as a core text for undergraduate modules in cognitive neuroscience. It can also be used as a key text on courses in cognition, cognitive neuropsychology, bio-psychology or brain and behavior. Those embarking on research will find it an invaluable starting point and reference.

*The Student's Guide to Cognitive Neuroscience, Third Edition* is supported by a companion website, featuring helpful resources for both students and instructors.

**Jamie Ward** is Professor of Cognitive Neuroscience at the University of Sussex, UK. He is the author of a number of books on social and cognitive neuroscience and on synaesthesia, and is the Founding Editor of the journal *Cognitive Neuroscience*.

# THE STUDENT'S GUIDE TO COGNITIVE NEUROSCIENCE

## Third Edition

## JAMIE WARD

**Ψ Psychology Press**
Taylor & Francis Group

LONDON AND NEW YORK

Third edition published 2015
by Psychology Press
27 Church Road, Hove, East Sussex, BN3 2FA

and by Psychology Press
711 Third Avenue, New York, NY 10017

*Psychology Press is an imprint of the Taylor & Francis Group, an informa business*

First edition published by Psychology Press 2006

Second edition published by Psychology Press 2010

*British Library Cataloguing in Publication Data*
A catalogue record for this book is available from the British Library

*Library of Congress Cataloging in Publication Data*
The student's guide to cognitive neuroscience/Jamie Ward.—
    Third edition.
    pages cm
    Includes bibliographical references and index.
    1. Cognitive neuroscience. I. Title.
    QP360.5.W37 2015
    612.8′233—dc23
    2014022744

ISBN: 978-1-84872-271-2 (hbk)
ISBN: 978-1-84872-272-9 (pbk)
ISBN: 978-1-315-74239-7 (ebk)

Typeset in Times
by Florence Production Ltd, Stoodleigh, Devon, UK

Printed by Bell and Bain Ltd, Glasgow

# Contents

# About the author

Jamie Ward is Professor of Cognitive Neuroscience at the University of Sussex, UK. He completed degrees at the University of Cambridge (1991–1994) and the University of Birmingham (1994–1997). He subsequently worked as a Research Fellow at the University of Sussex (1997–1999) and as Lecturer and Senior Lecturer at University College London (1999–2007). His principal research interest lies in the cognitive neuroscience of synesthesia, although he has published on many other topics, including frontal lobe function, memory, and disorders of reading and spelling. His research uses a number of methods in cognitive neuroscience, including human neuropsychology, functional imaging, EEG and TMS. His other books include *The Frog who Croaked Blue: Synesthesia and the Mixing of the Senses* and *The Student's Guide to Social Neuroscience*. He is the founding editor of the journal, *Cognitive Neuroscience*.

# Preface to the third edition

The motivation for writing this book came out of my experiences of teaching cognitive neuroscience. When asked by students which book they should buy, I felt that none of the existing books would satisfactorily meet their needs. Other books in the market were variously too encyclopedic, too advanced, not up-to-date or gave short shrift to explaining the methods of the field. My brief for writing this textbook was to provide a text that presents key ideas and findings but is not too long, that is up-to-date, and that considers both method and theory. I hope that it will be useful to both lecturers and students.

In writing a book on cognitive neuroscience I had to make a decision as to how much would be "cognitive" and how much would be "neuroscience." In my opinion, the theoretical underpinnings of cognitive neuroscience lie within the cognitive psychology tradition. Some of the most elegant studies using methods such as fMRI and TMS have been motivated by previous research in cognitive psychology and neuropsychology. The ultimate aim of cognitive neuroscience is to provide a brain-based account of cognition, and so the methods of cognitive neuroscience must necessarily speak to some aspect of brain function. However, I believe that cognitive neuroscience has much to learn from cognitive psychology in terms of which theoretically interesting questions to ask.

In Chapter 1, I discuss the current status of cognitive neuroscience as I see it. Some of the topics raised in this chapter are directly aimed at other researchers in the field who are skeptical about the merits of the newer methodologies. I suspect that students who are new to the field will approach the topic with open-mindedness rather than skepticism, but I hope that they will nevertheless be able to gain something from this debate.

Chapter 2 is intended primarily as a reference source that can be referred back to. It is deliberately pitched at a need-to-know level.

Chapters 3 to 5 describe in detail the methods of cognitive neuroscience. The aim of an undergraduate course in cognitive neuroscience is presumably to enable students to critically evaluate the field and, in my opinion, this can only be achieved if the students fully understand the limitations of the methods on which the field is based. I also hope that these chapters will be of use to researchers who are starting out in the field. This third edition has been updated to include the latest research tools (such as tDCS, transcranial direct current stimulation) and the latest research methodology (such as multi-voxel pattern analysis, MVPA, in fMRI research).

Chapters 6 to 16 outline the main theories and findings in the field. I hope that they convey something of the excitement and optimism that currently exists. Although no new chapters have been added, this third edition represents a substantial update. Chapter 7 is now rewritten to focus specifically on attention, rather than spatial cognition more generally. The content relating to working memory now appears in Chapter 9, "The Remembering Brain," rather than in the chapter on executive functions, and the "cognitive map" theory of the hippocampus (place cells, etc.) is integrated within the memory chapter, too. The hot-topic of embodied cognition is introduced in more detail and critically evaluated, notably in Chapter 10 (e.g. motor theories of speech perception), Chapter 11 (e.g. sensorimotor grounding of semantic features), and Chapter 15 (e.g. understanding others via simulation). Chapter 14, "The Executive Brain," has been substantially rewritten and reorganized to take into account newer theories concerning the organization of control systems in the prefrontal cortex.

Jamie Ward
jamiew@sussex.ac.uk
Brighton, UK, July 2014

CHAPTER 1

# Introducing cognitive neuroscience

## CONTENTS

Between 1928 and 1947, Wilder Penfield and colleagues carried out a series of remarkable experiments on over 400 living human brains (Penfield & Rasmussen, 1950). The patients in question were undergoing brain surgery for epilepsy. To identify and spare regions of the brain involved in movement and sensation, Penfield electrically stimulated regions of the cortex while the patient was still conscious. The procedure was not painful (the surface of the brain does not contain pain receptors), but the patients did report some fascinating experiences. When stimulating the occipital lobe one patient reported, "a star came down toward my nose." Upon stimulating a region near the central sulcus, another patient commented, "those fingers and my thumb gave a jump." After temporal lobe stimulation, another patient claimed, "I heard the music again; it is like the radio." She was later able to recall the tune she heard and was absolutely convinced that there must have been a radio in the operating theatre. Of course, the patients had no idea when the electrical stimulation was being applied—they couldn't physically feel it or see it. As far as they were concerned, an electrical stimulation applied to the brain felt pretty much like a mental/cognitive event.

This book tells the emerging story of how mental processes such as thoughts, memories and perceptions are organized and implemented by the brain. It is also concerned with how it is possible to study the mind and brain, and how we know what we know. The term **cognition** collectively refers to a variety of higher mental

A timeline for the development of methods and findings relevant to cognitive neuroscience, from phrenology to present day.

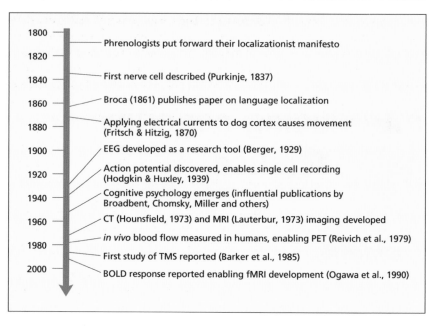

1800 — Phrenologists put forward their localizationist manifesto

1820 —

1840 — First nerve cell described (Purkinje, 1837)

1860 — Broca (1861) publishes paper on language localization

1880 — Applying electrical currents to dog cortex causes movement (Fritsch & Hitzig, 1870)

1900 — EEG developed as a research tool (Berger, 1929)

1920 — Action potential discovered, enables single cell recording (Hodgkin & Huxley, 1939)

1940 — Cognitive psychology emerges (influential publications by Broadbent, Chomsky, Miller and others)

1960 — CT (Hounsfield, 1973) and MRI (Lauterbur, 1973) imaging developed

1980 — *in vivo* blood flow measured in humans, enabling PET (Reivich et al., 1979)

First study of TMS reported (Barker et al., 1985)

2000 — BOLD response reported enabling fMRI development (Ogawa et al., 1990)

processes such as thinking, perceiving, imagining, speaking, acting and planning. **Cognitive neuroscience** is a bridging discipline between cognitive science and cognitive psychology, on the one hand, and biology and neuroscience, on the other. It has emerged as a distinct enterprise only recently and has been driven by methodological advances that enable the study of the human brain safely in the laboratory. It is perhaps not too surprising that earlier methods, such as direct electrical stimulation of the brain, failed to enter into the mainstream of research.

This chapter begins by placing a number of philosophical and scientific approaches to the mind and brain in an historical perspective. The coverage is selective rather than exhaustive, and students with a particular interest in these issues might want to read more deeply elsewhere (Wickens, 2015). The chapter then provides a basic overview of the current methods used in cognitive neuroscience. A more detailed analysis and comparison of the different methods is provided in Chapters 3 to 5. Finally, the chapter attempts to address some of the criticisms of the cognitive neuroscience approach that have been articulated.

# COGNITIVE NEUROSCIENCE IN HISTORICAL PERSPECTIVE

## Philosophical approaches to mind and brain

Philosophers as well as scientists have long been interested in how the brain can create our mental world. How is it that a physical substance can give rise to our sensations, thoughts and emotions? This has been termed the **mind–body problem**, although it should more properly be called the mind–brain problem, because it is now agreed that the brain is the key part of the body for cognition. One position is that the mind and brain are made up of different kinds of substance, even though they may interact. This is known as **dualism**, and the most famous proponent of this idea was René Descartes (1596–1650). Descartes believed that the mind was non-physical and immortal whereas the body was physical and mortal. He suggested that they interact in the pineal gland, which lies at the center of the brain and is now considered part of the endocrine system. According to Descartes, stimulation of the sense organs would cause vibrations in the body/brain that would be picked up in the pineal gland, and this would create a non-physical sense of awareness. There is little hope for cognitive neuroscience if dualism is true because the methods of physical and biological sciences cannot tap into the non-physical domain (if such a thing were to exist).

Even in Descartes' time, there were critics of his position. One can identify a number of broad approaches to the mind–body problem that still have a contemporary resonance. Spinoza (1632–1677) argued that mind and brain were two different levels of explanation for the same thing, but not two different kinds of thing. This has been termed **dual-aspect theory** and it remains popular with some current researchers in the field (Velmans, 2000). An analogy can be drawn to wave–particle duality in physics, in which the same entity (e.g. an electron) can be described both as a wave and as a particle.

An alternative approach to the mind–body problem that is endorsed by many contemporary thinkers is **reductionism** (Churchland, 1995; Crick, 1994). This position states that, although cognitive, mind-based concepts (e.g. emotions, memories, attention) are currently useful for scientific exploration, they will eventually be replaced by purely biological constructs (e.g. patterns of neuronal firings, neurotransmitter release). As such, psychology will eventually reduce to biology as we learn more and more about the brain. Advocates of this approach note that there are many historical precedents in which scientific constructs are abandoned when a better explanation is found. In the seventeenth century, scientists believed that flammable materials contained a substance, called *phlogiston*, which was released when burned. This is similar to classical notions that fire was a basic element along with water, air and earth. Eventually, this construct was replaced by an understanding of how chemicals combine with oxygen. The process of burning became just one example (along with rusting) of this particular chemical reaction. Reductionists believe that mind-based concepts, and conscious experiences in particular, will have the same status as phlogiston in a future theory of the brain. Those who favor dual-aspect theory over reductionism point out that an emotion will still *feel* like an emotion even if we were to fully understand its neural basis and, as such, the usefulness of cognitive, mind-based concepts will never be fully replaced.

## Scientific approaches to mind and brain

Our understanding of the brain emerged historically late, largely in the nineteenth century, although some important insights were gained during classical times. Aristotle (384–322 BC) noted that the ratio of brain size to body size was greatest in more intellectually advanced species, such as humans. Unfortunately, he made the error of claiming that cognition was a product of the heart rather than the brain. He believed that the brain acted as a coolant system: the higher the intellect, the larger the cooling system needed. In the Roman age, Galen (circa AD 129–199) observed brain injury in gladiators and noted that nerves project to and from the brain. Nonetheless, he believed that mental experiences themselves resided in the ventricles of the brain. This idea went essentially unchallenged for well over 1,500 years. For example, when Vesalius (1514–1564), the father of modern anatomy,

**KEY TERM**

**Phrenology**
The failed idea that individual differences in cognition can be mapped on to differences in skull shape.

published his plates of dissected brains, the ventricles were drawn in exacting detail, whereas the cortex was drawn crudely and schematically. Others followed in this tradition, often drawing the surface of the brain like the intestines. This situation probably reflected a lack of interest in the cortex rather than a lack of penmanship. It is not until one looks at the drawings of Gall and Spurzheim (1810) that the features of the brain become recognizable to modern eyes.

Gall (1758–1828) and Spurzheim (1776–1832) received a bad press, historically speaking, because of their invention and advocacy of **phrenology**. Phrenology had two key assumptions; first, that different regions of the brain perform different functions and are associated with different behaviors; and second, that the size of these regions produces distortions of the skull and correlates with individual differences in cognition and personality. Taking these two ideas

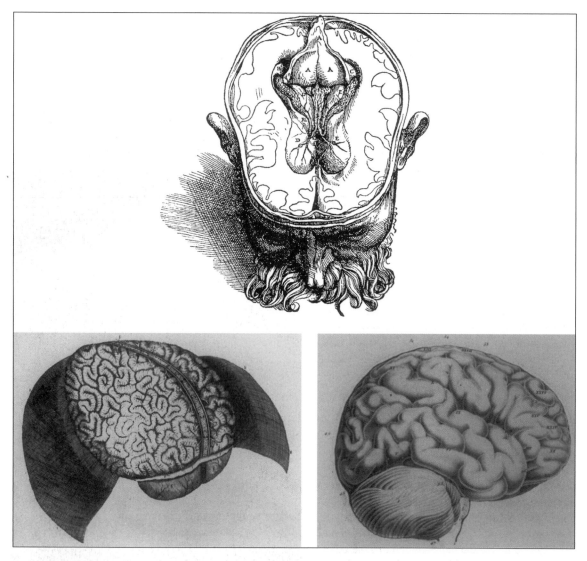

Drawings of the brain from Vesalius (1543) (top), de Viessens (1685) (bottom left) and Gall and Spurzheim (1810) (bottom right). Note how the earlier two drawings emphasized the ventricles and/or misrepresented the cortical surface.

in turn, the notion of **functional specialization** within the brain has effectively endured into modern cognitive neuroscience, having seen off a number of challenges over the years (Flourens, 1824; Lashley, 1929). The observations of Penfield and co-workers on the electrically stimulated brain provide some striking examples of this principle. However, the functional specializations of phrenology were not empirically derived and were not constrained by theories of cognition. For example, Fowler's famous phrenologist's head had regions dedicated to "parental love," "destructiveness," and "firmness." Moreover, skull shape has nothing to do with cognitive function.

Although phrenology was fatally flawed, the basic idea of different parts of the brain serving different functions paved the way for future developments in the nineteenth century, the most notable of which are Broca's (1861) reports of two brain-damaged patients. Broca documented two cases in which acquired brain damage had impaired the ability to speak but left other aspects of cognition relatively intact. He concluded that language could be localized to a particular region of the brain. Subsequent studies argued that language itself was not a single entity but could be further subdivided into speech recognition, speech production and conceptual knowledge (Lichtheim, 1885; Wernicke, 1874). This was motivated by the observation that brain damage can lead either to poor speech comprehension and good production, or good speech comprehension and poor production (see Chapter 11 for full details). This suggests that there are at least two speech faculties in the brain and that each can be independently impaired by brain damage. This body of work was a huge step forward in terms of thinking about mind and brain. First, empirical observations were being used to determine what the building blocks of cognition are (is language a single faculty?) rather than listing them from first principles. Second, and related, they were developing models of cognition that did not make direct reference to the brain. That is, one could infer that speech recognition and production were separable without necessarily knowing *where* in the brain they were located, or how the underlying neurons brought these processes about. The approach of using patients with acquired brain damage to inform theories of normal cognition is called **cognitive neuropsychology** and remains influential today (Chapter 5 discusses the logic of this method in detail). Cognitive neuropsychology is now effectively subsumed within the term "cognitive neuroscience," where the latter phrase is seen as being less restrictive in terms of methodology.

Whereas discoveries in the neurosciences continued apace throughout the nineteenth and twentieth centuries, the formation of psychology as a discipline at the end of the nineteenth century took the study of the mind away from its biological underpinnings. This did not reflect a belief in dualism. It was due, in part, to some pragmatic

**KEY TERMS**

**Functional specialization**
Different regions of the brain are specialized for different functions.

**Cognitive neuropsychology**
The study of brain-damaged patients to inform theories of normal cognition.

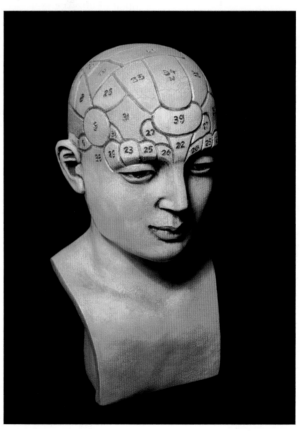

The phrenologist's head was used to represent the hypothetical functions of different regions of the brain.

**KEY TERMS**

**Information processing**
An approach in which behavior is described in terms of a sequence of cognitive stages.

**Interactivity**
Later stages of processing can begin before earlier stages are complete.

**Top-down processing**
The influence of later stages on the processing of earlier ones (e.g. memory influences on perception).

**Parallel processing**
Different information is processed at the same time (i.e. in parallel).

constraints. Early pioneers of psychology, such as William James and Sigmund Freud, were interested in topics like consciousness, attention and personality. Neuroscience has had virtually nothing to say about these issues until quite recently. Another reason for the schism between psychology and biology lies in the notion that one can develop coherent and testable theories of cognition that do not make claims about the brain. The modern foundations of cognitive psychology lie in the computer metaphor of the brain and the **information-processing** approach, popular from the 1950s onwards. For example, Broadbent (1958) argued that much of cognition consists of a sequence of processing stages. In his simple model, perceptual processes occur, followed by attentional processes that transfer information to short-term memory and thence to long-term memory (see also Atkinson & Shiffrin, 1968). These were often drawn as a series of box-and-arrow diagrams. The implication was that one could understand the cognitive system in the same way as one could understand the series of steps performed by a computer program, and without reference to the brain. The idea of the mind as a computer program has advanced over the years along with advances in computational science. For example, many cognitive models contain some element of interactivity and parallel processing. **Interactivity** refers to the fact that stages in processing may not be strictly separate and that later stages can begin before earlier stages are complete. Moreover, later stages can influence the outcome of early ones (**top-down processing**). **Parallel processing** refers to the fact that lots of different information can be processed simultaneously (serial computers process each piece of information one at a time). Although these computationally explicit models are more sophisticated than earlier box-and-arrow diagrams, they, like their predecessors, do not always make contact with the neuroscience literature (Ellis & Humphreys, 1999).

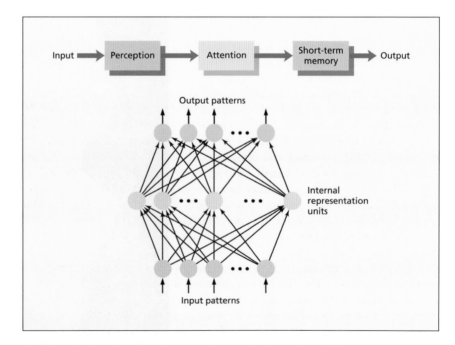

Examples of box-and-arrow and connectionist models of cognition. Both represent ways of describing cognitive processes that need not make direct reference to the brain.

## COMPUTATIONAL AND CONNECTIONIST MODELS OF COGNITION

In the 1980s, powerful computers became widely accessible as never before. This enabled cognitive psychologists to develop computationally explicit models of cognition (that literally calculate a set of outputs given a set of inputs) rather than the computationally inspired, but underspecified, box-and-arrow approach. One particular way of implementing computational models has been very influential; namely the **neural network**, connectionist or parallel distributed processing (PDP) approach (McClelland *et al.*, 1986). These models are considered in a number of places throughout this book, notably in the chapters dealing with memory, speaking and literacy.

Connectionist models have a number of architectural features. First, they are composed of arrays of simple information-carrying units called nodes. **Nodes** are information-carrying in the sense that they respond to a particular set of inputs (e.g. certain letters, certain sounds) and produce a restricted set of outputs. The responsiveness of a node depends on how strongly it is connected to other nodes in the network (the "weight" of the connection) and how active the other nodes are. It is possible to calculate, mathematically, what the output of any node would be, given a set of input activations and a set of weights. There are a number of advantages to this type of model. For example, by adjusting the weights over time as a result of experience, the model can develop and learn. The parallel processing enables large amounts of data to be processed simultaneously. A more controversial claim is that they have "neural plausibility." Nodes, activation and weights are in many ways analogous to neurons, firing rates and neural connectivity, respectively. However, these models have been criticized for being too powerful in that they can learn many things that real brains cannot (Pinker & Prince, 1988). A more moderate view is that connectionist models provide examples of ways in which the brain *might* implement a given cognitive function. Whether or not the brain actually *does* implement cognition in that particular way will ultimately be a question for empirical research in cognitive neuroscience.

## The birth of cognitive neuroscience

It was largely advances in imaging technology that provided the driving force for modern-day cognitive neuroscience. Raichle (1998) describes how brain imaging was in a "state of indifference and obscurity in the neuroscience community in the 1970s" and might never have reached prominence if it were not for the involvement of cognitive psychologists in the 1980s. Cognitive psychologists had already established experimental designs and information-processing models that could potentially fit well with these emerging methods. It is important to note that the technological advances in imaging not only led to the development of functional imaging, but also enabled brain lesions to be described precisely in ways that were never possible before (except at post mortem).

Present-day cognitive neuroscience is composed of a broad diversity of methods. These will be discussed in detail in subsequent chapters. At this juncture, it is useful to compare and contrast some of the most prominent methods. The distinction between *recording* methods and *stimulation* methods is crucial in cognitive neuroscience. Direct electrical stimulation of the brain in humans is now rarely carried out. The modern-day equivalent of these studies uses stimulation across the skull rather than directly to the brain (i.e. transcranially). This includes transcranial magnetic stimulation (TMS) and transcranial direct current stimulation (tDCS). These will be considered in Chapter 5, alongside the effect of organic brain lesions. Electrophysiological methods (EEG/ERP and single-cell recordings) and magnetophysiological methods (MEG) record the electrical and magnetic properties of neurons themselves. These methods are considered in Chapter 3. In contrast, functional imaging methods (PET and fMRI) record physiological changes associated with blood supply to the brain, which evolve more slowly over time. These are called hemodynamic methods and are considered in Chapter 4.

The methods of cognitive neuroscience can be placed on a number of dimensions:

* The **temporal resolution** refers to the accuracy with which one can measure *when* an event is occurring. The effects of brain damage are permanent and so this has no temporal resolution as such. Methods such as EEG, MEG, TMS,

**THE DIFFERENT METHODS USED IN COGNITIVE NEUROSCIENCE**

| Method | Method type | Invasiveness | Brain property used |
|---|---|---|---|
| EEG/ERP | Recording | Non-invasive | Electrical |
| Single-cell (and multi-unit) recordings | Recording | Invasive | Electrical |
| TMS | Stimulation | Non-invasive | Electromagnetic |
| tDCS | Stimulation | Non-invasive | Electrical |
| MEG | Recording | Non-invasive | Magnetic |
| PET | Recording | Invasive | Hemodynamic |
| fMRI | Recording | Non-invasive | Hemodynamic |

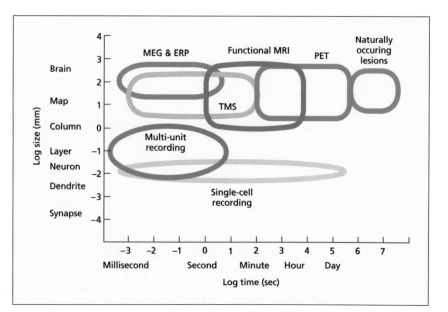

The methods of cognitive neuroscience can be categorized according to their spatial and temporal resolution.

Adapted from Churchland and Sejnowski, 1988.

and single-cell recording have millisecond resolution. fMRI has a temporal resolutions of several seconds that reflects the slower hemodynamic response.

- The **spatial resolution** refers to the accuracy with which one can measure *where* an event is occurring. Lesion and functional imaging methods have comparable resolution at the millimeter level, whereas single-cell recordings have spatial resolution at the level of the neuron.
- The *invasiveness* of a method refers to whether the equipment is located internally or externally. PET is invasive because it requires an injection of a radio-labeled isotope. Single-cell recordings are performed on the brain itself and are normally only carried out in non-human animals.

**KEY TERM**

**Spatial resolution**
The accuracy with which one can measure where an event (e.g. a physiological change) is occurring.

## DOES COGNITIVE PSYCHOLOGY NEED THE BRAIN?

As already noted, cognitive psychology developed substantially from the 1950s, using information-processing models that do not make direct reference to the brain. If this way of doing things remains successful, then why change? Of course, there is no reason why it should change. The claim is not that cognitive neuroscience is replacing cognitive psychology (although some might endorse this view), but merely that cognitive psychological theories can inform theories and experiments in the neurosciences and vice versa. However, others have argued that this is not possible by virtue of the fact that information-processing models do not make claims about the brain (Coltheart, 2004b; Harley, 2004).

Coltheart (2004b) poses the question: "Has cognitive neuroscience, or if not might it ever (in principle, or even in practice), successfully used data from cognitive neuroimaging to make theoretical decisions entirely at the cognitive level (e.g. to adjudicate between competing information-processing models of some cognitive system)?" (p. 21). Henson (2005) argues that it can in principle and that it does in practice. He argues that data from functional imaging (blood flow, blood oxygen) comprise just another dependent variable that one can measure. For example, there are a number of things that one could measure in a standard forced-choice reaction-time task: reaction time, error rates, sweating (skin conductance response), muscle contraction (electromyograph), scalp electrical recordings (EEG) or hemodynamic changes in the brain (fMRI). Each measure will relate to the task in some way and can be used to inform theories about the task.

To illustrate this point, consider an example. One could ask a simple question such as: Does visual recognition of words and letters involve computing a representation that is independent of case? For example, does the reading system treat "E" and "e" as equivalent at an early stage in processing or are "E" and "e" treated as different letters until some later stage (e.g. saying them aloud)? A way of investigating this using a reaction-time measure is to present the same word twice in the same or different case (e.g. radio-RADIO, RADIO-RADIO) and compare this with

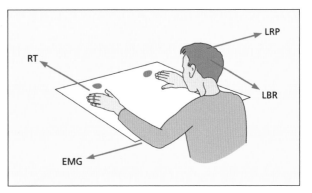

One could take many different measures in a forced-choice response task: behavioral (reaction time [RT], errors) or biological (electromyographic [EMG], lateralized readiness potential [LRP], lateralized BOLD response [LBR]). All measures could potentially be used to inform cognitive theory.

Adapted from Henson, 2005. By kind permission of the Experimental Psychology Society.

situations in which the word differs (e.g. mouse-RADIO, MOUSE-RADIO). One general finding in reaction-time studies is that it is faster to process a stimulus if the same stimulus has recently been presented. For example, if asked to make a speeded decision about RADIO (e.g. is it animate or inanimate?) then performance will be faster if it has been previously encountered. Dehaene *et al.* (2001) investigated this mechanism by comparing reaction-time measures with functional imaging (fMRI) measures. In this task, the first word in each pair was presented very briefly and was followed by visual noise. This prevents the participants from consciously perceiving it and, hence, one can be sure that they are not saying the word. The second word is consciously seen and requires a response. Dehaene *et al.* found that reaction times are faster to the second word when it follows the same word, irrespective of case. Importantly, there is a region in the left fusiform cortex that shows the same effect (although in terms of "activation" rather than response time). In this concrete example, it is meaningless to argue that one type of measure is "better" for informing cognitive theory (to return to Coltheart's question) given that both are measuring different aspects of the same thing. One could explore the nature of this effect further by, for instance, presenting the same

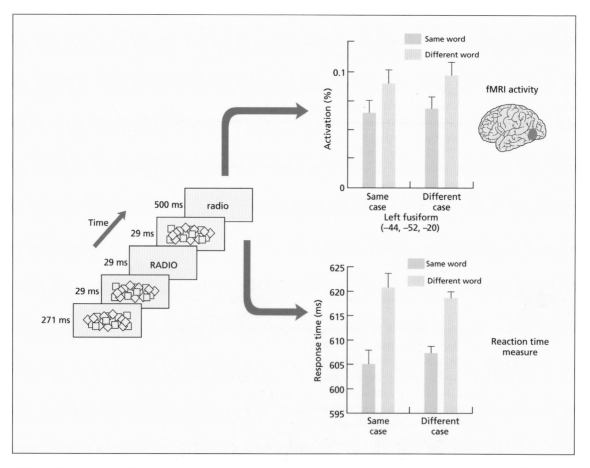

Both reaction times and fMRI activation in the left fusiform region demonstrate more efficient processing of words if they are preceded by subliminal presentation of the same word, irrespective of case.

Adapted from Dehaene *et al.*, 2001.

word in different languages (in bilingual speakers), presenting the words in different locations on the screen, and so on. This would provide further insights into the nature of this mechanism (e.g. what aspects of vision does it entail? Does it depend on word meaning?). However, both reaction-time measures and brain-based measures could be potentially informative. It is not the case that functional imaging is merely telling us *where* cognition is happening and not *how* it is happening.

Another distinction that has been used to contrast cognitive psychology and cognitive neuroscience is that between software and hardware, respectively (Coltheart, 2004b; Harley, 2004). This derives from the familiar computer analogy in which one can, supposedly, learn about information processing (software) without knowing about the brain (hardware). As has been shown, to some extent this is true. But the computer analogy is a little misleading. Computer software is written by computer programmers (who, incidentally, have human brains). However, information processing is not written by some third person and then inscribed into the brain. Rather, the brain provides causal constraints on the nature of information processing. This is not analogous to the computer domain in which the link between software and hardware is arbitrarily determined by a computer programmer. To give a simple example, one model of word recognition suggests that words are recognized by searching words in a mental dictionary one by one until a match is found (Forster, 1976). The weight of evidence from cognitive psychology argues against this serial search, and in favor of words being searched in parallel (i.e. all candidate words are considered at the same time). But *why* does human cognition work like this? Computer programs can be made to recognize words adequately with both serial search and parallel search. The reason why human information processing uses a parallel search and not a serial search probably lies in the relatively slow *neural* response time (acting against serial search). This constraint does not apply to the fast processing of computers. Thus, cognitive psychology may be sufficient to tell us the structure of information processing but it may not answer deeper questions about why information processing should be configured in that particular way.

## DOES NEUROSCIENCE NEED COGNITIVE PSYCHOLOGY?

It would be no exaggeration to say that the advent of techniques such as functional imaging have revolutionized the brain sciences. For example, consider some of the newspaper headlines that have appeared in recent years. Of course, it has been well known since the nineteenth century that pain, mood, intelligence, and sexual desire are largely products of processes in the brain. The reason headlines such as these are extraordinary is because now the technology exists to be able to study these processes *in vivo*. Of course, when one looks inside the brain one does not "see" memories, thoughts, perceptions, and so on (i.e. the stuff of cognitive psychology). Instead, what one sees is gray matter, white matter, blood vessels, and so on (i.e. the stuff of neuroscience). It is the latter, not the former, that one observes when conducting a functional imaging experiment. Developing a framework for linking the two will necessarily entail dealing with the mind–body problem either tacitly or explicitly. This is a daunting challenge.

Is functional imaging going to lead to a more sophisticated understanding of the mind and brain than was achieved by the phrenologists? Some of the newspaper

The media loves to simplify the findings of cognitive neuroscience. Many newspaper stories appear to regard it as counterintuitive that sex, pain and mood would be products of the brain.

## KEY TERMS

**Modularity**
The notion that certain cognitive processes (or regions of the brain) are restricted in the type of information they process.

**Domain specificity**
The idea that a cognitive process (or brain region) is dedicated solely to one particular type of information (e.g. colors, faces, words).

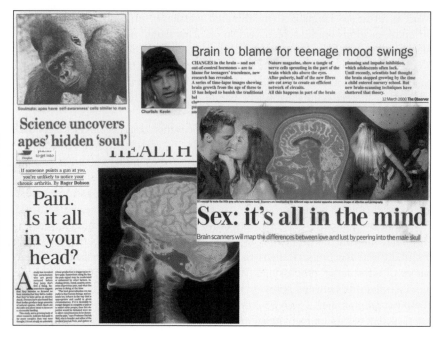

Sunday Times, 21 November 1999; Metro, 5 January 2001; The Observer, 12 March 2000; The Independent, 27 May 1999.

## IS THE BRAIN MODULAR?

The notion that the brain contains different regions of functional specialization has been around in various guises for 200 years. However, one particular variation on this theme has attracted particular attention and controversy—namely Fodor's (1983, 1998) theory of **modularity**. First, Fodor makes a distinction between two different classes of cognitive process: central systems and modules. The key difference between them relates to the types of information they can process. Modules are held to demonstrate **domain specificity** in that they process only one particular type of information (e.g. color, shape, words, faces), whereas central systems are held to be domain independent in that the type of information processed is non-specific (candidates would be memory, attention, executive functions). According to Fodor, one advantage of modular systems is that, by processing only a limited type of information, they can operate rapidly, efficiently and in isolation from other cognitive systems. An additional claim is that modules may be innately specified in the genetic code.

Many of these ideas have been criticized on empirical and theoretical grounds. For example, it has been suggested that domain specificity is not innate, although the means of acquiring it could be (Karmiloff-Smith, 1992). Moreover, systems like reading appear modular in some respects but cannot be innate because they are recent in evolution. Others have argued that evidence for interactivity suggests that modules are not isolated from other cognitive processes (Farah, 1994).

On balance, the empirical evidence does not favor this strong version of modularity. However, there is still an active debate over the organizing principles of the brain. For instance, the extent to which different regions of the brain are domain specific or are domain general is still debated (Fedorenko et al., 2013).

reports in the figure suggest it might not. One reason why phrenology failed is because the method had no real scientific grounding; the same cannot be said of functional imaging. Another reason why phrenology failed was that the psychological concepts used were naïve. It is for this reason that functional imaging and other advances in neuroscience do require the insights from cognitive psychology to frame appropriate research questions and avoid becoming a new phrenology (Uttal, 2001).

The question of whether cognitive, mind-based concepts will eventually become redundant (under a reductionist account) or coexist with neural-based accounts (e.g. as in dual-aspect theory) is for the future to decide. But for now, cognitive, mind-based concepts have an essential role to play in cognitive neuroscience.

## SUMMARY AND KEY POINTS OF THE CHAPTER

- The mind–body problem refers to the question of how physical matter (the brain) can produce mental experiences, and this remains an enduring issue in cognitive neuroscience.
- To some extent, the different regions of the brain are specialized for different functions.
- Functional neuroimaging has provided the driving force for much of the development of cognitive neuroscience, but there is a danger in merely using these methods to localize cognitive functions without understanding how they work.
- Cognitive psychology has developed as a discipline without making explicit references to the brain. However, biological measures can provide an alternative source of evidence to inform cognitive theory and the brain must provide constraining factors on the nature and development of the information-processing models of cognitive science.

## EXAMPLE ESSAY QUESTIONS

- What is the "mind–body problem" and what frameworks have been put forward to solve it?
- Is cognitive neuroscience the new phrenology?
- Does cognitive psychology need the brain? Does neuroscience need cognitive psychology?

Visit the companion website at www. psypress/cw/ward for:

- References to key papers and readings
- Video interviews on key topics with leading psychologists Wilder Penfield and Michael Gazzaniga, and philosopher Ned Block
- Multiple choice questions and interactive flashcards to test your knowledge
- Downloadable glossary

## RECOMMENDED FURTHER READING

- Henson, R. (2005). What can functional neuroimaging tell the experimental psychologist? *Quarterly Journal of Experimental Psychology*, 58A, 193–233. An excellent summary of the role of functional imaging in psychology and a rebuttal of common criticisms. This debate can also be followed in a series of articles in Cortex (2006, 42, 387–427).
- Shallice, T. & Cooper, R. P. (2011). *The organisation of mind*. Oxford, UK: Oxford University Press. The chapters on "conceptual foundations" deal with many of the issues touched on in the present chapter in more detail.
- Uttal, W. R. (2001). *The new phrenology: The limits of localizing cognitive processes in the brain*. Cambridge, MA: MIT Press. An interesting overview of the methods and limitations of cognitive neuroscience.
- Wickens, A. P. (2015). *A history of the brain: How we have come to understand the most complex object in the universe*. New York: Psychology Press. A good place to start for the history of neuroscience.

# CHAPTER 2

# Introducing the brain

## CONTENTS

It is hard to begin a chapter about the brain without waxing lyrical. The brain is the physical organ that makes all our mental life possible. It enables us to read these words, and to consider thoughts that we have never considered before—or even to create thoughts that no human has considered before. This book will scratch the surface of how this is all possible, but the purpose of this chapter is more mundane. It offers a basic guide to the structure of the brain, starting from a description of neurons and working up to a description of how these are organized into different neuroanatomical systems. The emphasis is on the human brain rather than the brain of other species.

## STRUCTURE AND FUNCTION OF THE NEURON

All **neurons** have basically the same structure. They consist of three components: a **cell body** (or soma), **dendrites**, and an **axon**. Although neurons have the same basic structure and function, it is important to note that there are some significant differences between different types of neurons in terms of the spatial arrangements of the dendrites and axon.

The cell body contains the nucleus and other organelles. The nucleus contains the genetic code, and this is involved in protein synthesis (e.g. of certain

## TEN INTERESTING FACTS ABOUT THE HUMAN BRAIN

(1) There are 86 billion neurons in the human brain (Azevedo *et al.*, 2009).

(2) Each neuron may connect with around 10,000 other neurons.

(3) If each neuron connected with every single other neuron, our brain would be 12.5 miles in diameter (Nelson & Bower, 1990). This is the length of Manhattan Island. This leads to an important conclusion—namely, that neurons only connect with a small subset of other neurons. Neurons may tend to communicate only with their neighbors, and long-range connections are the exception rather than the rule.

(4) The idea that we only use 10 percent of the cells in our brain is generally considered a myth (Beyerstein, 1999). It used to be thought that only around 10 percent of the cells in the brain were neurons (the rest being cells called glia), hence a plausible origin for the myth. This "fact" also turns out to be inaccurate, with the true ratio of neurons to glia being closer to 1:1 (Azevedo *et al.*, 2009). Glia serve a number of essential support functions; for example, they are involved in tissue repair and in the formation of myelin.

(5) The brain makes up only 2 percent of body weight.

(6) It is no longer believed that neurons in the brain are incapable of being regenerated. It was once widely believed that we are born with our full complement of neurons and that new neurons are not generated. This idea is now untenable, at least in a region called the dentate gyrus (for a review, see Gross, 2000).

(7) On average, we lose a net amount of one cortical neuron per second. A study has shown that around 10 percent of our cortical neurons perish between the ages of 20 and 90 years—equivalent to 85,000 neurons per day (Pakkenberg & Gundersen, 1997).

(8) Identical twins do not have anatomically identical brains. A comparison of identical and nonidentical twins suggests that the three-dimensional cortical gyral pattern is determined primarily by non-genetic factors, although brain size is strongly heritable (Bartley *et al.*, 1997).

(9) People with autism have large brains (Abell *et al.*, 1999). They also have large heads to accommodate them. There is unlikely to be a simple relationship between brain size and intellect (most people with autism have low IQ), and brain efficiency may be unrelated to size.

(10) Men have larger brains than women, but the female brain is more folded, implying an increase in surface area that may offset any size difference (Luders *et al.*, 2004). The total number of cortical neurons is related to gender, but not overall height or weight (Pakkenberg & Gundersen, 1997).

neurotransmitters). Neurons receive information from other neurons and they make a "decision" about this information (by changing their own activity) that can then be passed on to other neurons. From the cell body, a number of branching structures called dendrites enable communication with other neurons. Dendrites receive information from other neurons in close proximity. The number and structure of the dendritic branches can vary significantly depending on the type of neuron (i.e. where it is to be found in the brain). The axon, by contrast, sends information to other neurons. Each neuron consists of many dendrites but only a single axon (although the axon may be divided into several branches called collaterals).

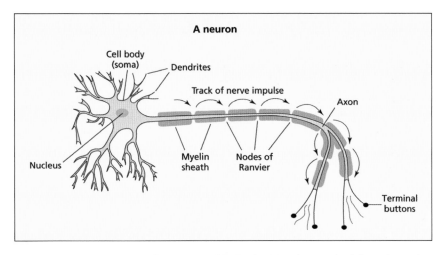

**A neuron**

Cell body (soma)

Dendrites

Track of nerve impulse

Axon

Nucleus

Myelin sheath

Nodes of Ranvier

Terminal buttons

Neurons consist of three basic features: a cell body, dendrites that receive information and axons that send information. In this diagram the axon is myelinated to speed the conduction time.

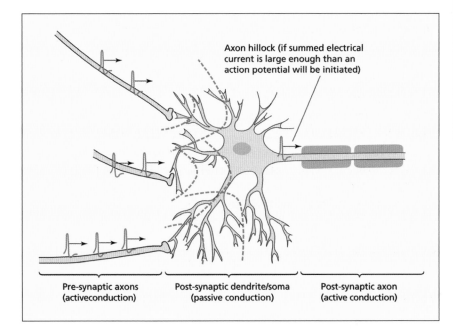

Axon hillock (if summed electrical current is large enough than an action potential will be initiated)

| Pre-synaptic axons (activeconduction) | Post-synaptic dendrite/soma (passive conduction) | Post-synaptic axon (active conduction) |

Electrical currents are actively transmitted through axons by an action potential. Electrical currents flow passively through dendrites and soma of neurons, but will initiate an action potential if their summed potential is strong enough at the start of the axon (called the hillock).

The terminal of an axon flattens out into a disc-shaped structure. It is here that chemical signals enable communication between neurons via a small gap termed a **synapse**. The two neurons forming the synapse are referred to as presynaptic (before the synapse) and postsynaptic (after the synapse), reflecting the direction of information flow (from axon to dendrite). When a presynaptic neuron is active, an electrical current (termed an **action potential**) is propagated down the length of the axon. When the action potential reaches the axon terminal, chemicals are released into the synaptic cleft. These chemicals are termed **neurotransmitters**. (Note that a small proportion of synapses, such as retinal gap junctions, signal electrically and not chemically.) Neurotransmitters bind to receptors on the dendrites or cell body of the postsynaptic neuron and create a synaptic potential. The synaptic potential is conducted passively (i.e. without creating an action potential) through the dendrites and soma of the postsynaptic neuron. If these passive currents are sufficiently strong when they reach the beginning of the axon in the postsynaptic neuron, then an action potential (an *active* electrical current) will be triggered in this neuron. It is important to note that each postsynaptic neuron sums together many synaptic potentials, which are generated at many different and distant dendritic sites (in contrast to a simple chain reaction between one neuron and the next). Passive conduction tends to be short range because the electrical signal is impeded by the resistance of the surrounding matter. Active conduction enables long-range signalingsignaling between neurons by the propagation of action potentials.

## Electrical signaling and the action potential

Each neuron is surrounded by a cell membrane that acts as a barrier to the passage of certain chemicals. Within the membrane, certain protein molecules act as gatekeepers and allow particular chemicals in and out under certain conditions. These chemicals consist, among others, of charged sodium ($Na^+$) and potassium ($K^+$) ions. The balance between these ions on the inside and outside of the membrane is such that there is normally a resting potential of $-70$ mV across the membrane (the inside being negative relative to the outside).

Voltage-gated ion channels are of particular importance in the generation of an action potential. They are found only in axons, which is why only the axon is capable of producing action potentials. The sequence of events is as follows:

1. If a passive current of sufficient strength flows across the axon membrane, this begins to open the voltage-gated $Na^+$ channels.
2. When the channel is opened, then $Na^+$ may enter the cell and the negative potential normally found on the inside is reduced (the cell is said to *depolarize*). At about $-50$ mV, the cell membrane becomes completely permeable and the charge on the inside of the cell momentarily reverses. This sudden depolarization and subsequent repolarization in electrical charge across the membrane is the action potential.
3. The negative potential of the cell is restored via the *outward* flow of $K^+$ through voltage-gated $K^+$ channels and closing of the voltage-gated $Na^+$ channels.
4. There is a brief period in which hyperpolarization occurs (the inside is more negative than at rest). This makes it more difficult for the axon to depolarize straight away and prevents the action potential from traveling backwards.

An action potential in one part of the axon opens adjacent voltage-sensitive $Na^+$ channels, and so the action potential moves progressively down the length of the axon, starting from the cell body and ending at the axon terminal. The conduction of the action potential along the axon may be speeded up if the axon is myelinated.

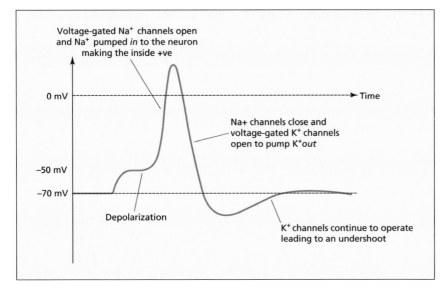

Voltage-gated Na+ channels open
and Na+ pumped *in* to the neuron
making the inside +ve

0 mV ········································→ Time

Na+ channels close and
voltage-gated K+ channels
open to pump K+*out*

−50 mV

−70 mV

Depolarization

K+ channels continue to operate
leading to an undershoot

The action potential consists of a number of phases.

**Myelin** is a fatty substance that is deposited around the axon of some cells (especially those that carry motor signals). It blocks the normal $Na^+/K^+$ transfer and so the action potential jumps, via passive conduction, down the length of the axon at the points at which the myelin is absent (called *nodes of Ranvier*). Destruction of myelin is found in a number of pathologies, notably *multiple sclerosis*.

## Chemical signaling and the postsynaptic neuron

When the action potential reaches the axon terminal, the electrical signal initiates a sequence of events leading to the release of neurotransmitters into the synaptic cleft. Protein *receptors* in the membrane of the postsynaptic neurons bind to the neurotransmitters. Many of the receptors are transmitter-gated ion channels (not to be confused with voltage-gated ion channels found in the axon). This sets up a localized flow of $Na^+$, $K^+$, or chloride ($Cl^-$), which creates the synaptic potential. Some neurotransmitters (e.g. GABA) have an inhibitory effect on the postsynaptic neuron (i.e. by making it less likely to fire). This can be achieved by making the inside of the neuron more negative than normal and hence harder to depolarize (e.g. by opening transmitter-gated $Cl^-$ channels). Other neurotransmitters (e.g. acetylcholine) have excitatory effects on the post-synaptic neuron (i.e. by making it more likely to fire). These synaptic potentials are then passively conducted as already described.

## How do neurons code information?

The amplitude of an action potential does not vary, but the number of action potentials propagated per second varies along a continuum. This rate of responding (also called the "spiking rate") relates to the informational "code" carried by that neuron. For example, some neurons may have a high spiking rate in some situations (e.g. during speech), but not others (e.g. during vision), whereas other

**KEY TERMS**

**Gray matter**
Matter consisting primarily of neuronal cell bodies.

**White matter**
Tissue of the nervous system consisting primarily of axons and support cells.

**Glia**
Support cells of the nervous system involved in tissue repair and in the formation of myelin (among other functions).

**Corpus callosum**
A large white matter tract that connects the two hemispheres.

**Ventricles**
The hollow chambers of the brain that contain cerebrospinal fluid.

neurons would have a complementary profile. Neurons responding to similar types of information tend to be grouped together. This gives rise to the functional specialization of brain regions that was introduced in Chapter 1.

If information is carried in the response rate of a neuron, what determines the *type* of information that the neuron responds to? The type of information that a neuron carries is related to the input it receives and the output it sends to other neurons. For example, the reason neurons in the primary auditory cortex can be considered to carry information about sound is because they receive input from a pathway originating in the cochlea and they send information to other neurons involved in more advanced stages of auditory processing (e.g. speech perception). However, imagine that one were to rewire the brain such that the primary auditory cortex was to receive inputs from the retinal pathway rather than the auditory pathway (Sur & Leamey, 2001). In this case, the function of the primary "auditory" cortex would have changed (as would the type of information it carries) even though the region itself was not directly modified (only the inputs to it were modified). This general point is worth bearing in mind when one considers what the function of a given region is. The function of a region is determined by its inputs and outputs. As such, the extent to which a function can be strictly localized is a moot point.

## THE GROSS ORGANIZATION OF THE BRAIN

### Gray matter, white matter, and cerebrospinal fluid

Neurons are organized within the brain to form white matter and gray matter. **Gray matter** consists of neuronal cell bodies. **White matter** consists of axons and support cells (**glia**). The brain consists of a highly convoluted folded sheet of gray matter (the cerebral cortex), beneath which lies the white matter. In the center of the brain, beneath the bulk of the white matter fibers, lies another collection of gray matter structures (the subcortex), which includes the basal ganglia, the limbic system, and the diencephalon.

White matter tracts may project between different cortical regions within the same hemisphere (called *association tracts*), may project between different cortical regions in different hemispheres (called *commissures*; the most important commissure being the **corpus callosum**) or may project between cortical and subcortical structures (called *projection tracts*).

The brain also contains a number of hollow chambers termed **ventricles**. These were incorrectly revered for 1,500 years as being the seat of mental life. The ventricles are filled with *cerebrospinal fluid* (CSF), which does serve some useful functions, albeit non-cognitive. The CSF carries waste metabolites, transfers some messenger signals, and provides a protective cushion for the brain.

### A hierarchical view of the central nervous system

Brain evolution can be thought of as adding additional structures onto older ones, rather than replacing older structures with newer ones. For example, the main visual pathway in humans travels from the retina to the occipital lobe, but a number of older visual pathways also exist and contribute to vision (see Chapter 6). These older pathways constitute the dominant form of seeing for other species such as birds and reptiles.

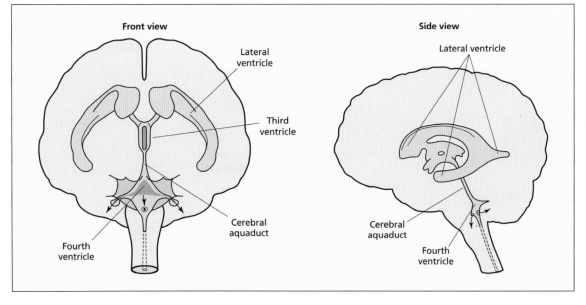

Association tract
(cortical within hemisphere)

Commisure
(cortical between hemisphere)

Projection tract
(cortical to subcortical)

There are three different kinds of white matter tract, depending on the nature of the regions that are connected.

Adapted from Diamond *et al.,* 1986. © 1986 by Coloring Concepts, Inc. Reprinted by permission of HarperCollins Publishers.

**Front view**

Lateral ventricle

Third ventricle

Cerebral aquaduct

Fourth ventricle

**Side view**

Lateral ventricle

Cerebral aquaduct

Fourth ventricle

The brain consists of four ventricles filled with cerebrospinal fluid (CSF): the lateral ventricles are found in each hemisphere, the third ventricle lies centrally around the subcortical structures, and the fourth ventricle lies in the brainstem (hindbrain).

## Terms of reference and section

There are conventional directions for navigating around the brain, just as there is a north, south, east, and west for navigating around maps. **Anterior** and **posterior** refer to directions toward the front and the back of the brain, respectively. These are also called *rostral* and *caudal*, respectively, particularly in other species that have a tail (caudal refers to the tail end). Directions toward the top and the bottom are referred to as **superior** and **inferior**, respectively; they are also known as **dorsal** and **ventral**, respectively. The terms anterior, posterior, superior, and inferior (or rostral, caudal, dorsal, and ventral) enable navigation in two dimensions: front–back and top–bottom. Needless to say, the brain is three-dimensional and so a further dimension is required. The terms **lateral** and **medial** are used to

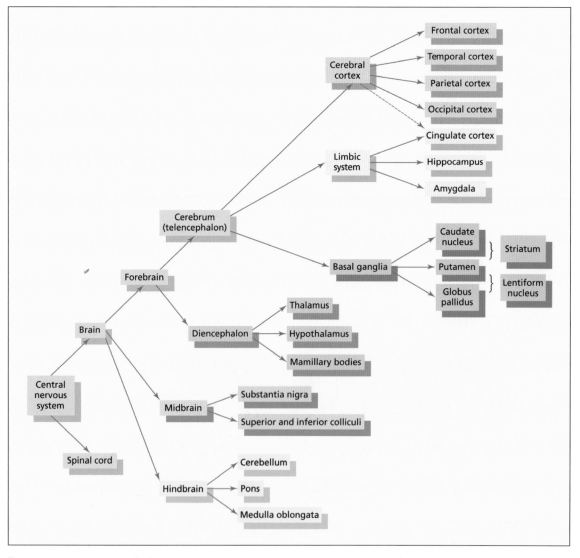

The central nervous system (CNS) is organized hierarchically. The upper levels of the hierarchy, corresponding to the upper branches of this diagram, are the newest structures from an evolutionary perspective.

refer to directions toward the outer surface and the center of the brain, respectively; although "medial" is ambiguous, because it is also used in another context. Although it is used to refer to the center of the brain, it is also used to refer to the middle of structures more generally. For example, the medial temporal gyrus lies on the lateral surface of the brain (not the medial surface). It is labeled medial because it lies midway between the superior and inferior temporal gyri.

The brain can be sectioned into two-dimensional slices in a number of ways. A *coronal* cross-section refers to a slice in the vertical plane through both hemispheres (the brain appears roundish in this section). A *sagittal* section refers to a slice in the vertical plane going through one of the hemispheres. When the sagittal section lies between the hemispheres it is called a *midline* or medial section. An *axial* (or horizontal) section is taken in the horizontal plane.

**KEY TERMS**

**Dorsal**
Towards the top.

**Ventral**
Towards the bottom.

**Lateral**
The outer part (cf. medial).

**Medial**
In or toward the middle.

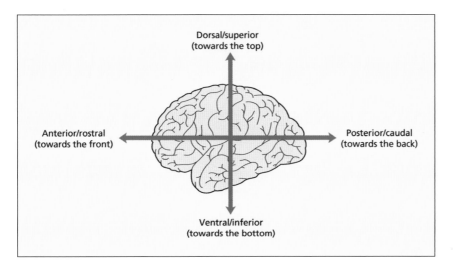

Terms of reference in the brain. Note also the terms *lateral* (referring to the outer surface of the brain) and *medial* (referring to the central regions).

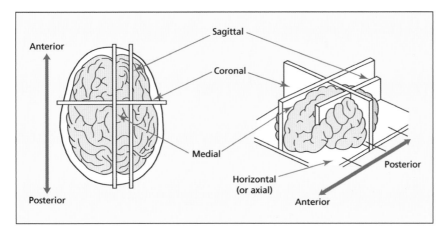

Terms of sections of the brain.

Adapted from Diamond *et al.,* 1986. © 1986 by Coloring Concepts Inc. Reprinted by permission of HarperCollins Publishers.

# THE CEREBRAL CORTEX

The cerebral cortex consists of two folded sheets of gray matter organized into two hemispheres (left and right). The surface of the cortex has become increasingly more convoluted with evolutionary development. Having a folded structure permits a high surface area to volume ratio and thereby permits efficient packaging. The raised surfaces of the cortex are termed **gyri** (or gyrus in the singular). The dips or folds are called **sulci** (or sulcus in the singular).

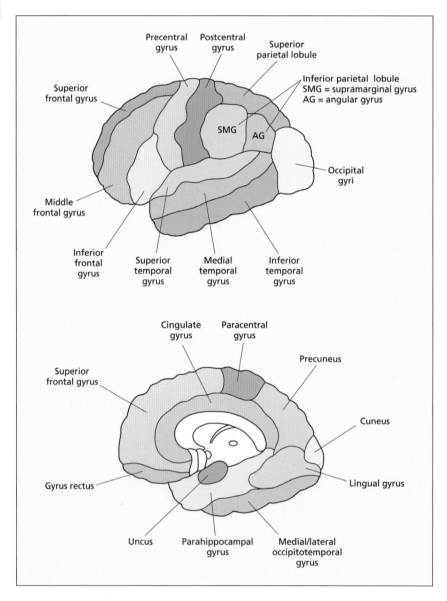

The main gyri of the lateral (top) and medial (bottom) surface of the brain. The cortical sulci tend to be labeled according to terms of reference. For example, the superior temporal sulcus lies between the superior and medial temporal gyri.

The cortex is only around 3 mm thick and is organized into different layers that can be seen when viewed in cross-section. The different layers reflect the grouping of different cell types. Different parts of the cortex have different densities in each of the layers. Most of the cortex contains six main cortical layers, termed the *neocortex* (meaning "new cortex"). Other cortical regions are the mesocortex (including the cingulate gyrus and insula) and the allocortex (including the primary olfactory cortex and hippocampus).

The lateral surface of the cortex of each hemisphere is divided into four lobes: the frontal, parietal, temporal and occipital lobes. The dividing line between the lobes is sometimes prominent, as is the case between the frontal and temporal lobes (divided by the lateral or *sylvian fissure*), but in other cases the boundary cannot readily be observed (e.g. between temporal and occipital lobes). Other regions of the cortex are observable only in a medial section, for example the cingulate cortex. Finally, an island of cortex lies buried underneath the temporal lobe; this is called the *insula* (which literally means "island" in Latin).

There are three different ways in which regions of cerebral cortex may be divided and, hence, labeled:

1. *Regions divided by the pattern of gyri and sulci.* The same pattern of gyri and sulci is found in everyone (although the precise shape and size varies greatly). As such, it is possible to label different regions of the brain accordingly.
2. *Regions divided by cytoarchitecture.* One of the most influential ways of dividing up the cerebral cortex is in terms of **Brodmann's areas**. Brodmann divided the cortex up into approximately 52 areas (labeled from BA1 to BA52), based on the relative distribution of cell types across cortical layers. Areas are labeled in a circular spiral starting from the middle, like the numbering system of Parisian suburbs. Over the years, the map has been modified.
3. *Regions divided by function.* This method tends only to be used for primary sensory and motor areas. For example, Brodmann areas 17 and 6 are also termed the primary visual cortex and the primary motor cortex, respectively. Higher cortical regions are harder (if not impossible) to ascribe unique functions to.

**KEY TERM**

**Brodmann's areas**
Regions of cortex defined by the relative distribution of cell types across cortical layers (cytoarchitecture).

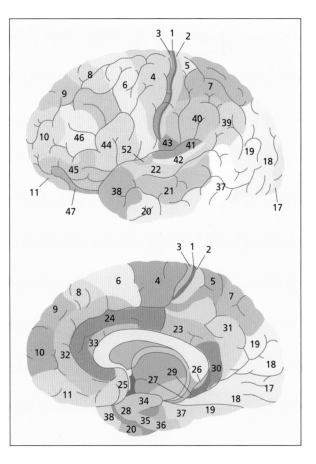

The Brodmann areas of the brain on the lateral (top) and medial (bottom) surface.

**KEY TERMS**

**Basal ganglia**
Regions of subcortical gray matter involved in aspects of motor control and skill learning; they consist of structures such as the caudate nucleus, putamen, and globus pallidus.

**Limbic system**
A region of subcortex involved in relating the organism to its present and past environment; limbic structures include the amygdala, hippocampus, cingulate cortex, and mamillary bodies.

**Thalamus**
A major subcortical relay center; for instance, it is a processing station between all sensory organs (except smell) and the cortex.

**Hypothalamus**
Consists of a variety of nuclei that are specialized for different functions that are primarily concerned with the body and its regulation.

# THE SUBCORTEX

Beneath the cortical surface and the intervening white matter lies another collection of gray matter nuclei termed the subcortex. The subcortex is typically divided into a number of different systems with different evolutionary and functional histories.

## The basal ganglia

The **basal ganglia** are large rounded masses that lie in each hemisphere. They surround and overhang the thalamus in the center of the brain. They are involved in regulating motor activity, and the programming and termination of action (see Chapter 8). Disorders of the basal ganglia can be characterized as hypokinetic (poverty of movement) or hyperkinetic (excess of movement). Examples of these include Parkinson's and Huntington's disease, respectively (see Chapter 8). The basal ganglia are also implicated in the learning of rewards, skills, and habits (see Chapters 9 and 15). The main structures comprising the basal ganglia are: the *caudate nucleus* (an elongated tail-like structure), the *putamen* (lying more laterally) and the *globus pallidus* (lying more medially). The caudate and putamen funnel cortical inputs into the globus pallidus, from which fibers reach into the thalamus. Different circuits passing through these regions either increase or decrease the probability and intensity of certain behaviors (e.g. voluntary movements).

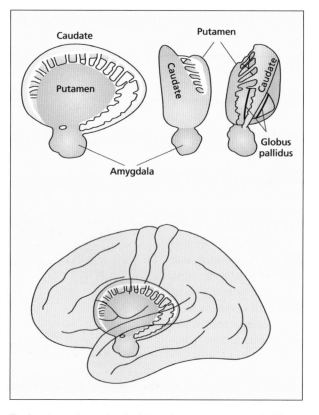

The basal ganglia are involved in motor programming and skill learning.

## The limbic system

The **limbic system** is important for relating the organism to its environment based on current needs and the present situation, and based on previous experience. It is involved in the detection and expression of emotional responses. For example, the *amygdala* has been implicated in the detection of fearful or threatening stimuli (see Chapter 15), and parts of the *cingulate gyrus* have been implicated in the detection of emotional and cognitive conflicts (see Chapter 14). The *hippocampus* is particularly important for learning and memory (see Chapter 9). Both the amygdala and hippocampus lie buried in the temporal lobes of each hemisphere. Other limbic structures are clearly visible on the underside (ventral surface) of the brain. The *mamillary bodies* are two small round protrusions that have traditionally been implicated in memory (Dusoir *et al.*, 1990). The *olfactory bulbs* lie on the under surface of the frontal lobes. Their connections to the limbic system underscore the importance of smell for detecting environmentally salient stimuli (e.g. food, other animals) and its influence on mood and memory.

## The diencephalon

The two main structures that make up the diencephalon are the thalamus and the hypothalamus.

The **thalamus** consists of two interconnected egg-shaped masses that lie in the center of the brain and appear prominent in a medial section. The thalamus is the main sensory relay for all senses (except smell) between the sense organs (eyes, ears, etc.) and the cortex. It also contains projections to almost all parts of the cortex and the basal ganglia. At the posterior end of the thalamus lie the *lateral geniculate nucleus* and the *medial geniculate nucleus*. These are the main sensory relays to the primary visual and primary auditory cortices, respectively.

The **hypothalamus** lies beneath the thalamus and consists of a variety of nuclei that are specialized for different functions primarily concerned with the body. These include body temperature, hunger and thirst, sexual activity, and regulation of endocrine functions (e.g. regulating body growth). Tumors in this region can lead to eating and drinking disorders, precocious puberty, dwarfism, and gigantism.

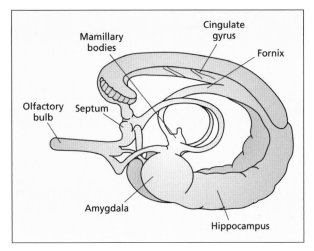

The limbic system.

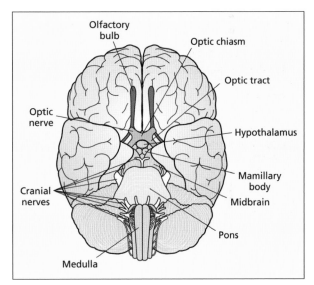

The ventral surface of the brain shows the limbic structures of the olfactory bulbs and mamillary bodies. Other visible structures include the hypothalamus, optic nerves, pons, and medulla.

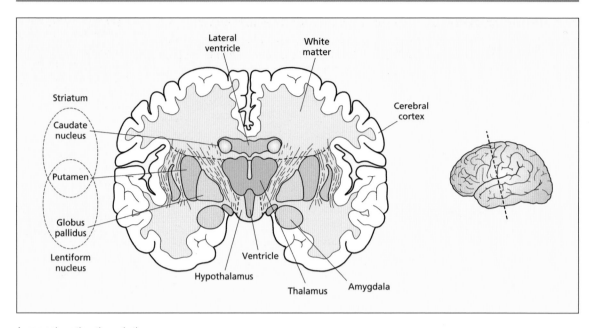

A coronal section through the amygdala and basal ganglia shows the thalamus and hypothalamus as prominent in the midline.

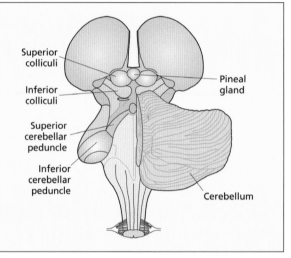

A posterior view of the midbrain and hindbrain. Visible structures include the thalamus, pineal gland, superior colliculi, inferior colliculi, cerebellum, cerebellar peduncle, and medulla oblongata (the pons is not visible but lies on the other side of the cerebellum).

## THE MIDBRAIN AND HINDBRAIN

The midbrain region consists of a number of structures, only a few of which will be considered here. The **superior colliculi** and **inferior colliculi** (or colliculus in singular) are gray-matter nuclei. The superior colliculi integrate information from several senses (vision, hearing, and touch), whereas the inferior colliculi are specialized for auditory processing. These pathways are different from the main cortical sensory pathways and are evolutionarily older. They may provide a fast route that enables rapid orienting to stimuli (flashes or bangs) before the stimulus is consciously seen or heard (Sparks, 1999). The midbrain also contains a region called the *substantia nigra*, which is connected to the basal ganglia. Cell loss in this region is associated with the symptoms of Parkinson's disease.

The **cerebellum** (literally "little brain") is attached to the posterior of the hindbrain via the cerebellar peduncles. It consists of highly convoluted folds of gray matter. It is organized into two interconnected lobes. The cerebellum is important for dexterity and smooth execution of movement. This function may be achieved by integrating motor commands with online sensory feedback about the current state of the action (see Chapter 8). Unilateral lesions to the cerebellum result in poor coordination on the same side of the body as the lesion (i.e. ipsilesional side). Bilateral lesions result in a wide and staggering gait, slurred speech (dysarthria), and eyes moving in a to-and-fro motion (nystagmus). The **pons** is a key link between the cerebellum and the cerebrum. It receives information from visual areas to control eye and body movements. The **medulla oblongata** protrudes from the pons and merges with the spinal cord. It regulates vital functions such as breathing, swallowing, heart rate, and the wake–sleep cycle.

## KEY TERMS

**Cerebellum**
Structure attached to the hindbrain; important for dexterity and smooth execution of movement.

**Pons**
Part of the hindbrain; a key link between the cerebellum and the cerebrum.

**Medulla oblongata**
Part of the hindbrain; it regulates vital functions such as breathing, swallowing, heart rate, and the wake–sleep cycle.

## SUMMARY AND KEY POINTS OF THE CHAPTER

- The neuron is the basic cell type that supports cognition. Neurons form a densely interconnected network of connections. Axons send signals to other cells and dendrites receive signals.
- Neurons code information in terms of a response rate. They only respond in certain situations (determined by the input they receive from elsewhere).
- Neurons are grouped together to form gray matter (cell bodies) and white matter (axons and other cells). The cortical surface consists of a folded sheet of gray matter organized into two hemispheres.
- There is another set of gray matter in the subcortex that includes the basal ganglia (important in regulating movement), the limbic system (important for emotion and memory functions) and the diencephalon (the thalamus is a sensory relay center and the hypothalamus is concerned with hemostatic functions).

## EXAMPLE ESSAY QUESTIONS

- How do neurons communicate with each other?
- Describe how electrical and chemical signals are generated by neurons.
- Compare and contrast the different functions of the forebrain, midbrain and hindbrain.

Visit the companion website at www. psypress/cw/ward for:

- References to key papers and readings
- Video interviews on key topics
- Links to the *Interactive Neuroanatomy* website and Harvard's *MRI Brain Atlas*
- Multiple choice questions and interactive flashcards to test your knowledge
- Downloadable glossary

## RECOMMENDED FURTHER READING

- Bear, M. F., Connors, B. W., & Paradiso, M. A. (2006). *Neuroscience: Exploring the brain* (3rd edition). Baltimore, MA: Lippincott Williams & Wilkins. A detailed book that covers all aspects of neuroscience. It is recommended for students whose degree contains significant neuroscience components. The book may be beyond the need of many psychology students.
- Crossman, A. R. & Neary, D. (2010). *Neuroanatomy: An illustrated colour text* (4th edition). Edinburgh: Harcourt Publishers. A good and clear guide that is not too detailed.
- Pinel, J. P. J. & Edwards, M. (2007). *A colorful introduction to the anatomy of the human brain: A brain and psychology coloring book* (2nd edition). New York: Pearson. An active way of learning your way around the brain.

# CHAPTER 3

# The electrophysiological brain

## CONTENTS

How is it possible that the world "out there" comes to be perceived, comprehended, and acted upon by a set of neurons operating "in here"? Chapter 2 introduced some of the basic properties of the neuron, including the fact that the rate of responding of a neuron (in terms of the number of action potentials or "spikes") is a continuous variable that reflects the informational content of that neuron. Some neurons may respond, say, when an animal is looking at an object but not when listening to a sound. Other neurons may respond when an animal is listening to a sound but not looking at an object, and still others may respond when both a sound and an object are present. As such, there is a sense in which the world out there is reflected by properties of the system in here. Cognitive and neural systems are sometimes said to create **representations** of the world. Representations need not only concern physical properties of the world (e.g. sounds, colors) but may also relate to more abstract forms of knowledge (e.g. knowledge of the beliefs of other people, factual knowledge).

Cognitive psychologists may refer to a *mental representation* of, say, your grandmother, being accessed in an information-processing model of face processing. However, it is important to distinguish this from its *neural representation*.

There is unlikely to be a one-to-one relationship between a hypothetical mental representation and the response properties of single neurons. The outside world is not copied inside the head, neither literally nor metaphorically; rather, the response properties of neurons (and brain regions) correlate with certain real-world features. As such, the relationship between a mental representation and a neural one is unlikely to be straightforward. The electrophysiological method of **single-cell recordings** has been used to investigate questions related to neural representations, and this method will be considered first in this chapter.

The other electrophysiological method that will be considered in this chapter is **electroencephalography (EEG)**. This is based on measurements of electrical signals generated by the brain through electrodes placed on different points on the scalp. Changes in electrical signal are conducted instantaneously to the scalp, and this method is therefore particularly useful for measuring the relative *timing* of cognitive events and neural activity. The method of **event-related potentials (ERP)** links the *amount* of change in voltage at the scalp with particular cognitive events (e.g. stimulus, response). It has also become increasingly common to link the *rate* of change of the EEG signal to cognitive processes (oscillation based measures) that also depend on the good temporal resolution of EEG.

ERP measurements have much in common with the main method of cognitive psychology, namely, the **reaction time** measure. It is important to note that the absolute time to perform a task is not normally the thing of interest in cognitive psychology. It is of little theoretical interest to know that one reads the word "HOUSE" within 500 ms (ms = millisecond). However, relative differences in timing can be used to make inferences about the cognitive system. For example, knowing that people are slower at reading "HoUsE" when printed in mIxEd CaSe could be used to infer that, perhaps, our mental representations of visual words are case-specific (e.g. Mayall *et al.*, 1997). The extra processing time for "HoUsE" relative to "HOUSE" may reflect the need to transform this representation into a more standard one. Other methods in cognitive neuroscience are sensitive to measures other than timing. For example, functional imaging methods (such as fMRI) have a better spatial resolution than temporal resolution (see Chapter 4). Lesion methods tend to rely on measuring error rates rather than reaction times (see Chapter 5). Methods such as transcranial magnetic stimulation (TMS) have both good spatial and temporal resolution (see Chapter 5). It is important to stress that all these methods converge on the question of *how* cognitive processes are carried out by the brain. Just because one method is sensitive to timing differences and another is sensitive to spatial differences does not mean that the methods just tell us *when* and *where*. The "when" and "where" constitute the data, and the "how" is the theory that accounts for them.

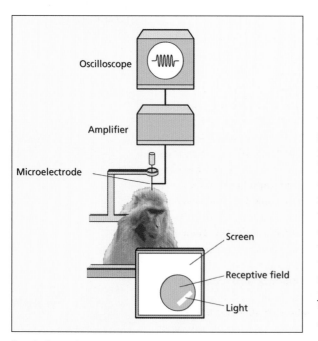

A typical experimental set-up for single-cell recording.

# IN SEARCH OF NEURAL REPRESENTATIONS: SINGLE-CELL RECORDINGS

## How are single-cell recordings obtained?

By measuring changes in the responsiveness of a neuron to changes in a stimulus or changes in a task, it is possible to make inferences about the building blocks of cognitive processing. The action potential is directly measured in the method of single-cell (and multi-unit) recordings. Single-cell recordings can be obtained by implanting a very small electrode either into the neuron itself (intracellular recording) or outside the membrane (extracellular recording) and counting the number of times that an action potential is produced (spikes per second) in response to a given stimulus (e.g. a face). This is an *invasive* method. As such, the procedure is normally conducted on experimental animals only. The electrodes are implanted during full anesthesia, and the recordings do not cause the animal pain. Extracellular recordings are the norm in the mammalian brain due to the small size of neurons. The method is occasionally conducted on humans undergoing brain surgery (see Engel *et al.*, 2005). It is impossible to measure action potentials from a single neuron noninvasively (i.e. from the scalp) because the signal is too weak and the noise from other neurons is too high.

An electrode may pick up on activity from multiple nearby neurons and, when used in this way, is referred to as **multi-cell (or multi-unit) recordings**. Special algorithms can then be applied to separate the combined signal into individual contributions from different neurons. Technology has now advanced such that it is possible to simultaneously record from 100 neurons in multi-electrode arrays.

## Distributed versus sparse coding

Hubel and Wiesel (1959) conducted pioneering studies of the early visual cortical areas (see Chapter 6 for detailed discussion). They argued that visual perception is hierarchical in that it starts from the most basic visual elements (e.g. small patches of light and dark) that combine into more complex elements (e.g. lines and edges), that combine into yet more complex elements (e.g. shapes). But what is the highest level of the hierarchy? Is there a neuron that responds to one particular stimulus? A hypothetical neuron such as this has been termed a **grandmother cell** because it may respond, for example, just to one's own grandmother (Bowers, 2009). The term was originally conceived to be multi-modal, in that the neuron may respond to her voice, and the thought of her, as well as the sight of her. It is now commonly referred to as a cell that responds to the sight of her (although from any viewpoint).

Rolls and Deco (2002) distinguish between three different types of representation that may be found at the neural level:

1. *Local representation*. All the information about a stimulus/event is carried in one of the neurons (as in a grandmother cell).
2. *Fully distributed representation*. All the information about a stimulus/event is carried in all the neurons of a given population.
3. *Sparse distributed representation*. A distributed representation in which a small proportion of the neurons carry information about a stimulus/event.

## KEY TERMS

**Event-related potential (ERP)**
The average amount of change in voltage at the scalp that are linked to the timing of particular cognitive events (e.g. stimulus, response).

**Reaction time**
The time taken between the onset of a stimulus/event and the production of a behavioral response (e.g. a button press).

**Multi-cell recordings (or multi-unit recordings)**
The electrical activity (in terms of action potentials per second) of many individually recorded neurons recorded at one or more electrodes.

**Grandmother cell**
A hypothetical neuron that just responds to one particular stimulus (e.g. the sight of one's grandmother).

Could there be a single neuron in our brain that responds to only one stimulus, such as our grandmother? These hypothetical cells are called "grandmother cells."

Several studies have attempted to distinguish between these accounts. Bayliss *et al.* (1985) found that neurons in the temporal cortex of monkeys responded to several different faces (from a set of five), albeit to different degrees. Similar results have been found with much larger sets of faces in both monkeys (Rolls & Tovee, 1995) and more recently in humans undergoing surgery for epilepsy (Quiroga *et al.*, 2005). The neurons typically respond to several different stimuli from within the same category (e.g. responding to several faces but no objects). This is inconsistent with a strict definition of a grandmother cell. However, they also showed a surprising degree of specificity. In the study on humans, Quiroga *et al.* (2005) recorded from neurons in parts of the brain traditionally implicated in memory rather than perception (i.e. medial temporal lobes). They found some neurons that responded maximally to celebrities such as Jennifer Aniston or Halle Berry, irrespective of the particular image used, clothes worn, etc. The "Halle Berry neuron" even responded to the sight of her name and to her dressed up as Catwoman, but not to other actresses dressed up as Catwoman. However, it is impossible to conclude that the neuron *only* responds to Halle Berry without probing an infinite number of stimuli. These studies speak against a fully distributed representation of personal identity and are more consistent with the notion of "sparse" coding at the top of the visual hierarchy.

Some neurons code for other aspects of a stimulus than facial identity. For example, consider the pattern of responding of a particular neuron taken from the superior temporal sulcus (STS) of an alert macaque monkey (Perrett *et al.*, 1992). The activity of the neuron when shown four different views of faces is compared with spontaneous activity in which no face is shown. The neuron responds strongly to a downward gaze, both with the eyes and the whole head, but not an upward or straight-ahead gaze. In this instance, the two stimuli that elicit the strongest response (head down and head forward with eyes down) do not resemble

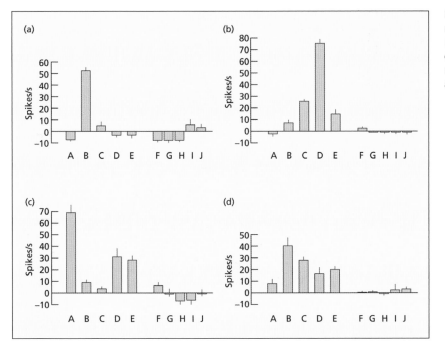

Four neurons (a, b, c, d) respond to different faces (A–E), but not different objects (F–J). They typically respond to several faces, albeit in a graded fashion.

Reprinted from Bayliss et al., 1985. © 1985, with permission from Elsevier.

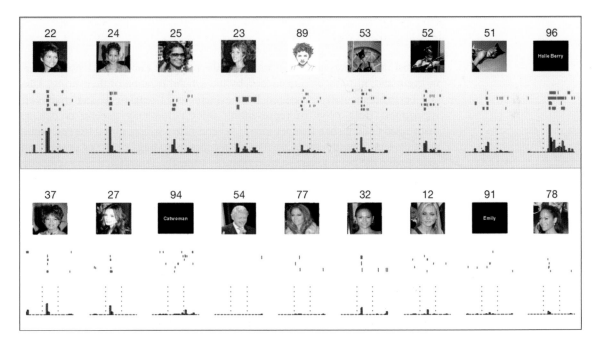

This neuron, recorded in the human medial temporal lobe, responds to Halle Berry (top panel) more than comparable stimuli (bottom panel). The response of the neuron is depicted in two ways. A raster plot (blue) depicts the firing of the neuron over time (represented left-to-right horizontally) by shading in when the neuron fires. Each row is a different recording with that stimulus. The histogram (red) sums together the number of times that the neuron fired at each time point.

From Quiroga et al., 2005.

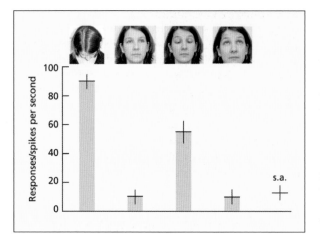

This neuron responds when gaze is oriented downwards. The activity of the neuron (spikes per second) is shown when presented with four faces and during spontaneous activity (s.a.).

Adapted from Perrett *et al.*, 1992.

each other physically, although they are related conceptually. Coding of gaze direction may be important for cognitive processes involved in interpreting social cues (eye contact is perceived as a threat by many species), or for orienting attention and action systems. Perhaps there is something interesting down there that would warrant our attention.

The studies described above can all be classified as **rate coding** of information by neurons in that a given stimulus/event is associated with an increase in the rate of neural firing. An alternative way for neurons to represent information about stimuli/events is in terms of **temporal coding**, in that a given stimulus/event is associated with greater synchronization of firing across different neurons. Engel *et al.* (1991) obtained multi-cell recordings from neurons in the primary visual cortex. This region contains a spatial map of the retinal image (see Chapter 6). If two regions were stimulated with a single bar of light, the two regions synchronized their neural firing. But, if the two regions were stimulated by two different bars of light, there was no synchronization even though both regions showed a response in terms of increased rate of firing. Temporal coding may be one mechanism for integrating information across spatially separated populations of neurons.

## Evaluation

Information is represented in neurons by the response rates to a given stimulus or event and, in some circumstances, by the synchronization of their firing. This can be experimentally measured by the methods of single-cell and multi-cell recordings. Both ways of representing information may depend on sparse distributed coding such that activity in several neurons is required to represent a stimulus (e.g. a particular face). The sparseness of coding conserves energy and may enable the brain to have a high memory capacity. Distributed representation may protect against information loss if synapses or neurons are lost. It may also allow the cognitive system to generalize and categorize (e.g. a novel stimulus that resembles a stored representation would partially activate this representation).

## ELECTROENCEPHALOGRAPHY AND EVENT-RELATED POTENTIALS

This section considers the basic principles behind the electrophysiological method known as electroencephalography (EEG). The following sections go on to consider some concrete examples of how EEG is used in contemporary cognitive neuroscience and contrast it with other methods used in cognitive psychology and cognitive neuroscience (principally the reaction-time measure).

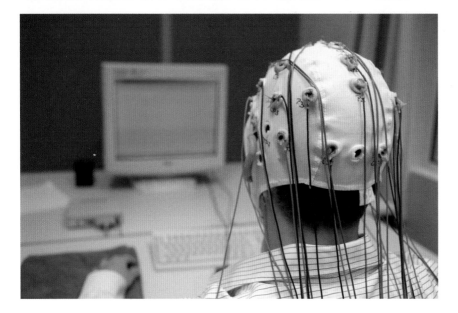

A participant in an EEG experiment.

AJ Photo / HOP AMERICAIN / Science Photo Library.

## How does EEG work?

The physiological basis of the EEG signal originates in the postsynaptic dendritic currents rather than the axonal currents associated with the action potential (Nunez, 1981). These were described as passive and active currents, respectively, in Chapter 2. Electroencephalography (EEG) records electrical signals generated by the brain through electrodes placed on different points on the scalp. As the procedure is non-invasive and involves recording (not stimulation), it is completely harmless as a method. For an electrical signal to be detectable at the scalp a number of basic requirements need to be met in terms of underlying neural firing. First, a whole population of neurons must be active in synchrony to generate a large enough electrical field. Second, this population of neurons must be aligned in a parallel orientation so that they summate rather than cancel out. Fortunately, neurons are arranged in this way in the cerebral cortex. However, the same cannot necessarily be said about all regions of the brain. For example, the orientation of neurons in the thalamus renders its activity invisible to this recording method.

   To gain an EEG measure one needs to compare the voltage between two or more different sites. A reference site is often chosen that is likely

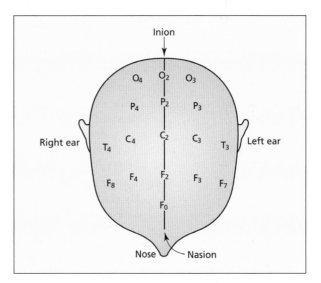

The 10–20 system of electrodes used in a typical EEG/ERP experiment.

to be relatively uninfluenced by the variable under investigation. One common reference point is the mastoid bone behind the ears or a nasal reference; another alternative is to reference to the average of all electrodes. The experimental electrodes themselves are often arranged at various locations on the scalp and often described with reference to the so-called 10–20 system of Jasper (1958). The electrodes are labeled according to their location (F = frontal, P = parietal, O = occipital, T = temporal, C = central) and the hemisphere involved (odd numbers for left, even numbers for right, and "z" for the midline). For example, the $O_2$ electrode is located over the right occipital lobe, and the $F_z$ electrode is located over the midline of the frontal lobes. It is important to stress that the activity recorded at each location cannot necessarily be attributed to neural activity near to that region. Electrical activity in one location can be detected at distant locations. In general, EEG/ERP is not best equipped for detecting the location of neural activity (see later for further discussion).

## Rhythmic oscillations in the EEG signal

The EEG signal, when observed over a sufficiently long timescale, has a wave-like structure. The EEG signal tends to oscillate at different rates (also called frequency bands) that are named after letters of the Greek alphabet: thus alpha waves reflect oscillations in the 7 to 14 Hz range, beta in the 15 to 30 Hz range, and gamma in the 30 Hz and above range (and so on). These oscillations arise because large groups of neurons tend to be in temporal synchrony with each other in terms of their firing (action potentials) and in terms of their slower dendritic potentials (which forms the basis of the EEG signal). It has long been established that different rates of oscillation characterize different phases of the sleep-wake cycle (for the detailed mechanisms see McCormick & Bal, 1997).

In recent decades, attempts have been made to link the relative amount of oscillations (the "power") in different bands to different kinds of cognitive function during normal wakefulness (Ward, 2003). This section will provide only a few examples from the literature to illustrate the general principle. For instance, increases in the alpha band have been linked to increased attention. More specifically, it has been linked to filtering out of irrelevant information. If participants are asked to ignore a region of space in which an irrelevant stimulus will later appear (a so-called distractor) then increases in the alpha band are found over electrode sites that represent that region of space (Worden et al., 2000). Alpha is also greater when attending to an internally generated image in which external visual input is unattended (Cooper et al., 2003). An "increase in the alpha band" means that neurons become more synchronized in their electrical activity specifically in the 7 to 14 Hz range. What is less clear is why this particular neural coding should be linked to this kind of cognitive mechanism rather than changes in any other frequency band.

By contrast, increases in the gamma band have been linked to perceptual integration of parts into wholes. This kind of mechanism is important for object recognition (e.g. deciding that a handle and hollowed cylinder is a single object—a mug), and the general process is referred to as binding or grouping. Rodriguez et al. (1999) presented participants with an ambiguous visual stimulus that could be perceived either as a face (parts bound into a whole) or a meaningless visual pattern (collection of separate parts). They found that increased gamma synchronization was linked to the face percept (Rodriguez et al., 1999).

Although gamma and delta have been linked to rather different functions (similarly for other frequency bands), it is inconceivable that there will be a one-to-one mapping between particular frequency bands and particular cognitive functions. Synchronization (or desynchronization) of alpha, gamma, and so on are linked to a wide range of cognitive functions and may come from different regions in the brain. However, it provides another tool within which to understand the different mechanisms that comprise cognition. Perhaps, most importantly, it suggests that there is more to cognition than the *amount* of brain "activity" (the standard interpretation of fMRI data) and suggests that the *synchronization* of brain activity (measurable in EEG because of its fast temporal resolution) has particular roles to play in cognition.

## Event-related potentials (ERPs)

The most common use of EEG in cognitive neuroscience is not in measurements of neuronal oscillations, but rather in the method known as ERP or event-related potentials. The EEG waveform reflects neural activity from all parts of the brain. Some of this activity may specifically relate to the current task (e.g. reading, listening, calculating), but most of it will relate to spontaneous activity of other neurons that do not directly contribute to the task. As such, the *signal-to-noise ratio* in a single trial of EEG is very low (the signal being the electrical response to the event and the noise being the background level of electrical activity). The ratio can be increased by averaging the EEG signal over many presentations of the stimulus (e.g. 50–100 trials), relative to the onset of a stimulus. In general, the background oscillatory activity (alpha, beta, etc.) will not be synchronised with

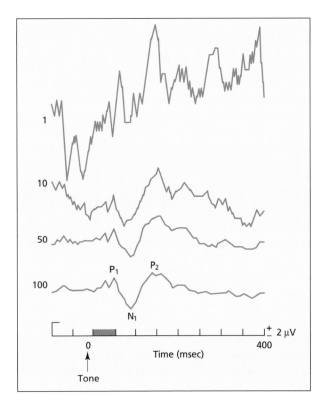

When different EEG waves are averaged relative to presentation of a stimulus (e.g. a tone), the signal-to-noise ratio is enhanced and an event-related potential is observed. The figure shows the mean EEG signal to 1, 10, 50, and 100 trials.

From Kolb and Whishaw, 2002. © 2002 by Worth Publishers. Used with permission.

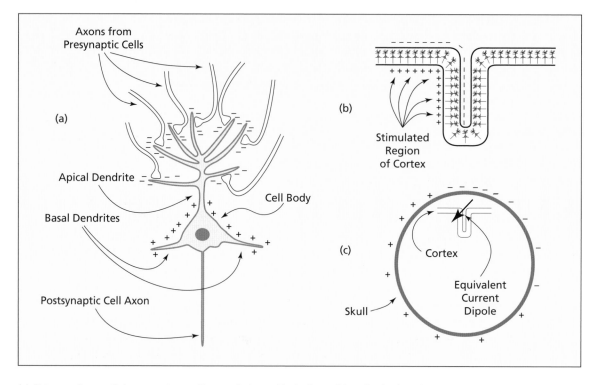

(a) Release of an excitatory neurotransmitter results in positively charged ions flowing into the post-synaptic neuron (and a net negativity in the extracellular region). (b) This sets up a dipole that may sum together with dipoles from surrounding neurons (which tend to be aligned in the same way). (c) This conducts to the scalp as a distribution of positive and negative charges. Changes in the negative or positive potential at a given site over time are the neural basis for the ERP signal.
From Luck & Girelli, 1998.

the onset of events and so these fluctuations are also averaged out. The results are represented graphically by plotting time (milliseconds) on the *x*-axis and electrode potential (microvolts) on the *y*-axis. The graph consists of a series of positive and negative peaks, with an asymptote at 0 μV. This is done for each electrode, and each will have a slightly different profile. The positive and negative peaks are labeled with "P" or "N" and their corresponding number. Thus, P1, P2, and P3 refer to the first, second, and third positive peaks, respectively. Alternatively, they can be labeled with "P" or "N" and the approximate timing of the peak. Thus, P300 and N400 refer to a positive peak at 300 ms and a negative peak at 400 ms (*not* the 300th positive and 400th negative peak!).

Whether a peak is positive or negative (its *polarity*) has no real significance in cognitive terms, nor does a positive peak reflect excitation and a negative peak inhibition. The polarity depends on the spatial arrangement of the neurons that are giving rise to the signal at that particular moment in time. Positive ions flow into the dendrites when an excitatory neurotransmitter is released leaving a net negative voltage in the extracellular space. This creates what is called a **dipole**. Dipoles from different neurons and different regions summate and conduct to the skull, and these give rise to the characteristic peaks and troughs of the ERP waveform. What is of interest in the ERP waveform, in terms of linking it to cognition, is the timing and amplitude of those peaks. This is considered in the next section.

**KEY TERM**

**Dipole**
A pair of positive and negative electrical charges separated by a small distance.

## SOME PRACTICAL ISSUES TO CONSIDER WHEN CONDUCTING EEG/ERP RESEARCH

### Where can a set of guidelines for conducting and reporting ERP experiments be found?

A detailed set of guidelines is provided by Picton *et al.* (2000) and is based on a consensus agreed by 11 leading laboratories in the field. This is recommended reading for all new researchers in the field.

### What behavioral measures should be obtained?

In almost all ERP experiments, participants are required to perform a task in which an overt behavioral response is required (e.g. a button press), and this can be analyzed independently (e.g. in terms of reaction times and/or error rates). One exception to this is ERP responses to unattended stimuli (e.g. ignored stimuli, stimuli presented subliminally). It is not possible to record vocal responses (e.g. picture naming) because jaw movements disrupt the EEG signal.

It is important that the initial hypothesis places constraints on the ERP component of interest (e.g. "the experimental manipulation will affect the latency of P300 component") rather than predicting non-specific ERP changes (e.g. "the experimental manipulation will affect the ERP in some way"). This is because the dataset generated from a typical ERP experiment is large and the chance of finding a "significant" result that is not justified by theory or reliable on replication is high.

### How can interference from eye movement be avoided?

Not all of the electrical activity measured at the scalp reflects neural processes. One major source of interference comes from movement of the eyes and eyelids. These movements occur at the same frequencies as important components in the EEG signal. There are a number of ways of reducing or eliminating these effects. One can instruct the participant not to blink or to blink only at specified times in the experiment (e.g. after making their response). The problem with this method is that it imposes a secondary task on the participant (the task of not moving their eyes) that may affect the main task of interest. It is also possible to discard or filter out the effect of eye movements in trials in which they have occurred (Luck, 2005).

## MENTAL CHRONOMETRY IN ELECTROPHYSIOLOGY AND COGNITIVE PSYCHOLOGY

**Mental chronometry** can be defined as the study of the time-course of information processing in the human nervous system (Posner, 1978). The basic idea is that changes in the nature or efficiency of information processing will manifest themselves in the time it takes to complete a task. For example, participants are faster at verifying that $4 + 2 = 6$ than they are to verify that $4 + 3 = 7$, and this is faster than verifying that $5 + 3 = 8$ (Parkman & Groen, 1971). What can be concluded from this? First of all, it suggests that mathematical sums such as these are not just stored as a set of facts. If this were so, then all the reaction times would be expected to be the same because all statements are equally true. It suggests, instead, that the task involves a stage in processing that encodes

> **KEY TERM**
>
> **Mental chronometry**
> The study of the time course of information processing in the human nervous system.

numerical size together with the further assumption that larger sums place more limits on the efficiency of information processing (manifested as a slower verification time). This provides one example of how it is possible to make inferences about the nature of cognitive processes from timing measures.

A task such as verification of sums is likely to involve a series of stages, including visual recognition of the digits, computing the sum and producing a response. The reaction time measure is the end product of all these stages. Sternberg (1969) developed a general method for dividing reaction times into different stages termed the **additive factors method**. His experiment involved a working memory task in which participants were given an array of one, two or four digits to hold in mind (e.g. 5, 9, 3, 2). They were then shown a single probe digit (e.g. 9) and asked to press one of two buttons (labeled "yes" and "no") to indicate whether this item had been in the previous array. Sternberg proposed that the task could be divided into a number of separate stages, including:

1.  *Encoding* the probe digit.
2.  *Comparing* the probe digit with the items held in memory.
3.  *Decision* about which response to make.
4.  *Responding* by executing the button press.

He further postulated that each of these stages could be independently influenced by different factors affecting the task. For instance, the encoding stage may be affected by the perceptibility of the probe digit (e.g. presenting it on a patterned background). The comparison stage may be affected by the number of items in the array (the more items in the array, the slower the task). He reasoned that, if different factors affect different stages of processing, then the effects should have additive effects on the overall reaction time, whereas if they affect the same processing stage, they should have interactive effects. The strength of this method is that one could then take an unknown factor (e.g. sleep deprivation, Parkinson's

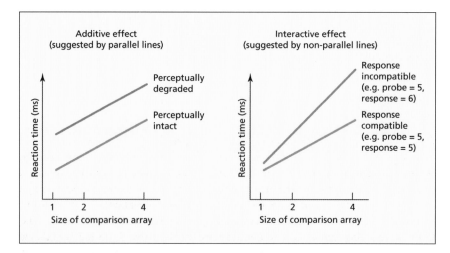

Sternberg's additive factors method assumes that if two variables affect different stages of processing then they should have an additive effect on the overall reaction time (left), but if two variables affect the same stage of processing then the factors should have an interactive effect (right). His task involved comparing a probe digit (e.g. 5) with an array of one, two, or four digits held in mind.

disease, reading ability) and determine whether this has an interactive effect on stimulus perceptibility (implying that the new factor affects perceptual encoding) or whether it has an interactive effect with the number of items in the array (implying the new factor affects the comparison stage) or both (implying the new factor has effects at multiple levels).

The additive factors approach has been very influential in cognitive psychology research, although it is to be noted that the assumptions do not always apply. For example, the model assumes that the stages are strictly sequential (i.e. later stages do not occur until earlier ones are complete), but this assumption is not always valid.

At this juncture it is useful to consider how the mental chronometry approach applies to the analysis and interpretation of ERP data. Whereas a reaction time consists of a *single* measure that is assumed to reflect different stages/components, an ERP waveform consists of a series of peaks and troughs that vary continuously over time. These peaks and troughs are likely to have some degree of correspondence with different cognitive stages of processing. For example, in the task described above, earlier peaks may reflect perceptual encoding and later peaks may reflect the comparison stage. One could then observe how the amplitude of those peaks varied, say, with the number of items to be compared. One could also observe whether a new variable (e.g. sleep deprivation) affected earlier or later peaks. The different peaks and troughs of the ERP signal have been referred to as *ERP components* (Donchin, 1981). There may not be a simple mapping between an ERP component and a cognitive component of a task. For example, a single cognitive component may reflect the action of several spatially separate neural populations (i.e. one cognitive component could affect several ERP components) or several cognitive components may be active at once and sum together, or cancel each other out, in the ERP waveform (i.e. several cognitive components affect a single ERP component). As such, some researchers prefer to use the more neutral term ERP *deflection* rather than ERP *component*.

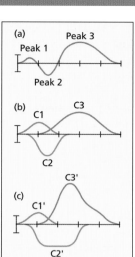

Graph (a) shows an observed ERP waveform and graphs (b) and (c) show two different sets of hidden components that could have given rise to it. This illustrates the point that there is not a one-to-one mapping between ERP components and the activity of underlying cognitive/neural components.

From Luck, 2005. © 2004 Massachusetts Institute of Technology by permission of the MIT Press.

## Investigating face processing with ERPs and reaction times

This chapter has already considered the neural representation of faces as measured by single-cell recordings. ERP studies have also investigated the way that faces are processed. A full model of face processing is discussed in Chapter 6, but a consideration of a few basic stages will suffice for the present needs. An initial stage consists of perceptual coding of the facial image (e.g. location of eyes, mouth), followed by a stage in which the facial identity is computed. This stage is assumed to map the perceptual code onto a store of known faces and represents the face irrespective of viewing conditions (e.g. lighting, viewing angle). (Note that this doesn't assume grandmother cells because facial identity could be computed by a population of neurons.) Finally, there may be a representation of the identity of the person that is not tied to any modality (e.g. responds to faces and names) and may enable retrieval of other types of knowledge (e.g. their occupation).

**KEY TERM**

**N170**
An ERP component (negative potential at 170 ms) linked to perceiving facial structure.

As with the single-cell results, there is evidence for an ERP component that is relatively selective to the processing of faces compared with other classes of visual objects. This has been termed the **N170** (a negative peak at 170 ms) and is strongest over right posterior temporal electrode sites (Bentin *et al.*, 1996). This component is uninfluenced by whether the face is famous or not (Bentin & Deouell, 2000) and is also found for cartoon "smiley" faces (Sagiv & Bentin, 2001). It is, however, reduced if the face is perceptually degraded (Schweinberger, 1996). The N250, by contrast, is larger for famous and personally familiar faces relative to unfamiliar faces (Herzmann, *et al.*, 2004) and responds to presentation of different images of the same person (Schweinberger *et al.*, 2002b). This suggests that it codes properties of the specific face rather than the specific image. Later, positive-going components (from 300 ms onwards) are also sensitive to the repetition and familiarity of specific person identities, and the effects generalize to names as well as faces (Schweinberger *et al.*, 2002a).

Having sketched out a plausible relationship between different components of the ERP waveform and different cognitive processes, it is possible to use these electrophysiological markers to adjudicate between different theories of face processing. One debate in the cognitive psychology literature concerns the locus of associative priming. **Associative priming** refers to the fact that reaction times are faster to a stimulus if that stimulus is preceded by a stimulus that tends to co-occur with it in the environment. For example, judging that the face of Mikhail Gorbachev (the last President of the Soviet Union) is familiar is performed faster if it immediately follows Boris Yeltsin's face (former President of Russia) or even Yeltsin's name (Young *et al.*, 1988). The fact that associative priming is found between names and faces might imply that the effect arises at a late stage of processing. However, there is evidence inconsistent with this. Using Sternberg's (1969) method, it has been found that associative priming interacts with stimulus degradation (Bruce & Valentine, 1986) and that associative priming interacts with how perceptually distinctive a face is (Rhodes & Tremewan, 1993). This would imply that associative priming has a perceptual locus such that perceiving Gorbachev's face also activates the perceptual face representation of Yeltsin. Schweinberger (1996) used ERP measures to determine the locus of associative priming of faces and names. ERP was suitable for addressing this question because it enables early and late

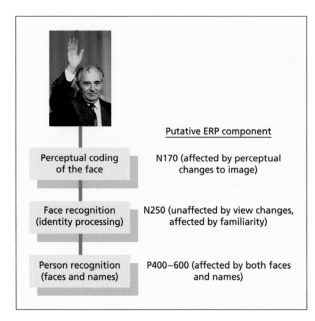

A simple model of several hypothetical stages involved in face processing together with their putative ERP manifestations.

Photo © Bernard Bisson and Thierry Orban/Sygma/Corbis.

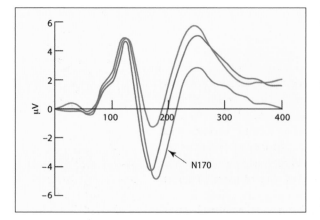

The N170 is observed for both human faces (purple) and animal faces (blue), but not other objects (green).

From Rousselet *et al.*, 2004. With permission of ARVO.

time points to be measured separately. He found that associative priming has a late effect (after 300 ms) on the ERP waveform that is more consistent with a post-perceptual locus. Effects of stimulus degradation were found under 150 ms. Schweinberger (1996) suggests that, in this instance, the Sternberg method may have led to an invalid conclusion because it assumes discrete stages.

## Endogenous and exogenous ERP components

Traditionally, ERP components have been classified as belonging to one of two categories. **Exogenous** components are those that appear to depend on the physical properties of a stimulus (e.g. sensory modality, size, intensity). These have also been called *evoked potentials*. **Endogenous** components, in contrast, appear to depend on properties of the task (e.g. what the participant is required to do with the stimulus). These can even occur in the absence of an external stimulus (e.g. if an expected stimulus does not occur; Sutton *et al.*, 1967). Exogenous components tend to be earlier than endogenous components.

Although the exogenous–endogenous classification is useful, it should be considered as a dimension rather than a true categorical distinction. To remain with the current example of face processing, consider the nature of the ERP waveform when viewing two repeated symbols that are horizontally spaced (e.g. + +). Typically, such symbols do not evoke the N170 response characteristic of face processing (Bentin *et al.*, 2002). However, if the symbols have previously been shown embedded in a face context (as eyes), then the pair of symbols do elicit the N170 response (Bentin *et al.*, 2002). Is this an endogenous or exogenous component? It is impossible to say. Although the N170 is normally taken as indicative of perceptual processing (an exogenous component), in this instance it is entirely dependent on the interpretive bias given.

## The spatial resolution of ERPs

The discussion so far has emphasized the importance of ERPs in the timing of cognition. The reason why the spatial resolution of this method is poor is given by the so-called **inverse problem**. If one had, say, three sources of electrical activity in the brain during a given task, and the magnitude and location of the activity were known, then it would be possible to calculate the electrical potential that we would expect to observe some distance away at the scalp. However, this is not the situation that is encountered in an ERP study; it is the inverse. In an ERP study, the electrical potential at the scalp is known (because it is measured), but the number, location, and magnitude of the electrical sources in the brain are unknown. Mathematically, there are an infinite number of solutions to the problem.

The most common way of attempting to solve the inverse problem involves a procedure called **dipole modeling**. This requires assumptions to be made about how many regions of the brain are critical for generating the observed pattern of scalp potentials. Attempts at dipole modeling with the N250 and N170 evoked

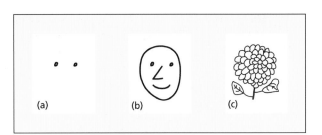

Two horizontally spaced symbols (the dots in a) do not elicit an N170 unless they have previously been presented in the context of a face (b). The participant's task was merely to count flowers (e.g. c), and so both the faces and "eyes" were irrelevant to the task.

From Bentin *et al.*, 2002. Reprinted by permission of Blackwell Publishing.

by face processing (see above) revealed probable loci in the fusiform gyrus and the posterior occipital region, respectively (Schweinberger *et al.*, 2002b). However, the most common way of obtaining good spatial resolution is to use a different method altogether, such as fMRI (see Chapter 4) or magnetoencephalography (MEG). (For similar results from fMRI concerning face processing, see Eger *et al.*, 2004.)

## WHY ARE CARICATURES EASY TO RECOGNIZE?

This caricature is instantly recognizable despite significant distortions. We are sometimes faster at recognizing caricatures than actual depictions. Why might this be?

Caricatures of faces are typically considered humorous and are often used for deliberate mockery or propaganda. As Richard Nixon's unpopularity grew during the Watergate scandal, so did his nose and jowls in published caricatures (see Rhodes, 1996). The paradox of caricatures is that the face is instantly recognizable despite being perceptibly wrong. In fact, people can sometimes be twice as fast at recognizing a caricature of a face as the same face undistorted (Rhodes *et al.*, 1987); the caricature appears to be more like the face than the face itself. What does this reveal about the way that faces are processed and represented?

First of all, it is important to clarify how caricatures are created. Caricatures exaggerate the distinctive features of an individual. Computer routines now exist that compare, for example, the size of an individual's nose with the average nose size. If the person has a larger than average nose, then this will be enlarged further in the caricature. If someone has a smaller than average nose, it will be shrunk in the caricature. It is also possible to morph a face to make it look more average (a so-called anti-caricature), and such faces are typically rated as more attractive than the real or caricatured face. One explanation for the effect of caricatures is to assume that our memory representations of faces are caricatured themselves; that is, we store the distinctive properties of a face rather than the face as it is. However, explanations such as these must assume that a "norm" or prototype face exists from which to infer what constitutes a distinctive feature. Another hypothesis is that it is the distinctiveness of caricatures per se that aids their recognition because there are fewer similar-looking competitor faces (Valentine, 1991). This account does not need to assume the existence of a face prototype, or that the stored representations themselves are caricatured. Research using ERPs is consistent with this view. Photographic caricatures of unfamiliar people lead, initially, to an enhancement of the N170 component relative to undistorted images or anti-caricatures (Kaufmann & Schweinberger, 2008). As this component is normally associated with perceptual coding of faces rather than memory of faces, it suggests that the effect is more likely to be due to perceptual distinctiveness than the way faces are coded in memory.

## Evaluation

Investigating the time-course of cognitive processes is an important method in cognitive psychology and cognitive neuroscience. Event-related potentials have excellent temporal resolution. This method has a number of benefits over and above reaction-time measurements: it provides a continuous measurement of changes over time (rather than a single timing measure) and it is, at least in theory, easier to link to neural processes in the brain. ERP also enables electro-physiological changes associated with unattended stimuli (that are not responded to) to be measured whereas a reaction-time measure always requires an overt behavioral response.

## MAGNETOENCEPHALOGRAPHY

The recording of magnetic signals, as opposed to electrical ones, generated by the brain has a much shorter history in cognitive neuroscience and still remains in its infancy (for reviews, see Papanicolaou, 1995; Singh, 2006). All electric currents, including those generated by the brain, have an associated magnetic field that is poten-tially measurable. However, the size of this field is very small relative to the ambient magnetic field of the earth. As such, the development of **magnetoencephalography (MEG)** had to wait for suitable technological advances to become a viable enterprise. This technological advance came in the form of superconducting devices termed SQUIDs (an acronym of Superconducting Quantum Interference Device). A whole-head MEG contains 200–300 of these devices. The apparatus used requires extreme cooling, using liquid helium, and isolation of the system in a magnetically shielded room. As such, the costs and practicalities associated with MEG are far greater than those needed for EEG. However, the biggest potential advantage of MEG over EEG is that it permits a much better spatial resolution.

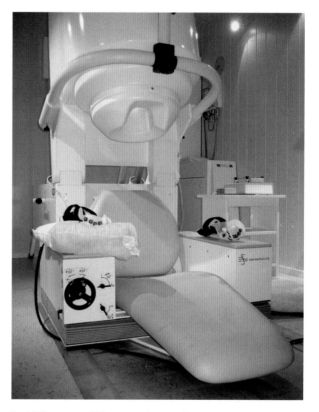

An MEG scanner. This extremely powerful machine measures the magnetic fields produced by electrical activity in the brain.

| MEG | EEG/ERP |
|---|---|
| • Signal unaffected by skull, meninges, etc. | • Signal affected by skull, meninges, etc. |
| • Poor at detecting deep dipoles | • Detects deep and shallow dipoles |
| • More sensitive to activity at sulci | • Sensitive to gyri and sulci activity |
| • Millisecond temporal resolution | • Millisecond temporal resolution |
| • Potentially good spatial resolution (2–3 mm) | • Poor spatial resolution |
| • Expensive and limited availability | • Cheaper and widely available |

### KEY TERM

**Magnetoencephal-ography (MEG)**
A noninvasive method for recording magnetic fields generated by the brain at the scalp.

Visit the companion website at www. psypress/cw/ward for videos on key topics covered in this chapter, a lecture by author Jamie Ward on *The Electrophysiological Brain*, references to key papers and readings, multiple choice questions and interactive glossary flashcards.

## SUMMARY AND KEY POINTS OF THE CHAPTER

- Neuronal activity generates electrical and magnetic fields that can be measured either invasively (e.g. single-cell recording) or noninvasively (e.g. EEG).
- Studies of single-cell recordings are based on measuring the number of action potentials generated and provide clues about how neurons code information, by measuring the specificity of their responses to external stimuli.
- When populations of neurons are active in synchrony they produce an electric field that can be detected at the scalp (EEG). When many such waves are averaged together and linked to the onset of a stimulus (or response), then an event-related potential (ERP) is obtained.
- An ERP waveform is an electrical signature of all the different cognitive components that contribute to the processing of that stimulus. Systematically varying certain aspects of the stimulus or task may lead to systematic variations in particular aspects of the ERP waveform. This enables inferences to be drawn about the timing and independence of cognitive processes.

## EXAMPLE ESSAY QUESTIONS

- How does the brain generate electrical signals, and how are these used in electrophysiological techniques?
- How do neurons code information?
- What is an "event-related potential" (or ERP) and how can it be used to inform theories of cognition?
- What have electrophysiological studies contributed to our understanding of how faces are represented and processed by the brain?

## RECOMMENDED FURTHER READING

- Dickter, C. L. & Kieffaber, P. D. (2014). *EEG methods for the psychological sciences*. London: Sage. Covers some material missed by Luck, including use of ERPLAB and frequency-based analysis.
- Luck, S. J. (2005). *An introduction to the event-related potential technique*. Cambridge, MA: MIT Press. This is the place to start if you are going to conduct research using EEG/ERPs.
- Senior, C., Russell, T., & Gazzaniga, M. S. (2006). *Methods in mind*. Cambridge, MA: MIT Press. Includes chapters on single-cell recording, EEG, and MEG.

# CHAPTER 4

# The imaged brain

## CONTENTS

If George Orwell had written *Nineteen Eighty-four* during our times, would he have put an MRI scanner in the Ministry of Truth? Could we ever really know the content of someone else's thoughts using functional imaging technology? This chapter will consider how functional imaging methods work, focusing in particular on fMRI (functional magnetic resonance imaging). This chapter is broadly divided into three parts. The first part considers how functional and structural brain imaging works, with particular reference to underlying neurophysiology. The second part considers methodological factors that are important in ensuring that the results obtained can indeed be meaningfully linked to cognitive theory. The third part covers how functional imaging data are analyzed to find regions of activation and considers some of the pitfalls in their interpretation. Finally, the chapter returns to the question of whether functional imaging could be used as an Orwellian-like mind reader.

**Structural imaging**
Measures of the spatial configuration of different types of tissue in the brain (principally CT and MRI).

**Functional imaging**
Measures temporary changes in brain physiology associated with cognitive processing; the most common method is fMRI and is based on a hemodynamic measure.

# STRUCTURAL IMAGING

One key distinction is the difference between **structural imaging** methods and **functional imaging** methods. Structural imaging is based on the fact that different types of tissue (e.g. skull, gray matter, white matter, cerebrospinal fluid) have different physical properties. These different properties can be used to construct detailed *static* maps of the physical structure of the brain. The most common structural imaging methods are computerized tomography (CT) and magnetic resonance imaging (MRI). Functional imaging is based on the assumption that neural activity produces local physiological changes in that region of the brain. This can be used to produce *dynamic* maps of the moment-to-moment activity of the brain when engaged in cognitive tasks.

## Computerized tomography

Computerized tomography (CT) scans are constructed according to the amount of X-ray absorption in different types of tissue. The amount of absorption is related to tissue density: bone absorbs the most (and so the skull appears white), cerebrospinal fluid absorbs the least (so the ventricles appear black), and the brain matter is intermediate (and appears gray). Given that CT uses X-rays, the person being scanned is exposed to a small amount of radiation.

CT scans are typically used only in clinical settings, for example to diagnose tumors or to identify hemorrhaging or other gross brain anomalies. CT cannot distinguish between gray matter and white matter in the same way as MRI, and it cannot be adapted for functional imaging purposes.

## Magnetic resonance imaging

Magnetic resonance imaging (MRI) was one of the most important advances in medicine made during the twentieth century. Its importance was recognized by the awarding of the 2003 Nobel Prize to its inventors—Sir Peter Mansfield and

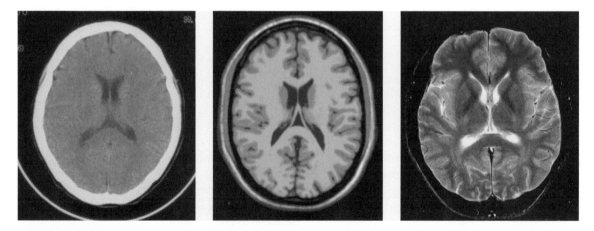

An example of CT (left), T1-weighted MRI (center), and T2-weighted MRI (right) scans of the brain. Note how the MRI scans are able to distinguish between gray matter and white matter. On the T1-weighted scan (normally used for structural images), gray matter appears gray and white matter appears lighter.

Paul Lauterbur. There are a number of advantages of this method over CT scanning, as summarized below:

- It does not use ionizing radiation and so is completely safe (people can be scanned many times).
- It provides a much better spatial resolution, which allows the folds of individual gyri to be discerned.
- It provides better discrimination between white matter and gray matter; this may enable early diagnosis of some pathologies, and can be used to explore how normal variation brain structure is linked to differences in cognitive ability.
- It can be adapted for use in detecting the changes in blood oxygenation associated with neural activity, and in this context is called functional MRI (fMRI).

## MRI physics for non-physicists

MRI is used to create images of soft tissue of the body, which X-rays pass through largely undistorted. Most human tissue is water-based and the amount of water in each type of tissue varies. Different types of tissue will thus behave in slightly different ways when stimulated, and this can be used to construct a three-dimensional image of the layout of these tissues (for an accessible, but more detailed description, see Savoy, 2002).

The sequence of events for acquiring an MRI scan is as follows. First, a strong magnetic field is applied across the part of the body being scanned (e.g. the brain). The single protons that are found in water molecules in the body (the hydrogen nuclei in $H_2O$) have weak magnetic fields. (Other atoms and nuclei also have magnetic moments, but in MRI it is the hydrogen nuclei in water that form the source of the signal.) Initially, these fields will be oriented randomly, but when the strong external field is applied a small fraction of them will align themselves with this. The external field is applied constantly during the scanning process. The strength of the magnetic field is measured in units called tesla (T). Typical scanners have field strengths between 1.5 and 3 T; the Earth's magnetic field is of the order of 0.0001 T.

When the protons are in the aligned state a brief radio frequency pulse is applied that knocks the orientation of the aligned protons by 90 degrees to their original orientation. As the protons spin (or *precess*) in this new state, they produce a detectable change in the magnetic field and this is what forms the basis of the MR signal. The protons will eventually be pulled back into their original alignment with the magnetic field (they "*relax*"). The scanner repeats this process serially by sending the radio wave to excite different slices of the brain in turn. With the advent of acquisition methods such as echo planar imaging, a whole brain can typically be scanned in about 2 s with slices of around 3 mm.

Different types of image can be created from different components of the MR signal. Variations in the rate at which the protons return back to the aligned state following the radio frequency pulse (called the T1 relaxation time) can be used to distinguish between different types of tissue. These T1-weighted images are typically used for structural images of the brain. In a T1-weighted image, gray matter looks gray and white matter looks white. When in the misaligned state, at

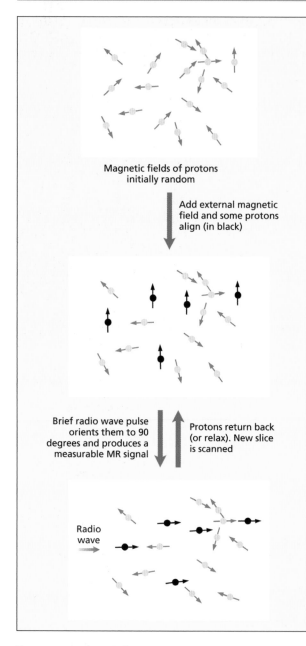

Magnetic fields of protons
initially random

Add external magnetic
field and some protons
align (in black)

Brief radio wave pulse
orients them to 90
degrees and produces a
measurable MR signal

Protons return back
(or relax). New slice
is scanned

Radio
wave

The sequence of events in
the acquisition of an MRI
scan.

90 degrees to the magnetic field, the MR signal also decays because of local interactions with nearby molecules. This is termed the T2 component. Deoxyhemoglobin produces distortions in this component and this forms the basis of the image created in functional MRI experiments (called a T2* image, "tee-two-star").

## FUNCTIONAL IMAGING

Whereas structural imaging measures the permanent characteristics of the brain, functional imaging is designed to measure the moment-to-moment variable characteristics of the brain that may be associated with changes in cognitive processing.

### Basic physiology underpinning functional imaging

The brain consumes 20 percent of the body's oxygen uptake; it does not store oxygen and it stores little glucose. Most of the brain's oxygen and energy needs are supplied from the local blood supply. When the metabolic activity of neurons increases, the blood supply to that region increases to meet the demand (for a review, see Raichle, 1987; but see Attwell & Iadecola, 2002). Techniques such as PET measure the change in blood flow to a region directly, whereas fMRI is sensitive to the concentration of oxygen in the blood. They are therefore referred to as hemodynamic methods.

## LINKING STRUCTURE TO FUNCTION BY IMAGING WHITE MATTER AND GRAY MATTER

Small scale differences (at the millimeter level) in the organization and concentration of white matter and gray matter can now be analyzed noninvasively using MRI. This is providing important clues about how individual differences in brain structure are linked to individual differences in cognition. Two important methods are **voxel-based morphometry**, or VBM, and **diffusion tensor imaging**, or DTI.

Voxel-based morphometry (VBM) capitalizes on the ability of structural MRI to detect differences between gray matter and white matter (Ashburner & Friston, 2000). VBM divides the brain into tens of thousands of small regions, several cubic millimeters in size (called voxels) and the concentration of white/gray matter in each voxel is estimated. It is then possible to use this measure to compare across individuals by asking questions such as these: If a new skill is learned, such as a second language, will gray matter density increase in some brain regions? Will it decrease in other regions? How does a particular genetic variant affect brain development? Which brain regions are larger, or smaller, in people with good social skills versus those who are less socially competent? Kanai and Rees (2011) provide a review of this method in relation to cognitive differences.

Diffusion tensor imaging (DTI) is different from VBM in that it measures the white matter connectivity between regions (Le Bihan *et al.*, 2001). (Note: VBM measures the *amount* of white matter without any consideration of how it is connected.) It is able to do this because water molecules trapped in axons tend to diffuse in some directions but not others. Specifically, a water molecule is free to travel down the length of the axon but is prevented from traveling out of the axon by the fatty membrane. When many such axons are arranged together it is possible to quantify this effect with MRI (using a measure called **fractional anisotropy**). As an example of a cognitive study using DTI, Bengtsson *et al.* (2005) found that learning to play the piano affects the development of certain white matter fibers. However, different fibers were implicated depending on whether the piano was learned during childhood, adolescence, or adulthood.

Visualization of a DTI measurement of a human brain. Depicted are reconstructed fiber tracts that run through the mid-sagittal plane.

Image by Thomas Schultz from http://upload.wikimedia.org/wikipedia/commons/8/82/DTI-sagittal-fibers.jpg.

### KEY TERMS

**Voxel-based morphometry (VBM)**
A technique for segregating and measuring differences in white matter and gray matter concentration.

**Diffusion tensor imaging (DTI)**
Uses MRI to measure white matter connectivity between brain regions.

**Fractional anisotropy (FA)**
A measure of the extent to which diffusion takes place in some directions more than others.

The brain is always physiologically active. Neurons would die if they were starved of oxygen for more than a few minutes. This has important consequences for using physiological markers as the basis of neural "activity" in functional imaging experiments. It would be meaningless to place someone in a scanner, with a view to understanding cognition, and simply observe which regions were receiving blood and using oxygen because this is a basic requirement of all neurons, all of the time. As such, when functional imaging researchers refer to a region being "active," what they mean is that the physiological response in one task is greater *relative* to some other condition. There is a basic requirement in all functional imaging studies that the physiological response must be compared with one or more baseline responses. Good experimental practice is needed to ensure that the baseline task is appropriately matched to the experimental task otherwise the results will be very hard to interpret.

It is also worth pointing out that hemodynamic methods are not measuring the activity of neurons directly but, rather, are measuring a downstream consequence of neural activity (i.e. changes in blood flow/oxygen to meet metabolic needs). This is to be contrasted with methods such as EEG (electroencephalography) and MEG (magnetoencephalography) that measure the electrical/magnetic fields generated by the activity of neurons themselves.

## Positron emission tomography

Positron emission tomography (PET) has been replaced by fMRI as the imaging method of choice. However, PET does still have a few advantages: radiolabelled pharmacological agents can be used to trace certain specific pathways, and it is less susceptible to signal distortion around the air cavities (e.g. sinuses, oral cavity) than fMRI. It is introduced briefly here, as many of the classic studies in functional imaging were based on this method.

PET uses a radioactive tracer injected into the bloodstream. The greater the blood flow in a region, the greater the signal emitted by the tracer in that region. The most commonly used tracers are oxygen-15, administered in the form of water, and fluorine-18, administered in the form of a glucose sugar. However, it is also possible to use other tracers. For example, it is possible to use radiolabeled neurotransmitters to investigate particular neural pathways and to study the effects of drugs on the brain. Volkow *et al.* (1997), for instance, were able to study how different aspects of cocaine abuse (e.g. euphoria, craving, restlessness) are implemented by different systems in the brain by administering a radiolabeled tracer with a similar profile to the drug.

When the tracer is in the bloodstream it converts back from the unstable radioactive form into the normal stable form. As it does so, it emits a particle (called a positron) that then collides with an electron, releasing two photons that can be detected by detectors positioned around the head, thus enabling a spatial image to be constructed. The positron travels 2–3 mm before collision. However, the need to average across participants in PET means that the effective spatial resolution is somewhat worse than this (about 10 mm). The spatial resolution refers to the accuracy with which one can measure *where* a cognitive event (or more accurately, a physiological change) is occurring.

In PET it takes 30 sec for the tracer to enter the brain and a further 30 sec for the radiation to peak to its maximum. This is the critical window for obtaining changes in blood flow related to cognitive activity. The temporal resolution of

PET is therefore around 30 sec. The temporal resolution refers to the accuracy with which one can measure *when* a cognitive event is occurring. Given that most cognitive events take place within a second, this is very slow indeed.

## Functional magnetic resonance imaging

Functional magnetic resonance imaging (fMRI) uses standard MRI equipment and, unlike PET, there is no need for ionizing radiation. As such, it means that participants can be retested in the scanner many times, if need be. Testing of a single participant can normally be completed in under an hour, allowing 30–40 min to complete the experiment and 10 min for a high-resolution structural MRI scan to be obtained.

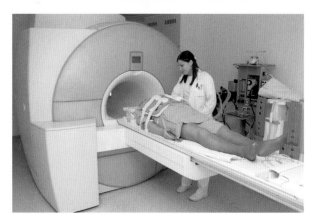

Over the last 10 years functional magnetic resonance imaging (fMRI) has overtaken PET scans in functional imaging experiments.

The component of the MR signal that is used in fMRI is sensitive to the amount of deoxyhemoglobin in the blood. When neurons consume oxygen they convert oxyhemoglobin to deoxyhemoglobin. Deoxyhemoglobin has strong paramagnetic properties and this introduces distortions in the local magnetic field. This distortion can itself be measured to give an indication of the concentration of deoxyhemoglobin present in the blood. This technique has therefore been termed **BOLD** (for blood oxygen-level-dependent contrast; Ogawa *et al.*, 1990). The way that the BOLD signal evolves over time in response to an increase in neural activity is called the **hemodynamic response function** (**HRF**). The HRF has three phases, as plotted and discussed below (see also Hoge & Pike, 2001):

1. *Initial dip.* As neurons consume oxygen there is a small rise in the amount of deoxyhemoglobin, which results in a reduction of the BOLD signal (this is not always observed in 1.5 T magnets).
2. *Overcompensation.* In response to the increased consumption of oxygen, the blood flow to the region increases. The increase in blood flow is greater than the increased consumption, which means that the BOLD signal increases significantly. This is the component that is normally measured in fMRI.

| PET | fMRI |
|---|---|
| • Based on blood volume | • Based on blood oxygen concentration |
| • Involves radioactivity (signal depends on radioactive tracer) | • No radioactivity (signal depends on deoxyhemoglobin levels) |
| • Participants scanned only once | • Participants scanned many times |
| • Temporal resolution = 30 sec | • Temporal resolution = 1–4 sec |
| • Effective spatial resolution = 10 mm | • Spatial resolution = 1 mm |
| • Must use a blocked design | • Can use either blocked or event-related design |
| • Sensitive to the whole brain | • Some brain regions (e.g. near sinuses) are hard to image |
| • Can use pharmacological tracers | |

The hemodynamic response function (HRF) has a number of distinct phases.

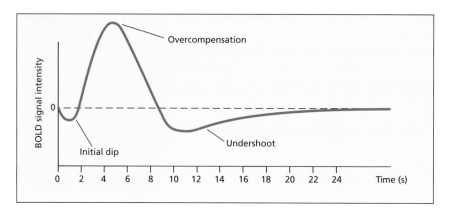

3.  *Undershoot*. Finally, the blood flow and oxygen consumption dip before returning to their original levels. This may reflect a relaxation of the venous system, causing a temporary increase in deoxyhemoglobin again.

The hemodynamic signal changes are small—approximately 1–3 percent with moderately sized magnets (1.5 T). The hemodynamic response function is relatively stable across sessions with the same participant in the same region, but is more variable across different regions within the same individual and more variable between individuals (Aguirre *et al.*, 1998).

The spatial resolution of fMRI is around 1 mm depending on the size of the voxel. The temporal resolution of fMRI is several seconds and related to the rather sluggish hemodynamic response. This allows the use of event-related designs (see later), but it is still slow compared with the speed at which cognitive processes take place. In fMRI the sluggishness of the hemodynamic response to peak and then return to baseline does place some constraints on the way that stimuli are presented in the scanning environment that differ from equivalent tasks done outside the scanner. However, it is not the case that one has to wait for the BOLD response to return to baseline before presenting another trial, as different HRFs can be superimposed on each other (Dale & Buckner, 1997). In general during

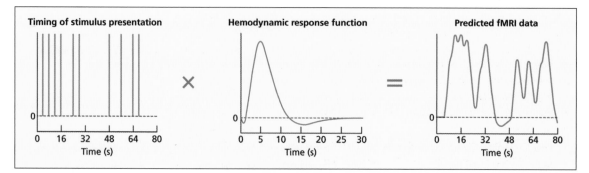

Unless the stimuli are presented far apart in time (e.g. every 16 sec) the predicted change in BOLD response will not resemble a single HRF but will resemble many superimposed HRFs. Statistically, the analysis is trying to find out which voxels in the brain show the predicted changes in the BOLD response over time, given the known design of the experiment and the estimated shape of the HRF. To achieve this there has to be sufficient variability in the predicted BOLD response (big peaks and troughs).

fMRI, there may be fewer trials that are more spaced out in time than standard cognitive testing, and it is common to have "null events" (e.g. a blank screen). These null events allow the BOLD signal to dip toward baseline, essentially providing the necessary variability in the signal needed for the analysis. In standard cognitive psychology experiments (e.g. using response time measures) the amount of data is effectively the same as the number of *trials and responses*. In the equivalent fMRI experiment, the amount of data is related to the number of *brain volumes* acquired rather than the number of trials or responses.

## FROM IMAGE TO COGNITIVE THEORY: EXPERIMENTAL DESIGN

### An example of cognitive subtraction methodology

One of the groundbreaking studies for establishing the use of functional imaging of cognition was that by Petersen *et al.* (1988), which was designed to look for brain regions specialized for the processing of written and spoken words. A consideration of this study provides a good introduction to the principle of **cognitive subtraction**. The idea behind cognitive subtraction is that, by comparing the activity of the brain in a task that utilizes a particular cognitive component (e.g. the visual lexicon) to the activity of the brain in a baseline task that does not, it is possible to infer which regions are specialized for this particular cognitive component. As has been noted, the brain is always active in the physiological sense and so it is not possible to infer from a single task which regions are dedicated to specific aspects of the task; a comparison between two or more tasks or conditions is always needed.

Let's consider the different processes involved with reading and understanding isolated written words. A simple model of written word recognition is given below, which forms the motivation for the imaging study to be described. The study by Petersen *et al.* (1988) was concerned with identifying brain regions involved with: (1) recognizing written words; (2) saying the words; and (3) retrieving the meaning of the words. To do this, the researchers performed a number of cognitive subtractions.

To work out which regions are involved with recognizing written words, Petersen *et al.* compared brain activity when passively viewing words (e.g. CAKE) with passively viewing a cross (+) (see diagram on the next page). The logic is that both experimental and baseline tasks involve visual processing (and so a subtraction should cancel this out), but only the experimental task involves visual word recognition (so this should remain after subtraction).

To work out which regions are involved with producing spoken words they compared passive viewing of written words (see CAKE) with reading aloud the word (see CAKE, say "cake"). In this instance, both experimental and baseline tasks involve visual processing of the word and word recognition (so subtracting

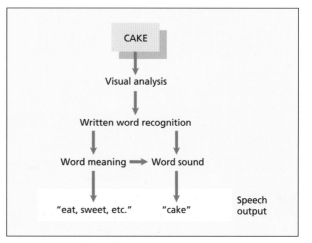

Basic cognitive stages involved in reading written words aloud and producing spoken semantic associates to written words.

should cancel these out), but only the experimental task involves spoken output (so activity associated with this should remain after subtraction).

To work out which regions are involved with retrieving the meaning of written words, they compared a verb-generation task (e.g. see CAKE, say "eat") with reading aloud (e.g. see CAKE, say "cake"). In this instance, both experimental and baseline tasks involve visual processing, word recognition and spoken output (so subtracting should cancel out the activity associated with these processes), but only the experimental task involves generating a semantic associate (so activity associated with this should remain after subtraction).

The results of these subtractions show activity in a number of different sites. Only the principal sites on the left lateral hemisphere are depicted in the diagram. Recognizing written words activates bilateral sites in the visual (striate) cortex as well as a site on the left occipitotemporal junction. Producing speech output in the reading aloud condition activates the sensorimotor cortex bilaterally, whereas verb generation activates the left inferior frontal gyrus. This last result has provoked some controversy because of an apparent discrepancy from lesion data; this is discussed later.

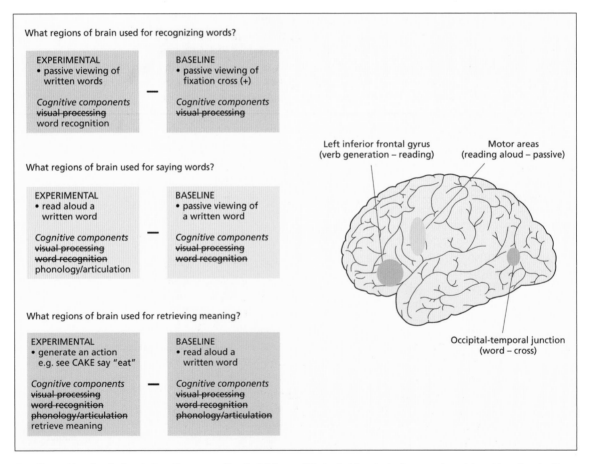

Cognitive subtraction is founded on the assumption that it is possible to find two tasks (an experimental and baseline task) that differ in terms of a small number of cognitive components. The results show several regions of activity, but only the main results on the left lateral surface are depicted here.

## Problems with cognitive subtraction

With the benefit of hindsight, there are a number of difficulties with this study, some of which are related to the particular choice of baseline tasks that were employed. However, there are also more general problems with the method of cognitive subtraction itself (Friston *et al.*, 1996). Consider the subtraction aimed at identifying brain regions associated with written word recognition. The assumption here was that both tasks involve visual processing but that one has the added component of word recognition. That is, one assumes that adding an extra component does not affect the operation of earlier ones in the sequence. This is referred to as the assumption of **pure insertion** (or pure deletion). It could be that the type or amount of visual processing that deals with written words is not the same as for non-linguistic vision. The fact that the visual information presented in the baseline task (viewing a cross, +) was simpler than in the experimental task makes this a real possibility. However, a more basic problem is common to all functional imaging experiments that employ this methodology. The addition of an extra component in the task has the potential to change the operation of other components in the task. That is, **interactions** are possible that make the imaging data, at best, ambiguous. The next sections consider other types of design that allow one to eliminate or even directly study these interactions.

The choice of baseline is crucial in imaging experiments and can have substantial impacts on the data that is obtained. Ideally, the baseline should be as similar to the experimental task as possible. For example, to find brain regions involved with producing spoken words, Petersen *et al.* (1988) compared reading aloud with viewing of written words. This is likely to involve several stages of processing. It will involve retrieving the word from the brain's store of vocabulary (the mental lexicon), preparing and executing a motor command (to speak) and also listening to what was said. The pattern of activity observed is therefore ambiguous with regards to linking a precise cognitive function with brain structure. Another baseline that could be used is to get the participant to articulate generic verbal responses, such as saying the word "yes" whenever a word comes up (Price *et al.*, 1996a). This would enable one to study the lexical retrieval component while factoring out the articulation and auditory feedback components.

In summary, functional imaging requires comparisons to be made between different conditions because the brain is always physiologically active. Regions of "activity" can only be meaningfully interpreted relative to a baseline, and the selection of an appropriate baseline requires a good cognitive theory of the elements that comprise the task. The simplest way of achieving this is the method of cognitive subtraction that compares activity in an experimental task with activity in a closely matched baseline task. However, the main problem with cognitive subtraction is that it assumes that a cognitive component can be added on to a task without changing the other components in the task (the problem of pure insertion). Adding a new component to a task may interact with existing components and this interaction may show up as a region of activity. Other types of experimental design that reduce this particular problem have been developed and are discussed in the next section.

**KEY TERM**

**Efference copy**
A motor signal used
to predict sensory
consequences of an
action.

# Cognitive conjunctions and factorial designs

The method of cognitive conjunction requires that one is able to identify a set of tasks that has a particular component in common. One can then look for regions of activation that are shared across several different subtractions rather than relying on a single subtraction. A baseline task (or tasks) is still required, but the problem of interactions can be reduced. This is because the interaction terms will be different for each pair of subtractions.

Let's consider one concrete example from the literature: why can't we tickle ourselves? Tactile sensations applied to the skin are rated as less ticklish if produced by oneself relative to if they are elicited by another person. The key to explaining this lies in the fact that it is possible to predict the sensory consequences of our own actions. The motor commands that we generate specify where and when the touch will occur and the manner of the touch (e.g. a rough or gentle tickle). This information can then be used to predict what the action will feel like. Thus a representation of the motor command (a so-called **efference copy**) is sent to the relevant sensory area, touch in this example, so that the perceptual system knows what to expect. This may help the brain to prioritize incoming sensory

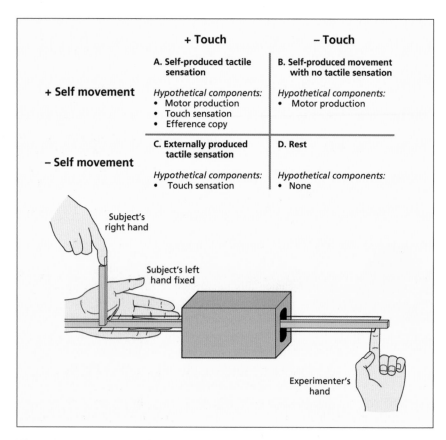

Why can't we tickle ourselves? Self-produced touches (condition A) are less tickly because we can predict their sensory consequences using an "efference copy" of the motor command.

Bottom diagram adapted from Blakemore *et al.*, 1998. © 1998 Elsevier.
Reproduced with permission.

information toward the most relevant stimuli in the environment. Being touched by someone or something else is arguably more important to the organism in terms of detecting potential threats than being touched by oneself.

To investigate this, Blakemore *et al.* (1998) set up a factorial design with two factors. The first factor was whether a tactile stimulus was felt; the second factor was whether the participants moved their arm. The experiment involved moving a felt rod that tickled the palm. The rod could be moved either by the experimenter or the participant. It could either make contact with the palm or miss it altogether. In total, this produced four experimental conditions, which have been labeled A to D in the figure.

Before going on to consider the neural basis of the less tickly sensation associated with condition A (hypothetically due to an efference copy), one can perform two cognitive conjunctions to identify regions involved in motor production and the tactile sensation per se. Consider the two pairs of subtractions, A − B and C − D. If one asks the question, "What regions do these subtractions have in common [i.e. (A − B) and (C − D)]?", then this can isolate regions involved in tactile sensation. The experiment found activity in the primary and secondary somatosensory cortex in the hemisphere opposite the hand that was stimulated. Consider the two pairs of subtractions, A − C and B − D. If one asks the question, "What regions do these subtractions have in common [i.e. (A − C) and (B − D)]?", then this can isolate regions involved in motor production. In this analysis, the experiment found several active regions, including primary motor, premotor and prefrontal regions. In terms of methodology, the key point to note is that both of these results are based on conjunctions between two different tasks and baselines and this is sufficient to minimize the problem of pure insertion faced by using a single subtraction alone.

However, these conjunction analyses do not enable one to analyze the neural basis of the efference copy or the reduced ticklishness when self-produced. To find this out, one can examine the interaction directly by performing the following analysis: (A − B) − (C − D). This effectively asks the question: is the difference between A and B more (or less) than the difference between C and D (an interaction is simply a difference of differences)? In the present example, it would ask whether the effect of touch is greater in the presence of self-movement than in the presence of other-movement. Blakemore *et al.* (1998) report that there was decreased activity in the somatosensory cortex. This is likely to be the neural correlate of reduced ticklishness. There were also changes in cerebellum activity that were not found in any other condition and were interpreted as the neural correlate of the efference copy that links self-movement with touch.

## Parametric designs

The main difference between a parametric design and a categorical design is that, in a parametric design, the variable of interest is treated as a continuous dimension rather than a categorical distinction (Friston, 1997). In intuitive terms, one is measuring *associations* between brain activity and changes in the variable of interest, rather than measuring *differences* in brain activity between two or more conditions. Thus, one is ultimately likely to use correlations (or similar) to analyze data collected using a parametric design.

Price *et al.* (1992) conducted an imaging study in which participants listened passively to lists of spoken words spoken at six different rates between 0 words

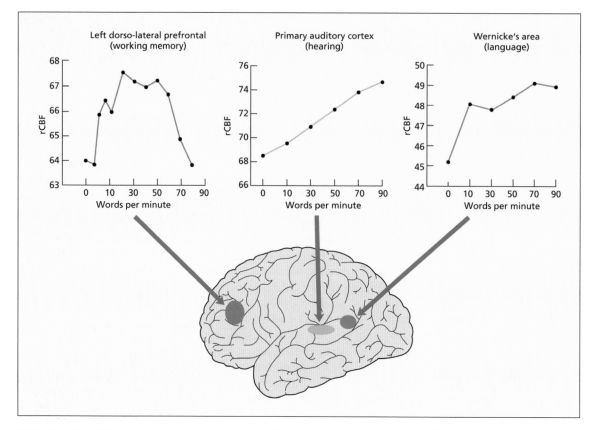

Different regions of the brain respond to changes in speech rate (words per minute, wpm) in different ways. Note that 0 wpm is equivalent to rest. rCBF = regional cerebral blood flow.

Adapted from Price *et al.*, 1992, and Friston, 1997.

per minute (i.e. silence, or rest) and 90 words per minute. The change in activity in various regions could then be correlated with the rate of speech. Note that in a parametric design such as this, a separate baseline condition is not necessary (the effects are evaluated globally across all levels of the factor). In terms of the results, a number of interesting findings were observed. In areas involved in auditory *perception* (e.g. the primary auditory cortex), the faster the speech rate, the greater the activity. However, in regions involved in non-acoustic processing of *language* (e.g. Wernicke's area), the activity was related to the presence of words irrespective of speech rate. In a region often associated with verbal *working memory* (the left dorsolateral prefrontal cortex), a more complex picture was found (Friston, 1997). Activity increased with speech rate but then decreased as the speech rate got faster (an inverted-U function). It suggests that the region has an optimal level at which it functions, beyond which it fails to keep up. This is consistent with the notion of working memory having a limited capacity. One interesting point to note is that, if the experimenters had compared 20 words per minute with 50 words per minute in a cognitive subtraction or a factorial design, this region would not have appeared to be implicated in the task.

# Functional integration

Most of the functional imaging studies described in this book could be labeled as studies of *functional specialization*. Functional specialization implies that a region responds to a limited range of stimuli/conditions and that this distinguishes it from the responsiveness of other neighboring regions. It is not strictly the same as *localization*, in that it is not necessary to assume that the region is solely responsible for performance on a given task or to assume that other regions may not also respond to the same stimuli/conditions (Phillips *et al.*, 1984). **Functional integration**, on the other hand, refers to the way in which different regions communicate with each other. This is likely to be essential for a full understanding of how cognition is linked to the brain, and also for dismissing claims that functional imaging is a new phrenology (Friston, 2002; Horwitz *et al.*, 1999).

The basic approach of functional integration is to model how activity in different regions is interdependent. This is used to infer the *effective connectivity* or *functional connectivity* between regions when performing a task (these methods use techniques such as structural equation modeling and principal components analysis, which are beyond the scope of the present discussion). If parametric designs correlate brain activity with some cognitive/behavioral measure, then designs employing functional integration correlate different regions of brain activity with each other. To give a concrete example, Friston and Frith (1995) conducted an imaging study with a 2 × 2 factorial design with task instruction as one factor (generate words beginning with "A" versus repeating letters) and subject group as the other factor (participants either had or had not been diagnosed as schizophrenic). Although both groups showed a number of similar frontal and temporal lobe activities, there was a strong correlation between activity in these regions in controls and a striking absence of correlation in the schizophrenics. Friston and Frith argued that schizophrenia is best characterized in terms of a failure of communication between distant brain regions (i.e. a functional disconnection).

One commonly used procedure for measuring functional integration does not use any task at all. These are known as **resting state paradigms**. Participants are merely asked to lie back and rest. In the absence of a task, the fluctuations in brain activity are little more than noise. However, in brain regions that are functionally connected the noise levels tend to correlate together. This has enabled researchers to identify sets of networks in the brain, consisting of spatially separated regions, for which fluctuations in activity tend to be shared (Damoiseaux *et al.*, 2006). For instance, one commonly studied network is called the **default mode network** of the brain and is implicated in internalized thoughts: for instance, it tends to be more active when *not* engaged in an experimental task (Raichle *et al.*, 2001). Differences in the way that these networks operate and are constructed are found in various conditions such as schizophrenia and autism (Buckner *et al.*, 2008).

## Event-related versus blocked designs

A separate issue as to the choice of experimental design (e.g. categorical versus parametric) is how the different stimuli will be ordered. Broadly speaking, there are two choices. First, stimuli that belong together in one condition could be grouped together. This is termed a **block design**. Second, different stimuli or conditions could be interspersed with each other. This is termed an **event-related design**. In an event-related design the different intermingled conditions are subsequently separated out for the purpose of analysis.

**KEY TERMS**

**Functional integration**
The way in which different regions communicate with each other.

**Resting state paradigm**
A technique for measuring functional connectivity in which correlations between several regions (networks) are assessed while the participant is not performing any tasks.

**Default mode network**
A set of brain regions that is more hemodynamically active during rest than during tasks.

**Block design**
Stimuli from a given condition are presented consecutively together.

**Event-related design**
Stimuli from two or more conditions are presented randomly or interleaved.

## SAFETY AND ETHICAL ISSUES IN FUNCTIONAL IMAGING RESEARCH

It is essential to be aware of the local regulations that apply in your own institution but the following points generally apply:

### What are the risks of taking part in functional imaging experiments?

The risks are small (PET) or negligible (fMRI). The risk from PET comes from the fact that it uses a small amount of radioactivity. The amount of radioactivity from a PET scan is equivalent to around 1–3 years of annual background radioactivity. fMRI does not use radiation and the same participants can take part in multiple experiments. Participants wear ear protectors, given that the scanner noise is very loud. Larger magnets (> 3 T) can be associated with dizziness and nausea, and participants need to enter the field gradually to prevent this.

### Are some people excluded from taking part in functional imaging experiments?

Before entering the scanner, all participants should be given a checklist that asks them about their current and past health. Pregnant women and children cannot take part in PET studies because of the use of radiation. People with metal body parts, cochlear implants, embedded shrapnel or pacemakers will not be allowed to take part in fMRI experiments. In larger magnets, eye make-up should not be worn (it can heat up, causing symptoms similar to sunburn) and women wearing contraceptive coils should not be tested. Before going into the scanner both the researcher and participant should put to one side all metal objects such as keys, jewelry and coins, as well as credit cards, which would be wiped by the magnet. Zips and metal buttons are generally okay, but metal spectacle frames should be avoided. It is important to check that participants do not suffer from claustrophobia as they will be in a confined space for some time. Participants have a rubber ball that can be squeezed to signal an alarm to the experimenter, who can terminate the experiment if necessary.

### What happens if a brain abnormality is detected during scanning?

There is always a very small possibility that a brain tumor or some other unsuspected abnormality could be detected during the course of the study. In such instances, the researcher has a duty to double-check this by inviting the participant back for a subsequent scan. Potential abnormalities are followed up by a neurologist (or a clinically qualified member of staff), who would inform the participant and their doctor, if needs be. Wolf et al. (2008) provide a set of ethics concerning the incidental discovery of abnormalities during non-clinical scanning.

### How can I find up-to-date details about safety in fMRI experiments?

The standard safety reference is by Shellock (2014), and updates can be found at: www.magneticresonancesafetytesting.com.

In fMRI, the advantage of block designs over event-related ones is that the method has more power; that is, it is more able to detect significant but small effects (Josephs & Henson, 1999). The advantage of event-related designs over blocked ones is that they enable a much wider range of experimental designs and are more closely related to the typical design structure of most cognitive psychology experiments. Certain types of empirical question can be adequately addressed only with event-related designs. In some instances, there is no way of knowing in advance how events should be grouped and so block designs are impossible. For example, one event-related fMRI study investigated participants in a tip-of-the-tongue state (Maril *et al.* 2001). In this state people are unable to retrieve a name (e.g. the capital of Peru) but have a strong certainty of knowing the answer. In a typical experiment, responses fall into three categories (known, unknown and tip-of-the-tongue). These are defined by each participant and cannot be blocked together at the outset. To give another example of events being defined by a participant, Ffytche *et al.* (1998) studied spontaneously occurring visual hallucinations in patients with progressive blindness. The patients lifted their finger when a hallucination occurred and lowered it when it disappeared. The neural signal in the "on" phase could then be contrasted with the "off" phase. Finally, some events cannot be blocked because the task requires that they are unexpected and occur infrequently.

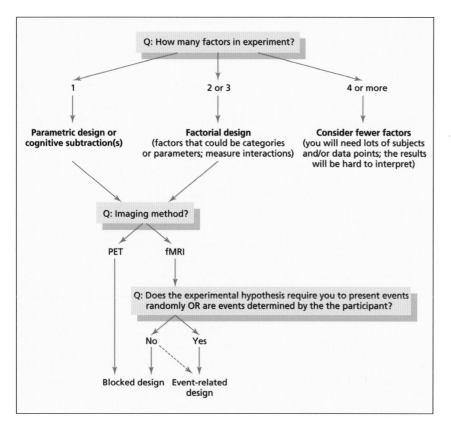

Setting up a functional imaging experiment requires asking oneself a number of questions, and making assumptions about the most appropriate method. This flowchart is intended to be useful rather than prescriptive.

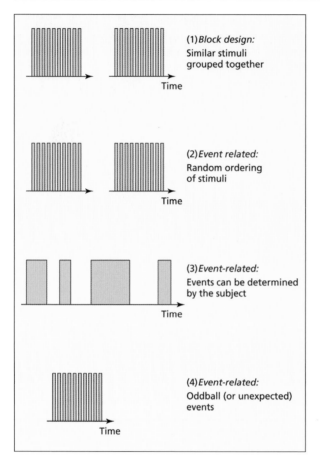

A comparison of block designs versus event-related designs. The purple and green bars could represent different types of stimuli, conditions or task.

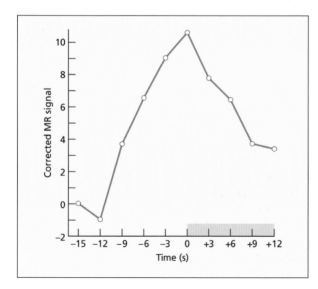

## Evaluation

A number of different methods are available for setting up experiments in functional imaging. The main consideration is that the method should be appropriate for the hypothesis being tested (and the level of detail of the hypothesis will vary considerably). Having said this, the diagram on p. 65 offers a number of general points to consider and some suggested outcomes. Note that different labs may have other established methods and that the field itself is developing new methods all the time.

## ANALYZING DATA FROM FUNCTIONAL IMAGING

The images of brains with superimposed colored blobs are the outcome of several stages of data processing and statistical analysis. In fact, these images are not literal pictures of the workings of the brain at all. What these images depict are the regions of the brain that are computed to be statistically significant given the type of design used. Functional imaging is a statistical science and, as such, is susceptible to error. Although different laboratories use different packages to analyze their data, the challenges faced in analyzing and interpreting functional imaging data are common to them all (for a detailed discussion, see Petersson *et al.*, 1999a, 1999b).

A central problem faced in the analysis of functional imaging data is how to deal with individual differences. Although the gross brain structure does not differ considerably from one person to the next, there are nevertheless significant individual differences in the size of gyri and the location of folds in the brain. For example, the

A hemodynamic response function related to the onset of visual hallucinations (at 0 s, shown by purple bar). This is derived by averaging together a number of hallucinations involving visual regions of the brain. Note how the brain activity precedes the onset of the conscious experience by as much as 12 s. An example of a reported hallucination is as follows: "colored shiny shapes like futuristic cars or objects found in the pyramids. The shapes contained edges within them and did not look like real objects."

From Ffytch *et al.*, 1998. Reprinted by permission of Macmillan Publishers Ltd. © 1998.

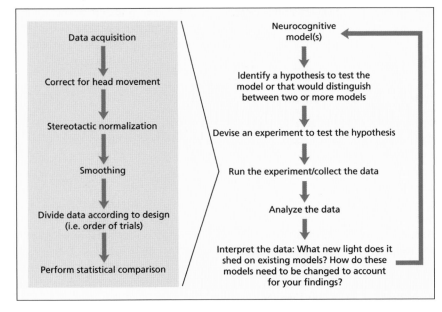

The main stages of analyzing data in a functional imaging experiment.

location of sulci can vary between people by a centimeter or more (Thompson *et al.*, 1996).

The most common way of dealing with individual differences is effectively to assume that they do not exist. Or, more properly put, individual differences needn't get in the way of making claims about general brain function. Individual differences are minimized by averaging data over many participants, and one is left with regions of activity that are common to most of us. Before this averaging process can occur, the data from each individual needs to be modified in a number of ways. First, each brain is mapped onto a standard reference brain (called **stereotactic normalization**). This is followed by a process called **smoothing**, which can enhance the signal-to-noise ratio and facilitates detection of common regions of activity across individuals. A flow diagram summarizes the sequence from initial hypothesis to data interpretation that typically occurs in a functional imaging experiment. These main stages will be considered in turn.

## Correction for head movement

Perhaps the biggest advantage of the fMRI technique over others is its good spatial resolution. It is able to identify differences in activity over millimeter distances (although this resolution still entails millions of neurons). However, there is a downside to this; namely, that small spatial distortions can produce spurious results. One key problem that has already been noted is that every brain differs spatially in terms of size and shape. The process of stereotactic normalization attempts to correct for this. A different problem is that each person's head might be aligned slightly differently in the scanner over time. If a person wriggles or moves the head in the scanner, then the position of any active region will also move around. This could either result in the region being harder to detect (because the activity is being spread around) or a false-positive result could be obtained (because head movements may appear to shift an active region between consecutive conditions). It is for this reason that the collected data are corrected for head movement (Brammer, 2001), which is minimized in the first place by physically restraining the head in position, and instructing participants to keep as still as possible.

## Stereotactic normalization

The process of stereotactic normalization involves mapping regions on each individual brain onto a standard brain. Each brain is divided up into thousands of small volumes, called **voxels** (volume elements). Each voxel can be given three-dimensional spatial coordinates (x, y, z). This enables every x, y, z coordinate on a brain to be mapped onto the corresponding x, y, z coordinate on any other brain. Basically, the template of each brain is squashed or stretched (by applying mathematical transformations that entail an optimal solution) to fit into the standard space. The standard space that is used to report functional imaging data across most laboratories in the world is provided by the brain atlas of Talairach and Tournoux (1988). Each point in the brain is assigned a three-dimensional x, y, z coordinate (commonly referred to as the **Talairach coordinates**) with the origin lying at a region called the anterior commissure (small and easily seen in most scans). The x-coordinate refers to left and right (left is negative and right is positive). The y-coordinate refers to front and back (front/anterior is positive and back/posterior is negative) and the z-coordinate refers to top and bottom (top is positive and bottom is negative). This atlas is based on anatomical data from a single post-mortem brain. However, rather than relying on comparisons to this single brain, many contemporary studies use a template based on an average of 305 brains provided by the Montreal Neurological Institute (Collins *et al.* 1994). This averaged template is then put into Talairach coordinates and used in favor of the single brain originally described in that atlas.

Smoothing spreads the activity across voxels—some voxels (e.g. D4) may be enhanced whereas others (e.g. L8) may be reduced.

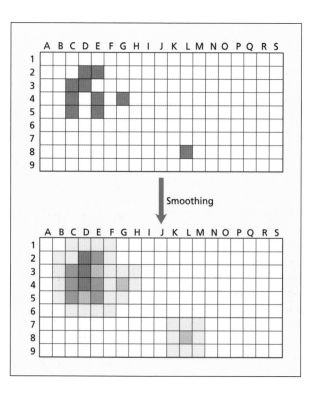

## Smoothing

After each brain has been transformed into this standard space, further stages of preprocessing *may* take place before a statistical analysis. The process of "smoothing" sounds like it could waste important information, but it is an important part of data manipulation. Smoothing spreads some of the raw activation level of a given voxel to neighboring voxels. The closer the neighbor is, the more activation it gets (the mathematically minded might be interested to know that the function used is a Gaussian or normal distribution centered on each voxel). In the figure, the darker the square, the more active it is. Consider voxel D4. Prior to smoothing, this voxel is inactive, but because it has many active neighbors the voxel gets "switched on" by the smoothing process. In contrast, consider voxel L8. This voxel is initially active but, because it has inactive neighbors, it gets "switched off" by the smoothing process. Smoothing thus enhances the signal-to-noise ratio. In this instance, one assumes that the signal (i.e. the thing of interest) corresponds to the larger cluster of activity and the noise is the isolated voxel. Neighboring voxels that are active mutually reinforce each other and the spatial extent (i.e. size) of the active region is increased. If the brain happened to implement cognition using a mosaic of non-adjacent voxels, then smoothing would work against detecting such a system. There are, however, some statistical techniques (such as multi-voxel pattern analysis, MVPA) that can be used to analyze this kind of neural representation that do not require smoothing (Norman *et al.* 2006). This is considered later.

As well as enhancing the signal-to-noise ratio, smoothing offers an additional advantage for analyzing groups of participants. Smoothing increases the spatial extent of active regions. As such, when averaging the activity across individuals there is a greater chance of finding common regions of activity. Of course, if individual differences are the focus of the study, then one may justifiably choose not to smooth the data at all.

## Statistical comparison

After the data have been stereotactically normalized, smoothed and corrected for head movement, it is possible to perform a statistical analysis. The standard way to do this is to ask the question: "Is the mean activity at a particular voxel in the experimental condition greater than in the baseline condition?" The same types of statistical test as would be employed in any psychology experiment can be used in functional imaging (e.g. a *t*-test to compare means). But there are complications. In most psychology experiments one would typically have, at most, only a handful of means to compare. In functional imaging, each brain slice is divided up into tens of thousands of voxels and each one needs to be considered. If one uses the standard psychology significance level of $P < 0.05$, then there would be thousands of brain voxels active just by chance. (Recall that the significance level represents the probability ($P$) at which one is willing to say that a result is more than just a chance occurrence. The value of 0.05 represents a 1 in 20 chance level.) How could one prevent lots of brain regions being active by chance? One could have a more conservative criteria (i.e. a lower significance level), but the danger is that this will not detect regions that are important (this is termed a type I error). An analogy here would be trying to count islands by lowering or raising the sea level. If the sea level is too high, there are no islands to observe. If the sea level is too low, there are islands everywhere. One could divide the nominal $P$ value (0.05) by the number of tests (i.e. voxels)—a so-called Bonferroni correction. A difficulty with this approach is that the activity at each voxel is not independent: neighboring voxels tend to have similar activity, particularly if smoothed. This has led to the development of sophisticated mathematical models of choosing a statistical threshold, based on spatial smoothness (so-called *random field theory*). This general method of correction is termed **Family Wise Error** (FWE). Other researchers generate thousands of random brain images (e.g. by permuting the data) and select a threshold (e.g. $P < 0.05$) based on random datasets. This method of correction is termed the **False Discovery Rate** (FDR). In this method a more conservative statistical threshold would be used for datasets in which lots of voxels are active than in a dataset in which only few voxels are active.

### KEY TERMS

**Family Wise Error (FWE)**
An approach for correcting for many statistical comparisons based on the number of tests being conducted.

**False Discovery Rate (FDR)**
An approach for correcting for many statistical comparisons based on the number of positive results obtained.

When reading papers that have used functional imaging methods, one sometimes observes that they report different significance levels that are "corrected" or "uncorrected." Why is this done and is it acceptable? A corrected level implies that a more conservative criterion has been used to prevent detecting lots of regions just by chance. However, if the interest is in *one* particular voxel, then it is possible to use an uncorrected significance level (e.g. the standard $P < 0.05$) because in this instance there are not multiple comparisons over lots of brain regions. Other procedures are used when investigating effects in a predetermined region covering several voxels (a so-called *small volume correction*).

## INTERPRETING DATA FROM FUNCTIONAL IMAGING

What does it mean to say that a brain region is active in a functional imaging experiment? Literally speaking, what this means is that the signal from that region (the BOLD signal in fMRI) is greater in one condition than in other conditions that are being compared (whether in a categorical design, parametric design or whatever). There are several reasons why a region may be active and not all of them are theoretically interesting. Importantly, it need not imply that the particular region is essential for the task. Alternative accounts include: an increase in signal could reflect the strategy that the participants happen to adopt, it could reflect use of some general mechanism (e.g. increased attention) that is not specific to the task, or it could reflect the fact that a region is receiving input but is not responding to the input (i.e. **inhibition**). These competing scenarios can only be ruled out with more rigorous experimentation. Chance occurrences can be ruled out by replicating the results and the necessity of a region for a task can be determined using lesion methods. This is discussed in more detail below.

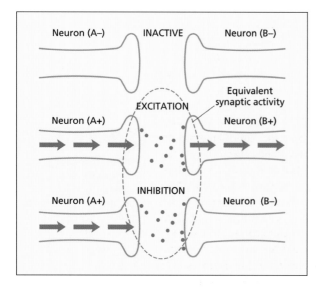

Excitatory and inhibitory synaptic connections both involve metabolic activity and thus an inhibited region could be mistakenly interpreted as a region of activity.

### Inhibition versus excitation

Functional imaging signals are assumed to be correlated with the metabolic activity of neurons, and synapses in particular (see Jueptner & Weiller, 1995). However, neurons can be metabolically active by virtue of both inhibitory interactions (when the presynaptic neuron is active, the postsynaptic neuron is switched off) and **excitations** (when the presynaptic neuron is active, the postsynaptic neuron is switched on). Most connections are excitatory in nature. Logothetis *et al.* (2001) demonstrated that the BOLD signal used in fMRI is more sensitive to the neuronal input into a region rather than the output from the region. Thus, regions that "listen" to other active regions but do not themselves respond to it could appear as areas of activation.

It is unclear whether functional imaging can distinguish between these two types of neural function since both are assumed to be associated with similar physiological changes.

## Activation versus deactivation

Activation and deactivation simply refer to the sign (positive or negative) of the difference in signal between two conditions. This is not to be confused with **excitation**/inhibition that refers to the nature of the mechanism by which neurons communicate. If the subtraction (Task A) – (Task B) is performed, there could be a set of regions that show a significant positive effect (i.e. "**activation**") because they are used more in Task A than in Task B, and there could also be a set of regions that show a significant negative effect (i.e. "**deactivation**") because they are more active in Task B than in Task A. Of course, if one had done the subtraction (Task B) – (Task A), then the same regions would be identified, but the positive and negative signs would merely swap. Thus, the terms activation and deactivation merely refer to whether there is a difference in signal between conditions and the direction of that difference. The question of *why* there is a difference is open to theoretical interpretation. If the baseline task is very different from the experimental conditions, the activations and deactivations may be very hard to interpret.

## Necessity versus sufficiency

In an intriguingly titled paper, "If neuroimaging is the answer, what is the question?", Kosslyn (1999) sets out some of the reasons why functional imaging has its limitations. One particular point that will be picked up on here is the notion that some of the regions that appear active may indeed be used during performance of the task but yet might not be critical to the task. For example, a region may appear to be active because of a particular strategy that the participants adopted, even though other strategies might be available. It could also be the case that the tasks being compared differ in some other, more general, way. For example, if one task is harder than the other it could demand more attention, and this demanding of attention would have its own neural correlate. Although paying more attention could certainly help with the performing of the task, it may not in and of itself be crucial for performing the task. As such, it has been claimed that functional imaging gives us a better idea of which regions may be sufficient for performing a particular task but not always which regions are crucial and necessary for performing a task.

The value of functional imaging data is likely to be enhanced when it is used in conjunction with other methods. One early benefit of functional imaging was mooted to be that it could replace lesion-based neuropsychology. However, this is unlikely to happen because the logic of inference is different in these two methods, as illustrated on p. 72. In lesion-based neuropsychology, the location of the lesion is manipulated (or selected for in a patient sample) and the resulting behavior is observed. In doing this, a causal connection is assumed between the lesion and the ensuing behavior. In functional imaging the reverse is true. In this instance, the task given to participants in the scanner is manipulated and changes in brain regions are observed. Although some of these changes are likely to be critically related to the performance of the task, other changes may be incidental to it. It is for this reason that functional imaging is unlikely to supplant the traditional lesion-based approach. The next section discusses in more detail how divergent results between imaging and neuropsychology could be reconciled.

**KEY TERMS**

**Activation**
An increase in physiological processing in one condition relative to some other condition(s).

**Deactivation**
A decrease in physiological processing in one condition relative to some other condition(s).

Functional brain imaging and lesion-deficit analysis of patients (or TMS, see Chapter 5) are logically different types of methodology. It is unlikely that one will supplant the other.

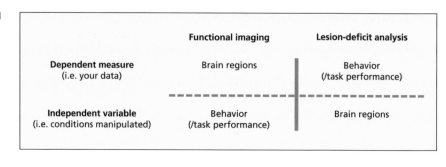

| | Functional imaging | Lesion-deficit analysis |
|---|---|---|
| **Dependent measure** (i.e. your data) | Brain regions | Behavior (/task performance) |
| **Independent variable** (i.e. conditions manipulated) | Behavior (/task performance) | Brain regions |

## WHY DO FUNCTIONAL IMAGING DATA SOMETIMES DISAGREE WITH LESION DATA?

There are two broad scenarios in which functional imaging data and lesion-deficit data can disagree. These are listed below, together with possible ways of resolving the disagreement, as described in the following box.

**Disagreement 1:** Imaging data imply that a brain region is used in a given task, but lesion data suggest that this region is not essential to the task (imaging +, lesion –)

Possible reasons for disagreement:

- The activated region reflects a particular strategy adopted by the participants that is not essential to performing the task.
- The activated region reflects the recruitment of some general cognitive resource (e.g. due to increased task difficulty, attention or arousal) that is not specific to the task.
- The activated region is being inhibited (i.e. switched off) rather than excited (i.e. switched on).
- The lesion studies have not been powerful enough to detect the importance of the region (e.g. too few patients, lesion not in correct location, tasks used with patients not the same as those used in imaging).

**Disagreement 2:** Imaging data imply that a brain region is not used in a given task, but lesion data suggest that this region is critical to the task (imaging –, lesion +)

Possible reasons for disagreement:

- If the experimental task and baseline task both depend critically on this region, then a comparison between them might produce an artifactual null result.
- It might be intrinsically hard to detect activity in this region of the brain (e.g. it is a very small region, it is in different places in different individuals or genuine activity produces a small signal change).
- The impaired performance after lesion reflects damage to tracts passing through the region rather than the synaptic activity in the gray matter of the region itself.

The above discussion thus highlights the fact that disagreements between results from functional imaging and results from lesion data could lie with imaging results, with the lesion results, or with both. There is no magic solution for resolving the disagreements except through more rigorous experimentation. Each method has some relative merit. As such, disagreements should be viewed as something that is potentially of theoretical interest rather than dismissed as a failure of one or other method (Henson, 2005). To provide a feel for how this might be achieved, the next section considers a concrete example from the literature.

## Having your cake and eating it

A small proportion of unfortunate people in later life start to lose the meanings of words and objects that they previously understood. This deterioration can spare, at least in the early stages, memory for events, calculation abilities, and syntax, among other things (e.g. Hodges *et al.*, 1992). These patients would probably be given a diagnosis of **semantic dementia**, because their functional lesion is primarily in the **semantic memory** system that stores the meaning of words and objects. Where are the anatomical lesions in these patients? Lesion studies based on voxel-based morphometry (VBM) have shown that the degree of semantic memory impairment is correlated with the amount of atrophy in the left anterior temporal lobe (Mummery *et al.*, 2000). Given this finding, it would be encouraging if functional imaging studies also activated this particular region when healthy (non-brain-damaged) people are given semantic memory tasks. However, this has not always been the case and a number of studies have reliably shown activation in a different region—the left inferior frontal gyrus (also referred to as the ventrolateral prefrontal cortex). How can these divergent results be explained? It will be argued that a more careful comparison of the tasks used can account for this divergence and reveals, in turn, more about how the brain supports semantic memory.

One of the first ever functional imaging studies of cognition tried to address the question of where semantic memories are stored. As already discussed, Petersen *et al.* (1988) compared brain activation in two tasks: verb generation (e.g. the participant sees CAKE and says "eat") and reading aloud (e.g. the participant sees CAKE and says "cake"). The verb-generation task is assumed to tap semantic memory more than the reading task. However, a comparison of the two tasks shows activity in regions of the left inferior frontal gyrus, but not in the same regions that are associated with semantic memory loss. Is the imaging data or the lesion data to be believed? Could it be the case that the left inferior frontal gyrus is really involved in semantic memory? To test this hypothesis, instead of taking a group of patients with semantic memory difficulties and asking where the lesion is, one would need to take a group of patients with selective lesions to the left inferior frontal gyrus and give them the

**KEY TERMS**

**Semantic dementia**
A progressive loss of information from semantic memory.

**Semantic memory**
Conceptually based knowledge about the world, including knowledge of people, places, the meaning of objects and words.

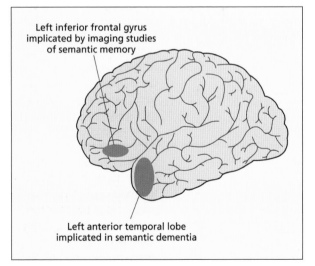

Left inferior frontal gyrus implicated by imaging studies of semantic memory

Left anterior temporal lobe implicated in semantic dementia

Studies of brain-damaged patients with semantic memory and imaging studies of semantic memory have not always highlighted the importance of the same regions.

same verb-generation task as the healthy people were given when they were scanned. As it turns out, such patients do have subtle but real difficulties with these tasks. Thompson-Schill *et al.* (1998) asked these patients to generate verbs that had either a low selection demand (e.g. scissors?), in which most people agree upon a verb (i.e. cut), and words with a high selection demand (e.g. cat?), which do not suggest an obvious single answer. The patients are impaired on the latter but not the former. More extensive imaging data on controls shows that the region is responsive to the difficulty of semantic memory retrieval (Thompson-Schill *et al.*, 1997, 1999). Thus, this disagreement is perhaps more apparent than real. The reason why patients with damage to the left inferior frontal gyrus do not show clinical symptoms of semantic memory impairment is because the region is involved in strategic retrieval operations from semantic memory when no obvious answer comes to mind. By contrast, the temporal regions may be the *store* of semantic information and lesions here can produce more devastating impairments of semantic knowledge. So why didn't these particular imaging studies activate regions that are putatively the store of semantic knowledge? One possibility could be the baseline that was used. Petersen *et al.* (1988) compared verb generation (their semantic task) with reading (their putatively non-semantic task). However, if word reading does depend on the semantic store, and there is in fact good evidence that it might (Woollams *et al.* 2007), then the two conditions would cancel each other out when subtracted away.

In this instance, an initial discrepancy between functional imaging and lesion data has resulted in a more complete understanding of how semantic memory is both stored and retrieved. This is a nice example of how the strengths of different methodologies can be combined in cognitive neuroscience.

## BRAIN-READING: IS "BIG BROTHER" ROUND THE CORNER?

This chapter started with the specter of functional imaging being used to reveal one's innermost thoughts to the outside world. It therefore seems appropriate to return to this interesting theme in light of the various points raised so far. It should by now be clear that the process of analyzing and interpreting data produced by functional imaging is not straightforward. It entails a number of stages, each with its own assumptions, rather than a literal reading of the MR signal. Nonetheless, the technology is still relatively new and the amount of progress that has already been made is substantial. Even at this early stage, there are serious studies exploring how functional imaging could be used as a lie detector and studies that try to predict the content of another person's thoughts at some basic level (for a review, see Haynes & Rees, 2006).

It is generally believed that different classes of objects (e.g. faces, places, words, tools) activate somewhat different regions of the brain. So is it possible to infer what someone is looking at from brain activity alone? A number of studies have attempted to guess, in a third-person way, what a person is observing (Haxby *et al.*, 2001) or imagining (O'Craven & Kanwisher, 2000) on a particular trial using only the concomitant neural activity. To achieve this, each person requires pretesting on a whole range of objects to determine the average response to that class of objects relative to some baseline (e.g. all the other objects). Rather than locating the peak area of activity (as in regular fMRI analysis), one can examine the *pattern* of activation over a distributed set of voxels to enable a more fine-

## COULD FUNCTIONAL IMAGING BE USED AS A LIE DETECTOR?

Lying appears to be a normal component of human social interaction. It is likely to be composed of several cognitive components. For example, it requires an understanding that other people can have states of mind that are different from one's own (so-called theory of mind). Lying also requires an ability to inhibit a truthful response and generate a plausible alternative response. Given this complexity, there will probably be no single "deception module" in the brain dedicated

Not all lies are as easy to detect.

specifically to lying. Nevertheless, there is every reason to believe that studying the brain during deception might lead to more reliable indices of lying than the traditional lie detector (or "polygraph"), given that the brain is the organ that produces the lie in the first place.

The traditional polygraph monitors a number of bodily responses, including sweating, respiration and heart rate, which are considerably downstream from the thought process that creates the lie. As these measures are associated with increased arousal generally (e.g. anxiety), they cannot exclusively detect guilt and their usage is highly questionable. Also, if a liar does not feel guilty there may be no strong arousal response.

A number of studies have used fMRI to measure the neural correlates of deception (Ganis et al., 2003; Langleben et al., 2002). When participants are asked to generate a spontaneous lie to a question (e.g. "Who did you visit during your vacation?", "Was that the card you were shown before?"), a number of regions are activated, including the anterior cingulate cortex. This region is of particular interest in this context, because it has been implicated in monitoring conflicts and errors (Carter et al., 1998) and also in generating the kinds of bodily response that formed the basis of the traditional polygraph (Critchley et al., 2003). However, not all types of deception may recruit this region. Ganis et al. (2003) found that, if participants memorized a lie in advance of being interviewed in the scanner, then this region was not involved, but regions involved in memory retrieval were involved. Thus, to conclude, although fMRI might have some use in lie detection it is unlikely to offer a simple solution to this complex and important real-world problem (Sip et al. 2007).

grained approach. This method is called MVPA or **multi-voxel pattern analysis** (for a review see Tong & Pratte, 2012). For example, Haxby et al. (2001) gave participants pictures from eight different types of category, including cats, houses, faces, and shoes. The neural activity from an individual trial was then compared to the previous known patterns of activity to determine the most probable category that was being viewed. This procedure could predict, given pairwise comparisons, what the person was seeing with 96 percent accuracy. The same regions of the brain are used, to some extent, when thinking about objects even when they are not physically seen. O'Craven and Kanwisher (2000) obtained comparable results on individual imagery trials. Other research has shown that activity in these

### KEY TERM

**Multi-voxel pattern analysis (MVPA)**
An fMRI analysis method in which distributed patterns of activity are linked to cognitive processes.

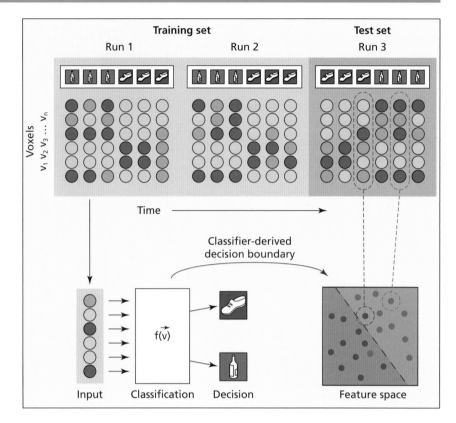

In MVPA experimental designs, participants are given certain tasks or stimuli (in this example seeing bottles or shoes) and a mathematical algorithm (a "classifier") trains itself to optimally discriminate between them based on the pattern of activity in the voxels (note: the actual spatial arrangement of voxels isn't crucial). In the next phase (testing), the participant is then given more tasks or stimuli (e.g. new images of shoes) and the algorithm must classify them. In this phase the participant's mind/brain is effectively being "read."

Adapted from Norman et al., 2006.

regions can be used to accurately predict semantic categories when reading words (Mitchell *et al.*, 2008) or when recalling previously seen images from memory (Polyn *et al.*, 2005).

The studies described thus far are limited in that they generate answers from a closed set of options (e.g. shoe compared with bottle). However, other studies have used this approach to generate an open ended set of responses. The primary visual cortex (also termed V1) has a particular functional layout such that it is a mosaic of small regions that are specialized for detecting lines of certain orientations and also for detecting light in particular locations. The grid of voxels used in fMRI may capture some of this patterning, and attempts have been made to reconstruct visual images (presented to a participant) based on the pattern of activity in this region. For instance, Miyawaki *et al.* (2008) used a 10 × 10 grid of pixels to train a classifier. Just as the classifier can search for voxels that "prefer" shoes over bottles, one can do the same for voxels that prefer brightness in, say, the top left of the grid as opposed to bottom right or for voxels that prefer horizontal over vertical orientations. From this simple training, it was possible to reconstruct letters and words that were presented to the participants. Attempts at

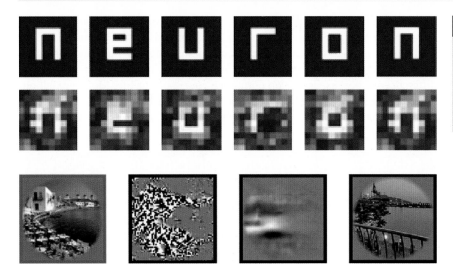

**KEY TERM**

**Vegetative state**
A disorder of consciousness in which patients with severe brain damage are in a state of partial arousal.

Can activity in the brain be used to reconstruct what image is being seen? In the top example, letters displayed in a 10 × 10 grid to the participants can clearly be read out from the pattern of brain activity. In the bottom example, the target image is shown on the left (red outline) and, to the right, are shown three attempts at image reconstruction from the pattern of activity (black outline). The first reconstruction uses an algorithm based on detecting local contrast. The second reconstruction uses the global (blurred) image characteristics. The final attempt involves finding a best match from a database of 6 million images (not including the target image).

Top, from Miyawaki et al., 2008. Bottom, from Naselaris et al., 2009.

generating more complex images using this method have more limited success but are good at finding a close match to a novel image from within a large database (Naselaris et al., 2009).

Much of the discussion has focused on brain decoding of external inputs. What about intentions and decisions that are, by their nature, internally driven? Patterns of activity in the prefrontal cortex can be used to predict (even before the person made their response) which of two tasks will be performed—in this study the decision was whether to add or subtract digits (Haynes et al., 2007). Brain activity when shown a series of goods predicts, above chance, subsequent purchasing decisions (Knutson et al., 2007). Finally, a remarkable set of studies have been performed on patients in a **vegetative state** who, because of their condition, are unable to produce verbal or motor responses (Monti et al., 2010; Owen et al., 2006). Some of these patients are able to understand sentences by complying with instructions such as "imagine navigating around your house" or "imagine playing tennis": these tasks have very different neural substrates related to spatial and motor imagery, respectively. Moreover, these different neural signatures can be used as a simple substitute for communication to answer questions such as "Is your father's name Alexander? (yes = imagine tennis, no = imagine your house)." As such, brain reading may ultimately have real clinical significance rather than being an instrument of a "Big Brother" state.

## Evaluation

In summary, brain imaging can be used to infer the *type* of stimulus that is being processed and simple cognitive decisions (e.g. add or subtract). However, it is unclear whether fMRI will ever be able to infer the *specific content* of thought. To infer, for example, whether someone in a scanner is thinking about his or her own cat or next-door's cat would require knowledge of how and where an individual stimulus is represented in the brain. We have all been exposed to different cats, houses, and so on during the course of our life. Moreover, all our brains differ in subtle ways. This presents a natural boundary on the imaging enterprise that technological developments alone are unlikely to resolve.

## SUMMARY AND KEY POINTS OF THE CHAPTER

- Structural imaging reveals the static physical characteristics of the brain (useful in diagnosing disease), whereas functional imaging reveals dynamic changes in brain physiology (that might correlate with cognitive function).
- Neural activity consumes oxygen from the blood. This triggers an increase in blood flow to that region (measured by PET) and a change in the amount of deoxyhemoglobin in that region (measured by fMRI).
- As the brain is always physiologically active, functional imaging needs to measure *relative* changes in physiological activity. The most basic experimental design in functional imaging research is to subtract the activity in each part of the brain while doing one task away from the activity in the same parts of the brain while doing a slightly different task. This is called cognitive subtraction.
- Other methods, including parametric and factorial designs, can minimize many of the problems associated with cognitive subtraction.
- There is no foolproof way of mapping a point on one brain onto the putatively same point on another brain because of individual differences in structural and functional anatomy. Current imaging methods cope with this problem by mapping individual data onto a common standard brain (stereotactic normalization) and by diffusing regions of significance (smoothing).
- A region of "activity" refers to a local increase in metabolism in the experimental task compared with the baseline, but it does not necessarily mean that the region is essential for performing the task. Lesion studies might provide evidence concerning the necessity of a region for a task.
- Functional imaging can be used to make crude discriminations about what someone is thinking and feeling and could potentially outperform traditional lie detectors. However, it is highly unlikely that they will ever be able to produce detailed accounts of another person's thoughts or memories.

## EXAMPLE ESSAY QUESTIONS

- What are the physiological processes that underpin fMRI? What determines the temporal and spatial resolution of this method?
- What is meant by the method of "cognitive subtraction" in functional imaging research? What problems does this method face?
- Is functional imaging ever likely to completely replace lesion methods for informing theories of cognition?
- If a brain region is shown to be "active" in a given task, does it mean that this region is critical for performing the task? If not, why not?
- Could functional imaging be used in lie detection? Could it be used to read someone else's thoughts and feelings?

## RECOMMENDED FURTHER READING

- Huettel, S. A., Song, A. W., & McCarthy, G. (2008). *Functional magnetic resonance imaging* (2nd edition). Sunderland, MA: Sinauer Associates. Thorough but generally accessible. This is recommended for the general reader.
- Jezzard, P., Matthews, P. M., & Smith, S. M. (2001). *Functional MRI: An introduction to methods*. Oxford, UK: Oxford University Press. An advanced text that is only recommended to those who have a very good understanding of the basics, or those who wish to know more about the math and physics of fMRI.
- Poldrack, R. A., Mumford, J. A., & Nichols, T .E. (2011). *Handbook of functional MRI data analysis*. Cambridge, UK: Cambridge University Press. For those getting hand-on experience of fMRI research.

Visit the companion website at www. psypress/cw/ward for:

- References to key papers and readings
- Video lectures and interviews on key topics with leading psychologists Geoffrey Aguirre, Thomas Insel and author Jamie Ward
- Multiple choice questions and interactive flashcards to test your knowledge
- Downloadable glossary

# CHAPTER 5

# The lesioned brain

## CONTENTS

Studies of humans who have been unfortunate enough to acquire brain damage have provided a rich source of information for cognitive neuroscientists. The basic premise behind the approach is that, by studying the abnormal, it is possible to gain insights into normal function. This is a form of "reverse engineering," in which one attempts to infer the function of a component (or region) by observing what the rest of the cognitive system can and can't do when that component (or region) is removed. In this way, lesions "carve cognition at its seams" (McCarthy & Warrington, 1990).

Patient-based neuropsychology has tended to take two broad forms. In one tradition, which I shall call *classical neuropsychology*, attempts have been made to infer the function of a given brain region by taking patients with lesions to that region and examining their pattern of impaired and spared abilities. This type of research has benefited greatly from the development of imaging methods that enable more accurate lesion localization and quantification. It also provides an important source of constraint on functional imaging data. In the second tradition, which I shall call *cognitive neuropsychology*, the pattern of spared and impaired abilities in and of themselves has been used to infer the building blocks of

## KEY TERMS

**Group studies**
In neuropsychology, the performance of different patients is combined to yield a group average.

**Single-case studies**
In cognitive neuropsychology, the data from different patients are not combined.

**Transcranial magnetic stimulation (TMS)**
Non-invasive stimulation of the brain caused by a rapidly changing electrical current in a coil held over the scalp.

**Transcranial direct current stimulation (tDCS)**
Non-invasive stimulation of the brain caused by passing a weak electrical current through it.

cognition—irrespective of where they are located in the brain. This approach has been particularly informative for guiding the development of detailed information-processing models and provides the cognitive framework that underpins much imaging research. The schism between these traditions has run deep. For example, many journals either tacitly or explicitly favor one approach over the other. Moreover, each tradition has tended to rely on its own methodology, with classical neuropsychology favoring **group studies** and cognitive neuropsychology favoring **single-case studies**. The development of cognitive neuroscience has led to something of a reconciliation of these traditions, and this textbook discusses both. The key point that one needs to bear in mind is this: the method one chooses should be appropriate to the question one is asking. It will be argued in this chapter that group studies are more appropriate for establishing lesion-deficit associations, whereas single-case studies are particularly helpful for establishing how cognitive processes might be subdivided.

Naturally occurring brain lesions are "accidents of nature" that occur because of stroke, tumor, head injury, or other types of brain damage. A complementary approach, that in many ways resembles the logic of the lesion method, involves magnetic stimulation of the intact brain to produce what has been described as "virtual lesions" (e.g. Pascual-Leone *et al.*, 1999). This method is called **transcranial magnetic stimulation (TMS)**. The method makes contact with the literature from the classical neuropsychology tradition with its emphasis on lesion location. However, it can also be used to test information-processing theories of cognition because it can provide information on the timing of cognitive processes. The method has a number of advantages over traditional lesion methods. A newer method is based on the principle of electrical stimulation and is termed **transcranial direct current stimulation (tDCS)** (Nitsche *et al.*, 2008). Like TMS it can be used to temporarily disrupt cognitive function (a virtual lesion approach). However, it can also be used to boost cognitive function which has important implications for rehabilitation as well as for exploring the brain basis of cognition.

## WAYS OF ACQUIRING BRAIN DAMAGE

Brain damage can be acquired in a number of ways, as summarized below:

### Neurosurgery

Operations are occasionally performed in cases of severe epilepsy in which the focus of the epileptic seizure is surgically removed. One of the most famous cases in neuropsychology, HM, had dense amnesia after part of his medial temporal lobe was surgically removed (see Chapter 9). Another surgical procedure formerly used to reduce epileptic seizures spreading across the brain was to sever the fibers of the corpus callosum. This operation was referred to as the **split-brain** procedure. Patients who have undergone this intervention have only mild impairments in daily living, but the impairments can be observed in laboratory conditions in which stimuli are presented briefly to each hemisphere (for a review, see Gazzaniga, 2000). Surgical intervention was also previously common in psychiatric patients (see the discussion on the prefrontal lobotomy in Chapter 14). In general, surgical procedures are only carried out in the absence of suitable pharmacological treatments.

## Strokes (or cerebrovascular accident; CVA)

Disruptions to the blood supply of the brain (called **strokes** or cerebrovascular accidents, CVA) can result in global or local death of neurons. If an artery ruptures, this leads to a hemorrhage and an increase in intracranial pressure (typically relieved by surgery). People born with **aneurysms** are more susceptible to rupture. These are localized regions of over-elastic artery that may balloon and rupture. Blood vessels may also become blocked if, for example, a fatty clot gets pushed from a large vessel into a smaller one (an *embolism*) or a stationary clot becomes large enough to block the vessel (*thrombosis*). Other vascular disorders include *angiomas* (tangled and tortuous blood vessels liable to rupture) and arteriosclerosis (hardening of the vessel walls).

## Traumatic head injuries

Whereas vascular disorders tend to affect older people, traumatic head injuries are the most common form of brain damage in people of less than 40 years of age. They are particularly common in young men as a result of road traffic accidents. Traumatic head injuries are classified in two ways, "open" or "closed," depending on whether the skull is fractured. Open head injuries often have more localized injuries; whereas closed head injuries have more widespread effects (as the brain ricochets in the skull) and often produce loss of consciousness.

## Tumors

The brain is the second most common site for tumors (after the uterus), and brain tumors are often spread from other parts of the body (these are called metastatic tumors). Tumors are caused when new cells are produced in a poorly regulated manner. Brain tumors are formed from supporting cells such as the meninges and glia (termed "meningioma" and "gliomas," respectively). Tumors adversely affect the functioning of the brain because the extra cellular material puts pressure on the neurons, disrupting functioning and possibly leading to cell death.

## Viral infections

A number of viruses target specific cells in the brain. These include herpes simplex encephalitis (HSE), human immunodeficiency virus (HIV), and Creutzfeldt-Jakob disease (CJD).

## Neurodegenerative disorders

Most western societies have a large ageing population that will, if anything, continue to get larger and older. In 1900, 4 percent of people were over the age of 65; in 2030, 20 percent of the population is estimated to be over 65. An increase in life expectancy is bringing about an increase in degenerative illnesses that affect the brain. By far the most common is dementia of the Alzheimer type (or DAT). This is associated with atrophy in a number of regions of the brain, with memory loss (amnesia) typically being the earliest noted symptom. Other neurodegenerative diseases include Parkinson's disease and Huntington's disease (see Chapter 8), Pick's disease (often the medical diagnosis in cases of semantic dementia), and multi-infarct dementia (caused by many small strokes that can be hard to distinguish from DAT).

# DISSOCIATIONS AND ASSOCIATIONS

In 1990, two very unusual patients came to the attention of Roberto Cubelli (Cubelli, 1991). One patient, CF, was unable to write any vowel letters and left gaps in their place ("Bologna" → B L GN). Another patient, CW, made spelling errors selectively on vowels (e.g. "dietro" → diatro); equivalent errors were not found in his spoken language. By contrast, Kay and Hanley (1994) report a different patient who made spelling errors selectively on consonants (e.g. "record" → recorg). The basic logic behind the cognitive neuropsychological approach is that a difficulty in one domain relative to an absence of difficulty in another domain can be used to infer the independence of these domains. In the case of the patients just discussed, the implication was that the brain has separate neural resources for the processing of written vowels relative to consonants. These neural resources need not lie in different locations of the brain (at least on a millimeter or centimeter scale), but might reflect two different populations of interspersed neurons. Note, also, that it is not clear that one can conclude that the *only* function of these neurons is the coding of consonants and/or vowels. The difference could be relative and, indeed, without testing a whole range of other stimuli (e.g. digits), it is unwise to conclude exclusivity of function. Nonetheless, it is reasonable to conclude that there are some neural resources predominantly implicated in written vowel processing relative to consonants and vice versa.

If a patient is impaired on a particular task (task A) but relatively spared on another task (task B), this is referred to as a **single dissociation**. If the patient performs entirely normally on task B compared with a control group, this has been termed a *classical* single dissociation, whereas if the patient is impaired on both tasks but is significantly more impaired on one task, this is referred to as a *strong* single dissociation (Shallice, 1988). In either of these instances, one inference is that task A and task B utilize different cognitive processes with different neural resources. However, other inferences could also be made.

It could be the case that both task A and task B use exactly the same cognitive/neural resources as each other, but task B requires more of this resource than task A (i.e. task B is harder). If brain damage depletes this resource, then task B may be relatively or selectively impaired. This has been referred to as a **task-resource artifact** (Shallice, 1988). Another explanation of a single dissociation is in terms of a **task-demand artifact** (Shallice, 1988). A task-demand artifact is when a single dissociation occurs because a patient performs one of the tasks suboptimally. For example, the patient may have misunderstood the instructions or have adopted an unusual strategy for performing the task. Task-demand artifacts

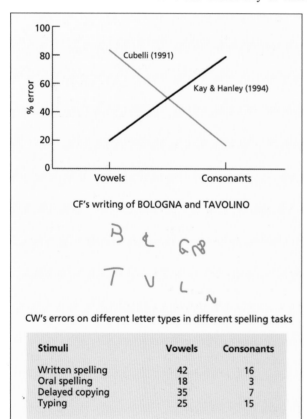

CF's writing of BOLOGNA and TAVOLINO

CW's errors on different letter types in different spelling tasks

| Stimuli | Vowels | Consonants |
|---|---|---|
| Written spelling | 42 | 16 |
| Oral spelling | 18 | 3 |
| Delayed copying | 35 | 7 |
| Typing | 25 | 15 |

Some patients produce spelling errors selectively on either consonants or vowels. This may imply separate neural resources for coding consonants and vowels.
Data from Cubelli, 1991.

can be minimized by assessing the patient's general intellectual functioning, giving clearer instructions or training, using ecologically valid tests, and repeating the same (or similar tests) on several occasions.

In general, almost all neuropsychological studies are aimed at proving that two or more tasks have different cognitive/neural resources and disproving the task-resource and task-demand explanations even if this is not explicitly stated in these terms. In the case of Cubelli's patients, a task-demand artifact can easily be ruled out because the same task (i.e. writing) was performed in both conditions. One of the most powerful ways of discounting a task-resource artifact is to document a **double dissociation**, which merely refers to two single dissociations that have a complementary profile of abilities. To remain with the current example, Kay and Hanley's patient could write vowels better than Cubelli's patient, whereas Cubelli's patient could write consonants better than Kay and Hanley's.

So far, the discussion has emphasized the importance of dissociations between deficits, but what about *associations* of deficits? For example, if for every patient that resembled Cubelli's there were 10, 20, or 100 times as many patients who had comparable **dysgraphia** for *both* consonants and vowels, then would this diminish the findings of the dissociation? Some researchers would suggest not. There are some theoretically uninteresting reasons why two symptoms may associate together, the main reason being that they are close together in the brain and so tend to be similarly affected by strokes (or whatever) in that region. For example, patients with difficulties in recognizing faces often have difficulties in perceiving colors, but this probably reflects neuroanatomical proximity rather than suggesting a "super-module" that is specialized for both. It is the (double) dissociations between the two that count from a theoretical point of view.

Needless to say, this particular viewpoint has attracted controversy. It has been argued that it is important to know how common a particular dissociation is in order to rule out that it hasn't been observed by chance (Robertson *et al.*, 1993). For example, if brain damage affects some written letters more than others in a random fashion, then it would still be possible to find patients who appear to have selective difficulties in writing vowels, but it would be a chance occurrence rather than meaningful dissociation. Other researchers have focused more on associations between symptoms (so-called **syndromes**) rather than dissociations. The use of the double dissociation itself has been subject to criticism (see Dunn & Kirsner, 2003). Some have argued that the use of double dissociation implies an endorsement of the notion of modularity (e.g. as specified by Fodor, 1983; see Chapter 1). However, it need not. Shallice (1988) discusses why this argument is wrong by setting up the following thought trap: if modules exist, then double dissociations are a reliable way of uncovering them; double dissociations do exist, therefore modules exist. The way

## KEY TERMS

**Single dissociation**
A situation in which a patient is impaired on a particular task (task A) but relatively spared on another task (task B).

**Task-resource artifact**
If two tasks share the same neural/cognitive resource but one task uses it more, then damage to this resource will affect one task more than the other.

**Task-demand artifact**
One task is performed worse than another because the task is performed sub-optimally (but not because some aspect of the task is compromised).

**Double dissociation**
Two single dissociations that have a complementary profile of abilities.

**Dysgraphia**
Difficulties in spelling and writing.

**Syndrome**
A cluster of different symptoms that are believed to be related in some meaningful way.

In a classical dissociation, performance on one task lies within the control range (shown by dotted lines). In a strong dissociation, both tasks fall outside the control range, but one task is significantly more impaired than the other.

From Shallice, 1988. © Cambridge University Press. Reproduced with permission.

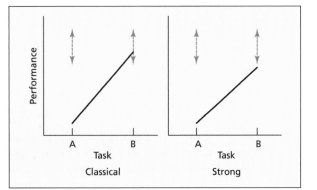

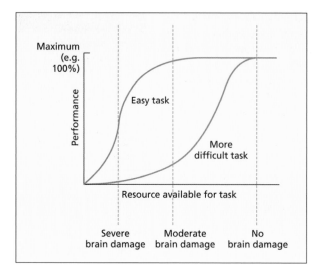

A task-resource artifact can arise because one task uses more of a cognitive/neural resource than the other (i.e. one task is harder). One could construe brain damage as depleting the amount of resource available. In this instance, at moderate brain damage the patient can still perform the easy task normally. A single dissociation need not reflect different cognitive/neural substrates for the tasks.

Adapted from Shallice, 1988.

out of this trap, however, is to ask the question: can non-modular systems produce double dissociations? It has been demonstrated that other types of cognitive architecture, such as interactive connectionist models, can produce double dissociations (Plaut, 1995). The reason why they do so is interesting. It reflects the fact that these systems also contain units that are functionally specialized for certain types of process/information, even though the system is interactive, and even though these units may respond (to a greater or lesser degree) to a range of stimuli.

Some have argued that the reliance on double dissociations is flawed because it requires the study of "pure" cases (Dunn & Kirsner, 2003). However, it need not (Shallice, 1979). First of all, one must be careful to state what is meant by a pure case. For example, imagine that the dysgraphic patients mentioned above also had amnesia. Would the fact that they were not "pure dysgraphic" exclude them from study? This might depend on the theoretical stance one adopts. If one's theoretical model assumes that writing and memory are independent (as most do), then studying writing in isolation is entirely feasible.

It is worth stating that finding a double dissociation between two patients on two tasks is only part of the neuropsychologist's toolkit. To interpret their spared and impaired performance, one requires evidence from a range of other relevant tasks. For example, to fully interpret the dysgraphic patients' impairments it would be interesting to know if they could copy vowels and consonants, or recognize them visually. The types of error that patients produce can also be an important source of information, irrespective of their performance level (i.e. how good or bad they are). For example, the independence of consonants and vowels was initially inferred from the types of errors made in dysgraphia (Caramazza & Miceli, 1990) and not from the double dissociation logic. The double dissociation is useful, but it is not a panacea.

## SINGLE-CASE STUDIES

### Caramazza's assumptions for theorizing in cognitive neuropsychology

Although the use of single cases of brain-damaged individuals to study normal cognitive/brain function began in the mid-nineteenth century, attempts to formalize the logic of this approach were lacking for many years. Caramazza provided one of the first serious attempts to do so in the 1980s (Caramazza, 1986, 1992; Caramazza & Badecker, 1989; Caramazza & McCloskey, 1988; McCloskey & Caramazza, 1988).He suggested that three underlying, and unstated, assumptions underpinned almost all neuropsychological studies to date:

1. *The fractionation assumption*. The first assumption is that damage to the brain can produce selective cognitive lesions. Note that the assumption is stated with reference to a lesion within a particular cognitive model and not to a lesion to a particular region of the brain (although the two may, of course, be correlated). Caramazza's arguments were concerned with using observations of brain-damaged individuals to inform theories of cognition (cognitive neuropsychology), not to localize cognitive processes in the brain (classical neuropsychology).

2. *The transparency assumption*. The **transparency assumption** states that lesions affect one or more components within the preexisting cognitive system, but they do not result in a completely new cognitive system being created. This assumption is needed because one wishes to study the abnormal in order to understand the normal, and not just to study the abnormal as an end in itself.

3. *The universality assumption*. The universality assumption is that all cognitive systems are basically identical.

**KEY TERM**

**Transparency assumption**
Lesions affect one or more components within the preexisting cognitive system but do not result in a completely new cognitive system being created.

Caramazza acknowledges that these assumptions may, under some situations, not hold true. It is a matter for empirical research to determine the extent to which they are true and, hence, the validity of any inference that can be drawn from the study of brain-damaged individuals. Critics have pointed to a number of potential difficulties with the assumptions. Kosslyn and van Kleek (1990) have suggested that whether selective cognitive impairments will be observed (the fractionation assumption) depends on the neural architecture. For example, selective deficits may be more likely if neurons performing a given operation are clustered together rather than distributed around the brain, and if the neurons are dedicated to one operation rather than shared by many operations. Nevertheless, selective cognitive impairments *can* be observed and so the fractionation assumption appears to hold true at one level, even if there are some cognitive processes that may be hard to uncover by the lesion method by virtue of an atypical neural architecture.

The transparency assumption is potentially the most problematic. Basically, one needs to assume that brain damage removes one component of cognition, but does not create, from scratch, a rearranged or different cognitive system. Examples of brain plasticity, and rehabilitation and recovery after brain damage, might at first appear to be convincing arguments against transparency. But they need not be. For example, imagine that a patient has severe problems in speaking after a stroke (i.e. aphasia) but that these problems ameliorate over time. This could be taken as *prima facie* evidence that the brain has somehow reorganized itself after the stroke. However, it could be that the preexisting cognitive model has just been reinstated rather than that a whole new way of performing the task has been created. As such, this would *not* be a violation of the transparency assumption. Plasticity at a neural level is a pervasive aspect of brain function (see also Chapter 9), and need not imply behavioral change or functional change. It is important to point out that the assumption is more likely to hold true for brain damage acquired during adulthood than childhood (Thomas & Karmiloff-Smith, 2002). It is also worth pointing out that the transparency assumption refers to the cognitive organization of the cognitive system and not necessarily its location. Consider the case of an epileptic child who has his left hemisphere removed and then learns to speak using the right hemisphere (Vargha-Khadem *et al.*, 1997a). Is that a violation of the transparency assumption? It could be, but it need not be. It depends on whether the new right hemisphere system is cognitively equivalent to the one in the left. The transparency assumption refers to the comparability between premorbid and postmorbid cognitive systems, and not on *where* such systems are located. Although the debate remains open about the validity of this assumption, a good rule of thumb is that the transparency assumption is less likely to be violated in adult relative to child cases, and when studied soon after injury relative to later in time (or if the cognitive profile after injury remains stable over time).

The universality assumption, that all cognitive systems are basically the same, may also be problematic to neuropsychology. But Caramazza has argued that it is equally problematic for other methods within cognitive neuroscience. Basically, one needs to assume that an individual (or individuals) are representative of the population at large in order to make generalizations to normal cognition. Individual differences, such as they are, are attributable to "noise" (e.g. variations in performance related to time) or other factors that may be related to the efficiency of the cognitive system (e.g. expertise) but need not reflect qualitative differences in the way the task is performed. Of course, if there are individual qualitative differences, then this is theoretically interesting. Finding a framework to explore and account for these differences is a challenge for cognitive neuroscience in general, rather than patient-based neuropsychology in particular. Caplan (1988), however, has argued that individual differences are more of a problem for single-case studies relative to other methods because this method gives exaggerated importance to exceptional findings. But this could be construed as the strength of this method rather than a weakness—assuming that the individual differences can be ascribed to something of theoretical interest rather than just "noise."

## The case for single-case studies

Caramazza and McCloskey (1988) have gone as far as to suggest that the single-case study is the *only* acceptable method in cognitive neuropsychology. The titles of the papers debating this position tell a story of their own. The original paper, entitled "The case for single patient studies" (Caramazza & McCloskey, 1988), was interpreted as the case against group studies. A subsequent paper, "The case against the case against group studies" (Zurif *et al.*, 1989), defended group studies on the grounds that "syndromes [i.e. associations of symptoms] are what the world gives us." This provoked a paper with a particularly amusing title: "Clinical syndromes are not God's gift to cognitive neuropsychology: A reply to a rebuttal to an answer to a response to the case against syndrome-based research" (Caramazza & Badecker, 1991). To understand this heated debate, it is necessary to take a step back and consider the argument as initially laid out.

Consider first the logic of testing participants in the non-brain-damaged population. One may recruit a sample of participants ($S_1$ to $S_n$) and make the assumption, valid or not, that they have broadly equivalent cognitive systems (M). One may then conduct an experiment (E), making the further assumption that all participants carry it out in equivalent ways (i.e. no task-demand artifacts), and derive a set of observations ($O_1$ to $O_n$). In this instance, it is argued that it is quite feasible to average the observations of the group because it is assumed that the only difference between the participants is "noise" (i.e. variations in performance over time, differences in speed or ability).

Consider next the situation in which one wishes to test a group of brain-damaged patients ($P_1$ to $P_n$). As before, it is assumed that each has (before their lesion) essentially the same cognitive system (M) and that each is given the same experiment (E) and complies with the experiment in the same way. However, each patient may have a different lesion to the cognitive system ($L_1$ to $L_n$) and so difference in observed performance may be attributable to differences in lesion rather than between-patient noise and, as such, averaging across patients is not possible. Determining where the lesion is in the cognitive system can only be determined on the basis of empirical observation of each case in turn. It is crucial to bear in mind the distinction between a lesion to a cognitive component (which is relevant to the discussion here) and an anatomical lesion. At present, there is no magic way of working out what the precise cognitive profile of a given patient will be from a structural lesion (except in the most general terms). Thus, establishing the cognitive impairment requires cognitive testing of individual patients.

What if one were to establish that a group of patients had identical lesions to the same component of the cognitive system, could one then average across the patients? Caramazza has argued that, although legitimate, the study becomes a series of single-case studies, not a group study, and so the unit of interest is still the single case. To establish that they had the same lesion, one would have to carry out the same set of experiments on each individually. As such, one would not learn any more from averaging the set of patients than could be learned from a single case itself. The objection is not against the idea of testing more than one patient per se, but rather averaging the results of many patients assumed (but not proven) to be equivalent.

| In a non brain-damaged population... | | | | | |
|---|---|---|---|---|---|
| Subjects | $S_1$ | $S_2$ | $S_3$ | $S_4$... | $S_n$ |
| Cognitive system | M | M | M | M | M |
| Experiment | E | E | E | E | E |
| Observations | $O_1$ | $O_2$ | $O_3$ | $O_4$... | $O_n$ |

| In a brain-damaged population... | | | | | |
|---|---|---|---|---|---|
| Subjects | $P_1$ | $P_2$ | $P_3$ | $P_4$... | $P_n$ |
| Cognitive system | M | M | M | M | M |
| Lesion | $L_1$ | $L_2$ | $L_3$ | $L_4$ | $L_n$ |
| Experiment | E | E | E | E | E |
| Observations | $O_1$ | $O_2$ | $O_3$ | $O_4$... | $O_n$ |

Caramazza has argued that it is possible to average observations ($O_1$ to $O_n$) across different non-braindamaged participants ($S_1$ to $S_n$) because they are assumed to have the same cognitive system (M) that performs the experiment (E) in comparable ways. The same logic may not apply to brain-damaged patients ($P_1$ to $P_n$) because each patient will have a different cognitive lesion (L), which cannot be known *a priori*.

From Caramazza & McCloskey, 1988.

The use of single cases is not peculiar to neuropsychology. For example, it is the mainstay of archaeology and anthropology. In 1974, Donald Johanson discovered a partial skeleton of a single primate, Lucy, from 3.18 million years ago, which had walked upright and had a small brain. Previous theories had suggested that brain enlargement preceded the ability to walk upright. This single case proved this not to be so. Note that Johanson did not have to provide a group of "Lucys" for his findings to be acceptable to the scientific community.

John Reader/Science Photo Library.

Some of the common objections against the use of the single-case study are that one cannot create a theory based on observations from only a single case, or that it is not possible to generalize from a single case. The counterarguments are that nobody is trying to construct whole new theories of cognition based on a single case. Theories, in neuropsychology and elsewhere, must account for a wide range of observations from different sources, both normal and brain-damaged. For example, cognitive models of reading are able to account for different observations found in skilled readers and also account for the different types of acquired dyslexia (drawn from several different single cases). They must also account for the pattern of performance (e.g. the types of error made) as well as the level of performance (i.e. following the logic of dissociations). Although nobody wishes to construct a theory based on a single case, observations from single cases constitute valid data with which to test, amend, and develop theory. As for the argument that it is not possible to generalize from a single case, the counterquestion would be "generalize to what?." It is entirely plausible to generalize from a single case to a model of normal cognition. It is, however, much harder to generalize from one single case to another single case. Two patients with a stroke may have very different cognitive profiles (i.e. one cannot generalize from one case to another), but it should nevertheless be possible for each particular case to generalize to some aspect of normal cognition.

## Evaluation

The argument presented above has emphasized the point that single-case studies are a valid methodology and they may have a particularly important role to play in determining what the components of cognitive systems are. The discussion has also argued that the term "lesion" can be construed both in terms of disruption to a component in a cognitive model, as well as a region of organic brain damage. Does this mean that group studies have no role to play at all? It will be argued that group studies do have an important role to play, and that they may be particularly suited to addressing different types of question from the single-case approach.

## GROUP STUDIES AND LESION-DEFICIT ANALYSIS

The introduction to this chapter discussed the historical schism that exists between cognitive neuropsychology, which is aimed at developing purely cognitive accounts of cognition, and classical neuropsychology, which is aimed at developing brain-based accounts of cognition. Both approaches fit well within a cognitive neuroscience framework. The cognitive neuropsychology tradition enriches the conceptual framework and provides a testable hypothesis about what the likely neural components of cognition are (although not necessarily where they are). The classical neuropsychology tradition provides important contrastive data with functional imaging. There are several reasons why regions may appear active or inactive in functional imaging tasks, and a region of activity need not imply that a region is critically involved in that particular task. Studies of patients with lesions in that area do enable such conclusions to be drawn. The lesions of patients, however, are typically large and rarely restricted to the region of interest. Thus, to be able to localize which region is critical for a given task, several patients may need to be considered.

## Ways of grouping patients

How does one decide the principle by which patients should be grouped in order to associate lesion sites with deficits? There are at least three approaches in the literature:

1.  *Grouping by syndrome*. Patients are assigned to a particular group on the basis of possessing a cluster of different symptoms. This approach is particularly common in psychiatric studies (e.g. of schizophrenia), but there are equivalent approaches in neuropsychology (e.g. the aphasia subtypes identified by Goodglass and Kaplan, 1972).
2.  *Grouping by cognitive symptom*. Patients are assigned to a particular group on the basis of possessing one particular symptom (e.g. auditory hallucinations; difficulty in reading nonwords). They may also possess other symptoms, but, assuming that the other symptoms differ from case to case, the method should be sensitive to the symptom under investigation.
3.  *Grouping by anatomical lesion*. Patients are selected on the basis of having a lesion to a particular anatomical region. This region may have been identified as interesting by previous functional imaging studies. This method need not require that patients have damage exclusively to the region of interest. The patients may have additional damage elsewhere, but, assuming that the other lesions differ from case to case, the method should be sensitive to the region in question (Damasio & Damasio, 1989).

There is no right or wrong way of deciding how to group patients, and to some extent it will depend on the precise question being addressed. The method of grouping cases by syndrome is likely to offer a more coarse level of analysis, whereas grouping according to individual symptoms may provide a more fine-grained level of analysis. In general, the syndrome-based approach may be more appropriate for understanding the neural correlates of a given disease pathology rather than developing theories concerning the neural basis of cognition.

The method of grouping patients by symptom (2 in the list above) and then finding out what regions of damage they have in common is relatively new. This is made feasible by new techniques that compare the location of lesions from MRI scans of different patients on a voxel-by-voxel basis thus producing a fine-grained statistical map of the likely lesion "hot spot" (Rorden & Karnath, 2004). For example, it has been used to separate out the different contributions of frontal regions in tests of executive function (Shammi & Stuss, 1999; Stuss *et al.*, 2002). One advantage of working forward from a symptom to a lesion location is that it could potentially reveal more than one region as being critically involved. For example, let's assume that a deficit can arise from damage to either region X or region Y. If one were to initially group patients according to whether they have damage to region X and test for a deficit (3 in the list above), then one could falsely conclude that region X is the key region that gives rise to this deficit and the method would not detect the importance of region Y. The main situation in which one would group patients by lesion site and

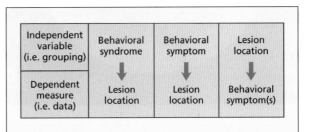

There are at least three different ways of grouping patients to carry out a lesion-deficit analysis.

## KEY TERMS

**Edema**
A swelling of the brain following injury.

**Diaschisis**
A discrete brain lesion can disrupt the functioning of distant brain regions that are structurally intact.

then test for the presence of a particular symptom (3 in the list above) is if one has a specific testable prediction about what the region is critical for (e.g. the region has been implicated by functional imaging studies).

## Caveats and complications

There are at least two caveats and complications that warrant further discussion. The first concerns the ability of current structural imaging techniques to identify lesions. The second concerns the inferences that can be drawn from lesion-deficit associations that can, if not articulated properly, lapse into neophrenology.

Damasio and Damasio (1989) discuss how certain types of neuropathology are more suited to lesion-deficit analysis than others, at least with current techniques. The most suitable lesions are those in which dead tissue is eventually replaced by cerebrospinal fluid. This is frequently the case in stroke (at least in the chronic rather than acute phase), in damage resulting from the herpes simplex encephalitis (HSE) virus and following neurosurgery. Identifying the site of a lesion caused by a tumor is particularly problematic when the tumor is *in situ*, but is less problematic once it has been excised. Certain tumors (e.g. gliomas) may infiltrate surrounding tissue and so have no clear boundary, and physical strain around the tumor may cause swelling (termed **edema**). This distorts the true size and shape of the brain tissue and may render neurons inoperative even if they are not destroyed. Similar arguments apply to the presence of leaked blood during hemorrhage, and the intracranial swelling associated with closed head injury. In general, reliable lesion images are best obtained 3 months after onset and when the neuropsychology testing is carried out at a similar time to the structural imaging (Damasio & Damasio, 1989).

On finding that a function (F) is disrupted following a lesion to region X, it is tempting to conclude that function F is located in region X or, worse still, that the purpose of region X is to implement F. These conclusions, and the second one in particular, are tantamount to endorsing a neophrenological view of brain structure–function relationship. Before jumping to such a conclusion, one would need to consider a number of other questions. Is this the only function of region X? Do other regions contribute to the performance of function F, or is this the only region that does so? On finding that a function (F) is disrupted following a lesion to region X, a more cautious conclusion is that region X is critical for performing some aspect of function F. This assertion does not assume that region X has a single function, or that function F has a discrete location. It is also important to note that even a very discrete brain lesion can disrupt the functioning of distant brain regions that are structurally intact; this is termed **diaschisis**. For example, structural lesions to the left frontal lobe can result in markedly

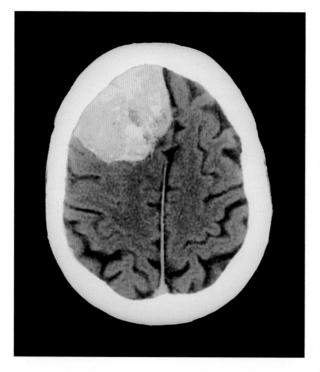

A tumor (here shown on a CT scan) can make it hard to estimate lesion size, and the distortion in the shape of the brain makes it hard to map onto a standard atlas.
Sovereign, ISM/Science Photo Library.

reduced activity in other distant regions (e.g. left inferior posterior temporal lobe) during a letter judgment task (Price *et al.*, 2001). This can occur even though this distant region is not lesioned and may function normally in other contexts. The implications are that damage to one region can disrupt the functioning of another, intact, region when these two regions work together to implement a particular cognitive function.

## Evaluation

Group studies of patients can be important for establishing whether a given region is critical for performing a given task or tasks. Two broad methods are favored, depending on the hypothesis being addressed. The first method involves establishing (on a case-by-case basis) whether a patient is impaired on a given task and then determining the lesion location(s). The second method involves selecting the group on the basis of a lesion to a predefined area and then establishing what functional deficits the group has. This second method is important for testing predictions derived from functional imaging research.

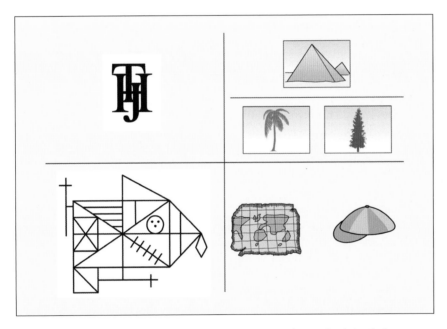

The purpose of a neuropsychological assessment is to ascertain a patient's level of functioning relative to that expected based on his or her premorbid functioning (Cipolotti & Warrington, 1995a). Some common neuropsychological tests are shown; clockwise from top left: patients with visual recognition problems find it hard to identify overlaid letters relative to non-overlaid ones (from BORB; Riddoch & Humphreys, 1995); patients with semantic memory impairments may find it hard to match the palm tree to the pyramid (Howard & Patterson, 1992); patients with aphasia may find it hard to decide whether things rhyme (from PALPA; Kay *et al.*, 1992); patients with memory problems may be able to copy but not remember this figure

From Rey, 1964. © International Universities Press Inc.

## ANIMAL MODELS IN NEUROPSYCHOLOGY

The two main methods that use non-human animals that are considered in this textbook are single-cell recordings (discussed in Chapter 3) and lesion methods. Both of these methods have been greatly assisted by structural MRI scanning enabling individual differences in each animal's brain anatomy to be taken into consideration when placing electrodes and lesions, and also for determining the extent of lesions in vivo. When non-human animals are used in this way, it is typically referred to as **behavioral neuroscience** rather than cognitive neuroscience. The implication of this difference in terminology is that humans think but animals behave, or, rather, we know that humans think but we can't be so sure about other animals.

Although lesion methods in humans rely on naturally occurring lesions, it is possible—surgically—to carry out far more selective lesions on other animals. Unlike human lesions, each animal can serve as its own control by comparing performance before and after the lesion. It is also common to have control groups of animals that have undergone surgery but received no lesion, or a control group with a lesion in an unrelated area. There are various methods for producing experimental lesions in animals (Murray & Baxter, 2006):

1. *Aspiration.* The earliest methods of lesioning involved aspirating brain regions using a suction device and applying a strong current at the end of an electrode tip to seal the wound. These methods could potentially damage both gray matter and the underlying white matter that carries information to distant regions.
2. *Transection.* This involves cutting of discrete white matter bundles such as the corpus callosum (separating the hemispheres) or the fornix (carrying information from the hippocampus).
3. *Neurochemical lesions.* Certain toxins are taken up by selective neurotransmitter systems (e.g. for dopamine or serotonin) and, once inside the cell, they create chemical reactions that kill it. A more recent approach involves toxins that bind to receptors on the surface of cells, allowing for even more specific targeting of particular neurons.
4. *Reversible "lesions."* Pharmacological manipulations can sometimes produce reversible functional lesions. For example, scopolamine produces a temporary amnesia during the time in which the drug is active. Cooling of parts of the brain also temporarily suppresses neural activity.

A family of macaque monkeys.

Studies of non-human animals have also enabled a more detailed anatomical understanding of the brain and, in particular, the anatomical connectivity between regions. In non-human animals, injecting the enzyme horseradish peroxidase into axons carries a visible tracer back to the cell bodies that send them. The tracer can be visualized at post-mortem. This enables one to ascertain which regions project to a given region (Heimer & Robards, 1981).

While the vast majority of neuroscience research is conducted on rodents, some research is still conducted on non-human primates. In many countries, including in the EU, neuropsychological studies of great apes (e.g. chimpanzees) are not permitted. More distant human relatives used in research include three species of macaque monkeys (rhesus monkey, cynomolgus monkey, and Japanese macaque) and one species of New World primate, the common marmoset. There are a number of difficulties associated with the use of animal models in neuropsychology, not least the concern for the welfare of the animals. Scientists working with these species must provide a justification as to why the research requires primates rather than other animals or other methods, and they must justify the number of animals used. It is also important to have careful breeding programs to avoid having to catch animals in the wild and to protect the animals from viruses. It is important to give them adequate space and social contact. Another disadvantage of animal models is that there are some human traits that do not have obvious counterparts in other species. Language is the most obvious such trait; consciousness is a more controversial one (see Edelman & Seth, 2009).

## TRANSCRANIAL MAGNETIC STIMULATION (TMS)

Attempts to stimulate the brain electrically and magnetically have a long history. Electric currents are strongly reduced by the scalp and skull and are therefore more suitable as an invasive technique on people undergoing surgery. In contrast, magnetic fields do not show this attenuation by the skull. However, the limiting factor in developing this method has been the technical challenge of producing large magnetic fields, associated with rapidly changing currents, using a reasonably small stimulator (for a historical overview, see Walsh and Cowey, 1998). Early attempts at magnetic stimulation were successful at eliciting phosphenes (Magnussen & Stevens, 1914), but this was probably due to stimulation of the retina rather than the brain (Barlow et al., 1947). It was not until 1985 that adequate technology was developed to magnetically stimulate focal regions of the brain (Barker et al., 1985). Since then, the number of publications using this methodology has increased rapidly. Typically, the effects of transcranial magnetic stimulation (TMS) are small, such that they alter reaction time profiles rather than elicit an overt behavior. But there are instances of the latter. For example, if the coil is placed over the region of the right motor cortex representing the hand, then the subject may

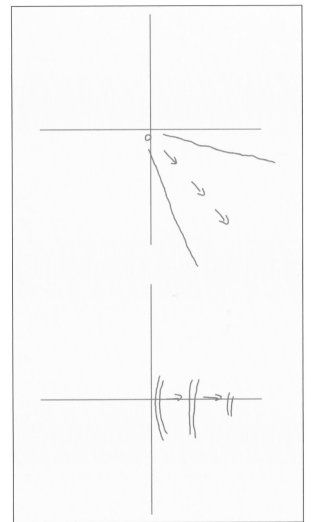

An example of two phosphenes produced by stimulating area V5/MT. Left hemisphere V5/MT stimulation produces right visual field phosphenes moving away from the center. The first was described as "movement of a single point in a static field" and the second as "drifting right, not continuous."

From Stewart et al., 1999. © 1999 Elsevier. Reproduced with permission.

experience a sensation or involuntary movement in the left hand (given that the right motor cortex sends movement signals to the left part of the body). If the coil is placed over the right visual cortex, then the subject may report visual sensations or "phosphenes" on the left side (given that the right visual cortex represents the left side of space). Even more specific examples have been documented. Stewart *et al.*, (1999) stimulated a part of the visual cortex dedicated to motion perception (area V5/MT) and reported that these particular phosphenes tended to move. Stimulation in other parts of the visual cortex produces static phosphenes.

## How does TMS work?

TMS works by virtue of the principle of electromagnetic induction that was first discovered by Michael Faraday. A change in electric current in a wire (the stimulating coil) generates a magnetic field. The greater the *rate of change* in electric current, the greater the magnetic field. The magnetic field can then induce a secondary electric current to flow in another wire placed nearby. In the case of TMS, the secondary electric current is induced, not in a metal wire, but in the neurons below the stimulation site. The induced electric current in the neurons is caused by making them "fire" (i.e. generate action potentials) in the same way as they would when responding to stimuli in the environment. The use of the term "magnetic" is something of a misnomer as the magnetic field acts as a bridge between an electric current in the stimulating coil and the current induced in the brain. Pascual-Leone *et al.* (1999) suggest that "electrodeless, noninvasive electric stimulation" may be more accurate, although it is a less catchy term.

A number of different designs of stimulating coil exist, and the shape of the coil determines how focused the induced current is. One of the most common designs is the figure-of-eight coil. Although the coil itself is quite big, the focal point of stimulation lies at the intersection of the two loops and is about 1 cm$^2$ in area. If you have access to TMS equipment, try holding the coil a few centimeters above your arm. When the pulse is released, you should feel a slight harmless twinge on a small area of skin that is representative of the area of direct stimulation of the brain.

## The "virtual lesion"

TMS causes neurons underneath the stimulation site to be activated. If these neurons are involved in performing a critical cognitive function, then stimulating them artificially will disrupt that function. Although the TMS pulse itself is very brief (less than 1 millisecond), the effects on the cortex may last for several tens of ms. As such, the effects of a single TMS pulse are quickly reversed. Although this process is described as a "virtual lesion" or a "reversible lesion," a more accurate description would be in terms of interference. The neurons are being activated both from an internal source (the task demands themselves) and an external source (the TMS) with the latter disrupting the former. Of course, if the region is not involved in the task, then interference would not occur in this way.

## WHAT IS THE "VISUAL" CORTEX OF A BLIND PERSON USED FOR?

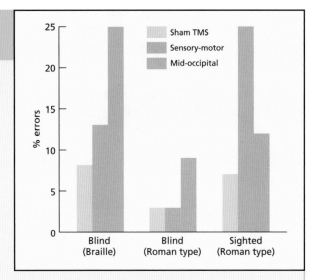

Could whole regions of the brain normally dedicated to one type of processing (e.g. vision) take on a completely different functional characteristic (e.g. touch)? A number of studies have investigated the functioning of the visual cortex (in the occipital lobes) in people who were blind from a very early age.

Sadato et al. (1996) conducted a brain imaging study demonstrating that early blind Braille readers showed activity in their primary visual cortex (V1) during Braille reading. This was not found for late blind or sighted individuals with their eyes closed. However, functional imaging methods can reveal increases in activity that may not be functionally critical. It could be, for instance, that the blind readers are *trying* to use the

TMS over mid-occipital "visual" cortex impairs tactile identification in the blind, but not in blindfolded sighted people, whereas TMS over sensorimotor (tactile) cortex impairs tactile discrimination in sighted individuals.

From Cohen et al., 1997. Reprinted by permission of Macmillan Publishers Ltd. © 1997.

visual cortex during Braille reading but that this activity is not actually contributing to task performance. To address this, lesion methods are appropriate. Given that early blind people with late brain damage restricted to occipital regions are rare (but see Hamilton et al., 2000), TMS avails itself as the most appropriate method.

Cohen et al. (1997) studied tactile identification of Braille letters in early blind individuals, and tactile identification of embossed letters in roman type in both early blind and (blindfolded) sighted individuals. When they placed their finger on the letter, a train of TMS pulses was delivered. The TMS was delivered to a number of sites, including the mid-occipital ("visual" cortex), the sensory-motor (tactile/motor cortex) and "air" as the control condition. For the blind participants, TMS over mid-occipital regions impaired tactile letter discrimination. This suggests that the "visual" cortex is used for touch in the early blind. Sighted people show disruption when TMS is applied over sensory-motor cortex. It is perhaps surprising that blind people do not additionally show an effect here. It could be that, because they are more skilled, they require a higher intensity of TMS for disruption to be induced. There is evidence for plasticity in somatosensory, as well as mid-occipital, regions in the blind as the region of the brain representing their reading fingers is enlarged by as much as two or three times (Pascual-Leone & Torres, 1993). Similar TMS studies have revealed cortical enlargements are found for skilled racquet players (Pearce et al., 2000), and cortical reductions found for limb amputees (Cohen et al., 1991). These suggest that level of use is critical for plasticity.

Is it likely that any brain region can substitute for the function of another? In this instance, the function of the brain region is largely the same (i.e. it makes fine-grained spatial discriminations) even though in one instance it responds to vision and in another to touch. However, more recent research suggests that the occipital cortex in blind individuals can support tasks of a very different nature (e.g. verb generation; Amedi et al., 2004).

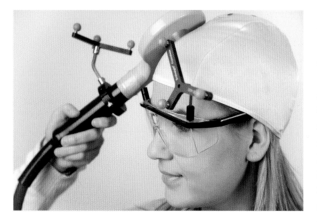

The coil is held against the participant's head, and a localized magnetic field is generated during performance of the task.

University of Durham/Simon Fraser/Science Photo Library.

TMS has a number of advantages over traditional lesion methods (Pascual-Leone *et al.*, 1999). The first advantage is that real brain damage may result in a reorganization of the cognitive system (a violation of the transparency assumption) whereas the effects of TMS are brief and reversible. This also means that within-subject designs (i.e. with and without lesion) are possible in TMS that are very rarely found with organic lesions (neurosurgical interventions are an interesting exception, but in this instance the brains are not strictly premorbidly "normal" given that surgery is warranted). In TMS, the location of the stimulated site can be removed or moved at will. In organic lesions, the brain injury may be larger than the area under investigation and may affect several cognitive processes.

| Advantages of TMS over organic lesions | Advantages of organic lesions over TMS |
| --- | --- |
| • No reorganization/compensation | • Subcortical lesions can be studied |
| • Can be used to determine timing of cognition | • Lesions can be accurately localized with MRI (effects of TMS are less well understood spatially) |
| • Lesion is focal | |
| • Lesion can be moved within the same participant | • Changes in behavior/cognition are more apparent |
| • Can study functional integration | |

Will TMS completely replace traditional neuropsychological methods? Probably not. For one thing, TMS is restricted in the sites that can be stimulated, i.e. those beneath the skull; stimulations elsewhere cannot be studied with TMS. Moreover, the spatial extent of the changes induced by TMS is not fully understood and it is possible that more distant brain structures receive stimulation if they are connected to the stimulation site (Paus, 1999). In contrast, organic lesion localization using MRI is more tried and tested. Another advantage of traditional neuropsychology is that the "accidents of nature" turn up some unexpected and bizarre patterns. For example, some patients can name body parts, but not point to named parts of their body (Semenza & Goodglass, 1985); and some patients can draw a bicycle, but not recognize a drawing of a bicycle (Behrmann *et al.*, 1994). Perhaps these sorts of pattern could also be observed with TMS, but nobody would think to look for them without the patient-based observations. Indeed, the effects of TMS "lesions" are often only observable through slowed reaction times and not through error rates or the externally observable behavior that characterizes most neurological deficits.

## Using TMS to study functional integration

The uses of TMS described so far come within the framework of functional specialization: i.e. trying to understand the functional contributions of particular regions to certain aspects of cognition. A complementary approach is functional integration; i.e. trying to understand how one region influences another or how one cognitive function influences another. One way in which this is achieved is by undergoing a session of focal TMS and then studying how this affects the communication between brain regions using fMRI (Bestmann & Feredoes, 2013). (Note: for safety reasons TMS cannot be done in the scanner itself). Another approach is to use TMS to examine competition between brain regions. If there are different processes competing in the brain, then eliminating one process from the competition (using TMS) might have a beneficial effect on the other.

The brain divides up the visual world into different attributes such as color, shape and motion and these different attributes are essentially represented in different regions of the brain (see Chapter 6 for discussion). One theoretical question is: "Do these regions compete with each other, and does attending to one attribute (e.g. motion) have positive or negative consequences for irrelevant attributes (e.g. color)?" To answer this question, Walsh *et al.* (1998b) presented participants with arrays of different shapes made up of different colors that were either moving or static. The task of the participants was to determine whether a prespecified target (e.g. a moving cross, a static cross, a green cross) was present or absent in the array as quickly as possible. TMS was delivered at area V5/MT (specialized for visual motion perception) at a number of different time intervals, but, for simplicity, the overall pattern across time only will be discussed here. In the first two examples, motion is needed to discriminate between targets and distractors because relying on shape alone will not help (some Xs move and some Xs are static). Unsurprisingly, a virtual lesion to V5/MT disrupts this visual search,

| Stimulus | Task | | Result |
|---|---|---|---|
| | Find moving X (arrows shows movement) | TMS at V5 | *Slower* RT to detect target (interference) |
| | Find the static X (arrows shows movement) | TMS at V5 | *Slower* RT to detect target (interference) |
| | Find the green X | TMS at V5 | *Faster* RT to detect target (facilitation) |

The participants must search for the presence or absence of a specified target (e.g. moving X) in an array of other items. TMS was applied over area V5/MT (involved in visual motion perception) at various points during search. If motion was relevant to the search task, then performance was impaired, but if motion was irrelevant to the search task, then performance was facilitated.

Adapted from Walsh *et al.*, 1998b.

as has been found for organic lesions to this area (McLeod *et al.*, 1989). The unexpected finding comes when there is no motion at all and the participants must find a target based on color and form (a green X). In this instance, a virtual lesion to V5/MT facilitates search efficiency. This suggests that different visual areas may compete with each other and eliminating an irrelevant visual area can improve the operation of relevant ones.

## Practical aspects of using TMS

When designing experiments using TMS (or when evaluating other people's choice of design), there are three main considerations: when to deliver the pulses, where to deliver the pulses, and selection of appropriate control conditions (for a good overview, see Robertson *et al.*, 2003). Finally, given that the brain is being stimulated, one must be fully aware of safety and ethical considerations when performing TMS experiments.

### *Timing issues—repetitive or single pulse?*

The issue of when to deliver the pulse is crucial to the success, or otherwise, of a TMS experiment. On rare occasions, the time taken for a stimulus to be registered in a given brain region is known by previous research using other techniques. For example, single-cell recordings suggest that it takes 100 ms for a visual stimulus to be registered in the primary visual cortex (area V1), and TMS studies in which a single pulse is delivered close to this critical window can render the subject effectively "blind" to the stimulus (Corthout *et al.*, 1999). On most occasions, information such as this will not be known. In this situation, there are a number of options. First, one could make the time of pulse delivery a variable in its own right. For example, if a stimulus is presented for 500 ms, the TMS pulse (or pulses) could be delivered in different time windows (0–50 ms, 50–100 ms, . . . 450–500 ms). This experimental design could thus provide important information about the timing of cognition, as well as providing information about the necessity of that region. An alternative solution is to use a train of pulses during the task (i.e. repetitive or rTMS). In this situation, the experiment becomes potentially more powerful in its ability to detect the necessity of a region, but it would not be possible to draw conclusions about timing because it would be unclear which pulse (or pulses) was critical. Whether or not single-pulse or rTMS is used is not only related to whether timing is an independent variable, but also to the nature of the task itself. Some tasks may require several pulses for TMS to exert interference. The reasons why this might be are not fully understood, but it is a general rule of thumb that TMS studies of perceptual processes have often used single-pulse

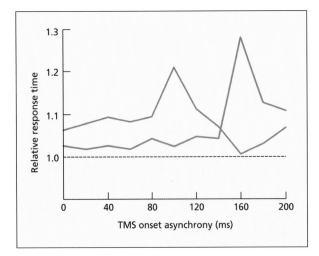

TMS can be used to establish *when* in a task a given region is critical. In this experiment, participants had to search for a visual target in an array that was either present or absent. TMS applied over the parietal lobes disrupted performance, but only in specific time windows, with present trials occurring earlier (100 ms; purple line) than absent trials (160 ms; green line). A temporal dissociation such as this could not be observed in patients with irreversible organic brain damage.

From Ashbridge *et al.*, 1997. © 1997 Elsevier. Reproduced with permission.

designs, whereas studies of "higher" cognition (e.g. memory, language) have often used rTMS (Walsh & Rushworth, 1999).

## How to hit the spot?

To conduct a TMS experiment, one needs to make some assumptions about which regions of the brain would be interesting to stimulate. In some instances, functional resolution is all that is needed. Just as with the arguments concerning classical versus cognitive neuropsychology, one may wish to establish that a given task/behavior can be selectively disrupted (in which case, the location of the stimulation site is not relevant to the type of conclusion drawn).

Positions on the head can be defined relative to landmarks, such as those used in the EEG system of electrode placement. Skull landmarks include the inion (a bony protrusion at the back of the skull), the anion (the bony ridge between the eyebrows), and the vertex (midway between the anion and inion, and midway between the ears). For example, one published way of approximately locating area V5/MT (dedicated to visual motion perception) is by marking a spot 5 cm in front of the inion, and 3 cm up from it (Walsh et al., 1998a). The spot can be physically marked by placing an X on the skin, or by marking the position on a taut swimming cap. If a precise location is not known before the study, then one could stimulate, say, six different spots lying in a $2 \times 3$ cm grid, drawn on a swimming cap relative to a fixed skull landmark. Different adjacent positions could then serve as control conditions in the analysis.

Structural and functional MRI can also be used to locate candidate regions of stimulation taking into account individual differences in brain anatomy and skull shape (this is called *frameless stereotaxy*). A structural or functional MRI scan can be obtained prior to TMS and then online digital registration (using specialist software) enables the position on the skull to be identified. Alternatively, the TMS could be performed prior to a structural MRI scan in which the stimulation sites used have been marked in such a way as to render them visible on the scan. Cod liver oil tablets, attached to the head, have been used previously (Hadland et al., 2001).

## What is the appropriate control condition?

Two possible control conditions for TMS experiments have already been considered. First, one can compare performance when the same region is stimulated in critical and non-critical time windows. Second, one can compare stimulation in critical and non-critical regions. Some consideration needs to be given to the selection of the non-critical region. Using regions adjacent to the critical region can provide extra clues about the spatial size of the region of interest. In studies in which there is good reason to believe that the cognitive function is lateralized, one could use the same site on the opposite hemisphere as a control. A further advantage in using the control conditions mentioned above is that peripheral effects of TMS can be minimized. These include the loud sound of the pulse and twitches caused by inadvertent stimulation of the facial nerves and muscles. The latter can be more pronounced at some sites and so using adjacent regions or opposite hemisphere regions would minimize this. "Sham TMS," in which the coil is held in the air rather than against the head, is not an ideal control condition, and having no TMS at all as a control condition is also not desirable.

Another control condition that can be used in TMS experiments is a task control. Thus, the same region can be stimulated at the same times, but with some aspect of the task changed (e.g. the stimuli, the instructions).

## Evaluation

TMS is an interesting addition to the cognitive neuroscientist's toolkit. It is able to ascertain the importance of a given region by stimulating that region during task performance. As such, it is related to other lesion methods that are used for establishing the importance of a given region, but it has certain advantages over the organic lesion method. The main advantage lies in the fact that the interference is short-lived and reversible. It can also be used to explore how regions interact with each other (functional connectivity) and shed light on the timing of cognitive processes.

## SAFETY AND ETHICAL ISSUES IN TMS RESEARCH

Researchers need to bear in mind a number of safety issues when conducting TMS experiments. It is essential to be aware of the local regulations that apply in your own institution, but the following points are likely to be important:

- The most recent safety and ethics guidelines come from a consensus of leading researchers in the field that offers guidance on issues such as the number and intensity of pulses (Rossi *et al.*, 2009).
- Whereas single-pulse TMS is generally considered to be safe, repetitive-pulse TMS carries a very small risk of inducing a seizure (Wassermann *et al.*, 1996). Given this risk, participants with epilepsy or a familial history of epilepsy are normally excluded. Participants with pacemakers and medical implants should also be excluded. Credit cards, computer discs and computers should be kept at least 1 m away from the coil.
- The intensity of the pulses that can be delivered is normally specified with respect to the "motor threshold"; that is, the intensity of the pulse, delivered over the motor cortex, that produces a just noticeable motor response (for a discussion of problems with this, see Robertson *et al.*, 2003).
- During the experiment, some participants might experience minor discomfort due to the sound of the pulses and facial twitches. Although each TMS pulse is loud (~100 dB), the duration of each pulse is brief (1 ms). Nonetheless, it is mandatory to protect the ears with earplugs or headphones. When the coil is in certain positions, the facial nerves (as well as the brain) may be stimulated, resulting in involuntary twitches (e.g. blinking, jaw clamping). Participants should be warned of this and told they can exercise their right to withdraw from the study if it causes too much discomfort.
- It is generally believed that a single session of TMS has no long-term consequences. However, repeated participation in experiments could conceivably have longer-term effects—either positive or deleterious. A number of studies report an *improvement* in mood in depressed individuals following repeated frontal lobe stimulation (George *et al.*, 1995). But this study involved repeated stimulation on a daily basis. Except in cases of therapeutic intervention, it is good practice not to test the same participants many times over a short interval.

# TRANSCRANIAL DIRECT CURRENT STIMULATION (tDCS)

The use of electrical currents to stimulate the brain has a long and checkered history, with the most notorious noninvasive method being electro-convulsive therapy (ECT) used to "treat" psychiatric illnesses. Unlike ECT, the method of transcranial direct current stimulation (tDCS) uses a very weak electric current. Direct current involves the flow of electric charge from a positive site (an anode) to a negative site (a cathode). In tDCS, a stimulating pad (either anodal or cathodal) is placed over the region of interest and the control pad is placed in a site of no interest (sometimes on the front of the forehead, or sometimes on a distant site such as the shoulders). After a period of stimulation (e.g. 10 min) a cognitive task is performed and this can be compared with sham stimulation, or anodal and cathodal stimulation can be directly contrasted. **Cathodal tDCS** stimulation tends to disrupt performance (i.e. it is conceptually equivalent to a virtual lesion approach) whereas **anodal tDCS** stimulation tends to enhance performance (Nitsche *et al.*, 2008). For example, anodal stimulation over visual cortex leads to an enhanced early visual ERP component (N100) and enhances the ability to detect weak visual stimuli, whereas cathodal stimulation has the opposite effects (Accornero *et al.*, 2007; Antal *et al.*, 2001).

Stagg and Nitsche (2011) provide a summary of the likely neurophysiological mechanisms. It is important to consider the immediate effects of direct current stimulation and the aftereffects separately. Animal models of direct current stimulation followed by single-cell recordings have shown that anodal stimulation increases the spontaneous firing rate of neurons whereas cathodal stimulation reduces the firing rate. The *immediate* effects of stimulation are believed to occur on the resting membrane potential rather than modulation at the synapse. However, the *aftereffects* of stimulation are likely to occur due to changes in synaptic plasticity influencing learning and perhaps affecting different neurotransmitter systems. Anodal stimulation affects the GABA system (this neurotransmitter has inhibitory effects) whereas cathodal stimulation affects the glutamate system (this neurotransmitter has excitatory effects).

The current safety guidelines recommend upper limits on the size of the current and the surface area of the stimulating electrodes (Nitsche *et al.*, 2003).

**KEY TERMS**

**Cathodal tDCS**
Decreases cortical excitability and decreases performance.

**Anodal tDCS**
Increases cortical excitability and increases performance.

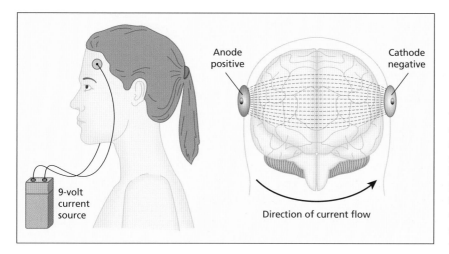

The method of tDCS uses a very weak electric current applied using stimulating pads attached to the scalp. Direct current involves the flow of electric charge from a positive site (an anode) to a negative site (a cathode).

Adapted from George and Aston-Jones.

If the current is concentrated on a small electrode, then it can cause skin irritation. However, unlike TMS, participants often cannot tell whether the machine is switched on or used as sham (there is no sound or twitching). As such there is very little discomfort.

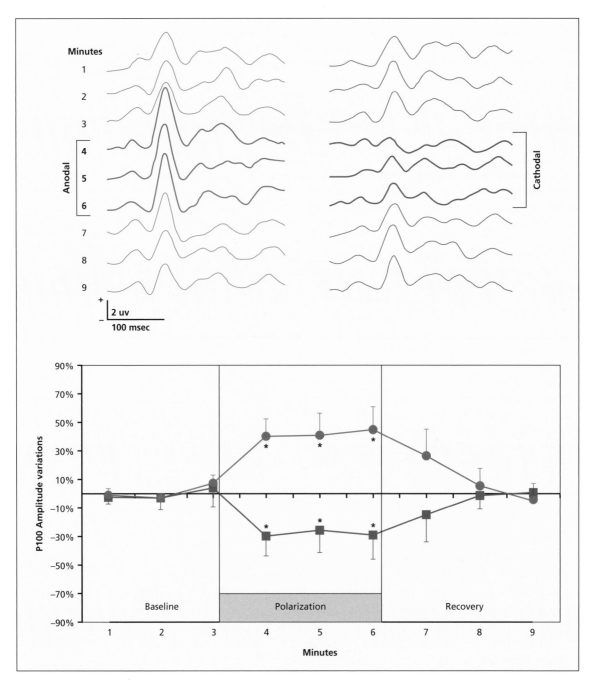

tDCS applied over the visual cortex (for 3 min) disrupts the amplitude of an ERP component (P100) elicited in response to viewing a black and white checkerboard. Anodal stimulation increases the amplitude, but cathodal stimulation reduces it.
From Accornero *et al.*, 2007.

Repeated sessions of anodal tDCS are becoming increasingly used for cognitive enhancement (of normal brains) and neurorehabilitation (of damaged brains). For instance, repeated sessions of tDCS over the primary motor cortex leads to increased cortical excitability and greater hand functionality in patients with motor impairments following stroke (Hummel *et al.*, 2005). In this study, the treatment was compared with sham and the procedure was double blind (i.e. neither participant nor experimenter knew which condition they were in). Other studies using anodal tDCS have reported improvements in language following stroke (Monti *et al.*, 2008) and improved working memory in patients with Parkinson's disease (Boggio *et al.*, 2006).

## SUMMARY AND KEY POINTS OF THE CHAPTER

- A double dissociation between two patients occurs when patient 1 is significantly better than patient 2 on task A, and patient 2 is significantly better than patient 1 on task B. The standard interpretation of this is that task A and task B utilize some different neural resources.
- The use of single cases has led to important insights into the way in which cognitive components are organized and may be fractionated.
- Group studies of patients are important for making links between lesion location and behavioral deficits, and provide an important source of converging evidence for functional imaging data.
- Transcranial magnetic stimulation (TMS) works by stimulating a region of cortex placed beneath a current-carrying coil. This stimulation temporarily interferes with ongoing cognitive activity in that region and, therefore, provides information about the necessity of that region for performing the task. This has been termed a "virtual lesion."
- Transcranial direct current stimulation (tDCS) has a poorer temporal and spatial resolution to TMS, but has the advantage of being able to facilitate cognitive function (anodal tDCS).

## EXAMPLE ESSAY QUESTIONS

- What assumptions must one accept to be able to draw inferences about normal cognition from adults with brain damage? Are these assumptions plausible?
- Critically evaluate the role of group studies in neuropsychological research.
- What are the advantages and disadvantages of using single cases to draw inferences about normal cognitive functioning?
- How have TMS and tDCS studies contributed to our knowledge of brain plasticity?
- Compare and contrast lesion methods arising from organic brain damage with TMS and tDCS.

Visit the companion website at www. psypress/cw/ward for:

- References to key papers and readings
- Video lectures and interviews on key topics with leading psychologists Elizabeth Warrington and author Jamie Ward, as well as demonstrations of and lectures on brain stimulation
- Multiple choice questions and interactive flashcards to test your knowledge
- Downloadable glossary

## RECOMMENDED FURTHER READING

- A special edition of *Cognitive Neuropsychology* (1988), Vol. 5, No. 5, is dedicated to methodological issues related to single-case and group studies in neuropsychology.
- A special section of the journal *Cortex* (2003), *39*(1), debates the use of dissociations in neuropsychology.
- Pascual-Leone, A., Davey, N. J., Rothwell, J., Wassermann, E. M., & Puri, B. K. (2002). *Handbook of transcranial magnetic stimulation*. London: Arnold. A detailed account of the methods and uses of TMS, with a strong clinical slant.
- Walsh, V. & Pascual-Leone, A. (2003). *Transcranial magnetic stimulation: A neurochronometrics of mind*. Cambridge, MA: MIT Press. A detailed account of the methods and uses of TMS, with a cognitive neuroscience slant.

# CHAPTER 6

# The seeing brain

## CONTENTS

Students who are new to cognitive neuroscience might believe that the eyes do the seeing and the brain merely interprets the image on the retina. This is far from the truth. Although the eyes play an undeniably crucial role in vision, the brain is involved in actively constructing a visual representation of the world that is not a literal reproduction of the pattern of light falling on the eyes. For example, the brain divides a continuous pattern of light into discrete objects and surfaces, and translates the two-dimensional retinal image into a three-dimensional interactive model of the environment. In fact, the brain is biased to perceive objects when there is not necessarily an object there. Consider the Kanizsa illusion (p. 108) —it is quite hard to perceive the stimulus as three corners as opposed to one triangle. The brain makes inferences during visual perception that go beyond the raw information given. Psychologists make a distinction between **sensation** and **perception**. Sensation refers to the effects of a stimulus on the sensory organs, whereas perception involves the elaboration and interpretation of that sensory stimulus based on, for example, knowledge of how objects are structured. This chapter will consider many examples of the constructive nature of the seeing brain,

Do you automatically perceive a white triangle that isn't really there? This is called the Kanizsa illusion.

## KEY TERMS

**Sensation**
The effects of a stimulus on the sensory organs.

**Perception**
The elaboration and interpretation of a sensory stimulus based on, for example, knowledge of how objects are structured.

**Retina**
The internal surface of the eyes that consists of multiple layers. Some layers contain photoreceptors that convert light to neural signals, and others consist of neurons themselves.

**Rod cells**
A type of photoreceptor specialized for low levels of light intensity, such as those found at night.

from the perception of visual attributes, such as color and motion, up to the recognition of objects and faces.

## FROM EYE TO BRAIN

The **retina** is the internal surface of the eyes that contains specialized photo-receptors that convert (or *transduce*) light into neural signals. The photoreceptors are made up of **rod cells**, which are specialized for low levels of light intensity,

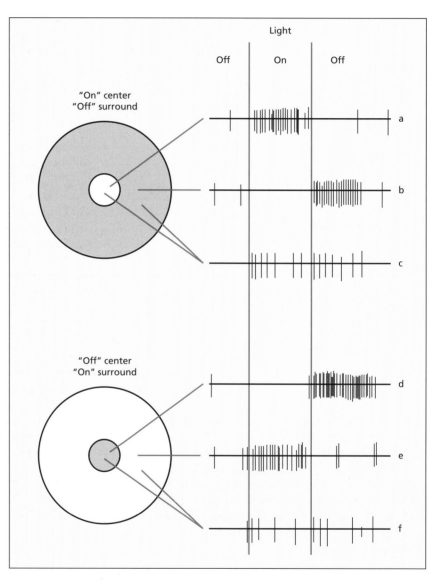

Receptive fields of two retinal ganglion cells. The cell in the upper part of the figure responds when the center is illuminated (on-center, a) and when the surround is darkened (off-surround, b). The cell in the lower part of the figure responds when the center is darkened (off-center, d) and when the surround is illuminated (on-surround, e). Both cells give on- and off-responses when both center and surround are illuminated (c and f), but neither response is as strong as when only center or surround is illuminated.

From Hubel, 1963.

such as those found at night, and **cone cells**, which are more active during daytime and are specialized for detecting different wavelengths of light (from which the brain can compute color).

There is already a stage of neural computation that takes place at the retina itself. Bipolar cells in the retina are a type of neuron that behave in one of two ways: detecting light areas on dark backgrounds (ON) or detecting dark areas on light backgrounds (OFF). A higher level of processing, by retinal ganglion cells, has a more complex set of on and off properties. Most retinal ganglion neurons have a particular characteristic response to light that is termed a *center-surround* receptive field. The term **receptive field** denotes the region of space that elicits a response from a given neuron. One intriguing feature of the receptive fields of these cells, and many others in the visual system, is that they do not respond to light as such (Barlow, 1953; Kuffler & Barlow, 1953). Rather, they respond to *differences* in light across their receptive field. Light falling in the center of the receptive field may excite the neuron, whereas light in the surrounding area may switch it off (but when the light is removed from this region, the cell is excited again). Other retinal ganglion cells have the opposite profile (on-center off-surround cells). Light over the entire receptive field may elicit no net effect because the center and surround inhibit each other. These center-surround cells form the building blocks for more advanced processing by the brain, enabling detection of, among other things, edges and orientations.

The output of the retinal ganglion cells is relayed to the brain via the *optic nerves*. The point at which the optic nerve leaves the eye is called the **blind spot**, because there are no rods and cones present there. If you open only one of your eyes (and keep it stationary), there is a spot in which there is no visual information. Yet, one does not perceive a black hole in one's vision. This is another example of the brain filling in missing information. The highest concentration of cones is at a point called the *fovea*, and the level of detail that can be perceived (or visual acuity) is greatest at this point. Rods are more evenly distributed across the retina (but are not present at the fovea).

## The primary visual cortex and geniculostriate pathway

There are a number of different pathways from the retina to the brain (for a review, see Stoerig and Cowey, 1997). The dominant visual pathway in the human brain travels to the **primary visual cortex** at the back, or posterior, of the brain, via a processing station called the lateral geniculate nucleus (LGN). The LGN is part of the thalamus which has a more general role in processing sensory information; there is one LGN in each hemisphere. The primary visual cortex is also referred to as V1, or as the striate cortex because it has a larger than usual stripe running

To find your blind spots, hold the image about 50 cm away. With your left eye open (right closed), look at the +. Slowly bring the image (or move your head) closer while looking at the + (do not move your eyes). At a certain distance, the dot will disappear from sight . . . this is when the dot falls on the blind spot of your retina. Reverse the process: Close your left eye and look at the dot with your right eye. Move the image slowly closer to you and the + should disappear.

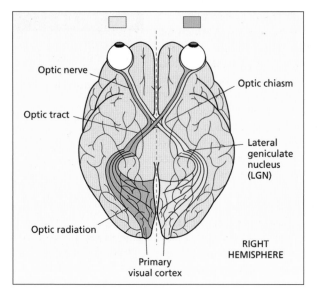

Connections from the retina to the primary visual cortex—the geniculostriate pathway.

From Zeki, 1993. © Blackwell Publishing. Reproduced with permission.

through one layer that can be seen when stained and viewed under a microscope. This particular route is called the geniculostriate pathway.

The neural representation in the lateral geniculate nucleus divides up information on the retinal surface in a number of interesting ways. Objects in the right side of space (termed the right visual field) fall on the left side of the retina of *both* eyes and project to the left lateral geniculate nucleus. The representation in the lateral geniculate nucleus thus contains information from both the left and right eyes. This information is segregated into the six different neuronal layers of this structure, three for each eye. The layers of the lateral geniculate nucleus are not only divided according to the eye (left or right) but contain a further subdivision. The upper four layers have small cell bodies and have been termed *parvocellular*, or P layers, whereas the lower two layers contain larger cell bodies and have been termed *magnocellular*, or M layers. Parvocellular cells respond to detail and are concerned with color vision. Magnocellular cells are more sensitive to movement than color and respond to larger areas of visual field (Maunsell, 1987). More recently a third type of cell (K or konio) has been documented in the LGN that lies between the magnocellular (magno) and parvocellular (parvo) layers (Hendry & Reid, 2000). These cells show much less functional specificity than magno and parvo cells and have a different pattern of connectivity.

The properties of neurons in the primary visual cortex were elucidated by pioneering work by David Hubel and Torsten Wiesel (1959, 1962, 1965, 1968,

## EYE-BRAIN MYTH 1

Do not make the mistake of believing that the retina of the left eye represents just the left side of space, and the retina of the right eye represents just the right side of space. (If you are still confused, close one eye and keep it fixed—you should be able to see both sides of space with a minor occlusion due to the nose.) Rather, the left side of the left eye and the left side of the right eye both contain an image of objects on the right side of space. The right side of the left eye and the right side of the right eye both contain an image of objects on the left side of space.

## EYE-BRAIN MYTH 2

If you think that the response of neurons on the retina or in the brain is like the response of pixels in a television screen, then think again. Some visual neurons respond when light is taken away, or when there is a *change* in light intensity across the region that they respond to. Other neurons in extrastriate areas respond only to certain colors, or movement in certain directions. These neurons often have very large receptive fields that do not represent a very precise pixel-like location at all.

1970a), for which they were awarded the Nobel Prize in Medicine in 1981. The method they used was to record the response of single neurons in the visual cortex of cats and monkeys. Before going on to consider their work, it might be useful to take a step backwards and ask the broader question: "What kinds of visual information need to be coded by neurons?" First of all, neurons need to be able to represent how light or dark something is. In addition, neurons need to represent the color of an object to distinguish, say, between fruit and foliage of comparable lightness/darkness but complementary in color. Edges also need to be detected, and these might be defined as abrupt changes in brightness or color. These edges might be useful for perceiving the shape of objects. Changes in brightness or color could also reflect movement of an object, and it is conceivable that some neurons may be specialized for extracting this type of visual information. Depth may also be perceived by comparing the two different retinal images.

The neurons in the primary visual cortex (V1) transform the information in the lateral geniculate nucleus into a basic code that enables all of these types of visual information to be extracted by later stages of processing. As with many great discoveries, there was an element of chance. Hubel and Wiesel noted that an oriented crack in a projector slide drove a single cell in V1 wild, i.e. it produced lots of action potentials (cited in Zeki, 1993). They then systematically went on to show that many of these cells responded only to particular orientations. These were termed **simple cells**. The responses of these simple cells could be construed as a combination of the responses of center-surround cells in the lateral geniculate nucleus (Hubel & Wiesel, 1962). The cells also integrate information across both eyes and respond to similar input to either the left or right eye. Many orientation-selective cells were found to be wavelength-sensitive too (Hubel & Wiesel, 1968), thus providing a primitive code from which to derive color.

Just as center-surround cells might be the building blocks of simple cells, Hubel and Wiesel (1962) speculated that simple cells themselves might be combined into what they termed **complex cells**. These are orientation-selective too, but can be distinguished from simple cells by their larger receptive fields and the fact that complex cells require stimulation across their entire length, whereas simple cells will respond to single points of light within the excitatory region. Outside of V1, another type of cell, termed **hypercomplex cells**, which can be built from the responses of several complex cells, was observed (Hubel & Wiesel, 1965). These cells were also orientation-sensitive, but the length was also critical. The receptive fields of hypercomplex cells may consist of adding excitatory complex cells, but with inhibitory complex cells located at either end to act as "stoppers." In sum, the response properties of cells in V1 enable more complex visual information (e.g. edges) to be constructed out of more simple information.

The take-home message of the work of Hubel and Wiesel is of a hierarchically organized visual system in which more complex visual features are built (bottom-up) from more simple ones. However, this is only half of the story. Information

## KEY TERMS

**Simple cells**
In vision, cells that respond to light in a particular orientation.

**Complex cells**
In vision, cells that respond to light in a particular orientation but do not respond to single points of light.

**Hypercomplex cells**
In vision, cells that respond to particular orientations and particular lengths.

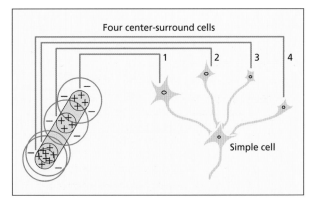

A simple cell in V1 responds to lines of particular length and orientation. Its response may be derived from a combination of responses from different cells with center-surround properties such as those located in the lateral geniculate nucleus.

From Zeki, 1993. © Blackwell Publishing. Reproduced with permission.

from more complex representations also propagates *down* the hierarchy. For instance, in the Kanizsa illusion there are cells in V2 (but not V1) that respond to the illusory "white edges" of the triangle (Von der Heydt *et al.*, 1984). This is assumed to reflect feedback information to V2 from regions in the brain that represent shapes and surfaces (Kogo & Wagemans, 2013).

## Cortical and non-cortical routes to seeing

To date, around ten different pathways from the eye to the brain have been discovered, of which the pathway via the lateral geniculate nucleus to V1 is the most well understood and appears to make the largest contribution to human visual perception (Stoerig & Cowey, 1997). The other routes are evolutionarily more ancient. Evolution appears not to have replaced these routes with "better" ones, but has retained them and added new routes that enable finer levels of processing or that serve somewhat different functions. For example, a visual route to the suprachiasmatic nucleus (SCN) in the hypothalamus provides information about night and day that is used to configure a biological clock (Klein *et al.*, 1991). Other routes, such as via the superior colliculus and inferior pulvinar, are important for orienting to stimuli (e.g. a sudden flash of light) by initiating automatic body and eye movements (Wurtz *et al.*, 1982). These latter routes are faster than the route via V1 and can thus provide an early warning signal; for instance, to threatening or unexpected stimuli. This can explain how it is possible to unconsciously turn to look at something but without realizing its importance until after orienting. More recently, an alternative pathway from the LGN (via the K-cells) to the cortex has been documented that projects to a part of the brain that

There are believed to be ten different routes from the retina to different regions of the brain.

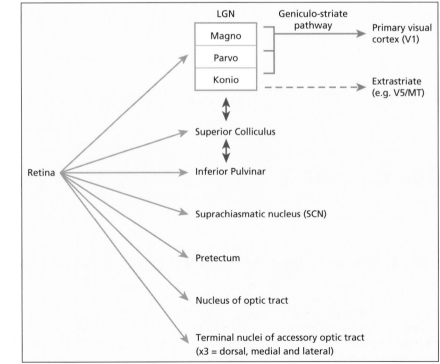

## EYE–BRAIN MYTH 3

The image on the retina and the representation of it in V1 are "upside down" with respect to the outside world. As such, one might wonder how the brain turns it the right way up. This question is meaningless because it presupposes that the orientation of things in the outside world is in some way "correct" and the brain's representation of it is in some way "incorrect." There is no "correct" orientation (all orientation is relative) and the brain does not need to turn things around to perceive them appropriately. The function of the seeing brain is to extract relevant information from the environment, not to create a carbon copy that preserves, among other things, the same relative top-to-bottom orientation.

is specialized for process of visual motion (area V5/MT) without first projecting to V1 (Sincich *et al.*, 2004). This may account for the fact that some patients with cortical blindness can still discriminate motion.

## Evaluation

The primary visual cortex (V1) contains cells that enable a basic detection of visual features, such as edges, that are likely to be important for segregating the scene into different objects. There is some evidence for a hierarchical processing of visual features such that responses of earlier neurons in the hierarchy form the building blocks for more advanced responses of neurons higher up in the hierarchy. A number of other routes operate in parallel to the geniculostriate route to V1. These may be important for early detection of visual stimuli, among other things.

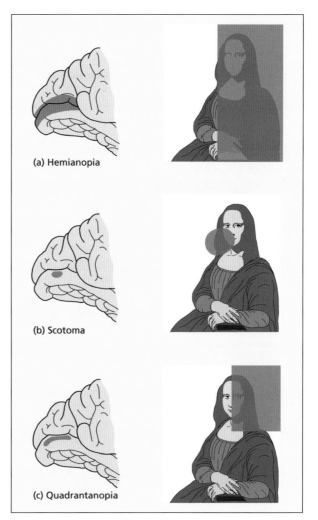

(a) Hemianopia

(b) Scotoma

(c) Quadrantanopia

Partial damage to the primary visual cortex (V1) can result in blindness in specific regions. This is because this region of the brain is retinotopically organized. Area V1 is at the back of the brain and on the middle surface between the two hemispheres.

Adapted from Zeki, 1993.

KEY TERMS

**Hemianopia**
Cortical blindness restricted to one half of the visual field (associated with damage to the primary visual cortex in one hemisphere).

**Quadrantanopia**
Cortical blindness restricted to a quarter of the visual field.

**Scotoma**
A small region of cortical blindness.

**Retinotopic organization**
The receptive fields of a set of neurons are organized in a such a way as to reflect the spatial organization present in the retina.

**Blindsight**
A symptom in which the patient reports not being able to consciously see stimuli in a particular region but can nevertheless perform visual discriminations (e.g. long, short) accurately.

# CORTICAL BLINDNESS AND "BLINDSIGHT"

Loss of one eye, or the optic nerve of that eye, results in complete blindness in that eye. The spared eye would still be able to perceive the left and right sides of space and transmit information to the left and right primary visual cortex. But what would be the consequences of *complete* damage to one side of the primary visual cortex itself? In this instance, there would be cortical blindness for one side of space (if the left cortex is damaged, then the right visual field would be blind, and vice versa). The deficit would be present when using either the left or right eye alone, or both eyes together. This deficit is termed **hemianopia** (or homonymous hemianopia). *Partial* damage to the primary visual cortex might affect one subregion of space. As the upper part of V1 (above a line called the calcarine fissure) represents the bottom side of space, and the lower part of V1 represents the top part of space—damage here can give rise to cortical blindness in a quarter of the visual field (so-called **quadrantanopia**). Blindness in a smaller region of space is referred to as a cortical **scotoma**. Note that the layout of visual information in V1 parallels that found on the retina. That is, points that are close in space on the retina are also close in space in V1. Areas such as V1 are said to be **retinotopically organized**.

The previous section described how there are several visual routes from the eye to the brain. Each of these routes makes a different contribution to visual perception. Taking this on board, one might question whether damage to the brain (as opposed to the eyes) could really lead to total blindness unless each and every one of these visual pathways coincidentally happened to be damaged. In fact, this is indeed the case. Damage to the primary visual cortex does lead to an inability to report visual stimuli presented in the corresponding affected region of space and can be disabling for such a person. Nevertheless, the other remaining visual routes might permit some aspects of visual perception to be performed satisfactorily in exactly the same regions of space that are reported to be blind. This paradoxical situation has been referred to as "**blindsight**" (Weiskrantz *et al.*, 1974).

Patients exhibiting blindsight deny having seen a visual stimulus even though their behavior implies that the stimulus was in fact seen (for a review, see Cowey, 2004). For example, patient DB had part of his primary visual cortex (V1) removed to cure a chronic and severe migraine (this was reported in detail by Weiskrantz, 1986). When stimuli were presented in DB's blind field, he reported seeing nothing. However, if asked to point or move his eyes to the stimulus then he could do so with accuracy, while still maintaining that he saw nothing. DB could perform a number of other discriminations well above chance, such as orientation discrimination (horizontal, vertical, or diagonal), motion detection (static or moving) and contrast discrimination (gray on black versus gray on white). In all these tasks DB felt as if he was guessing even though he clearly was not. Some form/shape discrimination was possible but appeared to be due to detection of edges and orientations rather than shape itself. For example, DB could discriminate between X and O, but not between X and △ and not between squares and rectangles that contain lines of similar orientation (but see Marcel, 1998).

How can the performance of patients such as DB be explained? First of all, one needs to eliminate the possibility that the task is being performed by remnants of the primary visual cortex. For example, there could be islands of spared cortex within the supposedly damaged region (Campion *et al.*, 1983). However, many patients have undergone structural MRI and it has been established that no cortex remains in the region corresponding to the "blind" field (Cowey, 2004). Another explanation is that light from the stimulus is scattered into other intact parts of the visual field and is detected by intact parts of the primary visual cortex. For example, some patients may be able to detect stimuli supposedly in their blind field because of light reflected on their nose or other surfaces in the laboratory (Campion *et al.*, 1983). Evidence against this comes from the fact that performance is superior in the "blindsight" region to the natural blind spot (found in us all). This cannot be accounted for by scattered light (see Cowey, 2004). Thus, the most satisfactory explanation of blindsight is that it reflects the operation of other visual routes from the eye to the brain rather than residual ability of V1. For instance, the ability to detect visual motion in blindsight might be due to direct projections from the LGN to area V5/MT that bypasses V1 (Hesselmann *et al.*, 2010).

This account raises important questions about the functional importance of conscious versus unconscious visual processes. If unconscious visual processes can discriminate well, then why is the conscious route needed at all? As it turns out, such questions are misguided because the unconscious routes (used in blindsight) are not as efficient and are only capable of coarse discriminations in comparison to the finely tuned discriminations achieved by V1 (see Cowey, 2004). At present, we do not have a full understanding of why some neural processes but not others are associated with conscious visual experiences. Nevertheless, studies of patients with blindsight provide important clues about the relative contribution and functions of the different visual pathways in the brain.

If a visually presented semi-circle abuts a cortical scotoma (the shaded area), then the patient might report a complete circle. Thus, rather than seeing a gap in their vision, patients with blindsight might fill in the gap using visual information in the spared field. If the semi-circle is presented inside the scotoma, it isn't seen at all, whereas if it is away from the scotoma, it is perceived normally.

Adapted from Torjussen, 1976.

Blindsight ≠ normal vision – awareness of vision

Blindsight = impaired vision + no awareness of vision

# FUNCTIONAL SPECIALIZATION OF THE VISUAL CORTEX BEYOND V1

The neurons in V1 are specialized for detecting edges and orientations, wavelengths and light intensity. These form the building blocks for constructing more complex visual representations based on form (i.e. shape), color and movement. Some of the principal anatomical connections between these regions are shown in the figure below. One important division, discussed in more detail in later chapters, is between the **ventral stream** (involved in object recognition and memory) and the **dorsal stream** (involved in action and attention). The ventral stream runs along the temporal lobes whereas the dorsal stream terminates in the parietal lobes.

The occipital cortex outside V1 is known as the *extrastriate cortex* (or prestriate cortex). The receptive fields in these extrastriate visual areas become increasingly broader and less coherently organized in space, with areas V4 and

## KEY TERMS

**Ventral stream**
In vision, a pathway extending from the occipital lobes to the temporal lobes involved in object recognition, memory and semantics.

**Dorsal stream**
In vision, a pathway extending from the occipital lobes to the parietal lobes involved in visually guided action and attention.

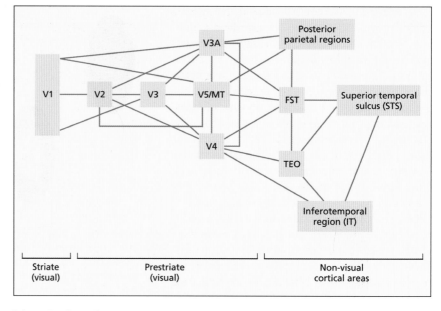

Information from V1 is sent in parallel to a number of other regions in the extrastriate cortex, some of which are specialized for processing particular visual attributes (e.g. V5/MT for movement). These extrastriate regions interface with the temporal cortex (involved in object recognition) and parietal cortex (involved in space and attention).

V5/MT having very broad receptive fields (Zeki, 1969). The extrastriate cortex also contains a number of areas that are specialized for processing specific visual attributes such as color (area **V4**) and movement (area **V5** or MT, standing for medial temporal). To some extent, the brain's strategy for processing information outside of V1 is to "divide and conquer." For example, it is possible to have brain damage that impairs color perception (cerebral **achromatopsia**) or movement perception (cerebral **akinetopsia**) that preserves other visual functions.

## V4: The main color center of the brain

Area V4 is believed to be the main color center in the human brain because lesions to it result in a lack of color vision, so that the world is perceived in shades of gray (Heywood *et al.*, 1998; Zeki, 1990). This is termed cerebral achromatopsia. It is not to be confused with color blindness in which people (normally men) have difficulty discriminating reds and greens because of a deficiency in certain types of retinal cells. Achromatopsia is rare because there are two V4 areas in the brain and it is unlikely that brain damage would symmetrically affect both hemispheres. Damage to one of the V4s would result in one side of space being seen as colorless (left V4 represents color for the right hemifield and vice versa). Partial damage to V4 can result in colors that appear "dirty" or "washed out" (Meadows, 1974). In people who have not sustained brain injury, area V4 can be identified by functional imaging by comparing viewing patterns of colored squares (so-called Mondrians, because of a similarity to the work of that artist) with their equivalent gray-scale picture (Zeki *et al.*, 1991). The gray-scale pictures are matched for luminance such that if either image were viewed through a black and white camera they would appear identical to each other.

Why is color so important that the brain would set aside an entire region dedicated to it? Moreover, given that the retina contains cells that detect different wavelengths of visible light, why does the brain need a dedicated color processor at all? To answer both of these questions, it is important to understand the concept of **color constancy**. Color constancy refers to the fact that the color of a surface is perceived as constant even when illuminated in different lighting conditions and even though the physical wavelength composition of light reflected from a surface can be shown (with recording devices) to differ under different conditions. For example, a surface that reflects a high proportion of long-wave "red" light will appear red when illuminated with white, red, green or any other type of light. Color constancy is needed to facilitate recognition of, say, red tomatoes across a wide variety of viewing conditions.

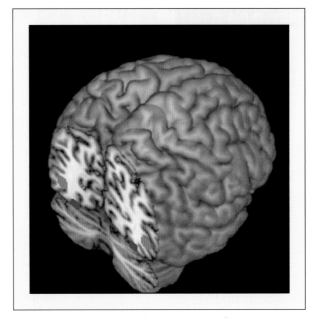

Area V5/MT (in red) lies near the outer surface of both hemispheres and is responsible for perception of visual motion. Area V4 (in blue) lies on the under surface of the brain, in each hemisphere, and is responsible for the perception of color. This brain is viewed from the back.

The derivation of color constancy appears to be the function of V4 (Zeki, 1983). Neurons in V4 may achieve this by comparing the wavelength in their receptive fields with the wavelength in other fields. In this way it is possible to compute the color of a surface while taking into account the illuminating conditions of the whole scene (Land, 1964, 1983). Cells in earlier visual regions (e.g. V1) respond only to the local wavelength in their receptive field and their response would change if the light source were changed even if the color of the stimulus was not (Zeki, 1983). Achromatopsic patients with damage to V4 are able to use earlier visual processes that are based on wavelength discrimination in the absence of color experience. For example, patient MS could tell if two equiluminant colored patches were the same or different if they abutted to form a common edge, but not if they were separated (Heywood *et al.*, 1991). This occurs because wavelength comparisons outside of V4 are made at a local level. Although earlier visual regions respond to wavelength, V4 has some special characteristics. The neurons in V4 tend to have larger receptive fields than earlier regions. Moreover, evidence from fMRI shows that voxels that are sensitive to one color (e.g. red) tend to have graded selectivity to perceptually neighboring colors (e.g. violets, yellows), but this is not found in earlier visual regions (Brouwer & Heeger, 2009). It suggests that V4 implements a relational coding between colors (analogous to a color wheel) that may also be helpful for color constancy.

It should be pointed out that V4 is not the only color-responsive region of the brain. For example, Zeki and Marini (1998) compared viewing of appropriately colored objects (e.g. red tomato) with inappropriate ones (e.g. blue tomato) and found activation in, among other regions, the hippocampus, which may code long-term memory representations.

## V5/MT: The main movement center of the brain

If participants in a PET scanner view images of moving dots relative to static dots, a region of the extrastriate cortex called V5 (or MT) becomes particularly active (Zeki *et al.*, 1991). Earlier electrophysiological research on the monkey had found that all cells in this area are sensitive to motion, and that 90 percent of them respond preferentially to a particular direction of motion and will not respond at all to the opposite direction of motion (Zeki, 1974). None were color-sensitive.

Patient LM lost the ability to perceive visual movement after bilateral damage to area V5/MT (Zihl *et al.*, 1983). This condition is termed akinetopsia (for a review, see Zeki, 1991). Her visual world consists of a series of still frames: objects may suddenly appear or disappear, a car that is distant may suddenly be seen to be near, and pouring tea into a cup would invariably end in spillage as the level of liquid appears to rise in jumps rather than smoothly.

More recent studies have suggested that other types of movement perception do not rely on V5/MT. For example, LM is able to discriminate biological from non-biological motion (McLeod *et al.*, 1996). The perception of **biological motion** is assessed by attaching light points to the joints and then recording someone walking/running in the dark. When only the light points are viewed, most people are still able to detect bodily movement (relative to a condition in which these moving lights are presented jumbled up). LM could discriminate biological from non-biological motion, but could not perceive the overall direction of movement. Separate pathways for this type of motion have been implied by functional imaging (Vaina *et al.*, 2001).

LM was able to detect movement in other sensory modalities (e.g. touch, audition), suggesting that her difficulties were restricted to certain types of visual movement (Zihl *et al.*, 1983). However, functional imaging studies have identified supramodal regions of the brain (in parietal cortex) that appear to respond to movement in three different senses—vision, touch, and hearing (Bremmer *et al.*, 2001).

### Evaluation

One emerging view of visual processing in the brain beyond V1 is that different types of visual information get parsed into more specialized brain regions. Thus, when one looks at a dog running across the garden, information about its color resides in one region, information about its movement resides in another and

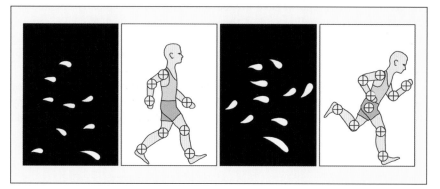

When this array of dots is set in motion, most people can distinguish between biological and non-biological motion.

## HOW DOES THE BRAIN RESPOND TO VISUAL ILLUSIONS?

When you look at the top figure do you have a sense of motion in the circles even though the image is static? This image is called the Enigma illusion. When you look at the bottom image do you see one vase or two faces? Does this image appear to spontaneously flip between one interpretation and the other, even though the image remains constant? Examples such as these reveal how the brain's perception of the world can differ from the external physical reality. This is, in fact, a normal part of seeing. Visual illusions are in many respects the norm rather than the exception, even though we are not always aware of them as such.

A functional imaging study has shown that parts of the brain specialized for detecting real movement (area V5/MT) also respond to the Enigma illusion (Zeki et al., 1993). A recent study suggests that the illusion is driven by tiny adjustments in eye fixation (Troncoso et al., 2008). An fMRI study using bi-stable stimuli such as the face-vase has shown how different visual and non-visual brain structures cooperate to maintain perceptual stability. The momentary breakdown of activity in these regions is associated with the timing of the subjective perceptual flip (Kleinschmidt et al., 1998). TMS over the right parietal lobes affects the rate of switch between bi-stable images with adjacent regions either promoting stability or generating instability (Kanai et al., 2011). This suggests different top-down biasing influences on perception.

Do you see movement in the image on the top when you stare at the center? Do you see a vase or faces on the bottom? How does the brain interpret such ambiguities?

Top image by Isia Levant, 1981, www.michaelbach.de/ot/mot_enigma/index.html

information about its identity (this is my dog rather than any dog) resides in yet another, to name but a few. The question of how these different streams of information come back together (if at all) is not well understood, but may require the involvement of non-visual processes related to attention (see Chapter 7).

**KEY TERMS**

**Structural descriptions**
A memory representation
of the three-dimensional
structure of objects.

**Apperceptive agnosia**
A failure to understand
the meaning of objects
due to a deficit at the
level of object perception.

**Associative agnosia**
A failure to understand
the meaning of objects
due to a deficit at the
level of semantic
memory.

# RECOGNIZING OBJECTS

For visual information to be useful it must make contact with knowledge that has been accumulated about the world. There is a need to recognize places that have been visited and people who have been seen, and to recognize other stimuli in the environment in order to, say, distinguish between edible and non-edible substances. All of these examples can be subsumed under the process of "object recognition." Although different types of object (e.g. faces) may recruit some different mechanisms, there will nevertheless be some common mechanisms shared by all objects, given that they are extracted from the same raw visual information.

The figure below describes four basic stages in object recognition that, terminology aside, bear a close resemblance to Marr's (1976) theory of vision:

1. The earliest stage in visual processing involves basic elements such as edges and bars of various lengths, contrasts and orientations. This stage has already been considered above.
2. Later stages involve grouping these elements into higher-order units that code depth cues and segregate surfaces into figure and ground. Some of these mechanisms were first described by the Gestalt psychologists and are considered below. It is possible that this stage is also influenced by top-down information based on stored knowledge. These visual representations, however, represent objects according to the observer's viewpoint and object constancy is not present.
3. The viewer-centered description is then matched onto stored three-dimensional descriptions of the structure of objects (**structural descriptions**). This store is often assumed to represent only certain viewpoints and thus the matching process entails the computation of object constancy (i.e. an understanding that objects remain the same irrespective of differences in viewing condition). There may be two different routes to achieving object constancy, depending on whether the view is "normalized" by rotating the object to a standard orientation.
4. Finally, meaning is attributed to the stimulus and other information (e.g. the name) becomes available. This will be considered primarily in Chapter 11.

Disorders of object recognition are referred to as visual agnosia, and these have been traditionally subdivided into **apperceptive agnosia** and **associative agnosia**, depending on whether the deficit occurs at stages involved in perceptual

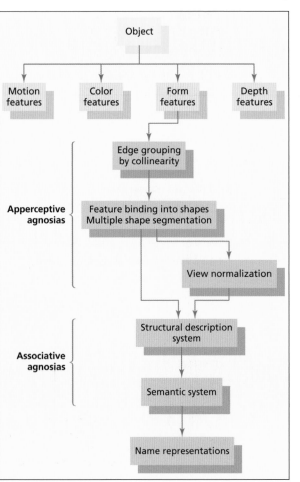

A simple model of visual object recognition.
From Riddoch and Humphreys, 2001.

processing or stages involving stored visual memory representations (Lissauer, 1890). This classification is perhaps too simple to be of much use in modern cognitive neuroscience. Models such as the one of Riddoch and Humphreys (2001) acknowledge that both perception and the stored properties of objects can be broken down into even finer processes. It is also the case that most contemporary models of object recognition allow for interactivity between different processes rather than discrete processing stages. This is broadly consistent with the neuroanatomical data (see earlier) of connections between early and late visual regions and vice versa.

## Parts and wholes: Gestalt grouping principles

In the 1930s, Gestalt psychologists identified a number of principles that explain why certain visual features become grouped together to form perceptual wholes. These operations form a key stage in translating simple features into three-dimensional descriptions of the world, essential for object recognition. The process of segmenting a visual display into objects versus background surfaces is also known as **figure–ground segregation**. The Gestalt approach identified five basic principles to account for how basic visual features are combined:

1. *The law of proximity* states that visual elements are more likely to be grouped if they are closer together. For example, the dots in (a) in the figure tend to be perceived as three horizontal lines because they are closer together horizontally than vertically.
2. *The law of similarity* states that elements will be grouped together if they share visual attributes (e.g. color, shape). For example, (b) tends to be perceived as vertical columns rather than rows, because elements in columns share both shape and color.
3. *The law of good continuation* states that edges are grouped together to avoid changes or interruptions; thus, (c) is two crossing lines rather than > and <.

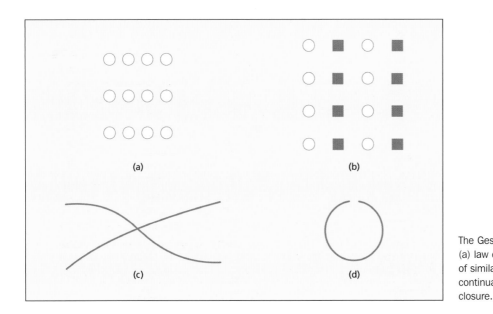

The Gestalt principles of (a) law of proximity, (b) law of similarity, (c) law of good continuation, and (d) law of closure.

4. *The law of closure* states that missing parts are "filled in"; thus (d) has circular properties in spite of the gap. This law, and the previous one, is important for recognizing objects that are partly occluded.

5. *The law of common fate* states that elements that move together tend to be grouped together. A good example of this comes from studies of biological motion perception (e.g. Johansson, 1973). Light points attached to bodily joints are perceived as movement of a single human figure when viewed in the dark.

Perceptual grouping occurs at multiple levels within the visual hierarchy (and via interactions between those levels). For instance, grouping of light points based on the known structure and dynamics of the human body occurs only at later stages of visual processing, in this case in the superior temporal sulcus (Grossman *et al.*, 2000). In other instances, there is evidence of grouping effects at the earliest stages of visual processing. Cells in V1 tuned to particular orientations fire more when these orientations are part of the figure than the ground as shown by animal single-cell electrophysiology (Lamme, 1995). Human fMRI shows that V1 as well as higher visual regions are sensitive to the law of good continuation (Altmann *et al.*, 2003). In general, whether grouping occurs early or late will depend on the nature of the stimulus and the extent to which it depends on stored knowledge of objects (e.g. shape of the human body) or less specific knowledge (e.g. the general properties of surfaces, such as occlusion).

## Case HJA: seeing the parts but not the whole

Perhaps the most detailed study of visual agnosia in the literature is case HJA, which was reported in a number of studies by Humphreys, Riddoch and colleagues (Humphreys & Riddoch, 1987; Riddoch *et al.*, 1999). HJA was a businessman who suffered a bilateral stroke that left him with severe difficulties in recognizing objects, but with preserved sensory discriminations of length, orientation, and position. A number of tests conducted on HJA support the conclusion that he has difficulty in integrating parts into wholes—a type of apperceptive agnosia on the simple model on p. 120. The evidence in support of this interpretation is

| HJA's spared abilities | HJA's impaired abilities |
| --- | --- |
| • He is able to copy drawings of objects that he cannot recognize, suggesting that he can "see" them at some level. | • He is unable to recognize pictures, but gives a reasonable description of their parts. For example, when shown a carrot: "The bottom point seems solid and the other bits are feathery. It does not seem logical unless it is some sort of brush." |
| • He is able to draw objects from memory, suggesting that he can access structural descriptions from memory, but not vision. | • When shown degraded pictures he does not benefit from Gestalt principles in the same way as other people do (Boucart & Humphreys, 1992). |
| • He is able to recognize objects from modalities other than vision and has good verbal knowledge about them. | • He is unable to perform an object decision task in which "novel" objects are created by recombining the parts of real objects. |

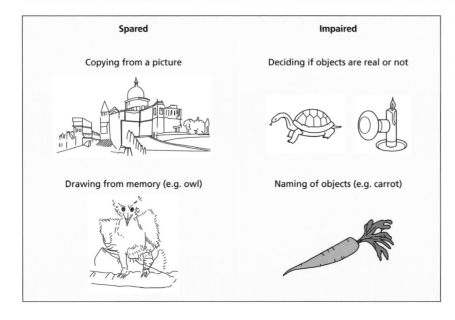

Spared

Copying from a picture

Drawing from memory (e.g. owl)

Impaired

Deciding if objects are real or not

Naming of objects (e.g. carrot)

HJA is impaired at deciding if objects are real or made up and naming objects. However, he can copy drawings and draw objects from memory.

Adapted from Humphreys and Riddoch, 1987 and Riddoch and Humphreys, 1995.

summarized in the table below. These results support the conclusion that HJA has difficulties in using perceptual grouping mechanisms to translate his intact perception of lines into more complex visual descriptions required to access stored knowledge. His visual system does not permit him to take advantage of Gestalt-based grouping mechanisms that support normal object recognition. Humphreys and Riddoch have termed this **integrative agnosia**. It isn't the case that no grouping at all occurs. There is evidence that local contours may be grouped together, for instance, based on the Gestalt principle of continuation (Giersch *et al.*, 2000). This is consistent with the claim that some forms of grouping, and figure–ground segmentation, occur at earlier stages in the visual stream (with these stages largely spared in HJA).

## Accessing structural descriptions: object constancy

One of the most important aspects of object recognition is to be able to recognize an object across different viewpoints and different lighting conditions—this is termed **object constancy**. It is generally agreed that object constancy is brought about by matching the constructed visual representation with a store of object descriptions in memory that carry information about the invariant properties of objects. One suggestion is that the brain stores only structural descriptions in the usual or canonical view, such that the principal axis is in view. Indeed, naming times for objects presented in usual views are faster (Palmer *et al.*, 1981). Clinical tests of object constancy typically involve identifying (i.e. naming) objects drawn from different angles, or matching together different instances of the same object.

A number of different ways in which this matching to memory process might occur have been put forward. Some researchers have argued that object constancy is achieved by matching features or parts of objects to structural descriptions (Biederman, 1987; Warrington & Taylor, 1973). Others have argued that the most important mechanism is more holistic and involves extracting the principal axis of an object (Marr & Nishihara, 1978). For example, if the principal axis of a

**KEY TERMS**

**Integrative agnosia**
A failure to integrate parts into wholes in visual perception.

**Object constancy**
An understanding that objects remain the same, irrespective of differences in viewing condition.

**KEY TERM**

**Object orientation agnosia**
An inability to extract the orientation of an object despite adequate object recognition.

tennis racket is viewed from a foreshortened angle it is harder to recognize. Others have suggested that both processes play a role (Humphreys & Riddoch, 1984; Warrington & James, 1986). The latter seems the most plausible based on the evidence reviewed below.

Some visual agnosic patients are able to recognize and name objects from the usual view, but are impaired at recognizing objects presented in unusual views (Humphreys & Riddoch, 1984; Warrington & Taylor, 1973). This typically occurs after damage to the right parietal lobe, which has a particularly important role in spatial processing. The parietal lobe may contain mechanisms that extract the principal axis from an object and then rotate the object to a standard view, thus facilitating matching. Patients with damage to this process would have to rely on a mechanism that is independent of the way that the object is viewed. Thus, in these patients, the route drawn on the right of the model on p. 120 is impaired and the one on the left is spared. Other patients may have more subtle damage to this route such that they do not appear to be visually agnosic in tests of object naming or matching, yet they are unable to decide on the correct orientation for an object or even decide whether two simultaneously presented objects have the same orientation (Harris *et al.*, 2001; Turnbull *et al.*, 2002). These striking cases of an inability to extract the orientation of an object despite adequate object recognition have been given the name **object orientation agnosia**. These patients appear to achieve object constancy by using a view-independent route that does not extract the orientation (or principal axis) of objects.

An alternative account for the advantage of usual views is that these are more familiar and have more robust neural representations (Karnath *et al.*, 2000; Perrett *et al.*, 1998), rather than suggesting two specialized routes. However, recent functional imaging evidence would appear to support the two-routes view, with different hemispheres implicated in each. This evidence is outlined below.

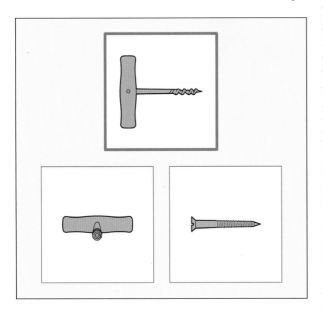

A test of object recognition that requires matching to an unusual view.

From Riddoch & Humphreys, 1995.

## Neural substrates of object constancy

The inferotemporal cortex (IT) takes its input from the geniculostriate pathway and appears to

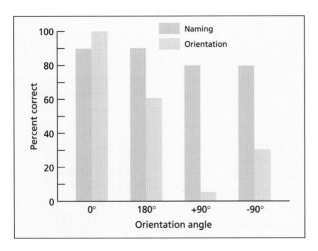

Patient EL with object orientation agnosia could produce the names of items presented in various orientations (green bars), but could not correctly judge whether an object was in its correct orientation (purple bars).

From Harris *et al.*, 2001. © The MIT Press. Reproduced with permission.

code the type of information important for object constancy. For example, single-cell recordings show that these cells respond to very specific object attributes, and have large receptive fields that almost always cover the fovea and typically extend to both hemifields (Gross, 1992; Gross *et al.*, 1972). Thus, the neurons tend to code for specific visual information but are less concerned with the location of the object—an ideal condition for computing object constancy.

An fMRI study used pairs of stimuli of the same object that differed in size, viewpoint, or exemplar in a similar vein to the clinical tests of object constancy discussed above (Vuilleumier *et al.*, 2002a). The logic behind the experiment is that the response of neurons tends to decrease over time if the same stimulus is repeated (priming). Thus, one can correlate reductions in fMRI signal with repetition of particular object attributes (i.e. whether "same" refers to the same viewpoint, the same size or the same type of object). It was found that the left inferotemporal (or fusiform) region responds irrespective of viewpoint or size, whereas viewpoint (but not size) was important for the comparable region in the right hemisphere. This is convincing evidence that there are at least two routes to object constancy—one that is sensitive to viewpoint and one that is not.

Other research using fMRI repetition priming confirms viewpoint-insensitive regions within inferotemporal cortex, but also finds regions within the parietal lobes that are sensitive to object viewpoint but not to object identity (Valyear *et al.*, 2006). The latter may enable acting upon objects.

## Category specificity in visual object recognition?

It has already been suggested that higher visual areas of the brain may be specialized for processing particular visual attributes such as color and motion. But are there higher visual areas of the brain that are specialized for recognizing different categories of object such as animals, faces, places, words and bodies? Chapter 1 outlined Fodor's (1983) theory that many cognitive functions are carried out by domain-specific modules. The term "domain-specific" refers to the fact that the module is hypothesized to process one, and only one, type of information (e.g. there may be a module that processes faces but not other types of stimuli). Evidence in favor of this strong position has been mustered from dissociations of spared and impaired performance in the recognition of different classes of object, and from the observation that different regions of the brain are optimized for responding to certain classes of stimuli. The notion that the brain represents different categories in different ways is termed **category specificity**. A parallel debate exists in the literature concerning whether the semantic representation of objects is represented categorically (see Chapter 11), as well as for the structural descriptions of objects. The alternative to the domain-specific hypothesis is that different categories of stimuli require somewhat different kinds of processing (e.g. words are recognized by parts, and faces recognized holistically), and that such differences may be relative rather than absolute.

This chapter discusses the domain-specific hypothesis with regards to faces; Chapter 12 discusses a similar proposal with regards to recognizing visual words (Dehaene *et al.*, 2002; Petersen *et al.*, 1990). However, it is worth noting that functional imaging studies have identified other regions that appear to be relatively specialized for the visual recognition of particular categories. These include the *parahippocampal place area* (PPA), which responds to scenes more than

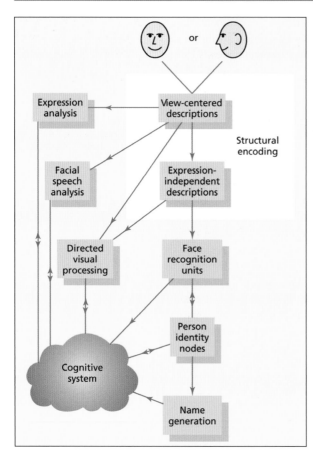

The Bruce and Young (1986) model of face recognition.
From Parkin, 1996.

objects (Epstein & Kanwisher, 1998), and the *extrastriate body area* (EBA), which responds to the human body more than to faces, scenes or objects (Downing *et al.*, 2001). Although these studies argue in favor of some degree of category specificity, it is unclear whether they support domain-specificity in the strong form (i.e. that the regions are only involved in recognizing stimuli from one category). The strongest evidence for domain specificity in object recognition so far has come from face processing, and this is considered next.

## RECOGNIZING FACES

Although faces are a type of visual object like any other, there is some reason to believe that the process of face recognition may be different from other aspects of object recognition. First of all, the goal in face recognition is normally to identify one particular face (e.g. "that is Barack Obama!") rather than categorizing a face as such (e.g. "that visual object is a face!"). Second, researchers have suggested that faces might be "special" either because of the type of processing they require or because they are a distinct category. Although there is good evidence to suggest that faces do have a different neural substrate from most other objects and can be disproportionately spared or impaired, the reasons why this is so remain a matter of controversy.

## Models of face processing

Bruce and Young (1986) proposed a cognitive model of face recognition that has largely stood the test of time. They assume that the earliest level of processing involves computation of a view-dependent structural description, as postulated for object recognition more generally. Following this, a distinction is made between the processing of familiar and unfamiliar faces. Familiar faces are recognized by matching to a store of face-based structural descriptions (which they term **face recognition units**). Following this, a more abstract level of representation, termed **person identity nodes**, accesses semantic (e.g. their occupation) and name information about that individual. A separate route (termed directed visual processing) was postulated to deal with unfamiliar faces. A number of other face-processing routes are postulated to occur in parallel to the route involved in recognizing familiar people. Evidence from neurological patients suggests that recognition of emotional expression, age, and gender is independent of familiar face recognition (Tranel *et al.*, 1988; for electrophysiological data, see Hasselmo *et al.*, 1989), as is the ability to use lip-reading cues (Campbell *et al.*, 1986).

### KEY TERMS

**Face recognition units (FRUs)**
Stored knowledge of the three-dimensional structure of familiar faces.

**Person identity nodes (PINs)**
An abstract description of people that links together perceptual knowledge (e.g. faces) with semantic knowledge.

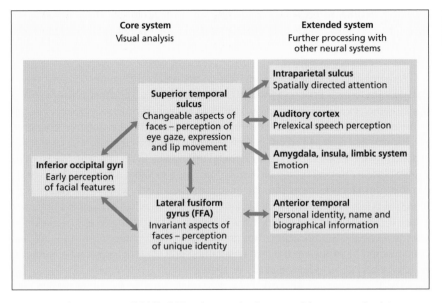

| Core system<br>Visual analysis | Extended system<br>Further processing with<br>other neural systems |
|---|---|

**Superior temporal sulcus**
Changeable aspects of faces – perception of eye gaze, expression and lip movement

**Intraparietal sulcus**
Spatially directed attention

**Auditory cortex**
Prelexical speech perception

**Amygdala, insula, limbic system**
Emotion

**Inferior occipital gyri**
Early perception of facial features

**Lateral fusiform gyrus (FFA)**
Invariant aspects of faces – perception of unique identity

**Anterior temporal**
Personal identity, name and biographical information

The model of Haxby *et al.* (2000) divides the neural substrates of face processing into a number of core mechanisms (relatively specialized for faces) and an extended system in which face processing makes contact with more general cognitive mechanisms (e.g. concerning emotion, language, action).

The model of Haxby *et al.* (2000) presents a neuroanatomically inspired model of face perception that contrasts with the purely cognitive account offered by Bruce and Young (1986). In their model, Haxby *et al.* (2000) consider the core regions involved in face perception to lie in the fusiform gyrus in humans (corresponding to the inferotemporal cortex identified in primates) and the superior temporal sulcus. The so-called **fusiform face area (FFA)** is assumed to be involved in recognizing familiar faces. The superior temporal sulcus (STS) is assumed to process dynamic aspect of faces (such as expression, and lip and gaze movements) that is common to familiar and unfamiliar faces alike. They also identify an "extended system" to denote other areas of the brain that receive inputs from the core face perception system but are not essential for face perception (e.g. regions supporting semantic knowledge of people).

## Evidence that faces are special

The Bruce and Young (1986) model has a number of similarities with models of object recognition, including distinctions between "apperceptive" and "associative" stages, and distinctions between view-independent and view-dependent codes.

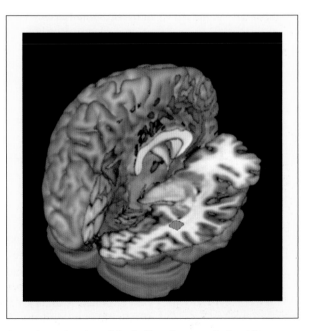

Approximate location of the fusiform face area in the right hemisphere, viewed from the back.

## KEY TERMS

**Prosopagnosia**
Impairments of face
processing that do not
reflect difficulties in early
visual analysis (also used
to refer to an inability to
recognize previously
familiar faces).

**Categorical perception**
The tendency to perceive
ambiguous or hybrid
stimuli as either one thing
or the other (rather than
as both simultaneously or
as a blend).

However, in other respects faces may differ from other objects. Broadly speaking, two lines of evidence have been presented to back up the claim. First, that faces have a distinct neural substrate; second (and related to the first), that faces can thus be selectively impaired.

Impairments of face processing that do not reflect difficulties in early visual analysis are termed **prosopagnosia** (Bodamer, 1947). The term prosopagnosia is also sometimes used specifically to refer to an inability to recognize previously familiar faces. As such, care must be taken to describe the putative cognitive mechanism that is impaired rather than relying on simple labeling. The case study reported by De Renzi (1986) had profound difficulties in recognizing the faces of people close to him, including his family, but could recognize them by their voices or other non-facial information. He once remarked to his wife: "Are you [wife's name]? I guess you are my wife because there are no other women at home, but I want to be reassured." In contrast, the patient could perform perceptual matching tests involving faces normally. Within the Bruce and Young (1986) model, his deficit would be located at the face recognition unit stage. The patient's ability to recognize and name other objects was spared.

The FFA responds to faces more than other stimuli, including bodies, and may be particularly important for recognizing known faces (Kanwisher *et al.*, 1997; Kanwisher & Yovel, 2006). It is for this reason that Kanwisher and colleagues have suggested that this is a strong candidate for domain-specificity (i.e. contains neurons that process only one particular kind of information). The FFA is found bilaterally, with a generally more robust response on the right. The region shows fMRI adaptation (reduced BOLD signal on repeated presentations) when the same face is repeated even if physical aspects of the image changes (see Kanwisher & Yovel, 2006). Unlike earlier regions in the occipital gyrus, that also demonstrate some face specificity, the FFA demonstrates categorical perception. **Categorical perception** refers to the tendency to perceive ambiguous or hybrid stimuli as either one thing or the other (rather than as both simultaneously or as a blend). Rotshtein *et al.* (2005) studied this using morphed images of Margaret Thatcher and Marilyn Monroe in an fMRI adaptation study. Physical differences in the image only affect fMRI adaptation when the participants' percept of the ambiguous face flips between Thatcher and Monroe.

## Why are faces special?

This section considers four accounts of why faces might be special. These accounts are not necessarily mutually exclusive and there might be several factors that contribute.

### Task difficulty

Faces are complex visual stimuli that are very similar to each other (e.g. they all consist of mouth, nose, eyes, etc.), so are faces special simply by virtue of added task difficulty relative to other kinds of objects? A number of reports of patients with visual agnosia without prosopagnosia would appear to speak against this view (Rumiati *et al.*, 1994). Farah *et al.* (1995a) attempted to address the issue of task difficulty directly by creating an object recognition task (using spectacle frames) of comparable difficulty to a face recognition task in controls (both tasks performed at 85 percent correct). They found that their prosopagnosic participant, LH, was impaired on the face task (62 percent), but not the frames task (92 percent), ruling out a task-difficulty explanation.

## Part-based compared with holistic perceptual processing

Perhaps faces are treated differently from other types of object because they require a special type of processing, rather than being special because they are faces as such. The most influential theory along these lines has been proposed by Farah (1990; Farah *et al.*, 1998). Her thesis is that *all* object recognition lies on a continuum between recognition by parts and recognition by wholes. Recognition of faces may depend more on holistic processing, whereas recognition of written words may depend on more part-based processing (e.g. identifying the sequence of letters in the word); recognition of most other objects lies somewhere in between. Farah's initial source of evidence came from a meta-analysis of cases with visual agnosia, prosopagnosia, and difficulties in visual word recognition (pure alexia; see Chapter 12). She found no convincing cases of isolated object agnosia (without prosopagnosia or alexia) or prosopagnosia with alexia (without object agnosia), supporting the claim that these lie on a continuum (Farah, 1990).

Subsequent to this, there have been reported cases of isolated object agnosia without prosopagnosia or alexia (Humphreys & Rumiati, 1998; Rumiati *et al.*, 1994), isolated object agnosia and alexia without prosopagnosia (Moscovitch *et al.*, 1997), and prosopagnosia and alexia without object agnosia (De Renzi & di Pellegrino, 1998). These cases support an alternative view in which there are separate stores of structural descriptions for objects, faces, and words rather than a continuum between two types of underlying perceptual processes (but see Farah, 1997).

Evidence from human fMRI (Harris & Aguirre, 2008) and monkey electro-physiology (Freiwald *et al.*, 2009) suggests that face-selective regions of the cortex respond to both whole faces and face parts.

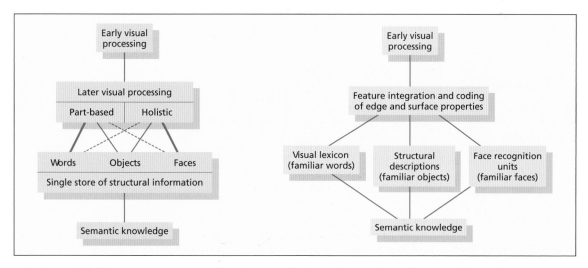

In Farah's model, differences between recognition of words, objects, and faces reflects different weightings of part-based versus holistic perception (left). Other models have suggested, on the basis of dissociations between object agnosia, prosopagnosia, and alexia, that there may be separate stores of structural knowledge for these categories (right).

## Visual expertise at within-category discrimination

A somewhat different account from that of Farah has been put forward principally by Gauthier and colleagues (Diamond & Carey, 1986; Gauthier & Logothetis, 2000; Gauthier & Tarr, 1997; Gauthier *et al.*, 1999). Their account has two key elements: (1) that faces require discrimination within a category (between one face and another), whereas most other object recognition requires a superordinate level of discrimination (e.g. between a cup and comb); and, consequently, that (2) we become "visual experts" at making these fine within-category distinctions through prolonged experience with thousands of exemplars. Like Farah's explanation, this account assumes that faces are special because of processing demands rather than because faces are a domain-specific category.

The evidence for this theory comes from training participants to become visual experts at making within-category discriminations of non-face objects, called "Greebles." As participants become experts they move from part-based to holistic processing, as has often been proposed for faces (Gauthier & Tarr, 1997). In addition, they have shown that Greeble experts activate the FFA (Gauthier *et al.*, 1999), and similar findings have been reported for experts on natural categories such as cars (McGugin *et al.*, 2012). In addition, Greeble recognition has a characteristic N170 ERP signal normally only found for faces (Rossion *et al.*, 2002). Gauthier and Logothetis (2000) reported similar training studies in monkeys and found that certain cells (claimed to be analogous to face cells) became sensitive to the whole configuration after training even though non-facial stimuli were used.

## Faces are a distinct category

Although it might indeed be the case that faces make different processing demands on certain perceptual mechanisms relative to other classes of stimuli, there is some evidence to suggest that these accounts are not sufficient to explain the whole picture. Some have argued that what is additionally required is the assumption that faces really are a distinct category and are represented as such in the adult brain. For example, there is evidence of dissociations between faces and other expert categories from ERP studies (Carmel & Bentin, 2002) and human neuropsychology (McNeil & Warrington, 1993; Sergent & Signoret, 1992). Sergent and Signoret (1992) reported a prosopagnosic patient, RM, who had a collection of over 5,000 miniature cars. He was unable to identify any of 300 famous faces, or the face of himself or his wife, or match unfamiliar faces across viewpoints. Nevertheless, when shown 210 pictures of miniature cars he was able to give the company name, and for 172 he could give the model and approximate year of manufacture. Thus, although the FFA may tend to represent within-category exemplars (Gauthier *et al.*, 2000), there could still be scope for finer-grained

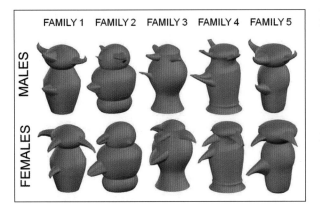

Examples of "Greebles." Greebles can be grouped into two genders and come from various families. To what extent does discriminating against Greebles resemble discriminating against faces?

Images provided courtesy of Michael J. Tarr (Carnegie Mellon University, Pittsburgh), see www.tarrlab.org.

categorical dissociations. McNeil and Warrington (1993) reported patient WJ, who was unable to distinguish previously familiar faces from unfamiliar ones. Following his stroke, he acquired a flock of 36 sheep, which testing revealed that he could distinguish from unfamiliar sheep. This case was taken to support the view that faces are a special category independent of the type of perceptual processing, but skeptics may argue that the sheep recognition task could be performed in different ways (e.g. recognizing markings rather than holistic configuration) or that the level of expertise is not matched (e.g. 36 sheep versus many thousands of faces).

## Evaluation

There is good evidence to suggest that face recognition can be spared or impaired relative to the recognition of other objects. To account for this, it might be necessary to assume that faces engage different types of perceptual mechanism related to holistic versus part-based processing and might require expert within-category discriminations. Whereas these accounts might be necessary to explain the data, they might not be sufficient. There remains some evidence to suggest that there is indeed a separate store of structural descriptions for familiar faces.

### THE MARGARET THATCHER ILLUSION

What is wrong with this face? Turn it upside down and have a look. In the so-called Thatcher illusion the holistic configuration of the face, in its inverted orientation, disrupts the ability to detect local anomalies in the stimulus such as an inversion of the eyes and mouth (Thompson, 1980). The success of the illusion is based on two properties of the face recognition system. First, that faces usually have an upright orientation and may be stored in the brain as such. This explains why the anomaly is detected upon inversion.

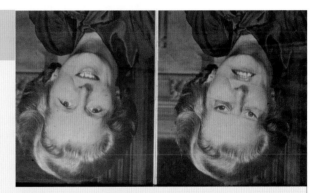

You should recognize this face instantly even if it is upside down. But what is wrong with the image? Turn it the right way up to find out.

From Thompson, 1980. © Pion Limited, London. Reproduced with permission.

Second, that faces are processed largely on the basis of surface features and global shape rather than piecemeal from parts.

For most adults, inverted faces are much harder to identify (Yin, 1969). But, prosopagnosic patients such as LH may show no advantage of upright over inverted faces, suggesting this information is lost (Farah et al., 1995b). Greeble experts tend to show an advantage for processing upright Greebles (Gauthier & Tarr, 1997). Infants show a preference for a "top heavy" configuration of facial features from birth but, beyond that, do not have a strong preference for how the parts themselves are oriented (Macchi Cassia et al., 2004).

## VISION IMAGINED

Close your eyes and imagine a horse galloping left-to-right through a green field and jumping over a fence. To what extent is this "visual imagery" task achieved by using the same mechanisms used to visually perceive objects, color, movement, and so on? At one extreme, imagining scenes such as these may not use any of the same mechanisms as seeing. But why would the brain develop separate mechanisms for seeing a horse and imagining the visual appearance of one? At the other extreme, imagining scenes could use exactly the same mechanisms as visual perception. This, of course, raises the question of how it is possible to distinguish between perception and imagination at all, and what prevents us from lapsing into hallucinatory delirium. As is often the case, the truth may lie somewhere between these extreme viewpoints.

A number of case studies have supported the conclusion that difficulties in visual imagery parallel difficulties in visual perception, such that selective impairments of color, objects, space, and so on tend to be found both in perception and in mental imagery. For example, Levine *et al.* (1985) document two patients. The first patient had both prosopagnosia and achromatopsia. This was accompanied by an inability to imagine previously known faces or the colors of objects. The other patient was impaired in spatial aspects of vision (e.g. poor visually guided reaching—optic ataxia). This was accompanied by difficulties in spatial imagery (e.g. poor descriptions of routes). Beauvois and Saillant (1985) also report a patient who could not imagine colors, given visual imagery strategies (e.g. "imagine a beautiful snowy landscape—what color is the snow?"), but could retrieve color "facts" from non-perceptual long-term memory (e.g. "what do people say when asked what color snow is?").

In contrast to these studies showing close imagery–perception parallels, Behrmann *et al.* (1994) report a study of patient CK that suggests that visual imagery and visual perception can be dissociated. CK was unable to recognize or name objects from vision, although he could recognize them by other means (e.g. touch), and a number of studies suggested that, like HJA, he had integrative agnosia. In contrast to his poor object recognition he could produce detailed drawings of objects from memory and describe the visual appearance of objects. This imagery–perception dissociation can be accounted for by assuming that CK has access to object structural descriptions top-down (i.e. from memory) but not bottom-up (i.e. from visual perception). Similar findings were initially reported for HJA (Humphreys & Riddoch, 1987). However, a subsequent study on HJA some 16 years later suggests that caution is warranted in postulating a strong separation of vision and imagery (Riddoch *et al.*, 1999). Although HJA could initially draw

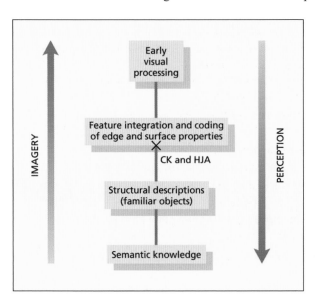

Imagery may involve some of the same structures as perception, but activated in the reverse ("top-down") direction. CK and HJA can use intact knowledge of object structure to perform the imagery task despite poor perceptual integration. But does imagery need to go back as far as early visual processing in V1?

accurately from memory, this ability receded over time (but his memory, in general, remained intact). Presumably, visual input is needed to maintain the structural descriptions over longer periods of time.

The studies above suggest that visual imagery for properties such as color and object shape is normally related to the ability to perceive those characteristics, although the two may occasionally be disconnected. A more controversial claim that has been made about mental imagery is that the primary visual cortex (V1) is necessary for it (Kosslyn *et al.*, 1995; 1999; 2001). Kosslyn *et al.* (1995) compared an imagery condition of visualizing objects of different sizes relative to a non-imagery baseline. They found that there was activity in V1 and, moreover, that the locus of activity was related to the size of the imagined stimulus. (Recall that V1 is retinotopically organized so that images that cover a large area on the retina will cover a large area on V1.) To establish the functional necessity of V1 for imagery, Kosslyn *et al.* (1999) conducted a TMS study on participants who were making imagery judgments about a previously learned array of line gratings (e.g. parallel lines of different width, length, and orientation). They found that TMS over V1 did indeed disrupt mental imagery.

How is it possible to reconcile the finding of Kosslyn and colleagues, suggesting that early perceptual processes are important for imagery, with other studies suggesting that later visual processes (e.g. those supporting color or object recognition) are the critical ones? The solution may lie in considering the *content* of the images. Kosslyn's experiments involved imagery for lines and retinal size for which V1 may be important, whereas other studies involved imagery for faces, objects, spatial location and colors, which are less likely to depend on V1 when activated top-down. Thus, the extent to which different perceptual regions are involved in imagery may be related to the different content of what is being imagined.

## SUMMARY AND KEY POINTS OF THE CHAPTER

- The primary visual cortex (V1) contains a spatial map based on the retinal image and detects edges and boundaries within the visual scene.
- The primary visual cortex may be necessary for conscious awareness of vision. Damage to this area can lead to a condition called blindsight, in which conscious experiences of vision are abolished, although some visual processing in the "blind" region is still computed by routes that bypass V1.
- Later visual regions are specialized for analyzing particular visual attributes such as color (area V4) and motion (area V5/MT).
- The ability to recognize objects from a wide variety of views (object constancy) may arise from matching visual features to a stored representation of objects or from mentally rotating the seen object to a standard viewpoint. Basic categorical recognition of objects implicates inferotemporal processing, whereas recognizing the orientation may involve the parietal lobes.

Visit the companion website at www. psypress/cw/ward for:

- References to key papers, readings and useful websites
- Videos including an interview with key psychologists Huber and Wiebel , BBC documentary *Brain Story—The Mind's Eye*, a patient's experience with visual agnosia, and a lecture with author Jamie Ward on *The Seeing Brain*.
- Multiple choice questions and interactive flashcards to test your knowledge
- Downloadable glossary

- The processing of faces relative to other objects may, to some degree, utilize different neural substrates and cognitive resources. Faces may make more demands on holistic processes, and typically require individuation of particular exemplars. It is also possible that faces are special because they are an evolutionarily salient category.
- Mental imagery utilizes many of the same resources as actually perceiving and, like vision itself, different types of image (e.g. of color, objects, lines) may have different neural substrates.

## EXAMPLE ESSAY QUESTIONS

- What is "blindsight"? What can studying blindsight tell us about the normal visual system?
- To what extent is the primary visual cortex (V1) necessary for visual perception?
- One function of the visual system is to extract constant properties of a stimulus independently from moment-to-moment fluctuations in viewing conditions. Explain how the brain achieves this, using the examples of color constancy and object constancy.
- Are faces "special"? If so, why?
- To what extent is visually imagining like visually perceiving?

## RECOMMENDED FURTHER READING

- Farah, M. J. (2000). *The cognitive neuroscience of vision*. Oxford, UK: Blackwell. This book provides excellent coverage of most topics covered in this chapter and a few vision-related topics covered elsewhere (e.g. space and attention; visual word recognition).
- Peterson, M. A. & Rhodes, G. (2003). *Perception of faces, objects and scenes: Analytic and holistic processes*. Oxford, UK: Oxford University Press. An up-to-date collection of papers that will be of interest to students wanting to pursue more advanced reading.
- Zeki, S. (1993). *A vision of the brain*. Oxford, UK: Blackwell. This is a thorough account of the neuroscience of vision from an historical and contemporary perspective. It is particularly strong on single-cell data and early stages of visual processing.

# CHAPTER 7

# The attending brain

## CONTENTS

**Attention** is the process by which certain information is selected for further processing and other information is discarded. Attention is needed to avoid sensory overload. The brain does not have the capacity to fully process all the information it receives. Nor would it be efficient for it to do so. As such, attention is often likened to a filter or a bottleneck in processing (Broadbent, 1958). There are some striking examples of this bottleneck in operation in the real world. Although we have a sense that our visual field is uniformly rich and expansive, research has shown that we often only attend to (and aware of) a small proportion of it at any moment. If we were watching a game of basketball and a man in a gorilla costume walked between the players, surely we would be aware of it? But if our attention were drawn to one aspect of the game (such as counting the number of passes), then there is a high probability (50 percent) that you would not notice it (Simons & Chabris, 1999). This phenomenon is termed **inattentional blindness**. A related phenomenon is **change blindness**, in which participants fail to notice the appearance/disappearance of objects between two alternating images separated with a brief blank screen (Rensink *et al.*, 1997). Similarly, people fail to notice when a person serving you in a shop briefly disappears from view and another person reappears to continue the interaction (Simons & Levin, 1998). Although both of these examples are metaphorically labeled as "blindness"

## KEY TERMS

**Attention**
The process by which certain information is selected for further processing and other information is discarded.

**Inattentional blindness**
A failure to be aware of a visual stimulus because attention is directed away from it.

**Change blindness**
A failure to notice the appearance/disappearance of objects between two alternating images.

**Salient**
Any aspect of a stimulus that, for whatever reason, stands out from the rest.

**Orienting**
The movement of attention from one location to another.

**Covert orienting**
The movement of attention from one location to another without moving the eyes/body.

When concentrating on counting the passes in a basketball game, many people fail to notice the arrival of the gorilla! This study shows that our awareness of the details of a visual scene can be very limited, particularly if our attention is focused on a demanding task.

they reflect the capacity limitations of our attentional systems rather than a fundamental limitation of vision. Indeed functional imaging suggests an involvement of parietal areas (lying outside the main visual system) in change detection (Beck *et al.*, 2001).

Whereas perception is very much concerned with making sense of the external environment, attentional processes lie at the interface between the external environment and our internal states (goals, expectations, and so on). The extent to which attention is driven by the environment (our attention being grabbed, so-called bottom-up) or our goals (our attention being sustained, so called top-down) can vary according to the circumstances. In most cases both forces are in operation and attention can be construed as a cascade of bottom-up and top-down influences in which selection takes place.

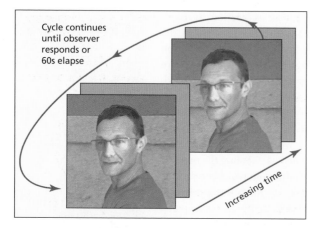

In change detection tasks, two different images alternate quickly (with a short blank in between). Participants often appear "blind" to changes in the image (here, the height of the wall) and this is linked to limitations in attentional capacity.

## SPATIAL AND NON-SPATIAL ATTENTIONAL PROCESS

In terms of visual attention, one of the most pervasive metaphors is to think about attention in terms of a spotlight. The spotlight may highlight a particular location in space (e.g. if that location contains a **salient** object). It may move from one location to another (e.g. when searching) and it may even zoom in or out (La Berge, 1983). The locus of the attentional spotlight need not necessarily be the same as the locus of eye fixation. It is possible, for example, to look straight ahead while focusing attention to the left or right when metaphorically "looking out of the corner of one's eyes." However, there is a natural tendency for attention and eye fixation to go together because visual acuity (discriminating fine detail) is greatest at the point of fixation. Moving the focus of attention is termed **orienting** and is conventionally divided into **covert orienting** (moving attention without moving the eyes or head) and **overt orienting** (moving the eyes or head along with the focus of attention). It is important not to take the spotlight metaphor too literally. For example, there is evidence to suggest that attention can be split between two non-adjacent locations without incorporating the middle locations (Awh & Pashler, 2000). The most useful aspects of the spotlight metaphor are to emphasize the notion of limited capacity (not everything is illuminated), and to emphasize the typically spatial characteristics of attention. However, there are non-spatial attentional processes too as described later.

Posner described a classic study to illustrate that attention operates on a spatial basis (Posner, 1980; Posner & Cohen, 1984). The participants were presented with three boxes on the screen in different positions: left, central, and right. The task of the participant was simply to press a button when they detected a target in one of the boxes. On "catch trials" no target appeared. At a brief interval before the onset of the target, a cue would also appear in one of the locations such as an increase in luminance (a flash). The purpose of the cue was to summon attention to that location. On some trials the cue would be in the same box as

Attention has been likened to a spotlight that highlights certain information or a bottleneck in information processing. But how do we decide which information to select and which to ignore?

the target and on others it would not. As such, the cue is completely uninformative with regards to the later position of the target. When the cue precedes the target by up to 150 ms, participants are significantly faster at detecting the target at that location. The cue captures the attentional spotlight and this facilitates subsequent perceptual processing at that location. At longer delays (above 300 ms) the reverse pattern is found: participants are slower at detecting a target in the same location as the cue. This can be explained by assuming that the spotlight initially shifts to the cued location, but if the target does not appear, attention shifts to another location (called "disengagement"). There is a processing cost in terms of reaction time associated with going back to the previously attended location. This is called **inhibition of return**.

How does the spotlight know where to go? Who controls the spotlight? In the Posner spatial cueing task, the spotlight is attracted by a sudden change in the periphery. That is, attention is externally guided and bottom-up. This is referred to as **exogenous orienting**. However, it is also possible for attention to be guided, to some degree, by the goals of the perceiver. This is referred to as **endogenous orienting**. As an example of this, La Berge (1983) presented participants with words and varied the instructions. In one instance, they were asked to attend to the central letter and on another occasion they were asked to attend to the whole word. When attending to the central letter participants were faster at making judgments about that letter but not other letters in the word. In contrast, when asked to attend to the whole word they were faster at making judgments about all the letters. Thus, the

## KEY TERMS

**Overt orienting**
The movement of attention accompanied by movement of the eyes or body.

**Inhibition of return**
A slowing of reaction time associated with going back to a previously attended location.

**Exogenous orienting**
Attention that is externally guided by a stimulus.

**Endogenous orienting**
Attention is guided by the goals of the perceiver.

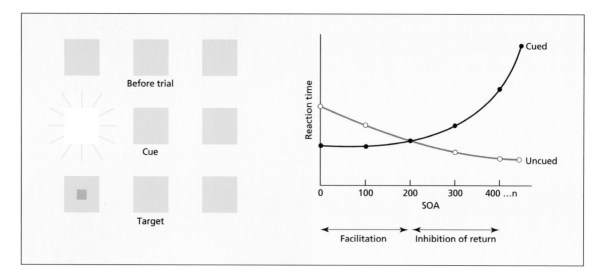

Participants initially fixate at the central box. A brief cue then appears as a brightening of one of the peripheral boxes. After a delay (called the "stimulus onset asynchrony," or SOA), the target then appears in the cued or uncued box. Participants are faster at detecting the target in the cued location if the target appears soon after the cue (facilitation) but are slower if the target appears much later (inhibition).

**Visual search**
A task of detecting the presence or absence of a specified target object in an array of other distracting objects.

attentional focus can be manipulated by the demands of the task (i.e. top-down). Another commonly used paradigm that uses endogenous attention is called **visual search** (Treisman, 1988). In visual search experiments, participants are asked to detect the presence or absence of a specified target object (e.g. the letter "F") in an array of other distracting objects (e.g. the letters "E" and "T"). As discussed in more detail later, visual search is a good example of a mix of bottom-up processing (perceptual identification of objects and features) and top-down processing (holding in mind the target and endogenously driven orienting of attention).

Examples of non-spatial attention mechanisms include object-based attention and time-based/temporal (not to be confused with temporal lobes) attentional processes. With regards to object-based attention, if two objects (e.g. a house and a face) are transparently superimposed in the same spatial location then participants can still selectively attend to one or the other. This has consequences for neural activity—the attended object is linked to a greater BOLD response in its corresponding brain region given that extrastriate visual cortex contains regions that respond differently to different stimuli (O'Craven *et al.*, 1999). So attending to a face will activate the fusiform face area, and attending to a house will

Do you see a face or a house? The ability to shift between these percepts is an example of object-based attention.

From Kanwisher & Wojciulik, 2000.

activate the parahippocampal place area even though both objects are in the same spatial location. It also has consequences for cognition: for instance, the unattended object will be responded to more slowly if it now becomes task-relevant (Tipper, 1985). With regards to Posner-style cueing tasks, research has shown that inhibition of return is partly related to the spatial location itself and partly related to the object that happens to occupy that location (Tipper *et al.*, 1991). If the object moves, then the inhibition can also move with the object rather than remaining entirely at the initial location.

The best example of attention also operating in a temporal domain comes from the **attentional blink** (Dux & Marois, 2009; Raymond *et al.*, 1992). In the attentional blink paradigm, a series of objects (e.g. letters) are presented in rapid succession (~10 per second) and in the same spatial location. The typical task is to report two targets that may appear anywhere within the stream which are

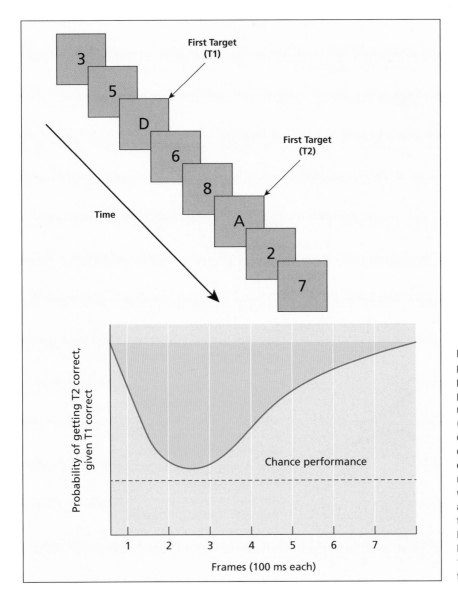

In the attentional blink paradigm, there is a fast presentation of stimuli and participants are asked to report which targets they saw (e.g. reporting letters among digits; "D and A" being the correct answer in this example). Participants fail to report the second target when it appears soon after an initial target. The initial target (T1) may take over our limited attentional capacity leading to an apparent "blindness" of a subsequent target (T2).

referred to as T1 and T2 (e.g. white letters among black; or letters among digits). What is found is that participants are "blind" to the second target, T2, when it occurs soon after the first target, T1 (typically 2–3 items later). This is believed to reflect attention rather than perception because it is strongly modulated by the task. The effect is found when participants are instructed to attend to the first target but not when instructed to ignore it (Raymond *et al.*, 1992).

## THE ROLE OF THE PARIETAL LOBES IN ATTENTION

This section considers the role of the parietal lobes (and to a lesser degree the frontal lobes) in attention. The frontal lobes are considered in more detail elsewhere with regards to action selection (Chapter 8), working memory (Chapter 9), and executive functions (Chapter 14). The first part of this section considers mechanisms of spatial attention and how this relates to the notion of a "where" pathway. The second part of the section considers hemispheric asymmetries in function considering both spatial and non-spatial attention processes. The final part considers the interplay between perception, attention, and awareness.

### The "where" pathway, salience maps, and orienting of attention

From early visual processing in the occipital cortex, two important pathways can be distinguished that may be specialized for different types of information (Ungerleider & Mishkin, 1982). A ventral route (or "what" pathway) leading into the temporal lobes may be concerned with identifying objects. In contrast, a dorsal route (or "where" pathway) leading in to the parietal lobes may be specialized for locating objects in space. The dorsal route also has an important role to play in attention, spatial or otherwise. The dorsal route also guides action toward objects and some researchers also consider it a "how" pathway as well as a "where" pathway (Goodale & Milner, 1992).

Single-cell recordings from the monkey parietal lobe provide important insights into the neural mechanisms of spatial attention. Bisley and Goldberg (2010) summarize evidence that a region in the posterior parietal lobe, termed **LIP (lateral intra-parietal area)**, is involved in attention. This region responds to external sensory stimuli (vision, sound) and is important for eliciting a particular kind of motor response (eye movements, termed **saccades**). Superficially then, it could be labeled as a sensorimotor association region. However, a closer inspection of its response properties reveals how it may play an important role in attention. First, this region does not respond to most visual stimuli, but rather has a sparse response profile such that it tends to respond to stimuli that are unexpected (e.g. abrupt, unpredictable onsets) or relevant to the task. When searching for a target in an array of objects (e.g. a red triangle), LIP neurons tend to respond more strongly when the

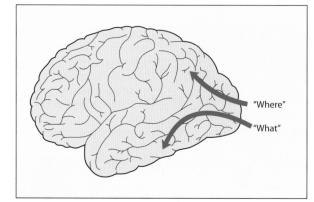

"Where"
"What"

Later stages of visual processing are broadly divided into two routes: a "what" pathway (or ventral stream) is involved in object perception and memory, whereas a "where" pathway (or dorsal stream) is involved in attending to and acting upon objects.

target lands in its receptive field than when a distractor (e.g. a blue square) does (Gottlieb *et al.*, 1998). So it isn't related to sensory stimulation per se. Moreover, sudden changes in luminance are a salient stimulus to these neurons (Balan & Gottlieb, 2009), analogous to how luminance changes drive attention in the Posner cueing task. As such, neurons in this region have characteristics associated with both exogenous and endogenous attention. It has been suggested that area LIP contains a **salience map** of space in which only the locations of the most behaviorally relevant stimuli are encoded (e.g.Itti & Koch, 2001). This is clearly reminiscent of the filter or spotlight metaphor of attention in cognitive models that selects only a subset of information in the environment.

In addition to representing the saliency of visual stimuli, neurons in LIP also respond to the current position of the eye (in fact, its responsiveness depends on the two sources of information being multiplied together). This information can be used to plan a saccade—i.e. overt orienting of attention. There is also evidence that they may support covert orienting. Lesioning LIP in one hemisphere leads to slower visual search in the contralateral (not ipsilateral) visual field even in the absence of saccades (Wardak *et al.*, 2004).

Spatial attention to sounds is also associated with activity in LIP neurons and this can also be used to plan saccades (Stricanne *et al.*, 1996). Thus, this part of the brain is multi-sensory. In order to link sound and vision together on the same salience map it requires the different senses to be spatially aligned or **remapped**. This is because the location of sound is coded relative to the angle of the head/ears, but the location of vision is coded (at least initially) relative to the angle of the eyes. Some neurons in LIP transform sound locations to be relative to the eyes so they can be used to plan saccades, instead of relative to the head/ears (Stricanne *et al.*, 1996).

In humans, using fMRI, presenting an arrow (an endogenous cue for spatial orienting) is associated with brief activity in visual cortical regions followed by sustained activity in posterior parietal lobes (including the likely homologue of

## KEY TERMS

**Salience map**
A spatial layout that emphasizes the most behaviorally relevant stimuli in the environment.

**Remapping**
Adjusting one set of spatial coordinates to be aligned with a different coordinate system.

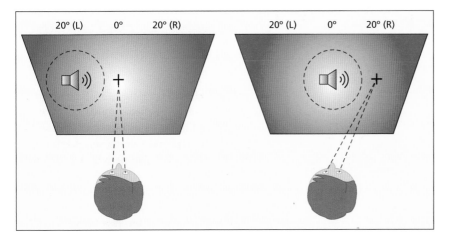

An example of an auditory neuron that responds to sounds that have been "remapped" into eye-centered coordinates. These neurons are found in brain regions such as LIP and the superior colliculus. This neuron responds to sounds about 20 degrees to the left of fixation irrespective of whether the sound source itself comes from the left (left figure) or centre of space (right figure). This enables orienting of the eyes to sounds.
From Stein & Stanford, 2008.

area LIP) and a frontal region called the **frontal eye field, FEF** (Corbetta *et al.*, 2000). This activity occurs irrespective of whether the required response is one of covert orienting of attention, a saccade, or a pointing response (Astafiev *et al.*, 2003). That is, it reflects a general orienting of attention. It may also not be spatially specific as a similar region is implicated in orienting attention between spatially superimposed objects (Serences *et al.*, 2004). Bressler *et al.* (2008) examined the functional connectivity among this network during presentation of a preparatory orienting stimulus (the spoken words "left" or "right") prior to a visual stimulus and concluded that, in this situation, the directionality of activation was top-down: that is, from frontal regions, to parietal regions, to visual occipital cortex. Of course, in other situations (an exogenous cue) it may operate in reverse.

According to Corbetta and Shulman (2002), this is only one of two major attentional networks involving the parietal lobes. They suggest that the dorsal stream should be reconsidered as split into two: a dorso-dorsal branch and a ventro-dorsal branch (for a related proposal see Rizzolatti & Matelli, 2003). They conceptualize the role of the dorso-dorsal stream in attention as one of orienting within a salience map (as described above) and involving the LIP and FEF. By contrast, they regard the more ventro-dorsal branch as a "circuit breaker" that interrupts ongoing cognitive activity to direct attention outside of the current focus of processing. This attentional disengagement mechanism is assumed to involve the temporoparietal region (and ventral prefrontal cortex) and is considered to be more strongly right lateralized. For instance, activity in this region is found when detecting a target (but not when processing a spatial cue) whereas activity in the LIP region shows a strong response to the cue (Corbetta *et al.*, 2000). Activity in the right temporoparietal region is enhanced when detecting an infrequent target particularly if it is presented at an unattended location (Arrington *et al.*, 2000). Downar *et al.* (2000) found that several frontal areas as well as the temporoparietal junction (TPJ) were activated when participants were monitoring for a stimulus change, independently of whether the change occurred in auditory, visual or tactile stimuli.

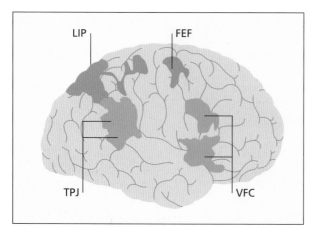

Corbetta and Schulman (2002) have suggested that there are two main attention-related circuits involving the parietal lobes: a dorso-dorsal circuit (involving LIP) that is involved in attentional orienting within a salience map; and a more ventral circuit (involving right TPJ) that diverts attention away from its current focus.

## Hemispheric differences in parietal lobe contributions to attention

The parietal lobes of the right and left hemispheres represent the full visual field (unlike early parts of visual cortex) but do so in a graded fashion that favors the contralateral side of space (Pouget & Driver, 2000). So the right parietal lobe shows a maximal responsiveness to stimuli on the far left side, a moderate responsiveness to the middle, and a weaker response to the far right side. The left parietal lobe shows the reverse profile. One consequence of this is that damage to the parietal lobes in one hemisphere leads to left-right spatially graded deficits in attention. For instance, damage to the right parietal lobe would lead to less attentional resources allocated to the far left side, moderate attentional resources to the midline, and

## WHY DO ACTORS MAKE A HIDDEN ENTRANCE FROM STAGE RIGHT?

The right parietal lobes of humans are generally considered to have a more dominant role in spatial attention than its left hemisphere equivalent. One consequence of this is that right-hemisphere lesions have severe consequences for spatial attention, particularly for the left space (as in the condition of "neglect"). Another consequence of right-hemisphere spatial dominance is that, in a non-lesioned brain, there is *over-attention* to the left side of space (termed pseudoneglect). For example, there is a general tendency for everyone to bisect lines more to the left of center (Bowers & Heilman, 1980). This phenomenon may explain why actors enter from stage right when they do not wish their entrance to be noticed (Dean, 1946). It may also explain why pictures are more likely to be given titles referring to objects on the left, and why the left side of pictures feels nearer than the right side of the same picture when flipped (Nelson & MacDonald, 1971). The light in paintings is more likely to come from the left side and people are faster at judging the direction of illumination when the source of light appears to come from the left (Sun & Perona, 1998). Moreover, we are less likely to bump into objects on the left than the right (Nicholls *et al.*, 2007). Thus, there is a general leftwards attentional bias in us all.

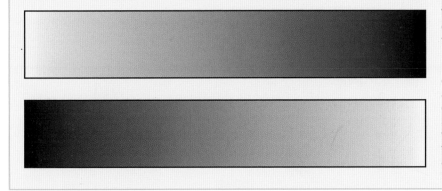

Which bar appears darker: the one on the top or the bottom? Most people perceive the bottom bar as being darker because of an attentional bias to the left caused by a right-hemisphere dominance for space/attention, even though the two images are identical mirror images.

near-normal attentional abilities on the right. This disorder is called **hemispatial neglect**, in which patients fail to attend to stimuli on the opposite side of space to the lesion. Neglect is normally far more severe following right hemisphere lesions, resulting in failure to attend to the left. This suggests that, in humans, there is likely to be a hemispheric asymmetry such that the right parietal lobe is more specialized for spatial attention than the left. Another possible way of conceptualising this is that the right parietal lobe makes a larger contribution to the construction of a salience map than the left side: resulting in a normal bias for the left side of space to be salient (a phenomenon termed **pseudo-neglect**, see BOX) and for the left side of space to be, therefore, particularly vulnerable to the effects of brain damage (neglect)

Parietal lobe lesions can also result in non-spatial deficits of attention. Husain *et al.* (1997) found that neglect patients had an unusually long "blind" period in the attentional blink task in which stimuli were presented centrally. Again, this can be construed in terms of both hemispheres making a contribution to the normal detection of salient stimuli (in this task, the second target in a rapidly changing stream). When one hemisphere is damaged then the attentional resource is depleted.

### KEY TERMS

**Hemispatial neglect**
A failure to attend to stimuli on the opposite side of space to a brain lesion.

**Pseudo-neglect**
In a non-lesioned brain there is over attention to the left side of space.

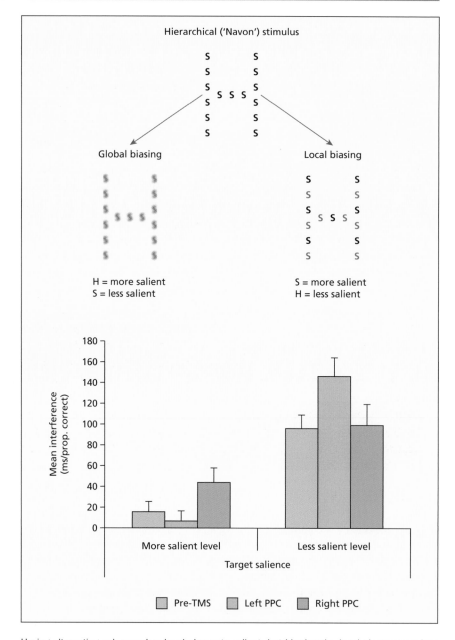

Having alternating colors makes local elements salient, but blurring the local elements makes the global shape more salient. TMS over the right posterior parietal cortex disrupts the ability to detect the more salient element (e.g. the local S in the right example, and the global "H" in the left example). TMS over the left posterior parietal cortex disrupts the ability to detect the less salient element (e.g. the global "H" in the right example, and the local S in the left example).

Graph from Mevorach et al., 2006.

## SPATIAL ATTENTION ACROSS THE SENSES—VENTRILOQUIST AND RUBBER HAND ILLUSIONS

In ventriloquism, there is a conflict between the actual source of a sound (the ventriloquist him or herself) and the apparent source of the sound (the dummy). In this instance, the sound appears to come from the dummy the dummy has associated lip movements whereas the lip movements of the ventriloquist are suppressed. In other words, the spatial location of the visual cue "captures" the location of the sound.

Why is it that sound tends to be captured by the visual stimulus but not vice versa? One explanation is that the ability to locate things in space is more accurate with vision than audition, so when there is a mismatch between them, the brain may default to the visual location. Witkin et al. (1952) found that sound localization was impaired in the presence of a visual cue in a conflicting location. Driver and Spence (1994) found that people are able to repeat back a speech stream (or "shadow") more accurately when lip movements and the loudspeaker are on the same side of space than when they are on opposite sides.

In the brain, there are multi-sensory regions such as in the superior temporal sulcus and intra-parietal sulcus that respond selectively to sound and vision when both occur at the same time or in the same location (Calvert, 2001). For instance, the superior temporal sulcus shows greater activity to synchronous audio-visual speech than asynchronous speech (Macaluso et al., 2004). However, when there is a *spatial* mismatch between the auditory and visual locations of synchronous speech then the right inferior parietal lobe is activated (Macaluso et al., 2004). This audio-visual spatial mismatch is found in the ventriloquist illusion and may involve the shifting or suppression of the heard location or, conversely, "grabbing" of spatial attention by the visual modality.

More bizarrely, there is an analogue of the ventriloquist effect in the tactile modality. Botvinick and Cohen (1998) placed participants' hand behind a hidden screen and placed a rubber hand on the visible side of the screen. Watching the rubber hand stroked with a paintbrush while their own (unseen) hand was stroked with a paintbrush could induce a kind of "out of body" experience. Participants report curious sensations such as, "I felt as if the rubber hands were my hands." In this instance, there is a conflict between the seen location of the (rubber) hand and felt bodily location of the real hand: the conflict is resolved by visual capture of the tactile sensation.

Mevorach and colleagues have proposed that the left and right parietal lobes have different roles in non-spatial attention: specifically the right hemisphere is considered important for attending to a salient stimulus, and the left hemisphere is important for suppressing a non-salient stimulus or "ignoring the elephant in the room" (Mevorach et al., 2010; Mevorach et al., 2006). Their non-spatial manipulation of saliency involved making certain elements of the display easier to perceive. For instance, a figure comprised of an "H" made up of small S's can be altered so that either the "H" is more salient (blurring the S's) or the S is more salient (using alternating colors). fMRI shows that the *left* intra-parietal sulcus is involved when the task is to focus on non-salient features (and ignore salient ones)—such as finding the local S's in a blurred global "H" (Mevorach et al., 2006). Disruption of this region using TMS (but not the right hemisphere region) interferes with the ability to do this task and disrupts the connectivity between this region and those in the occipital lobe that are presumably engaged in shape processing. By contrast, the *right* intraparietal cortex responds more when the task is to identify the salient features (and ignore the non-salient ones) and TMS to this region disrupts that task (Mevorach *et al.*, 2006). What is presently unclear is how these sorts of non-spatial selection mechanisms relate to the spatially specific deficits seen in neglect. One possibility is that neglect comprises a variety of attention-related deficits, some that are spatially specific (the defining symptoms of neglect) and some that are not. Whatever the relationship to neglect, there is an emerging consensus that attention itself can be fractionated into different kinds of mechanisms (Riddoch *et al.*, 2010).

## The relationship between attention, perception, and awareness

The terms "attention," "perception," and "awareness" are all common in everyday usage although most of us would be pushed to give a good definition of them in either lay or scientific terms. To begin with, a simple working definition may suffice (although more detailed nuances will be introduced later). Attention is a mechanism for the selection of information. Awareness is an outcome (a conscious state) that is, in many theories, linked to that mechanism. Perception is the information that is selected from and, ultimately, forms the content of awareness. Needless to say it is possible to be aware of, and attend to, things that are not related to perception (e.g. one's own thoughts and feelings) and it is assumed that broadly similar mechanisms operate here with, possibly, an additional prefrontal gating mechanism that switches the focus of attention between the external environment and inner thoughts (Burgess *et al.*, 2007).

Considering first the relationship between perception and attention, a number of studies have explored what happens in brain regions responsible for perception (e.g. in the visual ventral stream) when a stimulus is attended versus unattended. In general, when an object (e.g. a face) or a perceptual feature (e.g. motion) is attended then there is an increased activity, measured with fMRI, in brain regions that are involved in perceiving those stimuli relative to when they are unattended (Kanwisher & Wojciulik, 2000). This, however, also depends on how difficult the attention-demanding task is. For instance, Rees *et al.* (1997) instructed participants to attend to words (in a language-based task) and ignore visual motion in the periphery. The activity in the motion-sensitive area V5/MT was reduced when the language-based task was difficult compared with when it was easy. This is compatible with the notion of attention being a limited resource, with less of the resource available for (bottom-up) processing of irrelevant perceptual information when (top-down) task demands are high.

There is evidence that attention can affect activity in visual cortex (including in V1) even in the absence of a visual stimulus (Kastner *et al.*, 1999). This increase appears to be related to attended locations rather than attended features such as color or motion (McMains *et al.*, 2007). It is also related to attended modalities. Increases in BOLD activity are found in visual, auditory or tactile cortices when a stimulus is expected in that modality but is linked to decreases in the non-predicted modalities (Langner *et al.*, 2011). This may reflect increased neural activity prior to the presentation of the stimulus. In monkeys it has been shown that neurons increase the spontaneous firing rate in an attended location even in the absence of a visual stimulus (Luck *et al.*, 1997). In these examples in which no perceptual stimulation is present, it is clear that attention can sometimes

THE ATTENDING BRAIN 147

operate in the absence of awareness of perceptual stimuli (Koch & Tsuchiya, 2007).

The discussion above has centered on the links between perception and attention. What of the links between perception and awareness? Awareness, as typically defined, depends on participants' ability to report on the presence of a stimulus. This can be studied by comparing stimuli that are perceived consciously versus those perceived unconsciously (e.g. presented too briefly to be reported). In such studies, conducted with fMRI, a typical pattern of brain activity has two main features: firstly, there is greater activity in regions involved in perception (e.g. ventral visual stream) when participants are aware of a stimulus than unaware and, secondly, that there is a spread of activity to distant brain regions (notably the frontal-parietal network) in the aware state (see Dehaene *et al.*, 2006). It is this broadcasting of information that is often assumed to enable participants to be able to report on, or act on, the perceived information. Moreover, this network of regions

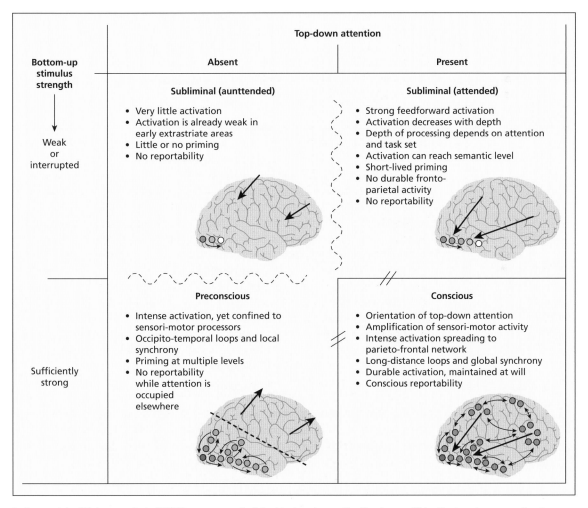

In the model of Dehaene *et al.* (2006), awareness is linked to top-down attention to a sufficiently strong sensory stimulus. This is associated with activity spreading to a frontal-parietal network. In contrast, non-aware conditions (e.g. attending to a very weak sensory signal, inattention to a strong sensory signal) are linked to varying levels of activity in sensory cortex alone. From Dehaene *et al.*, 2006.

in the frontal and parietal lobes are those typically implicated in studies of attention suggesting (to some researchers) that attention is the mechanism that gives rise to awareness of perception (Posner, 2012; Rees & Lavie, 2001). To give a concrete example, in the attentional blink paradigm activity in frontal and parietal regions discriminates between awareness versus unawareness of the second target (Kranczioch *et al.*, 2005). It has been suggested that, in these circumstances, attentional selection generates an all-or-nothing outcome (something that is consciously seen or unseen) from information that is essentially continuous in nature, i.e. perceived to *some* degree (Vul *et al.*, 2009).

This standard view of perception, attention and awareness is not universally accepted. One alternative viewpoint suggests that perceptual awareness can be sub-divided into two mechanisms: one relating to the *experience* of perceiving itself and one related to the *reportability* of that experience (Block, 2005; Lamme, 2010). These are often referred to as **phenomenal consciousness** and **access consciousness** respectively. In these models, the reportability of an experience is linked to the frontal-parietal network, but the actual experience of perceiving is assumed to lie within interactions in the perceptual processing network itself. For instance, there is evidence that the visibility of unattended stimuli is related solely to activity in the occipital lobe (Tse *et al.*, 2005). In this view, attention is still related to awareness, but only to some aspects of awareness (i.e. its reportability).

## Evaluation

This section has taken core ideas relating to the concept of attention (e.g. filtering irrelevant information, the spotlight metaphor, links to eye movements) and explained how these may be implemented in the brain. The parietal lobes has a key role due to it the fact that it interfaces between regions involved in executive control (top-down aspects of attention) and regions involved in perceptual processing (bottom-up aspects of attention). One of the emerging trends in the literature on attention, that has been driven largely by neuroscience evidence, is to consider attention in terms of separable but interacting component processes (e.g. orienting attention, disengaging attention, and so on). This is not surprising given that most other cognitive faculties (e.g. vision, memory) are now thought of in this way. However, it would be fair to say that there is less consensus over what the constituent components are (if any) in the attention domain. The next main section considers several specific models of attention that conform to the general principles discussed thus far.

## THEORIES OF ATTENTION

This section considers in more detail three influential theories in the attention literature: the Feature Integration Theory proposed by Treisman and colleagues; Biased Competition Theory proposed by Desimone, Duncan, and colleagues; and the Premotor Theory of Rizzolatti and colleagues.

### Feature integration theory

Feature integration theory (FIT) is a model of how attention selects perceptual objects and binds the different features of those objects (e.g. color and shape) into a reportable experience. Most of the evidence for it (and against it) has come from the visual search paradigm. Look at the two arrays of letters in the next figure. Your task is to try to find the blue "T" as quickly as possible.

Was the letter relatively easy to find in the first array, but hard to find in the second array? In the second case, did you feel as if you were searching each location in turn until you found it? In the first array, the target object (the blue "T") does not share any features with the distractor objects in the array (red Ts and red Ls). The object can therefore be found from a simple inspection of the perceptual mechanism that supports color detection.

According to FIT, perceptual features such as color and shape are coded in parallel and prior to attention (Treisman, 1988; Treisman & Gelade, 1980). If an object does not share features with other objects in the array it appears to **pop-out**. In the second array, the distractors are made up of the same features that define the object. Thus, the object cannot be detected by inspecting the color module alone (because some distractors are blue) or by inspecting the shape module alone (because some distractors are T-shaped). To detect the target one needs to bring together information about several features (i.e. a conjunction of color and shape). Feature-Integration Theory assumes that this occurs by allocating spatial attention to the location of candidate objects. If the object turns out not to be the target, then the "spotlight" inspects the next candidate and so on in a serial fashion.

Typical data from a visual search experiment such as the one conducted by Treisman and Gelade (1980) is presented on p. 150. The

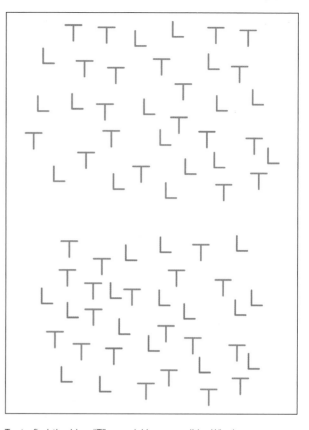

Try to find the blue "T" as quickly as possible. Why is one condition harder than the other? Feature-Integration Theory assumes that basic features are coded in parallel but that focused attention requires serial search. When the letter differs from others by a single feature, such as color, then it can be identified quickly by the initial stage of feature detection. When the letter differs from others by two or more features, then attention is needed to serially search.

dependent measure is the time taken to find the target (some arrays do not contain the target, but these data are not presented here). The variables manipulated were the number of distractors in the array and the type of distractor. When the target can only be found from a conjunction of features, there is a linearly increasing relationship between the number of distractors and time taken to complete the search. This is consistent with the notion that each candidate object must be serially inspected in turn. When a target can be found from only a single feature, it makes very little difference how many distractors are present, because it "pops out." If attention is not properly deployed, then individual features may incorrectly combine. These are referred to as **illusory conjunctions**. For example, if displays of colored letters are presented briefly so that serial search with focal attention cannot take place, then participants may incorrectly say that they had seen a red "H" when in fact they had been presented with a blue "H" and a red "E" (Treisman & Schmidt, 1982). This supports the conclusion arising from FIT that attention needs to be deployed to combine features of the same object correctly.

## KEY TERMS

**Pop-out**
The ability to detect an object among distractor objects in situations in which the number of distractors presented is unimportant.

**Illusory conjunctions**
A situation in which visual features of two different objects are incorrectly perceived as being associated with a single object.

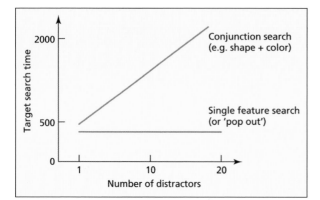

According to FIT, when a target is defined by a conjunction of features, search becomes slower when there are more items, because the items are searched serially. When a target is defined by a single feature it may "pop out"; that is, the time taken to find it is not determined by the number of items in the array.

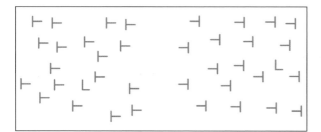

Searching for an "L" among "T" is hard if the "T" is rotated 180 degrees or 270 degrees (left), but easier if the "T" is rotated at 0 degrees or 90 degrees (right). It suggests that features in visual search consist of more than oriented lines, or that some form of feature integration takes place without attention.

TMS applied over the parietal lobe slows conjunction searches but not single-feature searches (Ashbridge *et al.*, 1997, 1999) and a functional imaging study has demonstrated parietal involvement in conjunction, but not single-feature searches (Corbetta *et al.*, 1995). Patients with parietal lesions often show a high level of illusory conjunction errors with brief presentation (Friedman-Hill *et al.*, 1995).

One difficulty with FIT is that there is no a priori way to define what constitutes a "feature." Features tend to be defined in a post hoc manner according to whether they elicit pop-out. For instance, it is generally assumed that the features consist of lines (e.g. vertical line, horizontal line) rather than letters (i.e. clusters of lines). However, some evidence does not support this assumption. For example, searching for an "L" among Ts is hard if the "T" is rotated at 180 or 270 degrees, and easier if the "T" is rotated at 0 or 90 degrees (Duncan & Humphreys, 1989). This occurs even though the basic features (horizontal and vertical lines) are equally present in them all. Duncan and Humphreys (1989) suggest that most of the data that FIT attempts to explain can also be explained in terms of how easy it is to perceptually group objects together rather than in terms of parallel feature perception followed by serial attention. They found that it is not just the similarity between the target and distractor that is important, but also the similarity between different types of distractor. This implies that there is some feature binding prior to attention and this contradicts a basic assumption of FIT.

Another issue is whether simple feature searches (e.g. a single blue letter among red letters) really occur without attention as assumed by FIT. An alternative position is that all visual search requires attention even in the case of pop-out stimuli. Wolfe (2003) argues that pop-out is not preattentive but is simply a stimulus driven (exogenous) cue of attention.

Finally, FIT is an example of what has been termed an **early selection** model of attention. Recall that the main reason for having attentional mechanisms is to select some information for further processing, at the expense of other information. According to early selection theories, information is selected according to perceptual attributes (e.g. color or pitch). This can be contrasted with **late selection** theories that assume that all incoming information is processed up to the level of meaning (semantics) before being selected for further processing. One of the most frequently cited examples of late selection is the **negative priming** effect (Tipper, 1985). In this figure, participants must name the red object and ignore the blue one. If the ignored object on trial N suddenly becomes the attended object on trial N+1, then participants are slower at naming it (called negative

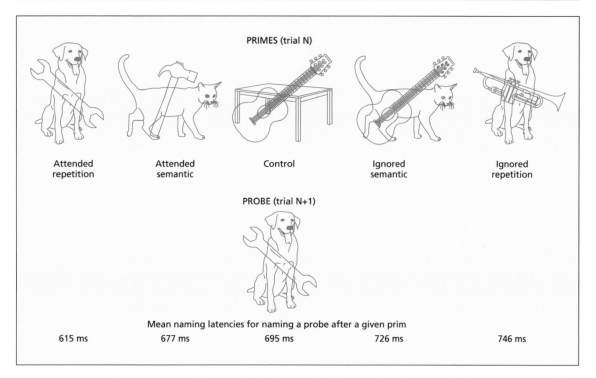

In this example, participants must name the red object and ignore the blue one. If an ignored object becomes an attended object on the subsequent trial, then there is cost of processing, which is termed negative priming.

priming). The effect can also be found if the critical object is from the same semantic category. This suggests that the ignored object was, in fact, processed meaningfully rather than being excluded purely on the basis of its color as would be expected by early selection theories such as FIT.

How can the evidence both for and against FIT be reconciled? The selection of objects for further processing may sometimes be early (i.e. based on perceptual features) and sometimes late (i.e. based on meaning), depending on the demands of the task. Lavie (1995) has shown that, when there is a high perceptual load (e.g. the large arrays typically used for visual search), then selection may be early, but in conditions of low load in which few objects are present (as in the negative priming task), then there is a capacity for all objects to be processed meaningfully consistent with late selection. Other findings have suggested that the process of feature binding may also operate at several levels (Humphreys *et al.*, 2000), with some forms of binding occurring prior to attention. This could account for the distractor similarity effects of Duncan and Humphreys (1989).

## Biased competition theory

The biased competition theory of Desimone and Duncan (1995) draws more heavily from neuroscience than from cognitive psychology. It explicitly rejects a spotlight metaphor of attention (inherent, for instance, in Feature Integration Theory). Instead "attention is an emergent property of many neural mechanisms working to resolve competition for visual processing and control of behavior." By "emergent property," Desimone and Duncan imply that attention isn't a dedicated module, but rather a broad set of mechanisms for reducing many inputs to limited outcomes and there is no clear division between attentive and preattentive stages. The Biased Competition Theory has been extended and updated by others in light of more recent evidence (Beck & Kastner, 2009; Knudsen, 2007).

One assumption of the model is that competition occurs at multiple stages rather than at some fixed bottleneck—i.e. neither early nor late selection but something more dynamic. This competition occurs first within the visual ventral stream itself in terms of the processing of visual features (colors, motion, etc.) and objects. For instance, single cell electrophysiology suggests that when two stimuli are presented in a single receptive field (e.g. two color patches presented in the receptive field of a neuron in V4) then the responsiveness of the neuron is less than the sum of its responsiveness to each stimulus in isolation (Luck et al., 1997). This is one way in which "competition" may be realized at the neural level.

In humans, the BOLD response in areas of the visual ventral stream to multiple stimuli presented together is less than the sum of its parts as determined by a control condition involving sequential presentation. This also depends on how spatially close together the different stimuli are (Kastner et al., 2001). Brain regions containing neurons with small receptive fields (e.g. V1) are only disrupted by competitors that are close by, but regions that have larger receptive fields (e.g. V4) are also disrupted by more distant competitors. As well as spatial proximity, the degree of competition depends on perceptual similarity of multiple stimuli within the field (Beck & Kastner, 2009). This may be the neural basis of early grouping effects and also pop-out. Certain perceptual representations may also tend to dominate in the competitive process by virtue of being familiar (e.g. spotting your partner in a crowd), or by virtue of being recently seen, and so on. Again, this does not require a special mechanism as such: it just requires that there is bias in the way these stimuli are represented that facilitates their selection (e.g. neurons fire more when expected or frequently encountered). Selection may also be biased by top-down signals. When a receptive field contains an experimentally defined target and an irrelevant distractor then the neural response resembles that to the target alone suggesting some filtering out of the distractor (Moran & Desimone, 1985).

Another key assumption of this theory is that attention is not deployed serially, but rather perceptual competition occurs in parallel. Serial processing, by contrast, is assumed to arise from competition at the response level rather than perceptual processing (e.g. from the fact that it is only possible to fixate one location at a time). (This idea is linked closely to the Premotor Theory of Attention discussed in the next section). Neurons recorded in monkey V4 during visual search tasks are activated in parallel (i.e. irrespective of whether it is being currently attended/fixated) whenever a target feature (e.g. color) falls in the receptive field (Bichot et al., 2005). This occurs for both simple feature (i.e. pop-out) and conjunction searches. However, there is also an enhanced response when the target is selected for a saccade suggesting serial processing linked to motor responses. Whereas Feature-Integration Theory assumes either parallel *or* serial search (depending on the nature of the targets), the Biased Competition Theory suggests both kinds of mechanisms act together.

The Biased Competition Model also accounts for spatial and non-spatial attention within the same model. The differences between spatial and non-spatial attention was originally assumed to be due to different anatomical origins of the biasing signals rather than reflecting different mechanisms per se. The posterior parietal cortex was thought to be the origin of spatial biases (e.g. effects of arrows in orienting attention) and prefrontal cortex may code task-related biases (find the blue X). However, other research has suggested that the same frontal and parietal regions support both spatial and non-spatial search cues (Egner *et al.*, 2008).

Damage to the parietal lobe not only produces neglect it may also lead to a curious symptom called **extinction** (Riddoch *et al.*, 2010). When a single stimulus is presented briefly to either the left or the right of fixation, patients with parietal lesions tend to accurately report them. But when presented with two stimuli at the same time, the patient may report seeing the object on the right but not the object on the left (in the case of right parietal damage). Thus the patient has not lost the ability to see the left side of space, nor have they lost the ability to attend to the left side of space per se, but they have lost the ability to attend to (and be aware of) the left side of space when there is a competitor on the right.

Similar effects are found for the Posner-cueing task as a result of parietal lobe lesions (Posner & Petersen, 1990). For patients with right parietal lobe lesions, they are able to initially orient attention to either the left or right side of space as a result of a prestimulus flash of light on either the left or right. However, while they are able to shift attention from a cue on the left (their neglected side) to a target on the right (their "good" side) they are impaired in the reverse scenario (shifting from the "good" to neglected side). While this could be explained by damage to a special attention mechanism relating to dis-engaging attention (Posner & Petersen, 1990) it could be explained by biased competition: it is easy to orient to the "bad" side of space when competition is low (i.e. to the initial cue), but harder to orient to the "bad" side following a salient visual stimulus on the "good" side.

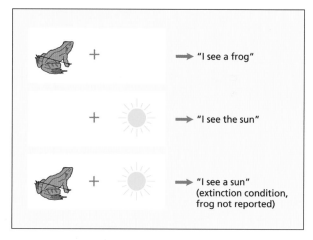

Neglect patients may fail to notice the stimulus on the left when two stimuli are briefly shown (called extinction), but notice it when it is shown in isolation. It suggests that attention depends on competition between stimuli.

## The premotor theory of attention

The premotor theory of attention assumes that the orienting of attention is nothing more than preparation of motor actions (Rizzolatti *et al.*, 1987, 1994). As such, it is primarily a theory of spatial attention. The theory encompasses both overt orienting, in which actual movement occurs, and covert orienting. The latter is assumed to reflect movement that is planned but not executed.

The initial evidence for the theory came from a spatial cueing task (Rizzolatti *et al.*, 1987). The set-up used four spatial locations arranged left to right (1, 2, 3 and 4) and a centrally fixated square. Within the central square, a digit would appear that would indicate where a target was likely to appear (with 80 percent certainty). A flash would then appear in one of the four boxes and the participant simply had to press a button as soon as it was detected. Participants were slower when the cue was misleading, forcing them to shift attention. However, they found that costs in response times were not only related to whether attention had to shift per se, but also whether attention had to *reverse* in direction. So a shift of attention from position 2 (left) to position 1 (far left) had a small cost whereas a shift from

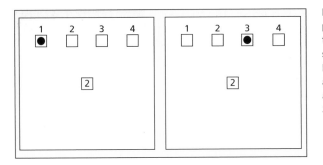

In the study of Rizzolatti *et al.* (1987), a centrally presented digit indicates where a target stimulus is likely to appear (in this case, position 2), but it may sometimes appear in an unattended location (as shown here, in positions 1 or 3). Although positions 1 and 3 are equidistant from the expected location, participants are faster at shifting attention to position 1 than position 3. Why might this be?

position 2 (left) to a rightward location (position 3) had a larger cost (and similarly a shift from 3 to 4 was less costly than from 3 to 2). The same results were also found for vertical alignments of the four positions so the findings do not relate to processing differences across hemispheres. The basic finding is hard to reconcile with a simple "spotlight" account, because the spotlight is moved the same distance in both scenarios. They suggest instead that the pattern reflects the programming of eye movements (but not their execution as overt movements were not allowed). Specifically, a leftwards eye movement can be made to go further leftwards with minimal additional processing effort, but to change a leftwards movement to a rightwards movement requires a different motor program to be set up and the original one discarded.

The term "premotor" refers to the claim that attention is a preparatory motor act and is not referring to the premotor cortical region of the brain (discussed in Chapter 8). The theory does, however, make strong neuroanatomical predictions: namely that the neural substrates of attention should be the same as the neural

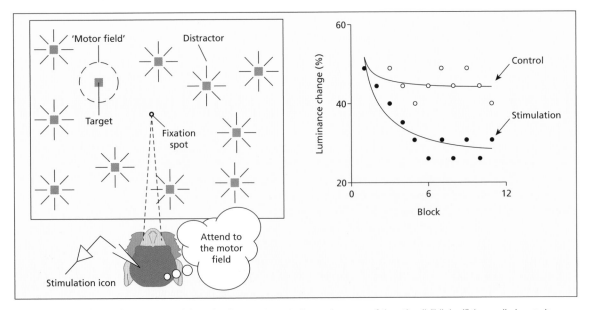

In Moore and Fallah (2001) the task of the animal was to press a lever when one of the stimuli "blinked" (a small change in luminance). They were better at doing the task when a part of the brain involved in generating eye movements was stimulated than in a no-stimulation control condition (even though no eye movements occurred), provided the light stimulus fell in the appropriate receptive field. This is consistent with the idea that attending to a region of space is like a virtual movement of the eyes.

Left image from www.nature.com/neuro/journal/v5/n9/fig_tab/nn0902–819_F1.html. Right image from Moore and Fallah, 2001.

substrates for motor preparation (particularly eye movements). As discussed previously, there is evidence to support this view from single-cell recordings (Bisley & Goldberg, 2010) and human fMRI (Nobre *et al.*, 2000). There is also intriguing evidence from brain stimulation studies. Electrical stimulation of neurons in the frontal eye fields (FEF) of monkeys can elicit reliable eye movements to particular locations in space. Moore and Fallah (2001) identified such neurons and then stimulated them at a lower intensity such that no eye movements occurred (the animal continued to fixate centrally). However, the animals did show enhanced perceptual discrimination of a stimulus presented in the location where an eye-movement would have occurred. This suggests that attention was deployed there and is consistent with the idea that covert orienting of attention is a non-executed movement plan.

The premotor theory of attention has not been without criticism. Smith and Schenk (2012) argue that it fails as a general theory of attention and may only be valid in certain situations (e.g. exogenous orienting of attention to, say, flashes of

## SEEING ONE OBJECT AT A TIME: SIMULTANAGNOSIA AND BALINT'S SYNDROME

The idea that one could perceive an object but not its location is highly counterintuitive, because it falls outside of the realm of our own experiences. However, there is no reason why the functioning of the brain should conform to our intuitions. Patients with **Balint's syndrome** (Balint, 1909, translated 1995) typically have damage to both the left and the right parietal lobes and have severe spatial disturbances. Patients with Balint's syndrome may notice only one object at a time: this is termed **simultanagnosia**. For example, the patient may notice a window, then, all of a sudden, the window disappears and a necklace is seen, although it is unclear who is wearing it. In terms of the two visual streams idea, it is as if there is no "there" there (Robertson, 2004). Within the Biased Competition Theory it could be regarded as an extreme form of perceptual competition due to a limited spatial selection capacity. Within Feature Integration Theory, it can be construed as an inability to bind features to locations and, hence, to each other. Recall that if a blue "H" and a red "E" are presented very quickly to normal participants, then illusory conjunction errors may be reported (e.g. red "H"). Balint's patients show these errors even when they are free to view objects for as long as they like (Friedman-Hill *et al.*, 1995). In addition

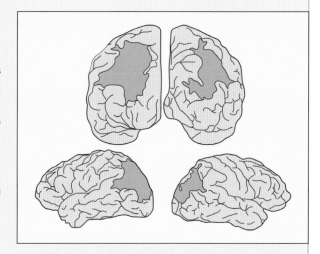

RM has extensive damage to both the left and right parietal lobes and severe difficulties in perceiving spatial relationships (top diagrams are viewed from the back of the brain; bottom diagrams are viewed from the side). RM was unable to locate objects verbally, or by reaching or pointing (Robertson *et al.*, 1997). In contrast, his basic visual abilities were normal (normal 20/15 visual acuity, normal color vision, contrast sensitivity, etc.). He was impaired at locating sounds, too.

to simultanagnosia, patients typically have problems in using vision to guide hand actions (optic ataxia; considered in Chapter 8) and fail to make appropriate eye movements (optic apraxia).

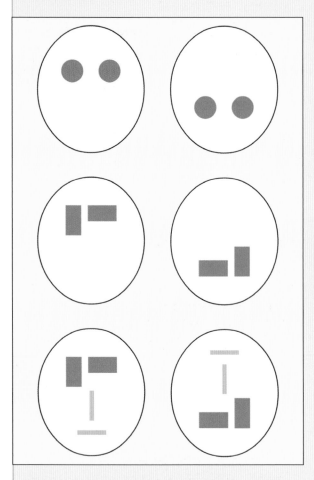

To say that Balint's patients can recognize single objects leads to some potential ambiguities. Consider a face. Is a face a single object or a collection of several objects (eyes, nose, mouth, etc.) arranged in a particular spatial configuration? A number of factors appear to determine whether parts are grouped together or not. Humphreys *et al.* (2000) showed that, in their Balint's patient, GK, parts are likely to be grouped into wholes if they share shape, if they share color, or if they are connected together. This suggests that some early feature binding is possible prior to attention. Another factor that determines grouping of parts into wholes is the familiarity of the stimulus and how a given stimulus is interpreted (so-called top-down influences). Shalev & Humphreys (2002) presented GK with the ambiguous stimuli on the left. When asked whether the two circles were at the top or bottom of the oval he was at chance (55 percent). He performed the task well (91 percent) when asked whether the eyes were at the top or bottom of the face.

Under what circumstances is a face perceived as a whole or as a collection of parts? Patient GK can identify the location of the ovals when he is told that they are the eyes of a face, but not if he thinks of them just as circles inside an oval. The former judgment may use his intact ventral route for identifying faces/objects, whereas the latter may use the impaired dorsal route for appreciating the location of the circles relative to another. GK was also better at making location judgments about the rectangles when other face-like features were added.

light). For instance, patients with chronic lesions of the FEF have a saccadic deficit but no deficit of endogenous attention in covert orienting tasks involving, say, arrow cues (Smith *et al.*, 2004).

## Evaluation

Although there are many theories of attention, three prominent ones have been considered here. Feature Integration Theory and the Premotor Theory are necessarily limited in scope in that they are specifically theories of *spatial* attention, whereas the Biased Competition Theory has the advantage of offering a more general account. Feature Integration Theory has been successful in explaining much human behavioral data in visual search. Biased Competition Theory offers a more neuroscientific account of this data in which competition arises at multiple levels (e.g. perceptual crowding, and response competition) and attention is synonymous with the selection function of this overall system. The Premotor Theory offers an interesting explanation as to how attention can be considered as a combination of both "where" (spatial) and "how" (motor) functions of the dorsal stream.

## NEGLECT AS A DISORDER OF SPATIAL ATTENTION AND AWARENESS

Patients with neglect (also called hemispatial neglect, visuospatial neglect or visual neglect) fail to attend to stimuli on the opposite side of space to their lesion—normally a right-sided lesion resulting in inattention to the left side of space.

### Characteristics of neglect

There are a number of common ways of testing for neglect. Patients may omit features from the left side when drawing or copying. In tests of **line bisection**, patients tend to misplace the center of the line toward the right (because they underestimate the extent of the left side). The bias in bisection is proportional to the length of the line (Marshall & Halligan, 1990). **Cancellation tasks** are a variant of the visual search paradigms already discussed, in which the patients must search for targets in an array (normally striking them through as they are found). They will typically not find ones on the right. Some of these tasks may be passed by some neglect patients but failed by others, the reasons for which

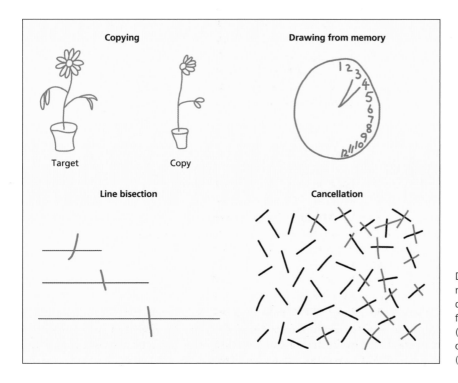

Different ways of assessing neglect include copying, drawing from memory, finding the center of a line (line bisection), and crossing out targets in an array (cancellation).

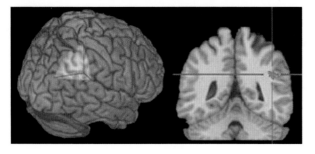

Neglect is associated with lesions to the right inferior parietal lobe. This photo shows the region of highest overlap of the lesions of 14 patients.

have only recently started to become clear (Halligan & Marshall, 1992; Wojciulik *et al.*, 2001). In extreme cases, neglect patients may shave only half of their face or eat half of their food on the plate.

Mort *et al.* (2003) examined the brain regions critical for producing neglect in 35 patients and concluded that the critical region was the right angular gyrus of the inferior parietal lobe, including the right temporoparietal junction (TPJ). Functional imaging studies of healthy participants performing line bisection also point to an involvement of this area in that particular task (Fink *et al.*, 2000); as do the results from a TMS study (Fierro *et al.*, 2000). While there is good consensus over the role of this region in neglect, it is not the only region that is implicated. For instance, Corbetta and Schulman (2011) argue that the right posterior parietal cortex, containing salience maps, may tend to be functionally deactivated (due to its connectivity with the damage right TPJ) despite not being structurally damaged. Others have argued that neglect itself can be fractionated into different kinds of spatial processes with differing neural substrates, as considered later.

## Neglect and the relationship between attention, perception, and awareness

It is important to stress that neglect is not a disorder of low-level visual perception. A number of lines of evidence support this conclusion. Functional imaging reveals that objects in the neglected visual field still activate visual regions in the occipital cortex (Rees *et al.*, 2000). Stimuli presented in the neglected field can often be detected if attention is first cued to that side of space (Riddoch & Humphreys, 1983). This also argues against a low-level perceptual deficit. The situations in which neglect patients often fare worse are those requiring voluntary orienting to the neglected side and those situations in which there are several stimuli competing for attention. Although the primary deficit in neglect is related to attention, not perception, it does lead to deficits in *awareness* of the perceptual world.

Neglect is not just restricted to vision, but can apply to other senses as well. This is consistent with evidence presented earlier that the parietal lobes have multi-sensory characteristics. Pavani *et al.* (2002) have shown that neglect patients show a right-skewed bias in identifying the location of a sound (but note that they are not "deaf" to sounds on the left). Extinction can also cross sensory modalities. A tactile (or visual) sensation on the right will not be reported if accompanied by a visual (or tactile) stimulus on the left, but will be reported when presented in isolation (Mattingley *et al.*, 1997).

Patients with neglect can be shown to process information in the neglected field to at least the level of object recognition. The ventral "what" route seems able to process information "silently" without entering awareness, whereas the dorsal "where" route to the parietal lobe is important for creating conscious experiences of the world around us. Vuilleumier *et al.* (2002b) presented brief pictures of objects in left, right, or both fields. When two pictures were presented simultaneously the patients extinguished the one on the left and only reported the

**HOW IS A "LACK OF AWARENESS" IN NEGLECT DIFFERENT FROM LACK OF AWARENESS IN BLINDSIGHT?**

| Neglect | Blindsight |
|---|---|
| • Lack of awareness is not restricted to vision and may be found for other sensory modalities | • Lack of awareness is restricted to the visual modality |
| • Whole objects may be processed implicitly | • Implicit knowledge is restricted to basic visual discriminations (direction of motion; but see Marcel, 1998) |
| • Lack of awareness can often be overcome by directing attention to neglected region | • Lack of awareness not overcome by directing attention to "blind" region |
| • Neglected patients often fail to voluntarily move their eyes into neglected region | • Blindsight patients do move their eyes into "blind" region |
| • Neglected region is egocentric | • Blind region is retinocentric |

one on the right and when later shown the neglected stimuli they claimed not to remember seeing them (a test of explicit memory). However, when later asked to identify a degraded picture of the object, their performance was facilitated, which suggests that the extinguished object was processed unconsciously. Other lines of evidence support this view. Marshall and Halligan (1988) presented a neglect patient with two depictions of a house that were identical on the non-neglected (right) side, but differed on the left side such that one of the two houses had flames coming from a left window. Although the patients claimed not to be able to perceive the difference between them, they did, when forced to choose, state that they would rather live in the house without the flames! This, again, points to the fact that the neglected information is implicitly coded to a level that supports meaningful judgments being made.

## Different types of neglect and different types of space

Space, as far as the brain goes, is not a single continuous entity. A more helpful analogy is to think of the brain creating (and perhaps storing) different kinds of "maps." Cognitive neuroscientists refer to different spatial reference frames to capture this notion. Each reference frame ("map") may have its own center point (origin) and set of coordinates. Similarly there may be ways of linking one map to another—so-called remapping. It has already been described how neurons may remap the spatial position of sounds from a head-centered reference frame to an eye-centered reference frame (so-called retinocentric space). This enables sounds to trigger eye movements. The same can happen for other combinations: for instance, visual receptive fields may be remapped so that they are centered on the position of the hands rather than the position of the eyes (facilitating hand-eye coordination during manual actions). The parietal lobes can perform remapping because they receive postural information about the body as well as sensory information relating to sound, vision and touch (Pouget & Driver, 2000).

The main clinical features of neglect tend to relate to **egocentric space** (reference frames centered on the body midline) and it is these kinds of spatial attentional disorders that are linked to brain damage to the right temporoparietal region (Hillis *et al.*, 2005). However, neglect is also linked to other kinds of spatial reference frames, as outlined below. Although this could be conceptualized as losing particular kinds of spatial representations, another way of thinking about it is in terms of attention deficits created by disrupting competition at different levels of processing.

### Perceptual versus representational neglect

Bisiach and Luzzatti (1978) established that neglect can occur for spatial mental images and not just for spatial representations derived directly from perception. Patients were asked to imagine standing in and facing a particular location in a town square that was familiar to them (the Piazza del Duomo, in Milan). They were then asked to describe the buildings that they saw in their "mind's eye." The patients often failed to mention buildings in the square to the left of the Duomo. Was this because of loss of spatial knowledge of the square or a failure to attend to it? To establish this, the patients were then asked to imagine themselves at the opposite end of the square, facing in, and describe the buildings. In this condition, the buildings that were on the left (and neglected) are now on the right and are reported, whereas the buildings that were on the right (and reported previously) are now on the left and get neglected. Thus, spatial knowledge of the square is not lost but is unavailable for report. Subsequent research has established that this so-called representational neglect forms a double dissociation with neglect of perceptual space (Bartolomeo, 2002; Denis *et al.*, 2002). The brain appears to contain different spatial reference frames for mental imagery and for egocentric perceptual space. The hippocampus is often considered to store an **allocentric** map of space (the spatial relationship of different landmarks to each other, rather than relative to the observer), but the parietal lobes may be required for imagining it from a given viewpoint (Burgess, 2002).

The Piazza del Duomo in Milan featured in a classic neuropsychological study. When asked to imagine the square from one viewpoint, patients with neglect failed to report buildings on the left. When asked to imagine the square from the opposing viewpoint they still failed to report buildings on the left, even though these had been correctly reported on the previous occasion. It suggests a deficit in spatial attention rather than memory.

Image from http://en.wikipedia.org.

## Near versus far space

Double dissociations exist between neglect of near space (Halligan & Marshall, 1991) versus neglect of far space (Vuilleumier *et al.*, 1998). This can be assessed by line bisection using a laser pen and stimuli in either near or far space, even equating for visual angles. Near space appears to be defined as "within reach," but it can get stretched! Berti and Frassinetti (2000) report a patient with a neglect deficit in near space but not far space. When a long stick was used instead of a laser pointer, the "near" deficit was extended. This suggests that tools quite literally become fused with the body in terms of the way that the brain represents the space around us. This is consistent with single-cell recordings from animals suggesting that visual-receptive fields for the arm get spatially stretched when the animal has been trained to use a rake tool (Iriki *et al.*, 1996).

## Personal and peripersonal space

Patients might show neglect of their bodily space. This might manifest itself as a failure to groom the left of the body or failure to notice the position of the left limbs (Cocchini *et al.*, 2001). This can be contrasted with patients who show neglect of the space outside their body, as shown in visual search type tasks, but not the body itself (Guariglia & Antonucci, 1992).

The orientation of the body and the orientation of the world can have independent effects on neglect, suggesting that these are also coded separately. Calvanio *et al.* (1987) displayed words in four quadrants of a computer screen for the patients to identify. When seated upright, patients showed left neglect. However, when lying down on their side (i.e. 90 degrees to upright), the situation was more complex. Performance was determined both relative to the left–right dimension of the room and the left–right dimension of the body.

## Within objects versus between objects (or object-based versus space-based)

Look at the figures to the right (from Robertson, 2004). Note how the patient has attempted to draw all of the objects in the room (including those on

The patient makes omission errors on the left side of objects irrespective of the object's position in space.

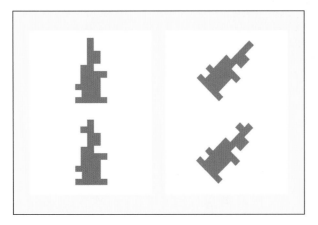

Are these objects the same or different? The critical difference lies on the left side of the object but, in the slanted condition, on the right side of space.

the left) but has distorted or omitted the left parts of the objects. Similarly, the patient has failed to find the As on the left side of the two columns of letters even though the right side of the left column is further leftwards than the left side of the right column. This patient would probably be classed as having object-based neglect.

The object in question may be more dynamically defined according to the current spatial reference frame being attended. Driver and Halligan (1991) devised a task that pitted object-based coordinates with environmentally based ones. The task was to judge whether two meaningless objects were the same or not. On some occasions, the critical difference was on the left side of the object but on the right side of space, and the patient did indeed fail to spot such differences.

Written words are an interesting class of object, because they have an inherent left to right order of letters. Patients with left object-based neglect may make letter substitution errors in reading words and nonwords (e.g. reading "home" as "come"), whereas patients with space-based (or between object) neglect may read individual words correctly but fail to read whole words on the left of a page. In one unusual case, NG, the patient made neglect errors in reading words that were printed normally but also made identical errors when the words were printed vertically, printed in mirror image (so that the neglected part of the word was on the opposite side of space) and even when the letters were dictated aloud, one by one (Caramazza & Hillis, 1990a). This strongly suggests that it is the internal object frame that is neglected.

Neglect within objects is linked to brain damage in different regions than that associated with neglect of egocentric space; in particular, it seems to be linked to ventral stream lesions including to the white matter (Chechlacz et al., 2012). This raises the interesting possibility that this form of neglect represents a disconnection between object-based perceptual representations and more general mechanisms of attention.

## Evaluation

Although the cardinal symptom of neglect is a lack of awareness of perceptual stimuli, neglect is best characterized as a disorder of attention rather than perception. This is because it tends to be multi-sensory in nature, the deficit is more pronounced when demands on attention are high (e.g. voluntary orienting, presence of competing stimuli), and there is evidence that neglected stimuli are perceived (albeit unconsciously and perhaps less detailed). However, neglect is a heterogeneous disorder and this may reflect the different ways in which space is represented in the brain. Basic attention processes (involving competition and selection) may operate across different spatial reference frames giving rise to the different characteristics of neglect.

## SUMMARY AND KEY POINTS OF THE CHAPTER

- Attention is the process by which certain information is selected for further processing and optimizes efficiency by preventing sensory overload.
- This is a dynamic system in which there is an interaction between top-down (task relevant) and bottom-up (sensory driven) influences, and in which selection can operate at multiple levels (perceptual, semantic, response-based).
- The parietal lobes may transform sensory-based maps of space (e.g. retinocentric coordinates) into various egocentric (viewer-centered) maps of space. These maps contain a sparse code of the perceptual environment in which salient features predominate (either due to bottom-up or top-down constraints).
- The orienting of attention (at least from bottom-up, exogenous cues) taps mechanisms involved in preparing eye movements.
- Attended relative to unattended stimuli are associated with greater activity in the neural system involved in perceiving that stimulus (e.g. visual ventral stream) and with activity in a frontoparietal network. The latter is normally linked to conscious awareness of perceptual stimuli.
- There is evidence for different attention-related mechanisms in the parietal lobes (e.g. contrasting posterior parietal versus temporoparietal; or left and right hemispheres) although it is less clear how these different mechanisms normally operate together.
- Studies of neglect have been important for establishing that space is represented at several different levels within the brain.

## EXAMPLE ESSAY QUESTIONS

- How has evidence from neuroscience changed the way that cognitive science thinks about attention?
- Can any theory account for spatial and non-spatial aspects of attention?
- What is the relationship between attention, perception, and awareness?
- What is the relationship between orienting attention and moving the eyes?
- What have studies of human brain damage contributed to our understanding of attention and its neural basis?

Visit the companion website at www. psypress/cw/ward for:

- References to key papers, readings and useful websites
- Videos including interviews with key psychologists Geoff Boynton and Marlene Behrmann, examples and accounts of change blindness and hemispatial neglect, and a lecture with author Jamie Ward on *The Spatial Brain*
- Multiple choice questions and interactive flashcards to test your knowledge

## RECOMMENDED FURTHER READING

- Mangun, G. R. (2012). *The neuroscience of attention*. Oxford, UK: Oxford University Press. An excellent set of chapters written by leading experts in the field.
- Posner, M. I. (2011). *The cognitive neuroscience of attention* (2nd edition). New York: The Guilford Press. An edited book with chapters at the cutting edge of research. Recommended for students who want to find out about more advanced topics.
- Styles, E. A. (2006). *The psychology of attention* (2nd edition). Hove, UK: Psychology Press. This book is a good introduction to attention that explains difficult ideas in a straightforward way. It covers neglect, but otherwise does not focus on cognitive neuroscience findings.

# CHAPTER 8

# The acting brain

## CONTENTS

Action is our way of interfacing with the world, and our means of putting all our goals and desires into practice. Action has traditionally been viewed as the endpoint of cognition. Having perceived an object and made a cognitive decision about what to do with it, we may then, depending on our goals, act toward it. Findings from cognitive neuroscience have radically shaken up this viewpoint. For example, in some situations it is possible to accurately act toward objects that have not been consciously seen. In addition, it has been claimed that not only is our action system equipped to produce our own actions, it may also be used to understand the actions of others—an important part of social cognition. Moreover, the processes that generate and control actions also appear to generate and control thought and cognition more generally. These ideas will also be explored in this chapter, together with an overview of more traditional areas of research on the "acting brain," such as Parkinson's disease, the role of the basal ganglia and tool use.

### KEY TERMS

**Degrees of freedom problem**
There are potentially an infinite number of motor solutions for acting on an object.

**Motor programs**
Stored routines that specify certain motor parameters of an action (e.g. the relative timing of strokes).

# A BASIC COGNITIVE FRAMEWORK FOR MOVEMENT AND ACTION

A simple model of movement and action is presented below and is unpacked in more detail throughout the chapter. Note that the model is hierarchically organized. At the highest level, there is action planning based on the goals and intentions of the individual. At the lowest level, there are the perceptual and motor systems that interface with the external world. Action can be considered to be an outcome of all these processes that work together in a concerted fashion, combining the needs of the person with the current environmental reality. As such, the term "action" needs to be contrasted with the physical *movement* of the body that ensues. Movements can sometimes occur in the absence of cognition. A reflex movement generated, say, when a hand goes near a flame occurs in the absence of a centrally generated command.

There are a number of computational problems faced when performing an action. Imagine a task of turning off a light switch. There are potentially an infinite number of motor solutions for completing the task in terms of the angles of the joints and their trajectories through space. This has been termed the **degrees of freedom problem** (for a discussion, see Haggard, 2001). There are likely to be physical constraints on the solution (e.g. to minimize the torque on joints), but there could also be cognitive constraints too (e.g. to minimize the amount of planning).

It is probably not the case that actions are calculated from scratch each time one needs to be performed. Most theories of action postulate the existence of generalized **motor programs** (Schmidt, 1975). This may simplify the computations (and computational speed) underlying movement. For example, in producing a tennis serve the different movement components may be linked

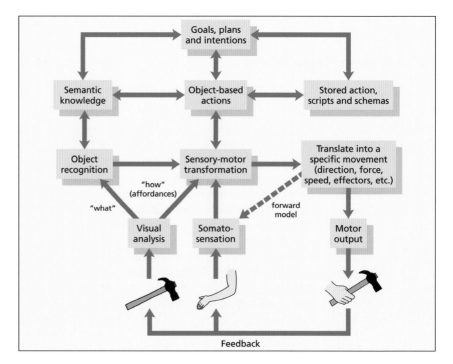

A very basic cognitive framework for understanding movement and action.

together. Motor programs may code general aspects of the movement (e.g. the timing of different components) rather than the actual means of performing the movement (e.g. the joints and muscles). One commonly cited example is the fact that handwriting does not change when different effectors are used (e.g. writing with feet) or when the amplitude is changed (e.g. writing on a blackboard versus a notebook). Different objects in the environment may also be linked to different motor programs that reflect their cultural usage: for instance, the way that chopsticks are manipulated or scissors are used. Object–action associations typically have to be learned, but they can also be lost as a result of brain damage.

Most actions are directed toward externally perceived objects, particularly via vision. After early visual analysis, two routes diverge into different streams specialized for object recognition (the "what" or ventral stream) and object location (the "how," "where" or dorsal stream). This was covered in Chapter 7. One aspect that is particularly relevant to the present topic is how this visual information is integrated with somatosensory information. **Somatosensation** refers to a cluster of perceptual processes that relate to the skin and body, and includes touch, pain, thermal sensation and limb position. The position of the limbs in space is computed by receptors in the muscles and joints, and this is termed **proprioception**. Information concerning the location of objects coded on the surface of sensory receptors (e.g. on the retina) is insufficient to permit interaction with that object unless the position of the sensory receptors themselves is taken into account (e.g. gaze direction and head position). As such, there is a need to co-register these two different types of information into a common spatial reference frame. In the context of action, this process will be referred to as **sensorimotor transformation** although more generally it is referred to as remapping.

The way in which the goals, plans and intentions of an individual are represented in the brain is the least understood aspect of the action system. The difficulty lies in explaining the intentions of an individual without recourse to what psychologists have termed a **homunculus**. We all have a sense in which "I" make a decision to go somewhere or "I" intend to make tea. The homunculus problem is that there is no "I" in the brain that makes all these decisions (the word homunculus literally means "little man"); the "I" is simply a product of the firing of neurons.

Note that, in this simple framework, there are bi-directional arrows to and from the "goals, plans and intentions." This implies that the system may also be used to observe and understand the actions and intentions of other people, as well as to generate one's own actions. This may be vital for learning skills by observation and may form an important component of comprehending actions.

## THE ROLE OF THE FRONTAL LOBES IN MOVEMENT AND ACTION

The frontal lobes take up around a third of the cortical area and comprise a number of functionally and anatomically separate regions. Moving from the posterior to the anterior of the frontal lobes, their function becomes less specific to movement and action. The more anterior portions are involved in the control of behavior irrespective of whether it results in an overt action (i.e. in aspects of thought such as planning, reasoning and working memory). Given this hierarchical organization, it is useful to consider the roles of the different frontal regions separately.

## Primary motor cortex

The **primary motor cortex** (in the precentral gyrus, Brodmann's area 4, BA4) is responsible for execution of all voluntary movements of the body. Most other frontal regions are related to action planning, irrespective of whether actions are actually executed. Different regions of the primary motor cortex represent different regions of the body—that is, it is *somatotopically organized*. The left hemisphere is specialized for movements of the right side of the body and the right hemisphere is specialized for movements of the left side of the body (although the division is not as strict as once believed; Tanji *et al.*, 1998). Thus, damage to one hemisphere as a result of, say, stroke could result in a failure to move the other side of the body—**hemiplegia**. Note that some parts of the body, such as the hands, have a particularly large representation because of the need for fine levels of movement control.

The relationship between the activity of individual neurons and resultant limb movement is understood in some detail. Studies of the firing of single cells in the primary motor cortex show that activity for each neuron is highest for a particular direction of movement (the preferred direction) and it decreases gradually with directions further and further away (for reviews, see Georgopoulos, 1997; Georgopoulos *et al.*, 1986). Different neurons "prefer" different directions, and the firing is genuinely related to the direction of movement rather than the spatial location of the endpoint. Thus, a neuron would fire equivalently with different starting and ending positions assuming the direction is the same (Georgopoulos *et al.*, 1985).

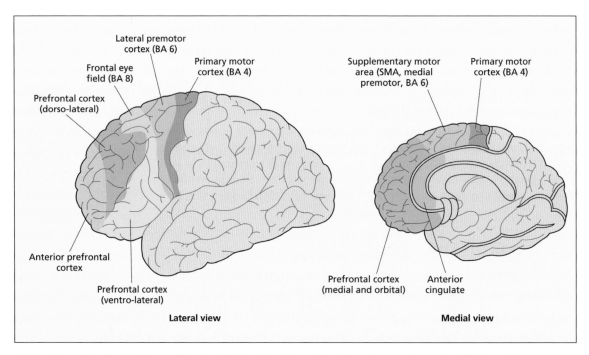

Anatomical and functional divisions of the frontal lobes. Broadly speaking, the primary motor cortex initiates voluntary movements, the premotor regions are involved in online coordination of movements; and the prefrontal regions plan and select actions according to goals.

One computational issue raised by these findings is this: how do the neurons decide on a single movement to execute given that lots of different neurons with lots of different preferred movements will be active at a given point in time? One possible solution could be that the most active neuron(s) at that point in time is the one that dictates the actual movement (i.e. a winner-takes-all solution). This idea is unsatisfactory, because movements tend to be very precise whereas the coding of preferred direction is broad (e.g. a neuron with a preferred direction of 70 degrees would still respond strongly at 60 and 80 degrees). This idea also turns out to be empirically incorrect. The direction of the resultant movement appears to be computed by summing together the vectors (i.e. degree of activity multiplied by preferred direction) of a whole population of neurons (the so-called **population vector**).

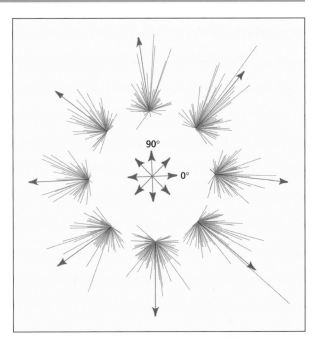

Each line represents the preferred direction of many neurons in the primary motor cortex, and their length represents the amount of firing. The population vector, calculated for eight different directions, is the gray line and this predicts the direction of movement.

From Georgopoulos.et al., 1983, with kind permission of Springer Science and Business Media.

## Frontal eye fields

Voluntary movement of the eyes is not determined by the primary motor cortex but by a separate region of the frontal lobes known as the frontal eye fields (FEFs, Brodmann's area 8). Stimulation of this region in monkeys with microelectrodes results in movement of the eyes (Bruce *et al.*, 1985). The separation of body and eyes may reflect the different nature of the input signals that guide movement: eye movement is primarily guided by external senses (vision and hearing) whereas skeletal-based movements rely more heavily on proprioceptive information concerning position of the limbs (derived from parietal regions). Studies in monkeys shows that the FEF is activated rapidly (within 100 ms) following a visual stimulus (Lamme & Roelfsema, 2000). Moreover, electrical stimulation of the FEF can

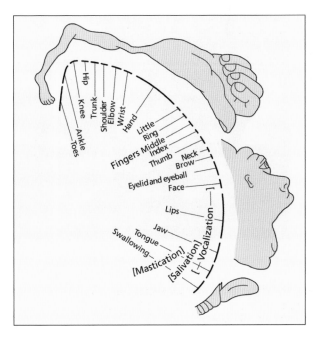

The primary motor cortex controls movement in different parts of the body. Areas governing different parts of the body are arranged spatially (somatotopic organization) but do not strictly reflect the spatial arrangement of the body.

From Penfield and Rasmussen, 1950.

enhance activity within primary visual cortex in the presence of a visual stimulus and it can increase activity in higher (extrastriate) visual regions even in the absence of a visual stimulus (Ekstrom *et al.*, 2008). This is another example, of the action system influencing cognition (in this case, visual attention) rather than being a mere endpoint of cognition.

## COULD NEURAL ACTIVITY IN THE PRIMARY MOTOR CORTEX BE USED TO GUIDE A PROSTHETIC LIMB?

The direction of resulting limb movement can be computed from measurements in fewer than 100 cells (Salinas & Abbott, 1994). This holds out the promise of being able to use this information to guide an artificial limb in patients with amputated or paralyzed limbs (Chapin, 2004). In recent years, this has been demonstrated in a small number of human patients. One study demonstrated that two tetraplegic patients could exert some control over the speed and direction of movement of a computer cursor based on recording of motor cortical activity from 96 neurons in the dominant hand area (Kim *et al.*, 2008). The patients in this study had an inability to move all four limbs arising from brainstem stroke and motor neuron disease. Subsequent studies have shown that tetraplegic patients are able to move a robotic arm for reaching and grasping including, in one case, to drink from a bottle (Hochberg *et al.*, 2012).

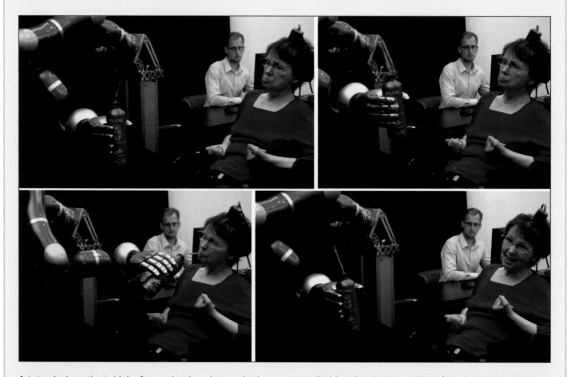

A tetraplegic patient drinks from a bottle using a robotic arm controlled by electrical recordings from her primary motor cortex.

From Hochberg *et al.*, 2012. © Nature.

## Lateral and medial premotor cortex

The area immediately in front of the primary motor cortex is termed the **premotor cortex**. In contrast to the primary motor cortex, electrical stimulation of the premotor cortex does not result in movement per se, but rather modulates the activity of the primary motor cortex (Shimazu et al., 2004). Many studies have drawn attention to the different roles played by the lateral premotor cortex and the medial premotor cortex (also known as the **supplementary motor area, SMA**) (Goldberg, 1985; Passingham, 1988). Whereas the lateral premotor cortex has been associated with acting objects in the environment (e.g. reaching for a coffee cup), the SMA has conversely been associated with dealing with spontaneous, well-learned actions, particularly action sequences that do not place strong demands on monitoring the environment (e.g. playing a familiar tune on a musical instrument). This functional difference reflects the different anatomical connections of these regions. The lateral premotor cortex receives visual signals via the parietal cortex (the so-called dorsal route in vision), whereas the medial premotor cortex (SMA) receives strong proprioceptive signals concerning the current position of the limbs.

In one experiment, TMS was delivered to three frontal regions in three conditions: "simple" button presses (pressing the same key over and again), "scale" button presses (pressing consecutive buttons as in a musical scale), and "complex" button presses (as in playing a prelearned musical piece). TMS over the SMA disrupted the sequence in the "complex" condition only, whereas TMS over the primary motor cortex affected both "complex" and "scale" action sequences; TMS over the lateral prefrontal cortex had no effects (Gerloff et al., 1997). Gerloff et al. (1997) suggested that the SMA has a critical role in organizing forthcoming movements in complex motor sequences that are rehearsed from memory and fit into a precise timing plan.

If the SMA is important for implementing internally generated actions, the lateral premotor region is more important for producing movements based on external contingencies (e.g. "pull a handle if the light is blue, rotate it if it is red"). In the monkey, lesions in this area prevent these kinds of associations being formed but without loss of basic sensory or motor abilities

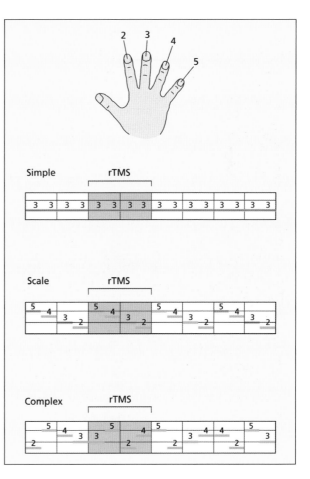

Gerloff et al. (1997) contrasted three different types of action sequence: repetitive movements of the same finger (top), a regular pattern of finger movements as in a scale (middle), and an irregular memorized pattern of finger movements (bottom). Only the latter condition was disrupted by TMS applied over the supplementary motor area. This suggests that this region is critical for coordinating complex learned movement patterns.

(Passingham, 1988). Single-cell recordings in the monkey also show that neurons in the lateral premotor region respond when movement is required to an external cue, but not to spontaneous movements from memory, whereas the opposite is true for the SMA (Halsband *et al.*, 1994). Lateral premotor regions are also considered to contain a "vocabulary" of actions (e.g. tearing, grasping) that have both a sensory and motor component (Rizzolatti *et al.*, 1996). These will be discussed later in terms of mirror neurons and sensorimotor transformation.

## Prefrontal contributions to action

Prefrontal regions lie to the front of premotor regions and are principally involved in planning and higher aspects of the control of action. Unlike premotor and motor regions, prefrontal regions are involved extensively in higher cognition more generally rather than action specifically. Premotor regions have a primary role in preparing actions (to internally or externally triggered events), while the prefrontal region mediates their selection and maintains the goal of the action. For example, recordings of single neurons in the monkey prefrontal cortex show that they may respond to the rule that is being followed (e.g. "match the triangles" or "match the circles") rather than the mechanics of the movement being performed (White & Wise, 1999). Similarly, when monkeys are trained to move a cursor through a maze using joystick movements, prefrontal neurons respond to the predicted sensory consequences (e.g. cursor moves up) rather than the limb movements per se (Mushiake *et al.*, 2006). The primary motor cortex shows the opposite pattern.

The study of Frith *et al.* (1991) provides a good illustration of prefrontal function in humans. Participants were required to generate finger movements that were either predetermined (i.e. move the finger that is touched) or in which the participant could freely choose which finger to move. Note that the actual motor response is identical in both tasks. Nevertheless, the dorsolateral prefrontal cortex showed greater activation in the free choice task, suggesting that it is involved in "willed" or intentional aspects of action (for a review, see Jahanshahi and Frith, 1998). Its role may extend to the open-ended selection of responses more generally. Similar activation was found when participants were asked to generate any word from a specified letter ("S" or "F") in contrast to producing a predetermined word (Frith *et al.*, 1991).

The function of the prefrontal cortex is by no means specific to action. For instance, it is involved in holding things in mind (working memory) and in the control of cognition/behavior (executive functions). Nevertheless, one of the

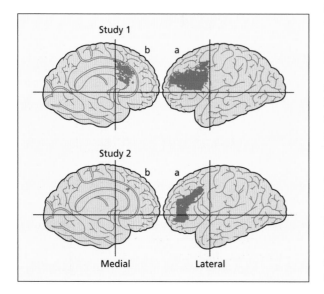

Activation in the (a) left dorsolateral prefrontal cortex and (b) anterior cingulate, when participants generate words beginning with S or F relative to being given the words (top), and when participants choose which finger to move relative to being instructed which to move (bottom). These regions may be important for response selection and willed action.

Redrawn from Frith *et al.*, 1991. Royal Society of London.

most influential models of executive function (the SAS model of Norman and Shallice, 1986) was initially put forward to explain action errors and, as such, will be introduced next.

## Evaluation

The movement and action system of the frontal lobes is hierarchically organized. The *primary motor cortex* is essential for the execution of voluntary movements. The *premotor cortex* is important for the preparation of actions, and may be functionally subdivided into actions that are elicited by external cues (lateral premotor) or that are internally generated (medial premotor, SMA). The *prefrontal cortex* is involved in the selection of actions and their corresponding goals.

**KEY TERMS**

**Perseveration**
Repeating an action that has already been performed and is no longer relevant.

**Utilization behavior**
Impulsively acting on irrelevant objects in the environment.

## PLANNING ACTIONS: THE SAS MODEL

Damage to prefrontal regions does not impair the movement or execution of actions per se. Instead the actions themselves become poorly organized and do not necessarily reflect the goals and intentions of the individual. For example, a patient with damage to the prefrontal cortex may repeat an action that has already been performed and is no longer relevant (called **perseveration**), or might act impulsively on irrelevant objects in the environment (called **utilization behavior**). An example of this, in the acute phase of a stroke, was described by Shallice *et al.* (1989, p. 1588):

the patient was found early in the morning wearing someone else's shoes, not apparently talking or responding to simple commands, but putting coins into his mouth and grabbing imaginary objects. He went around the house, moving furniture, opening cupboards and turning light switches on and off.

Norman and Shallice (1986; see also Cooper & Shallice, 2000) proposed a model to explain goal-driven action. The model is called the SAS or "Supervisory Attentional System" and has subsequently been applied to explain the control of cognition more generally. One of the key distinctions that they make is between actions that are performed automatically (with minimal awareness) versus actions that require attention and some form of online control. For example, when driving it may be possible to change gears, stop at traffic lights, turn corners, and so on in a kind of "autopilot" mode. In fact, drivers often have no recollection of having gone through traffic lights, even though they know that they must have done so. These actions may be using well-learned

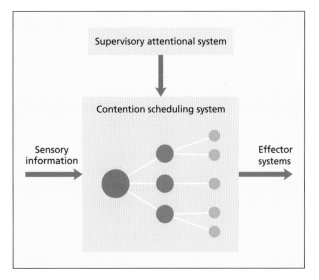

In the supervisory attentional system (SAS) model, contention scheduling selects the most active schema. The activation of schemas depends partly on the environment (derived from sensory input) and partly on the biasing influence of current and future goals (derived from the SAS component).
From Humphreys and Forde, 1998.

## KEY TERMS

**Schema**
An organized set of stored information (e.g. of familiar action routines).

**Contention scheduling**
The mechanism that selects one particular schema to be enacted from a host of competing schemas.

**Frontal apraxia**
Failure in tasks of routine activity that involve setting up and maintaining different subgoals, but with no basic deficits in object recognition or gesturing the use of isolated objects (also called action disorganization syndrome).

schemas and are assumed not to require SAS control. By contrast, imagine that you are required to reverse into a narrow space, or that you are diverted down an unfamiliar route. Situations such as these may require an interruption of automatic behavior or setting up a novel action sequence and these are assumed to require intervention of the SAS.

The SAS model contains a number of different components. Familiar actions and action routines may be stored as schemas. For example, specific objects (e.g. chopsticks, hammer) may have their own action schema (in this case, a motor program). Specific tasks (e.g. making tea) may be stored as a hierarchical collection of schemas (sometimes called scripts). In many respects, this organization of actions into abstract scripts and object-based schemas is akin to the distinction between syntax and word-based knowledge in language and, as with language, there is a debate about the extent to which action-based semantics and syntax are separable (Patriot *et al.*, 1996; Zanini *et al.*, 2002).

**Contention scheduling** is the mechanism that selects one particular schema to be enacted from a host of competing schemas. The idea of competition between schemas is the key part of this model. Schemas can be activated by objects in the environment (e.g. a hammer will activate its own particular schema). Schemas also receive biasing top-down activation from the SAS system that represents information about the needs of the person. If these two sources of activation are summed, then the most appropriate schema (i.e. that satisfies the current needs and is consistent with the environmental reality) should have the highest activation. This schema will then be selected by the contention-scheduling mechanism and translated into a specific action. As such, there is no need for a special entity with decision-making powers (i.e. a homunculus) as the decision to act is directly determined by the activation levels of schemas.

The action errors made by patients with prefrontal lesions can be explained by this model if one assumes that there is an imbalance in the type of information that enters into the contention-scheduling process. Utilization behavior can be accounted for by assuming that schemas are activated solely by environmental cues without any SAS regulation. Repetition of the same action (perseveration) is accounted for by assuming that activated schemas are not deactivated when they are no longer relevant to the current goal, or that the goal itself is not changed once it has been successfully accomplished.

Damage to the frontal lobes can also lead to what some researchers have termed **frontal apraxia** (Schwartz *et al.*, 1995), or action disorganization syndrome (Humphreys & Forde, 1998). This is characterized by failure in tasks of routine activity (e.g. making tea) that involve setting up and maintaining different subgoals (e.g. boil kettle, add sugar), but with no basic deficits in object recognition or gesturing the use of isolated objects. This disorder has been variously explained as damage to the scripts themselves (Humphreys & Forde, 1998), to the online maintenance of scripts (Sirigu *et al.*, 1995) or to some combination of these (Schwartz *et al.*, 1995). In many ways, the errors of these patients reflect those associated with "lapses of attention" in us all. Reason (1984) documented many everyday action slips, including putting a match in the mouth and striking the cigarette instead of vice versa.

## Evaluation

Damage to the prefrontal cortex does not prevent movement, but instead can produce actions that are disorganized, inappropriate, and/or unintentional. This set of behaviors has frequently been characterized as a dysexecutive syndrome. The syndrome affects the control of thoughts as well as actions and can be accounted for within the SAS model. This model makes an important distinction between automatic actions and those requiring attention and online control.

## OWNERSHIP AND AWARENESS OF ACTIONS

Our voluntary actions appear, at least introspectively, to have at least two elements: an intention/decision to act, and the execution of that action. The fact that one holds in mind an intention to act enables some degree of ownership to be asserted over that action. It also provides the foundation for the notion of having social responsibility for one's actions. However, the concept of intentions is not straightforward to pin down in neuroscientific terms, and there is even some evidence that appears to suggest that our conscious intentions occur after a decision (unconscious) to act has been made.

Libet *et al.* (1983) recorded EEG activity from the scalp above the primary motor cortex and the SMA when participants simply pressed a key "whenever they felt the urge to." The exact time at which the key was pressed could be recorded from an electrical signal from the wrist movement. In addition, participants reported the time at which they were first aware of wanting to move. This was achieved by noting the position of a hand on a gradually rotating clock face. Libet and colleagues found that the EEG activity (or readiness potential) started several hundred milliseconds before the participants reported an intention to act. The results appeared to suggest that the brain had made an unconscious commitment to act before participants experienced a conscious intention to act. One strong interpretation is that "free will" (i.e. the feeling that "I" decide my own actions) is something of an illusion.

Haggard and Eimer (1999) identified which particular cognitive mechanism is likely to be associated with the conscious intention. In their variation of the experiment, the subject could freely choose either a left or right response, resulting in a lateralized readiness potential over the opposite hemisphere. Their results suggested that awareness of intentions is related to selection of a specific movement (left or right) rather than a generalized intention to act. This finding is also consistent with the data discussed above that suggest that willed action may be functionally related to response selection in conditions in which the response is essentially arbitrary (e.g. which finger to move) or is drawn from an open-ended set of responses (e.g. which word to say) (Frith *et al.*, 1991; Jahanshahi & Frith, 1998). Even after an urge to move, however, the participant may not be fully committed to act and may still be able to suppress the action (Brass & Haggard, 2007). This suggests the operation of a late checking mechanism. An altogether different account of the findings of Libet *et al.* (1983) has recently been offered by Schurger *et al.* (2012). They suggest that the urge to act in this experiment occurs when normal random fluctuations in motor activity happen to cross a threshold, but that the earlier build-up neither reflects an unconscious intention nor a commitment to act.

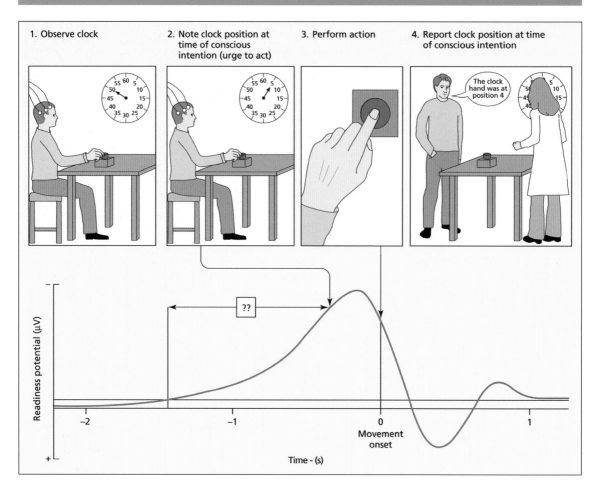

1. Observe clock

2. Note clock position at time of conscious intention (urge to act)

3. Perform action

4. Report clock position at time of conscious intention

The clock hand was at position 4

??

Readiness potential (µV)

−2

−1

0
Movement onset

1

Time - (s)

The motor cortex generates a readiness potential long before the participant declares an intention to act. This challenges the classical Cartesian view that the mind controls the brain.

Redrawn from Haggard (2008. Reprinted by permission of Macmillan Publishers Ltd. © 2008.

**KEY TERM**

**Forward model**
A representation of the motor command (a so-called efference copy) is used to predict the sensory consequences of an action.

One way in which a sense of ownership over actions could be maintained is by predicting the sensory outcomes of our actions. One influential class of model, which links together action intention with action outcome, is **forward models** (Wolpert *et al.*, 1995). A simplistic example appears on p. 165 with respect to somatosensation (similar pathways may exist for other senses). The main assumption is that a representation of the motor command (a so-called efference copy) is used to predict the sensory consequences of an action. For example, tickling oneself feels less ticklish than being tickled by another person, because we can use our own motor commands to predict what the sensation will feel like (Blakemore *et al.*, 1998). The motor command when one tickles oneself can be used to predict what the sensation will feel like (and, hence, it is possible to compensate for it). Another example comes from eye movements. When we move our eyes the visual world appears static rather than moving, even though the image on the retina changes considerably. In this instance the motor commands to move the eyes is used to predict (and compensate for) changes in visual input. These may arise via interactions between frontally based action systems, and structures such as the cerebellum (Wolpert *et al.*, 1998) and superior colliculus (for sensory consequences of eye movements, see Wurtz, 2008).

## THE ANARCHIC (OR "ALIEN") HAND SYNDROME

the pathological hand of these patients is seen to wander involuntarily, and to perform purposeless movements. Often the arm levitates spontaneously, sometimes with tentacular movements of the fingers

(Marchetti & Della Sala, 1998)

when G.C. had a genital itch, the right hand scratched it vigorously, in view of other people, causing considerable embarrassment to the patient, who tried to stop the right hand with her left. . . . The patient considered the left hand to be the one she could trust . . . while the right hand was the untrustworthy one that "always does what it wants to do."

(Della Sala et al., 1991, p. 1114)

The anarchic (or alien) hand syndrome. The eponymous protagonist of the film *Dr. Strangelove* is a type of "mad scientist," whose eccentricities include a severe case of alien hand syndrome—his right hand, clad in an ominous black leather glove, occasionally attempts to strangle him.

© Sunset Boulevard/Corbis Sygma.

In the anarchic or "alien" hand syndrome, the hand and arm of a patient may produce an action such as grasping an object or interfering with the activities of the other hand that the patient regards as *unintentional*. Although unintentional, the patient typically acknowledges that the arm and action belong to them. Some of suggested that the terms "anarchic" and "alien" should refer to situations in which the patient does and does not, respectively, acknowledge them as their own (Della Sala et al., 1991). In common use, the term "alien" is used to denote both scenarios.

Assal et al. (2007) examined the neural basis of voluntary and alien movements using fMRI in a patient with a right parietal lesion and left alien hand. Alien hand movements were associated with activity in the right primary motor cortex. Voluntary hand movements also activated this region but additionally recruited a wider network of action-related regions (right premotor, left prefrontal cortex) suggesting that these are crucial for the feeling of intentionality over actions.

## ACTION COMPREHENSION AND IMITATION

There are broadly two ways in which to reproduce the actions of another person. The first way involves a shallow level of analysis. It is possible to reproduce an action via sensorimotor transformations that do not make any inferences about the goals and intentions of the actor; this is *mimicry*. The second way involves observing the action, computing the goals and intentions of the actor and then reproducing the actions oneself based on the goal. This is **imitation** proper and it implies a deeper level of processing of the observed action. Aside from imitation, another situation in which goals are shared between individuals is in *joint action*; for example, when several people are lifting a heavy object or several people are operating different parts of a machine (Sebanz et al., 2006).

### KEY TERM

**Imitation**
The ability to reproduce the behavior of another through observation.

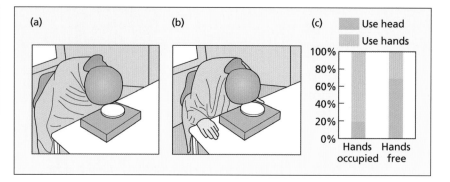

Infants imitate the goal of actions rather than the motor aspects of actions. If the experimenter presses a button with his or her head because their arms are occupied, the infants "copy" the action by using their hands rather than heads—i.e. they appear to infer that the experimenter would have used his or her hands to achieve the goal had they been free.

From Gergely *et al.*, 2002. Reprinted by permission of Macmillan Publishers Ltd. © 2002.

There is evidence to suggest that humans tend to reproduce the actions of others by representing the goal state rather than by mimicry, particularly when the action is more complex. Wohlschlager *et al.* (2003) found that, when asked to "copy" the actions of another, there is a tendency to reproduce the goal of the action (e.g. putting an object in a cup) rather than the means of the action (e.g. which particular arm is used). Infants appear to imitate based on goals too (Gergely *et al.*, 2002). In this study, the infants watched an adult press a button on a table by using their forehead. In one condition, the adult's hands and arms are bound up under a blanket, and in the other condition the adult's hands are free. When the adult's hands are free, the infants copy the action directly—they use their foreheads too. But when the adult's hands are not free, the infants imitate the goal but not the action, i.e. the infants use their hands rather than their head. The implication is that the infants understand that the goal of the action is to press the button, and they assume that the adult would have used his or her hands had they been free.

Despite the fact that we use the verb "to ape" to refer to imitation and mimicry, other primate species tend not to spontaneously imitate or do so only for rewards such as food. After considerable training, chimpanzees (Custance *et al.*, 1995), but not macaque monkeys (Mitchell & Anderson, 1993), are capable of learning a "do-as-I-do" game to produce complex arbitrary actions (e.g. grab thumb of other hand). Chimpanzees raised in captivity tend to imitate the goals of an action rather than simply reproducing the same movement with the same body part (Buttelmann *et al.*, 2007) in an adaptation of the human infant study by Gergely *et al.* (2002).

## Mirror neurons

One of the most fascinating discoveries in cognitive neuroscience over the last decade has been of the **mirror-neuron** system. Rizzolatti and colleagues found a group of neurons in the monkey ventral premotor cortex (area F5) that respond both during the performance *and* the observation of the same action (di Pellegrino *et al.*, 1992; Rizzolatti *et al.*, 1996). Thus, the response properties of mirror neurons disregard the distinction between self and other. It responds to actions performed by the experimenter or another monkey as well as to actions performed by itself. The response properties of these neurons are quite specific. They are often tuned to precise actions (e.g. tearing, twisting, grasping) that are goal-directed. They do *not* respond to mimicked action in the absence of an object, or if the object moves robotically without an external agent. This suggests that it is the purposeful nature of the action rather than the visual/motoric correlates that is critical. By contrast, other regions such as superior temporal sulcus (STS), also respond to specific movements of body parts but have a purely visual component (Perrett *et al.*, 1989).

Moreover, mirror neurons respond if an appropriate action is implied as well as directly observed. Umiltà and colleagues (2001) compared viewing of a whole action with viewing of the same action in which a critical part (the hand–object interaction) was obscured by a screen. Their findings suggest that the premotor cortex contains abstract representations of action intentions that are used both for planning one's own actions and interpreting the actions of others.

The evidence above is derived from non-human primates. What is the evidence that humans possess such a system? The human analogue of area F5 is believed to be in Broca's area (specifically, in Brodmann's area 44) extending into the premotor area (Rizzolatti *et al.*, 2002). This region is activated by the observation of hand movements, particularly when imitation is required (Iacoboni *et al.*, 1999), and also the observation of lip movements within the human repertoire (e.g. biting and speaking, but not barking; Buccino *et al.*, 2004). Moreover, TMS applied over the primary motor cortex increases the amplitude of motor-evoked potentials elicited in the hands/arms when participants also observed a similar action (Strafella & Paus, 2000). This suggests that action observation biases activity in the primary motor area itself.

Subsequent research has found mirror neurons in other parts of the macaque brain, but they do not necessarily have the same functional properties as those described in the premotor cortex. The primary motor cortex itself contains neurons with motor and visual properties but they respond to the mechanics of particular movements (by showing tuning to preferred directions of

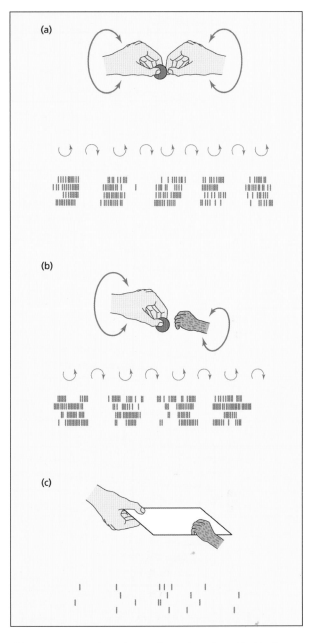

This neuron responds to the rotating action of an object in the experimenter's hands (a) or when the monkey rotates the object held by the experimenter (b), but not during grasping without rotation (c). Notice that the neuron is even sensitive to the direction of rotation (responding counter-clockwise, not clockwise).

Adapted from Rizzolatti *et al.*, 1996.

> ## WIDER IMPLICATIONS OF THE MIRROR-NEURON SYSTEM
>
> - Did human language evolve from hand gestures? The human homologue of monkey area F5 is Broca's area (Rizzolatti & Arbib, 1998)—an area traditionally associated with language.
> - Are mirror neurons important for being able to empathize with others, by internally simulating their behavior (Gallese, 2001)?
> - Do individuals with particular difficulties in understanding others (e.g. autistic people) have impaired mirror-neuron systems? Dapretto *et al.* (2006) present fMRI evidence to suggest that autistic people have lower activity in the mirror system when imitating and observing expressions, but others have questioned whether this can explain the range of autistic behaviors (Southgate & Hamilton, 2008).

movement) rather than more abstract features such as goals (Dushanova & Donoghue, 2010). In contrast, mirror neurons in the parietal lobe tend to be more sensitive to the wider context in which an action is situated, for instance responding to a grasping action differently depending on whether the subsequent goal is to eat it or put it in a container (Bonini *et al.*, 2010).

## ACTING ON OBJECTS

This chapter has, so far, only considered in detail the role of the frontal lobes in some of the highest levels of action processing—namely, action planning and organization, the intention to act and comprehending the actions and intentions of others. The remaining sections will deal with topics related to how specific actions are put into place and enacted. This involves, among other things, an appreciation of where things are in space and what certain objects (e.g. tools) can be used for. The parietal lobes appear to be specialized for this type of information.

### "What" versus "how": the dorsal and ventral streams reconsidered

Ungerleider and Mishkin (1982) first described two routes of visual processing, which they labeled the "what" route (or ventral stream from occipital to temporal) and the "where" route (or dorsal stream from occipital to parietal). Goodale and Milner (1992; Milner & Goodale, 1995) have offered a somewhat different characterization of these routes in terms of "what" versus "how." In doing so, they placed an emphasis on output requirements (identification verses action) rather than input requirements (identity versus location). As they noted, we do not reach to locations in space but to objects. These arguments over labeling are not critical to the present discussion, and the term sensorimotor captures both the "how" and "where" nature of the dorsal stream adequately.

Damage to dorsal versus ventral streams has different consequences for action. First of all, consider damage to the ventral route, running along the inferior temporal lobes. Patient DF has visual agnosia that impairs her ability to recognize objects from vision, despite intact basic visual processes. Milner and colleagues (1991a) presented DF with a letter box in which the orientation of the slot could be rotated. DF had difficulty in matching the orientation of the slot to visually presented alternatives. However, when asked to post a letter she was able to reach toward the slot and orient her hand appropriately. This suggests a dissociation between visual perception (based on the impaired ventral stream) and visual control of action (using the spared dorsal stream). When DF was given a more complex T-shaped object and slot, she was still fairly accurate, but she did make some errors, which tended to be at 90 degrees. This suggests that her action is driven by orientation of a single edge. Thus the dorsal route cannot adequately integrate different edges into whole objects (Goodale *et al.*, 1994).

Turning next to impairments of the dorsal stream—some patients with damage to the parietal lobe have deficits in acting toward objects in space. However they do not (unlike DF) have problems in recognizing single objects. **Optic ataxia** is a symptom arising from damage to the occipitoparietal junction (Karnath & Perenin, 2005). These patients are unable to accurately reach toward objects under visual guidance. Perenin and Vighetto (1988) argue that this reflects a failure to transform visual perceptual information into appropriate motor commands.

For example, when acting toward an oriented slot their hands may be oriented incorrectly or they may miss the slot altogether (a double dissociation with the visual agnosia patient, DF). The deficits would sometimes be restricted to a particular hand (typically the hand opposite the side of the lesion) or even a particular hand when it was in a particular half of space. The latter suggests that it is unlikely to be purely motoric (because the "bad" hand functions well in the "good" side of space) or purely visual (because the "good" hand functions well in the "bad" side of space) but due to a failure to integrate the two (when the "bad" hand is in the "bad" side of space).

Action deficits may depend on the type of action required. For example, grasping may require greater processing of object-based properties than reaching or pointing (Jeannerod, 1997). Neglect patients with damage to the dorsal stream may show a rightward bias when asked to point to the center of a rod, but, if asked to pick the rod up between thumb and forefinger, they may do so in the center of the rod (Robertson *et al.*, 1995). In this instance, the act of grasping may lead to more efficient processing of the object coordinates than reaching.

Interestingly, dissociations between vision for action and visual perception have been found in the normal population. Certain *visual illusions*, such as the Ponzo or railway track illusion and the Titchener circles illusion, result in physically

**KEY TERM**

**Optic ataxia**
An inability to use vision to accurately guide action, without basic deficits in visual discrimination or voluntary movement per se.

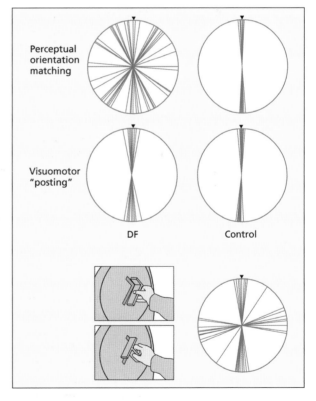

Can the hand "see" better than the eye? Patient DF can accurately post objects through slots even though she cannot report the orientation of the slots from vision. With more complex objects (e.g. T-shaped), she appears to use single orientations to guide action.

Adapted from Milner *et al.*, 1991a and Goodale *et al.*, 1994.

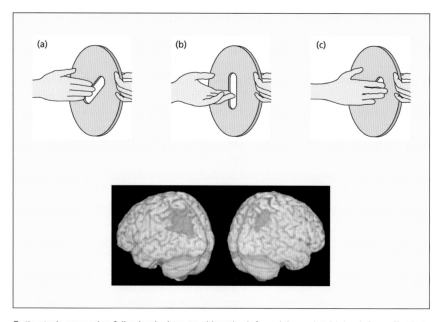

Optic ataxia may arise following lesions to either the left or right parietal lobe (often affecting the opposite hand), and results in both misreaching (c) and hand posture problems (b); the correct solution is shown in (a). It reflects an inability to link visual and motor information together.

Top: from Perenin and Vighetto, 1988. Reprinted by permission of Oxford University Press. Bottom: from Karnath and Perenin, 2005. Reprinted by permission of Oxford University Press.

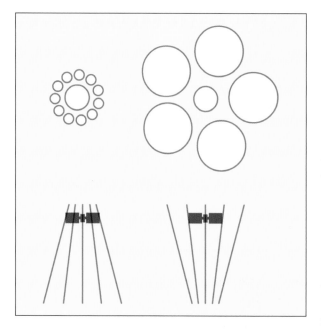

The Titchener circle (above) and Ponzo (railway track; below) illusions affect perception but not action. When a subject is asked to pick up the central circle or horizontal rod, the grip aperture more closely resembles the true rather than the distorted size.

identical objects being perceived as different in size. If one is asked to pick up the size-distorted object (e.g. a poker chip in the Titchener illusion), then the grip aperture between thumb and finger is not influenced by the illusion (Aglioti *et al.*, 1995; Jackson & Shaw, 2000).

In summary, evidence from brain-damaged individuals points to specialized visual mechanisms that guide action. Studies of single-cell recordings in primates shed light on the nature of the underlying mechanisms at the neural level.

## Neural mechanisms of sensorimotor transformation

Different types of information need to be linked to enable sensorimotor transformation. This section will consider three broad ways in which neurons code information relevant to this process. Most of the evidence comes from primate single-cell recordings.

## Neurons that code specific types of actions

The neurons located in area F5 of the macaque are interesting not only for their mirror properties (i.e. they represent the actions of both self and others), but also for the specificity of the actions they represent. The specificity of coding varies and is often referred to as strictly congruent or broadly congruent depending on the size of the repertoire of actions that they respond to. Rizzolatti and Luppino (2001) describe them in terms of an action vocabulary, including grasping, holding and tearing. For example, a neuron that responds to performed finger movements for grasping may not discharge for scratching. Other neurons may be specialized for different types of hand shaping (e.g. precision grip, whole-hand prehension). The advantage of having a stored repertoire is that the brain does not have to compute certain aspects of the action each time, and may also enable certain types of action to become associated with familiar objects.

## Neurons that code action-relevant properties of objects

Murata *et al.* (2000) studied neurons in an area of the parietal lobe, called **anterior intraparietal area** (**AIP**), in which neurons respond selectively to certain shapes (e.g. cylinder, sphere, cube), sizes and orientations. Representations such as these provide a potentially suitable interface for the more general motor vocabulary in areas such as the frontal lobe. This region has anatomical connections both to motor regions of the frontal lobes (including the premotor area and frontal eye fields) and, importantly to inferotemporal cortex of the visual ventral stream which is involved in object recognition (Borra *et al.*, 2008). This suggests that it is well placed to act as a key hub in tool use.

Similar neural mechanisms may be found in humans, although the situation is likely to be more complex because of the large range of man-made manipulable objects that we use. In this instance, the use of familiar objects could be seen as the learning of action parameters within the parietal-frontal network (Wolpert & Ghahramani, 2000). An fMRI study in humans has also identified the AIP area as coding object shape for actions (Culham, 2004). The region shows greater activity for grasping relative to reaching and does not respond to two-dimensional object images. Using a tool to grasp, instead of using the hand itself in the normal way, also activates area AIP and premotor cortex in humans (Jacobs *et al.*, 2010). Given that these neural regions code relatively abstract properties of an action (rather than the actual movement mechanics) they may enable transfer of skills from hand to tool.

## Neurons that code sensory information across different modalities

Chapter 7 discussed how certain neurons, in the parietal lobes and elsewhere, respond to information from different senses particularly when they represent the same region of space. With regards to action, it may be particularly important to integrate visual and proprioceptive information about the location of the body. Graziano (1999) identified neurons in the macaque premotor regions that respond to both the felt position of the arm (irrespective of whether the arm was covered or in view) and the visual position of the arm (irrespective of whether it was the monkey's own arm or a stuffed arm in that position). If the arm was moved, then

**KEY TERM**

**Anterior intraparietal area (AIP)**
A part of intra-parietal sulcus that responds, in particular, to manipulable shapes or 3D objects.

This patient has one real arm and a phantom limb that is immobile (i.e. the amputated arm feels as if it still exists and feels paralyzed). When the patient looks in the mirror it creates the illusion that the amputated arm has returned and can move again.

## HOW TO MOVE A PHANTOM LIMB

Almost everyone who has a limb amputated will experience a **phantom limb**—a vivid sensation that the limb is still present and, in some cases, painful (for a fascinating review, see Ramachandran and Hirstein, 1998). Phantom limbs can be explained by plasticity in the brain. The neurons in the brain that previously used to respond to stimulation of the limb may instead be stimulated by activation in nearby regions of cortex (perhaps representing other parts of the body). This gives rise to an illusory sensation that the limb has returned.

The nature of the phantom differs significantly from one patient to another. Some report being able to move the phantom (e.g. it may appear to be gesturing). The motor cortex presumably doesn't "know" that the limb is missing and continues to send commands. For other patients, the limb may be immobile and potentially painful (this may relate to whether the limb was paralyzed prior to amputation). Ramachandran and Rogers-Ramachandran (1996) report a clever experiment, based on visual feedback, which enables such patients to reexperience movement in the phantom and, in some cases, alleviate pain. The patient puts the intact arm into a box with a mirrored side so that a second hand can be seen reflected in the position where the phantom is felt. When asked to move both hands they can experience movement in the phantom based on the visual feedback. This study illustrates the point that sensory (touch and vision) and motor information is highly integrated in the brain.

the visual receptive field would move too. This suggests that vision was coded relative to the body. This facilitates interaction with the external world irrespective of changes in eye fixation. Similar neurons are also found in a region of the parietal lobe known as the ventral intraparietal area, or VIP (Graziano *et al.*, 2000)

The studies noted above provide the building blocks for a theory of how sensory and motor systems may be interfaced. But, of course, the *meaning* of objects is going to be as critical for determining how and when they are used. This is likely to be especially important for humans. Whereas other species may use objects found in their natural environments as tools, humans have created for themselves a wide range of manipulable objects to perform specific functions, each with specific associated actions. The next section considers how these may be represented in the brain.

## KEY TERM

**Phantom limb**
The feeling that an amputated limb is still present.

# Tool use

A number of evolutionary developments appear to have facilitated the skilled use of tools found in modern man. First, there is the freeing of the hands by walking upright rather than on all fours that occurred around 6 million years ago. Second, there is the development of the hands themselves, in which the thumb has become much longer in humans relative to chimps. This facilitates a precision grip, such as that used in picking up a peanut. Finally, there is the corresponding development of the brain in terms of the disproportionate amount of space dedicated to representing the hands. It is hard not to underestimate the impact that tool use has had in terms of human beings' mastery of the environment, from the deserts to the poles. Note that the term **tool** is used broadly, not only to encompass hammers and chisels, but also cups, pencils and so on. What distinguishes tools from other classes of object (e.g. cats, clouds, carpets) is the fact that they have specific gestures and functions associated with them.

Tools, like other classes of object, are represented in the brain at several levels:

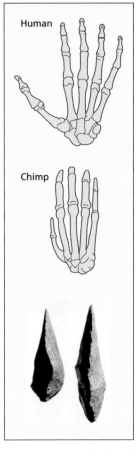

The thumb of humans has evolved to be considerably longer than that of the chimp's, enabling precision grip. Acheulean tools dating from 1.5 million years ago found in central-East Africa.

Stone tools: John Reader/Science Photo Library.

- A stored visual representation of the shape of the object that is computed by the visual ventral stream (or inferotemporal cortex, IT, in monkeys).
- A semantic representation of the object linked to medial and anterior temporal lobes.
- A volumetric representation of the tool that has both visual and motoric components related to grasping. This may correspond to area AIP in the parietal lobes (discussed previously).
- A motor-based component that stores the conventional gestures associated with the tool.

It is the latter that distinguishes tools from most other objects. A number of lines of evidence suggest that the store of object-based actions is located in the left inferior parietal lobe. Chao and Martin (2000) compared activity (fMRI) when viewing tools relative to other classes of objects and found activity in both the left inferior parietal lobe and Broca's area. Rumiati and colleagues (2004) examined object-based action more directly by asking participants to generate actions while being scanned. They used the factorial design depicted below, in which participants were presented with either static objects or actions (without

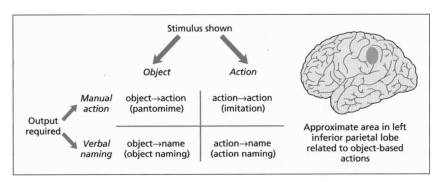

Rumiati et al. (2004) compared the brain activity when participants were asked to generate actions or name actions from either an object or action. They found a region in the left inferior parietal lobe that appears specific to object-based action in their "pantomime" condition.

**KEY TERM**

Tool
An object that affords certain actions for specific goals.

KEY TERMS

**Ideomotor apraxia**
An inability to produce
appropriate gestures
given an object, word or
command.

**Affordances**
Structural properties of
objects imply certain
usages.

the object) and were required to either gesture the appropriate action or produce the name of it. Producing an action from a static picture of an object (called *pantomiming*) was found to be particularly associated with the left inferior parietal lobe and a left lateral premotor region, after controlling for other factors (e.g. object recognition).

Consistent with the imaging data, some patients with damage to the left parietal lobe may be unable to produce appropriate actions on command given either an object (e.g. an iron), a word (e.g. "iron") or a command (e.g. intransitive gestures such as "waving goodbye"). These patients are traditionally classified as having **ideomotor apraxia** (Gonzalez Rothi *et al.*, 1991; Liepmann, 1905). When assessing for ideomotor apraxia, it is important to establish whether the patient can copy meaningless actions (e.g. holding the left palm upwards). Failure on such a task would imply a more general deficit of sensorimotor transformation that is not strictly related to the learned use of objects (Schwoebel *et al.*, 2004).

An important debate in the literature concerns the extent to which semantic representations of objects are critical for the production of object-related gestures. Semantic representations specify abstract conceptual knowledge of words and objects that are neither sensory nor motoric in nature. Some studies have reported surprisingly good use of pantomiming or performance of routine actions in the face of poor semantic knowledge (Beauvois, 1982; Lauro-Grotto *et al.*, 1997). This poses a challenge to a simple model in which retrieval of actions is contingent on the retrieval of semantic knowledge, because this would predict that loss of semantic knowledge of objects should produce a comparable difficulty in generating actions for those objects.

There are a number of ways of modifying this basic model to account for this and these different options need not be mutually exclusive. First, one could fractionate semantic knowledge itself into separate stores with a separate, impaired, store of functional knowledge in these patients (Beauvois, 1982). A second possibility is to suggest that there is a direct route from the structural descriptions of objects to their actions that bypasses semantic memory altogether (Riddoch *et al.*, 1989). Evidence for this comes from the fact that disrupting regions involved in core aspects of semantic memory (anterior temporal lobes) using TMS does not interfere with decisions about how tools are manipulated (how held, how moved) but does interfere with judgments about their functions (e.g. for eating, cutting). Conversely, TMS over the left inferior parietal lobes produces the opposite pattern (Ishibashi *et al.*, 2011).

A third possibility is that there could be a mechanism that links together sensory and motor properties of objects that is independent of their conventional usage. For example, semi-spherical shapes may imply a container, a handle may imply grasping and a sharp edge may imply cutting. Gibson (1979) has referred to these as **affordances**. Patients with semantic dementia lose their semantic knowledge of objects but are still able to act on objects using affordances. The degree of semantic impairment (as assessed via naming and matching tasks, e.g. match a bottle to a glass) was found to be related to the level of impairment in tool use for those same items (Hodges *et al.*, 2000). Despite being unable to produce conventional actions, many errors suggested intact affordances. For example, one patient correctly held the scissors by the handle rather than the blade but did so bimanually (plausibly correct) rather than unimanually (conventionally correct). The patients could copy actions performed by the experimenter and use novel tools (e.g. the test of Goldenberg and Hagmann, 1998). This suggests that

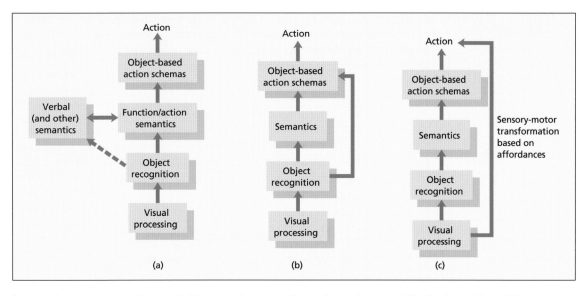

Some patients can gesture the use of objects despite poor understanding and naming ability for those objects. This can be explained in three ways: fractionated semantic knowledge (a), direct links between stored object and action representations (b), or affordances related to non-arbitrary correspondences between visual features and motor commands (c).

the deficits were truly object related. These object-based affordances may account for the fact that many ideomotor apraxic patients perform better when given the actual objects rather than producing the actions simply from memory.

### Is left hemispheric dominance for tool use related to language laterality or handedness?

One long-standing question is why object-based actions should reside predominantly in the left hemisphere of humans (no such bias has been found in other primates). One possibility dating back to the work of Liepmann (1905) is that it reflects the fact that the majority of people are right-handed for tool use. Recent functional imaging studies of left-handers have shed light on this. Regions of the *left* hemisphere involved in tool use (area AIP and ventral premotor cortex) are activated to the same degree in left-handers and right-handers, irrespective of which hand is used, and irrespective of whether the action involves tool use or hand-based grasping (Martin *et al.*, 2011). However, left-handers do show more bilateral activity in the equivalent right hemispheric regions. This suggests that handedness is a factor, but it is not simply the case that left-handed and right-handed people are mirror images of each other in terms of brain activity when they use tools.

One possibility is that the apparent bilateral pattern in left-handers is due to differences in language dominance rather than handedness itself. Left-handers tend to show more variability in which hemisphere is dominant for language production (either right, left, or mixed dominance), whereas right-handers are almost always left-hemispheric dominant (Rasmussen & Milner, 1977). When left-handers are assessed for language dominance (assessed by silently generating words) then parietal regions relating to praxis (assessed by generating gestures to words, e.g. "cutting") tend to be lateralized to the language dominant hemisphere

(Kroliczak *et al.*, 2011). Thus language rather than handedness per se seems to be the main determinant of hemispheric asymmetry for tool use. It is less clear which aspects of language (speech production, conceptual knowledge, etc.) are most relevant to the association.

## Evaluation

The human brain contains a store of object-dependent actions that may reside in the left inferior parietal lobe and are impaired in ideomotor apraxia. These actions may normally be accessed from semantic representations of objects, but actions can often be inferred from the non-arbitrary relationship between the structures of tools and the functions they serve (affordances).

# PREPARATION AND EXECUTION OF ACTIONS

## Role of subcortical structures in movement and action

The chapter so far has concentrated on cortical influences on action and movement. However, subcortical structures have an important role to play particularly with regards to the preparation and execution of actions. These structures may be important for setting the particular parameters of the movement, such as the force and duration of movement and for controlling the movement in progress. One imaging study that highlights the different roles of cortical and subcortical structures was conducted by Krams and colleagues (1998). In one condition, participants were shown a hand position, given 3 sec to *prepare*, and were then asked to *execute* it (PE condition). In another condition, they were required to *execute* it as soon as it was shown (E condition), and in the final experimental condition they were asked to *prepare* but not to execute (P condition). (The baseline condition was viewing the hand movement without preparation or execution.) The cerebellum and basal ganglia were found to be more active when both preparation and execution were required (PE relative to P; also PE relative to E). In contrast, the prefrontal cortex including Broca's area was more active when merely preparing to produce observed movements (P relative to PE; also P relative to E).

The figure below summarizes the two main types of cortical-subcortical loop involved in the generation of movement. One loop passes through the basal ganglia and the other through the cerebellum. These loops have somewhat different functions. The *cerebellar loop* is involved in the coordination of movements. It may utilize a copy of the cortical motor commands to ensure that the desired movement occurs accurately and occurs at the desired time (Ohyama *et al.*, 2003). For example, it is physiologically active during coordination tasks that require one movement to be synchronized with another (Ramnani *et al.*, 2001). Moreover, patients with cerebellum lesions produce tremulous movements that suggest that they are unable to use information about the progress of the movement to update the initiated motor program (Haggard *et al.*, 1995). Given this role, it is perhaps not surprising that the cerebellum connects strongly with lateral premotor and parietal regions involved in sensorimotor transformation.

The basal ganglia "loop" actually consists of around five different loops. Each loop has essentially the same architecture (a set of interconnected excitatory and

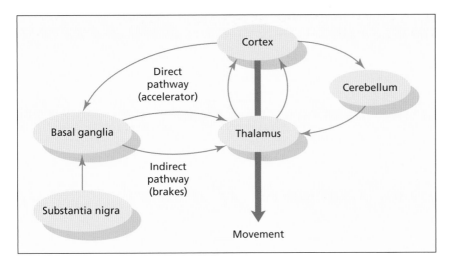

Two main types of subcortical loop are involved in movement generation. The cerebellar loop (green) coordinates the timing and trajectory of movement using sensory and motor information. The basal ganglia motor circuit (purple) regulates the excitability of frontal motor structures (SMA) and biases the likelihood of movement and the nature of the movement (e.g. the force).

inhibitory pathways) but projects to somewhat different structures in the basal ganglia and in the cortex (Alexander & Crutcher, 1990). Of primary relevant here is the so-called motor circuit that passes through dorsal regions of the basal ganglia and projects to premotor areas and particularly strongly to the SMA. Other loops target different regions of the frontal lobes and pass through different structures in the basal ganglia and the thalamus: for instance, an oculomotor circuit projects strongly to the frontal eye fields (FEF); a limbic circuit passes through more ventral regions of the basal ganglia and projects to the orbitofrontal cortex, amygdala and anterior cingulate; and other loops project to the lateral prefrontal cortex. These different circuits modulate different aspects of behavior. The prefrontal loop relates to the control of cognition, the oculomotor circuit relates to the control of eye movements, and the limbic circuit is linked to reward-based learning. The motor circuit itself appears to be particularly important for the initiation and execution of internally generated movements (more so than cued movements), sequencing of actions, and procedural learning. It is to be noted that the basal ganglia do not generate the signals to execute a movement (this is achieved from connections from the primary motor cortex down the brainstem to the spinal cord). They function, instead, to modify activity in frontal motor structures and influence the probability of movement and the nature of the movement (e.g. its amplitude).

The spinal cord makes connections between the brain and the muscles and controls simple reflexive movements (e.g. to avoid sudden injury). Unlike the other actions considered so far, reflexes can't be construed as cognitively based. As well as these descending fiber tracts, the spinal cord also contains ascending fibers that provide sensory feedback about the state of the body and the fate of the executed movement. For example, Patient GO lost these pathways from a severe peripheral sensory disease (Rothwell *et al.*, 1982). Although he could make accurate quick movements with appropriate force, his lack of sensory feedback meant that he was unable to sustain motoric tasks. For example, when carrying a suitcase he would quickly drop it unless he continually looked down to see it was there.

# Hypokinetic disorders of the basal ganglia: Parkinson's disease

**Parkinson's disease** affects about 0.15 percent of the total population and has a mean age of onset at around 60 years. It was first described by James Parkinson in 1817 in his "Essay on the shaking palsy." No single cause has yet been found, although in some cases a genetic link has been suggested. However, the neuropathologic signs of the disease are well understood. Dopaminergic brain cells are lost in the pathways linking the substantia nigra and basal ganglia (Brooks *et al.*, 1990). Dopamine agonists therefore tend to be used in the treatment of Parkinson's disease.

To understand the symptoms of Parkinson's disease it is necessary to understand the nature of the basal ganglia motor circuit in more detail. First of all, it is important to recall the nature of inhibitory and excitatory pathways. Imagine that two brain structures, "A" and "B," connect such that "A" connects to "B" (A → B). If the connection is inhibitory, then greater activity in "A" produces less activity in "B." If the connection is excitatory, then greater activity in "A" produces more activity in "B." The loops connecting the basal ganglia and thalamus consist of a mix of inhibitory and excitatory connections that combine together to form two complementary routes: a direct route that promotes action (increases activity in the cortex) and an indirect route that inhibits action (decreases activity in the cortex) (DeLong, 1990). These direct and indirect routes act like an accelerator and brake in the initiation of action. Lesions of the connections between the substantia nigra and the basal ganglia in Parkinson's disease have a net effect of increasing the output of the indirect pathway (the brakes) and decreasing the output on the direct pathway (the accelerator). The net result is a poverty of self-initiated movement.

Not all types of movement and action are affected equally in Parkinson's disease. For example, an ordinarily immobile patient may walk or run normally in situations of risk such as fire, and the shuffling gait can be improved by provision of lines on the floor over which the patients must step (Martin, 1967).

Michael J. Fox was diagnosed with young-onset Parkinson's disease in 1991. Upon disclosing his condition to the public in 1998, he has since committed himself to the campaign for increased Parkinson's research in a bid to uncover a cure.

© Lucas Jackson/Reuters/Corbis.

This suggests that there is not a simple movement failure, but that there is a failure in self-initiating the action that can to some extent be overcome by external cues. The motor programs themselves also appear to be preserved. For example, signatures and handwriting style are preserved even though the kinematics are impaired such that writing is very slow and shrunken in size (a symptom called *micrographia*; McLennan *et al.*, 1972). One common finding is that patients with Parkinson's disease are relatively spared at initiating actions in which the response is determined by some property of the stimulus (e.g. left finger if stimulus green, right finger if stimulus red), but significantly impaired on simple reaction time tasks (e.g. press a single button, or any button, when the stimulus appears) (Evarts *et al.*, 1981). How are we to account for the relatively spared actions? Recall that there is an additional

## MOTOR SYMPTOMS OF PARKINSON'S DISEASE

Symptoms include the following (Beradelli *et al.*, 2001):

- akinesia (lack of spontaneous movement)
- bradykinesia (slowness of movement)
- decay of movement sequences (walking degenerates to a shuffle)
- failure to scale muscle activity to movement amplitude
- failure to weld several movement components into a single action plan
- rigidity
- tremor (when stationary).

subcortical route that bypasses the basal ganglia altogether and goes via the cerebellum (note: this is not to be confused with the direct and indirect pathways, both of which go through the basal ganglia). This route may be more involved in actions specified by environmental cues, whereas the routes through the basal ganglia are more involved with self-initiated actions associated with the supplementary motor area (SMA). Functional imaging studies have shown that patients with Parkinson's disease have reduced frontostriatal activation during self-initiated action but can show normal activation in externally triggered actions (Jahanshahi *et al.*, 1995).

The pattern of spared and impaired action in patients with Parkinson's disease is also found in cognitive tasks with minimal motor requirements. This is perhaps not surprising since the lesioned pathway (from the substantia nigra to the basal ganglia) contributes to loops other than the motor circuit. Patients with Parkinson's disease perform poorly on tasks of executive function that involve the self-initiation of cognitive strategies (Taylor *et al.*, 1986). Brown and Marsden (1988) used a variant of the Stroop test in which the subject must either name the INK color (e.g. say "red" when the written word *green* is printed in red ink) or the WORD color (e.g. say "green" when the written word *green* is printed in red ink). Participants would either have to spontaneously switch between naming the ink and naming the color or they would receive a written cue (INK or WORD) before each trial. The patients with Parkinson's disease were impaired on the uncued self-initiated trails but not the cued trials.

## Hyperkinetic disorders of the basal ganglia: Huntington's disease and Tourette's syndrome

If Parkinson's disease is characterized as a poverty of spontaneous movement (**hypokinetic**), then a number of disorders exist that can be characterized as an excess of spontaneous movement (**hyperkinetic**). **Huntington's disease** is a genetic disorder with a well-characterized neuropathology (MacDonald *et al.*, 2003). The symptoms consist of dance-like, flailing limbs (chorea) and contorted postures. The symptoms arise in mid-adulthood and degenerate over time. Many of those condemned in the Salem witch trials of 1692 are now believed to have suffered from the illness. Huntington's disease arises because of depletion of inhibitory neurons in the early part of the indirect pathway linking the basal ganglia with the thalamus (Wichmann & DeLong, 1996). The net effect of this lesion is that the output of the indirect pathway (the brakes) is reduced, whereas the output of the direct pathway (the accelerator) remains normal. This shift in the balance of power promotes movement in general.

**Tourette's syndrome** is characterized by excessive and repetitive actions such as motor tics or vocalizations. Functional imaging (fMRI) of children with Tourette's revealed a correlation between tic severity and activation of the substantia nigra and cortical, striatal and thalamic regions in the direct ("accelerator") pathway during a cognitive task (Baym et al., 2008). The prefrontal cortex also tends to be more activate in people with Tourette's relative to controls in complex motor and cognitive tasks (Jackson et al., 2011) and this is typically interpreted as a compensatory mechanism to try to control the tics.

Tourette's syndrome has similar characteristics and co-morbidity with **obsessive-compulsive disorder** or OCD (Sheppard et al., 1999). This consists of repetitive thoughts (obsessions) and/or actions (compulsions) such as cleaning, counting or checking. The actions in OCD are clearly more complex than tics and are, to some degree, voluntary in nature despite being unwanted and inappropriate. The currently available evidence implicates the limbic circuit of the basal ganglia (projecting to orbitofrontal cortex) in OCD rather than the motor circuit which contributes to the movement disorders in Parkinson's and Huntington's disease. Patients with OCD have increased functional connectivity (measured with fMRI) between the orbitofrontal cortex and regions in the ventral basal ganglia (Harrison et al., 2009). The orbitofrontal cortex is involved in behavioral flexibility and responding to negative feedback. Patients with OCD show less activity in their orbitofrontal cortex when learning that a previously rewarded response is no longer rewarded (Chamberlain et al., 2008).

---

## SYMPTOMS OF TOURETTE'S DISEASE

Symptoms include:

- motor tics (e.g. eye blinks, neck movements)
- echolalia (repeating someone else's words)
- palilalia (repeating one's own words)
- coprolalia (production of obscenities).

---

### Evaluation

A number of circuits involving the cortex (notably frontal) and subcortical structures are critical for the initiation and execution of movement. One circuit, involving the cerebellum, is involved in coordinating the movement once initiated. Another circuit, involving the basal ganglia, is involved in establishing self-initiated movements. The basal ganglia loop contains two parallel pathways known as the direct and indirect pathway that promote or reduce cortical excitability. Disruptions in the direct and indirect pathways are implicated in a number of movement-related disorders including Parkinson's disease, Huntington's disease, and Tourette's syndrome.

## SUMMARY AND KEY POINTS OF THE CHAPTER

- Action can be considered an outcome of a number of processes working together in a concerted fashion. These processes include selection and maintenance of goals; the identification of objects in the environment and translation of their visuospatial properties into motor commands; preparing movements; and executing and online control of movements.
- The prefrontal cortex is involved in the highest stages of action planning and cognitive control in general. The SAS model provides a good account of action selection and its breakdown following frontal lobe damage.
- The lateral premotor cortex may be involved both in the preparation of action (particularly toward external objects) and in observing the actions of others (using "mirror neurons"). This may be important for imitation and skill learning.
- Visual processing of objects contains both a ventral stream (involved in explicit object recognition) and a dorsal stream. The dorsal stream codes action-relevant properties of objects (e.g. their absolute size, position in egocentric space).
- The dorsal stream terminates in the parietal lobes, and parieto-frontal networks are responsible for developing action plans based on the current external reality and the goals of the individual (sensorimotor transformation).
- Humans use a vast range of tools. Tool use may be achieved by retrieving stored knowledge of objects and their actions via semantic memory, or may be partially achieved using "affordances" based on sensorimotor properties of objects. A difficulty in using objects is referred to as apraxia.
- The preparation and execution of action is influenced by two main subcortical circuits involving: (1) the cerebellum and (2) the basal ganglia. The cerebellar loop is involved in the online coordination of movement by comparing intended motor acts with sensory outcomes.
- The basal ganglia regulate action via a balance of action-promoting and action-inhibiting pathways, and are particularly involved in self-generated actions (prepared in the supplementary motor area). Parkinson's and Huntington's diseases can be explained as a disruption of this balance, leading to a poverty or excess of movement.

Visit the companion website at www. psypress/cw/ward for:

- References to key papers and readings
- Video interviews on key topics with leading psychologists Giacomo Rizzolatti, Niels Birbaumer and Ann Graybiel
- Multiple choice questions and interactive flashcards to test your knowledge
- Downloadable glossary

## EXAMPLE ESSAY QUESTIONS

- What is the role(s) of the frontal lobes in action?
- What are mirror neurons and how has their discovery changed the way that people think about action?
- How are object-related actions stored and retrieved?
- How are vision and action integrated in the brain?
- Compare and contrast the role of the cerebellum and the basal ganglia in action.

## RECOMMENDED FURTHER READING

- Goodale, M. A. & Milner, A. D. (2004). *Sight unseen*. Oxford, UK: Oxford University Press. A very good and accessible account of the role of vision in action.
- Haggard, P., Rossetti, Y., & Kawato, M. (2008). *Sensory-motor foundations of higher cognition (Attention and performance XXII)*. Oxford, UK: Oxford University Press. A set of chapters written by experts with good coverage of areas such as imitation, action intention, and so on.
- Morsella, E., Bargh, J. A., & Gollwitzer, P. M. (2008). *Oxford handbook of human action*. Oxford, UK: Oxford University Press. A very comprehensive set of chapters again focussing on action rather than movement.
- Rizzolatti, G., Sinigaglia, C., & Anderson, F. (2007). *Mirrors in the brain*. Oxford, UK: Oxford University Press. An accessible account of mirror neurons and their wider implications.

# CHAPTER 9

# The remembering brain

CONTENTS

The ability to learn and remember has several evolutionary advantages. It enables one to predict future outcomes on the basis of experience and adapt to new situations. One can learn to avoid situations previously associated with threat, or to return to locations where food has previously been found. **Plasticity** refers to the brain's ability to change as a result of experience and, while greatest during childhood, plasticity persists throughout life. At a neural level, plasticity occurs by changing the pattern of synaptic connectivity between neurons. Given that the whole brain is capable of such changes, one could regard learning and memory to be a feature of the brain as a whole rather than a specialized module or faculty. Indeed there are no instances in which memory is completely lost or abolished. Even amnesic patients can learn and remember certain things. Although the whole brain may make contributions to learning and memory, it is crucial to recognize that different regions contribute in different ways. Some regions may be specialized for learning and remembering words, other regions specialized for learning and remembering visual objects, and other regions may be especially important for recollecting episodes from one's life. The latter is the traditional sense in which the word "memory" is used, but there is far more to memory than that.

The general approach of this chapter is to consider different types of memory, how they are implemented in the brain and how they interact. The chapter begins by considering the distinction between long-term and short-term or working memory. The chapter then considers different types of long-term memory and discusses amnesia in terms of this theoretical framework. It then goes on to discuss whether the hippocampus has a time-limited role, whether there are separate neural substrates for familiarity and recollection and the cognitive/neural mechanisms of forgetting. Finally, the chapter discusses frontal lobe contributions to memory.

## SHORT-TERM AND WORKING MEMORY

The labels "short-term" and "long-term" appear to suggest that there could be different types of memory evoked for different periods of time with, perhaps, separate stores for things that happened a few days ago relative to several years ago. This is a popular misconception. It is not how psychologists distinguish between short- and long-term memory. **Short-term memory (STM)** is defined as memory for information currently held "in mind" and has limited capacity. **Long-term memory (LTM)** refers to information that is stored; it need not be presently accessed or even consciously accessible. The long-term store is considered to have essentially unlimited capacity within the inherent confounds of the brain. According to this definition, memory for things that happened several hours, days, or years ago are all stored within long-term memory.

This section will begin by considering the evidence for different kinds of limited-capacity short-term memory stores, and their neural basis. The second part of this section will consider the concept of working memory and, in particular, the role of prefrontal cortex in maintenance and manipulation of information.

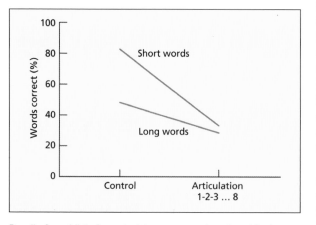

Recall of word lists from short-term memory is reduced for longer words and affected by articulatory suppression.

Data from Baddeley et al., 1975.

### Phonological short-term memory

Short-term memory is often used as an abbreviated term for phonological short-term memory or verbal working memory. The capacity limitation of phonological short-term memory is typically investigated with span tasks, in which participants are read a sequence of, say, digits, and must repeat them back immediately or after brief retention. Miller (1956) argued that humans have a span of seven items plus or minus two (i.e. between five and nine items). He argued that the seven items are meaningful "chunks" of information rather than words or syllables. For example, familiar dates such as "1812" may be one chunk, but "5297" may be four single-digit chunks. However, others have argued that chunking is relying on long-term memory to recode information and that the true capacity limitation is lower, around four (Cowan, 2001). Evidence against Miller's proposal comes from research showing that the capacity limitation is related to phonological characteristics of the stimuli and not merely their meaningfulness. Span length is lower when lists of words are polysyllabic (e.g. "skeleton, binocular, . . ."; Baddeley *et al.*, 1975) or when they are phonologically similar (e.g. "map, can, cap, mat . . ."; Baddeley, 1966). Another factor that may influence span is the opportunity to rehearse the material. Span is reduced if participants are asked to silently mouth irrelevant speech (e.g. saying "the, the, the . . ." or "1, 2, 3 . . .") while encoding a list (Baddeley *et al.*, 1984). This is termed **articulatory suppression**.

Baddeley argues that span tasks involve at least two components: a phonological store and a rehearsal mechanism based on subvocal articulation that refreshes the store. Articulatory suppression impairs the latter. Collectively, he terms the store and rehearsal mechanism the "phonological loop" or the "articulatory loop" (Baddeley *et al.*, 1984). Neuroscience of this process consider the loop in terms of reciprocal activation between speech perception processes and mechanisms of speech production (Buchsbaum & D'Esposito, 2008; Jones *et al.*, 2004). This is considered in more detail in Chapter 11, "The Speaking Brain."

## Visuo-spatial short-term memory

It has been proposed that there is a limited-capacity short-term memory system for visuo-spatial information that is analogous to the one involving phonological information described above (Logie, 1995). One simple test, often termed the "Corsi blocks," involves tapping a sequence of squares/blocks that the participant must then reproduce. Typical performance on such a task is to accurately maintain sequences of up to five (Della Sala *et al.*, 1999). Another approach is to display an array of objects and then retain this over a brief delay period (several seconds). Memory can then be probed via recognition (was this object present?), change detection (is the array the same?), or cued recall (what object was at this location?). Luck and Vogel (1997) displayed arrays of different colored squares or arrays of different line orientations. In both cases, memory deteriorates when holding in mind more than four items. The interesting comparison was when conjunctions of features had to be remembered (i.e. an oriented *and* colored line). Even though the conjunction involves holding twice as many features in mind, it was found that memory performance was not halved but remained constant; that is, around four feature conjunctions could be remembered. They even extended this finding to a quadruple feature condition: 16 features distributed across four objects can be retained as accurately as four features distributed across four objects. The explanation is that the capacity limitation relates to visual objects/locations rather than visual features.

What is the neural basis of visuo-spatial STM? There is evidence that holding in mind an object, over a delay period, involves sustaining activity in regions of the brain involved in object perception. Ranganath *et al.* (2004) examined visual short-term memory for images of faces or places using fMRI. In delayed-matching to sample, participants were shown a face/place (for 1 sec) and asked to keep it in mind (for 7 sec) followed by a test stimulus (is it the same or different item?). Holding in mind a face or place sustains activity in parts of the ventral stream specialized for perceiving faces and places respectively (this reveals itself in the sluggish BOLD response ~6 sec later). In delayed paired associates, a similar

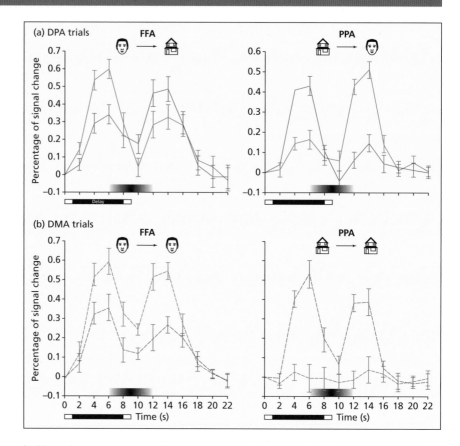

In this study a visual stimulus (face or house, presented for 1 sec) must either be held in STM to be recognized after a delay (DMS, delayed matching to sample) or an associated item from the other category must be held in STM (DPA, delayed paired associates). Activity is measured in parts of the brain sensitive to faces (FFA, fusiform Face Area) or places (PPA, Parahippocampal Place Area) in response to seeing and holding in mind faces (blue lines) or places (red lines). The key part of the figure is the delay period: physically occurring between 1 and 8 sec (black bar) but manifest in the BOLD response between 6 and 12 sec.

From Ranganath *et al.*, 2004.

procedure was used except that participants had previously learned to pair particular place and face images together (e.g. face A paired with place A). This time, BOLD activity relating to the delay period reflected the type of stimulus being recalled rather than the one just presented. However, these visual regions alone do not account for visual STM. These regions are functionally connected to frontal and parietal regions during the delay period (Gazzaley *et al.*, 2004). Moreover, distracting stimuli presented in the delay period (e.g. irrelevant faces when trying to hold in mind a face) disrupts connectivity in that network as well as disrupting visual STM (Yoon *et al.*, 2006).

Functional imaging studies using arrays of simple visual objects (e.g. colored shapes), in the Luck and Vogel (1997) tradition, show the importance of regions in the posterior parietal cortex (intra-parietal sulcus) that are also implicated in visuo-spatial attention (Todd & Marois, 2004). fMRI activity in this region, together with regions involved in visual perception, are related to individual differences in capacity (Todd & Marois, 2005).

# The concept of working memory

The concept of **working memory** is essentially an extension of the one already described for short-term memory. The key difference is that working memory emphasizes a wider role in cognition (reasoning, comprehension, etc.), whereas short-term memory is often taken to imply a more passive retention of material. One of the most influential models is that proposed by Baddeley and Hitch (1974; Baddeley, 1986). This original model consists of three components. The phonological consists of a limited-capacity phonological store, together with a mechanism for refreshing it (based on subvocal rehearsal). A comparable system is postulated in the visual domain and termed the visuospatial sketchpad. Collectively, the phonological loop and visuospatial sketchpad are considered to be "slave systems." They can be contrasted with the third component: the central executive. The central executive coordinates the slave systems, and cognition in general, specifying task goals, initiating and terminating cognitive routines and so on. It is the interaction between the flexible executive system and the more specific processing routines that is the essential characteristic of a working memory. Subsequently, a third slave system—the episodic buffer—was added to the model for maintaining and manipulating information from episodic long-term memory (Baddeley, 2000).

Working memory models such as those of Baddeley and colleagues propose that information (e.g. words) gets transferred or copied into a separate dedicated system (e.g. a phonological short-term memory store) which may then be acted on by an executive system. The alternative approach is to "cut out the middle man" and suggest that there are no short-term stores, but that working memory is, instead, just the temporary activation of long-term memories (including perceptual representations of words and objects) by a prefrontal/executive system (Cowan, 2001; D'Esposito, 2007). There are some advantages to this approach: it is a simpler explanation, and it can be used to account for working memory for all kinds of information (e.g. touch, smell) and not just those for which separate slave systems are assumed to exist. The challenge for those models that regard working memory as temporary activation of long-term memory is to explain where capacity limitation comes from in the first place. (Note: This is not a problem for traditional models, because capacity limitation is an intrinsic property of short-term stores; for instance, by having four or seven "slots".) One explanation is that the more items that are simultaneously activated in a long-term memory store, the more interference there is between them and the less precision there is (e.g. "mop" may become confusable with "map" when holding multiple other words in mind, but not when holding one word in mind). In visual STM, for instance, knowing the exact location of an object in a just-seen array becomes increasingly less precise as the array size increases, but doesn't immediately become error-prone when the array size reaches a "magic-number" of four objects (Bays & Husain, 2008).

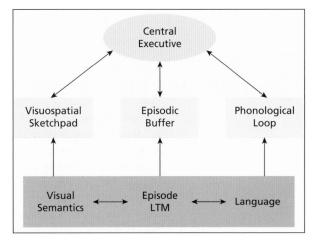

Baddeley's (2000) model of working memory was revised to incorporate three kinds of short-term systems (blue) that interface with long-term memory (shown in green).

The evidence from cognitive neuroscience is consistent with the view that working memory involves temporary activity in parts of the brain involved in long-term storage of objects, words and episodes (D'Esposito, 2007). The study of Ranganath *et al.* (2004), shown on p. 198, is one good example of this. As noted by Baddeley (2012) studies of this kind do not disprove additional short-term stores, but it does support the idea that working memory and long-term memory are not completely distinct.

Other evidence that is consistent with this view is that the integrity of working memory is important for long-term learning of new material. Earlier theories, such as the influential model of Atkinson and Shiffrin (1968), had proposed that working memory was crucial for long-term learning, but this wasn't supported by the evidence that was available at that time. For example, brain-damaged patients with phonological short-term memory impairments can learn to associate familiar pairs of words together (Warrington & Shallice, 1969). Subsequent research has focused on learning new material (rather than new combinations of old material) and shown that brain-damaged patients with phonological short-term memory impairments struggle to learn new words, such as when learning new vocabulary (Baddeley, 1993; Baddeley *et al.*, 1988). Moreover, individual differences in phonological short-term memory predict learning of toy names in children (Gathercole & Baddeley, 1990). There were no differences in their ability to attach familiar names (e.g. Michael, Peter) to toys, but differences occurred for made-up names (e.g. Piekle, Meater). Similarly, when brain-damage disrupts visuo-spatial STM it can impair the ability to learn new visual information, such as new faces (Hanley *et al.*, 1991). Thus, problems in short-term memory efficiency have negative consequences for long-term learning. (As discussed later, the reverse isn't necessarily true; i.e. that problems in long-term learning are necessarily accompanied by reduced working memory capacity.)

## Working memory and the frontal lobes

The prefrontal cortex within the frontal lobes is widely recognized as playing a crucial role in working memory. Most models tend to assume that the main storage site of information is not within the frontal lobes themselves but in the posterior cortex, and that the function of the prefrontal cortex is to keep this information active and/or manipulate the active information according to current goals.

In Baddeley's (1986) model, for instance, the notion of the central executive is effectively synonymous with models of prefrontal functioning. Goldman-Rakic's (1992, 1996) account also regards the prefrontal cortex as implementing a working memory system and draws primarily on animal lesion studies and single-cell recordings. Lesions to the lateral prefrontal cortex can impair the ability to hold a stimulus/response in mind over a short delay (Butters & Pandya, 1969). In one delayed response task, monkeys were presented with a box in a particular location on the screen. The box then disappeared and the monkey was required to hold the location "in mind." After a delay, they were then required to look at where the target was previously displayed. Single-cell recordings from monkeys show that some dorsolateral prefrontal neurons respond selectively during the delay period, suggesting that this is the neural mechanism for holding locations in mind (Funahashi *et al.*, 1989).

Goldman-Rakic (1996) argued that there is a division between the content of information processed in dorsolateral and ventro-lateral regions, but that the same

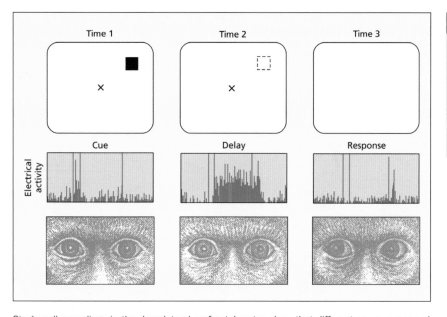

Single-cell recordings in the dorsolateral prefrontal cortex show that different neurons respond to (a) studying in a target location, (b) holding it "in mind" during a delay, and (c) responding to the removal of a cue by moving the eyes to that location.

From Goldman-Rakic, 1992. Reprinted with permission of Patricia J. Wynne. www.patriciawynne.com.

types of process are used for both. Specifically, she suggests that ventral regions support working memory for objects and dorsal regions support spatial working memory (that is, the dorsal and ventral visual stream is manifested at the level of executive functions). Recent evidence is inconsistent with this view. Rao *et al.* (1997) report that individual neurons can change their responsiveness from being object based to being location based as the demands of the task change, irrespective of whether they are located in dorsolateral or ventrolateral regions.

Petrides (1996, 2000, 2005) offers an alternative account of working memory to that of Goldman-Rakic. He argues that the dorsolateral and ventrolateral prefrontal regions should be distinguished by the fact that they are engaged in different types of process and not that they are specialized for different types of material (e.g. spatial versus object based). This is a hierarchical model of working memory. In this model, the ventrolateral prefrontal cortex is responsible for activating, retrieving and maintaining information held in the posterior cortex. The dorsolateral prefrontal region is responsible when the information held within this system requires active manipulation (e.g. ordering of information). Petrides and Milner (1982) found that patients with prefrontal lesions were impaired on a test of working memory termed the **self-ordered pointing task**. The patients were presented with

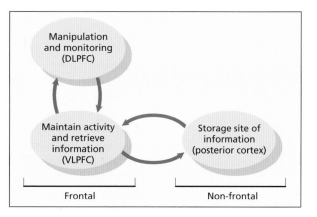

A hierarchical model of working memory in which ventrolateral prefrontal cortex (VLPFC) activates and maintains information, and the dorsolateral prefrontal cortex (DLPFC) manipulates that information.

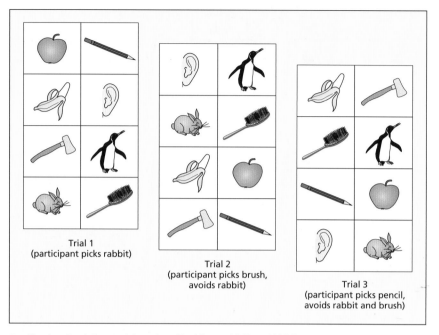

Trial 1
(participant picks rabbit)

Trial 2
(participant picks brush,
avoids rabbit)

Trial 3
(participant picks pencil,
avoids rabbit and brush)

A self-ordered pointing task based on Petrides and Milner (1982). Participants are required to point to a new object on each trial and, as such, must keep an online record of previous selections.

an array of eight words or pictures and, on the first trial, required to pick any one. On the second trial, they were asked to pick a different one from the first; on the third trial, they must pick a different one again and so on. As such, they must maintain and update an online record of chosen items. Similar studies on monkeys suggest the critical region to be the dorsolateral prefrontal cortex (Petrides, 1995). In a human functional imaging study, Owen *et al.* (1996) found that short-term retention of spatial locations was associated with ventrolateral activity. However, if they had to maintain and update a record of which locations had been marked and avoid these, then dorsolateral activity was found.

## Evaluation

Short-term memory systems have two essential features: a capacity limited storage system and a mechanism for refreshing and maintaining activity in that system. The latter mechanism is invariably linked to activity within lateral prefrontal cortex. The nature of the store itself is more controversial and could either be a separate memory system (with capacity limitation deriving primarily from the size of that system) or temporary activation of long terms stores (e.g. for words) or perceptual resources (e.g. for visual patterns), with capacity limitation arising solely from interference between active items. Evidence from cognitive neuroscience suggests some role for the latter. In addition, there are mechanisms for manipulating, rather than just maintaining, information that is held in mind (the idea of "working" memory) that has been linked in particular to the function of the dorsolateral region of the prefrontal cortex.

# DIFFERENT TYPES OF LONG-TERM MEMORY

Just as short-term memory may have several components (e.g. visuo-spatial, phonological), long-term memory may be further subdivided into different components. This has been termed the multiple memory systems approach (Nyberg & Tulving, 1996).

One distinction that can be made is whether the memories are consciously accessible or not; termed **declarative memory** and **non-declarative memory**, respectively (Squire *et al.*, 1993) or, alternatively, **explicit memory** and **implicit memory**, respectively. Non-declarative memory can be thought of as consisting of several subdomains.

**Procedural memory** refers to memory for skills such as riding a bike. It is not consciously accessible in the sense that the contents of the memory are not amenable to verbal report. Evidence suggests that the basal ganglia are important for the learning of procedural skills and habits (Packard & Knowlton, 2002). Perceptual representation systems are those used for perceiving sounds, words, objects, and so on (Schacter, 1987). They are memory systems in the sense that they store knowledge of the perceptual world and are capable of learning. Evidence for perceptual learning comes from priming studies. Priming refers to the fact that information is easier to access if it has recently been encountered. For example, people are more likely to complete a word fragment such as H__SE as HORSE if that word has recently been encountered. This is assumed to reflect the fact that the perceptual representation of the word is more accessible the second time around (Tulving & Schacter, 1990). Schacter *et al.* (1990) showed participants a sequence of unfamiliar objects. Although all objects were unfamiliar, some were plausible three-dimensional configurations, whereas others were impossible configurations. When shown a second time, participants were instructed to make a possible–impossible judgment. Priming was found (i.e. faster response times) only for the possible configurations, and not for the impossible configurations. This suggests that our perceptual systems have learned to distinguish plausible objects and that this is the source of priming in tests of implicit memory. The neural signature of priming appears to be reduced activity on the second presentation relative to the first (Schacter & Badgaiyan, 2001). Imaging studies (Schacter & Badgaiyan, 2001) and a report of a patient with occipital lobe lesion (Gabrieli *et al.*, 1995) are consistent with the notion that priming involves brain regions involved in perception.

Within declarative or explicit memory, Tulving (1972) has proposed the influential distinction between episodic and semantic memory. **Semantic memory** is conceptually based knowledge about the world, including knowledge of people, places, the meaning of objects and words. It is culturally shared knowledge. By contrast, **episodic memory** refers to memory of specific events in one's own life. The memories are specific in time and place. For example, knowing that Paris is the capital of France is semantic memory, but remembering a visit to Paris or remembering being taught this fact is episodic memory. Episodic memory has a first-person characteristic to it, i.e. the memories involve oneself as an observer/participant. For this reason, it is also known as autobiographical memory. Facts about oneself (e.g. addresses, the name of your spouse) are normally regarded a semantic memory, and are usually called personal semantic memory.

There is good evidence for multiple memory systems, but there is nevertheless likely to be some overlap between them. This will be outlined in subsequent sections.

## KEY TERMS

**Declarative memory**
Memories that can be consciously accessed and, hence, can typically be declared.

**Non-declarative memory**
Memories that cannot be consciously accessed (e.g. procedural memory).

**Explicit memory**
See declarative memory.

**Implicit memory**
See non-declarative memory.

**Procedural memory**
Memory for skills such as riding a bike.

**Semantic memory**
Conceptually based knowledge about the world, including knowledge of people, places, the meaning of objects and words.

**Episodic memory**
Memory of specific events in one's own life.

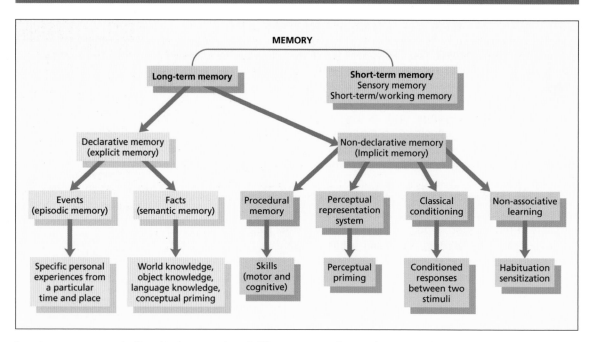

Long-term memory can be thought of as a number of different systems. But are the systems fully independent or do they depend on each other to some extent?

From Gazzaniga et al., 2002. © 2002 W. W. Norton & Company, Inc. Reproduced with permission.

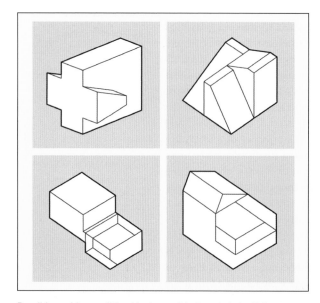

Possible and impossible objects used in the study by Schacter et al. (1990). Only possible objects show priming effects, suggesting that priming taps a perceptual store of known objects.

© 1990 American Psychological Association. Reproduced with permission.

# AMNESIA

One of the most famous patients in the neuropsychological literature is HM (Corkin, 2002). HM began to experience epileptic seizures at the age of ten and, by the time of leaving high school, his quality of life had deteriorated to a point where surgeons and family decided to intervene surgically. The procedure involved removing the medial temporal lobes, including the hippocampus, bilaterally (Scoville & Milner, 1957). What the surgeons did not foresee was that HM would develop one of the most profound amnesias on record. Several decades after the operation, it was observed that HM "does not know where he lives, who cares for him, or where he ate his last meal. His guesses as to the current year may be off by as much as 43 years. . . . In 1982 he did not recognize a picture of himself that had been taken on his fortieth birthday in 1966" (Corkin, 1984, p. 255). On his death, HM was identified as Henry Molaison (1926–2008) and his brain has been preserved in histological sections.

Global amnesics have memory problems both in terms of learning new information (**antero-**

grade memory impairment) and remembering information prior to their brain damage (**retrograde memory** impairment). HM's retrograde deficit extends back to age 16 (11 years before his surgery) and his anterograde deficit is extremely severe (Sagar *et al.*, 1985). It is to be noted that amnesia is a heterogeneous disorder, with patients differing both in terms of severity and also in some qualitative respects (Spiers *et al.*, 2001b). This may reflect different sites of damage in and around the medial temporal lobe. It is also to be noted that HM's lesion affected several regions, not just the hippocampus.

HM's amnesia was a result of neurosurgery. However, in most people amnesia arises as a result of stroke, head injury or viral infection (notably herpes simplex encephalitis). One particularly common cause of amnesia ensues from long-term alcoholism and may be related to thiamine deficiency. This is termed **Korsakoff's syndrome**, or Korsakoff's amnesia. Korsakoff's syndrome is associated with pathology of the midline diencephalon, including the dorsomedial thalamus and the mamillary bodies (Parkin & Leng, 1993).

## KEY TERMS

**Anterograde memory**
Memory for events that have occurred after brain damage.

**Retrograde memory**
Memory for events that occurred before brain damage.

**Korsakoff's syndrome**
Amnesia arising from long-term alcoholism.

## Preserved and impaired memory in amnesia

Within the framework of different types of memory outlined above, which type of memory appears to be disturbed in amnesia? Is it indeed possible to impair one particular aspect of long-term memory without there being consequences to the other systems? This section considers four different types of memory in turn.

### Episodic memory

Amnesic patients are impaired on tests of episodic memory both for events related to their own lives (autobiographical memory) and other types of episode (e.g. learning lists of words). Learning of new material is normally assessed on test batteries such as the Wechsler Memory Scale (Wechsler, 1984). This contains tests of recall and recognition for verbal and visual material. Amnesia is clinically defined as poor performance on memory tests relative to that expected based on their IQ scores. Knowledge of events and facts pertaining to their life prior to the onset of amnesia (i.e. in the retrograde period) can be assessed with tests such as

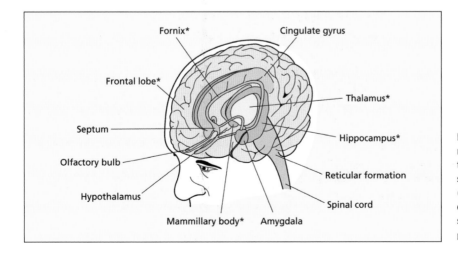

Damage to a number of regions in the medial temporal lobes and surrounding structures (marked with an asterisk) can produce an amnesic syndrome.
From Parkin, 2001.

## AMNESIA AT THE MOVIES

Amnesia has been a favorite topic in Hollywood since the earliest days of cinema (no fewer than ten silent movies on the topic were made) and continues to inspire film-makers today (for a thorough review, see Baxendale, 2004). Rich socialites may become caring mothers after falling from a yacht (*Overboard*, 1987), trained assassins may forget their vocation and become stalked themselves (*The Bourne Identity*, 2002; *The Long Kiss Goodnight*, 1996), and others just require a second bump on the head to be restored to their former selves (*Tarzan the Tiger*, 1922).

The 2001 film *Memento* chronicles the story of Leonard, an ex-insurance investigator who can no longer build new memories, as he attempts to find the perpetrator of a violent attack which caused his post-traumatic anterograde amnesia and left his wife dead. The attack is the last event he can recall.
© Corbis Sygma.

Clinical amnesia tends to affect both memory for events that happened prior to injury (retrograde memory) and learning of new information (anterograde memory), although relatively selective impairments can be found. In movie amnesia, the extent of retrograde or anterograde amnesia is often very pure. For example, Leonard from the film *Memento* (2000) has total anterograde memory loss but no loss of retrograde memory (he can even remember sustaining the injury). The film vividly captures the fact that he is stuck in the present, relying purely on his retrograde memory and memory aids (notes, photos, tattoos). In one scene, he is trying to hold in mind a clue (in working memory) and searching for a pen to write it down. But, as soon as he is distracted and stops rehearsing, the clue disappears from his mind as if it was never there. Whereas the portrayal is generally accurate, his description of it as a "short-term memory problem" is not.

Selective difficulties in retrograde amnesia have been noted in the academic literature, but there is controversy as to whether these have organic or psychogenic origin related to extreme stress (Kopelman, 2000). Fortunately for Hollywood scriptwriters, psychogenic amnesia can arise after committing a violent crime (Schacter, 1986). *The Bourne Identity* (2002) offers one example of focal retrograde amnesia in the movies. It is not clear whether the character's amnesia is organic or psychogenic. According to one reviewer: "Its protagonist, who's found floating off the coast of Marseilles with two bullets in his back and the number of a Zurich safe-deposit box in some sort of laser body-implant, has no idea who he is. But he has somehow retained lightning martial-arts reflexes, fluency in a handful of languages, and the wired instincts of a superspy." These skills would indeed be expected to be preserved in amnesics.

Many films portraying amnesia show a loss of identity or a change in personality. This is not what is found in amnesia of neurological origin, in which one's sense of identity is preserved (although perhaps frozen in time). For instance, amnesic patients are able to accurately reflect on their own personality traits as corroborated by the ratings of family members (Klein *et al.*, 2002). Personality changes can indeed arise from brain damage but are normally associated with a different pathology from amnesia (namely, orbitofrontal regions) or with psychiatric illness.

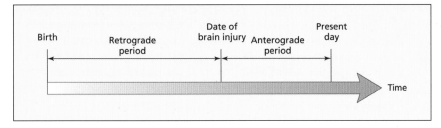

Amnesia normally consists of a severe impairment in anterograde memory, with a more variable impairment in retrograde memory (shading represents degree of impairment).

the Autobiographical Memory Interview (Kopelman *et al.*, 1990). The degree of retrograde memory loss can vary significantly between patients (Kapur, 1999). It is debatable whether retrograde memory loss can exist without any anterograde impairment in cases of organic amnesia (Kopelman, 2000), although this pattern is reported in amnesia arising from psychiatric illness and "mental breakdown" (Kritchevsky *et al.*, 2004).

## Short-term memory

One of the most consistent findings in the literature is that short-term memory in tasks such as digit span is spared (Baddeley & Warrington, 1970). Milner (1971) noted an occasion in which HM held on to a number for 15 min by continuously rehearsing it and using mnemonic strategies. A minute or so after stopping, he had no recollection of being asked to remember a number.

More recently it has been claimed that short-term memory problems are found in amnesia when holding in mind (or even perceiving) one particular kind of information: specifically the 3D layout of large-scale scenes (Hartley *et al.*, 2007). This may point to a particularly important role of the hippocampus in processing spatial environments that may, to some degree, be separable from other memory functions.

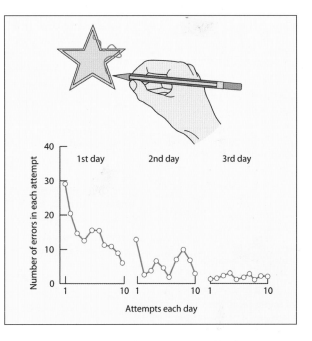

Patient HM was able to learn mirror drawing over a 3-day period, despite no apparent memory for having performed the task before.

From Blakemore, 1977. © Cambridge University Press. Reproduced with permission.

## Procedural and perceptual (implicit) memory

When given new tasks requiring visuomotor coordination, such as drawing around a shape when the hand is viewed in a mirror, then performance is initially poor but improves with practice. The same is true of amnesic patients (Milner, 1966). Thus, procedural knowledge appears to be spared. The same is true of other implicit memory tasks that do not have a strong motor component. Knowlton *et al.* (1994) devised a weather prediction game in which geometric shapes predict weather patterns with a partial degree of certainty (60–85 percent predictive).

Participants often feel that they are guessing although they exhibit learning over 50–100 trials. That is, there is evidence of implicit learning. Amnesic patients also show normal learning despite poor declarative memory for the stimuli, whereas patients with Parkinson's disease show the reverse dissociation consistent with a role of the basal ganglia in learning of habitual responses (Knowlton *et al.*, 1996).

Graf *et al.* (1984) tested implicit memory for words. The amnesics were given lists of words to read (e.g. DEFEND) and, at test, were presented with fragments (e.g. DEF___). They were asked either to recall the word previously shown or to generate the first word that came to mind. The latter was considered an implicit test of memory insofar as the participants were not directly asked a memory question. They found that amnesics performed normally under the implicit testing procedure (i.e. they showed priming) but not given explicit memory instructions. Within the framework proposed by Schacter (1987), this would be accounted for within the perceptual representation system for words.

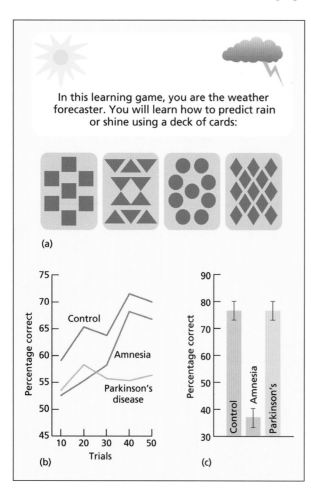

(a)

(b)

(c)

Four cue cards are presented in varying combinations and the participant must predict rain or shine (a). After repeated exposure, both controls and amnesics learn to predict, but Parkinson's patients do not (b). When given a test of explicit memory about the test, the amnesic patients perform badly, but the Parkinson's patients perform well (c).

Adapted from Knowlton *et al.*, 1996.

## Semantic memory

At first sight, amnesic patients appear to retain their knowledge of vocabulary and the world. This was initially taken as evidence that semantic memory is intact in amnesic patients (Parkin, 1982). However, a more complex picture has emerged over the years. One critical issue is the age at which the information was acquired. Most semantic knowledge is acquired within the first few years of life, whereas episodic memory develops later and is acquired throughout the lifespan. Given that amnesia tends to preserve relatively older memories (Ribot, 1882), could the apparent sparing of semantic knowledge reflect its early acquisition? To address this question, a number of studies have investigated knowledge of vocabulary (Verfaellie *et al.*, 1995) and famous people (Parkin *et al.*, 1990) that came into the public domain in the years prior to the onset of amnesia. These studies show amnesics to be impaired (see also Westmacott and Moscovitch, 2002). There is at least one case on record in which retrograde semantic memory is reported to be intact in the face of severe retrograde amnesia (Warrington & McCarthy, 1988). However, the patient was primarily assessed on tasks such as choosing the familiar name/face from an array, rather than supplying actual semantic details. As such, both semantic and episodic memory appear to be impaired in the retrograde period.

The discussion above pertains to the retention of previously learned semantic facts by amnesics. Can amnesics acquire new vocabulary after they become amnesic (i.e. in the anterograde period)? For patient HM (Gabrieli *et al.*, 1988) and many other amnesics (Manns *et al.*, 2003b), the answer appears to be "no." But this is by no means common to all amnesics. One amnesic is even reported to have learned a second language, Italian, following the onset of her anterograde amnesia (Hirst *et al.*, 1988). Others have acquired information about famous people, public events and new vocabulary after becoming amnesic (Kitchener *et al.*, 1998). However, there is one important caveat to bear in mind when considering these studies. Namely, it could be the case that both semantic and episodic memory are impaired, but that semantic memory is less vulnerable, because it can be learned through repetition and multiple events. There is evidence that new semantic memories may be acquired but perhaps at a slower rate (Holdstock *et al.*, 2002). If tissue surrounding the hippocampus, such as the entorhinal cortex, is spared, then semantic learning may be possible although not necessarily normal (Vargha-Khadem *et al.*, 1997b; Verfaellie *et al.*, 2000).

## Accounting for the memory deficits in amnesia

To summarize the preceding sections: amnesic patients have impaired episodic memory, typically in both retrograde and anterograde periods. In contrast they have generally spared short-term memory, procedural memory and perceptual priming (a type of implicit memory). Tulving and colleagues (1988) regard amnesia specifically as a difficulty with episodic memory. However, semantic memory is impaired in amnesia including after focal hippocampal lesions, even though it is often less vulnerable to damage than episodic memory (Holdstock *et al.*, 2002; Manns *et al.*, 2003b). New semantic memories may be formed by repetition learning that is not dependent on the hippocampus. As such, Squire and colleagues suggest that amnesia is a deficit in declarative memory (Manns *et al.*, 2003b, Squire, 1992). This explanation offers the most satisfactory description of the pattern of preservation and impairment.

Accounts of amnesia purely in terms of damage to a memory system (whether it be declarative or episodic) are clearly insufficient, in that they offer no account of the function of that system or the underlying mechanisms. One common mechanistic explanation of amnesia is in terms of a deficit of **consolidation** (Squire, 1992). Consolidation is the process by which moment-to-moment changes in brain activity are translated into permanent structural changes in the brain (e.g. by forming new neural connections). One challenge for explaining amnesia in terms of consolidation is in accounting for the fact that amnesia doesn't just affect new learning, but also retrograde loss of memories: a solution to this is to assume that consolidation takes place gradually such that unconsolidated memories are lost after a lesion to the hippocampus. A related account is that the hippocampus (and MTL) is involved in the permanent storage of certain kinds of memory in addition to supporting consolidation. Finally, an alternative suggestion is that the hippocampus (and MTL) are specialized for processing particular kinds of information that are of crucial importance to declarative memory. One kind of information might be contextual cues (Mayes, 1988). Memory for context closely relates to Tulving's (1972) definition of episodic memory as being specifiable in time ("when did the event occur?") and place ("where did the event occur?"), although context can incorporate other types of situational information too. A more specific idea along these lines is that the hippocampus is particularly important for spatial processing both for providing spatial context to past events, but also for using past experiences for orienting within ones current environment (Burgess *et al.*, 2002). These ideas are unpacked in detail in the next section, drawing not only on evidence from amnesic patients, but also from other methodologies.

## Evaluation

Accounting for the learning and memory that amnesics *can* do is as important as understanding what they can't remember. The results broadly support a multiple memory systems view of the brain in which declarative memory is particularly affected in amnesics. Episodic memories may be special by virtue of the fact that they contain rich contextual detail. These contextual details may be linked together by structures in the medial temporal lobe, including the hippocampus, and may gradually be consolidated over time. Newly learned semantic facts may initially be context dependent but become less so over time. This view of amnesia has been refined over the years as a result of more being learned about the function of different structures in the medial temporal lobe and their interaction with other brain regions. These are considered in subsequent sections.

## FUNCTIONS OF THE HIPPOCAMPUS AND MEDIAL TEMPORAL LOBES IN MEMORY

This section considers in more detail the role that the hippocampus (and surrounding regions) plays in consolidation, in the permanent storage of memories, and in large-scale spatial memory. The extent to which different theories can account for the empirical data will be discussed.

## Consolidation

The initial formation of memories involves an increase in the probability that a postsynaptic neuron will fire in response to neurotransmitters released from presynaptic neurons. In the laboratory, this has been studied by applying brief, high-frequency stimulation to presynaptic neurons. The induced change in responsiveness of the postsynaptic neuron is termed **long-term potentiation** (or LTP) and was first reported by Lømo (1966). In awake rats, the effects are sustained over weeks. This process is accompanied by rapid modification of existing synaptic proteins, followed by synthesis of new proteins that leads to a modified synapse (Pittenger & Kandel, 2003). The time course of this process can be assessed by injecting chemicals that inhibit protein synthesis at various stages after learning and is found to occur within an hour (Agranoff *et al.*, 1966). This synaptic consolidation, although originally studied in the hippocampus, turns out to be a universal property of the nervous system.

Dudai (2004) distinguishes between two types of consolidation: a fast *synaptic consolidation* that may occur anywhere in the nervous system (and based on LTP), and a slower *system consolidation* that may be related particularly to the hippocampus and declarative memory. In rats, this can be studied by lesioning the hippocampus at various stages after learning (Kim & Fanselow, 1992). These studies suggest that, in rats, it takes around one month for system consolidation to be complete. In humans, evidence from retrograde amnesia suggests that the process may take years.

One of the most consistently reported findings in the amnesia literature is that recall of events in the retrograde period shows a temporal gradient such that memories from earlier in life are easier to recall than those later in life. This has been termed **Ribot's law**, after its discoverer (Ribot, 1882). For example, Butters and Cermak (1986) reported the case of a college professor, PZ, who became amnesic a couple of years after writing his auto-biography. When tested for his ability to recollect events from his life, a clear temporal gradient was found, with more remote memories spared. The most common explanation for this phenomenon is in terms of consolidation theory—namely, that the older the event, the more consolidated it is and the less dependent on the hippocampus it is (Squire, 1992; Squire & Bayey, 2007). In effect, the memory is slowly transferred from the hippo-campus to the cortex. However, other explanations for the temporal gradient exist.

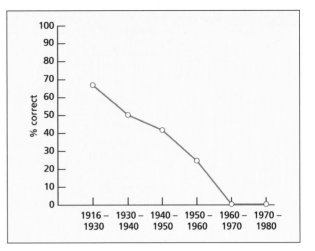

PZ was an eminent scientist (born 1914) who developed amnesia 2 years after writing his autobiography. His ability to recall events from his past life showed a clear temporal gradient.

From Butters and Cermak, 1986. © Cambridge University Press. Reproduced with permission.

The mechanism by which this transfer of information occurs is not well understood but is assumed to involve the hippocampal formation sending synaptic messages to neocortical neurons that promote consolidation mechanisms in the neocortex itself. It has been suggested that "replaying" memories during sleep (and possibly during relaxed wakefulness) is involved in this process. Neural recordings in rats suggest that patterns of activity in the hippocampus and visual cortex that occurred during a previous waking event are reactivated, in the same temporal order, during certain phases of sleep (Ji & Wilson, 2007).

A number of connectionist models have been developed to mimic long-term consolidation of declarative memory. The model of McClelland *et al.* (1995) provides a computational motivation for having a slow transfer mechanism. They

### KEY TERMS

**Ribot's law**
The observation that memories from early in life tend to be preserved in amnesia.

## DIFFERENT EXPLANATIONS FOR TEMPORAL GRADIENTS IN AMNESIA

1. The temporal gradient can arise because the stimuli are not carefully matched across decades (i.e. the stimuli for more remote decades are easier) (Sanders & Warrington, 1971).
2. The apparent loss of retrograde knowledge is anterograde amnesia in disguise. Alcoholics who subsequently go on to develop Korsakoff's amnesia may not have fully encoded the memories in the first instance. This cannot, of course, account for all cases but it may account for some.
3. Older memories become more semantic-like and less episodic with the passing of time, because they get rehearsed more often. They become more like stories than memories (Cermak & O'Connor, 1983).
4. Each time an old event is remembered, this creates a new memory for that event. The older the event, the greater the number of traces and the more resilient to brain damage it will be (Nadel & Moscovitch, 1997).
5. The hippocampus has a time-limited role and the more consolidated the memory is, the less dependent on the hippocampus it is (Squire, 1992).

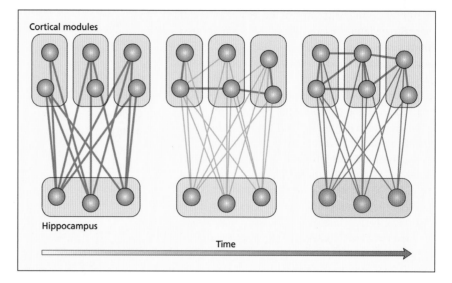

In models that assume a time-limited role for the hippocampus in memory consolidation, the hippocampus initially acts to bind together different aspects of memory (e.g. perceptual, affective, linguistic components) represented in disparate regions of the brain. Over time, these different aspects of the memory trace may be linked as part of a corticocortical network that is largely independent of the hippocampus. Active units/connections are shown in red.

From Frankland and Bontempi, 2005. Reprinted by permission from Macmillan Publishers Ltd. © 2005.

argue that adding a new memory to the neocortex straightaway would significantly distort old memories by a process called catastrophic interference. In their model, the hippocampus learns rapidly and then integrates this information gradually to enable efficient learning without disrupting existing memory structures. For instance, in order for the model to acquire new conceptual knowledge such as "a penguin is a flightless bird" this information would need to be represented separately (as an "episode") in order to prevent it disrupting existing knowledge structures ("birds can fly"). By developing the network gradually both the general rule and the exceptions to it are able to co-exist in long-term memory.

Other evidence in support of the standard consolidation model comes from patients with semantic dementia who have lesions to the anterior temporal lobes but typically spare the hippocampus (Mummery *et al.*, 2000). This is assumed to be part of the storage site after memories have been consolidated. However, these patients do not have intact episodic memory across all time spans and show a reversed temporal gradient to that found in amnesia: namely, better recent than remote memory (Nestor *et al.*, 2002). Although these patients have impoverished language as well as memory, they can be tested using the same cue words for different time periods (e.g. "think of a memory related to a restaurant in 2000–2005, or 1960–1970") or using famous faces (Hodges & Graham, 1998). The explanation for the reversed gradient is that in these patients, memories for recent events have not yet been fully transferred from the hippocampus to the neocortex and so are relatively intact. In contrast, in patients with hippocampal damage (including Alzheimer's dementia) it is recent memories that are lost or otherwise not consolidated.

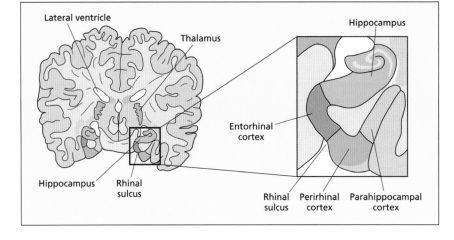

The different regions of the medial temporal lobe.

It is to be noted that the standard consolidation model doesn't make a distinction between the consolidation of episodic and semantic memories: both are grouped under the umbrella of declarative memory and are assumed to depend (initially) on the hippocampus and (subsequently) on the neocortex. However, other structures within the medial temporal lobe may have different roles to play. It has been suggested that the entorhinal cortex supports the acquisition of semantic memory, as is demonstrated in amnesic patients with damage to the hippocampus but relative sparing of this region (Vargha-Khadem *et al.*, 1994; Verfaellie *et al.*, 2000). The entorhinal cortex is the major input and output portal between the hippocampus and the neocortex. Healthy older participants shown faces acquired from different time periods during fMRI suggests that the entorhinal cortex may consolidate over decades, whereas the hippocampus consolidates over years

(Haist *et al.*, 2001). Other research has suggested that the extent of retrograde amnesia is linked to the size of the entorhinal and parahippocampal lesion, but not of the hippocampus itself (Yoneda *et al.*, 1994). Findings such as these suggest that the standard consolidation theory needs to be further refined. However, others have gone further than a simple refinement and suggested that entirely different theories of hippocampal/MTL function are needed.

## Multiple trace theory

In contrast to the standard model of consolidation, others have argued that the hippocampus is involved in some permanent aspects of memory storage (Nadel & Moscovitch, 1997). The term "permanent" doesn't mean that nothing is ever forgotten, only that its role in supporting memory is not time-limited. In the earlier version of the multiple-trace theory, Nadel and Moscovitch (1997) argued that the temporal gradients found

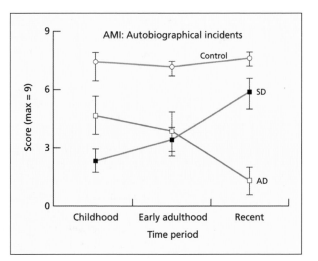

Semantic dementia patients (SD) show a reverse temporal gradient from that found in amnesics with Alzheimer's disease (AD). This has been used as evidence to support a time-limited role of the hippocampus in memory consolidation.

Reprinted from Nestor *et al.*, 2002. © 2002, with permission from Elsevier.

within amnesia were due to multiple memory traces of the event being created whenever an event is retrieved (and laid down in different parts of the medial temporal lobes); so older events are protected from brain damage because of these multiple traces. They cite as evidence in support of their theory the fact that not all amnesic patients show temporal gradients and are impaired, instead, for all remote memories (Cipolotti *et al.*, 2001). They suggest that this is more consistent with the hippocampus playing a permanent role in memory storage, as they regard it as improbable that the brain would evolve a mechanism that takes a lifetime to consolidate memories. Other initial evidence in support of their theory came from fMRI studies showing no difference in medial temporal lobe activity comparing recall of autobiographical events from the recent past relative to the remote past as would be expected if it had a time-limited role (Gilboa *et al.*, 2004). More recent fMRI research has been able to differentiate sub-fields within the hippocampus and suggests that some regions respond to both recent (2 weeks) and remote (10 years) recall of autobiographical memories, and other regions respond to remote but not recent memories, but regions responding more to recent than remote were not found (Bonnici *et al.*, 2013).

The multiple-trace theory has been revised and refined considerably since it was originally described (see Winocur *et al.*, 2010). In particular, the proponents of the model have articulated a clearer description of what kinds of memories are dependent on the hippocampus: namely, contextualized memories but not schematic memories. These relate, approximately, to the concepts of episodic memory (= contextualized) and semantic memory (= schematic) although not exactly. For instance, some recently acquired semantic knowledge may be linked to the context in which it was learned (e.g. memory of the classroom setting) and hence depend on the hippocampus. By contrast, some episodic events may have been retold so many times as to be schematic in nature and largely disconnected from their original context (and hence not depend on the hippocampus). The model assumes that schematic memories depend on regions such as the neocortex (supporting most semantic memories), but could also include procedural learning (dependent on the basal ganglia), and so on. Different medial temporal lobe regions may also make differential contributions to these processes. One fMRI study concluded that the entorhinal cortex computes the similarities between events (schematic, semantic-like), whereas certain regions in the hippocampus compute the discriminating features of events (contextual, episodic-like) (Bakker *et al.*, 2008).

In this theory, the process of system consolidation should be construed as *transforming* memories over time (from contextualized to schematic; although the initial contextual memories need not be lost) and not *transferring* them, unchanged, from one brain region to another. Insofar as the hippocampus has any bias toward the recent past, this is assumed to reflect the fact that recent memories contain more detailed contextual cues than remote ones (e.g. try to recall your last holiday and then compare it to a holiday when you were around 6 years old). In fact, the hippocampus has been shown to be involved in imagining future events (Addis *et al.*, 2007; Hassabis *et al.*, 2007) which is consistent with a more general role in binding contextual features rather than simply making past events durable. There is some direct evidence that hippocampus-dependent memories may be transformed rather than merely transferred. In rats, conditioned fear associations to stimuli show a temporal gradient depending on the interval between learning and hippocampal lesion. However, the conditioned associations become less sensitive to context manipulations over time suggesting that the nature of the memories are altered rather than simply transferred (Winocur *et al.*, 2007). A complete definition as to what kind of information constitutes "context" is presently lacking. However, one key element is generally considered to be spatial context (i.e. where the event occurred). This is based on evidence, considered below, that the hippocampus stores large-scale maps of space.

## Cognitive map theory

In the 1970s, a number of lines of evidence led to the hypothesis that the hippocampus contains a spatial map of the environment (O'Keefe & Nadel, 1978). O'Keefe (1976) planted electrodes into the hippocampus of rats that subsequently explored an enclosed environment. The firing rate of the neuron was measured when the rat was located at various points in the box. It was found that a given neuron only responded strongly when the rat was at a particular location. Neurons showing this pattern of firing are referred to as **place cells**. Given that each neuron responds to a given place, when a collection of neurons are considered together they could function as a map of the environment. Subsequent research has found that place cells are more complex than originally thought. The responses of place cell are often highly context sensitive. For example, if the environment is substantially changed (e.g. the box is white instead of black), then the place that the neuron codes can also change substantially (Anderson & Jeffery, 2003). It suggests that place cells are not coding space in isolation but integrate space with other kinds of contextual cues—this is likely to be crucial for memory more generally.

It is to be noted that the kind of map (and hence the kind of spatial memory) encoded by the hippocampus is different in kind to that typically studied in tests of visuo-spatial short-term memory (e.g. arrays of colored objects on a screen). Specifically, it relates to the spatial arrangement of landmarks in an environment that can be navigated around (allocentric space). Other brain regions, notably, the parietal lobes may code maps of space that are egocentric (i.e. coded relative to the observer) that serve largely perceptual and motor functions.

**KEY TERMS**

**Place cells**
Neurons that respond when an animal is in a particular location in allocentric space (normally found in the hippocampus).

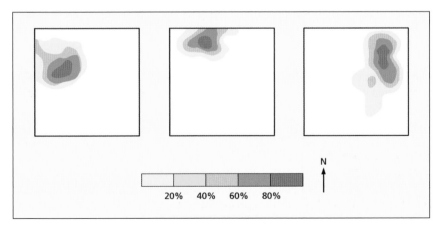

The firing rate of three different cells (the darker the shade, the more likely it is to respond). The data is obtained using single-cell recordings from the rat hippocampus.

Adapted from Chakraborty *et al.*, 2004.

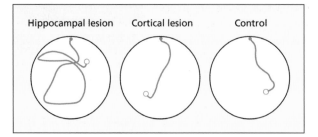

The route taken by a typical rat in the Morris water maze. The control rat and ones with cortical lesions can remember the location of the submerged platform and go directly there, whereas the hippocampal-lesioned rats find the platform by trial and error.

From Morris *et al.*, 1982. Reprinted by permission from Macmillan Publishers Ltd. © 1982.

Further evidence that the hippocampus stores a spatial map of the environment comes from lesion studies of rats using the Morris water maze (Morris *et al.*, 1982). If a rat is placed in a container filled with milky water in which there is a submerged platform, then the rat will, by trial and error, eventually find the platform (rats are good swimmers!). As the water is milky, the platform is not visible and the rat must learn the route. If the rat is placed in the environment again, it will remember the location and swim there directly without trial and-error meandering. If, however, the hippocampus is lesioned, then the rat is unable to learn the location of the platform and relies once more on trial and error.

Most of the evidence cited above comes from studies of rats. But what is the evidence, if any, that the human hippocampus contains a spatial map? Single-cell recordings in the primate (Rolls *et al.*, 1997) and human (Ekstrom *et al.*, 2003) hippocampus suggest that place cells are to be found in these species. However, there is at least one crucial difference from the rodent place cells. In rodents, the place cells respond when the animal is in that physical location. Many human and primate place cells can also respond to the mental location of the animal (e.g. if they attend to a particular location in space that differs from their current physical location).

Functional imaging and lesion studies in humans have provided converging evidence that the hippocampus stores large-scale allocentric maps of the environment. In humans, there also appears to be a greater lateralization of this function than in rodents. The right hippocampus seems to be particularly important for spatial memory, whereas the left hippocampus appears to be more specialized for remembering and storing other contextual details. Hartley *et al.* (2003) found that finding one's way through the virtual town activated the right hippocampus relative to a baseline task of following a visible trail. Spiers *et al.* (2001a) used a similar paradigm in groups of patients with either left or right hippocampal damage. The patients had to learn to navigate through the town. During their exploration they would collect different objects from different characters in different locations. Their memory was assessed by map drawing, together with forced-choice recognition of locations, characters and objects. The patients with right hippocampal damage were impaired on navigation, map drawing and scene recognition. In contrast, the patients with left hippocampal damage had problems in remembering who gave them the objects, and the order and location in which they were received.

Is the involvement of the hippocampus in spatial memory time-limited (as predicted by the standard consolidation model) or does the hippocampus store permanent spatial maps (as predicted by the cognitive map theory and multiple-trace theory)? There is some evidence that amnesic patients can find their way around old neighborhoods despite being unable to learn to find their way in new ones (Rosenbaum *et al.*, 2000). This supports the standard consolidation model. However, others have suggested that this preserved spatial memory appears to be schematic and lacking detail and so there may still be a role for the hippocampus (Winocur *et al.*, 2010). Consistent with this, a London taxi-driver who suffered bilateral damage of the hippocampi retained a broad knowledge of the city (the main roads) but not detailed knowledge including the side roads (Maguire *et al.*, 2006).

There is evidence that other regions within the medial temporal lobes also contribute to orienting within spatial environments. The entorhinal cortex (at least in rats) also contains cells that fire when the animal is in certain locations within a particular environment, but rather than responding to a single location they respond to multiple locations within a repeating, triangular grid-like structure (Hafting *et al.*, 2005). They are referred to as **grid cells**. Their function is not fully known but they may enable links between visuo-spatial and locomotive spatial signals. The parahippocampal complex, by contrast, contains visual representations of scenes and landmarks (Epstein & Kanwisher, 1998). Finally, the perirhinal cortex is linked to memory and perception of complex objects (Murray & Bussey, 1999) and is also linked to semantic memory (Davies *et al.*, 2004). Bachevalier and Nemanic (2008) report a lesion study in the macaque showing that parahippocampal lesions impair memory for the locations of objects in an array, whereas perirhinal lesions impaired learning about object features. Although this summary presents the briefest discussion of the wider contribution of MTL regions outside the hippocampus, there are several key points to note. The first is that while the function of all of these regions could reasonably be subsumed within the umbrella label of "declarative memory" that to do so would be an over-simplification. These regions show an interesting specificity in the type of information that they process. What is less clear is whether these regions are involved in both learning and storage, and how they interact with other regions of the brain.

## DOES DRIVING A TAXI INCREASE YOUR GRAY MATTER?

London taxi drivers are required to sit an exam (called "the knowledge") in which they are given two locations within the city and must generate a plausible route. Maguire *et al.* (2000) studied the gray matter volume of cab drivers (using voxel-based morphometry) and found that the volume in the right hippocampus is greater than in IQ-matched individuals. Could it be that the taxi drivers choose their occupation because they have better spatial memories (and bigger hippocampi)? It turns out that the amount of time spent in the job correlates with the volume of the region. This suggests that this region may expand with usage and argues

London taxi drivers must learn the best route to travel between any two points in the city. This is linked to an increased size of the hippocampus.

against a predisposition influencing the choice of occupation. This has subsequently been confirmed with a longitudinal study of the brain volume of the hippocampi of London taxi drivers as they acquire detailed knowledge of the city layout (Woollett & Maguire, 2011).

## Evaluation

Initial research on amnesia arising from medial-temporal lobe lesions suggested a wide-ranging impairment in declarative memory. While later research has not completely over-turned this conclusion it has suggested a far more intricate picture. This new understanding has arrived through a more detailed consideration of anatomical structures other than the hippocampus, and through carefully controlled studies of the function of the hippocampus. One function of the hippocampus that is universally accepted is its role in system consolidation. What is less clear is how this process should be conceptualized (e.g. transferring memories, transforming memories). Another key line of controversy is whether the hippocampus permanently stores certain kinds of information (e.g. that are required for detailed episodic remembering) and/or is specialized for processing certain kinds of information (e.g. spatial maps) that are crucial for some kinds of memory more than others (reliving memories as scenes from the past).

## THEORIES OF REMEMBERING, KNOWING, AND FORGETTING

### Recall versus recognition and familiarity versus recollection

This chapter has, thus far, concentrated on different types of memory *systems*. But to what extent do different types of memory *tasks* use different memory systems? Within the domain of explicit tests of memory (i.e. in which participants are directly asked to remember), the main tasks used are tests of **recognition memory** and tests of **recall**. In typical tests of recall, participants may be shown a list of words and asked to recall them in any order (free recall), in the order given (serial recall) or given a prompt (e.g. "one of the words begins with W," cued recall). In typical tests of recognition memory, participants may be shown a list of words and then, at test, asked to decide whether a given word was previously presented on that list (single probe recognition) or shown two words and asked to decide which one was previously presented in the list (forced choice recognition). Some typical results are shown in the figure at the top of p. 219.

Mandler (1980) proposed that recognition memory consists of two distinct mechanisms and that this could account for its general advantage over tests of recall. One mechanism, **familiarity**, is considered to be context free and the recognized item just feels familiar. The other mechanism, **recollection**, is context dependent and involves remembering specific information from the study episode. Tests of recall are considered almost exclusively to be dependent on recollection. Recollection and familiarity are associated with different "feelings" or conscious states. These have been called "remembering" and "knowing," respectively (Gardiner, 2000; Tulving, 1985). Recollection, in particular, has been described as "mental time travel," in which contextual detail is placed in a personal past (Wheeler *et al.*, 1997).

If amnesia reflects a deficit of contextual information, then it would be expected that they would be more reliant on familiarity and that recognition memory may be less impaired than recall. However, in most amnesics this is not the case (Kopelman & Stanhope, 1998). It is important to note that most amnesics have damage to several regions in and around the medial temporal lobes and if the mechanisms supporting familiarity and recollection are separate but nearby, then deficits in both could well be the norm. A number of reports of patients with very selective damage to the hippocampus do, however, support the notion that recollection can be specifically impaired (Aggleton & Brown, 1999; Bastin *et al.*, 2004). Mayes and colleagues have documented the remarkable patient, YR (Mayes *et al.*, 2001, 2002, 2004). Not only was YR's recognition memory for single items (e.g. words, pictures) spared but she could recognize previously seen stimulus pairs provided they were of the same kind (e.g. word–word, object–object) but *not* if they were of a different kind (e.g. object–location, word–object, face–name). It is suggested that associations between different kinds of material are recollection-based and depend on the hippocampus, whereas associations between stimuli of the same kind can also be performed by the perirhinal cortex and may be familiarity-based (Mayes *et al.*, 2007). Therefore lesions of the hippocampus may spare performance on the latter tests, despite the tests falling within the remit of declarative memory.

In contrast to the position that familiarity and recollection are different processes, some have argued that they are just stronger and weaker forms of the same process (Wixted & Stretch, 2004) or that the processes involved in familiarity are a subset of those involved in recollection. For example, recollection may require the additional use of frontal mechanisms (Manns *et al.*, 2003a; Squire *et al.*, 2004). There is some problematic evidence for these accounts. Ranganath *et al.* (2004) conducted an fMRI study that shows hippocampal activity in recollection, whereas familiarity selectively activated an adjacent region of cortex, called the perirhinal cortex. A more recent single-case study of a human patient with a perirhinal lesion but spared hippocampus demonstrated impaired familiarity but spared recollection (Bowles *et al.*, 2007). This supports the idea that familiarity and recollection have partly separable neural processes.

Eichenbaum *et al.* (2007) offer an account of how recollection and familiarity depend on different regions within the medial temporal lobes and relates it specifically to the kinds of information that these regions are specialized for processing. Specifically, perirhinal cortex is assumed

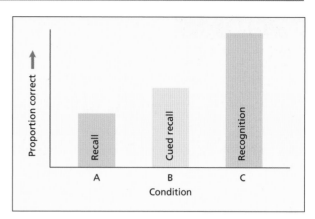

Typical results from different types of memory test. From Parkin, 1999.

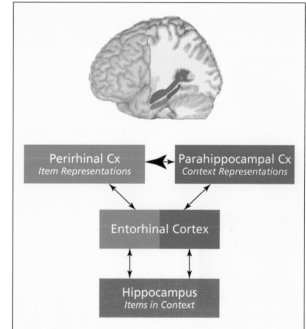

In Eichenbaum *et al.*'s (2007) model, the perirhinal cortex is assumed to process item representations (important for familiarity), the parahippocampal cortex is assumed to process "context" (including scene perception) and the hippocampus binds items in context (important for recollection).

**KEY TERM**

**Levels-of-processing account**
Information that is processed semantically is more likely to be remembered than information that is processed perceptually.

to process item representations (important for familiarity), the parahippocampal cortex is assumed to process "context" (including scene perception) and the hippocampus binds items in context (important for recollection).

## Why do we forget things?

Forgetting may be important for efficient use of memory, rather than a design fault. Access to previous information needs to be prioritized so that the most relevant information is retrieved. One needs to remember where, for example, the car is parked today not where it was parked last week. It may be adaptive to lose information for some episodes, or to blend information from different episodes together (e.g. to be able to remember where one *tends* to park the car). Explanations of why we forget have tended to be divided into the stages of encoding, storage or retrieval (for a more unitary account of forgetting, see Wixted, 2004). Each of these may be relevant to some degree.

If information is not processed adequately at encoding it may be forgotten. The **levels-of-processing account** of memory states that information that is processed semantically is more likely to be remembered than information that is processed perceptually (Craik & Lockhart, 1972). For example, if participants are asked to generate an adjective for a list of words (e.g. house → big) relative to generating a rhyme (house → mouse) or counting letters (house → 5), they are much more able to later recall those words (Eysenck, 1974). Regions in the frontal lobes may be important for selecting the attributes to attend to at encoding (Kapur *et al.*, 1994). Some studies have examined forgetting due to encoding directly. Wagner *et al.* (1998b) scanned participants when they were studying a list of words that were subsequently tested in a recognition memory test. Following the test, they then went back and looked at the brain activity during encoding to ask the question: does the brain activity at encoding predict which items are later going to be recognized and which will be forgotten? Activity in left temporal (parahippocampal) and a left ventrolateral prefrontal site at encoding was predictive of later recognizing versus forgetting. The frontal activity may relate to selection of features to encode, whereas the medial temporal activity reflects actual memory formation. Electrode recordings in humans have shown that synchronous firing of neurons in hippocampal and surrounding cortical regions predicts subsequent memory versus forgetting (Fell *et al.*, 2001). An amnesic patient has been shown to demonstrate normal frontal lobe activity at encoding despite having no subsequent memory (see Buckner *et al.*, 1999).

Distinguishing between forgetting due to loss from storage versus a failure of retrieval is very hard in practice. This is because information that appears inaccessible may subsequently be remembered (implying it was never really lost),

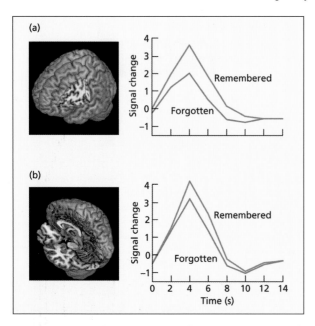

Activity at encoding in (a) left ventrolateral prefrontal cortex and (b) left parahippocampal region predicts whether the word is likely to be subsequently remembered or forgotten.

or information may appear accessible when certain tests are used (e.g. implicit tests) but not others. If one accepts a multiple memory systems view, then it is conceivable that memories can be lost from one store but not other stores.

Tulving (1983) has argued that the extent to which there is contextual similarity between the retrieval attempt and the initial encoding phase predicts the likelihood of remembering versus forgetting. This has been termed the **encoding specificity hypothesis**. Godden and Baddeley (1975) taught people lists of words either on land or underwater (when diving), and tested their recall either on land or underwater. Recall was better when learning and test were in the same location (land–land, sea–sea) relative to when they differed (land–sea, sea–land). Similarly, alcoholics may hide objects when drunk, forget where they are when sober, but remember the location again on a subsequent binge (Goodwin *et al.*, 1969). In these experiments, forgetting appears to reflect retrieval difficulties rather than storage difficulties.

What type of mechanism gives way to forgetting things that have already been encoded? Two broad explanations exist: passive mechanisms such as trace decay (memories spontaneously weaken), or active mechanisms such as interference and inhibition (memories weaken through interactions with each other or with strategic control processes). Although trace decay is hard to rule out altogether, there is good evidence for more active forgetting mechanisms. Anderson *et al.* (1994) devised a memory paradigm consisting of three phases. In the first phase, participants study lists of words associated with several different category labels (e.g. fruit–orange, fruit–banana). In the second phase, they rehearse some of the associations (e.g. fruit–orange) but not others (e.g. fruit–banana). In the test phase they are given the category labels (e.g. fruit–) and asked to generate the initial studied words. Performance on unstudied exemplars (e.g. banana) was worse than for studied items in the second phase and, crucially, was worse than that expected if the second phase had been omitted altogether. Anderson *et al.* (1994) argue that the act of retrieval causes active inhibition of similar competing memories. This has been termed **retrieval-induced forgetting**. To return to the car analogy, remembering where one parked the car today may actively inhibit memories for where it was parked on other days.

The previous section suggested that in some situations memories can *automatically* be inhibited, leading to forgetting, but can memories be inhibited *voluntarily*? Can we choose to forget? Experiments using the **directed forgetting** paradigm suggest that it is possible. In directed forgetting experiments, participants are read two lists of words. In the experimental condition, after the first list they are told that this was a practice block and the list can be forgotten. In the control condition, they are told that the first list needs to be remembered. After both lists have been presented they are instructed to recall from both lists even though they had previously been instructed to forget them. Recall is generally worse for the words given forget instructions (Bjork, 1998). Conway and Fthenaki (2003) found that lesions to the right frontal lobe disrupted the ability

**KEY TERMS**

**Encoding specificity hypothesis**
Events are easier to remember when the context at retrieval is similar to the context at encoding.

**Retrieval-induced forgetting**
Retrieval of a memory causes active inhibition of similar competing memories.

**Directed forgetting**
Forgetting arising because of a deliberate intention to forget.

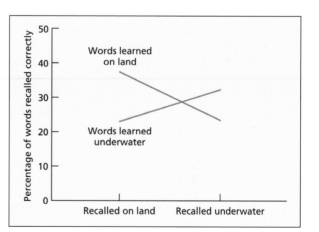

Words are better remembered if they are both learned and recalled in the same context.

From Baddeley, 1990.

**Constructive memory**
The act of remembering construed in terms of making inferences about the past, based on what is currently known and accessible.

**False memory**
A memory that is either partly or wholly inaccurate but is accepted as a real memory by the person doing the remembering.

to do direct forgetting but retrieval induced forgetting remained intact. This demonstrates a dissociation between voluntary or strategic forgetting, on the one hand, and automatic or rehearsal-based forgetting, on the other. Anderson *et al.* (2004) conducted an fMRI study in which pairs of words (e.g. jaw–gum, steam–train) were learned and then, at test, cue words (e.g. jaw–, steam–) were presented and participants were instructed either to remember the associate or not remember it. Not-remembering instructions relative to remembering instructions were linked to activity in the left and right dorsolateral prefrontal cortex. Remembering relative to not-remembering instructions were linked to activity in the hippocampus.

## Memory distortions and false memories

One pervasive metaphor for memory is in terms of a store of memory traces, and the act of remembering involves the retrieval of traces from the store (see Roediger, 1980). This metaphor is misleading: the past is not, by and large, represented in different brain structures from those concerned with dealing with the present. The alternative view is that the act of remembering can be construed as making inferences about the past based on what is currently known and accessible. This contrasting approach to the storehouse metaphor is termed the **constructive memory** approach (Schacter *et al.*, 1998). Studies based on the constructive memory approach have tended to rely on evidence of memory distortions, or false memories, rather than forgetting. A **false memory** is a memory that is either partly or wholly inaccurate, but is accepted as a real memory by the person doing the remembering.

Roediger and McDermott (1995) developed a paradigm that could induce high levels of false recall and false recognition in non-clinical populations. At study, participants are read lists of words (e.g. bed, night, tired . . .) that are semantically related to a critical word that is never presented (e.g. sleep). At test, participants claim to remember many of the critical words. They do so with high confidence and will attribute recollective experience to the false recognition (not just familiarity). If some of the lists are presented in male and female voices they will state that the critical word "sleep" was heard in a particular voice, even if the instructions encourage them not to guess (Payne *et al.*, 1996).

How can these results be explained? One explanation is that the critical word is implicitly activated at encoding through a semantic network (Underwood, 1965). However, it is not clear why this would result in a feeling of remembering as opposed to familiarity. Another explanation is that participants consciously think about the critical word ("sleep") at encoding and subsequently confuse thinking for hearing. One problem for this theory is that false recognition can be induced using abstract shapes presented at study that are based on a non-presented prototype (Koutstaal *et al.*, 1999). It is unlikely that participants would consciously generate other abstract shapes at study. A more satisfactory explanation is that false recognition/recall occurs because the features of the non-presented item reactivate the stored features relating to true events (Schacter & Slotnick, 2004). Evidence for this comes from the observation of hippocampal activity in both true and false recognition observed by fMRI (Cabeza *et al.*, 2001). In some situations, amnesic patients with hippocampal lesions may be less susceptible to false memories (because they are unable to store the information that gives rise to

Try reading aloud these lists of words to a friend and then ask them to recall as many of them as possible. Do they misremember hearing the words "sleep," "foot," and "bread"? (Lists taken from Roediger and McDermott, 1995.)

| | | |
|---|---|---|
| bed | shoe | butter |
| rest | hand | food |
| awake | toe | eat |
| tired | kick | sandwich |
| dream | sandals | rye |
| wake | soccer | jam |
| snooze | yard | milk |
| blanket | walk | flour |
| doze | ankle | jelly |
| slumber | arm | dough |
| snore | boot | crust |
| nap | inch | slice |
| peace | sock | wine |
| yawn | smell | loaf |
| drowsy | mouth | toast |

the distortion) giving them paradoxically better memory than controls (Mullally *et al.*, 2012).

There are some brain differences between true and false recognition. If words are initially presented on either the left or right side, then a contralateral ERP component is subsequently observed for true but not false memories (Fabiani *et al.*, 2000). Moreover, in an fMRI study involving abstract shapes, activity in early visual regions was found for true but not false memories (Slotnick & Schacter, 2004). Why don't participants use this sensory signal to avoid false recognition? It is possible that the difference between true and false memories lies within implicit memory systems and makes little contribution to the conscious memory evaluation.

## THE ROLE OF THE PREFRONTAL CORTEX IN LONG-TERM MEMORY

Fletcher and Henson (2001) offer a simple and effective way of characterizing the role of prefrontal cortex in long-term memory: namely "working with memory." This is obviously a

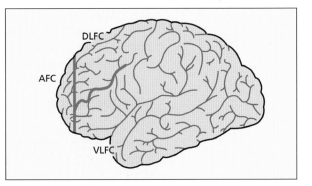

A number of researchers have made a distinction between the separate functions of the ventrolateral (VL), dorsolateral (DL) and anterior frontal (AF) cortex of the lateral frontal lobe.

From Fletcher and Henson, 2001. Reproduced with permission of Oxford University Press.

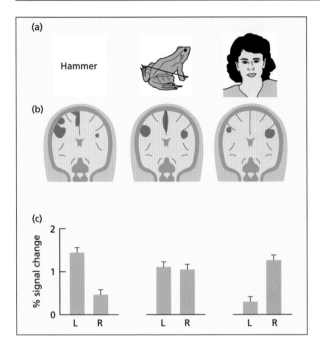

Attending to verbal and non-verbal stimuli at memory encoding has different consequences for left and right prefrontal activity.

Reprinted from Kelley et al., 1998. © 1998 with permission from Elsevier.

play-on-words with its parallel function in the short-term memory domain, i.e. working memory. Working memory and working-with-memory should not be thought of as separate brain mechanisms: both require maintaining and manipulating information that is currently accessible but differ only in whether that information is attributed to past or present events.

## Memory encoding

The ventrolateral PFC has been linked to long-term memory encoding which, in broader cognitive terms, may be a by-product of its role in selecting and maintaining information within working memory (the left ventrolateral region being synonymous with Broca's area). As already noted, activity in this region predicts subsequent remembering relative to forgetting (Wagner et al., 1998b). This region is associated with levels-of-processing manipulations in which semantic versus shallow processing of a stimulus is compared using functional imaging (Kapur et al., 1994). The left hemisphere may be important during verbal encoding, and the right hemisphere may be important when pictures or faces are presented (Wagner et al., 1998a).

The dorsolateral PFC is implicated in manipulating (e.g. ordering) information in working memory (Petrides, 2005). In memory encoding this region (along with ventrolateral PFC) is activated more when presented with structured (e.g. 2468) versus unstructured (e.g. 3972) digit strings (Bor et al., 2004). During encoding of words, dorsolateral prefrontal cortex (DLPFC) activation was predictive of subsequent semantic clustering during free recall (e.g. recalling names of fruit together; Long et al., 2010). Similarly, when participants were asked to reorder a set of words at encoding (versus passively rehearse) then activity in dorsolateral PFC predicted subsequent long-term memory for those reordered items, but ventral regions predicted long-term memory on both reordered and rehearsed trials (Blumenfeld & Ranganath, 2006).

## Monitoring and memory retrieval

In addition to its role in encoding, Fletcher and Henson (2001) suggest that the dorsolateral PFC (particularly in the right hemisphere) is involved in evaluating what has been retrieved from long-term memory—so-called monitoring. This also relates to the concept of source memory and recollective experience discussed in more detail below.

Retrieval demands can vary, depending on the type of retrieval cue provided (e.g. free recall, cued retrieval or recognition) and/or the amount of information that needs to be retrieved (e.g. the amount of contextual information). Activity in the dorsolateral region, particularly on the right, is greatest when the retrieval cue is minimal (e.g. free recall; Fletcher *et al.*, 1998); is greatest when context must be recollected compared with simple recognition (Henson *et al.*, 1999b); and is greatest when confidence in memory judgments are low irrespective of whether the stimulus was indeed old or new (Henson *et al.*, 2000). Maril *et al.* (2001) found that activity was greatest in the right DLPFC when participants were in a tip-of-the-tongue state (induced by cues such as: Chinatown + director, Iraq + capital), relative to when they were certain that they did not know the answer, or when the solution was accessible to them. This also suggests that activity in the region is related to uncertainty (in the tip-of-the-tongue state) rather than retrieval success or failure.

## Experiential states

As noted previously, recognition memory is associated with different kinds of experiential states termed familiarity and recollection. These are frequently discussed in terms of the contributions of different structures within the medial temporal lobes, but prefrontal regions may contribute too. For instance, prefrontal cortex may be responsible for making decisions based on the information that resides in medial temporal structures (and linking other kinds of information such as schemas, reward outcomes, etc.). Consistent with this, fMRI activity in the hippocampus was found to predict an implicit measure of memory (amount of time looking at old/new items), whereas activity in prefrontal cortex was linked to conscious recollection judgments (Hannula & Ranganath, 2009). In one recognition memory test using fMRI, participants were asked to judge whether they remember any context detail, or whether they know that they have seen it before but do not recollect context (Henson *et al.*, 1999a). A left anterior frontal region was associated with "remember" responses and explained as retrieval of contextual detail, whereas a right dorsolateral frontal region was associated with "know" responses and explained as greater memory monitoring due to lack of certainty.

## Source monitoring

**Source monitoring** is the process by which retrieved memories are attributed to their original context; for example, whether the event was seen or imagined, whether the story was told by Tim or Bob, whether the event happened in the morning or evening, and so on. This is closely related to the process of recollection that has already been considered. However, Johnson and colleagues argue that placing an event in context involves an active evaluation process rather than directly retrieving information that specifies the origin of the memory (Johnson, 1988; Johnson *et al.*, 1993). Moreover, the evaluation is based on qualitative characteristics of the information retrieved, such as the level of perceptual, temporal, spatial, semantic and affective information. External events contain richer spatial, temporal, affective and perceptual detail than mental events (thoughts, imagination), whereas the latter may contain information about cognitive strategies.

To give an example from this literature, Johnson *et al.* (1988) asked participants to distinguish between memories of heard and imagined words. One group of participants heard some words in the experimenter's voice and was asked to imagine another set of words in the experimenter's voice. These participants made more source confusions than another group who heard words in the

How can we distinguish between memories for heard words and memories for imagined words? Source monitoring involves an active evaluation of the quality and content of the retrieved information.

experimenter's voice and were asked to imagine another set of words in their own voice. Encoding of more perceptually distinct features can aid source monitoring (deciding whether a word was heard or imagined) even if the perceptual features are imagined.

Information relating to source may be contained in regions throughout the brain that processes perceptual, semantic and affective information. Within the medial temporal lobes, research using fMRI suggests that the hippocampus (and parahippocampal cortex) may be differentially activated by source recognition and the perirhinal cortex by item recognition (Davachi *et al.*, 2003).

Brain lesions to the prefrontal cortex also disrupt source monitoring. These patients have difficulties in putting memories in their spatial and temporal context despite having generally good recognition memory (Janowsky *et al.*, 1989; Milner *et al.*, 1991b). Prefrontal lesions may also impair source memory for spatial context even when the patients claim to have subjective "remember" experiences (Duarte *et al.*, 2005). Damage to the parietal lobes, by contrast, does not impair source monitoring but these patients tend to lack confidence in their memory judgments (Simons *et al.*, 2010) perhaps due to having lower imagery of remembered events.

## Memory for temporal context

It may be that different regions within the PFC contribute to source memory in different ways. For instance, one claim is that the orbitofrontal cortex is particularly specialized for temporal context. Remembering when something happened (or which happened more recently) may require a different kind of cognitive mechanism, because memories do not come conveniently time-stamped. Evaluating temporal context may rely on other strategies such as memory strength or associations between temporally adjacent items. Patients with lesions in the orbitofrontal cortex may have problems in temporal source monitoring, but not spatial source monitoring or deficits in standard tests of memory recognition/recall (Duarte *et al.*, 2010). Functional imaging suggests that the region is involved in successful *encoding* of temporal context but not necessarily its retrieval (Duarte *et al.*, 2010).

Lesions in the orbitofrontal region are also associated with a neurological symptom called **confabulation** (Gilboa & Moscovitch, 2002). Confabulating patients generate false memories either spontaneously or when prompted. For example, when one patient was asked about the Falklands war, she spontaneously described a fictitious holiday to the islands (Damasio *et al.*, 1985). She pictured herself strolling with her husband, and buying local trinkets in a store. When asked

**KEY TERMS**

**Confabulation**
A memory that is false and sometimes self-contradictory without an intention to lie.

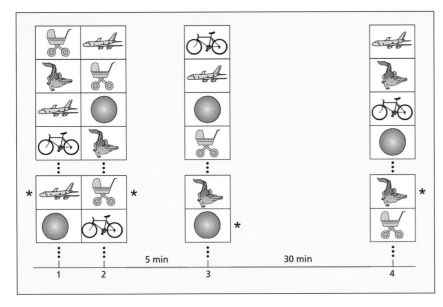

In the task devised by Schnider, participants must remember whether an item was previously presented in the *current* list (marked by *). However, some items are repeated between lists too (e.g. the crocodile appears on several lists) and confabulating patients have particular difficulties with these items.

From Schnider and Ptak, 1999. Reprinted by permission from Macmillan Publishers Ltd.

by the experimenter what language they speak there, she confidently replied: "Falklandese, what else?" One theory is that confabulation is related to temporal context confusion, such that confabulated memories represent blends of information from real memories (including, perhaps, memories for news and film clips) across different time periods (Schnider, 2003; Schnider & Ptak, 1999; Schnider *et al.*, 2000). Schnider argues that the deficient mechanism is one of inhibiting irrelevant memories rather than context retrieval per se. Evidence from this comes from a number of studies in which confabulators are compared with non-confabulating amnesics. The task of the patients is to detect whether a word or picture has previously been presented before in the current list. If patients producing spontaneous confabulations are given a word that was on a previous list but that is new to the current list, then they incorrectly state that it was in fact on the current list. This may be consistent with a wider role of this region in tasks such as extinction learning (i.e. learning that a previously rewarded stimulus should no longer be responded to).

## Evaluation

A useful metaphor for the functions of the prefrontal cortex in long-term memory is "working with memory." At encoding, this relates closely to the purported role of these regions in working memory: with ventrolateral regions supporting selection/maintenance and dorsolateral regions supporting manipulation (e.g. ordering to-be-remembered items). At retrieval, the prefrontal cortex may be involved in monitoring and evaluation of the contents of memory including confidence judgments, experiential states, and source monitoring.

## SUMMARY AND KEY POINTS OF THE CHAPTER

- Traditionally, short-term memory (STM) has been considered as distinct from long-term memory (LTM), although an alternative view regards STM as the temporary activation of LTM. Working memory involves the manipulation of information held within STM and is linked to dorsolateral regions of the prefrontal cortex.

- Long-term memory can be divided into explicit and implicit memory (or declarative/non-declarative), according to whether the content of memory is amenable to conscious report. Explicit memory consists of knowledge of facts (semantic memory) and events (episodic memory). Implicit memory consists primarily of skills and habits (procedural memory) and perceptual knowledge.

- Amnesia can arise from damage to medial temporal lobes, including the hippocampus. It results in selective impairment of declarative memory, leaving implicit memory intact. Both semantic and episodic memory is impaired in amnesia, although the extent of semantic memory impairment is variable.

- Amnesia is typically explained as a deficit in consolidation (i.e. forming of permanent new connections) and produces difficulties in acquiring new declarative memories (anterograde impairment) and retrieving old memories that were not fully consolidated at time of injury (retrograde impairment). It is generally believed that the hippocampus has a time-limited role in consolidation that gives rise to a temporal gradient when damaged (remote memories are spared more than recent memories).

- Recognition memory is generally believed to have two components: recollection (context-dependent) and familiarity (context-independent).

- Although the medial-temporal lobes are, collectively, involved in supporting declarative memory there are important differences between these structures. While the hippocampus is linked to contextual (and particularly spatial) associations, the perirhinal cortex is linked to object memory, the entorhinal cortex to gist memory, and the parahippocampal cortex to scene memory.

- Forgetting can occur because items are not processed deeply enough at encoding and/or because they fail to get consolidated. Forgetting can also occur because of retrieval failure. There is evidence that memory retrieval can actively inhibit other memories.

- The lateral frontal lobes have an important role to play in: (a) maintaining information in working memory; (b) selecting information in the environment to focus on (important for encoding); (c) providing cues and strategies to enable memory retrieval; and (d) evaluating the content of memories (as in "source monitoring").

## EXAMPLE ESSAY QUESTIONS

- Contrast the role of the hippocampus in memory with that of other structures in the medial temporal lobes.
- Is short-term memory distinct from long-term memory? Is short-term memory needed for long-term learning?
- What types of memory are typically impaired in amnesia?
- Are semantic and episodic memory separate memory systems?
- Does the hippocampus have a time-limited role in memory consolidation?
- What is the role of the frontal lobes in memory?

## RECOMMENDED FURTHER READING

- Baddeley, A., Eysenck, M. W., & Anderson, M. (2009). *Memory*. Hove, UK: Psychology Press. A very good starting point, with a focus on cognition rather than neuroscience.
- Tulving, E. & Craik, F. I. M. (2005). *The Oxford handbook of memory*. Oxford, UK: Oxford University Press. Good coverage in all areas.
- Eichenbaum, H. (2012). *The cognitive neuroscience of memory* (2nd edition). Oxford, UK: Oxford University Press. Detailed and up-to-date coverage from molecules to animal models to human studies.

Visit the companion website at www. psypress/cw/ward for:

- References to key papers and readings
- Video interviews on key topics with leading psychologists Larry Squire and Alan Baddeley, as well as a documentary clip featuring a densely amnesiac patient and a lecture with author Jamie Ward on *The Remembering Brain*
- Links to online tests demonstrating implicit memory and testing your own memory capacity
- Multiple choice questions and interactive flashcards to test your knowledge
- Downloadable glossary

# CHAPTER 10

# The hearing brain

## CONTENTS

Sound originates from the motion or vibration of an object; for example, the vibration of the vocal chords, the plucking of a violin string, or the passing of an overhead aircraft. This manifests itself in the surrounding medium, normally air, as changes in pressure in which molecules are alternately squeezed together and stretched apart. The human auditory system is capable of detecting a huge range of changes in air pressure, from around 0.00002 to more than 100 Pascals. However, the role of the hearing brain is not merely to detect such changes. As with vision and other perceptual systems, the goal of hearing is not to create a literal depiction of the outside world, but rather to construct an internal model of the world that can be interpreted and acted upon. This model is constructed not only from ongoing sensory information but also from previous sensory experiences. In vision, a tomato will not be perceived to change color when it is moved from indoor lighting to outdoor lighting (even if the wavelength reflected from it has changed). Hearing operates on the same principles. The hearing brain is also concerned with extracting "constancy" out of an infinitely varying array of sensory input and it will actively interpret the sensory input. For example, we

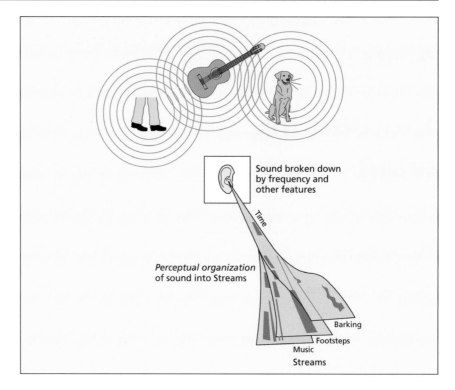

In our noisy environments, our ears often encounter several sounds at once. But, it is the job of the brain (not the ears!) to figure out how many different sound sources (or "streams") there are and what they correspond to. This will depend both on the incoming sensory information and learned knowledge about sounds (e.g. melodies of music, the pitch range of voices).

recognize a familiar tune when presented in a different key and we can recognize a familiar voice in a wide range of acoustic environments (in person, on the telephone, shouting over a megaphone). The hearing brain also uses stored knowledge to supplement the auditory input. If one is listening to a familiar song, such as The Rolling Stone's "Satisfaction," but there are gaps of 2–5 sec in the song ("I can't get no _____"), then auditory cortical areas are more active during the gaps, relative to unfamiliar songs (Kraemer *et al.*, 2005). Our musical and lyrical knowledge can fill in silent gaps in heard songs (or almost silent, given that there is the scanner background noise).

One difference that does exist between the auditory and visual senses is their sensitivity to temporal and spatial information. The auditory system is exquisitely tuned to detect temporal information, such as rapid changes in frequency that characterize certain speech sounds, and in grouping information together over time, such as in extracting melody from music. The different time intervals associated with "dots" and "dashes" in Morse Code are much easier to process when heard than seen (Saenz & Koch, 2008). In contrast, it is generally much easier to locate an object in space with vision than with hearing (Bertelson & Aschersleben, 1998).

This chapter will start by considering how sounds are processed by the early auditory system up to the primary and secondary auditory cortex. It will then go on to consider in more detail how the brain extracts features from the auditory scene, and divides up the auditory world into different streams (e.g. corresponding to different sound sources), and different kinds of information (e.g. "what" versus "where"). The final part of the chapter will consider auditory perception for three different classes of stimuli: music, voices, and speech.

## THE NATURE OF SOUND

One of the simplest sounds has a sinusoid waveform (when pressure change is plotted against time) and these sounds are termed **pure tones**. Pure tones have a characteristic **pitch** that is related to the frequency of the sound wave (measured in Hertz, i.e. vibrations per second). The human auditory system responds to sound frequencies between 20 Hz and 20,000 Hz. The intensity of the sound (i.e. its amplitude when considered as a sine wave) is related to the subjective experience of **loudness**. In perception, it is crucial to make a distinction between the physical properties of a stimulus and their perceived characteristics. Thus, in vision, there is a close relationship between the wavelength of light (a physical property) and color (a psychological property), but the two things are not the same. It is possible to see color without its associated wavelength, as in after-images, and it is possible to process wavelength without perceiving color, as in cerebral achromatopsia. Similarly, in hearing, although pitch is related to the frequency of sounds and loudness is related to the intensity (or amplitude) of sounds. Pitch and loudness are regarded as psychological features of sounds, whereas frequency and intensity are physical properties. For example, the pitch of a low frequency sound appears to get lower if it is made louder and the pitch of a high-frequency sound appears to get higher if it is made louder (Stevens, 1935). Although amplitude and frequency might be independent physical properties of sound waves, the subjective properties most closely associated with them (pitch and loudness) are not processed by the brain in a completely independent way.

In everyday life, pure tones are seldom heard. However, many sounds can be described in terms of combinations of superimposed sinusoids of different frequencies, intensities and phases. For example, musical notes typically contain

## KEY TERMS

**Pure tones**
Sounds with a sinusoid waveform (when pressure change is plotted against time).

**Pitch**
The perceived property of sounds that enables them to be ordered from low to high.

**Loudness**
The perceived intensity of the sound.

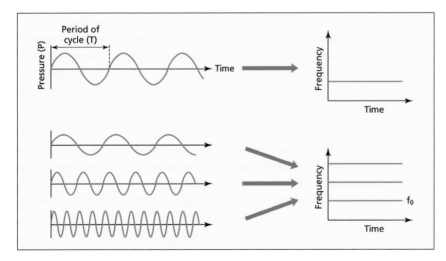

A pure tone (top) consists of sinusoidally varying pressure. Many naturally occurring sounds, such as musical tones (bottom), consist of a regular series of sinusoids of different frequencies. The perceived pitch is related to the lowest frequency in the series (the fundamental frequency, $f_0$).

## KEY TERMS

**Fundamental frequency**
The lowest frequency component of a complex sound that determines the perceived pitch.

**Missing fundamental phenomenon**
If the fundamental frequency of a complex sound is removed, then the pitch is not perceived to change (the brain reinstates it).

**Timbre**
The perceptual quality of a sound enables us to distinguish between different musical instruments.

**Cochlea**
Part of the inner ear that converts liquid-borne sound into neural impulses.

**Basilar membrane**
A membrane within the cochlea containing tiny hair cells linked to neural receptors.

**Primary auditory cortex**
The main cortical area to receive auditory-based thalamic input.

a series of regularly spaced sinusoids. Thus, a piano note of 220 Hz can be described in terms of sinusoids at 220 Hz, 440 Hz, 660 Hz, and so on. The lowest component (in this example 220 Hz), termed the **fundamental frequency** ($f_0$), typically determines the perceived pitch of a musical note. However, if the fundamental frequency is missing from the series (e.g. a tone made up of 440 Hz, 660 Hz, 880 Hz, etc.), then the pitch is still perceived as equivalent to 220 Hz. This is termed the **missing fundamental phenomenon** and is an example of pitch constancy, i.e. two notes with completely different physical characteristics (i.e. a single note of 220 Hz compared with a series of sinusoids at 440 Hz, 660 Hz, 880 Hz, etc.) can have the same perceived pitch.

The relative intensity levels of the different sinusoid components of musical sounds are important for discriminating between the same notes played on different musical instruments i.e. **timbre** (pronounced "tamber"). Timbre, like pitch, is a psychological characteristic of a sound. White noise can be thought of as an infinite sum of sinusoids of every frequency.

## FROM EAR TO BRAIN

The ear contains three main parts: the outer, middle, and inner ear. The outer ear contains the pinna (pinnae in plural), or earlobes, and the auditory canal. Reflections of the sound wave within the folds of the pinna and within the auditory canal can amplify certain sounds and are important for locating a sound source. The middle ear converts airborne vibrations to liquid-borne vibrations with minimal loss of energy. A series of three tiny bones (malleus, incus, and stapes; also called hammer, anvil, and stirrup) transfers the mechanical pressure on the eardrum, at the end of the airborne auditory canal, to a smaller membrane, called the oval window, in the fluid-filled **cochlea**. The inner ear contains chambers that are important both for the senses of hearing (the cochlea) and balance (including the semicircular canals). The cochlea converts liquid-borne sound into neural impulses. A membrane within the cochlea, termed the **basilar membrane**, contains tiny hair cells linked to receptors. Sound induces mechanical movement of the basilar membrane and the hair cells on it. These movements induce a flow of ions through stretch-sensitive ion channels, that initiates neural activity (release of neurotransmitters). The basilar membrane is not uniform but has different mechanical properties at either end (e.g. von Bekesy, 1960). The end nearest the oval window is narrower and stiffer, and shows a maximal deflection to high-frequency sounds. The end nearest the center of its spiral shape is wider and more elastic and shows a maximal deflection to low frequency sounds. As such, different parts of the membrane are sensitive to different frequencies of sound. But note that sounds originating from different parts of space do not stimulate different parts of the membrane (as occurs in the analogous scenario of light stimulating photoreceptors in the eye). The location of sound sources needs to be inferred from other kinds of information (e.g. differences between the signals in the ears).

There are four or five synapses in the auditory pathway from the ear to the brain, starting with projections from the auditory nerve to the cochlear nuclei in the brainstem, and ending with projections from the medial geniculate nucleus to the **primary auditory cortex**, also called A1 or the "core" region (the main cortical area to receive auditory-based thalamic input). The primary auditory cortex is located in Heschl's gyrus in the temporal lobes and is surrounded by adjacent

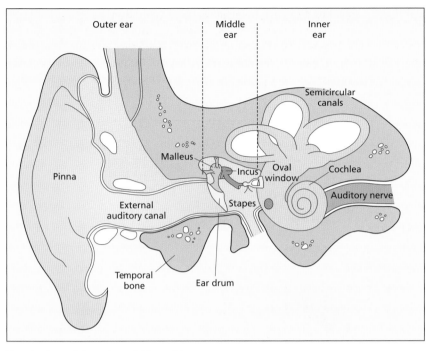

The structure of the outer, middle and inner ear.

secondary auditory cortical areas called the **belt** and **parabelt regions** (Kaas *et al.*, 1999). These secondary regions also receive some input from the medial geniculate nucleus and, hence, damage to the primary auditory cortex does not produce complete deafness but does lead to problems in identifying and locating sounds (Musiek *et al.*, 2007). This ascending pathway is not a passive transmission of information from the ear but, rather, is involved in the active extraction and synthesis of information in the auditory signal. For example, while the cochlear nucleus has 90,000 neurons, the medial geniculate nucleus has 500,000 and the auditory cortex has 100,000,000 (Worden, 1971). In addition, there are descending, top-down, pathways that go as far back as the cochlea itself (Rasmussen, 1953) and may be important in auditory attention.

The early auditory system can be said to have a **tonotopic organization**. Just as different parts of the basilar membrane respond maximally to different sound frequencies, neurons within the auditory nerve respond maximally to certain sound frequencies more than others. Moreover, the nerve bundle is orderly such that neurons responding to higher frequencies are located on the periphery

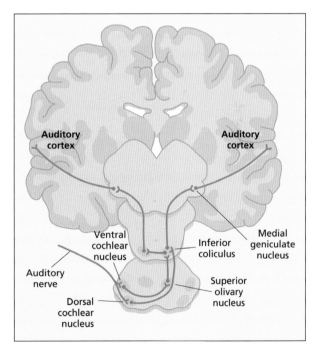

This ascending auditory pathway is not a passive transmission of information from the ear but, rather, is involved in the active extraction and synthesis of information in the auditory signal.

From Gazzaniga *et al.*, 2002. © 2002 W. W. Norton & Company Inc. Reproduced with permission.

and those responding to lower frequencies more centrally (Kiang *et al.*, 1965). To some extent, this organization is carried upwards to the early cortical stages. In both humans (Formisano *et al.*, 2003) and other animals (Merzenich *et al.*, 1973) there is evidence that the central region of the primary auditory cortex responds to lower frequencies and the outer regions, on both sides, to higher frequencies.

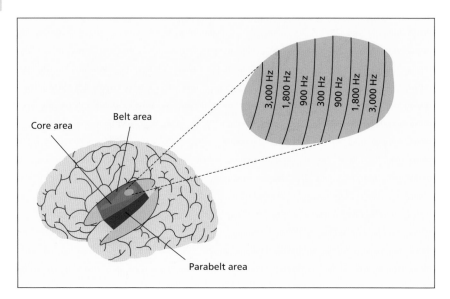

The primary auditory cortex lies on the medial surface of both the left and right temporal lobes and is organized tonotopically (i.e. different regions process different frequencies). It is surrounded by secondary auditory cortex (termed belt and parabelt) that processes more complex aspects of the sound and provide the starting point for separate "what" and "where" routes.

Adapted from Goldstin, 2012.

## DOING HEARING RESEARCH IN A NOISY MRI SCANNER

The noise from an MRI scanner is significant (up to 130 dB, i.e. similar to a jet engine take-off). The scanner noise may not only mask the auditory stimulus of importance, it could also change the nature of the auditory task by requiring attentive strategies to actively filter out the background noise. One solution that is now commonly used is to use so-called **sparse scanning** (Hall *et al.*, 1999). In this method, scanning is temporarily suspended for a few seconds so that an auditory stimulus can be displayed against a silent background and then scanning restarts. This method is possible because of the slow time it takes for the hemodynamic response function to reach a peak (about 6 sec after stimulus onset).

| COMPARISONS BETWEEN THE AUDITORY AND VISUAL SYSTEMS | | |
|---|---|---|
| | **Auditory system** | **Visual system** |
| Thalamocortical route | Medial geniculate nucleus projects to primary auditory cortex | Lateral geniculate nucleus projects to primary visual cortex |
| Organizing principle of early neural processing | Tonotopic organization (orderly mapping between sound frequency and position on cortex) | Retinotopic organization (orderly mapping between position on retina and position on cortex) |
| Temporal and spatial sensitivity | Temporal > Spatial | Spatial > Temporal |
| Functional specialization of feature processing | Less well documented in the auditory domain | Well documented for color and movement |
| Higher-order context-dependent pathways | Evidence for separate auditory pathways for "what" versus "where"/"how" | Evidence for separate visual pathways for "what" versus "where"/"how" |

# BASIC PROCESSING OF AUDITORY INFORMATION

Beyond the early auditory cortical areas, there are many other routes and regions of the brain involved in auditory processing. The precise network of regions used depends on the stimulus content (e.g. human speech, voices, music, environmental noises) and the current context (e.g. whether one needs to understand speech, identify a speaker or locate a sound source). These will be considered in the sections below.

## Feature processing in the auditory cortex

Just as visual perception involves the processing of different features (color, shape, movement, texture), so too does auditory perception, although the features differ (e.g. pitch, loudness, tempo). As with vision, there is some evidence of hierarchical processing of auditory feature information such that earlier cortical regions (e.g. the "core" region containing the primary auditory cortex) codes for more simple features and later cortical regions (e.g. the belt and parabelt) codes more complex information that could be thought of, to some extent, as conjunctions of simple features. Unlike vision, the evidence for modular-like organization of auditory features is less well established. But there is some evidence for a potential "pitch region" that responds to the psychological variable of pitch (i.e. how the note is perceived) as opposed to the physical properties of the sound (such as the frequency). This region, outside of primary auditory cortex, responds to perceived pitch, as in the missing fundamental illusion, rather than actual frequency (Bendor & Wang, 2005).

Kaas *et al.* (1999) present a summary of how more complex auditory features are constructed in a hierarchical fashion from core → belt → parabelt regions. Single-cell recordings in primates show that the neurons in the core region respond to narrowly defined frequencies (e.g. responding maximally to a pure tone of 200 Hz), whereas cells in the belt region respond to a broader band of frequencies (e.g. responding to noise between 200 Hz and 300 Hz; Kosaki *et al.*, 1997). This is consistent with the view that the neurons in the belt region sum together activity from many frequency-selective neurons in the core region; for example, by

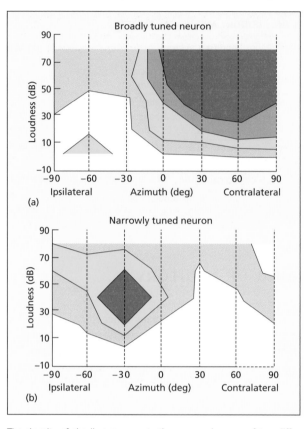

(a)

(b)

The density of shading represents the responsiveness of two different neurons in auditory cortex to sounds of different loudness levels presented in different regions of space. Neuron (a) responds to sounds over a broad range of loudness level and in various parts of space, whereas neuron (b) is more finely tuned to a particular loudness level and a particular part of space.

From Clarey *et al.*, 1994. Reprinted with permission of APS.

summing together activity from neurons tuned to respond to 200 Hz, 205 Hz, 210 Hz, 215 Hz, and so on to 300 Hz. This can be considered analogous to the way that simple cells in vision sum together information from center-surround cells (see p. 111).

More recently, cells have been documented in primary auditory cortex that possess something akin to center-surround properties (Tian *et al.*, 2013). Recall that, in vision, on-off center-surround cells respond when a light is projected ON to the *center* of the receptive field and also responds when a projected light is switched OFF the *surround* of the receptive field. In hearing, the response properties are defined according to the range of frequencies that a neuron responds to (rather than spatial position) but a similar principle applies. For instance, a neuron that responds when a sound of 3–6 kHz is ON may also respond when a sound of 6–9 kHz (i.e. an adjacent frequency band) is switched OFF.

Neurons in the belt region will also respond to other more complex tones, such as vocalizations, more vigorously than with pure tones (Rauschecker *et al.*, 1995). These sounds may be characterized by sudden shifts in frequency, such as abrupt onsets in speech (e.g. the /p/phoneme) or warbling or twitter calls in other species.

Indeed some neurons do not respond to fixed frequencies but only to changes in frequency and even the direction of change of frequency (Kajikawa *et al.*, 2008; Whitfield & Evans, 1965). This could be considered analogous to complex cells in vision, which respond to movement and movement direction.

Neurons of the auditory cortex do not just respond to frequency-related information, they also respond to particular loudness levels and particular spatial locations. Clarey *et al.* (1994) recorded from neurons in the cat primary auditory cortex using noise bursts but varying loudness and sound location. Some neurons respond only to particular loudness levels, and some neurons respond only to particular locations (typically contralaterally, so sounds presented on the left of space are more strongly processed in the right auditory cortex and vice versa). More than a third of neurons respond to particular loudness levels *and* particular locations; for example, a neuron may produce a maximal response both if the sound is between 30 and 50 dB and if it is located between 20 and 40 degrees on a particular side of space.

## "What" versus "where"

Within the auditory cortical areas, there is some degree of specialization for "what" versus "where." That is, some neurons/regions are relatively specialized for coding the content of the sound (irrespective of where it is coming from), and other neurons/regions are relatively specialized for coding where the sound is coming from (irrespective of what is heard). This may form the starting point for two separate routes to non-auditory regions. Rauschecker and Tian (2000) found that neural responses in the anterior belt region showed a high degree of specialization for monkey calls (irrespective of their location), whereas the posterior belt region showed greatest spatial selectivity. They speculated that this may form the starting point for two routes: a dorsal route involving the parietal lobes that is concerned with locating sounds, and a ventral route along the temporal lobes concerned with identifying sounds. Functional imaging evidence from humans is largely consistent with this view (Barrett & Hall, 2006). For sounds that can be reproduced (e.g. speech in humans), one additional suggestion is that the auditory dorsal route acts as a "how" route—i.e. the auditory signal interfaces with motor representations in parietal and frontal cortex rather than spatial ones. Recent evidence from structural and functional imaging suggests that this dorsal route may (at least partially) segregate into separate "where" and "how" streams rather than existing as a single stream with a dual how/where function (Isenberg *et al.*, 2012).

There are two broad solutions for identifying where a sound is located:

1.  *Inter-aural differences*. If a sound is lateralized it will tend to arrive at one ear before the other (inter-aural time difference) and will be less intense at the farthest ear because it lies in the "shadow" of the head (inter-aural intensity difference). Frequency-selective neurons in the core and belt regions adjust their responsiveness according to the inter-aural loudness differences and inter-aural time differences (Brugge & Merzenich, 1973). For example, a neuron that is selective for a particular frequency may be more responsive, i.e. generate more action potentials, when the left ear is played the sound slightly before the right ear but may reduce its responsiveness if the right ear hears the sound first.

## KEY TERMS

**Head-related transfer function (HRTF)**
An internal model of how sounds get distorted by the unique shape of one's own ears and head.

**Planum temporale**
A part of auditory cortex (posterior to primary auditory cortex) that integrates auditory information with non-auditory information, for example to enable sounds to be separated in space.

2. *Distortions of the sound wave by the head and pinnae.* To test the role of the pinnae in sound localization, Batteau (1967) placed microphones into the "ear canal" of casts of actual pinnae while playing sounds to these artificial ears from different locations. When participants listen to these recordings, using headphones (i.e. so the sound isn't distorted by their own pinnae), they are able to localize the sounds. They cannot do so if the recordings were taken without the artificial ears attached. Moreover, performance is improved if sounds are recorded from participants' own ear shapes rather than a generic ear (Wenzel et al., 1993). The brain develops an internal model of how sounds get distorted by the unique shape of one's own ears and head (called a **head-related transfer function**, HRTF) and it is able to use this knowledge to infer the likely location. Griffiths and Warren (2002) propose that a region called the **planum temporale**, lying posterior to the primary auditory cortex, is involved in integrating the sensory input with the learned head-related transfer function for different parts of space. In fMRI, this region responds more to sounds that appear to be subjectively located outside the head rather

The sound arrives at the left ear first (inter-aural time difference) and is more intense in the incoming ear (inter-aural intensity difference).

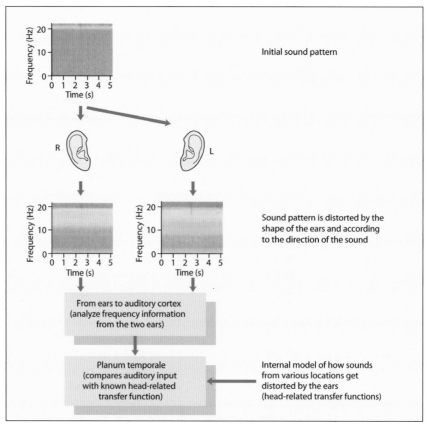

The shape of the ears distorts incoming sounds in predictable ways that depend on the location of the sound. The brain contains an internal model of how the sounds get distorted (head-related transfer function) and it can link the model with the auditory input to infer the location of a sound.

Adapted from Griffiths and Warren, 2002.

than the same sounds perceived to be internal, as occurs when listening to most sounds played through headphones (Hunter *et al.*, 2003). Whereas inter-aural differences only provide information about the left-right (or azimuthal) location of a sound, distortions of the auditory input by the pinnae can be used to locate sounds in both the left–right direction and the top–bottom direction (Batteau, 1967).

The computations described above can be used to locate sounds relative to the head (i.e. an egocentric coding of space). However, to determine the actual location of the sound source (i.e. in allocentric space), one also needs to know the current orientation and tilt of the head. A sound that is 10 degrees to the left of the head could actually be directly in front of the person if the head happens to be oriented at 10 degrees to the right. As such, auditory information needs to be combined with bodily postural information. Evidence from EEG suggests that information about the orientation of the head relative to the body affects auditory processing within 200 ms (Schechtman *et al.*, 2012). Top-down information from the motor/proprioceptive system can therefore influence early auditory processing.

## Auditory memory and auditory stream segregation

Visual objects generally extend through time and are available for reinspection. Auditory objects (e.g. a spoken word or musical phrase) tend not to hang around to be reinspected. Most models of hearing postulate an important role of a sensory memory store to integrate auditory information over brief time intervals (a few seconds). This auditory memory is assumed to be tapped by all kinds of heard material, i.e. it should not be confused with the verbal short-term memory store that is considered speech-specific. Perhaps the best developed model of auditory memory is that proposed by Näätänen and colleagues (Näätänen *et al.*, 2001), who regard the primary function of this memory system to lie in early **auditory stream segregation**. Complex auditory scenes such as a cocktail party or an orchestral performance can be divided into different streams (or "objects") according to, say, their pitch, melody, instrumentation or location in space.

Much of the evidence in this area comes from studies of a human ERP component termed the **mismatch negativity** (**MMN**). The mismatch negativity occurs when an auditory stimulus deviates from previously presented auditory stimuli (Näätänen *et al.*, 1978). It occurs between 100 and 200 ms after the onset of the deviant sound, and its main locus appears to be within the auditory cortex (Alho, 1995). The most simple example is a sequence of tones in which one tone has a deviant pitch (e.g. A-A-A-A-B where A = 1,000 Hz, B > 1,000 Hz). This is illustrated in the figure on p. 242. In one sense, the MMN can be considered as a "low level" phenomenon, because it occurs in the absence of attention. It is found in some comatose patients several days before waking (Kane *et al.*, 1993) and when the stimulus is presented to the unattended ear of healthy participants (Alho *et al.*, 1994). However, the MMN is also found for more complex auditory patterns, suggesting a more sophisticated underlying mechanism. It is found if a descending tone sequence suddenly ascends in pitch or remains constant (Tervaniemi *et al.*, 1994), or if the repetitive stimulus consists of varying pairs of *descending* tones, so there is no physical standard, and the deviant stimulus consists of a pair of *ascending* tones (Saarinen *et al.*, 1992). Thus, the auditory memory must code rather abstract properties of the auditory stimuli. Schechtman *et al.* (2012) also showed that an MMN can be elicited by spatial deviants suggesting that similar neural mechanisms underpin early stream segregation in both the frequency and spatial domain (a finding that is backed up by evidence from fMRI and MEG; Schadwinkel & Gutschalk, 2010). There is evidence that the MMN is generated anterior to the primary auditory cortex but may also involve an inferior frontal component; these regions may be linked to deviance detection and attentional orienting respectively (Tse & Penney, 2008).

Auditory stream segregation is unlikely to be limited to the auditory cortex. Parietal regions may be important too. Although the parietal cortex is seen as being an end-point of the "where" pathway it is to be noted that its role in auditory stream segregation is not solely spatial in nature but rather serving a more general role in binding and attention. Cusack (2005) used a perceptually ambiguous auditory stimulus of two alternating tones of different frequency that could either be interpreted as a single stream (like the "clip, clop, clip, clop" of a horse) or as two streams ("clip . . . clip . . ." overlaid on ". . . clop . . . clop"). That is, the stimuli in the two conditions were physically identical but associated with different percepts. This contrasts with the MMN approach, which always uses perceptually different repeated and deviant sounds that may be easier to segregate at a sensory level. This manipulation found activity in the right intra-parietal sulcus for two streams relative to one. This region has been implicated in binding different features together in vision (e.g. color and shape) and could possibly play a similar role in hearing. Indeed, patients with unilateral neglect (who typically have damage near this right parietal region) have difficulty in comparing auditory features if they are segregated into different auditory streams but not if they belong to the same stream (Cusack *et al.*, 2000).

The parietal lobes are also likely to play an important role in solving the classical **cocktail party problem** in which a single stream (a speaker) must be attended among competing streams (with different acoustic and spatial properties). Kerlin *et al.* (2010) used EEG to show that selectively attending to speech in a multi-talker environment is linked to increased power of low frequency neural oscillations from the auditory cortex in addition to oscillatory changes over parietal sites in the alpha range. Alpha oscillations, in visual attention, have been linked to suppression of irrelevant information (Worden *et al.*, 2000). Hill and Miller (2010) used fMRI to show that attending to a speaker, from a group of three,

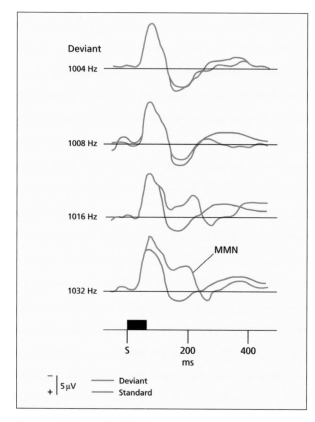

If a standard tone of 1,000 Hz is played repetitively (purple line) but with an occasional deviant tone that is more than 1000 Hz (green lines), then there is a distinct EEG event-related potential detected at the scalp that is termed the mismatch negativity, MMN. This has been attributed to an auditory memory component and the MMN is also found for some more complex auditory patterns.

activates a frontoparietal network linked to attention. However, attending to the location of the speaker versus attending to the pitch of the speaker was linked to different biases within the network: specifically, there was greater activity in the intra-parietal sulcus for speaker location but greater activity in the superior temporal sulcus when attending to speaker pitch.

## MUSIC PERCEPTION

Although music can rightfully be described as a form of art, this does not mean that it is purely a product of cultural learning. Many aspects of music perception have a biological basis and can be said to be "innate" in the same way as some argue language to be innate (Peretz, 2006). Namely, that it is a universal phenomenon (all known human cultures, past and present, have had it) and it emerges early in life without formal training (but with exposure to an appropriate environment). At this point, it is important to emphasize a distinction between music perception and music production. Music production typically requires many years of formal training (although it need not, as in singing or tapping/clapping a rhythm). In contrast, all of us, with the possible exception of those who are "tone deaf" (see later), are able to perceive and appreciate music and are avid consumers of music.

Music can be said to have a number of essential features (Dowling & Harwood, 1986). First, musical systems tend to be based on a discrete set of pitch levels. The infinite set of different pitches that the brain perceives become parsed into a finite set of musical notes. For example, the Western musical scale is made up of seven repeating notes (A to G, forming an octave when the first note is repeated), with intermediate semi-tones (the flats and sharps). Second, these different notes are combined to form perceptible groups and patterns. The way that these notes are grouped together is not arbitrary but depends on certain properties of the auditory system, such as those involved in auditory stream segregation. For example, notes that are similar in pitch or have similar durations may be grouped together. Some notes when played together "sound right" (consonance) or clash (dissonance) and this may depend on the physical relationship between the notes. For example, two notes that are double in fundamental frequency (e.g. 220 Hz and 440 Hz) have the lowest dissonance and this has a special status in musical systems. In the Western musical system, this doubling corresponds to the same note an octave apart.

Is the right hemisphere to music as the left hemisphere is to language? Although this hypothesis is interesting, it is also misleading as neither music nor language can be considered as single faculties. There is evidence that the right hemisphere may be more dominant for the processing of pitch-related information. However, the left hemisphere is also important for certain aspects of music. Alcock *et al.* (2000b) report that pitch abilities are more affected by right-hemispheric lesions but timing abilities are more affected by left-hemispheric lesions.

Peretz and Coltheart (2003) outlined a basic cognitive model of music processing that emphasizes different components of musical processing. The first distinction that they make is between processes that are shared between music and speech (shown in the figure below in blue) and those that are potentially specific to music (shown in green). Thus, listening to someone singing "Happy Birthday" would evoke at least two routes: one concerned with the words and one

**KEY TERM**

**Amusia**
An auditory agnosia in which music perception is affected more than the perception of other sounds.

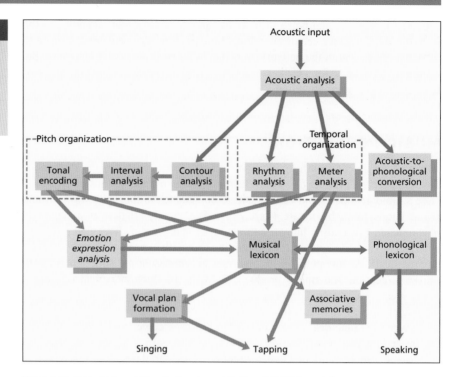

The model of musical cognition by Peretz and Coltheart (2003) contains separate processes for the lyrics versus melody and rhythm of music, as well as a further sub-division between processes for temporal organization (such as rhythm) and pitch-based organization (including melody).

From Peretz and Coltheart, 2003. By permission of Macmillan Publishers Ltd.

concerned with the music. Within the domain of music, they then make a distinction between *pitch organization* (which includes pitch relations between notes) and *temporal organization*, including rhythm (the tempo of beats) and meter (the way beats are grouped). Much of the evidence for this model has come from people with an acquired or congenital **amusia**.

## Memory for tunes

Some brain-damaged patients are unable to recognize previously familiar melodies despite being able to recognize songs from spoken lyrics, and being able to recognize voices and environmental sounds. For example, case CN was a non-musician who suffered bilateral temporal lobe damage (Peretz, 1996). Although she had some difficulties with pitch perception, her most profound difficulty was in identifying previously familiar tunes and, as such, her damage was attributed to a memory component of music (the "musical lexicon" in the model above). Subsequent studies show that CN can identify intonation from speech, which requires analysis of pitch contours but not knowledge of tunes (Patel *et al.*, 1998). In contrast to CN, some brain-damaged patients can lose the ability to recognize spoken words but are still able to recognize tunes (Mendez, 2001).

There is evidence that memory for familiar tunes is stored as part of semantic memory rather than episodic memory (although the latter may be used for recently learned tunes). Patients with semantic dementia, who have general impairments

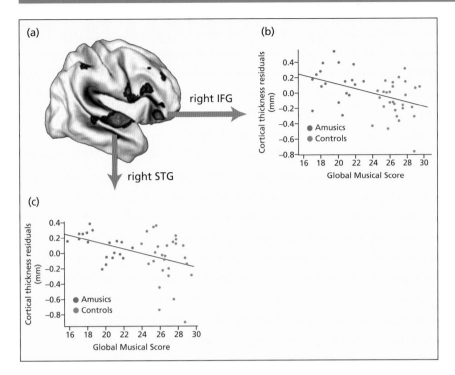

A right hemisphere frontotemporal network is linked to structural abnormalities in congenital amusia. Increased gray matter is correlated with lower combined scores on a battery of six tests of musical cognition.

From Hyde *et al.*, 2007.

in semantic memory, have difficulty in recognizing previously familiar tunes and the degree of impairment is linked to the amount of damage in the right anterior temporal lobes (Hsieh *et al.*, 2011). By contrast, patients with Alzheimer's disease (which is characterized by a more profound deficit in episodic memory) tend to have only mild impairments (Hsieh *et al.*, 2011).

## Rhythm

Disorders of rhythm can occur independently of disorders of pitch. Di Pietro *et al.*, (2004) report a case of acquired amusia who could process pitch-based melody but could not identify rhythm from auditory input. He could do so from visual input, suggesting the problem wasn't in general time perception. Members of the KE family with a congenital speech disorder (see Chapter 16) also have problems in rhythm production and rhythm perception but perform as well as controls in pitch-based melody production and melody perception (Alcock *et al.*, 2000a). The KE family is known to have structural abnormalities within the basal ganglia.

Evidence from functional imaging of normal listeners, implicates interactions between the auditory system and the motor system in both rhythm perception and production. Passive listening to regular rhythms, relative to irregular ones, is linked to activity in the premotor cortex, supplementary motor area and the cerebellum (Bengtsson *et al.*, 2009). Tapping to a rhythm in which the beat varies in its audibility is linked to connectivity differences between auditory (posterior superior temporal) and premotor regions—with louder beats linked to stronger audio-motor functional connectivity (Chen *et al.* 2006). Activity in the basal ganglia is greatest when participants have to maintain a beat relative to the initial finding of the beat (Grahn & Rowe, 2013).

## Pitch

Some people have good perception and production of rhythm but are impaired on pitch-based aspects of music. One recently studied group is those individuals who are said to be "**tone deaf**" or have so-called **congenital amusia**, because there is no known neurological cause such as brain damage. This can occur in up to 4 percent of the population and is not associated with difficulties in other domains, such as general intelligence (Ayotte *et al.*, 2002). It is associated with right-hemisphere abnormalities in white and gray matter density, both in right the auditory cortex and the right inferior frontal gyrus (Hyde *et al.*, 2007). Hyde and Peretz (2004) presented participants with a series of five notes in which the fourth note was either out of pitch or out of time. Tone-deaf participants could detect the timing but not the pitch violations.

Another line of research has examined whether the pitch processing difficulties in congenital amusia are selective to music or affect pitch processing of other sounds, notably in speech. In tests involving fine-grained discriminations of syllables varying in pitch, there is evidence of impairment but it is not as severe as for musical sounds (Tillmann *et al.*, 2011). Similarly, they have difficulty in discriminating pitch shifts in sentences but—interestingly—are able to imitate pitch shifts during sentence repetition (Hutchins & Peretz, 2012). This is consistent with separate pathways for translating sounds into motor commands (spared) versus extracting higher-level perceptual features (impaired). In most Western languages, shifts in pitch are related to prosody (e.g. adding emphasis) and intonation (at the sentence-level) rather than comprehension. By contrast, many Eastern languages are tonal in nature which means that, say, a rising or falling pitch could denote completely different words. Congenital amusia is also found in speakers of Mandarin Chinese and many of these people also have difficulties in discriminating lexical tones as well as the pitch of musical sounds (Nan *et al.*, 2010). Zatorre and Baum (2012) argue that while music and speech share common mechanisms in pitch processing, there are important differences too. In speech, pitch is processed on a continuous scale and *relative* changes in pitch are important (e.g. a rise in pitch may imply a question, but the rise does not have to be of a given amount). In music, pitch is arranged into discrete notes and a small change of the pitch of a note in a melody can be perceived as "wrong" even if the relative pitch contour of the music is the same. Zatorre and Baum (2012) argue that there are separate neural substrates for coarse pitch changes (more important for speech) and fine-grained pitch changes (more important for music). They claim that the latter is more dependent on the right hemisphere network and this tends to be selectively impaired in congenital amusia.

## Melody and musical syntax

The model of Peretz and Coltheart (2003) contains different stages of pitch processing in music that are concerned with the general up–down structure (contour analysis), the precise relationship between successive notes (interval analysis) and, finally, the construction of **melody** (tonal encoding). In most music, the melody follows certain regularities in which only some notes are "allowed." Determining the set of possible notes for a given melody is what Peretz and Coltheart mean by tonal encoding. As well as allowing certain notes and not others, some notes are more probable at certain points in the melody than others. This rule-like aspect of music has been referred to as musical syntax (Koelsch & Siebel, 2005). Whereas both random pitch sequences and tonal melodies activate the bilateral auditory cortex and surrounding temporal regions (Patterson *et al.*, 2002), musical syntactic deviations are associated with activation of inferior frontal regions (Maess *et al.*, 2001). This tends to be bilateral and stronger on the right but includes Broca's area on the left, which has, historically, been considered as specific to language. Brain

The music for movies such as *Jaws* and *Psycho* is designed to create a sense of fear. Would a patient with damage to the amygdala, who can't recognize fear from faces, be able to identify scary music?

© DLILLC/Corbis.

lesions in this area disrupt an event-related potential component measured using EEG (the ERAN, Early Right Anterior Negativity) that is linked to processing of musical syntactic deviations (Sammler *et al.*, 2011). This may not be the only region that processes musical syntax. Intracranial electrophysiological recordings also highlight the importance of left anterior superior temporal regions in the processing of both musical and linguistic syntax in addition to the inferior frontal gyrus (Sammler *et al.*, 2013).

## Timbre

One notable omission from the model of Peretz and Coltheart (2003) is timbre. This perceptual quality of a sound enables us to distinguish between different musical instruments. The same note played on a cello and a saxophone will sound very different even if they are matched for pitch and loudness. Different instruments can be distinguished partly on the basis of how the note evolves over time (e.g. the attack and decay of the note) and partly on the basis of the relative intensity of the different frequency components of the note. Timbre perception is particularly affected by lesions of the right temporal lobe and can be dissociated from some aspects of pitch-related perception such as melody (Samson & Zatorre, 1994).

## Music and emotion

Music has a special ability to tap into our emotional processes. This may rely on certain musical conventions such as happy music tending to be a faster tempo than sad music; happy being in major keys, and sad being in minor keys; dissonance between notes to create tension; musical syntactic deviations to create "surprise"; and fast and regular to create scary music (think *Jaws*). A native African group, the Mafa, have been shown to be able to recognize happy, sad and fear in Western music despite no cultural exposure to these musical styles (Fritz *et al.*, 2009).

## WHAT IS THE FUNCTION OF MUSIC?

Every human culture, past and present, is believed to have had music. But what evolutionary function could music serve?

Unlike language, the function of music is less obvious. Music gives people a huge amount of enjoyment but, while humans prefer music over silence, the reverse is true of other primates (McDermott & Hauser, 2007). But enjoyment, in itself, does not explain its existence from a Darwinian point of view: namely, in what ways does music promote survival of our species? Darwin's (1871) own answer to this question is that human musical tendencies are derived from a system for attracting mates. Another answer to the problem is that music exists because it brings people together and creates social cohesion, both of which lead to survival benefits (Huron, 2001). A third suggestion, made in *The Singing Neanderthals* (Mithen, 2005), is that music is a precursor to language. Steven Pinker (1997) takes the contrary view by arguing that language was the precursor to music (rather than music the precursor to language) and that music, while being immensely enjoyable, does not have an adaptive function. As he puts it: "Music is auditory cheesecake. It just happens to tickle several important parts of the brain in a highly pleasurable way, as cheesecake tickles the palate." Although it is hard to establish the direction of cause and effect, there is now evidence of a close link between the structure of speech and music. For instance, it is suggested that the cross-cultural tendency to have around 12 discrete notes in a musical scale derives from the number of formants in spoken vowels (Schwartz et al., 2003), and that major/minor musical modes reflect emotional prosody in human vocalisation (Bowling et al., 2012). Although other primates do not show a preference for *human* music over silence (McDermott & Hauser, 2007) they do show a preference for music when it is derived from the structure of their own vocalizations (Snowdon & Teie, 2010).

Functional imaging shows that emotional music activates the same circuitry as other emotional stimuli and even the brain's reward circuitry (Blood & Zatorre, 2001; Koelsch et al., 2006). This suggests that music can be a powerful motivator like sex, food and drugs, although the function of music, in evolutionary terms, remains unknown. Patients with acquired difficulties in emotion processing, such as in recognizing fearful faces, may show comparable deficits in recognizing scary music (Gosselin et al., 2007).

# VOICE PERCEPTION

Voices, like faces, convey a large amount of socially relevant information about the people around us. It is possible to infer someone's sex, size, age and mood from their voice. Physical changes related to sex, size and age affect the vocal apparatus in systematic ways. Larger bodies have longer vocal tracts and this leads to greater dispersion of certain frequencies (the formants found, for example, in human vowels and dog growls are more dispersed in larger animals). Adult men have larger vocal folds (17–25 mm) than adult women (12.5–17.5 mm), resulting in a lower pitched male voice. One can also infer the current emotional state (angry, sad, etc.) from a voice even in an unfamiliar language (Scherer *et al.*, 2001). Familiar people can also be recognized from their voice but this is generally more difficult than recognizing them from their face (Hanley *et al.*, 1998). Individual differences in the shape and size of the vocal apparatus (teeth, lips, etc.) and resonators (e.g. nasal cavity), together with learned speaking style (e.g. accent), create a unique voice signature. Similarly to models of face perception, it has been suggested that there are multiple parallel routes for processing a voice: one route is involved in recognizing speaker identity, one in extracting affective information, and one relating to extracting speech content (Belin *et al.*, 2011).

Belin *et al.* (2000) claimed to have identified a voice-selective area in the human brain. They found three regions in the bilateral superior temporal sulcus that respond to vocal sounds (speech and non-speech such as laughs) more than non-vocal sounds of comparable acoustic complexity, and including other sounds produced by humans such as clapping. Further research has suggested that these different regions may be sensitive to different aspects of voice. In particular, the right superior temporal region anterior to auditory cortex (i.e. in the auditory "what" pathway) appears to be important for speaker identity (Belin & Zatorre, 2003; Warren *et al.*, 2006). TMS over this region disrupts the ability to detect the presence of a briefly heard voice, but not loudness judgments of the same stimuli (Bestelmeyer *et al.*, 2011). A recent fMRI study with macaque monkeys has identified a homologous region that responds not only to vocalizations from their own species but is also affected by changes in identity between different vocalizers (Petkov *et al.*, 2008).

One case study, of developmental origin, was unable to identify familiar voices of personal acquaintances or famous people despite being able to recognize their faces and despite being able to extract other important information from voices including their sex and emotional state (Garrido *et al.*, 2009). Interestingly, fMRI of healthy participants shows that identifying a speaker from his or her voice activates face-selective regions,

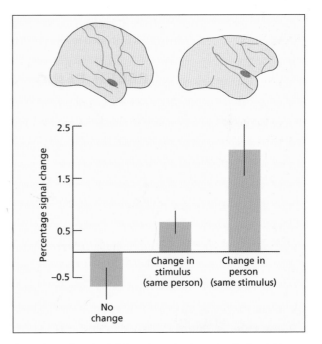

Approximate location of the voice-selective region in the right temporal lobe of humans (left) and macaques (right). This region responds more, in terms of fMRI BOLD signal, when the speaker changes (but the syllable/vocalization is the same) than when the syllable/vocalization changes (but the speaker is the same).

Reprinted from Scott, 2008. © 2008, with permission from Elsevier.

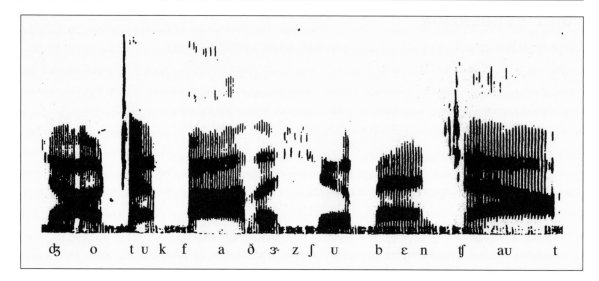

In the spectrogram, time is plotted along the x-axis and frequency along the y-axis, with intensity represented by darkness. There are no gaps between words but certain consonants (e.g. "b") block the flow of air and produce gaps. Vowels are represented by bands of horizontal stripes (called formants). The spectrogram represents "Joe took father's shoe bench out."

From Tartter, 1986. © Vivien Tartter. Reprinted with kind permission of the author.

although interpreting what the speaker says does not (von Kriegstein *et al.*, 2005). Thus, although face and voice information is theoretically separable, the two are often activated together when the person is known.

## SPEECH PERCEPTION

At what stage of processing, if any, does the brain treat speech sounds differently from other kinds of auditory stimuli? This question often reduces to identifying the stage in speech processing that is left lateralized. Wernicke (1848–1905), one of the earliest researchers to consider this question, believed that sensory speech processing was bilateral but that the left advantage arose through connections with the left motor–speech system (cited in Hickok and Poeppel, 2004). Functional imaging studies have shown that the primary auditory cortex of both left and right hemispheres responds equally to speech and other types of auditory stimuli (Binder *et al.*, 2000). This suggests divergence at a later cortical stage. Beyond auditory cortex, humans begin to show a greater left hemisphere responsiveness for speech relative to non-speech along the so-called what route of the temporal lobes. For example, Scott *et al.* (2000) report increased activity in a left temporal region in intelligible relative to unintelligible speech of comparable acoustic complexity. The right hemisphere homologue did not show this preference but was more responsive to dynamic pitch variation. This is consistent with the notion that the left hemisphere is specialized for processing rapid temporal change, and the right hemisphere extracts more melodic aspects (Zatorre *et al.*, 2002). Moreover, a specific type of acquired auditory agnosia called **pure word deafness** is found following damage to the left hemisphere (Takahashi *et al.*, 1992). These patients are able to identify environmental sounds and music but not speech. The patients are able to produce speech but heard speech appears to be "too fast" or "distorted."

# The nature of the speech signal

To appreciate the difficulties faced by the auditory system during speech perception, consider a typical **spectrogram** for the sentence "Joe took father's shoe bench out." A spectrogram plots how the frequency of sound (on the vertical $y$ axis) changes over time (on the horizontal $x$ axis) with the intensity of the sound represented by level of darkness. The first thing to notice is that, although there are gaps in the spectrogram, these typically correspond to the articulation of certain consonants (e.g. "t", "b", "f") rather than gaps occurring between words. Although we are used to seeing gaps between words in written language, they do not exist in speech (one famous example being "I scream" versus "ice-cream," which have the same sound). Thus, segmenting the speech stream into words will rely on stored knowledge of possible words as well as some auditory cues (e.g. stress patterns).

Another difficulty is that the same words can have very different acoustic properties depending on the person producing them. Male and female speakers have different pitch ranges, and speakers have different accents, talking speeds, and so on. This is the familiar problem of extracting constant information from sensory input that can vary infinitely.

Looking again at the spectrogram, it appears as if some speech sounds have very different characteristics from others. The basic segments of speech are called phonemes and, perhaps surprisingly, fewer than 100 phonemes describe all the languages of the world. The International Phonetic Alphabet (IPA) contains one written symbol for each phoneme; English contains around 44 phonemes. It is important not to confuse phonemes with letters. For example, the TH and SH in "thin" and "shin" are single phonemes (θ and ∫ in IPA) that are typically represented by two letters. Phonemes are more formally defined as minimal contrastive units of spoken language. To understand what this means, hold your hand very close to your mouth and say the words "pin" and "peg." Did you notice that the "p" sound of pin was more associated with an outward expulsion of air (called aspiration)? These are two **allophones** of the single "p" phoneme. Although they are physically different, the difference is irrelevant for recognizing the words. In some languages, the presence or absence of aspiration may signify a change in meaning. In Thai, "paa" aspirated means "to split"; whereas "paa" unaspirated means "forest." These are separate phonemes in Thai, but allophonic variants in English.

The different acoustic properties of phonemes can be related back to the way they are articulated. Vowels are produced with a relative free flow of air, modified by the shape (high, middle, low) and position (front, center, back) of the tongue. In the spectrogram, this free flow is represented as a series of horizontal stripes (called **formants**). Consonants typically place more constriction on the flow of air, sometimes blocking it completely as in phonemes such as "b" and "d". Other consonants differ by **voicing**. Hold your voice box when saying "zzzz" compared with "ssss". In the first instance, you should feel your vocal chords vibrating. On a spectrogram, this can be seen as a series of closely spaced vertical lines.

One way in which the brain deals with variability in the acoustic input is by using categorical perception. Categorical perception refers to the fact that continuous changes in input are mapped on to discrete percepts. For example, the syllables "da" and "ta" are identical except that the phoneme "t" is unvoiced ("d" and "a" are voiced). It is possible to experimentally manipulate the onset of voicing along a continuum from 0 ms (perceived as "da") to 80 ms (perceived as "ta"). But what happens at intermediate values such as 30 ms? Is a third type of sound perceived?

## KEY TERMS

**Spectrogram**
Plots the frequency of sound (on the $y$-axis) over time (on the $x$-axis) with the intensity of the sound represented by how dark it is.

**Allophones**
Different spoken/acoustic renditions of the same phoneme.

**Formants**
Horizontal stripes on the spectrogram produced with a relative free flow of air (e.g. by vowels).

**Voicing**
Vibration of the vocal cords that characterizes the production of some consonants.

No, listeners will always perceive it as one phoneme or the other, albeit to varying degrees of certainty (Eimas, 1963). Categorical perception also provides one way of dealing with variability in the acoustic signal due to **co-articulation**. Co-articulation refers to the fact that the production of a phoneme (and, hence, the sound of that phoneme) is influenced by the preceding and proceeding phonemes.

## HEARING LIPS AND SEEING VOICES—THE MCGURK ILLUSION

Although we may not think of ourselves as good lip-readers, we all are capable of using this visual information to supplement what we hear. Visual cues from lip-reading are particularly important when the auditory input becomes less reliable, such as in noisy settings (Sumby & Pollack, 1954). Normally it is advantageous to combine information from two or more different senses. However, if the information contained in the two senses is discrepant, then the brain may generate a misperception or illusion based on its "best guess" solution. One striking example of this is the so-called **McGurk illusion** (McGurk & MacDonald, 1976). To create the illusion, one needs to dub together a separate auditory stream saying

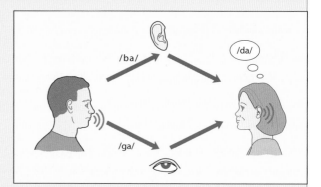

In the McGurk Illusion, the listener perceives a different syllable from that produced because of a mismatch between hearing and vision. At what stage in the auditory pathway might this illusion arise?

Reprinted from Calvert et al., 2000. © 2000, with permission from Elsevier.

one thing (e.g. "baba") with visual lip-movements saying another thing (e.g. "gaga"). Participants often subjectively report hearing a third syllable—in this example, it is "dada." Close your eyes and you hear the correct auditory stimulus ("baba"), open them again and you hear the illusory stimulus ("dada"). At what point in the auditory or speech perception pathway does the illusion arise? At present there are two main candidates. One proposal is that the illusion arises from the *multisensory perception* of speech. The left (posterior) superior temporal region is known to respond to speech and the sight of meaningful lip movements. Applying TMS to this region temporarily reduces the susceptibility to the illusion (Beauchamp et al., 2010) and people who are particularly prone to perceiving the illusion (relative to those who are not) show greater activity in this region to mismatching audio-visual stimuli during fMRI (Nath & Beauchamp, 2012). An alternative proposal is that the illusion arises from activating the *motor system* for speech production (including inferior frontal cortex/premotor regions and the insula). Skipper et al. (2007) found, using fMRI, that an illusory "da" stimulus (made up of auditory "ba" and visual "ga") resembles a real "da" stimulus (made up of auditory "da" and visual "da") in motor regions. Other research suggests that these regions are involved in the categorical perception of ambiguous (audio-only) syllables (Lee et al., 2012). The different roles of these two regions (superior temporal sulcus compared with inferior frontal gyrus) and their relative importance in giving rise to the illusion requires further clarification, but one suggestion is that it is the nature of the coupling between these regions that determines whether the illusion occurs (Keil et al., 2012).

# The motor theory of speech perception

It has already been suggested that speech perception involves matching an infinitely varying acoustic signal to a finite number of stored representations in the brain. But what is the nature of these stored representations and how exactly does this process occur? One possibility is that the auditory signal is matched on to motor representations for producing one's own speech rather than matching to an acoustic template. This is the motor theory of speech perception (Liberman & Mattingly, 1985; Liberman & Whalen, 2000). In this account, phonemes are recognized by inferring the articulatory movements that would have been necessary to produce these sounds. The motor commands must be abstract insofar as one can understand speech without literally having to echo it back.

The motor theory of speech perception has enjoyed a renaissance in recent years owing to the discovery of mirror neurons in the premotor and inferior frontal cortices (including parts of Broca's area). These neurons respond when the subject makes a gesture (e.g. a movement of the hands or mouth). That is, they have motor properties, but they can also respond to the sight and sound of gestures in other people, so they have perceptual properties too (Rizzolatti & Craighero, 2004). One claim is that human language evolved from initially relying on hand-based gestures (i.e. a visuo-motor language like modern sign language) to ultimately involving vocalized gestures (i.e. speech, a predominantly audio-motor language) (Corballis, 2002; Rizzolatti & Arbib, 1998).

The strongest form of the motor theory of speech perception would predict that damage to these motor/mirror regions in humans would result in severe difficulties in speech perception (as well as production). However, this is not the case. Patients with lesions in this area have the mildest of impairments in speech perception as assessed by tasks such as syllable discrimination (Hickok *et al.*, 2011). This suggests that auditory-related regions alone can support efficient perception of speech sounds. But there is evidence, nonetheless, that motor representations may make some contribution to speech perception. Virtual lesions using TMS suggest that the premotor region only contributes to speech perception when the auditory signal is hard to disambiguate (D'Ausilio *et al.*, 2012). Similarly, there is evidence from fMRI that the motor/mirror system tends to be more activated when a phoneme (presented against noise) is perceived correctly relative to when it is misperceived (Callan *et al.*, 2010). The pattern of activity in these regions tracks categorical judgments when presented with a blend between a "ba" and a "da" syllable (Lee *et al.*, 2012). That is, motor representations of speech may be important when the auditory signal is uncertain. In such cases the motor system appears to make contact with the auditory system via the dorsal, rather than ventral, auditory route (Chevillet *et al.*, 2013).

Motor representations may also be important for perceptual learning. Listening to phonemes belonging to another language is not sufficient to bring them under the jurisdiction of the left hemisphere auditory system—one also needs to produce the phonemes in speech in order to trigger left-lateralized speech perception (Best & Avery, 1999).

# Auditory ventral and dorsal routes for "what" and "how"

The general distinction between an auditory ventral route ("what") and an auditory dorsal route ("where") was introduced earlier in the chapter. One further claim

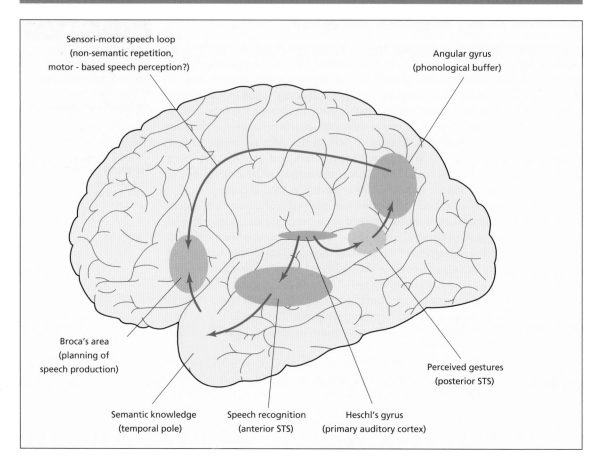

Sensori-motor speech loop
(non-semantic repetition,
motor - based speech perception?)

Angular gyrus
(phonological buffer)

Broca's area
(planning of
speech production)

Perceived gestures
(posterior STS)

Semantic knowledge
(temporal pole)

Speech recognition
(anterior STS)

Heschl's gyrus
(primary auditory cortex)

There may be two routes for perceiving and repeating speech: one that is based on lexical-semantic processing and one that is based on auditory-motor correspondence. These have been termed the ventral "what" route and the dorsal "how" route, respectively.

is that, for speech sounds, there is a further branch within the dorsal pathway that comprises a "how" route that links speech sounds with motor representations for producing speech (Hickok & Poeppel, 2004; Rauschecker & Scott, 2009).

The "what" stream runs anteriorly along the temporal lobe and the more speech-like (or intelligible) the auditory stimulus is then the more anterior the activity tends to be when measured with fMRI (Scott & Wise, 2004). The next chapter considers in detail the neural basis for linguistic aspects of speech processing (i.e. word recognition, semantics, syntax). The "how" stream runs posteriorly along the superior temporal lobe and the inferior parietal lobe (including the angular gyrus). The parietal and frontal parts of this pathway are assumed to be connected by the white matter tract known as the **arcuate fasciculus**. The posterior STS region is a multi-sensory region that is known to respond to the sight of speech as well as to hearing speech sounds (Calvert *et al.*, 2001). Single cell recordings from monkeys in this region show neurons that respond to both the sight and sound of the same vocalisation (Barraclough *et al.*, 2005). That is, the representation in the posterior STS could be regarded as the perceptual equivalent of a speech gesture. This can be contrasted with representations in the premotor cortex which are both perceptual and motoric in nature (Kohler *et al.*, 2002).

**KEY TERM**

**Arcuate fasciculus**
A white matter bundle that connects the temporoparietal region to the frontal lobes.

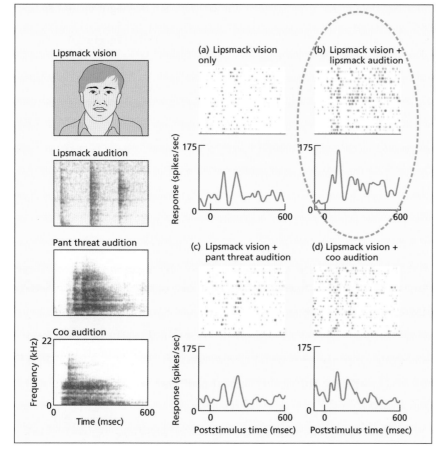

Single-cell recordings in the monkey STS show increased firing when the same vocalization is both seen and heard. This suggests that the region is not a purely visual one, but integrates across hearing and vision.

From Barraclough et al. (2005). © 2005 by the Massachusetts Institute of Technology. Reproduced with permission.

The function of the "what" pathway is universally agreed upon: i.e. it is involved in processing the meaningful content of speech (and, in parallel, the identity of the speaker). The function of the "how" pathway is less clearly agreed upon. As already noted, some have argued that the "how" route is important for speech perception. This view is controversial (Lotto *et al.*, 2009). Another suggestion, not commonly held, is that the "how" route functions to regulate turn-taking during a conversation (Scott *et al.*, 2009). A more generally agreed upon function of the "how" route is that it is involved in the learning and memory of auditory-verbal material. This may include both the long-term learning of novel phonemes and words, and the short-term retention (or "rehearsal") of verbal material. In terms of longer-term learning, activity in the left angular gyrus and left inferior frontal region is linked to learning to understand degraded speech (Eisner *et al.*, 2010). The posterior STS and left inferior frontal gyrus also shows reduced BOLD activity (i.e. less neural effort over time) when learning auditory nonwords via silent rehearsal (Rauschecker *et al.*, 2008). Hickok and Poeppel (2004) have suggested that the how route may be the neuroanatomical basis for the **articulatory loop** (or phonological loop) proposed by Baddeley (1986; Baddeley *et al.*, 1984). This system is a short-term memory store for verbal material and the information in the store is refreshed by subvocal articulation, as

**KEY TERM**

**Articulatory loop**
A short-term memory store for verbal material that is refreshed by subvocal articulation.

in the example of retaining a phone number between looking it up and dialing. Indeed, left parietal regions have been implicated in implementing a phonological memory store in both human neuropsychology and functional imaging (Buchsbaum *et al.*, 2011).

Repetition of speech places significant demands on verbal working memory and, as such, seems to depend heavily on the "how" route. Of course, the ventral "what" route can support repetition of single words and perhaps certain meaningful phrases but verbatim repetition of longer sequences and repetition of meaningless material will depend on the "how" route. Lesions along the "how" pathway, particularly in the posterior STS and angular gyrus, tend to result in deficits in repetition but good auditory comprehension (Baldo *et al.*, 2012; Kuemmerer *et al.*, 2013). Inter-individual differences in the ability to repeat complex auditory nonwords is linked to the functional connectivity between the angular gyrus (involved in short-term memory) and the hippocampus (involved in long-term learning) (McGettigan *et al.*, 2011).

## SUMMARY AND KEY POINTS OF THE CHAPTER

- As with visual perception, hearing involves extracting features (e.g. loudness, pitch) out of the sensory signal that may be useful for segregating the input into different "objects" (e.g. separating out speakers in a noisy room).
- Cells within the (secondary) auditory cortex may have differing degrees of specialization for the content of the sound ("what") versus the location of the sound ("where"). This may be the starting point for an auditory dorsal/where pathway to the parietal lobes and a ventral/what pathway along the temporal lobes (predominantly left lateralized for speech).
- Music perception involves a number of different mechanisms: such as rhythm/timing, pitch perception, and melody (or pitch pattern perception). These different components have partially separate neural substrates as revealed by fMRI and lesion-based studies.
- There is some evidence for a specialized region in the (predominantly right) temporal lobe that is specialized for recognizing voices.
- Speech recognition involves extracting categorical information from sensory input that can vary infinitely (e.g. due to speaker differences in pitch, accent, articulation). This may be achieved via acoustic processing (matching the sounds on to stored auditory templates) and possibly via motor processing (matching the sounds on to stored articulation templates).
- Speech recognition (and speech repetition) may involve both a ventral what route (via semantics) and a dorsal how route for unfamiliar words and verbatim repetition (possibly corresponding to the use of the "articulatory loop").

## EXAMPLE ESSAY QUESTIONS

- In what ways are the challenges faced by the auditory system similar to and different from those faced by the visual system?
- What have studies using single-cell recordings contributed to our knowledge of how auditory information is represented in the brain?
- What is the evidence for separate "what," "where," and "how" routes in hearing?
- Does music perception rely on different brain mechanisms from the perception of other auditory stimuli?
- Why is speech perception different from music perception?
- What is the evidence for a motor component to speech perception?

## RECOMMENDED FURTHER READING

- Moore, B. C. J. (2003). *Introduction to the psychology of hearing* (5th edition). San Diego, CA: Academic Press. This offers a good overview of basic processes in hearing, but for more recent studies based on neurophysiology, Kaas *et al.* (1999) is recommended.
- For music perception, a good overview paper is Stewart, L., von Kriegstein, K., Warren, J. D., & Griffiths, T. D. (2006). Music and the brain: Disorders of musical listening. *Brain, 129*, 2533–2553. For more detailed articles, the following book is recommended: Peretz, I. & Zatorre, R. J. (2003). *The cognitive neuroscience of music*. Oxford, UK: Oxford University Press.
- Moore, B. C. J, Tyler, L. K., & Marslen-Wilson, M. (2008). The perception of speech: From sound to meaning. Special issue of *Philosophical Transactions of the Royal Society of London B, 363*, 917–921. A very good selection of papers on speech perception.

Visit the companion website at www. psypress/cw/ward for:

- References to key papers and readings
- Video lectures and interviews on key topics with leading psychologists Daniel Levitin, Oliver Sachs, and author Jamie Ward
- Multiple choice questions and interactive flashcards to test your knowledge
- Downloadable glossary

# CHAPTER 11

# The speaking brain

The ability to produce, perceive, and comprehend speech is a remarkable human achievement. In the most simplistic terms, spoken language is concerned with transferring ideas from one person's head to another person's head with the common physical link being the vibration of molecules in the air. It involves the transformation of thoughts into sentences and words and, ultimately, a series of articulatory commands sent to the vocal apparatus. These sound waves then produce mechanical changes on the cochlea (part of the inner ear) of the listener. These are perceived as speech and the words, sentences and meaning are inferred from this input. Speech recognition and speech production are often studied separately from each other, and it can be helpful to think about them as separate tasks. However, it is important to recognize that the driving force behind human language is to communicate ideas to the people around us. Outside of the laboratory, speech production normally only exists when someone else is around to engage in the complementary process of speech recognition. This social aspect of language implies that we are able to deduce what other people know, what they believe and what they do not know. It is highly questionable whether the vocalizations of other animals could be said to be "true language" in this sense.

The previous chapter considered early auditory processing of speech. This chapter will consider how familiar spoken words are recognized and how the meaning of words and sentences are derived before, finally, considering the process of speech production.

A simple schematic diagram showing some of the main stages in speech production (left) and speech comprehension (right).

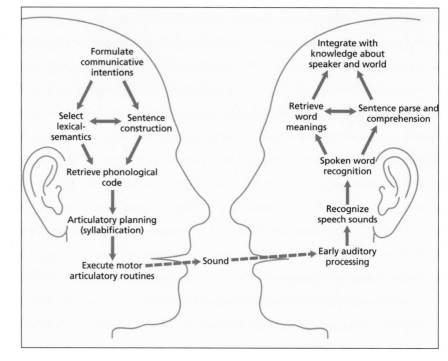

## DO NON-HUMAN ANIMALS HAVE LANGUAGE?

The idea of being able to talk to the animals, Dr. Doolittle style, is a captivating one. Other species are clearly able to communicate with each other. For example, bees perform a dance that signals the location of nectar, and vervet monkeys produce calls when faced with a threatening stimulus. But are these communication systems related to human language? The question of animal language is an important one because it focuses discussion on what language actually is and where it came from.

Many attempts at teaching language to other animals have relied on training them to associate symbols with objects and actions. The main difficulty with these studies is that, although animals are capable of learning associations, it is not clear that they have a conceptual level of understanding. For example, pigeons can be trained to respond in different ways, pecking once or twice, to pictures of trees or water (Herrnstein et al., 1977). But do they understand how trees relate to other concepts such as plants and bark, and could they use pecking to communicate the idea of a tree in the absence of a picture?

What about closer evolutionary neighbors, such as the chimpanzee? The chimp, Washoe, was taught American Sign Language and learned around 200 signs (Gardner et al., 1989). Moreover, there was evidence of overgeneralizations (e.g. using "hurt" for tattoo), and the combining of words for unfamiliar objects (e.g. "water bird" for duck). The system was also spontaneously acquired by Washoe's adopted son. The problem with these studies is that many signs are iconic rather than arbitrary (e.g. "give" is represented by an inward hand motion) and it is not clear how often Washoe produced random or inappropriate word combinations. Some have argued that the ability to

The pygmy chimp Kanzi learned to communicate using written "lexigrams." In what ways is this different from or similar to human language?

Based on Savage-Rumbaugh et al., 1983.

Kanzi using "lexigrams" to communicate.
From Savage-Rumbaugh & Lewin, 1994.

generate an infinite number of meaningful word combinations is the uniquely human component of language (Hauser et al., 2002).

Savage-Rumbaugh and colleagues adopted a different approach with their bonobo or pygmy chimp, Kanzi (e.g. Savage-Rumbaugh et al., 1986). Kanzi learned how to use arbitrary written symbols to communicate, and could select the symbols given human speech. There was evidence that the symbols were used flexibly (e.g. selecting "strawberry" to indicate wanting strawberries, the location of strawberries, or the object itself) and evidence of appreciation of word order (e.g. "Kanzi chase X" versus "X chase Kanzi"). This research has, however, been criticized on the grounds that Kanzi's utterances were mainly food requests that may have been learned through reward and that would not be found in a natural setting (Seidenberg & Petitto, 1987). Thus, while non-human animals may have some of the basic cognitive prerequisites for language it is doubtful that they possess anything akin to the human capacity (Hauser et al., 2002).

# SPOKEN WORD RECOGNITION

It is generally assumed that spoken word recognition entails matching some aspect of an acoustic form to a stored set of spoken words that comprise the set of known words in the speaker's vocabulary. This store of words is known as the **phonological lexicon** (or speech input lexicon), and the matching process itself is called **lexical access**. This process can be broken down in terms of a number of potentially distinct issues. First, what is the nature of the perceptual code that is used to access the stored set of words, and in what format are the stored speech forms themselves stored? Second, how is the matching process itself achieved? Are many different candidates considered together or one at a time? Is the process purely perceptual or does the semantic context matter?

## KEY TERMS

**Phonological lexicon**
A store of the abstract speech sounds that make up known words.

**Lexical access**
The process of matching a perceptual description of a word on to a stored memory description of that word.

# What are the access units for spoken word forms?

Linguists have traditionally placed great emphasis on the importance of phonemes in the representation of speech. Phonemes are categorical representations that distinguish between the sounds of different words. Thus, /r/ and /l/ are different phonemes in English but not Japanese. Even though /r/ and /l/ have certain acoustic and articulatory properties in common, they are considered as separate categories in languages that make this phonemic distinction. Some models of spoken word recognition also place great emphasis on the role of a phonemic code, as in the case of the motor theory of speech recognition (Liberman & Mattingly, 1985; Liberman & Whalen, 2000). However, other cognitive neuroscientists have taken a more skeptical approach and have argued that phonemes may just be useful descriptions of the structure of language rather than something that is actually implemented in real cognitive/neural systems. For example, in some models, acoustic features of speech (e.g. voicing, stops, formant frequencies) are considered to access the spoken word forms directly without an intermediate phonemic description (Marslen-Wilson & Warren, 1994).

The evidence for a phonemic level in lexical access is equivocal. Some patients with acquired speech recognition problems are able to comprehend spoken words but are poor at explicitly discriminating between phonemes (e.g. are "ta" and "da" different?), whereas others show the opposite dissociation (Miceli et al., 1980). Indeed, the ability to explicitly segment speech into phoneme segments appears to be predicted by literacy levels, particularly for alphabetic scripts, rather than spoken language ability (Petersson et al., 2000). This suggests that explicit phonemic awareness is not critical for speech recognition, although it remains to be determined whether such units are computed implicitly. In Hickok and Poeppel's (2004) model, explicit phoneme segmentation is captured by the dorsal route, whereas spoken word comprehension is performed by the ventral route. Recall from Chapter 10, that the ventral route is primarily concerned with speech comprehension, i.e. the process of translating between an acoustic input and a semantic output, whereas the dorsal route is concerned with more motoric aspects of speech (as well as locating sound sources), i.e. the process of translating an acoustic input into a motor output.

If not phonemes, then what are alternative perceptual access codes for spoken word recognition? Some researchers have argued that syllables may be critical (Mehler et al., 1981), whereas others have emphasized the importance of stress patterns (Cutler & Butterfield, 1992). In English, nouns tend to be stressed on the first syllable and this can be used by the speech recognition system to infer likely word boundaries (consider the nouns *EN*voy and *DE*coy, and compare with verbs such as en*JOY* and de*CAY,* in which stress is assigned to the second syllable). Models of speech recognition that are more neurobiologically inspired are based on the idea that different neurons respond to acoustic information that varies on different time scales (Luo & Poeppel, 2012). In primate electrophysiology, some neurons may respond preferentially to relatively rapid changes in the auditory signal (20–80 ms range), whereas others may respond preferentially to changes occurring over medium (150–300 ms) and longer (500–1,000 ms) time scales (see DeWitt & Rauschecker, 2012). In human speech, these time scales may correspond approximately to acoustic features of phonemes, syllables and stress patterns

## LINGUISTIC TERMINOLOGY MADE SIMPLE

**Phoneme**
A minimal unit of speech that serves to distinguish between meanings of words. In English, /r/ and /l/ are different phonemes because this sound difference can convey differences in word meaning (e.g. between "rip" and "lip"). In languages such as Japanese, this is not so and /r/ and /l/ are variants of a single phoneme.

**Syllable**
Clusters of phonemes that are centered on a vowel sound. The vowel forms the *nucleus* of the syllable. The vowel may optionally be preceded by consonant sounds (termed the syllable *onset*), and may optionally be followed by more consonants (termed the syllable *coda*). The vowel and coda collectively make up the *rime* of the syllable. The words "mark," "market," and "marquetry" have one, two, and three syllables, respectively.

**Stress**
An increase in the activity of the vocal apparatus of a speaker that aids segmentation of the speech stream into words.

**Morpheme**
The smallest meaningful unit in the grammar of a language. For example, "unladylike" has four syllables and three morphemes (un + lady+ like). "Dogs" has one syllable but two morphemes (dog+ s). Both "unladylike" and "dogs" are one word.

**Word**
Words occupy an intermediate position in size between a morpheme and a phrase. A word is sometimes defined as being the minimal possible unit in a reply.

**Syntax**
The rules (or grammar) that specify how words can be combined into sentences in a given language.

**Semantics**
Broadly defined as the meaning of linguistic expressions, but also defined as the meaning of particular words (lexical-semantics) or the meaning of objects, words and other types of stimuli (semantic memory).

**Pragmatics**
The way in which language is used in practice, such as implied or intended meaning (e.g. "Can't you read?" may be used as a rhetorical question that does not require an answer).

**Prosody**
Melodic aspects of spoken language such as stress, intonation (e.g. rising pitch to indicate a question), and emotion (e.g. slow and low to imply sadness).

**Nouns**
"The" words, which imply *things*, such as "the computer," "the idea."

**Verbs**
"To" words, which imply an *action*, such as "to buy," "to think," "to eat."

**Adjectives**
Words used descriptively such as "big," "soft," "easy."

**Pronoun**
A word that can substitute for a noun (e.g. "I," "you," and "him"). In the sentence "Mr. Rice spoke to Tom and offered him a job," "him" is the pronoun; it takes the place of "Tom."

**Preposition**
Indicates a connection, between two other parts of speech, such as "to," "with," "by" or "from."

**Function words**
**(or closed class words)**
Words that have little lexical meaning but instead serve to express grammatical relationships with other words within a sentence (e.g. pronouns, prepositions, "the," "and").

(respectively) that dominate in purely cognitive models of speech recognition. De Witt and Rauschecker (2012) suggest, based on a meta-analysis of fMRI studies of speech recognition, that these different time scales are implemented in the auditory ventral stream in a hierarchical fashion from short-to-long durations and from posterior-to-anterior along the superior temporal lobes. As such, multiple features of the acoustic signal (varying in temporal duration, and psycholinguistic unit size) are likely to contribute to word recognition rather than being reliant on a single source of information (e.g. phonemic).

## The cohort model

Although the precise nature of the mechanism by which spoken word recognition takes place is still debated, there is general consensus that it involves competition between similar sounding words (McQueen & Cutler, 2001). The most influential model in this area is the **cohort model** of Marslen-Wilson and Tyler (1980; Marslen-Wilson, 1987). The acoustic information required to identify a word is revealed over time. The central idea of this model is that a large number of spoken words are, in parallel, initially considered as candidates but that words get eliminated as more evidence accumulates. For example, on hearing the sound "e" all words beginning with this sound would become active. This is termed the cohort of words. But as more information is revealed (e.g. "ele"), then the cohort gets whittled down to fewer words (e.g. "elephant," "electricity") until a point is reached ("eleph") in which the evidence is consistent with only a single word. This is termed the **uniqueness point**. Thus the start of a word, particularly the first syllable, has an exaggerated importance. Indeed, listeners are better at detecting speech distortions when they occur prior to the uniqueness point, and the time taken to recognize a word depends on how early or late the uniqueness point occurs (Marslen-Wilson, 1987).

The uniqueness point is a structural property of the word, but do linguistic factors such as word frequency and imageability influence recognition? Considering word frequency, it is the case that not all candidates in a cohort behave equivalently. For example, the ambiguous onset "spee" is compatible with "speed," "speech," "species," and so on. However, studies of reaction time priming show that infrequent words (e.g. "species") get activated less (Zwitserlood, 1989). This suggests an early effect of word frequency. The imageability of a word also affects spoken word recognition but only for highly competitive cohorts (Tyler *et al.*, 2000). **Imageability** is a semantic property of a word that relates to the extent to which a word's meaning can evoke sensory images. An fMRI study shows that imageability and degree of cohort competition interact in a posterior region of the superior temporal gyrus—a region implicated in relatively early speech processing (Zhuang *et al.*, 2011). As such, selection from the cohort is not a purely bottom-up process (i.e. not determined solely by the perceptual input).

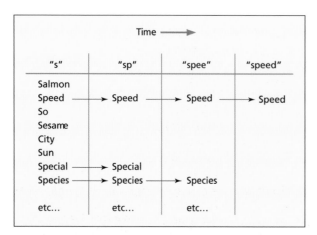

In the cohort model of spoken word recognition, all words that are initially consistent with the acoustic information become active in parallel. As more acoustic information is revealed, the size of the cohort is dwindled until a unique match can be made.

# Word recognition in context: the N400

The cohort model was primarily developed to explain the recognition of single spoken words. However, words are normally spoken in the context of a discourse rather than in isolation. This raises the important question as to how these different aspects of spoken word recognition are related: i.e., recognizing the form of a spoken word, retrieving its meaning, and linking word meaning to the wider meaning of the utterance.

One ERP component has been particularly informative for addressing this issue: the **N400**, so called because it reflects a negative peak at around 400 ms after the onset of a word (Kutas & Hillyard, 1980; for a review see Kutas & Federmeier, 2011). The amplitude of the N400 depends critically on whether a given word is appropriate to the wider context. Thus, the sentence "I take coffee with milk and dog" elicits a large N400 to the contextually anomalous word "dog" relative to the same sentence ending with

The N400 response to the critical word in three types of sentence: semantically coherent and correct ("the Dutch trains are *yellow*"; green line), semantically coherent but incorrect ("the Dutch trains are *white*"; brown line), semantically incoherent ("the Dutch trains are *sour*"; black line).

From Hagoort *et al.*, 2004. Reprinted with permission from AAAS.

the semantically appropriate word "sugar" (or a different sentence in which "dog" is an appropriate ending). The N400 is found either when a word is semantically anomalous, as in "the Dutch trains are sour" (trains cannot be tasted), or conflicts with known facts about the world, as in "the Dutch trains are white" (Dutch people know they are yellow) (Hagoort *et al.*, 2004). This suggests that word-knowledge and world-knowledge are both brought to bear on this process rather than representing two separate processing stages. Words need not be presented in sentence form for the N400 to be elicited. For example, given a semantically ambiguous word such as "bank," an N400 is elicited for the third word in triplets such as "river–bank–money," but not "finance–bank–money" (Titone & Salisbury, 2004). This result also suggests that the N400 reflects global context (operating over all three words) and not local context, given that the last two words are identical in both triplets.

The N400 is found for written words presented one at a time as well as spoken words (and, indeed, for other meaningful stimuli besides words). As such, it is not critically dependent on perceptual processes. Nevertheless, the N400 tends to emerge earlier for spoken words than written words (Holcomb & Neville, 1990). This is perhaps surprising given that spoken words are heard piecemeal over time. It suggests that the semantic context interacts with lexical access even before the spoken word can be uniquely discriminated. Several studies support this interpretation. Van den Brink *et al.* (2001) compared sentences with highly probable endings ("It was a pleasant surprise to find that the car repair bill was only 17 *dollars*") to those with contextually inappropriate endings including those that shared initial (e.g. "dolphin"), not final (e.g. "scholar") phonemes. In this example, "scholar" is linked to an earlier onset of the N400 than "dolphin." This reflects the mismatch between the heard and expected initial phonemes. Finally, van den Brink *et al.* (2006) varied the uniqueness point of the critical spoken word.

### KEY TERM

**N400**
An event-related component in EEG found when a word meaning appears out of context or unexpectedly.

**Amodal**
Not tied to one or more perceptual systems.

**Symbol grounding problem**
The problem of defining concepts without assuming some preexisting knowledge.

Despite the fact that words with an early uniqueness point could be identified 100 ms faster than the other words, the N400 did not shift in time. Thus, the language system does not have to "wait" for the uniqueness point to be reached before it can generate an N400, and, hence, lexical access and contextual integration are not two separate and discrete stages in speech recognition.

# SEMANTIC MEMORY AND THE MEANING OF WORDS

## Amodal versus grounded concepts

On encountering a word such as "lion" one is able to retrieve many associated properties, such as the fact that it is an animal, has four legs, is a native of Africa and is a carnivore. Collectively, such properties are considered to comprise the meaning of the word. According to most theories, this same knowledge base is consulted irrespective of whether the spoken word is heard, the written word is seen, or if a lion itself is seen, heard, or just merely thought about. In other words, semantic memory is often considered to be **amodal** or abstract. The notion that semantic memory is based on amodal representations (or "symbols") has dominated cognitive psychology for almost a century. However, this is by no means universally accepted and it encounters several problems.

This problem associated with representing the meaning of words as abstract symbols is well exemplified by Searle's (1980, 1990) Chinese room argument. In this philosophical thought-experiment, Searle asks us to imagine a computer that can process Chinese symbols to the extent that it can answer questions posed to it in Chinese such that these answers are sufficient to fool a native speaker. However, he claims that such a computer would not understand the meaning of Chinese. Taking the argument further, nor would a person locked in a room who processed Chinese using the same algorithm. The "mental lexicon" metaphor also falls into the same trap. It is often stated that the brain implements something akin to a dictionary (the mental lexicon)—i.e. a store of all the known words, how they sound, their grammatical usage (noun, verb, etc.), their meaning, and

It is often claimed that our brain contains a "mental lexicon," which, like a dictionary, specifies the properties of a word, such as how it is pronounced, its grammatical class (e.g. noun, verb), and its meaning(s).

so on. The problem with defining words in terms of other words, like a dictionary, is that it is an entirely circular process. When looking up a dictionary definition of, say, "power" one may get "strength or force exerted" and when looking up "force" one gets the definition "power made operative against resistance" and "strength" defined as "a source of power or force." In short, it is impossible to get a satisfactory definition for any given word without knowing the meaning of some other words in advance. This is termed the **symbol grounding problem** in linguistics.

One way of breaking the circle is if there are some concepts that are not defined in terms of each other but are "grounded" by universals in the environment and our interactions with them (such as shared perceptual and motor experiences). So, for instance, the meaning of words such as "pull" or "kick" could be grounded by the actions of our motor system, and "sweet" and "green" could be grounded by our perceptual experiences of the world. Thus, our conceptual knowledge of "green" may be derived from the associated sensory experiences rather than some abstract definition (e.g. knowing the likely wavelengths of light that correspond to green)—although the latter could be represented within semantic memory too. Grounded concepts could either be learned or innate, with some theories advocating one position or the other (see Barsalou, 2008). Certain abstract concepts may also be grounded in the same way. For instance, the proposal that the meaning of numbers has a spatial component (see Chapter 13) can be regarded as an example of grounding, as can the proposal that emotions can be defined in terms of contextualized bodily feelings (see Chapter 15). The term **embodied cognition** is used to refer to the use of the body (its movement, or internal state) to represent meaning and can be considered as a sub-field within grounded cognition (Barsalou, 2008; Wilson, 2002).

The contemporary landscape of models of semantic memory spans virtually the entire range of possibilities from amodal to fully grounded. In fully grounded models (Allport, 1985; Martin, 2007; Martin & Chao, 2001), the collection of different semantic features that make up a concept reside solely in the different information channels from which they were acquired. So, for instance, the semantic memory of a telephone would reside partly in auditory regions (for what it sounds like), visual regions (for what it looks like), action-related regions (for how to use it), and so on. The different domains of knowledge would be inter-connected as a network such that activating one property (e.g. the sound of a telephone) triggers activity in other parts of the network (e.g. its associated actions and appearance)— a process termed pattern-completion. In these accounts, retrieving information

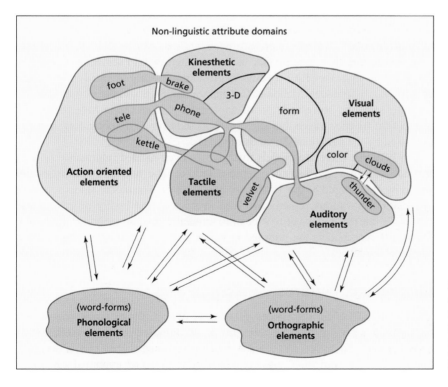

In Allport's (1985) model, concepts are distributed over many different domains of knowledge.

The hub-and-spoke model is a hybrid model of semantic memory which contains both amodal representations (assumed to lie in the anterior temporal lobes; the "hub") and representations that are grounded in sensory and motor systems (the "spokes").

Adapted from Patterson et al., 2007.

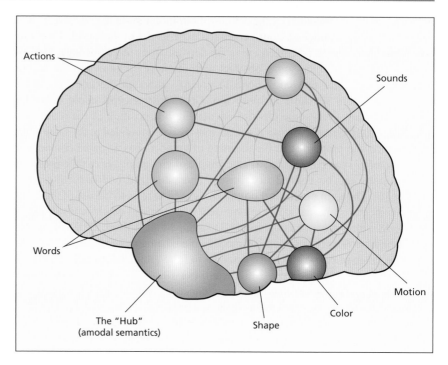

from semantic memory involves many of the same processes that are involved in mental imagery. There is evidence consistent with this. For instance, on encountering a sentence such as: "The ranger saw the eagle in the sky," participants are subsequently faster at naming a picture of an eagle (priming) but, crucially, they are even faster at naming a picture of an eagle with outstretched wings than one that is perched with folded wings (Zwaan et al., 2002).

On the other extreme, there are accounts that can be classed as weakly grounded in that they assume that the core system within semantic memory is amodal but that modality-specific representations are evoked more as a downstream by-product (Mahon & Caramazza, 2008). So, in the example above, the core semantic representation of an "eagle" would *not* include perceptual image(s) of its appearance, but such images could (in a non-obligatory way) be generated by the particular demands of the task.

In between, there are models that give an even-handed importance to both abstract and grounded semantic representations. The **hub-and-spoke model** would be an example of this (Patterson et al., 2007). The model stores semantic information in various regions involved in sensory and bodily processes (the "spokes") but these connect to a central, amodal, semantic system ("the hub"). These different models are returned to below in more detail and in light of the empirical evidence.

## Hierarchies, features, and categories

Whether amodal or fully grounded, all theories of semantic memory propose that the meaning of words (and objects, etc.) is decomposed into a constellation of basic features. These features are assumed to be linked together via a network. For example, the word "lion" may connect with features such as animal, carnivore,

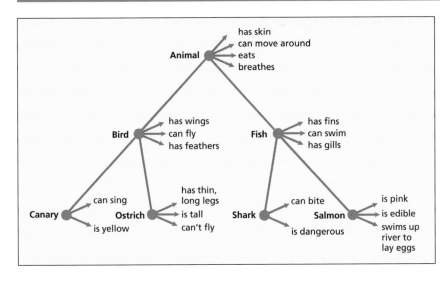

In the Collins and Quinlan (1969) model, semantic features are organized hierarchically with super-ordinate information accessed first. Subsequent models have retained the idea that knowledge may consist of a network of interconnected features but do not make the assumption of hierarchical organization.

Reprinted from Collins & Quinlan, 1969. © 1969, with permission from Elsevier.

etc.; the feature "animal" may connect with eats, breathes, reproduces, etc.; "breathes" connects with lungs, and so on. This network enables generalizations and novel inferences to be made. So, for instance, a question such as "does a giraffe have kidneys?" can be answered with a high degree of confidence despite the fact that this semantic proposition has (almost certainly) never been encountered before.

Although all models propose that concepts are comprised of a constellation of constituent features, models of semantic memory differ in terms of:

- What format do the features take: e.g. amodal versus grounded?
- How are the features organized: hierarchical versus non-hierarchical?
- Is category information (e.g. "is an animal") represented in addition to feature-level information (e.g. "has eyes"), or are categories purely emergent properties of features?

To give one concrete example, the early influential model of Collins and Quinlan (1969) assumed a hierarchical organization. Moreover, features in this model are regarded as amodal symbols. So the feature of salmon, "is pink," should be construed as representing information that is *about* color rather than the alternative claim that the information is stored using a visually based code. There is some evidence that supports the hierarchical nature of the model. Participants are faster at classifying a robin as a bird than an animal, because the latter requires going further up in the hierarchy (which takes additional processing time). However, there are also problems with the model. For example, not all concepts have clear hierarchies (e.g. the difference between truth, justice, and law). Second, apparent effects of distance within the hierarchy could also be explained by how frequently two words or concepts co-occur (Wilkins, 1971). For example, robin and bird may co-occur together more than robin and animal.

There is some evidence that these different kinds of super-ordinate and sub-ordinate information have different neural substrates. The lateral temporal lobes are widely recognized as having an important role in semantic memory, and constitute the ventral "what" route of speech processing (Hickok & Poeppel, 2004).

Rogers *et al.* (2006) found that different parts of the lateral temporal lobes were activated depending on the specificity of the information. There was a posterior to anterior gradient from less specific information (e.g. animal), intermediate specificity (e.g. bird) to more specific information (e.g. robin). This may explain why some studies of lexical semantics have highlighted posterior temporal regions (Hickock & Poeppel, 2004), whereas others implicate more anterior temporal regions (Mummery *et al.*, 2000). Both could be correct, depending on the type of information (super-ordinate, sub-ordinate) being evaluated. Patients with damage centered on the anterior temporal lobes tend to retain the ability to make super-ordinate classifications (e.g. "animal," "bird") but struggle more with item and sub-ordinate level classifications (e.g. "dog," "Labrador") (Rogers & Patterson, 2007). This supports the evidence from functional imaging that more anterior regions of the temporal lobes are activated by more finer-grained semantic judgments (e.g. Rogers *et al.*, 2006).

Another property of the Collins and Quinlan (1969) model is that categories are explicitly represented in the semantic network (e.g. as an "animal node" or "fish node"). Some contemporary models also endorse the view that, at least some, semantic categories are explicitly represented. Caramazza and Shelton (1998) put forward an evolutionarily based proposal that at least some categories are hard-wired. The categories proposed were animals, plant life (e.g. fruit and vegetables), conspecifics (other humans) and possibly tools. The alternative way of thinking about categories is to view them as emergent properties that come about because similar concepts tend to share similar features. For instance, animals tend to have lots of correlated features (i.e. features that tend to co-occur) such as presence of eyes, mouth, self-initiated movement, and so on. Man-made objects, on the other hand, tend to have distinctive relations between their shape and function (e.g. sharp edges and cutting). Computational simulations of semantic features of objects and animals tend not to result in a uniform network (i.e. different features associated to each other with roughly equal weightings) but rather a "lumpy" structure in which some features tend to be closely connected with each other but hardly connected at all to other sets of features in the network (Devlin *et al.*, 1998; Tyler & Moss, 2001). This has implications for how semantic memory is likely to be implemented in the brain. In general, the wiring in the brain tends to minimize the amount of long-range connections in favor of so-called small-world networks in which local connectivity dominates (Sporns *et al.*, 2004). One reason for this is the physical pressure for space limited by the size of the cranium (with longer connections requiring more space). Translating this principle into semantic memory, one would expect that correlated classes of features (e.g. those relevant to tools or animals) would tend not be uniformly distributed across the brain but would tend to be clustered together—i.e. that the "lumpy" structure is found not only in terms of patterns of connectivity but also in terms of different regions of the brain being specialized for representing different kinds of semantic feature.

## Category specificity in semantic knowledge

This section considers evidence that different kinds of semantic features (and/or categories) are represented in different regions of the brain. This can be considered using evidence from both lesion methods (selective patterns of semantic deficit) and functional imaging. At this point, it may be useful to attempt to clarify the difference between a "feature" and a "category." In general, the term feature implies that it is a property of an exemplar (e.g. "is green," "has eyes") and the term category denotes the set of exemplars. To some extent, the delineation between these terms can be a little arbitrary. For instance, consider the domain of color. Color is typically regarded as a semantic feature (e.g. of fruit, vegetables, animals) but, of course, it can also be regarded as a category within its own right.

## The sensory-functional distinction

Two publications in the early 1980s triggered an enduring debate on the neural organization of semantic categories (for a review, see Capitani *et al.*, 2003). Warrington and McCarthy (1983) documented a patient with acquired brain damage who had preserved knowledge for animals, foods and flowers relative to inanimate objects. The following year, Warrington and Shallice (1984) reported four patients with the opposite profile. These patients were impaired at comprehending pictures and words, in naming pictures, and matching pictures and words. To account for this pattern, Warrington and Shallice (1984) proposed the **sensory–functional distinction**. They suggested that certain categories may depend critically on certain types of knowledge: animals and fruit and vegetables may be defined more by their sensory properties (color, shape, four legs, etc.), whereas inanimate objects, particularly tools, may be defined by their functions.

In the original versions of the theory, there was no commitment that sensory and functional semantic properties would depend on perceptual and action-based regions of the brain (the assumption was that the semantic features were amodal). However, others have subsequently made this claim (e.g. the "sensorimotor" account; Martin & Chao, 2001). Functional imaging shows that different regions of temporal cortex show selective activity for tool movement versus human movement and, moreover, that the same regions are implicated in naming tools versus animals (Beauchamp *et al.*, 2002). Results such as these are intriguing but they can potentially be interpreted in different ways. For example, it could be the case that sensorimotor areas are activated top-down by other regions that form the core conceptual knowledge base, or that category-specific effects can arise at multiple levels within the cognitive system (e.g. at both modality-specific object recognition stages and amodal conceptual levels; Humphreys & Forde, 2001).

The sensory–functional account has been challenged by a number of lines of evidence. Brain-damaged patients with animate category-specific deficits are not necessarily impaired at answering sensory relative to functional questions about animals or objects (Funnell & DeMornay Davies, 1996; Lambon Ralph *et al.*, 1998). Conversely, some patients do present with selective difficulties in comprehending sensory properties but yet do not show the predicted category-specific impairments (Coltheart *et al.*, 1998). This suggests that sensory knowledge and animal knowledge can be independently impaired. This supports the general idea that semantic memory is not

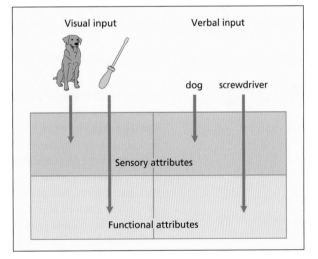

It has been argued that semantic memory may be organized along the lines of functional versus sensory features, rather than categorically along the lines of animals, tools, food, etc.

From Humphreys and Forde, 2001. © Cambridge University Press. Reproduced with permission.

homogeneous (i.e. it is "lumpy"), but does not support the specific idea that the category of animals emerges from a close dependence on knowledge of sensory features.

## Beyond the sensory-functional distinction

Subsequent models (e.g. Martin, 2007; Patterson *et al.*, 2007; Warrington & McCarthy, 1987) have retained the basic assumption that semantic memories for words are distributed over many different domains of knowledge (such as action-based, shape-based, movement-based, and so on) but have moved away from the notion that the features are divided into a dichotomy (such as sensory-functional). Evidence in support of this comes from a consideration of other categories beyond animals and tools.

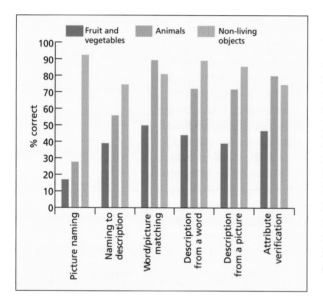

Patient RS had a particular difficulty with fruit and vegetables relative to other categories in a wide range of tasks.

From Samson and Pillon, 2003.

## Food

A number of studies have shown that impairments in understanding fruit and vegetables can dissociate from relative sparing of animals and man-made objects (Hart *et al.*, 1985; Samson & Pillon, 2003). In the case reported by Samson and Pillon (2003), the deficit extended to manufactured foods and the deficit was found in all comprehension tasks and when different types of semantic attribute were probed. The patient could choose the correct color given a black and white drawing, suggesting that there was no severe loss of sensory features (at least for color). They argued that food is represented categorically in support of Caramazza and Shelton (1998).

## Colors

Luzzatti and Davidoff (1994) report a patient who was able to name colors but could not retrieve colors given black and white line drawings (e.g. of a tomato). The fact that the patient was able to name actual colors rules out a perceptual deficit, or a loss of the words themselves. Functional imaging also supports the contention that perceiving and knowing about colors are distinct (Chao & Martin, 1999). Another patient was impaired at comprehending the color of objects but had spared form, size and function knowledge (Miceli *et al.*, 2001). Interestingly, the patient showed no category specificity (e.g. for fruits and vegetables). Thus, it is possible to have selective difficulties in particular knowledge domains (e.g. color) that do not reveal themselves as other category effects.

## Body parts

Some patients have relatively preserved knowledge of body parts relative to other living categories (Shelton *et al.*, 1998). Conversely, other patients present with difficulties in understanding body parts. Patients with **autotopagnosia** are unable to localize body parts on themselves, on pictures or on others, and their errors appear to be conceptual (Semenza, 1988; Semenza & Goodglass, 1985). For example, they might point to their elbow instead of their knee or their ear instead of their eye. In this instance, the deficit is often restricted to one particular aspect of body-part knowledge—namely, their location. It is not due simply to an inability to localize per se or a sensorimotor deficit (e.g. they can demonstrate normal location of gloves and ties) or a gross loss of category knowledge (e.g. they can say that the mouth is used for eating, and name pictures of body parts). In the case of body parts, it seems as if different features are represented differently (e.g. bodily location versus function) rather than behaving as an isolatable category in which all the relevant features are affected.

## Actions and verbs

Action concepts tend to map most closely on to the grammatical category of verbs. Logically, it appears possible to have action concepts that are not encoded with respect to a single word. For example, there is no single word for the action concept of "put the kettle on." Moreover, the meaning of verbs may encompass other types of information, such as the manner of execution (e.g. kicking done with the legs not arms), the type of object acted on (e.g. lifting implies an object acted on, but smiling does not), and intentions. Many verbs have no concrete action at all (e.g. to obey, to think). As such, it is helpful to think of action concepts as constituting part of semantic memory and verbs as constituting a grammatical property of words. The empirical evidence largely supports the distinction between grammatical and conceptual properties of verbs/actions (Druks, 2002; Shapiro & Caramazza, 2003). However, others have sought to explain differences in nouns and verbs purely in semantic terms. Bird *et al.* (2000) asked the question, "Why is a verb like an inanimate object?" The answer, according to this group, is that verbs and tools both load on to the functional side of the sensory–functional distinction. In support of this, lesion studies suggest an overlap in left parietofrontal regions involved in both action and tool comprehension (Tranel *et al.*, 2003). Moreover, event-related fMRI shows that verbs such as "lick," "pick" and "kick" activate regions that overlap with or are next to the corresponding part of the motor cortex—mouth, fingers, and legs (Hauk *et al.*, 2004). However, studies that directly compare action concepts against the noun/verb distinction do show independent contributions. One ERP study contrasted word attributes (abstract, high visual, high visual + motor) and grammatical class (noun, verb) and found

Some aphasic patients are impaired at naming verbs presented as pictorial actions.

From Druks and Masterson, 2000.

---

**KEY TERM**

**Proper name anomia**
Severe difficulties in retrieving proper names.

independent effects with no interaction (Kellenbach *et al.*, 2002). TMS research has shown that retrieval of both nouns and verbs associated with actions is disrupted by stimulation of motor areas but the same does not apply to non-action words (Oliveri *et al.*, 2004). In summary, action concepts appear to be a relatively specialized category but this does not map on to the difference between nouns and verbs in a straightforward way.

## Proper names

Proper names such as "Michael Jackson," "Paris" and "Lassie" denote particular instances, whereas corresponding common nouns such as "pop star," "city," and "dog" denote a class of entities. As with other categories, it is important to be clear whether any category specificity reflects damage to a conceptual system rather than word retrieval or grammatical mechanisms. Some patients have severe difficulties in retrieving proper names (called **proper name anomia**) but can comprehend them, suggesting the difficulty is not in semantics (Semenza & Zettin, 1988). However, other cases have been reported in which the deficit appears to reflect semantics (Bredart *et al.*, 1997). Ellis *et al.* (1989) report a patient who, after a right temporal lobectomy, was unable to name or understand "singular objects" such as famous people, famous animals, famous buildings, and brand names. There were no difficulties with animals per se or other categories. The opposite dissociation has been reported (Van Lancker & Klein, 1990). So are proper names represented categorically within the semantic system? This account seems too simplistic, because dissociations within the domain of proper names have been reported. Some cases have impaired semantic knowledge of people but not places (Miceli *et al.*, 2000), whereas others have the opposite effect (Lyons *et al.*, 2002).

## Numbers

The conceptual representation of numbers is dealt with in Chapter 12. However, it is interesting to note at this juncture that there is a double dissociation between spared numbers and impairments of other concepts (Cappelletti *et al.*, 2002), and impaired numbers but spared knowledge of other concepts (Cipolotti *et al.*, 1991). It is often argued that the representation of number knowledge is a true categorical distinction (Dehaene *et al.*, 2003).

## Semantic dementia as damage to an amodal hub?

Much of the evidence presented above supports the general view of semantic memory as a distributed network of specialized clusters. As one review has put it: "The search for the neuroanatomical locus of semantic memory has simultaneously led us nowhere and everywhere" (Thompson-Schill, 2003). However, there is one neurodegenerative condition that appears to affect semantic memory relatively selectively (sparing other cognitive functions) and globally (affecting almost all domains of knowledge)—semantic dementia. It tends to affect all semantic categories and features (albeit with some variability across patients). As noted in previous chapters, this is linked to atrophy of the temporal poles (Mummery *et al.*, 2000). This suggests that there is one region of the brain that is particularly important for the storage of semantic memories, even if many other regions of the brain have a role to play.

Patterson *et al.* (2007) explain semantic dementia in terms of damage to an amodal semantic store (termed the "hub") which acts to bind together different grounded features (termed the "spokes"). Why is an amodal hub needed at all? According to this model, the hub enables exceptional items to be categorized (e.g. penguin, ostrich) and enables superficially different entities to be grouped together (e.g. a prawn and scallop as seafood). Patients with semantic dementia are able to categorize pictures relatively accurately when the exemplars are typical (e.g. categorizing a dog as an animal) but struggle with atypical category members (e.g. failing to categorize an ostrich as a bird; Patterson, 2007). When asked to select semantic features, they are biased toward choosing the typical category answer. For instance, they may match green with carrot because most vegetables are green (Rogers *et al.*, 2007). In short, patients with semantic dementia are able to make category distinctions based on feature probabilities, but not based on conventional knowledge which incorporates exceptions-to-the-rule and learned taxonomies. This suggests that there may be a specialized mechanism for implementing the latter and may depend on interactions with medial temporal lobe structures (involved in long-term learning and memory, including semantic memory) and the nearby temporal poles (damaged in semantic dementia).

| Item | Sept 1991 | Mar 1992 | Sept 1992 | Mar 1993 |
|---|---|---|---|---|
| Bird | – | – | – | Animal |
| Chicken | – | – | Bird | Animal |
| Duck | – | Bird | Bird | Dog |
| Swan | – | Bird | Bird | Animal |
| Eagle | Duck | Bird | Bird | Horse |
| Ostrich | Swan | Bird | Cat | Animal |
| Peacock | Duck | Bird | Cat | Vehicle |
| Penguin | Duck | Bird | Cat | Part of animal |
| Rooster | Chicken | Chicken | Bird | Dog |

*Top*: when shown a picture and asked to reproduce it after a delay of only a few seconds, patients with semantic dementia tend to reproduce typical features of the category (e.g. four-legs, tails) but omit atypical features of the particular exemplar (e.g. the hump, flippers). *Bottom*: when naming animals they also tend to generate more typical category members as their impairment progresses with time.

From Patterson *et al.*, 2007.

## Evaluation

Several models of semantic memory have been introduced in this section so far. The present section aims to directly contrast them and relate them back to the evidence. One issue relates to the question of whether different semantic features tend to be clustered together anatomically and whether knowledge of semantic categories (e.g. animals) depends on the integrity of certain kinds of features more than others. A second issue relates to the nature of the conceptual representations: are they amodal or grounded in sensory, motor and affective processes?

With regards to the first issue, evidence from patients with impaired semantic memory after brain damage suggest that it is possible to impair quite specific domains of knowledge such as the location of body parts, and the colors of objects. It is also possible to selectively impair categories such as animals, food, and action words. Evidence from functional imaging and TMS in normal participants adds support to the view that different kinds of semantic features tend to have different anatomical loci. Some models of semantic memory have assumed that semantic categories are derived solely by the kinds of features they depend upon: the most prominent being models based on the sensory-functional distinction (Farah & McClelland, 1991; Warrington & Shallice, 1984). However, the empirical evidence suggests that it is possible to impair features and categories separately. This does not support the view that categories depend entirely on correlated features. So how are semantic categories represented in the brain if not as an emergent property of the kinds of features that comprise them? One proposal is that certain categories are innately given (Caramazza & Shelton, 1998). Another proposal, relating to the hub-and-spoke model (Patterson *et al.*, 2007), is that category structures are learned but belong to a separate system (the hub) to that which represents the content-based features (at the end of the spokes).

The second key issue introduced at the outset is whether semantic features are amodal or are grounded in sensory, motor, and bodily states. It would be fair to see that imaging methods have changed the intellectual landscape over the last 20 years and previous models, derived primarily from neuropsychological investigations, have had to incorporate the new findings. Specifically brain regions that are traditionally classified as being important for perception and action also appear to be involved in supporting some aspects of semantic memory. Researchers who had previously advocated a solely amodal semantic system (Caramazza *et al.*, 1990) have now incorporated these findings (Mahon & Caramazza, 2008). However, incorporating this new evidence does not necessarily entail the abandonment of the idea of an amodal store of semantic concepts. Mahon and Caramazza (2008) maintain that an amodal system is at the core of semantic memory but that

## LOOKING BACK ON NINETEENTH-CENTURY MODELS OF SPEECH AND APHASIA

Paul Broca (1861) is credited with providing the first scientific evidence that specific cognitive functions can be localized in the brain, although this idea had been around for some time (e.g. in the earlier phrenology movement). His patient, Leborgne, lost the ability to produce speech and his utterances consisted of "tan, tan, tan . . ." Broca concluded that there is a dedicated language center in the brain.

Wernicke (1874) documented a different type of aphasia in which the patient was fluent but had difficulties comprehending speech. He divided the spoken forms of words into separate input and output centers termed "auditory images" and "motor images," respectively.

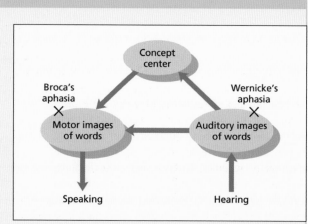

The Lichtheim model of speech and aphasia links together Wernicke's and Broca's area via direct and indirect routes.

Damage to the auditory images was assumed to impair speech perception and was associated with **Wernicke's aphasia**. Damage to the motor images was assumed to impair speech production and was associated with **Broca's aphasia**. Perhaps the most influential model of speech and aphasia to derive from the classical nineteenth-century research is that of Lichtheim (1885). His basic idea survived at least 100 years in various guises (Goodglass & Kaplan, 1972). Lichtheim maintained Wernicke's distinction between auditory and motor centers and argued that they are linked by two routes: both directly and indirectly via a concept center (equivalent to semantic memory). These separate routes were based on Lichtheim's observations that some aphasic patients have repetition disorders but adequate comprehension.

In some respects, the Lichtheim model still has a contemporary resonance. For example, the notion of separate speech input and output lexicons is still incorporated in most models (Shallice, 1988) as is the notion that there are both semantic and auditory-verbal routes to repetition (Butterworth & Warrington, 1995). The most significant challenges to the Lichtheim model have come from the observation that Broca's and Wernicke's aphasia are not well characterized as selective disorders of output and input. Broca's aphasics often have problems in comprehension as well as production (Caramazza & Zurif, 1976). Wernicke's aphasics also have difficulties in output as well as input. They tend to produce made-up words or neologisms: "A bun, bun (BULL) . . . a buk (BULL) is cherching (CHASING) a boy or skert (SCOUT) . . ." (Ellis *et al.* 1983). In fact, some have argued that these are meaningless syndromes that have no real modern-day relevance (Badecker & Caramazza, 1985). Furthermore, the functions associated with the regions termed Broca's area and Wernicke's area tend to be manifold and do not always map on to the functions that one would expect from the aphasic subtypes. Articulation deficits are not associated with damage to Broca's area (Dronkers, 1996); this suggests it is not a speech motor store. Wernicke's area comprises a number of functional regions involved in perception of non-speech as well as speech (Wise *et al.*, 2001) and involved separately in comprehension and in acoustic/phonological analysis (Robson *et al.*, 2012).

information spreads from this core system, perhaps bi-directionally, to regions involved in perception and action. This spreading activation may provide a "dressing" to conceptual processing that enriches it with detail but, they argue, that the amodal system is needed to maintain invariance of concepts in the face of significant variability in superficial details. For instance, the word/concept "dog" can be instantiated from Chihuahua through to Rhodesian Ridgeback. The diametrically opposite view holds that semantic concepts are not fixed but are dynamically constructed from the information presented at the time and constructed solely from perceptual, motor and bodily processes but situated in previous experience with those constructs (Barsalou, 2008). In this view, a separate amodal semantic system is superfluous to needs. However, this fully grounded view of semantics faces a challenge from the neuropsychological evidence from semantic dementia (Patterson *et al.*, 2007). The fact that relatively circumscribed damage to the brain (in the temporal poles) can impair almost all kinds of semantic concepts does not sit well with the proposal that semantic memory is based solely on a network of perceptual, motor and affective information distributed around the brain. The hub-and-spoke model is a compromise between other positions in that it assumes an amodal semantic hub together with a distributed network of (grounded) semantic features (Patterson *et al.*, 2007). It offers a good account of the full range of empirical data but is, arguably, is a less parsimonious view of semantic memory than its rival accounts.

# UNDERSTANDING AND PRODUCING SENTENCES

The preceding section has already introduced the notion that words carry not only information about meaning (semantics) but that they also carry information about syntactic roles (grammatical classes such as nouns and verbs). The syntactic properties of words will determine the order and structure of the words within a sentence, i.e. **syntax**. This enables the listener to figure out who is doing what to whom. Consider the three sentences below. Sentences A and B have different meanings but the same syntax, whereas sentences A and C have the same meaning but different syntax:

A: The boy hit the girl.
B: The girl hit the boy.
C: The girl was hit by the boy.

In general, empirical evidence suggests that processing the meaning of sentences uses similar neural resources to processing the meaning of single words (Friederici, 2012). However, there is far stronger evidence to suggest the processing of *syntax* of sentences is, at least partially, separable from the processing of semantics and also from other general resource demands such as working memory. This evidence is considered below.

## The role of Broca's area in sentence processing

One controversial claim is that there is a dedicated syntactic processor that is involved in both sentence comprehension and sentence production and that this is associated with the syndrome of Broca's aphasia (and/or with damage to Broca's area). This particular aspect of Broca's aphasia is termed **agrammatism**, meaning "loss of grammar." The typical presenting symptoms are halting, telegraphic speech production that is devoid of function words (e.g. of, at, the, and), bound morphemes (e.g. –ing, –s) and often verbs. For example, given the "cookie theft" picture (see left) to describe, one patient came out with "cookie jar ... fall over ... chair ... water ... empty ..." (Goodglass & Kaplan, 1983). The standard nineteenth-century view of Broca's aphasia was in terms of a loss of motor forms for speech. This fails to explain the agrammatic characteristic that is observed. Moreover, subsequent studies show that articulatory deficits are caused by lesions elsewhere (Dronkers, 1996) and even Broca's own cases had more extensive lesions, suggesting they may have had multiple deficits (Marie, 1906).

The nineteenth-century view that Broca's aphasics had better comprehension than production endured until the 1970s. However, many seemingly complex sentences such as "The bicycle that the boy is holding is broken" can be comprehended just from the content words and with minimal knowledge of syntax (bicycle ...

Sentence production abilities in aphasia have been assessed by giving patients complex pictures such as the "cookie theft" to describe.

From Goodglass and Kaplan, 1972.

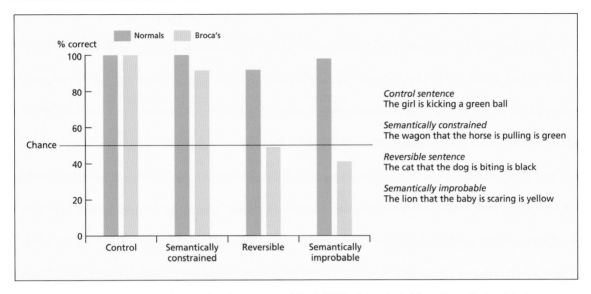

In a group study of so-called Broca's aphasics, Caramazza and Zurif (1976; data adapted from Figure 3) found that participants had particular problems in comprehending sentences on a picture–sentence matching task when the subject and object of the verb were determined from syntax and not from semantics.

boy . . . hold . . . broke). It was only when these patients were given sentences in which syntax was crucial to comprehension that disorders became apparent. For example, "The boy is eating the ice-cream" is semantically constrained by the fact that ice-creams do not eat boys, whereas a sentence such as "The boy is chasing the girl" cannot be unambiguously interpreted by the semantics of constituent words alone. Caramazza and Zurif (1976) showed that Broca's aphasics are impaired on the latter type of sentence only.

There are several important caveats to the aforementioned lines of evidence: some of them are methodological and some are theoretical. Given the paucity of appropriate imaging techniques in the 1970s and 1980s, the diagnosis of Broca's aphasia depended on a checklist of symptoms (such as agrammatic speech) rather than on the basis of brain damage localized to Broca's region. This generated a rather muddied picture that has only been clarified in recent times. First, it led to the erroneous assumption that agrammatic symptoms necessarily arose from damage to that region. Other studies that carefully map lesion location support the conclusion that parts of Broca's area are important for sentence comprehension (Tyler *et al.*, 2011). However, it is not the only part of the brain important for syntax. Damage to the temporal lobes has been found to be at least as important in sentence comprehension as Broca's area (Dronkers *et al.*, 2004). Patients with lesions in this area often have difficulties with a wide range of sentences, but do not necessarily have difficulty in comprehending single words. In fact,

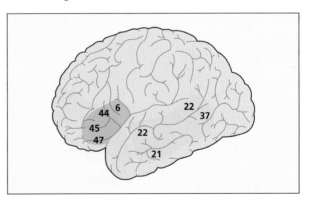

Areas of the brain important for sentence processing. Broca's area (in red) is traditionally defined as Brodmann areas 44 and 45. Temporal lobe regions (shown in blue) are also important in sentence processing.

Reprinted from Friederici (2002). © 2002, with permission from Elsevier.

they often meet the checklist-based diagnostic criteria of Broca's aphasia. Thus, sentence processing is comprised of different mechanisms supported by different regions: a key fact that was missed by earlier lines of research.

The contemporary view of Broca's area is that it is multi-functional and can be divided into (at least) two functional sub-divisions. The posterior division consists of BA44 (extending into the premotor area, BA6) and the anterior division consists of BA45 (extending into BA47).

BA44 is often considered to be involved in processing of hierarchical structures and sequencing of behavior in general (Friederici, 2011, 2012; Newman *et al.*, 2003). This includes, but is not limited to, the syntactic dependency of words in sentences. It is also often assumed to be involved in higher-level motor planning of speech linked to the audio-motor dorsal route of speech perception (Hickok & Poeppel, 2004) or, possibly, a mirror system for speech and other gestures (Rizzolatti & Arbib, 1998). It is higher-level insofar as it does not contain the actual motor programs for speech (Broca's original proposal). Of course, motor production of speech does involve hierarchical dependencies (phrase-level prosody, syllables, and phonemes) that may draw upon similar computational mechanisms as syntactic processing (for which the relevant units are grammatical categories such as nouns, verbs, and prepositions). With regards to syntax itself, Friederici *et al.* (2006b) found increasing activity in BA44 with increasing syntactic complexity; the latter being defined according to whether the word orderings were typical or atypical syntactic constructions in German. In a related study, artificial grammars were constructed using nonsense syllables and artificial syntactic structures rather than using real words and naturally occurring syntax (Friederici *et al.*, 2006a). So, instead of using grammatical categories (such as nouns and verbs), arbitrary categories were created (e.g. category A = vowels containing "i," category B = versus vowels containing "u") and different syntactic rules learned concerning the order in which A and B may occur (with rules differing in terms of hierarchical complexity). After exposure to grammatical sequences (a learning phase), participants judged whether a sequence was grammatical/ungrammatical (a test phase). Grammaticality judgments at test were was linked to activity in BA44 and the degree of activity modulated by syntactic complexity. One specific suggestion as to how this region might operate is that it generates predictive (feedforward) signals to other parts of the brain (in the case of sentences, to the temporal cortex) as to what kind of word is expected

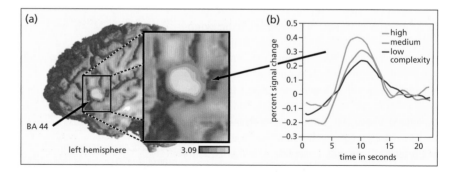

Processing of sentences, comprising real words, shows increasing activity in a region of Broca's area according to the degree of syntactic complexity.
Adapted from Friederici *et al.*, 2006b.

(e.g. a noun versus a verb) as well as monitoring (feedback) whether the prediction was obtained (Friederici, 2012).

The anterior portion of Broca's area (BA45, extending into BA47) is often considered to have rather different functions: specifically relating to working memory and the control of semantic memory. These are clearly important functions for sentence processing but are not directly related to syntax per se. In fMRI studies, judging a words grammatical class activates BA44 but judging its concreteness (a semantic property) activates the more anterior BA45 region (Friederici *et al.*, 2000). Applying TMS over Broca's region can produce a double dissociation between the processing of meaning (synonym judgments) versus phonology (deciding if two words sound the same) when two written words are presented, with impaired semantic judgments linked to more anterior stimulation (Gough *et al.*, 2005).

## Is syntax independent from semantics?

Evidence from patients with acquired brain-damage points to some separation between syntax and semantics. Patients with semantic dementia gradually lose the meaning of individual words but they still produce sentences that are grammatical, albeit lacking in content (e.g. "I've been worried to death thinking, trying, I am going to try and think with you today . . . I think of things, I can't often say . . . er . . . say what to say"; Hodges *et al.* 1994). Comprehension tests on semantic dementia patients also suggest that they can decide whether a sentence is grammatical or not even if it contains words that they apparently do not understand (e.g. is the following grammatical: "Are the boys fix the radio?"; Rochon *et al.*, 2004). However, some aspects of syntax may depend on the integrity of the semantics of particular words; for example, when a word is grammatically singular but conceptually plural (e.g. "the *label* on the bottles" refers to more than one label; Rochon *et al.*, 2004).

In normal sentence comprehension, the process of assigning a syntactic structure to words is termed **parsing**. One key debate in the literature concerns the extent to which parsing is based solely on the syntactic properties of words (so-called structure-driven parsing; Frazier & Rayner, 1982) or is additionally influenced by semantic properties of words (so-called discourse-driven parsing; MacDonald *et al.*, 1994). Evidence in favor of single initial computation of sentence structure comes from **garden-path sentences**, in which the early part of a sentence biases a syntactic interpretation that turns out to be incorrect. The classic example of this is given by Bever (1970):

The horse raced past the barn fell.

In this example, the word "fell" comes as a surprise unless one parses the sentence as "The horse {THAT} raced past the barn {WAS THE ONE THAT} fell." The fact that there is any ambiguity at all suggests that not all possible sentence constructions are considered (consistent with a structure-driven parse). However, in some instances semantics does appear to bias the way that the sentence is parsed (consistent with a discourse-driven parse). For example, being led up the garden path can often be avoided if the ambiguous sentence is preceded by supporting context (Altmann *et al.*, 1994). Consider the following sentence:

### KEY TERM

**P600**
An event-related brain potential (ERP) typically associated with the processing of grammatical anomalies.

The fireman told the man that he had risked his life for to install a smoke detector.

This sentence is less likely to lead down the garden path if preceded by context such as (Altmann *et al.*, 1994):

A fireman braved a dangerous fire in a hotel. He rescued one of the guests at great danger to himself. A crowd of men gathered around him. The fireman told the man that he had risked his life for to install a smoke detector.

On balance, it seems that the setting up of a sentence structure is, to some degree, dependent on both syntactic and contextual factors. Some researchers have taken this evidence as far as to state that syntactic and semantic processes are completely interwoven (McClelland *et al.*, 1989). However, studies of brain-damaged individuals (see above) and imaging/ERP methods (see below) speak against such a strong interpretation. It appears that certain aspects of syntax and lexical-semantics can be dissociated from each other.

There is an event-related brain potential (ERP) that is associated with processing grammatical anomalies such as the unexpected word in a garden-path sentence or an overtly ungrammatical sentence (Gouvea *et al.*, 2010). It is termed the **P600** because it is a positive deflection occurring at around 600 ms after word onset. This can be contrasted with N400, introduced earlier, which has been linked to the processing of semantic anomalies (irrespective of whether it is in a sentence context). More generally, the N400-P600 distinction supports the idea that syntax and semantics are separable. The P600 is still found when contrasting ungrammatical relative to grammatical sentences even when both are semantically meaningless (Hagoort & Brown, 1994) such as "The boiled watering can *smokes* the telephone in the cat" (grammatical) versus "The boiled watering can *smoke* the telephone in the cat" (ungrammatical). The most common cognitive interpretation of the P600 is that it reflects syntactic reanalysis

The P600 is found ~600 ms after a syntactically anomalous (or hard-to-process) word is presented. In this example the P600 is greater for "smoke" than "smokes" in the sentence "The boiling watering can smokes/smoke the telephone in the cat.

From Hagoort, 2008.

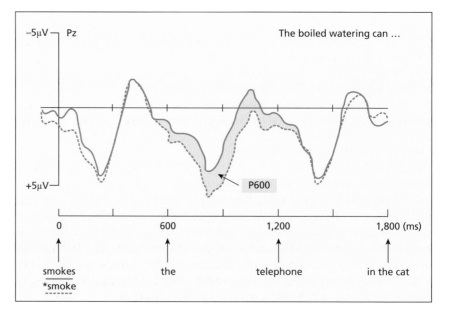

of the sentence. However, it can also be found for (non-garden path) grammatical sentences that are difficult to parse suggesting it is involved in syntactic analysis generally rather than reanalysis in particular (Kaan *et al.*, 2000).

Friederici (2011, 2012) argues for two levels of processing syntax: one based on local syntactic structures at the phrase level (e.g. determining whether a phrase is based on a noun or verb), and one operating on more global sentence structure (e.g. determining who is doing what to whom). In ERP studies, syntactic violations at the local level are detectable within an early (150–200msec) time window, whereas the latter occurs later and is linked to the P600 (Hahne & Friederici, 1999).

Functional imaging studies of normal participants suggest somewhat different roles for anterior and posterior temporal cortex and Broca's area that may correspond to differences between semantics and syntax, and also the interface between them. Pallier *et al.* (2011) presented sentences of increasing structure made up of either content words (which have lexical-semantics) or nonwords (e.g. "I tosieve that you should begept . . ."). The anterior temporal cortex responded to the presence of word meaning (relative to nonwords) but not the size of the syntactic structure. Both Broca's area and the posterior superior temporal sulcus showed the opposite profile. They argued that the posterior temporal lobes may be the integration site for semantics (originating in the anterior temporal regions) and syntax (within Broca's region). Other fMRI studies show that Broca's area is active when processing hierarchical/syntactic relationships among nonlinguistic symbols (Bahlmann *et al.*, 2008) but that the posterior temporal lobes are only activated when the stimulus material are related to language. This supports the view that this is a syntax-semantics integration site (see Friederici, 2012).

## Is syntax independent from working memory?

Increasing syntactic complexity tends to be linked to greater working memory loads. As such, distinguishing between syntax and working memory is not straightforward. It has even been claimed that the only contribution of Broca's area to sentence comprehension is its role in working memory (Rogalsky & Hickok, 2011).

Brain-damaged patients with phonological short-term memory deficits (markedly reduced digit span) can produce and comprehend many sentences adequately (Caplan & Waters, 1990; Vallar & Baddeley, 1984), suggesting a dissociation between the two, but others show clear deficits when syntactically complex sentences are presented (Romani, 1994). In the study by Romani (1994) the comprehension problems were not found when reading text (enabling reinspection to correct parsing) but were found for spoken sentences and when written words were presented one-by-one (which prevent reinspection and, hence, reanalysis of syntax).

In an fMRI study, Makuuchi *et al.* (2009) independently manipulated working memory and syntactic complexity. The working memory manipulation related to the number of intervening items between the subject of the sentence and the associated verb, whereas the syntax manipulation consisted of the presence/ absence of hierarchical syntactic structure (embedding). The effect of syntactic complexity was found in the posterior portion of Broca's area (BA 44). The effect of working memory was found in an adjacent, but distinct, region of Broca's area and was also linked to activity in the parietal lobes. Such frontoparietal systems are characteristic of working memory systems in general. Analysis of the

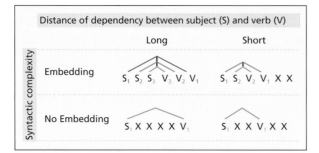

The experimental design of Makuuchi *et al.* (2009) varied working memory (short or long distance between a verb and its subject) and syntactic complexity (presence or absence of embedding). An example sentence for a long embedded sentence is "Maria (S1), die (S2) Hans, der (S3) gut aussah (V3) liebte (V2) Johann geküsst hatte (V1)" (translated as "Maria who loved Hans who was good looking kissed Johann"). An example of a long non-embedded sentence is "Achim (S1) den großen Mann gestern am späten Abend gesehen hatte (V1)" (translated as "Achim saw the tall man yesterday late at night").

functional connectivity between the two frontal regions (i.e. the extent to which their activity is correlated) revealed greater cooperation when processing the demanding embedded sentences.

## Evaluation

Broca's region appears to serve multiple functions in sentence processing. It is involved in processing hierarchical dependencies (e.g. syntactic trees) between words in a sentence. However, this may be a more general function that is not specific to language. In addition, it is important for verbal working memory which is needed for processing longer and more complex sentences. It is also important for placing words into context by retrieving or manipulating information in semantic memory. Again, this function is not specific to sentence processing—it is useful for memory (deep encoding) and reasoning (problem solving).

Although Broca's region is important for sentence processing it is not the only region of the brain to be so. It works in concert with other regions of the brain notably the anterior and posterior temporal lobes that are important for processing the meaning of words and sentences. Evidence for the partial separability of syntax and semantics comes from patient studies (showing dissociations in ability), from human electrophysiology (showing temporal dissociations such as the N400 and P600 components), and from fMRI (showing different but overlapping neural substrates).

## RETRIEVING AND PRODUCING SPOKEN WORDS

Speech production, in natural situations, involves translating an intended idea into a sentence structure and retrieving and producing the appropriate words. To study this process in the laboratory, one standard method has been to study the retrieval of single words in isolation upon presentation of a picture or word definition. Both of these tasks are assumed to initiate semantic processes. A number of variables affect how easy a word is to retrieve as measured using naming reaction times or error rates (Barry *et al.*, 1997). These are summarized on p. 286. Most, if not all, of these variables can be construed as factors affecting not only spoken word retrieval but also processing of single words in other contexts (e.g. in speech recognition, and reading and spelling). A number of broad questions will be considered in this section. How many stages are there in retrieving spoken words, and are the stages discrete or interactive? What type of information is retrieved—syntactic, semantic, morphological, syllabic, phonemic, and so on?

The type of information that needs to be retrieved in speech production is normally divided into three kinds. First, one must select a word based upon the meaning that one wishes to convey. This process is called **lexicalization**. This process is heavily constrained by knowledge of the listener (related to pragmatics). For example, the words "it," "horse," "stallion," and "animal" could, to some

## EARLY SIGNS OF DEMENTIA IN THE LANGUAGE USE OF IRIS MURDOCH

Iris Murdoch's last novel, *Jackson's Dilemma*, was considered by both critics and her family to be something of a puzzle, in that it departed significantly in style from her previous novels. Whereas this could conceivably reflect a deliberate shift due to artistic motivations, a more likely scenario is that Murdoch was already in the early stages of Alzheimer's disease. This is known to affect memory and result in word-finding difficulties. The novel was published in

Iris Murdoch; 1919–1999.
© Sophie Bassouls/Sygma/Corbis.

1995, just before her diagnosis. To investigate the changes, text from the last novel was compared with two of her earlier ones. The results found that, whereas the use of syntax and overall structure did not change, her vocabulary had changed such that she had a more restricted range of words, particularly relying more on higher frequency words than before (Garrard *et al.*, 2005). Text analyses such as these, based on letters or diary entries, could possibly be developed in the future to lead to early diagnostic tools for diseases such as dementia of the Alzheimer's type.

extent, all be used to convey the same concept. Second, at least in the context of producing sentences, the grammatical properties of a word must be retrieved and specified. This includes grammatical class (e.g. noun, verb, adjective) and, in many languages, the gender of the word. Finally, the actual form of the word in terms of its constituent syllables, phonemes and articulatory patterns needs to be retrieved. There is general consensus across different models that these are the kinds of information that need to be retrieved. However, individual models differ in terms of the nature of the mechanisms (e.g. whether different stages interact).

## Studies of speech errors

Observations of everyday speech errors have been useful in constraining theories of word retrieval (Garrett, 1992). Speech errors tend to swap words for words, morphemes for morphemes, phonemes for phonemes, and so on. This provides evidence for the psychological reality of these units. Considering the word level, it is possible to substitute words of similar meaning as in a semantic error, such as saying "dog" for cat. One variant of this error is the **Freudian slip**. Freud believed that speakers repress their true thoughts during conversation, and these could be revealed by inadvertent speech errors (Ellis, 1980). For example, the former British Prime Minister, Tony Blair, mistakenly referred to "weapons of mass *distraction*" (rather than destruction) in a parliamentary debate on the 2003 invasion of Iraq. It is also the case that word substitutions tend to preserve grammatical class, such that nouns swap for nouns, and verbs for verbs, as in the

### KEY TERM

**Freudian slip**
The substitution of one word for another that is sometimes thought to reflect the hidden intentions of the speaker.

**SYCHOLINGUISTIC PREDICTORS OF THE EFFICIENCY OF SINGLE-WORD PROCESSING**

| Variable | Description | Possible explanation |
|---|---|---|
| Word frequency | More common words in the language are easier to retrieve and recognize | The strength of connections to words may be increased each time they are encountered (Jescheniak & Levelt, 1994) or the threshold for activating the word may be lowered by each experience (Morton, 1969) |
| Imageability (or concreteness) | Concrete words are easier to retrieve and recognize than abstract words | Concrete (or high imageability words) have richer semantic representations (Jones, 2002) |
| Age-of-acquisition | Words acquired earlier in life (e.g. doll) are at an advantage relative to late acquired words (e.g. wine) | Initially, a network will adjust itself to accommodate any pattern it encounters, but after adding more and more patterns the ability of the system to adjust further is diminished (reduced plasticity) (Ellis & Lambon Ralph, 2000) |
| Recency | More recently encountered words have an advantage | Exposure to a word may increase the strength of the connections to the word, or lower the threshold for activating the word. **Repetition priming** refers to the fact that a word seen previously will be identified faster on a subsequent occasion soon after |
| Familiarity | More familiar items are at an advantage relative to less familiar ones | Related to the variables of word frequency and age-of-acquisition, but also dependent on the individual experience of the speaker |

**KEY TERM**

**Repetition priming**
A stimulus seen previously will be identified faster on a subsequent occasion.

Shortly after being exposed for having multiple affairs, Tiger Woods had to withdraw from The 2010 Players Championship because of a bulging disc in his neck. A journalist reporting on this famously substituted the word "disc" for a rather embarrassing word. What kind of cognitive mechanisms contributed to this slip?

example "guess whose *mind* came to *name*?" (Garrett, 1992). Moreover, affixation of morphemes may occur independently of retrieval of word stems (Fromkin, 1971), as illustrated by the example "I random*ed* some sampl*y*" (instead of "I sampled some randomly"). In this instance, the suffix morphemes (–ed, –y) were stranded while the stem morphemes (random, sample) swapped.

A final type of word error is where the error has a similar phonological form to the intended word (e.g. historical → "hysterical") (Fay & Cutler, 1977). These are also called **malapropisms** after the character Mrs. Malaprop (in Sheridan's play *The Rivals*, 1775) who made many such errors. These errors are typically used to support the notion that there is competition between similar words during normal word retrieval, rather than a single word selected immediately. Sometimes the exchange will be between phonemes, and it is generally the case that the exchanged phonemes will occupy the same position in the word (e.g. first consonants swap with each other, vowels swap with each other; Dell *et al.*, 1997). One example of this is **spoonerisms**, in which initial consonants are swapped (e.g. "you have *hissed* all my *mystery* lectures"). Errors in **inner speech** (saying things in one's head) tend to involve word-level exchanges but not exchanges between similar phonemes suggesting that inner speech is not a full mental simulation of the speech production process (Oppenheim & Dell, 2008).

Another common, naturally occurring disruption of speech production is the **tip-of-the-tongue phenomenon** (Brown, 1991; Brown & McNeill, 1966). In a tip-of-the-tongue state the person knows, conceptually, the word that he or she wishes to say, but is unable to retrieve the corresponding spoken form for output. It generally produces a "feeling of knowing" and can be intensely frustrating. These states can be elicited by giving people definitions or pictures of relatively infrequent words. For example, "a navigational instrument used in measuring angular distances, especially the altitude of the sun, moon and stars at sea" (the answer being *sextant*). Although the word may be elusive, other types of information may be available. For example, speakers of languages such as Italian often know the gender of a word (Vigliocco *et al.*, 1997), and speakers often know the approximate length of the word or the number of syllables (Brown & McNeill, 1966). These results suggest that words are not retrieved in an all-or-nothing manner, but, rather, that different aspects of a word can become available at different stages and relatively independently from each other.

Patients with **anomia** as a result of brain damage have severe word-finding difficulties. This is strongly reminiscent of the normal tip-of-the-tongue state, but in pathological proportions. This symptom can arise from two very different types of impairment. First, it may be a result of a semantic difficulty that results in a failure to distinguish between different concepts and, consequently, a difficulty in specifying the precise word to be retrieved (Caramazza & Hillis, 1990b). Second, other patients may know exactly which word they want to produce, but are unable to retrieve the associated phonological information to articulate it (Kay & Ellis, 1987).

## Discrete or interactive stages in spoken word retrieval?

The most influential models of spoken word retrieval divide the process of getting from a conceptual level of representation to a phonological word form into two steps. Further stages may be involved in translating this into motor commands. Consider the model put forward by Levelt and colleagues (for reviews, see Levelt, 1989, 2001). The first stage of their model involves retrieving a modality-independent word-level entry that specifies the syntactic components of the word (e.g. its grammatical class). These are termed **lemma** representations. Thus, this first stage involves lexicalization together with retrieval of syntactic features. The second stage involves retrieval of what they term a **lexeme** representation. Retrieval of the lexeme makes available the phonological code that drives articulation. This lemma–lexeme division accounts for some of the key findings in the speech production literature. First, it offers an account of the tip-of-the-tongue phenomenon by postulating that the lemma may be activated but the lexeme is not active (or is not fully active). Second, it offers a way of distinguishing between words with identical forms that differ in meaning (e.g. "bank"

**KEY TERMS**

**Malapropisms**
A speech error that consists of a word with a similar phonological form to the intended word.

**Spoonerisms**
A speech error in which initial consonants are swapped between words.

**Inner speech**
Use of words or images without audible or physical speaking.

**Tip-of-the-tongue phenomenon**
A state in which a person knows, conceptually, the word that he or she wishes to say but is unable to retrieve the corresponding spoken form.

**Anomia**
Word-finding difficulties.

**Lemma**
A modality-independent, word-level entry that specifies the syntactic components of the word.

**Lexeme**
The phonological code that drives articulation.

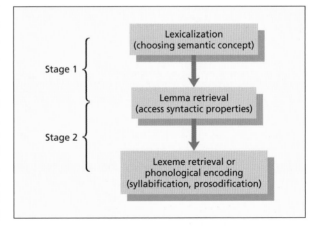

In Levelt's model, word retrieval takes place in two stages. The stages are discrete such that the second stage does not begin until the first stage is complete, and so phonological factors cannot influence word selection.

as in money or river) and/or grammatical class (the "watch"/to "watch"). These stimuli have different lemmas but a single lexeme. Using these stimuli, Jescheniak and Levelt (1994) found that word-frequency effects are related to the frequency of lexemes and not lemmas.

The question of whether these stages are discrete or interact is a source of particular controversy. Levelt's model proposes that they are discrete in that lexeme retrieval does not begin until lemma selection is complete. In contrast, other models have assumed that partial phonological processing can occur prior to selection of a lemma being complete and, moreover, that this information can feed back up to influence lemma selection itself. Thus, if one is trying to say "sheep," then the process of lemma selection may activate a host of other semantic candidates, including "goat." If this information reaches the lexeme level, then one may expect activation of words such as "goal," because this is phonologically similar to the semantic associate "goat." But if "sheep" is completely selected and "goat" is completely unselected before the second stage begins, then no such priming of "goal" should occur. Indeed, it appears that "sheep" does not prime "goal," even though it does prime "goat" (Levelt *et al.*, 1991). This evidence supports Levelt's discrete stages (but see Dell & O'Seaghdha, 1991).

However, there is some evidence that, on balance, is easier to account for with an interactive rather than discrete stage model. This includes the presence of so-called *mixed errors* that are both semantically and phonologically similar to the intended word (Dell & Reich, 1981). Examples of these include saying "rat" for cat, and "oyster" for lobster. If it were coincidental, then we would have to assume that "rat" is a semantic error for cat that just so happens to sound like it. However, these errors occur too often to be coincidences (Dell & Reich, 1981). In interactive models such as that of Dell's (1986), they occur because lemma selection arises out of both top-down semantic activation and bottom-up phonological activation. For the discrete stages model to account for this, it must assume that mixed errors are not generated more than expected by chance but they are just harder to detect and correct. These models assume that there is a monitoring device that checks for speech errors and that mixed errors are more likely to slip through the monitor. This explanation is plausible but *post hoc*.

The Levelt model has been criticized in other ways. Caramazza and Miozzo (1997) found that in tip-of-the-tongue states it is sometimes possible to report grammatical gender information without knowing the first phoneme (lemma access without lexeme access), but that it is also possible to know the first phoneme without knowing grammatical gender (lexeme access without lemma access). The latter should not be found if lemma retrieval were a prerequisite for access to phonological information. The authors argue in favor of the distinction between phonological and grammatical retrieval (similarly to Levelt and Dell) but argue against the idea that one is contingent upon the other. Furthermore, they present neuropsychological evidence to suggest that the organization of grammatical knowledge (putatively at a lemma level) is not amodal but is duplicated in both phonological and written modalities (Caramazza, 1997). For example, patient SJD had a selective difficulty in writing verbs relative to nouns but had no difficulty with producing spoken nouns and verbs (Caramazza & Hillis, 1991). Remarkably, the deficit was still found when the lexeme was the same. For example, SJD could write CRACK when dictated the spoken word and given the written sentence fragment *There's a ____ in the mirror* (noun form), but not *Don't ____ the nuts in here* (verb form). They suggest that grammatical information is

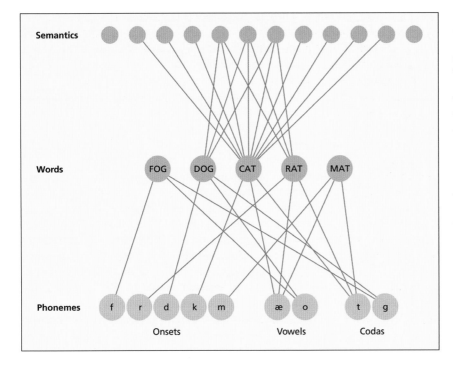

Dell's model contains three layers that are fully interactive: a layer of semantic features, a layer of words (or lemmas); and a phonological layer (in this version, it consists of different parts of the syllable). Mixed errors, such as cat → "rat" arise because of similarity both at the semantic and the phonological level. Models that do not allow interactive activation from phonology up to words have difficulty accounting for such errors.

Reprinted from Levelt, 1999. © 1999, with permission from Elsevier.

independently represented in speaking and spelling, contrary to the notion of a single amodal lemma articulated by Levelt or colleagues.

In summary, there is good evidence for a separation between grammatical and phonological knowledge of single words, but the precise organization of this knowledge is a matter of continued debate.

## Articulation: closing the communication loop

This chapter began with a simple model of spoken language in which ideas are shared between a speaker and a listener. Having started at the speech perception end of this loop and considered semantic and syntactic processes, and word retrieval, the final stage to be considered is articulation itself.

As noted earlier, phonemes can be described in terms of a limited set of articulatory gestures such as voicing (i.e. vibration of vocal chords) and place of articulators (e.g. tongue against teeth or against palate). However, in spite of this, many believe that the phoneme is not the basic unit of articulation. Others have argued that the basic unit of articulation is the syllable—at least for common syllables that may function as overlearned motor patterns (Levelt & Wheeldon, 1994). In connected speech there must be a mechanism that segments the phonological code into syllables across adjacent morphemes and adjacent words. This process has been called *syllabification*. For example, the phrase "he owns it" consists of three syllables ("he," "own," "zit"), in which the final consonant of the word "owns" becomes the onset of the following syllable.

Broca's area was once thought to be critical for articulation. This is now disputed. Patients with articulation disorders typically have damage to the basal ganglia and/or the insula cortex, but not necessarily Broca's area (Dronkers, 1996; but see Hillis *et al.*, 2004). Damage to the insula can result in difficulties in shaping the vocal tract, known as **apraxia for speech** (Dronkers, 1996). People with apraxia for speech know what it is that they want to say and have normal muscle tone of the speech articulators, but distort the production of consonants, vowels, and prosody. This is sometimes perceived by others as sounding like a foreign accent (Moen, 2000). The difficulties with prosody reflect poor coordination of the articulators rather than a primary deficit in prosody that is sometimes found following right hemisphere lesions (Pell, 1999).

fMRI studies of articulation relative to speech perception show activity of the insula and frontal–motor regions, but not Broca's area (Wise *et al.*, 1999). However, others have suggested that Broca's area has an important role in the planning stages of syllabification in both overt and covert speech production, even if the motor commands themselves do not reside there (Indefrey & Levelt, 2004). Note also that regions within Broca's area are also implicated in audio-motor transformations of speech as part of the dorsal "how" route of speech perception and as part of a "mirror system" for speech. This may contribute to speech *production* in various ways. For instance, it may contribute to the repetition of heard speech, and, indeed, facilitatory forms of TMS over Broca's area improves the accuracy of repetition of foreign (i.e. meaningless) speech (Restle *et al.*, 2012). In addition, when we produce self-generated speech we can hear our own words, and it has been suggested that this audio-motor loop is involved in auditory monitoring of ongoing speech production (Hickok, 2012).

As with all forms of voluntary movements, speech production ultimately depends upon the primary motor cortex (M1) to initiate movement of the mouth, jaw, and tongue. More recently, a region of M1 has been identified by fMRI that responds selectively to movement of the glottal folds of the larynx relative to the other articulators (Brown *et al.*, 2008).

The cerebellum and left basal ganglia lesions may also be crucial for efficient articulation. Damage to these regions can result in impaired muscular contractions known as **dysarthria** (Kent *et al.*, 2001).

## SUMMARY AND KEY POINTS OF THE CHAPTER

- Recognizing spoken words involves a process of competition and selection between similar sounding words, as in the "cohort model."
- The meaning of words may be represented as a network of distributed semantic features, but there is controversy as to how these features are internally organized and whether the features are amodal or are part of a wider network that supports perception and action.
- Deficits in syntax (word order) can occur largely, although perhaps not completely, independently from deficits in semantics (word meaning) and vice versa. However, there is little evidence for a single "syntax module" that is disrupted in aphasic disorders, such as agrammatism or that arises specifically from lesions to Broca's area.
- Producing spoken words involves retrieving different kinds of information: semantic, grammatical, and phonological. Evidence from tip-of-the-tongue, anomia, and everyday speech errors suggests that

some information can be retrieved in the absence of other types of information.

- There is controversy as to whether word-level (or "lemma") information and phonological-level (or "lexeme") information are retrieved as two discrete stages in time or interactively, such that the second stage begins before the first stage is complete.

Visit the companion website at www. psypress/cw/ward for:

- References to key papers and readings
- Video lectures and interviews on key topics with leading psychologists Angela Friederici, Alfonso Caramazza, Karalyn Patterson, and author Jamie Ward
- Multiple choice questions and interactive flashcards to test your knowledge
- Downloadable glossary

## EXAMPLE ESSAY QUESTIONS

- How is auditory input mapped on to our stored knowledge of spoken words?
- Does speech perception use mechanisms involved in speech production?
- How do studies of the N400 and P600 shed light on the cognitive architecture of language processing?
- Does semantic memory depend on brain systems specialized for perception and action?
- What is the role of Broca's region in language?
- Do models of word retrieval require discrete stages corresponding to semantics, grammar, and phonology?

## RECOMMENDED FURTHER READING

- Harley, T. A. (2008). *The psychology of language: From data to theory* (3rd edition). Hove, UK: Psychology Press. A good place to start for more detailed background information about the cognitive psychology of language, but little focus on brain-based accounts.
- Hickok, G. & Poeppel, D. (2004). Towards a new functional anatomy of language. Special edition of *Cognition*, 92, 1–270. An excellent collection of papers that is particularly strong on speech recognition.
- Friederici, A. D. (2011). The brain basis of language processing: From structure to function. *Physiological Reviews*, 91(4), 1357–1392. A thorough and up-to-date review.
- Patterson, K., Nestor, P. J., & Rogers, T. T. (2007). Where do you know what you know? The representation of semantic knowledge in the human brain. *Nature Reviews Neuroscience*, 8(12), 976–987. A good summary of theories of semantic memory and its neural basis.

# CHAPTER 12

# The literate
# brain

## CONTENTS

The ability to read and write is essentially a cultural invention, albeit one of enormous significance. It enables humans to exchange ideas without face-to-face contact and results in a permanent record for posterity. It is no coincidence that our historical knowledge of previous civilizations is derived almost entirely from literate cultures. Literacy, unlike speaking, requires a considerable amount of formal tuition. As such, literacy provides cognitive neuroscience with an interesting example of an "expert system." Learning to read and write may involve the construction of a dedicated neural and cognitive architecture in the brain. But this is likely to be derived from a core set of other skills that have developed over the course of evolution. These skills include visual recognition, manipulation of sounds, and learning and memory. However, it is inconceivable that we have evolved neural structures specifically for literacy, or that there is a gene specifically for reading (Ellis, 1993). Literacy is too recent an invention to have evolved specific neural substrates, having first emerged around 5,000 years ago. Moreover, it is by no means universal. Universal literacy has only occurred in Western societies over the last 150 year, and levels of literacy in developing countries have only changed substantially over the last 40 years (UN Human Development Report, 2011). Of course, the brain may acquire, through experience, a dedicated neural structure for literacy, but this will be a result of *ontogenetic development* (of the individual) rather than *phylogenetic development* (of the species).

This chapter considers how skilled adult literacy relates to other cognitive domains such as visual recognition and spoken language; how a complex skill such as reading can be broken down into a collection of more basic mechanisms; and how the skills of reading and spelling may relate to each other. Evidence will be primarily drawn from adults who have already become experts at reading and spelling, including acquired disorders of reading and spelling.

## THE ORIGINS AND DIVERSITY OF WRITING SYSTEMS

Writing has its historical origins in early pictorial representation. The point at which a picture ceases to be a picture and becomes a written symbol may relate to a transition between attempting to depict an object or concept rather than representing units of language (e.g. words, phonemes, morphemes). For example, although Egyptian hieroglyphs consist of familiar objects (e.g. birds, hands), these characters actually denote the sounds of words rather than objects in themselves. As such, this is a true writing system that is a significant step away from the pictorial depictions of rock art.

The diversity of written language.

Different cultures appear to have made this conceptual leap independently of each other (Gaur, 1987). This accounts for some of the great diversity of writing systems. The earliest writing system emerged between 4,000 and 3,000 BC, in what is now southern Iraq, and was based on the one-word–one-symbol principle. Scripts such as these are called **logographic**. Modern Chinese and Japanese **Kanji** are logographic, although they probably emerged independently from the Middle Eastern scripts. Individual characters may be composed of a number of parts that suggest meaning or pronunciation, but the arrangement of these parts is not linear like in alphabetic scripts.

Other types of script represent the sounds of words. Some writing systems, such as Japanese **Kana** and ancient Phoenician, use symbols to denote syllables. Alphabetic systems are based primarily on mappings between written symbols and spoken phonemes. All modern alphabets are derived from the one used by the Phoenicians; the Greeks reversed the writing direction to left–right at some point around 600 BC.

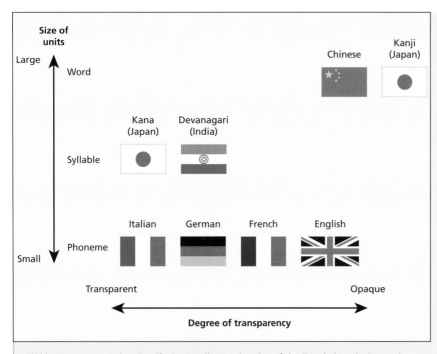

Writing systems can be classified according to the size of the linguistic unit denoted (phoneme, syllable, word) and the degree of regularity (or transparency) between the written and spoken forms. From Dehaene, 2010, p. 117

The term **grapheme** is normally used to denote the smallest meaningful unit of written language, analogous to the term "phoneme" in spoken language. In languages such as English, this corresponds to individual letters (Henderson, 1985), although the term is also often used to refer to letter clusters that denote phonemes (e.g. in the latter definition, the word THUMB would have three graphemes: TH, U, and MB, corresponding to the phonemes "th," "u," and "m").

It is important to note that not all alphabetic scripts have a very regular mapping between graphemes and phonemes. Such languages are said to be **opaque**. Examples include English and French (consider the different spellings for the words COMB, HOME, and ROAM). Not all irregularities are unhelpful. We write CATS and DOGS (and not CATS and DOGZ), and PLAYED and WALKED (not PLAYED and WALKT) to preserve common morphemes for plural and past tense, respectively. However, other irregularities of English reflect historical quirks and precedents (Scragg, 1974). For example, KNIFE and SHOULD would have been pronounced with the "k" and "l" until the seventeenth century. Moreover, early spelling reformers changed spellings to be in line with their Greek and Latin counterparts (e.g. the spelling of DETTE was changed to DEBT to reflect the Latin "debitum"). Other languages, such as Italian and Spanish, have fully regular mappings between sound and spelling; these writing systems are said to be **transparent**.

# VISUAL WORD RECOGNITION

## Cognitive mechanisms of visual word recognition

One of the earliest findings in the study of visual word recognition was the fact that there is little processing cost, in terms of reaction times, for recognizing long relative to short words (Cattell, 1886). Of course, reading a long word out loud will take longer than reading a short word aloud, and the preparation time before saying the word is also related to word length (Erikson *et al.*, 1970). But the actual *visual* process of recognizing a word as familiar is not strongly affected by word length. This suggests a key principle in visual word recognition—namely, that the letter strings are processed in parallel rather than serially one by one. Recognizing printed words is thus likely to employ different kinds of mechanisms from recognizing spoken words. All the information for visual word recognition is instantly available to the reader and remains so over time (unless the word is unusually long and requires an eye movement), whereas in spoken word recognition the information is revealed piecemeal and must be integrated over time.

Visual word recognition also appears to be greater than the sum of its parts (i.e. its constituent letters) in so far as patterns across several letters are also important. If one is asked to detect the presence of a single letter (e.g. R) presented briefly, then performance is enhanced if the letter is presented in the context of a word (e.g. CARPET), or a nonsense letter string that follows the combinatorial rules of the language (e.g. HARPOT) than in a random letter string (e.g. CTRPAE) or even a single letter in isolation (Carr *et al.*, 1979; Reicher, 1969). This is termed the **word superiority effect**. It suggests that there are units of representation corresponding to letter clusters (or known letter clusters comprising words themselves) that influence the visual recognition of letters and words. Intracranial EEG recordings suggest that word and word-like stimuli are distinguished from consonant strings after around 200 ms in the mid-fusiform cortex (Mainy *et al.*, 2008). Scalp EEG recordings reveal a similar picture but suggest an interaction between visual processes and lexical-semantic processes such that stimuli with typical letter patterns can be discriminated at around 100 ms (e.g. SOSSAGE compared with SAUSAGE), but with words differing from nonwords at 200 ms (Hauk *et al.*, 2006). This later effect was interpreted as top-down activity from the semantic system owing to the EEG source being located in language rather than visual regions.

The evidence cited above is often taken to imply that there is a role of top-down information in visual word recognition. Stored knowledge of the structure of known words can influence earlier perceptual processes (McClelland & Rumelhart, 1981; Rumelhart & McClelland, 1982). Although this view is generally recognized, controversy still exists over the extent to which other higher-level processes, such as meaning, can influence perceptual processing. One commonly used task to investigate word recognition is **lexical decision** in which participants must make a two-way forced choice judgment about whether a letter string is a word or not. Non-words (also called pseudo-words) are much faster to reject if they do not resemble known words (Coltheart *et al.*, 1977). For example, BRINJ is faster to reject than BRINGE.

According to many models, the task of lexical decision is performed by matching the perceived letter string with a store of all known letter strings that

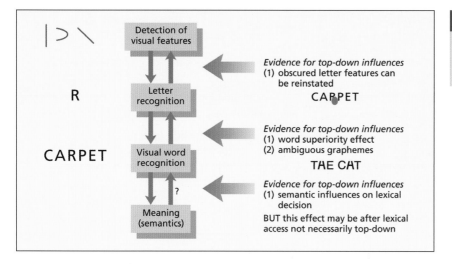

**KEY TERM**

**Visual lexicon**
A store of the structure of known written words.

A basic model of visual word recognition showing evidence in favor of top-down influences.

comprise words (Coltheart, 2004a; Fera & Besner, 1992; Morton, 1969). This store is referred to as the **visual lexicon** (also the orthographic lexicon). Under this account, there is no reason to assume that meaning or context should affect tasks such as lexical decision. However, such effects have been reported and could potentially provide evidence for semantic influences on word recognition.

Meyer and Schvaneveldt (1971) used a modified lexical decision in which pairs of words were presented. Participants responded according to whether both letter strings were words or otherwise. Semantically related pairs (e.g. BREAD and BUTTER) were responded to faster than unrelated pairs (e.g. DOCTOR and BUTTER). A number of potential problems with this have been raised. The first concerns the nature of the lexical decision task itself. It is possible that it is not a pure measure of access to the visual lexicon but also entails a post-access checking or decision mechanism. This mechanism might be susceptible to semantic influences, rather than the visual lexicon itself being influenced by top-down effects (Chumbley & Balota, 1984; Norris, 1986). Moreover, it has been argued that these effects may not be truly semantic at all. If participants are asked to associate a word with, say, BREAD, they may produce BUTTER but are unlikely to produce the word CAKE, even though it is semantically related (similarly, ROBIN is more likely to elicit HOOD as an associate than BIRD). Shelton and Martin (1992) found that associated words prime each other in lexical decision, but not other semantically related pairs. This suggests that the effect arises from inter-word association, but not top-down semantic influence.

## The visual word form area

As already noted, most models of visual word recognition postulate a dedicated cognitive mechanism for processing known words (a visual lexicon). Although these models have been formulated in purely cognitive terms, it is a short logical step to assume that a dedicated cognitive mechanism must have a dedicated neural architecture. This was postulated as long ago as 1892 (Dejerine, 1892), although it is only in recent times that its neural basis has been uncovered.

## CHARACTERISTICS OF THE VISUAL WORD FORM AREA

- Responds to learned letters compared with pseudo-letters (or false fonts) of comparable visual complexity (Price *et al.*, 1996b)
- Repetition priming suggests that it responds to both upper and lower case letters even when visually dissimilar (e.g. "a" primes "A" more than "e" primes "A") (Dehaene *et al.*, 2001)
- Subliminal presentation of words activates the area, which suggests that it is accessed automatically (Dehaene *et al.*, 2001)
- Electrophysiological data comparing true and false fonts suggests that the region is activated early, at around 150–200 ms after stimulus onset (Bentin *et al.*, 1999)

A number of functional imaging studies have been reported that argue in favor of the existence of a so-called visual word form area, VWFA (Dehaene & Cohen, 2011; Petersen *et al.*, 1990). This area is located in the left mid occipitotemporal gyrus (also called fusiform gyrus). Some of the response characteristics of this region to visual stimuli are listed on the next page. Meaningless shapes that are letter-like do not activate the region. This suggests that the neurons have become tuned to the visual properties of known letters and common letter patterns (Cohen *et al.*, 2002). This particular region of the brain lies along the visual ventral stream, and neurons in this region are known to respond to particular visual features (e.g. shapes, junctions) and have large receptive fields (i.e. do not precisely code for location of objects).

The visual word form area also responds to nonwords made up of common letter patterns as well as to real words, although the degree of this activity may be task dependent (e.g. reading versus lexical decision; Mechelli *et al.*, 2003; see also Fiebach *et al.*, 2002). The responsiveness to nonwords has cast some doubt over whether this region is actually implementing a visual lexicon (i.e. a store of known words). One reason a neural implementation of a visual lexicon could respond to nonwords, at least to some degree, as well as real words is because nonwords can only be classified as such after a search of the visual lexicon has failed to find a match (Coltheart, 2004a). Thus, a neural implementation of a visual lexicon could be activated by the search process itself, regardless of whether the search is successful or not (i.e. whether the stimulus is a word or nonword). Dehaene and colleagues (2002) initially argued that the VWFA contains a prelexical representation of letter strings, whether known or unknown. Subsequent evidence led them to refine this to include several different sized orthographic chunks including words themselves (Dehaene & Cohen, 2011). For instance, the BOLD activity in the VWFA is unaffected by the length of real words suggesting that the letter pattern might be recognized as a single chuck (Schurz *et al.*, 2010). The same isn't found for nonwords which implies that their recognition is not holistic. Moreover, BOLD activity in the VWFA differentiates real words from the same-sounding nonwords (e.g. taxi versus taksi; Kronbichler *et al.*, 2007). This suggests that word-based activity is indeed orthographic rather than phonological.

Given that visual recognition of letters and words is a culturally dependent skill, why should it be the case that this same part of the brain becomes specialized for recognizing print across different individuals and, indeed, across different

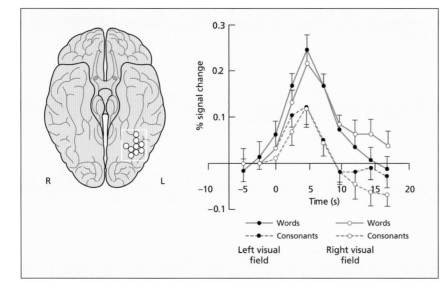

The visual word form area is located on the rear under-surface of the brain, primarily in the left hemisphere. It responds to written words more than consonant strings, and irrespective of whether they are presented in the left or right visual field.

Reprinted from McCandliss et al., 2003. © 2003, with permission from Elsevier.

writing systems (Bolger et al., 2005)? Possible answers to this question come from studies examining the function of the VWFA in illiterate people and also in people who do not read visually (Braille readers). Dehaene et al. (2010) compared three groups of adults using fMRI: illiterates, those who became literate in childhood, and those who became literate in adulthood. They were presented with various visual stimuli such as words, faces, houses, and tools. Literacy ability was correlated with increased activity of the left VWFA, and there was a tendency for literacy to reduce the responsiveness of this region to faces (which displaced to the right hemisphere). The basic pattern was the same if literacy was acquired in childhood or adulthood. In another fMRI study, congenitally blind individuals were found to activate the left VWFA when reading Braille relative to touching other kinds of object (Reich et al., 2011). Thus the VWFA is not strictly visual but may preferentially process certain types of shape. The tendency for it to be predominantly left-lateralized may arise from the need for it to establish close ties with the language system. Indeed literates, relative to illiterates, show greater top-down activation of the VWFA in response to processing speech (Dehaene et al., 2010). Further evidence that the laterality of the VWFA is dependent on the location of the speech system comes from studies of left-handers. Whereas right-handers tend to have left lateralization for speech production, left-handers show more variability (some on the left, others on the right or bilateral). In left-handers, the lateralization of the VWFA tends to correlate with the dominant lateralization of speech observed in the frontal lobes (Van der Haegen et al., 2012). This again suggests that the development of a putatively "visual" mechanism is linked to important nonvisual influences.

Other researchers have argued that the existence of the visual word form area is a "myth", because the region responds to other types of familiar stimuli, such as visually presented objects and Braille reading, and not just letter patterns (Price & Devlin, 2003, 2011). These researchers argue that this region serves as a computational hub that links together different brain regions (e.g. vision and speech) according to the demands of the task. This, of course, is not completely

Visual word recognition can be considered as a hierarchy that progresses from relatively simple visual features (e.g. based on processing of contrast and line orientation), to shape recognition, to culturally-tuned mechanisms that, for instance, treat E and e as equivalent. It is still debated as to what sits at the very top of the hierarchy: it may consist of whole words (i.e. a lexicon) or common letter patterns.

From Dehaene *et al.*, 2005. *Trends in Cognitive Science*.

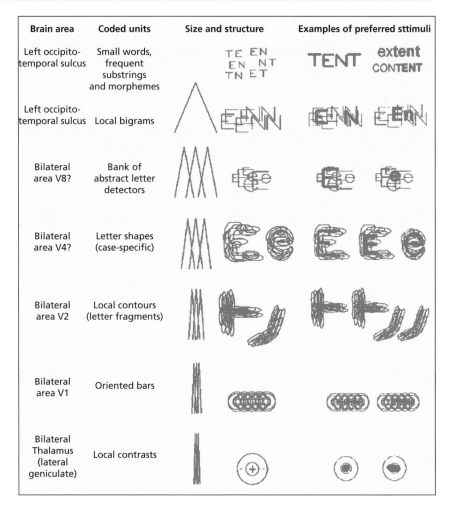

| Brain area | Coded units | Size and structure | Examples of preferred sttimuli |
|---|---|---|---|
| Left occipito-temporal sulcus | Small words, frequent substrings and morphemes | | |
| Left occipito-temporal sulcus | Local bigrams | | |
| Bilateral area V8? | Bank of abstract letter detectors | | |
| Bilateral area V4? | Letter shapes (case-specific) | | |
| Bilateral area V2 | Local contours (letter fragments) | | |
| Bilateral area V1 | Oriented bars | | |
| Bilateral Thalamus (lateral geniculate) | Local contrasts | | |

incompatible with the view described by others: i.e. that the region becomes tuned to certain stimuli over others and interacts with the language system (bidirectionally).

Other support for the idea that the VWFA is important for visual word recognition in particular, rather than visual perception or language in general, comes from neuropsychological evidence. It has also been argued that damage to this region produces a specific difficulty with reading—namely, pure alexia or letter-by-letter reading (Pflugshaupt *et al.*, 2009). This is considered in the next section.

## Pure alexia or "letter-by-letter" reading

Imagine that a patient comes into a neurological clinic complaining of reading problems. When shown the word CAT, the patient spells the letters out "C," "A," "T" before announcing the answer—"cat." When given the word CARPET, the patient again spells the letters out, taking twice as long overall, before reading the word correctly. While reading is often accurate, it appears far too slow and laborious to be of much help in everyday life. Historically, this was the first type of acquired dyslexia to be documented and it was termed **pure alexia** to emphasize the fact that reading was compromised without impairment of spelling, writing or verbal language (Dejerine,1892). It has been given a variety of other names, including "letter-by-letter reading" (Patterson & Kay, 1982), "word form dyslexia" (Warrington & Shallice, 1980) and "spelling dyslexia" (Warrington & Langdon, 1994).

Pure alexia is an example of a type of **peripheral dyslexia**. Peripheral dyslexias are believed to disrupt processing up to the level of computation of a visual word form (Shallice, 1988) and also include various spatial and attentional disturbances that affect visual word recognition (Caramazza & Hillis, 1990a; Mayall & Humphreys, 2002). This stands in contrast to varieties of **central dyslexia** that disrupt processing after computation of a visual word form (e.g. in accessing meaning or translating to speech). These will be considered later on in this chapter.

The defining behavioral characteristic of pure alexia is that reading time increases proportionately to the length of the word (the same is true of nonwords), although not all patients articulate the letter names aloud. This is consistent with the view that each letter is processed serially rather than the normal parallel recognition of letters in visual word recognition. At least three reasons have been suggested for why a patient may show these characteristics:

1. It may be related to more basic difficulties in visual perception (Farah & Wallace, 1991).
2. It may relate to attentional/perceptual problems associated with perceiving more than one item at a time (Kinsbourne & Warrington, 1962a).
3. It may relate specifically to the processing of written stimuli within the visual word form system or "visual lexicon" (Cohen & Dehaene, 2004; Warrington & Langdon, 1994; Warrington & Shallice, 1980).

As for the purely visual account, it is often the case that patients have difficulty in perceiving individual letters even though single-letter identification tends to outperform word recognition (Patterson & Kay, 1982). Some patients do not have low-level visual deficits (Warrington & Shallice, 1980), but, even in these patients, perceptual distortions of the text severely affect reading (e.g. script or "joined-up" writing is harder to read than print). Deficits in simultaneously perceiving multiple objects are not always present in pure alexia, so this cannot account for all patients (Kay & Hanley, 1991). Other studies have argued that the deficit is restricted to the processing of letters and words. For example, some patients are impaired at deciding whether two letters of different case (e.g. "E," "e") are the same, but can detect real letters from made-up ones, and real letters from their mirror image (Miozzo & Caramazza, 1998). This suggests a breakdown of more abstract orthographic knowledge that is not strictly visual.

Many researchers have opted for a hybrid account between visual deficits and orthography-specific deficits. Disruption of information flow at various stages, from early visual to word-specific levels, can result in cessation of parallel letter reading and adoption of letter-by-letter strategies (Behrmann *et al.*, 1998; Bowers *et al.*, 1996). These latter models have typically used "interactive activation" accounts in which there is a cascade of bottom-up and top-down processing (see the figure on p. 297). This interactive aspect of the model tends to result in

## KEY TERMS

**Pure alexia**
A difficulty in reading words in which reading time increases proportionately to the length of the word.

**Peripheral dyslexia**
Disruption of reading arising up to the level of computation of a visual word form.

**Central dyslexia**
Disruption of reading arising after computation of a visual word form (e.g. in accessing meaning, or translating to speech).

Some scripts are particularly difficult for letter-by-letter readers. Note the perceptual difficulty in recognizing "m" in isolation.

From Warrington and Shallice, 1980. Reproduced with permission of Oxford University Press.

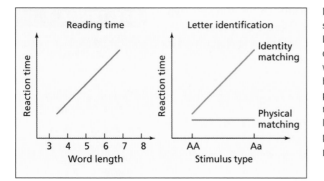

In pure alexia (or letter-by-letter reading), reading time is slow and laborious and is strongly affected by word length (see graph on the left). Patients often have difficulty in determining whether two letters are the same when they differ by case (e.g. slow at judging that A–a have the same identity, but not at judging that A–a are physically different; see graph on the right). The disorder results in a difficulty in parallel processing of abstract letter identities, but it is still debated whether the primary deficit is visual or reading-specific.

Data adapted from Kay and Hanley, 1991.

similar behavior when different levels of the model are lesioned. Another line of evidence suggests that the flow of information from lower to higher levels is reduced rather than blocked. Many pure alexic patients are able to perform lexical decisions or even semantic categorizations (animal versus object) for briefly presented words that they cannot read (Bowers *et al.*, 1996; Shallice & Saffran, 1986). For this to occur, one needs to assume that there is some partial parallel processing of the letter string that is able to access meaning and lexical representations, but that is insufficient to permit conscious visual word recognition (Roberts *et al.*, 2010).

## Evaluation

There is good evidence that there is a region within the mid-fusiform cortex that responds relatively more to word and word-like stimuli than other kinds of visual object. Although located within the "visual" ventral stream, neither its precise function nor anatomical location are strictly visual. Instead it is a region that

## WHAT DO STUDIES OF EYE MOVEMENT REVEAL ABOUT READING TEXT?

Eye movement is required when reading text, because visual acuity is greatest at the fovea and words in the periphery are hard to recognize quickly and accurately. However, the control of eye movements in reading clearly has two masters: visual perception and text comprehension (Rayner & Juhasz, 2004; Rayner, 2009). The eyes move across the page in a series of jerks (called saccades) and pauses (called **fixations**). This stands in contrast to following a moving target, in which the eyes move smoothly. To understand this process in more detail, we can break it down into two questions: How do we decide where to land during a saccade? How do we decide when to move after a fixation?

First, reading direction affects both the movement of saccades and the extraction of information during fixation. English speakers typically have left-to-right reading saccades and absorb more information from the right of fixation. It is more efficient to consider upcoming words than linger on previously processed ones. The eyes typically fixate on a point between the beginning and middle of a word (Rayner, 1979), and take information concerning three or four letters on the left and 15 letters to the right (Rayner *et al.*, 1980). Hebrew readers do the opposite (Pollatsek *et al.*, 1981).

The *landing position* within a word may be related to perceptual rather than linguistic factors. The predictability of a word in context does not influence landing position within the word (Rayner et al., 2001), nor does morphological complexity (Radach et al., 2004). Whether or not a word is *skipped* altogether seems to depend on how short it is (a perceptual factor) (Rayner & McConkie, 1976) and how predictable it is (a linguistic factor) (Rayner et al., 2001). The frequency of a word and its predictability do influence the *length of time fixated* (Rayner & Duffy, 1986). Similarly, the length of time fixated seems to depend on morphological complexity (Niswander et al., 2000).

Several detailed models have been developed that attempt to explain this pattern of data (in addition to making new testable predictions) that take into account the interaction of perceptual and linguistic factors (Pollatsek et al., 2006; Reilly & Radach, 2006).

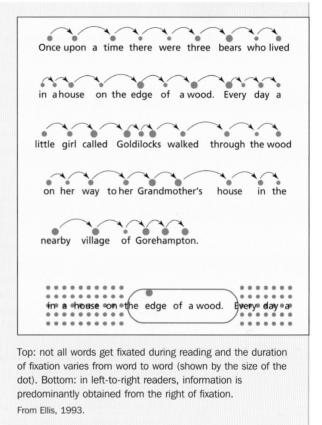

Top: not all words get fixated during reading and the duration of fixation varies from word to word (shown by the size of the dot). Bottom: in left-to-right readers, information is predominantly obtained from the right of fixation.

From Ellis, 1993.

connects vision to the wider language network and also multi-modal shape processing. Whether the region stores known words (i.e. implements a visual lexicon) in addition to letter patterns remains a matter of debate as the presence of word-specific effects could be related to top-down effects (e.g. from the semantic system) rather than reflecting a store of word forms.

## READING ALOUD: ROUTES FROM SPELLING TO SOUND

There are, broadly speaking, two things that one may wish to do with a written word: understand it (i.e. retrieve its meaning from semantic memory) or say it aloud (i.e. convert it to speech). Are these two functions largely separate or is one dependent on the other? For instance, does understanding a written word require that it first be translated to speech (i.e. a serial architecture)? This possibility

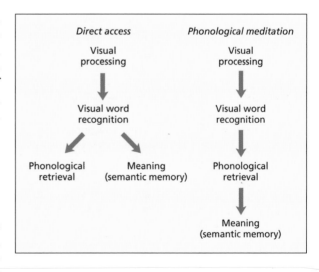

Do we need to access the spoken forms of words in order to understand them? In the model on the left, phonological retrieval may accompany silent reading but is not essential for it. In the model on the right, phonological mediation is essential for comprehension of text.

**KEY TERMS**

**Phonological mediation**
The claim that accessing the spoken forms of words is an obligatory component of understanding visually presented words.

**Homophone**
Words that sound the same but have different meanings (and often different spellings), e.g. ROWS and ROSE.

has sometimes been termed **phonological mediation**. The alternative proposal is that understanding written words and transcoding text into speech are two largely separate, but interacting, parallel processes. The evidence largely supports the latter view and has given rise to so-called dual route architectures for reading, which are discussed in this section.

Many studies that have examined the interaction between word meaning and phonology have used as stimuli **homophones** (words with the same phonology but different spelling, e.g. ROWS and ROSE) or pseudo-homophones (nonwords that are pronounced like a real word; e.g. BRANE). Van Orden (1987; Van Orden *et al.*, 1988) reported that normal participants are error-prone when making semantic categorizations when a stimulus is homophonic with a true category member (e.g. determining whether ROWS is a FLOWER). This was taken as evidence that mapping between visual words and their meaning requires phonological mediation (i.e. that understanding text depends on first accessing the spoken form of a word). This evidence certainly speaks against the alternative view of two separate and *noninteracting* processes. However, it is consistent with the notion of separate but interacting routes. For instance, some acquired aphasic patients who make phonemic errors during reading, naming, and spontaneous speech are capable of understanding the meaning of written homophones even if they have no idea whether the words ROWS and ROSE would sound the same if read loud (Hanley & MacDonell, 1997). This suggests intact access from text-to-meaning together with impaired access from text-to-speech.

The most influential models of reading aloud are based on a dual-route model of reading initially put forward by Marshall and Newcombe (1973). The key features of this model are: (1) a semantically based reading route in which visual words are able to access semantics directly; and (2) a phonologically based reading route that uses known regularities between spelling patterns and phonological patterns (e.g. the letters TH are normally pronounced as "th") to achieve reading. This route is also called grapheme–phoneme conversion.

Before going on to consider later developments of the model, it is important to state the key properties of the standard, traditional dual-route model (Morton, 1980; Patterson, 1981; Shallice *et al.*, 1983). In the traditional model, the phonologically based route is considered to instantiate a procedure called grapheme–phoneme conversion, in which letter patterns are mapped onto corresponding phonemes. This may be essential for reading nonwords, which, by definition, do not have meaning or a stored lexical representation. Known words, by contrast, do have a meaning and can be read via direct access to the semantic system and thence via the stored spoken forms of words. Of course, many of these words could also be read via grapheme–phoneme conversion, although in the case of words with irregular spellings it would result in error (e.g. YACHT read as "yatched"). The extent to which each route is used may also be determined by speed of processing—the direct semantic access route is generally considered faster. This is because it processes whole words, whereas the grapheme–phoneme conversion route processes them bit-by-bit. The semantic route is also sensitive to how common a word is—known as word frequency (and not to be confused with "frequency" in the auditory sense). Reading time data from skilled adult readers is broadly consistent with this framework. High-frequency words (i.e. those that are common in the language) are fast to read, irrespective of the sound–spelling regularity. For low-frequency words, regular words are read faster than irregular ones (Seidenberg *et al.*, 1984).

## Profiles of acquired central dyslexias

The dual-route model predicts that selective damage to different components comprising the two routes should have different consequences for the reading of different types of written material. Indeed this appears to be so. Some patients are able to read nonwords and regularly spelled words better than irregularly spelled words, which they tend to pronounce as if they were regular (e.g. DOVE pronounced "doove" like "move," and CHAOS pronounced with a "ch" as in "church"). These patients are called **surface dyslexics** (Patterson *et al.*, 1985; Shallice *et al.*, 1983). Within the dual-route system it may reflect reliance on grapheme–phoneme conversion arising from damage to the semantic system (Graham *et al.*, 1994) or visual lexicon itself (Coltheart & Funnell, 1987). In the figure below, they use the red route for reading, which enables nonwords and regularly spelled words to be read accurately. The green route may still have some level of functioning that supports high-frequency words. As such, these patients typically show a frequency × regularity interaction. That is, high-frequency words tend to be read accurately no matter how regular they are, but low frequency words tend to be particularly error prone when they are irregular (see figure on p. 306).

Another type of acquired dyslexia has been termed **phonological dyslexia**. These patients are able to read real words better than nonwords, although it is to be noted that real word reading is not necessarily 100 percent correct (Beauvois & Derouesne, 1979). When given a nonword to read, they often produce a real word answer (e.g. CHURSE read as "nurse"), and more detailed testing typically reveals that they have problems in aspects of phonological processing (e.g. auditory rhyme judgment) but that they can perceive the written word accurately (Farah *et al.*, 1996; Patterson & Marcel, 1992). As such, these patients are considered to have difficulties in the phonological route (grapheme–phoneme conversion) and are reliant on the lexical–semantic route. In the figure on the right they rely on green route for reading and have limited use of the red route.

Another type of acquired dyslexia exists that resembles phonological dyslexia in that real words are read better than nonwords, but in which real word reading is more error-prone and results in a particularly intriguing type of error—a semantic error (e.g. reading CAT as "dog"). This is termed **deep dyslexia** (Coltheart *et al.*, 1980). The

A dual-route model of reading. The standard lexical–semantic and grapheme–phoneme conversion routes are shown in green and red respectively. Grapheme-phoneme conversion is a slower route that can accurately read nonwords and regularly spelled words. The lexical–semantic route is faster and can read all known words (whether regular or irregularly spelled) but is more efficient for common, high-frequency words.

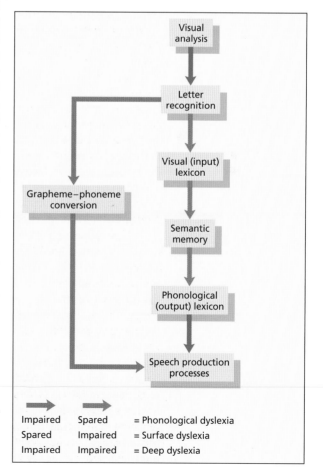

| | | |
|---|---|---|
| Impaired | Spared | = Phonological dyslexia |
| Spared | Impaired | = Surface dyslexia |
| Impaired | Impaired | = Deep dyslexia |

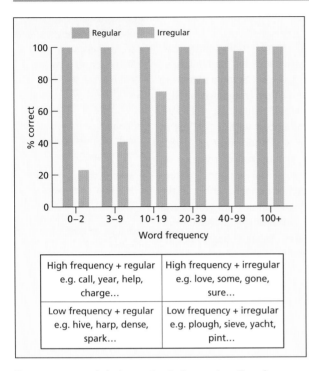

| High frequency + regular e.g. call, year, help, charge… | High frequency + irregular e.g. love, some, gone, sure… |
|---|---|
| Low frequency + regular e.g. hive, harp, dense, spark… | Low frequency + irregular e.g. plough, sieve, yacht, pint… |

Frequency → regularity interaction in the word reading of a semantic dementia patient and examples of words falling into these categories.

Reprinted from Ward et al., 2000. © 2000, with permission from Elsevier.

patients also have a number of other characteristics, including a difficulty in reading low imageability (e.g. truth) relative to high imageability (e.g. wine) words. Within the original dual-route model, this was explained as damage to grapheme–phoneme conversion and use of the intact semantic pathway (Marshall & Newcombe, 1973). However, this explanation is clearly inadequate, because it predicts that the semantic route is normally very error-prone in us all, and it fails to predict that patients with deep dyslexia have comprehension problems on tests of semantic memory that do not involve written material (Shallice, 1988). The most common way of explaining deep dyslexia is to assume that *both* reading routes are impaired (Nolan & Caramazza, 1982). The lexical–semantic route is degraded such that similar concepts have effectively become fused together and cannot be distinguished from one another, and the absence of grapheme-phoneme conversion prevents an alternative means of output.

A number of studies have reported patients who can read words aloud accurately but have impaired nonword reading and impaired semantic knowledge (Cipolotti & Warrington, 1995b; Coslett, 1991; Funnell, 1983; Lambon Ralph et al., 1995). So how are these patients able to read? The problem with nonwords implies a difficulty in grapheme–phoneme conversion, and the problem in comprehension and semantic memory implies a difficulty in the lexical–semantic route. One might predict the patients would be severely dyslexic—probably deep dyslexic. To accommodate these data, several researchers have argued in favor of a "third route" that links the visual lexicon with the phonological lexicon but does not go through semantics (Cipolotti & Warrington, 1995b; Coltheart et al., 1993; Coslett, 1991; Funnell, 1983).

There are several alternative accounts to the "third route" that have been put forward to explain good word reading in the face of impaired semantic knowledge. Woollams et al. (2007) noted that these cases, when observed in the context of semantic dementia, do tend to go on to develop word-reading problems (particularly for irregular spellings) as their semantic memory gets worse. They suggest that an intact semantic system is always needed for reading these words, but people differ in the extent to which they rely on one route more than the other. Those who rely more on the semantic route before brain damage will show the largest disruption in reading ability when they go on to develop semantic dementia. An alternative to the third route is provided by the *summation hypothesis* (Hillis & Caramazza, 1991; Ciaghi et al., 2010). The summation hypothesis states that lexical representations in reading are selected by summing the activation from the semantic system and from grapheme–phoneme conversion. Thus patients with partial damage to one or both of these routes may still be able to achieve relatively proficient performance at reading, even with irregular words. For example, in trying to read the irregular word *bear*, a degraded semantic system may activate a number of candidates including bear, horse, cow, etc. However, the grapheme–phoneme conversion system will also activate, to differing, a set of lexical candidates that are phonologically similar ("beer," "bare," "bar," etc.). By combining these two sources of information, the patient should be able to arrive at the correct pronunciation of "bear," even though neither route may be able to select the correct entry by itself. This prediction was tested by Hillis and Caramazza (1991). Their surface dyslexic/dysgraphic participant was able to read and spell irregular words for which he had partial understanding (e.g. superordinate category) but not irregular words for which no understanding was demonstrated.

## What has functional imaging revealed about the existence of multiple routes?

The initial motivation for postulating two (or more) routes for reading was cognitive, not neuroanatomical. Nevertheless, functional imaging may provide an important source of converging evidence to this debate—at least in principle (for reviews, see Fiez & Petersen, 1998; Jobard *et al.*, 2003; Cattinelli *et al.*, 2013). Of course, functional imaging measures the activity of regions only in response to particular task demands, and so it does not provide any direct evidence for actual anatomical routes between brain regions.

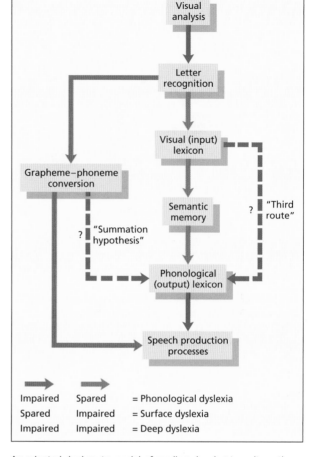

An adapted dual-route model of reading showing two alternative modifications to the model (blue lines). These modifications have been proposed by some researchers to account for the fact that some acquired dyslexic patients can read irregular words that they cannot understand. They bypass semantic memory.

Aside from the mid-fusiform (or VWFA) region already considered, a number of other predominantly left-lateralized regions are consistently implicated in fMRI studies of reading and reading-related processes such as lexical decision. These include the inferior frontal cortex (including Broca's area); the inferior parietal lobe; and several anterior and mid-temporal lobe regions. These are considered in turn.

### Inferior frontal lobe (Broca's area)

This region is implicated in fMRI studies of reading, as well as in language processing in general (see Chapter 11). Some have suggested that the inferior frontal lobe does not have a core role to play in single-word reading, but is instead related to general task difficulty (Cattinelli *et al.*, 2013). However, others have suggested that it has a specific role in converting graphemes to phonemes (Fiebach *et al.*, 2002). This is because this region is activated more by low frequency words

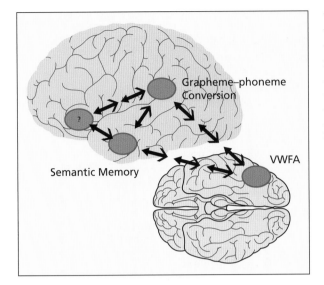

Key areas identified in brain imaging studies and their possible functions. Note that the anatomical routes (and intermediate processing stages) are largely unknown and are shown here as illustrative possibilities. The role of the inferior frontal lobe (Broca's area) in reading is uncertain but may contribute to both semantically based reading and reading via phonological decoding. It may also bias the reading strategy that is adopted (according to the task).

with an irregular spelling (Fiez *et al.*, 1999). These words are the hardest to read via that system, and the assumption is that more cognitive effort manifests itself as greater BOLD activity. An alternative way of interpreting increased activity for low frequency irregular words is by assuming that a greater BOLD response for these items provides evidence for more semantic support being offered by this region (rather than reflecting the grapheme–phoneme conversion routine working harder). Indeed, some studies have made this alternative claim (Jobard *et al.*, 2003). It is possible that both claims could be true if different sub-regions were contributing to both reading routes. Heim *et al.* (2005) suggest that BA45 is involved in semantic retrieval (e.g. during lexical decision), but BA44 supports grapheme–phoneme conversion. Patients with damage to the wider inferior frontal region make more errors on nonwords than real regular words, but additionally struggle with low-frequency irregular words (Fiez *et al.*, 2006). That is, the pattern is neither a specific profile of surface dyslexia or of phonological dyslexia but a mix of the two. This suggests that the region does indeed serve multiple functions during reading rather than being specifically tied to one process/route.

### Inferior parietal lobe

The inferior parietal lobe consists of two anatomical regions: the supramarginal gyrus, which abuts the superior temporal lobes; and the angular gyrus, lying more posteriorly. Both have long been linked to language. The supramarginal gyrus was historically linked to Wernicke's area (and phonological processing in particular). The angular gyrus has been linked to verbal working memory (Paulesu *et al.*, 1993) and binding semantic concepts (Binder & Desai, 2011). With particular reference to reading, it has been suggested that the left supramarginal gyrus is implicated in grapheme–phoneme conversion. It tends to be activated more by nonwords than words, and evidence from intracranial EEG (Juphard *et al.*, 2011) and fMRI (Church *et al.*, 2011) suggest that reading of longer nonwords is linked to longer duration of EEG activity and increased BOLD signal. These findings suggest piecemeal processing of letter string rather than holistic recognition. An excitatory (rather than inhibitory) version of TMS over this region facilitates nonword reading (Costanzo *et al.*, 2012), whereas inhibitory TMS impairs phonological (but not semantic) judgments about written words (Sliwinska *et al.*, 2012). Finally, patients with semantic dementia hyper-activate this region, relative to controls, when attempting to read low frequency irregular words (Wilson *et al.*, 2012). These words tend to be regularized by these patients (e.g. SEW read as "sue") suggesting that they, but not controls, may utilize this region to read these words (i.e. to compensate for their inability to read the words using semantics).

*Anterior and mid-temporal lobe*

These regions of the brain are strongly implicated in supporting semantic memory. Within models of reading, one would therefore expect that they would contribute to the reading-via-meaning route (i.e. mapping orthography to phonology via semantics). The mid-temporal cortex is a region that tends to be activated, during fMRI, in semantic relative to phonological processing of written words (Mechelli *et al.*, 2007). Gray matter volume in this region, and the anterior temporal pole, measured by VBM correlates with ability in reading of irregular words in aphasic patients (Brambati *et al.*, 2009). Finally, patients with semantic dementia, who invariably present with surface dyslexia, have lesions in this area (Wilson *et al.*, 2009).

In summary, the evidence from functional imaging suggests that different brain regions are involved in reading via grapheme–phoneme conversion (left supra-marginal gyrus) and reading via meaning (anterior and mid-temporal lobes). This evidence generally supports the dual-route notion but does not—at present—discriminate well between different versions of it. Other regions (e.g. left inferior frontal lobe) have an important role in reading but serve an unclear function, as they do not clearly map onto a construct within current cognitive models of reading.

## Is the same reading system universal across languages?

The dual-route model is an attractive framework for understanding reading in opaque languages such as English, in which there is a mix of regular and irregular spelling-to-sound patterns. But to what extent is this model likely to extend to languages with highly transparent mappings (e.g. Italian) or, at the other extreme, are logographic rather than alphabetic (e.g. Chinese)? The evidence suggests that the same reading system is indeed used across other languages, but the different routes and components may be weighted differently according to the culture-specific demands.

Functional imaging suggests that reading uses similar brain regions across different languages, albeit to varying degrees. Italian speakers appear to activate more strongly areas involved in phonemic processing when reading words, whereas English speakers activate more strongly regions implicated in lexical retrieval (Paulesu *et al.*, 2000). Studies of Chinese speakers also support a common network for reading Chinese logographs and reading Roman-alphabetic tran-scriptions of Chinese (the latter being a system, called pinyin, used to help in teaching Chinese; Chen *et al.*, 2002). Moreover, Chinese logographs resemble English words more than they do pictures in terms of the brain activity that is engendered, although reading Chinese logographs may make more demands on brain regions involved in semantics than reading English (Chee *et al.*, 2000). The latter is supported by cognitive studies showing that reading logographs is more affected by word imageability than reading English words (Shibahara *et al.*, 2003). Imageability refers to whether a concept is concrete or abstract, with concrete words believed to possess richer semantic representations. Thus, it appears that Chinese readers may be more reliant on reading via semantics but that the reading system is co-extensive with that used for other scripts.

Although Chinese is not alphabetic, whole words and characters can nevertheless be decomposed into a collection of parts. There is evidence to suggest that there is a separate route that is sensitive to part-based reading of Chinese characters that is analogous to grapheme–phoneme conversion in alphabetic scripts.

Cases of surface dyslexia have been documented in Japanese (Fushimi *et al.*, 2003) and Chinese (Weekes & Chen, 1999). Reading of Chinese logographs and Japanese Kanji can be influenced by the parts that comprise them. These parts have different pronunciations in different contexts, with degree of consistency varying. This is broadly analogous to grapheme–phoneme regularities in alphabetic scripts. Indeed, the degree of consistency of character–sound correspondence affecting reading of both words and nonwords is particularly apparent for low-frequency words. The results suggest that there are nonsemantic routes for linking print with sound even in scripts that are not based on the alphabetic principle. Conversely, phonological dyslexia has been observed in these scripts, adding further weight to the notion that the dual-route model may be universal (Patterson *et al.*, 1996; Yin & Weekes, 2003). Similarly, surface dyslexia (Job *et al.*, 1983) and phonological dyslexia (De Bastiani *et al.*, 1988) have been observed in Italian, even though this reading system is entirely regular and could, in principle, be achieved by grapheme–phoneme correspondence alone. As with English and Chinese, Italian also shows a word frequency × regularity interaction for reading aloud in skilled adult readers (Burani *et al.*, 2006).

## Evaluation

The dual-route model of reading presently remains the most viable model of reading aloud. It is able to account for skilled reading, for patterns of acquired dyslexia, and for difference in regional activity observed in functional imaging when processing different types of written stimuli. The model also extends to written languages that are very different from English. However, the precise nature of the computations carried out still remains to be fully elucidated.

## SPELLING AND WRITING

Spelling has received less attention than the study of reading. For example, there is a paucity of functional imaging studies dedicated to the topic (but see Beeson *et al.*, 2003). The reasons for this are unclear. Producing written language may be less common as a task for many people than reading; it may also be harder. For example, many adult developmental dyslexics can get by adequately at reading but only manifest their true difficulties when it comes to spelling (Frith, 1985). However, the study of spelling and its disorders has produced some intriguing insights into the organization of the cognitive system dedicated to literacy.

## A model of spelling and writing

First, it is important to make a distinction between the process of selecting and retrieving a letter string to be produced, and the task of physically producing an output. The latter task may take various forms such as writing, typing, and oral spelling. The term "spelling" can be viewed as an encompassing term that is neutral with respect to the mode of output.

As with reading, dual-route models of spelling have been postulated (for a review, see Houghton & Zorzi, 2003). In spelling the task demands are reversed, in that one is attempting to get from a spoken word or a concept to an orthographic one. As such, the names of some of the components are changed to reflect this. For example, phoneme–grapheme conversion is a hypothesized component of spelling, whereas grapheme–phoneme conversion is the reading equivalent.

The principal line of evidence for this model comes from the acquired **dysgraphias**. In surface dysgraphia, patients are better at spelling to dictation regularly spelled words and nonwords, and are poor with irregularly spelled words (e.g. "yacht" spelled as YOT) (Beauvois & Derouesne, 1981; Goodman & Caramazza, 1986a). This is considered to be due to damage to the lexical–semantic route and reliance on phoneme–grapheme conversion. Indeed, these cases typically have poor comprehension characteristic of a semantic disorder (Graham *et al.*, 2000). In contrast, patients with phonological dysgraphia are able to spell real words better than nonwords (Shallice, 1981). This has been explained as a difficulty in phoneme–grapheme conversion, or a problem in phonological segmentation itself. Deep dysgraphia (e.g. spelling "cat" as D-O-G) has been reported too (Bub & Kertesz, 1982). As with reading, there is debate concerning whether there is a "third route" that directly connects phonological and orthographic lexicons that by-passes semantics (Hall & Riddoch, 1997; Hillis & Caramazza, 1991). It is important to note that all of these spelling disorders are generally independent of the modality of output. For example, a surface dysgraphic patient would tend to produce the same kinds of errors in writing, typing, or oral spelling.

## The graphemic buffer

The **graphemic buffer** is a short-term memory component that holds on to the string of abstract letter identities while output processes (for writing, typing, etc.) are engaged (Wing & Baddeley, 1980). As with other short-term memory systems, the graphemic buffer may be mediated by particular frontoparietal networks (Cloutman *et al.*, 2009). The term "grapheme" is used in this context to refer to letter identities that are not specified in terms of case (e.g. B versus b), font (**b** versus b), or modality of output (e.g. oral spelling versus

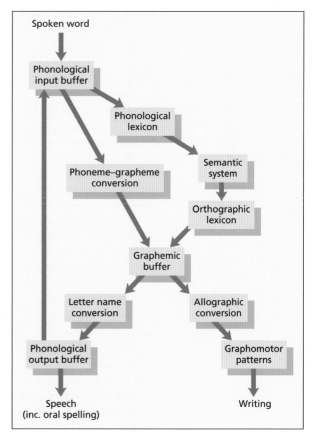

A dual-route model of spelling.

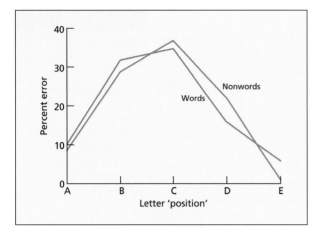

Patient LB had graphemic buffer damage and produced spelling errors with both words and nonwords. The errors tended to cluster around the middle of the word.

Reprinted from Caramazza et al., 1987. © 1987, with permission from Elsevier.

writing). Another important feature of the graphemic buffer is that it serves as the confluence of the phoneme–grapheme route and the lexical–semantic spelling route. As such, the graphemic buffer is used in spelling both words and nonwords.

Wing and Baddeley (1980) analyzed a large corpus of spelling errors generated by candidates sitting an entrance exam for Cambridge University. They considered letter-based errors that were believed to reflect output errors ("slips of the pen") rather than errors based on lack of knowledge of the true spelling (e.g. the candidate had correctly spelled the word on another occasion). These errors consisted of letter transpositions (e.g. HO*SR*E for HORSE), substitutions (e.g. HO*P*SE for HORSE), omissions (e.g. HOSE for HORSE), and additions (HOR*E*SE for HORSE). These errors were assumed to arise from noise or interference between letters in the graphemic buffer. One additional characteristic of these errors is that they tended to cluster in the middle of words, giving an inverted U-shaped error distribution. Wing and Baddeley speculated that letters in the middle have more neighbors and are thus susceptible to more interference.

The most detailed example of acquired damage to the graphemic buffer is patient LB (Caramazza *et al.*, 1987; Caramazza & Miceli, 1990; Caramazza *et al.*, 1996). In some respects, the errors could be viewed as a pathological extreme of those documented by Wing and Baddeley (1980). For example, spelling mistakes consisted of single-letter errors and were concentrated in the middle of words. In addition, equivalent spelling errors were found irrespective of whether the stimulus was a word or nonword, and irrespective of output modality. This is consistent with the central position of the graphemic buffer in the cognitive architecture of spelling. In addition, word length had a significant effect on the probability of an error. This is consistent with its role as a limited capacity retention system.

There is evidence to suggest that the information held in the graphemic buffer consists of more than just a linear string of letter identities (Caramazza & Miceli, 1990). In particular, it has been argued that consecutive double letters (e.g. the BB in RABBIT) have a special status. Double letters (also called geminates) tend to be misspelled such that the doubling information migrates to another letter (Tainturier & Caramazza, 1996). For example, RABBIT may be spelled as RABITT. However, errors such as RABIBT are conspicuously absent, even though they exist for comparable words that lack a double letter (e.g. spelling BASKET as BASEKT). This suggests that our mental representation of the spelling of the word RABBIT does not consist of R-A-B-B-I-T but consists of R-A-B[D]-I-T, where [D] denotes that the letter should be doubled. Why do double letters need this special status? One suggestion is that, after each letter is produced, it gets inhibited to prevent it getting produced again and to allow another letter to be processed (Shallice *et al.*, 1995). When the same letter needs to be written twice in a row, a special mechanism is required to block this inhibition.

# Output processes in writing and oral spelling

There is evidence for separate written versus oral letter name output codes in spelling. Some patients have damage to the letter names that selectively impairs oral spelling relative to written spelling (Cipolotti & Warrington, 1996; Kinsbourne & Warrington, 1965). The task of oral spelling is likely to be closely linked with other aspects of phonological processing (for a review, see Ward, 2003). In contrast, some patients are better at oral spelling than written spelling (Goodman & Caramazza, 1986b; Rapp & Caramazza, 1997). These peripheral dysgraphias take several forms and are related to different stages, from specification of the abstract letter to production of pen strokes.

Ellis (1979, 1982) refers to three different levels of description for a letter. The grapheme is the most abstract description that specifies letter identity, whereas an **allograph** refers to letters that are specified for shape (e.g. case, print versus script), but not motor output, and the **graph** refers to a specification of stroke order, size and direction. Damage to the latter two stages would selectively affect writing over oral spelling. Patients with damage to the allographic level may write in mIxeD CaSe, and have selective difficulties with either lowercase writing (Patterson & Wing, 1989) or upper-case writing (Del Grosso *et al.*, 2000). They also tend to substitute a letter for one of similar appearance (Rapp & Caramazza, 1997). Although this could be taken as evidence for confusions based on visual shape, it is also the case that similar shapes have similar graphomotor demands. Some researchers have argued that allographs are simply pointers that denote case and style but do not specify the visual shape of the letter (Del Grosso Destreri *et al.*, 2000; Rapp & Caramazza, 1997). Rapp and Caramazza (1997) showed that their patient, with hypothesized damage to allographs, was influenced by graphomotor similarity and not shape when these were independently controlled for. Other dysgraphic patients can write letters far better than they can visually imagine them (Del Grosso Destreri *et al.*, 2000) or can write words from dictation but cannot copy the same words from a visual template (Cipolotti & Denes, 1989). This suggests that the output codes in writing are primarily motoric rather than visuospatial.

The motor representations for writing themselves may be damaged ("graphs" in the terminology above). Some patients can no longer write letters but can draw,

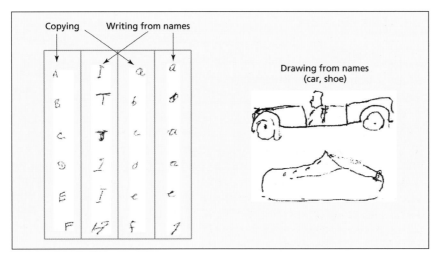

Drawing from names (car, shoe)

Patient IDT was unable to write letters to dictation, but could draw pictures on command and copy letters. This ability rules out a general apraxic difficulty.

Reproduced from Baxter and Warrington, 1986. © 1986, reproduced with permission from BMJ Publishing Group Ltd.

## THE UNUSUAL SPELLING AND WRITING OF LEONARDO DA VINCI

The writing of Leonardo da Vinci is unusual in terms of both content and style. In terms of content, there are many spelling errors. This suggests that he may have been surface dyslexic/dysgraphic (Sartori, 1987). In terms of style, his handwriting is highly idiosyncratic and is virtually unreadable except to scholars who are familiar with his style. Da Vinci wrote in mirror-reversed script, such that his writing begins on the right side of the page and moves leftward.

Was Leonardo da Vinci surface dysgraphic? Why did he write mirror-distorted letters from right to left? An example of this is shown here in his *Codex on the Flight of Birds*? (circa 1505).

© Luc Viatour GFDL/CC.

The letters themselves were mirror-image distortions of their conventional form. This has been variously interpreted as a deliberate attempt at code (to retain intellectual ownership over his ideas), as proof that he was no mere mortal (for either good or evil) or as being related to his left-handedness. It is well documented that da Vinci was a left-hander and a small proportion of left-handed children do spontaneously adopt such a style. An alternative is that he was born right-handed but sustained an injury that forced him to write with his left hand. Natural right-handers are surprised at how easy it is to write simultaneously with both hands, with the right hand writing normally and the left hand mirror-reversed (for discussion, see McManus, 2002).

As for his spelling errors, Sartori (1987) argues that da Vinci may have been surface dysgraphic. The cardinal feature of this disorder is the spelling of irregular words in a phonetically regular form. Although Italian (da Vinci's native language) lacks irregular words, it is nevertheless possible to render the same phonology in different written forms. For example, *laradio* and *l'aradio* are phonetically plausible, but conventionally incorrect, renditions of *la radio* (the radio). This type of error was commonplace in da Vinci's writings, as it is in modern-day Italian surface dysgraphics (Job *et al.*, 1983). It is, however, conspicuously absent in the spelling errors of normal Italian controls.

copy and even write numbers, which suggests that the difficulty is in stored motor representations and not action more generally (Baxter & Warrington, 1986; Zettin *et al.*, 1995).

Although the stored codes for writing may be motoric rather than visual, vision still has an important role to play in guiding the online execution of writing. Patients with **afferent dysgraphia** make many stroke omissions and additions in writing (Cubelli & Lupi, 1999; Ellis *et al.*, 1987). Interestingly, similar error patterns are found when healthy individuals write blindfolded and have distracting motor activity (e.g. tapping with their non-writing hand) (Ellis *et al.*, 1987). It suggests that these dysgraphic patients are unable to utilize sensorimotor feedback even though basic sensation (e.g. vision, proprioception) is largely unimpaired.

Patient VB is described as having "afferent dysgraphia," which is hypothesized to arise from a failure to utilize visual and motor feedback during the execution of motor tasks, such as writing. Similar errors are observed in normal participants when feedback is disrupted by blindfolding and when producing an irrelevant motor response.

From Ellis *et al.*, 1987.

## DOES SPELLING USE THE SAME MECHANISMS AS READING?

Given the inherent similarities between reading and spelling, one may wonder to what extent they share the same cognitive and neural resources. Many earlier models postulated the existence of separate lexicons for reading and spelling (Morton, 1980). However, the evidence in favor of this separation is weak. In fact, there is some evidence to suggest that the same lexicon may support both reading and spelling (Behrmann & Bub, 1992; Coltheart & Funnell, 1987). Both of these studies reported patients with surface dyslexia and surface dysgraphia who showed item-for-item consistency in the words that could and could not be read or spelled. These studies concluded that this reflects loss of word forms from a lexicon shared between reading and spelling.

There is also some evidence to suggest that the same graphemic buffer is employed both in reading and spelling (Caramazza *et al.*, 1996; Tainturier & Rapp, 2003). However, graphemic buffer damage may have more dire consequences for spelling than reading, because spelling is a slow process that makes more demands on this temporary memory structure than reading. In reading, letters may be mapped on to words in parallel and loss of information at the single-letter level may be partially compensated for. For example, reading EL??HANT may result in correct retrieval of "elephant" despite loss of letter information (where the question marks represent degraded information in the buffer). However, attempting to spell from such a degraded representation would result in error. Patients with graphemic buffer damage are particularly bad at reading nonwords, because this requires analysis of all letters, in contrast to reading words in which partial information can be compensated for to some extent (Caramazza *et al.*, 1996). Moreover, their errors show essentially the same pattern in reading and spelling,

### KEY TERM

**Afferent dysgraphia**
Stroke omissions and additions in writing that may be due to poor use of visual and kinesthetic feedback.

including a concentration at the middle of words. This suggests that the same graphemic buffer participates in both reading and spelling.

Functional imaging studies of writing activate a region of the left fusiform that is the same as the so-called visual word form area implicated in reading. For example, this region is active when writing English words from a category examplar relative to drawing circles (Beeson *et al.*, 2003), and when writing Japanese Kanji characters (Nakamura *et al.*, 2000). Brain-damaged patients with lesions in this region are impaired at both spelling and reading for both words and nonwords (Philipose *et al.*, 2007). The functional interpretation of this region is controversial (see above) and may reflect a single lexicon for reading and spelling, a common graphemic buffer, or possibly a multi-modal language region. In each case, it appears that reading and spelling have something in common in terms of anatomy.

## Evaluation

Not only is the functional architecture of spelling very similar to that used for reading, there is also evidence to suggest that some of the cognitive components (and neural regions) are shared between the task. There is evidence to suggest sharing of the visual/orthographic lexicon and of the graphemic buffer. However, the evidence suggests that the representation of letters used in writing is primarily graphomotor and that this differs from the more visuospatial codes that support both reading and imagery of letters.

## SUMMARY AND KEY POINTS OF THE CHAPTER

- The recognition of letters within words occurs automatically and in parallel, and is supported by knowledge of the structure of the language (i.e. which letters tend to go together).
- Evidence of top-down effects from semantics down to visual word recognition remains controversial. Most of the evidence that apparently supports this position is also consistent with post-access decision mechanisms and lexical–lexical priming.
- A region in the left fusiform gyrus responds to familiar letter strings more than false letters or consonant strings. This has been termed the "visual word form area," although it might also respond, to some degree, to other types of stimuli.
- Evidence from acquired dyslexia suggests that there are at least two routes used in reading words aloud: a sublexical route that translates graphemes into phonemes (impaired in phonological dyslexia) and a lexical–semantic route (impaired in surface dyslexia).
- There is evidence to suggest that many of the components involved in reading (e.g. graphemic buffer) are also involved in spelling.
- Letter representations used in spelling and writing exist at several levels: an abstract graphemic level, a level that specifies case and style (allograph), and a level that specifies the abstract motor commands (the graph level).

## EXAMPLE ESSAY QUESTIONS

- Is there a "visual lexicon" or a "visual word form area" that is used to support visual word recognition?
- What is the evidence for top-down influences in visual word recognition?
- How many routes are there for reading a word aloud?
- To what extent is the cognitive/neural architecture for reading and spelling common to speakers of different languages?
- Does spelling use the same cognitive mechanisms as reading?

## RECOMMENDED FURTHER READING

- Dehaene, S. (2010). *Reading in the brain: The new science of how we read*. London: Penguin Books. An accessible introduction written by a leading cognitive neuroscientist.
- Sandak, R. & Poldrack, R. A. (2004). *The cognitive neuroscience of reading: A special issue of scientific studies of reading*. London: Taylor & Francis. A good collection of review papers.
- Snowling, M. & Hulme, C. (2005). *The science of reading: A handbook*. Oxford, UK: Blackwell. Very thorough, but also accessible. It also contains chapters on spelling. A strong recommendation.

Visit the companion website at www. psypress/cw/ward for:

- References to key papers and readings
- Video lectures and interviews on key topics with leading psychologists Stanislas Dehaene, Dorothy Bishop, and author Jamie Ward, as well as an example of acquired dyslexia (termed pure alexia) following a stroke
- Multiple choice questions and interactive flashcards to test your knowledge
- Downloadable glossary

# CHAPTER 13

# The numerate brain

## CONTENTS

Numbers are everywhere: prices, distances, percentages, bus routes, and so on. Even most illiterate cultures have developed systems of trading and counting. This chapter is not concerned with algebra or calculus; it is concerned with a core set of numerical abilities that seem to be common to almost all humans from infants to the elderly, from the unschooled to the mathematical prodigy. It is to be noted that a basic level of numerical competence is found in *almost all* individuals. Some people with a condition known as **dyscalculia** (or acalculia) lack a basic understanding of numbers. This difficulty may be a result of brain damage (i.e. numerical competence is lost) or may be of developmental origin (i.e. numerical competence is never gained). The study of dyscalculic individuals has led to important insights into numerical cognition.

Numerical ability can certainly be promoted, or held back, by cultural quirks and inventions. Surprisingly, the **place value system** of numerical notation was not introduced into Europe until the twelfth century, having been invented by Indian scholars and passed on to Arab traders (as was the notation for zero). The place value notation means that the quantity is determined by its place in the written string—thus the "1" in 41, 17 and 185 all mean something different. In our base-10 system, they refer to 1, 10, 100 or $10^0$, $10^1$, $10^2$. Adding together two numbers (e.g. 41 + 17) basically involves little more than adding together the numbers in each place, carrying over if appropriate (7 + 1 is 8, and 4 + 1 is 5, so the answer is 58). Imagine performing multiplication or addition in Roman numerals that is not based on place value (e.g. XXXXI + XVII = LVIII). Scientific

An understanding of number is crucial for many day-to-day activities.

progress has undoubtedly benefited from cultural transmission of mathematical knowledge, such as place value, but there appears to be an aspect of numerical cognition that is independent of culture.

This chapter begins by summarizing the evidence that almost all humans and many other animals have a basic understanding of number. It then goes on to consider: how numbers are represented in the brain; where number meaning is represented in the brain; and the extent to which numerical cognition depends upon other cognitive systems (e.g. memory and language). Finally, the chapter contrasts two influential models of numerical cognition from the literature and weighs up the evidence from cognitive neuroscience that speaks to these models.

## UNIVERSAL NUMERACY?

Becoming skilled at mathematics in the modern world certainly requires learning of arbitrary notations and their meaning (e.g. +, −, >, Π, √), as well as specific procedures (e.g. for calculating the circumference of a circle). Over and above this acquired knowledge, humans and other species appear to have a more basic set of numerical abilities that enable them to estimate quantity and perform basic calculations. It is in this more fundamental sense that numeracy can be said to be universal.

### Infants

Cognition in infants has often been studied by a procedure called habituation. Infants like to look at novel things and will become disinterested if they are given the same thing to look at (i.e. they habituate). Antell and Keating (1983) found that babies just a day old can discriminate between small numbers. If the babies are shown a series of three dots, in different configurations, they soon lose interest (they **habituate**). If they are then shown configurations of two dots, then their interest increases (they dishabituate). If two dots are shown for a while, and then three dots (or one dot), then the same type of pattern is found. Is this result really to do with number or any new stimulus? Strauss and Curtis (1981) found comparable results in slightly older infants if different objects are used in each array (three keys, three combs, three oranges, etc. changing to two objects, or vice versa). This suggests that it is the number of objects that they habituate to and not the objects themselves. Simple arithmetic in infants has been studied using a paradigm called *violation of expectancy*. Infants

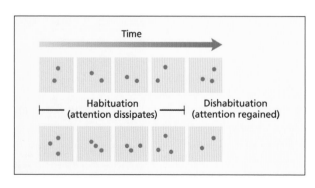
Babies lose interest when different displays are shown containing the same number (they habituate), but their interest increases when shown a display of a different number (dishabituation). This has been taken as evidence for an early appreciation of numbers.

look longer at unexpected events. Wynn (1992) devised a puppet show using this principle to demonstrate simple addition and subtraction. For example, two puppets go behind a screen, but when the screen is removed only one puppet is present (an unexpected event; $1 + 1 = 1$) or two characters go behind the screen and when the screen is removed two puppets are present (an expected event; $1 + 1 = 2$).

## The unschooled

Nunes *et al.* (1993) studied the numerical abilities of street children in Brazil, who had little or no formal training in math. For example, one boy, when asked the cost of ten coconuts priced at 35 centavos, was able to come up with the correct answer, albeit using unusual methods: "Three will be one hundred and five; with three more it will be two hundred and ten; I need four more . . . that's three hundred and fifteen. I think it is three hundred and fifty." In this instance, the boy seems to decompose the multiplier ($10 = 3 + 3 + 3 + 1$), use stored facts ("$3 \times 35 = 105$") and keep track of the sum. The idea of "adding zero" to 35 when multiplying by 10 may be meaningless in the world of coconuts (Butterworth, 1999).

## Cavemen

Archaeological evidence suggests that Cro-Magnon man, around 30,000 years ago, kept track of the phases of the moon by making collections of marks on bones (Marshack, 1991).

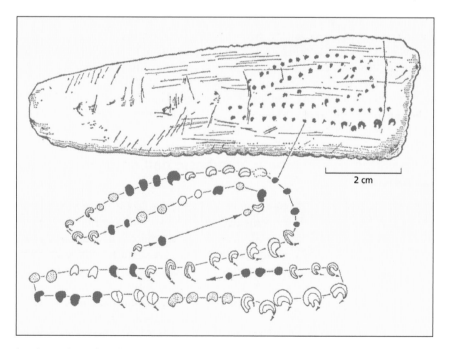

In a bone plaque from Dordogne, France, there were 24 changes in the type of pitting made in the 69 marks. According to Marshack, the changes in technique may correspond to different phases of the moon (e.g. crescent-shaped, full or dark)

Drawing after Marshack, 1970. Notation dans les gravures du paléolithique supérieur, Bordeaux: Delmas.

**KEY TERM**

**Counting**
The process of putting each item in a collection in one-to-one correspondence with a number or some other internal/external tally.

*Other species*

Monkeys in the wild are able to compute $1 + 1$ and $2 - 1$, as demonstrated by a violation of expectancy paradigm (Hauser *et al.*, 1996). After being trained to order sets of collections from 1 to 4, monkeys generalize this skill, without further training, to sets of 5 to 9 (Brannon & Terrace, 1998). Similarly, after basic training in responding to different quantities they are able to perform approximate addition (Cantlon & Brannon, 2007). For example, they can add together 3 dots and 5 dots presented consecutively by pointing to the approximately correct array size. The skill that does require extensive training, however, is learning our arbitrary language-based symbols for numbers (Washburn & Rumbaugh, 1991).

Having summarized the evidence for basic numerical abilities common to almost all humans and common to other species, the next section considers how number meaning is represented in the brain.

## THE MEANING OF NUMBERS

A telephone number is a number (or, rather, a numerical label), but it is not a quantity. The phone number 683515 is not larger than the phone number 232854. The meaning of numbers has been variously referred to as magnitude, quantity (Dehaene, 1997) or numerosity (Butterworth, 1999). Number meaning is abstract. It is "threeness" that links together three animals, three oranges, three ideas, and three events. Number meaning is also assumed to be independent of the format used to denote it (e.g. 3, III, "three," "*trois*" or three fingers). Integer numbers or whole numbers are properties of a collection. Two collections can be combined to yield a single collection denoted by a different number. Similarly, each collection (or each integer number) can be construed as being composed of smaller collections combined together. **Counting** involves putting each item in the collection in one-to-one correspondence with a number or some other internal/external tally ("one, two, three, four, five, six—there are 6 oranges!") (Gelman & Gallistel, 1978). Most fractions can be explained in terms of collections. Thus 6/7 refers to 6 parts of a collection of 7. Other types of number (e.g. zero, infinity, negative numbers) are harder to grasp and are learned later, if at all.

### Processing non-symbolic numbers: collections and quantities

Experimental studies involving judgments of the size of collections typically use arrays of dots and can be broadly divided into two domains: those that require an exact assessment of number (e.g. "there are 8") versus those that require a relative, or approximate, assessment of number (e.g. "there are about 8," "there are more blue dots than yellow dots"). These different kinds of task may recruit different kinds of cognitive processes and different brain mechanisms.

Considering relative assessments of number, a standard paradigm is to present two arrays of dots and instruct/train participants to respond to either the larger or smaller set. Typically the size of the dots is varied so that the two arrays are equated for factors such as overall surface area (i.e. so the judgment is based on discrete quantities rather than a continuous quantity). The advantage of this paradigm is that it can be adapted for use in a wide variety of animals from fish (Agrillo *et al.*, 2012) to primates (Washburn & Rumbaugh, 1991), and also humans at all stages of development (Xu & Spelke, 2000). One common finding is that the ability to perform the task decreases with increasing set sizes, even when the ratio is constant. Thus, it is harder to discriminate sets of 20:30 dots than sets of 10:15 even though the ratio is 2:3 in both cases. The standard explanation is that the system for processing numbers is less precise (or less efficient) the larger the set size that is considered. In addition, larger ratios are also easier to discriminate (e.g. 2:5 relative to 2:3). Individual differences in performance on this task (in ninth grade children) are correlated with math achievement in school, and extends back to Kindergarten (Halberda *et al.*, 2008). Moreover, the ability to discriminate which of two sets is larger is worse in children with developmental dyscalculia (Piazza *et al.*, 2010). As such, this basic numerical system may act as a start-up kit for culturally embedded mathematics. Whether the start-up system is specific to countable, discrete quantities or also extends to uncountable, continuous quantities such as size remains to be determined (Henik *et al.*, 2012).

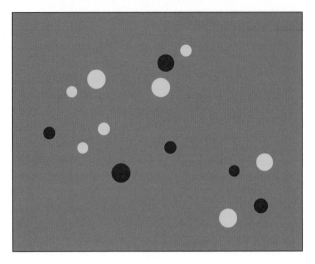

Which set is larger: blues or yellows? When presented too briefly to count (200 ms), then school children differ in their ability to perform the task and this correlates with SATs (Standard Assessment Tests) scores in mathematics.

Adapted from Halberda *et al.*, 2008.

The alternative approach is to require participants to determine exact quantities: for instance to state how many dots are present, or to respond when exactly N dots are present (the latter being more appropriate for other species).

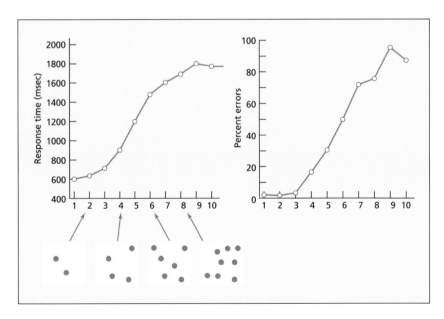

The ability to state how many objects are in an array may occur automatically for small arrays (< 4; called subitizing) but occurs serially for larger arrays (> 4; called counting). In this version of the experiment the arrays were presented briefly (200 ms).

**KEY TERMS**

**Subitizing**
The capacity to enumerate an exact quantity of objects without counting them.

**Distance effect**
It is harder to decide which of two numbers is larger when the distance between them is small (e.g. 8–9 relative to 2–9).

**Size effect**
It is easier to state which number is larger when the numbers are small (e.g. 2 and 4) relative to large (e.g. 7 and 9) even when the distance between them is the same.

These tasks require matching of a stimulus to some internal standard of number (linguistic or nonlinguistic). In humans, when participants are asked to state (verbally) the size of a collection, then there appears to be a difference between small numbers (up to 3 or 4) and larger numbers (beyond 4). Specifically, people are just as fast when there are 1, 2, 3 or 4 items in an array (i.e. no decrease in efficiency with increasing size of number), but above that they slow down proportionally to the number of items in the collection (Mandler & Shebo, 1982). This has typically been explained in terms of two separate mechanisms: (1) a rapid ability to enumerate, in parallel, a small collection of objects that is independent of language (termed **subitizing**) and (2) a slower, serial, mechanism that is dependent on language (counting) or resorting to approximation. The claim is not that collections above 4 cannot be processed without language, but, rather, that numbers above 4 can only be processed approximately rather than exactly in the absence of language (Dehaene, 1997) (for a different view see Gelman & Butterworth, 2005). Subitizing reflects a separate mechanism that doesn't simply reflect the general advantage for small numbers (Revkin *et al.*, 2008) and has been linked to different neural substrates, namely within the visual ventral stream rather than parietal cortices (Vuokko *et al.*, 2013).

## Processing number symbols: digits and words

Symbolic, or linguistic, representations of number consist of words and digits (e.g. 7 or "seven"). Although these are superficially very different to collections of dots, there is evidence that similar kinds of cognitive processes are used for symbols as for dots. Moyer and Landauer (1967) conducted a seminal study investigating how symbolic number magnitude is represented. Participants had

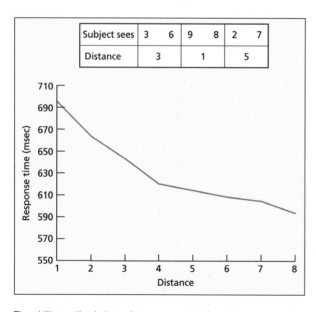

| Subject sees | 3 | 6 | 9 | 8 | 2 | 7 |
|---|---|---|---|---|---|---|
| Distance | | 3 | | 1 | | 5 |

to judge which of two numbers was the larger (e.g. 5 compared with 7). They noted two important effects on the pattern of response times. The **distance effect** refers to the fact that it is much easier (i.e. faster reaction time) to decide which number is larger when the distance between two numbers is large (e.g. 2 or 9) relative to small (e.g. 8 or 9). This suggests that number magnitude is retrieved, rather than, say, the relative order of numbers (since 2 and 8 both come before 9). The **size effect** refers to the observation that it is easier to judge which of two numbers is larger when the numbers are small (e.g. 3 or 5) compared with when they are large (e.g. 7 or 9), even when the distance between them is equal. This, of course, resembles the findings with dot arrays described earlier. The result implies that the mental representations of larger numbers are less robust (or "fuzzier") even in the symbolic domain.

The ability to discriminate between two numbers increases as the numerical distance between them increases—the so-called distance effect.

From Butterworth, 1999. © Palgrave-Macmillan. Reproduced with permission of the author.

Other studies suggest that symbolic and non-symbolic representations of number converge on to a single (abstract) number meaning system. Koechlin *et al.* (1999b) asked participants to decide whether a stimulus was greater than or less than 5. The stimulus consisted of Arabic numerals (e.g. 7), number words (e.g. SEVEN) or dot patterns (which participants were asked to estimate, not count). Crucially, before each trial a very brief (66 ms) additional stimulus was presented that the participants could not consciously report seeing—a prime. The prime was either greater or less than 5. If the prime and stimulus were on the same side of 5, then performance was enhanced. The fact that this occurs rapidly across different codes suggests that these codes access a single system for number meaning.

Finally, some cultures do not have a large range of number words. In certain Amazonian and Australian Aboriginal societies, there are no number names beyond around 3 (e.g. "1,2, many"). To what extent can they process larger numbers for which there is no symbolic representation? The Munduruku, in Amazonia, are able to divide a large collection into half by placing items into two piles one-at-a-time (McCrink *et al.*, 2013). They can also compare approximate sizes of collections as well as a Western control group (e.g., 20 compared with 15), and perform exact arithmetic on small numbers (e.g. 3 stones minus 1 stone = 2 stones) but *not* exact arithmetic on larger numbers, for which they lack a number name (Pica *et al.*, 2004). Thus, when adding 5 stones and 7 stones they might choose an answer that is approximately 12 (e.g. 11, 12 or 13) but not a distant number (e.g. 8 or 20). Thus, although symbolic and nonsymbolic representations of number are normally closely tied they are not equivalent and can serve different functions in numerical cognition. Symbolic representations permit exact and approximate quantification, whereas nonsymbolic representations permit approximate quantification (except for small numbers).

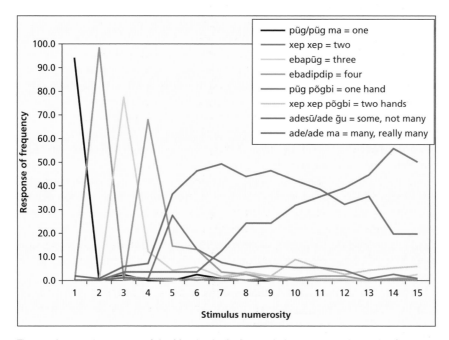

The number naming system of the Munduruku in Amazonia becomes very imprecise for numbers larger than 4. How does this affect their ability to understand numbers?

From Pica *et al.*, 2004.

# Neural substrates of number meaning

Evidence from electrophysiological single-cell recordings in nonhuman primates has revealed the existence of neurons that are tuned to the number of objects. These neural representations may enable core numerical abilities in many species and, in humans, may become linked to (and modified by) symbolic representations of number (Nieder & Dehaene, 2009). One type of neuron responds more strongly the more objects that there are (Roitman et al., 2007). Another type, so-called **number neurons**, appear to be selectively tuned to particular numbers; for instance responding to 4 objects more than to 3 or 5 (for a review see Nieder, 2013).

The standard procedure used in these studies involves recording from neurons while the monkey performs a number discrimination task of deciding whether two consecutively presented arrays contain the same number of dots. One important finding is that the degree of response selectivity of the neuron is related to numerical size, and this may be the neural basis of the size effect in reaction time studies that has already been discussed (Nieder & Miller, 2004). For example, a neuron that responds maximally to four dots will respond very little to three or five dots, but a neuron tuned to detect ten dots will respond quite strongly to nine or eleven dots. The number neurons tended to be found in both regions of the parietal lobes (notably the intraparietal sulcus, IPS) and the prefrontal cortex in the macaque. Some number neurons maintain the same tuning preference irrespective of whether dots were presented simultaneously, as an array, or after sequential presentation, one-by-one (Nieder et al., 2006). Certain number neurons may also respond to a particular number of sounds as well as visual stimuli (Nieder, 2012). Diester and Nieder (2007) trained monkeys to associate dot arrays with written digits, and found number neurons that responded both to a particular set size and its corresponding symbol. Interestingly, these neurons tended to be in the prefrontal cortex rather than intraparietal sulcus. In human fMRI, a frontal-to-parietal shift in BOLD activity is found contrasting children and adults when performing magnitude comparisons on pairs of digits (Ansari et al., 2005). That is, children tend to activate the prefrontal cortex more in this task, whereas adults tend to activate the intraparietal sulcus more. One possibility is that the intraparietal sulcus contains the core number meaning system (present from an early age and in other species) that, in humans, becomes progressively tuned to symbolic representations of numbers via education and/or language.

Evidence from adult human functional imaging also points to the particular importance of the intraparietal sulcus. This region is more active when people perform calculations relative to reading numerical symbols (Burbaud et al., 1999), and in number comparison relative to number reading (Cochon et al., 1999). The degree of activation of the region shows a distance effect for both digits and number words (Pinel et al., 2001), and is sensitive to subliminal priming when the "unseen" prime and seen stimulus differ in quantity (Dehaene et al., 1998b). This suggests that the region is the anatomical locus for many of the cognitive effects already discussed. Most of the studies cited above used Arabic numbers or number names. Another study with dot patterns showed habituation of the neural response to the number of items in an array, analogous to behavioral studies of human infants (Piazza et al., 2004). The same region of the brain is activated by numbers across different cultures and writing systems (Tang et al., 2006). Both the intraparietal sulcus and frontal regions show fMRI adaptation

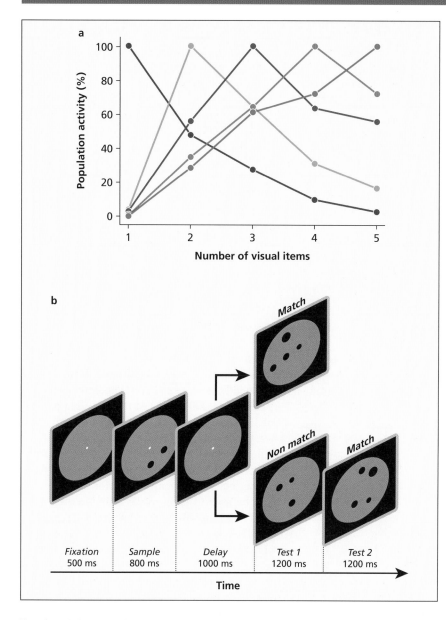

Top: the relative level of activity of number neurons that are selectively tuned to respond to between 1 and 5 items. Notice how the tuning to smaller numbers is more precise (narrower curves). Bottom: A typical experiment in which a monkey must decide whether two sets of dots are matched in quantity or not. The activity of individual neurons is recorded during the task.

From Nieder, 2013.

effects when the same number is repeated and irrespective of notation (Piazza *et al.*, 2007).

Dyscalculia also tends to be linked to dysfunction of the parietal lobes. Acquired dyscalculia has, for a century, been linked to left hemispheric lesions (Gertsmann, 1940; Grafman *et al.*, 1982) which more recent studies have localized to the left intraparietal region (Dehaene *et al.*, 1998a). However, studies of

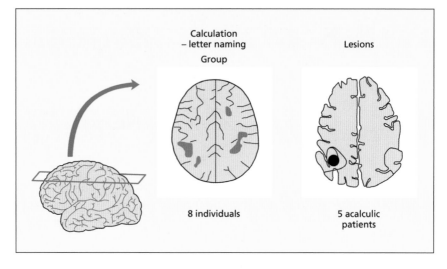

There is converging evidence from neuropsychology and functional imaging for the role of the parietal lobes in number meaning (particularly the left parietal lobe).

Left figure from Cochon et al., 1999. © 1999 MIT Press. Reproduced with permission. Right figure reprinted from Dehaene et al., 1998a. © 1998, with permission from Elsevier.

structural differences in developmental dyscalculia point to differences in the left and/or right intraparietal sulcus (Isaacs et al., 2001; Rotzer et al., 2008). Moreover, evidence from TMS (Cohen Kadosh et al., 2007) and brain imaging (Pinel et al., 2001) suggest that the right parietal lobe also plays an important role in normal number processing. Acquired dyscalculic patients with left hemispheric lesions may still have some numerical abilities that are presumably supported by the intact right hemisphere: for instance they may be able to give approximate answers (e.g. 5 + 7 = "13 roughly"; Warrington, 1982) or detect the falsehood of 2 + 2 = 9, but not 2 + 2 = 5 (and with the precision decreasing with increasing number size; Dehaene & Cohen, 1991). In a patient with a "split brain" (by severing the fibers of the corpus callosum), Cohen and Dehaene (1996) were able to present numbers to each hemisphere in isolation. When digits were presented to the right hemisphere the patient tended to give answers that were approximately correct (e.g. 5 read as "six"), but the left hemisphere could read them accurately. This patient wasn't dyscalculic under normal viewing conditions, but the hemispheric disconnection enables the two hemispheres to be studied in relative isolation. Thus although both hemispheres appear to be important for number it may be the case that the number representations in the left hemisphere are more exact, and this is assumed to reflect interactions

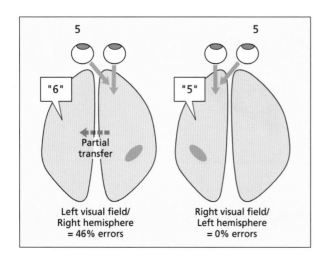

Severing of the fibers of the corpus callosum results in a lack of cortical transfer between the left and right hemispheres (but subcortical routes enable some transfer of information between hemispheres). By presenting stimuli briefly to the left or right of a centrally fixated point, it is possible to study the operation of each hemisphere in isolation. Cohen and Dehaene (1996) reported a split-brain patient who could accurately read digits presented briefly to the left hemisphere, but produced errors when they were presented to the right hemisphere. However, the errors were not random. They consisted of numerical approximations.

with the language system (Nieder & Dehaene, 2009). There is a strong correlation between the lateralization of the left superior temporal sulcus response to language and the left intraparietal sulcus response to arithmetic (Pinel & Dehaene, 2010). However, this study was in right-handers and it would be important to extend the research to left-handers for whom language lateralization is more variable.

That language is important for the development of skilled numeracy is not doubted, but this does not mean that skilled numeracy in adults is dependent on the integrity of language. This is again revealed through patients with acquired brain lesions. Rosser *et al.* (1995) documented a severely aphasic patient, HAB, who was only able to utter a few phrases such as "I do not know" and was unable to comprehend most spoken and written words. By contrast, he could accurately add, subtract and select the larger of two three-digit numbers. Similarly, patients with semantic dementia who lose the meaning of many words retain good numerical cognition (Cappelletti *et al.*, 2002). This disorder is linked to atrophy of the temporal lobes, whereas number meaning is linked to parietal function which tends to be spared by this disorder. Finally, there is undoubtedly a large working memory component involved in calculation that may depend on the complexity of the task (the number of stages) and the need to hold things "in mind" (e.g. when carrying over) (Furst & Hitch, 2000; Logie *et al.*, 1994). However, it seems unlikely that working memory deficits alone can account for acquired dyscalculia. Butterworth *et al.* (1996) report a brain-damaged patient with a digit span of 2. That is, the patient can repeat back single digits, pairs of digits, but not triplets of digits (most people have a digit span of 7). However, he was in the top 37 percent of the population for mental arithmetic. These included questions such as adding together two three-digit numbers ("one hundred and twenty-eight plus one hundred and forty-nine"). This suggests that mental arithmetic is not critically dependent on the articulatory loop component of working memory.

The fact that the intraparietal sulcus appears to play a particularly important role in numerical cognition does not mean that this is the only function supported by this region or, for that matter, that other regions of the brain are not involved in understanding number. Shuman and Kanwisher (2004) compared discrimination of dot patterns with tasks such as color discrimination and found that the region was sensitive to both. They concluded that the intraparietal sulcus is not domain-specific for numbers. This does not necessarily mean that numbers do not have a specialized neural substrate, but rather that the region also contains neurons engaged in other types of activities. Indeed in the macaque data, as few as 20 percent of the neurons in the region were tuned to particular set sizes (Nieder & Miller, 2004).

## Is number meaning discrete or continuous?

Most of the evidence cited above concerns discrete, countable quantities. But what about continuous, uncountable quantities such as length, area, and weight or other ordered dimensions such as brightness and loudness? There is now convincing evidence that the number system is involved in processing this kind of information (at least, when judgments of magnitude are required). What is less clear is the nature of that relationship: for instance, whether continuous or discrete quantity processing is evolutionarily older, or whether one type of information is mapped

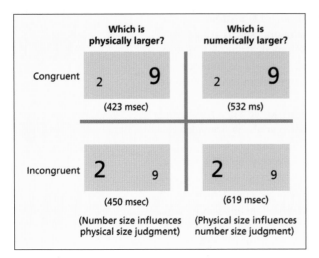

If physical size and numerical size are incongruent, then participants are slower at judging which number is physically or numerically larger. This is evidence that the meaning of a number is accessed automatically.

Adapted from Girelli et al., 2000.

to the other (e.g. discrete quantity transformed to a continuous scale), or which is more relevant to everyday (culture-bound) mathematics.

Evidence from cognitive psychology shows that processing single digits (discrete quantities) and processing continuous dimensions such as physical size (Henik & Tzelgov, 1982) interact with each other. For instance, interference (in terms of slower response times) is found if the numerical size of digits conflicts with the physical font size (Henik & Tzelgov, 1982); e.g. 5 versus 7. This is found both when participants must judge which is numerically larger and which is physically larger. Comparable interference effects are found for number and lightness (Cohen Kadosh & Henik, 2006) and many other dimensions (Bueti & Walsh, 2009). There is evidence from fMRI and TMS that these kinds of interaction between number and physical magnitude processing involve the intraparietal sulcus (Cohen Kadosh et al., 2012; Cohen Kadosh et al., 2008). Other studies have found that the intraparietal sulcus responds to comparisons of angles and line lengths as well as numbers (Fias et al., 2003). A more recent fMRI study reported that the right intraparietal sulcus and prefrontal cortex were activated both when processing discrete quantity (number of dots) and a continuous variable, the duration of time (Dormal et al., 2012). Connectivity analyses revealed that the right intraparietal sulcus was functionally coupled to the left intraparietal sulcus only in the discrete quantity task suggesting some possible differences at the network level between discrete and continuous.

The fMRI data, due to their limited spatial resolution, could potentially be explained by two different populations of neurons within the same region: one coding discrete quantity and one coding continuous quantity. However, evidence from single-cell recordings in the macaque speaks against that view. Tudusciuc and Nieder (2007) showed monkeys either four lines of different length or arrays of 1 to 4 dots. They found that neurons in the intraparietal sulcus that discriminate between length (continuous quantity) also discriminate between the number of dots (as discrete quantities). Vallentin and Nieder (2010) recorded neurons in the prefrontal cortex that were tuned to the ratio of pairs of lengths rather than absolute lengths. For instance, some neurons would respond when the line lengths were in a 1:4 ratio and others were tuned to a 1:2 or 3:4 ratio.

There are several theoretical positions that account for the link between discrete and continuous quantity processing. Walsh (e.g., Bueti & Walsh, 2009; Walsh, 2003) has put forward the ATOM model ("A Theory of Magnitude"). He argues that number processing has piggy-backed on to earlier brain adaptations involved in the processing of time, space and other forms of magnitude such as speed. These are functionally related to the dorsal (or "how") visual stream. In a similar vein, Dehaene (1997) has referred to the number meaning system in terms of a **mental number line** (following Moyer & Landauer, 1967). The mental number line consists of a single logarithmically compressed analogue scale (where

## KEY TERM

**Mental number line**
An internal analogue/continuous scale (like a line) used for comparing both discrete and continuous quantities.

the term "analogue" denotes a continuous scale) which is used for comparing both discrete and continuous quantities. Logarithmic compression implies that larger numbers are more similar (i.e. "closer together" on the line). One motivation for proposing this is the size effect which is found for both symbolic and nonsymbolic numbers and whether continuous or discrete. The analogy to a spatial line is deliberate and, in the next section, evidence will be considered of a close link between numbers and space.

It is important to note that there is not a universal consensus that there is a necessary relationship between the processing of discrete number and other quantities. It has been found that the bilateral intraparietal sulcus responds more strongly to the processing of discrete rather than continuous quantities when the two are directly compared (Castelli *et al.*, 2006), but this, in itself, does not mean that it has no role in processing continuous quantity. There are also some apparent dissociations between these domains in acquired dyscalculic patients. For instance, patient CG had effectively lost all number meaning beyond 4, but she could make size judgments (which object is bigger?), measure judgments (is a kilometer longer than a mile?) and judgments of more (e.g. could you get more coffee beans or salt grains into a cup?) (Cipolotti *et al.*, 1991). However, these kinds of tasks may relate more to semantic memory (i.e. long-term stored knowledge of objects) rather than online magnitude processing that is arguably computed in the intraparietal sulcus. It would be important for future research to document whether the deficit in (acquired and developmental) dyscalculia extends to the processing of continuous quantity.

**Easy discriminations**

Length:  ———  v  ———

Number:  3  v  5

**Hard discriminations**

Length:  ———————  v  ———————

Number:  7  v  9

Is deciding which number is bigger equivalent to deciding which line is longer? A size effect is found for both, i.e. it is harder to decide which line/number is longer/larger as the line/number increases in size (even if the difference between lines/numbers is the same).

## What is the relationship between numbers and space?

As noted before, numbers and spatial processes appear to be located in adjacent if not over-lapping regions of the parietal cortex (Hubbard *et al.*, 2005). One strong theoretical position is that number meaning is itself represented using some sort of spatial code, and the original mental number line proposal can be considered to be one instantiation of this (Dehaene, 1997; Moyer & Landauer, 1967). A weaker proposal is that number and space are distinct entities that, nonetheless, tend to interact with one another. The ATOM model can be considered an example of such a claim (Walsh, 2003). Before returning to these models it is important to summarize the key lines of evidence for number-space associations:

- When people are asked to make judgments about numbers (e.g. odd/even judgments), they are faster with their left hand for small numbers, but faster with their right hand for larger numbers—the **SNARC effect** (Spatial Numerical Association of Response Codes; Dehaene *et al.*, 1993). The direction of the number-space association may be influenced by reading direction and counting habits (Shaki *et al.*, 2012). Bilateral TMS over the posterior parietal lobe reduces the SNARC effect (Rusconi *et al.*, 2007).

**KEY TERM**

**SNARC effect (Spatial-numerical association of response codes)**
If people are asked to make judgments about numbers (e.g. odd/even judgments), they are faster with their left hand for small numbers but faster with their right hand for large numbers.

- Small numbers presented in the center of the screen (e.g. 1 and 2) orient attention to the left, but larger numbers (e.g. 8 and 9) orient attention to the right (Fischer *et al.*, 2003).

- Generating "random" numbers while turning the head from side to side is associated with smaller numbers, on average, generated from left turns (Loetscher *et al.*, 2008).

- An Amazonian tribe (the Munduruku) with very limited number vocabulary and no formal mathematical education understand number–space mappings (Dehaene *et al.*, 2008). When given a line (with end points marked as array sizes of 1 or 10 dots), they map the position of intermediate numbers (e.g. 6 dots) using a logarithmic scale. In a Western sample, education leads to linearization of number-space associations for small numbers (1–10), but not larger numbers (1–100).

- Patients with visuospatial neglect (but who are not dyscalculic) show spatial biases in number bisection (e.g. "what number is midway between 11 and 19? . . . 17") as if they are ignoring the left side of number space (Zorzi *et al.*, 2002).

- Some people report habitually visualizing numbers in particular visuospatial configurations, normally oriented from left to right. These are called **number forms** or number–space synaesthesia, and their functioning is linked with activity in the intraparietal sulcus and prefrontal cortex assessed with fMRI (Tang *et al.*, 2008).

In almost all of the examples above, there is evidence that the number-space associations are quite flexible and, in some cases, can even be reversed. This suggests that the number-space associations are generated on-the-fly according to current task demands (albeit influenced by prior habits, such as reading direction) rather than reflecting a fixed spatial coding of number magnitude. For instance, the association between left-right space and small-large magnitude can be reversed if participants are primed to think of a clock face (for which numbers 1–5 are on the right; Bachtold *et al.*, 1998) or if a response label for LEFT is placed on the right side of space and the label RIGHT is placed on the left side of space (Gevers *et al.*, 2010). Neglect during number bisection is related to spatial working memory deficits and is linked to right frontal lesions (Doricchi *et al.*, 2005). This again suggests that number-space associations are constructed via attention and working memory rather than stored in a spatial code. TMS over this region, in healthy participants, disrupts number-space correspondences when making a left/right response to categorize a number as lesser/greater than 5 (Rusconi *et al.*, 2011).

Another line of evidence that suggests that number-space associations are not tied specifically to quantity processing, is that similar affects are found for other sequences that do not represent quantities such as the alphabet or the months of the year. For instance, in certain tasks "January"

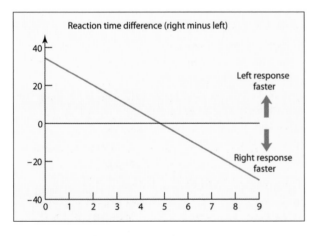

People are faster at making judgments about small numbers with their left hand and faster at making judgments about large numbers with their right hand.

Adapted from Dehaene et al., 1993.

## COUNTING WITH FINGERS, BODIES, AND BASES

To count beyond a small number of items, one may need a method to keep track of how many items have been counted so far. These may consist of external aids such as systems of tallying (e.g. the marks found on ancient bones) or internal aids such as linguistic symbols (written numerals and number names).

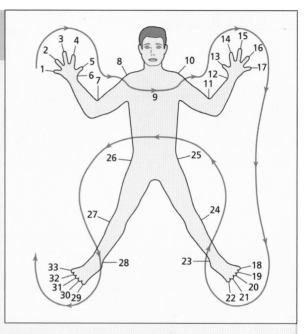

The number system of the Torres Strait islanders is based on body parts.

Adapted from Ifrah, 1985.

Given a large cultural diversity, humans appear to have developed a restricted number of ways of counting, in part, independently from each other. Two of the most common themes are (1) use of body parts and (2) use of base systems. Many cultures use fingers and other body parts to keep track of how many items have been counted. It is probably no coincidence that the word "digit" can refer both to numbers and to fingers and toes. In other cultures, such as those found in Papua New Guinea, the relationship is more explicit (Lancy, 1983). The Yupno have no specialized number names, but use the names of body parts to count and represent numbers. Thus, "one" is the left little finger and "thirty-three" is the penis. In Kilenge, body parts can be combined and also act as bases. Thus 5 is "hand," 10 is "two hands," and 20 is "man." These terms can be combined such that 30 is "a man and two hands."

Many non-trading cultures have little practical need to represent large numbers. But the question of how large numbers are to be represented when, say, body parts are exhausted seems to have been solved using bases. Bases are derived from a core property of numbers that is culturally independent—namely, that any given number (except 1 and 0) can be decomposed into a collection of collections. In our base-10 system, the number "35" refers to 3 collections of 10 and 5 collections of 1. Cultures such as the ancient Maya and the modern Basque language use base-20, with subunits of 5. Vestiges of a base-20 system can be heard in some European languages (77 in French is "soixante-dix-sept," literally "sixty and seventeen"). Base-60, with subdivisions of 10 units, was used by Babylonians and is retained in our measurement of angles and time.

Does a tendency to use body parts for counting have any brain-based explanation? Gerstmann (1940) observed that damage to the left parietal lobe can produce not just acalculia, but also finger agnosia—an inability to identify individual fingers by touch (Kinsbourne & Warrington, 1962b). Together with agraphia and left–right disorientation, these were collectively called **Gerstmann's syndrome**. The different symptoms of this syndrome have now been shown to dissociate from each other (Benton, 1977). Nevertheless, the fact that evolution may have placed the representation of the body and fingers and number meaning close by may be evidence for a close evolutionary relationship (Rusconi et al., 2005).

is responded to faster by a left-sided response and "December" is responded to faster by a right-sided response (Gevers *et al.*, 2003). Patients with neglect tend to show spatial biases for these sequences too (Zorzi *et al.*, 2006). In general, spatial associations to months or the alphabet tend to be found when the task requires thinking about the order rather than non-order-based judgments (Dodd *et al.*, 2008). This again suggests that the associations are created by the task itself (via spatial working memory and attention) rather than storing these sequences in a fixed spatial code.

## Evaluation

Different kinds of number tend to be processed in similar ways. Non-symbolic processing of numbers (e.g. dot arrays) show striking similarities across species (distance and size effects) and, in humans, processing of number symbols (e.g. digits) show comparable effects. Single-cell recordings from the parietal and frontal lobes of macaques suggest a likely neural substrate for this effect: namely, neurons that respond to some numbers more than others, but with a general tendency for larger numbers to be linked to less specificity in terms of the neural response. There is evidence that continuous quantities and discrete quantities are processed similarly, although not necessarily identically. Similarly, it is clear that both the left and the right hemispheres of humans (notably the left and right intraparietal sulcus) are involved in numerical cognition, but with some differences between them (e.g. greater left hemispheric specialization for exact number). There are close links between the processing of space and the processing of number, but the evidence falls short of the stronger claim that numbers are represented in a spatial code.

## MODELS OF NUMBER PROCESSING

A number of detailed models have been proposed that aim to capture much of the empirical data gathered on numerical cognition. In this section, two models will be considered in detail, although references to other models will be made when appropriate.

The first model is that proposed by McCloskey and colleagues (McCloskey, 1992; McCloskey *et al.*, 1985). This is the earlier of the two models and it offers a purely cognitive account of number processing without making specific claims about the neural architecture. A number of key features are worth noting. First, a distinction is made between specific number formats (both in input and output) and an abstract, internal, semantic representation. The format-specific codes are used for recognizing and producing numerical symbols. The semantic representation codes magnitude information. It also plays a critical role in transcoding and all forms of calculation. Calculation itself could be decomposed into different types of facts and procedures (e.g. separate stores and procedures for addition, subtraction, multiplication and division). **Transcoding** is the means by which one symbol is translated into another of a different type. It encompasses processes such as reading (written symbols to verbal ones), writing (verbal labels to written symbols) and others (e.g. from a written label to a hand gesture).

The second model to be considered is the Triple-Code Model proposed by Dehaene and colleagues (Dehaene, 1997; Dehaene & Cohen, 1995; Dehaene *et al.*, 1998a). The triple codes refer to: (1) a semantic magnitude representation;

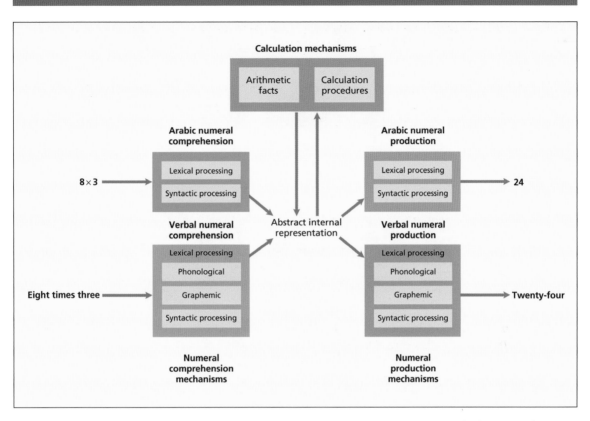

McCloskey's Model (1992) contains separate stores for calculation procedures, and separate stores for format-specific codes (e.g. Arabic numbers, number names). These are linked together via an amodal semantic representation of number.

Reprinted from McCloskey, 1992. © 1992 with permission from Elsevier.

(2) a verbal store of arithmetical facts; and (3) a visual representation for recognizing numerals and that acts as a "workbench" for performing certain calculations. Predictions are made at both a cognitive and neuroanatomical level. Considering each component in turn: the semantic magnitude representation is assumed to lie (bilaterally) in the intraparietal sulcus. The verbal store is used to comprehend and produce spoken number names and is also a repository for learned arithmetical facts and tables (e.g. "two and two is four"). This is assumed to be based in the left angular gyrus (Dehaene *et al.*, 2003), which is in a separate region of the parietal lobe to number meaning. The visual code is used for recognizing and producing Arabic numerals, and may lie bilaterally in the fusiform gyrus (Dehaene, 1997). It also consists of a visuospatial workspace for conducting multi-digit operations (e.g. 256 + 142). Unlike the McCloskey Model, it is possible to produce verbal numbers from visual numbers (3 → "three"), and vice versa ("three" → 3), without going through a central semantic bottle-neck. Dehaene's triple-code model also suggests that not all calculations are carried out semantically. In particular, he argues that simple multiplications and additions may be retrieved as "facts" from the verbal code. More complicated sums (e.g. multi-digit addition) may be accomplished visually or using visual images. Both of these are residues of how the material was initially acquired; for example, the rote repetition of multiplication tables (for a more extreme variant of this proposal, see Campbell, 1994).

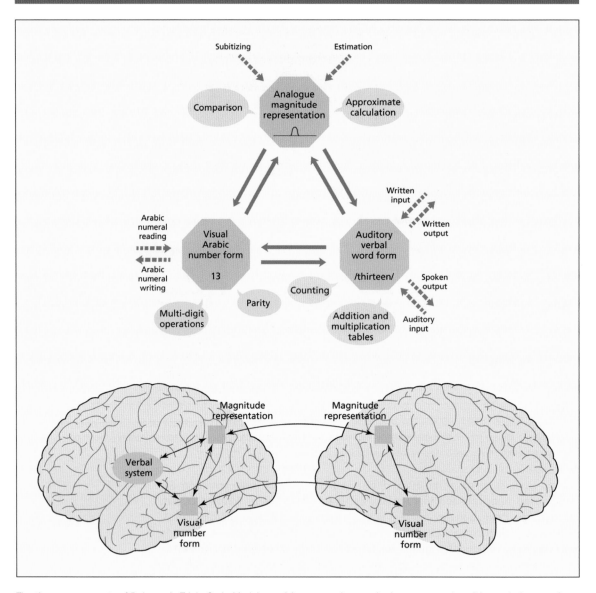

The three components of Dehaene's Triple-Code Model are: (a) a semantic magnitude representation; (b) a verbal store of arithmetical facts; and (c) a visual representation for recognizing numerals and a "workbench" for performing certain calculations. Top: functional components; and bottom: their approximate anatomical locations.

From: top, Dehaene, 1992; bottom, Dehaene & Cohen, 1995.

To contrast these two models, evidence will be drawn from three aspects of numerical cognition: the representation of number meaning (again), the nature of the processes that underpin different aspects of calculation (addition, subtraction, etc.) and mechanisms of transcoding between different numerical formats.

## Base-10 units or mental number line

Both models assume that there is a central semantic store of number magnitudes that is independent of specific number formats (e.g. numeral, number name, dots).

| The McCloskey Model | Dehaene's Triple-Code Model |
|---|---|
| • Cognitive model | • Cognitive and neuroanatomical model |
| • Number size is represented as base-10 units (divisible into 10s, 100s, 1,000s, etc.) | • Number size is represented in a logarithmically compressed form (larger numbers harder to discriminate) |
| • Separate routines or stores for arithmetical operations $(+, -, /, \times)$ | • No separate routines or stores for arithmetical operations $(+, -, /, \times)$ |
| • Abstract (semantic) representations used for all calculations | • Some calculations are independent of number semantics (e.g. multiplication is verbal fact retrieval) |
| • Transcoding performed semantically | • Transcoding may be performed without semantics |

However, the internal structure of this magnitude representation differs between the two models. The McCloskey Model assumes that the semantic number representation consists of separate representations for units (0–9), tens, hundreds, thousands, and so on. Thus, the semantic representation mirrors the way that numbers are denoted in the place-value system. In the Dehaene Triple-Code Model, the semantic number representation consists of the logarithmically compressed mental number line (mentioned previously). There is no division into hundreds, tens, and so on. Some evidence for this came from a study by Dehaene *et al.* (1990). They asked participants to decide whether a two-digit number was smaller or larger than a reference number (e.g. 65). Participants were faster at rejecting 51 than 59, and the difference in reaction time was logarithmically determined. If the judgment had been made purely on comparing tens (i.e. fifty-something with sixty-something), then no difference would have been predicted. More recent studies using this paradigm have questioned these results. Nuerk *et al.* (2001) note that, in the 51 versus 65 comparison, both the digits representing tens and units lead to the same answer (5 < 6 and 1 < 5), whereas there is incompatibility in the case of 59 versus 65 (5 < 6 but 9 > 5). In a series of experiments, they propose that information about tens and units is independently available, in support of the McCloskey Model. They propose a hybrid model containing both logarithmic compression and separate tens and unit representations.

## Calculation: multiplication, addition, subtraction, and division

According to Dehaene's Triple-Code Model, simple multiplication relies on retrieving facts from the verbal store just like any other word or phrase. Subtraction tends not to be learned in this rote fashion, and may make more demands on the number semantic representation. Addition can be performed in both ways— simple additions are likely to have been verbally learned by rote but can also be easily computed using the number semantic representation. In support of this, Delazer and Benke (1997) report a patient with a left parietal tumor who could recite and produce multiplication facts, but had severely impaired knowledge of numbers (e.g. unable to add 13 + 9; unable to get 103 using poker chips with values of 100, 50, 10, 5, 1). By contrast, the severely aphasic patient, HAB, could still perform many calculations, but his multiplication (part of the verbal store in the Triple-Code Model) was performed atypically (Rosser *et al.*, 1995). For example, 9 × 5 was done by converting it into an addition problem 18 + 18 + 9 = 45 [i.e. 9 × (2 + 2 + 1)]. These studies support the conclusion that multiplication facts are stored in verbal form.

Other evidence has been brought to bear on this. First, difficulties in multiplication and subtraction form a double dissociation. Patients have been reported with greater difficulties in multiplication relative to subtraction (Cohen & Dehaene, 2000; Dehaene & Cohen, 1997; Van Harskamp & Cipolotti, 2001). The reverse dissociation has also been reported (Delazer & Benke, 1997; Van Harskamp & Cipolotti, 2001; Van Harskamp *et al.*, 2002). In healthy participants, Lee and Kang (2002) found that simultaneous phonological rehearsal delayed multiplication more than subtraction, and that holding a visuospatial image in mind delayed subtraction, but not multiplication. In functional imaging experiments, the left angular gyrus (the putative "verbal code") shows more activity in multiplication than subtraction (Cochon *et al.*, 1999), and is more involved in simple addition (below 10) than complex addition (above 10) (Stanescu-Cosson *et al.*, 2000). Whereas *learning* a new multiplication fact activates the inferior prefrontal cortex and bilateral intraparietal sulcus, *retrieving* that fact involves the left angular gyrus in the parietal lobes (Ischebeck *et al.*, 2006). Subtraction, on the other hand, did not show the shift to the angular gyrus.

It is also important to stress that the McCloskey Model predicts dissociations between different aspects of calculation, but it does so in a different way. Calculation facts may be stored separately from procedural knowledge and number meaning, but no claims are made about whether some types of arithmetical operation are more "verbal" or "semantic" than others. Under the McCloskey Model, double dissociations between multiplication and subtraction merely reflect damage to distinct stores of knowledge (Dagenbach & McCloskey, 1992). There should be as many patterns of selective disruption as there are facts and operations.

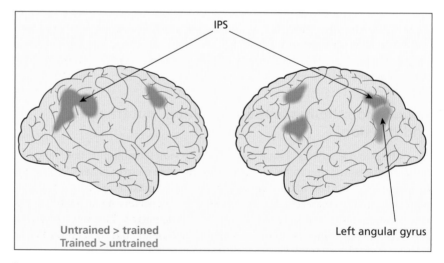

Learning new multiplication problems (red) versus retrieving previously learned problems (green) involves different brain regions.

Adapted from Ischebeck *et al.*, 2006.

# Transcoding: reading, writing, and saying numbers

Both the McCloskey and Dehaene models assume the existence of format-specific (and culturally dependent) codes for representing numbers, including Arabic numerals and written and spoken number names (8, "eight," EIGHT). These input and output codes may be selectively impaired. Anderson *et al.* (1990) report a patient who could still read and write numbers, but not letters or words, and Cipolotti (1995) reports the opposite dissociation. Ferro and Botelho (1980) report a patient who was unable to read (or use) mathematical operators (e.g. +) except when presented verbally (e.g. "plus"). On the spoken output side, McCloskey *et al.* (1986) argue for a distinction between lexical and syntactic processes in number production. Patient HY's reading errors preserved the syntactic class (i.e. units, tens, hundreds . . .), but not the position within the class (e.g. 5 becomes "seven," but not "fifteen"), whereas patient JG's errors preserved the position in the class, but not the syntactic class itself (e.g. 5 becomes "fifteen," but not "seven"). The production rules for writing Arabic numbers are somewhat different. Cipolotti *et al.* (1994) report a written "syntactic" deficit in which the patient failed to apply an overwriting-from-the-right rule. Thus, "one thousand nine hundred and forty-five" was written as 1000,945. While these studies illuminate the workings of the number input and output processes, the key distinction between the models under consideration is whether these processes are directly connected (e.g. Triple-Code) or whether they must pass through a semantic bottle-neck (the McCloskey Model).

| HY's reading of Arabic numbers | JG's reading of Arabic numbers |
| --- | --- |
| 5 → *seven* | 916 → *nineteen* hundred sixteen |
| 17 → *thirteen* | 912 → nine hundred *twenty* |
| 317 → three hundred *fourteen* | 620 → six hundred *two* |

The two models make different predictions about transcoding (e.g. from Arabic digits to spoken number names). McCloskey (1992) regards the relationship between Arabic and verbal forms to be too irregular to be implemented by non-semantic transcoding procedures, at least for languages such as English (but for one account, see Power & Dal Martello, 1997). For example, the written digit 2 can be verbally rendered as "two," "twelve" or "twenty" depending on the context in which it is used (e.g. 2, 12, 20). The same cannot always be said of other languages. Chinese children must learn the numbers up to 10, but thereafter it is easy. Thus, 12 is literally translated as "ten-two" in Chinese and 21 is "two-ten-one." Not surprisingly, Chinese-speaking children outperform their English-speaking counterparts when learning to count (Miller & Stigler, 1987). In English, reading Arabic numbers does appear to use number semantics. For example, reading a digit aloud (e.g. 6) will facilitate reading of a similar-sized number (e.g. 5) relative to a more distant number (e.g. 9) (Brysbaert, 1995). However, the question is not whether transcoding *can* go via semantics (as this is uncontested), but rather whether it *must* go through semantics.

A number of studies have provided empirical evidence for a direct route between Arabic numeral recognition and verbal output that bypasses number semantics (Cipolotti, 1995; Cipolotti & Butterworth, 1995; Cipolotti *et al.*, 1995;

Why do Chinese-speaking children find learning to count easier than speakers of many other languages?

Seron & Noel, 1995). For example, the patient reported by Cipolotti and Butterworth (1995) could perform sums and subtractions up to six digits with 98 percent accuracy, but made errors on half of the Arabic numbers that he was asked to read. When asked to write "seventy thousand," he wrote 17,000, but when asked to add "56,748 + 13,252," he wrote 70,000. He read 4,070 as "four hundred thousand and seventy" and wrote "four thousand and seventy" as 1,070; yet, given 2,561 + 1,509, he could write 4,070. To explain this, Cipolotti and Butterworth added direct transcoding routes to the model of McCloskey, thus making it, in this respect, similar to that proposed in the Dehaene Triple-Code Model.

## Evaluation

In summary, whereas some evidence from studies of number processing favors the Dehaene model over the McCloskey Model, other evidence favors the McCloskey Model over the Dehaene model. In terms of representation of number meaning, an analogical "mental number line" may be a necessary part of number meaning (as put forward by Dehaene), but may not be the only aspect of it.

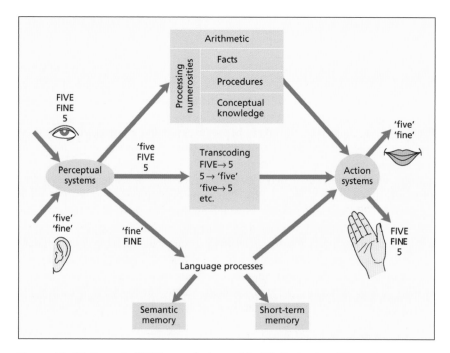

The model of Butterworth (1999) extends the model of McCloskey by adding separate transcoding routes that are independent of number meaning and calculation procedures.

From Butterworth, 1999. © Palgrave-Macmillan. Reproduced with permission of the author.

## THE MAKING OF MATHEMATICAL GENIUS

> Genius is ninety-nine percent perspiration and one percent inspiration.
> (Albert Einstein)

Although many would be happy to label Einstein a genius, the extent to which this reflects hard work or innate skill could be debated endlessly. "Genius" is a notoriously difficult word to define, but some scientific progress has been made in understanding the neural basis of unusual ability. The mathematical prodigy Gamm took part in a functional imaging study by Pesenti and colleagues (2001) while performing incredible calculations. For example, Gamm was able to divide prime numbers up to 60 decimal places (e.g. 31/61), and calculate the fifth root of numbers (e.g. $\sqrt[5]{8547799037}$). The regions of his brain that were activated included those involved in calculation and those involved in memory retrieval (control participants, given easier tasks, activated only the former). Gamm

Albert Einstein, 1879–1955.
© Bettmann/Corbis.

appears to have committed many number "facts" into long-term memory (he trained himself for 6 years for up to 4 hours per day) and uses these to reduce the high demands placed upon working memory during calculation. Observations of other prodigious calculators support this conclusion. Wim Klein can extract the thirteenth root of a 100-digit number in 2 min. To help him, he has learned the logarithm of all the integers up to 150 (Smith, 1983). Another prodigy, Aitken, solved the problem $777^2$ by decomposing it to a simpler multiplication and a square: $[(777 + 23) \times (777-23)] + 23^2$. He had memorized all the squares from 1 to 100 (Gardner, 1990). In the case of Gamm and associates, it appears that their skills reflect perspiration more than inspiration. It is interesting to note that Einstein was almost certainly unable to perform these calculations and, conversely, it is a moot point as to whether Gamm is a "genius." Perhaps other factors are needed to explain the kind of ability possessed by Einstein (Witelson et al., 1999).

It would be premature to state that there is no genetic contribution to numerical ability at all. Genetic factors may certainly contribute to numerical disability (Bruandet et al., 2003). The interaction between genes, environment and brain is likely to be complex. For example, autistic children may develop an unusual zeal for numbers that reflects a difficulty in socialization rather than a "gift" for numbers (Hermelin & O'Connor, 1986). Differences in motivation (as opposed to differences in some innate ability) can themselves be a product of genes and can result in a change in the environment that one creates for oneself.

In terms of the representation of specific calculation procedures (addition, subtraction, multiplication, division), the McCloskey Model predicts that these different domains may be selectively impaired, whereas the Triple-Code model predicts that impairments in calculation will tend to be either "semantic" (affecting subtraction strongly) or "verbal" (affecting multiplication strongly). There is evidence in favor of both positions. In terms of transcoding from Arabic to verbal forms, evidence favors both a semantic and an asemantic route (in line with the triple-code model of Dehaene).

Aside from the specific details and predictions of the models, it is worthwhile noting that the two models are conceptually different in the way that they approach numerical cognition. Dehaene's model attempts an explanatory account of *why* different types of numerical knowledge happen to be represented in a particular way (e.g. multiplication is different from subtraction because they tap different types of number-based representations). In contrast, the McCloskey model offers a more descriptive account of different aspects of numerical cognition (e.g. multiplication and subtraction differ because they are assumed to be different in kind). Although the empirical evidence does not unequivocally support one model over the other, it is perhaps not surprising that the general approach taken by Dehaene has had far more influence in the field.

## SUMMARY AND KEY POINTS OF THE CHAPTER

- Knowledge of numbers is a basic and near-universal aspect of cognition. It is aided by language and cultural knowledge, but is not directly dependent on these.
- Number meanings can be selectively impaired by brain damage (dyscalculia) and may have a dedicated neural substrate (including the intraparietal sulcus).
- Magnitude comparisons using either nonsymbolic (e.g. dot arrays) or symbolic (e.g. digits) representations of number became harder with increasing magnitude and this may reflect a broader tuning of number-specific neurons with increasing magnitude.
- There is a similarity in the way that the brain handles countable (discrete) and uncountable (continuous) quantities and both tend to evoke concomitant spatial associations.
- Different types of calculation procedure (subtraction, addition, multiplication, division) may be selectively impaired by brain damage and may, to some extent, draw on different kinds of code depending whether they are learned as verbal facts or calculated on the fly.
- Transcoding between Arabic numerals and number names may be mediated both semantically and nonsemantically.

## EXAMPLE ESSAY QUESTIONS

- To what extent is knowledge of number a product of innate endowment or cultural factors?
- Does knowledge of numbers have a separate neural substrate? Can it be selectively impaired?
- "Numerical cognition is performed by the left hemisphere." Discuss.
- Is language essential or helpful for understanding numbers?
- Compare and contrast the models of numerical cognition proposed by Dehaene and McCloskey.
- What is the evidence that humans possess a "mental number line"?

## RECOMMENDED FURTHER READING

- Campbell, J. I. D. (2005). *The handbook of mathematical cognition.* Hove, UK: Psychology Press. An extensive set of papers on the topic written by different experts in the field. More advanced readings.
- Cohen Kadosh, R. & Dowker, A. (in press). *The Oxford handbook of numerical cognition.* Oxford, UK: Oxford University Press. Up-to-date advanced readings on a wide selection of topics.
- Nieder, SA. & Dehaene, S. (2009). Representation of number in the brain. *Annual Review of Neuroscience, 32,* 185–208. An excellent summary of contemporary findings.

Visit the companion website at www. psypress/cw/ward for:

- References to key papers and readings
- Video lectures and interviews on key topics with leading psychologists Brian Butterworth and author Jamie Ward, as well as a video demonstrating innate number sense in infants
- Multiple choice questions and interactive flashcards to test your knowledge
- Downloadable glossary

# CHAPTER 14

# The executive brain

## CONTENTS

The **executive functions** of the brain can be defined as the complex processes by which an individual optimizes his or her performance in a situation that requires the operation of a number of cognitive processes (Baddeley, 1986). A rather more poetic metaphor is that the executive functions are the brain's conductor, which instructs other regions to perform, or be silenced, and generally coordinates their synchronized activity (Goldberg, 2001). As such, executive functions are not tied to one particular domain (memory, language, perception, and so on) but take on a role that is meta-cognitive, supervisory, or controlling. Executive functions have traditionally been equated with the frontal lobes, and difficulties with executive functioning have been termed as "frontal lobe syndrome." More accurately, executive functions are associated with the *prefrontal cortex* (PFC) of the frontal lobes, and it is an empirically open question as to whether all aspects of executive function can be localized to this region.

    The concept of executive functions is closely related to another distinction with a long history in cognitive science—namely, that between automatic and controlled behavior (e.g. Schneider & Shiffrin, 1977). This distinction has already been encountered in another context, namely, the production of actions. When driving a car, one may accelerate, change gear, and so on, in an apparently "autopilot" mode. But if the traffic is diverted through an unfamiliar route, then one would need to override the automatic behavior and exert online control. This is often assumed to require the use of executive functions (Norman & Shallice, 1986). The same logic may also apply in situations that lack motor output, i.e. in the online control of thoughts and ideas. This provides humans (and possibly other species) with a remarkable opportunity; namely, to mentally simulate scenarios and think through problems "in the mind" without necessarily acting them out. It is hardly surprising, therefore, that some theories of executive function are effectively synonymous with aspects of *working memory* (Baddeley, 1996; Goldman-Rakic, 1992, 1996). The notion of working memory has been discussed elsewhere (see Chapter 9) and can be thought of as consisting of a network of both storage components (often related to the posterior cortex) and control processes (typically related to prefrontal cortex).

Two other general points are in need of mention in this preamble. First, the extent to which behavior is "automatic" (i.e. not requiring executive function) versus "controlled" (i.e. requiring executive function) may be a matter of degree rather than all or nothing. Even when generating words in fluent conversation, some degree of executive control may be exerted. For example, one may need to select whether to say the word "dog," "doggy," "Fido," or "Labrador" depending on pragmatic context, rather than relying on, say, the most frequent word to be selected. Second, one must be cautious about falling into the trap of thinking that controlled behavior requires an autonomous controller. This is the so-called homunculus problem (think of a little man inside your head making your decisions, and then imagine another little man in his head making his decisions, and so on). Control may be an outcome of multiple competing biases rather than the presence of a controller. Decisions may arise out of an interaction of environmental influences (bottom-up processes) and influences related to the motivation and goals of the person (top-down processes). The sight of a cream cake may trigger an "eat me" response, but whether one does eat it may depend on whether one is hungry or dieting.

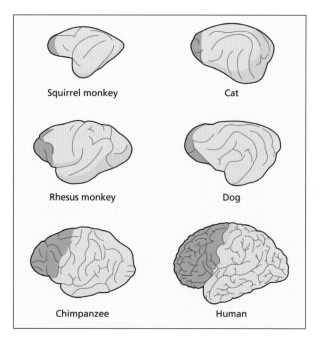

Enlargement of frontal cortex shows an evolutionary progression (the brains are not drawn to scale). In humans, this region occupies almost a third of the cortical volume.

Adapted from Fuster, 1989.

This chapter first considers the major anatomical divisions within the prefrontal cortex. The subsequent section outlines the main types of cognitive tests that are believed to depend critically on the functioning of the prefrontal cortex. The chapter then considers different possible functional organizations of the prefrontal cortex: for instance, different functional roles for the lateral versus orbital surfaces; different functional roles for posterior versus anterior portions of the lateral surface; and hemispheric differences. Before discussing executive functions, it is worthwhile to review the anatomy of the prefrontal cortex.

## ANATOMICAL AND FUNCTIONAL DIVISIONS OF THE PREFRONTAL CORTEX

The most basic anatomical division within the prefrontal cortex is that between the three different cortical surfaces. The *lateral* surface of the prefrontal cortex lies anterior to the premotor areas (Brodmann's area 6) and the frontal eye fields (in Brodmann's area 8). This surface lies closest to the skull. The *medial* surface of the prefrontal cortex lies between the two hemispheres and to the front of the corpus callosum and the anterior cingulate cortex. In terms of anatomy, the anterior cingulate is not strictly part of the prefrontal cortex, but it does have an important role to play in executive functions and, as such, will be considered in this chapter. The *orbital* surface of the prefrontal cortex lies above the orbits of the eyes and the nasal cavity. The orbitofrontal cortex is functionally, as well as anatomically, related to the ventral part of the medial surface (termed ventromedial prefrontal cortex) (Öngür & Price, 2000). The terms orbito- and ventromedial-PFC are sometimes used inter-changeably when finer anatomical divisions are not necessary.

The prefrontal cortex has extensive connections with virtually all sensory systems, the cortical and subcortical motor system and structures involved in affect and memory. There are also extensive connections between different regions of the prefrontal cortex. These extensive connections enable the coordination of a wide variety of brain processes. The lateral prefrontal cortex is more closely associated with sensory inputs than the orbitofrontal cortex. It receives visual, somatosensory and auditory information, as well as receiving inputs from multi-modal regions that integrate across senses. In contrast, the medial and orbital prefrontal cortex is more closely connected with medial temporal lobe structures critical for long-term memory and processing of emotion.

Aside from these gross anatomical divisions, a number of researchers have developed ways of dividing different regions into separate areas of functional specialization. These correspond approximately, although not exactly, with different Brodmann areas (e.g. Fletcher & Henson, 2001; Petrides, 2000; Stuss *et al.*, 2002). These include areas on the figure on the following page as ventrolateral (including Brodmann's areas 44, 45, and 47), dorsolateral (including Brodmann's areas 46 and 9), the anterior prefrontal cortex (Brodmann's area 10) and the anterior cingulate. These terms are sufficient to capture most of the functional distinctions discussed in this chapter, but it is to be noted that not all researchers regard the prefrontal cortex as containing functionally different subregions.

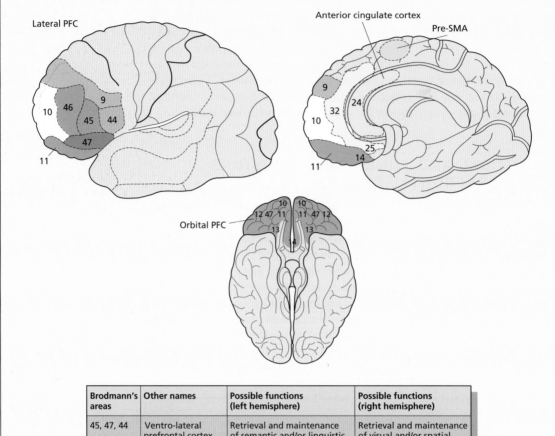

| Brodmann's areas | Other names | Possible functions (left hemisphere) | Possible functions (right hemisphere) |
|---|---|---|---|
| 45, 47, 44 | Ventro-lateral prefrontal cortex (VLPFC) | Retrieval and maintenance of semantic and/or linguistic information (Area 44 + 45 on left also called Broca's area) | Retrieval and maintenance of visual and/or spatial information |
| 46,9 | Dorso-lateral prefrontal cortex (DLPFC) | Selecting a possible range of responses, and suppressing inappropriate ones; manipulating the contents of working memory | Monitoring and checking of information held in mind, particularly in conditions of uncertainty; vigilance and sustained attention |
| 10 | Anterior prefrontal cortex; frontal pole; rostral prefrontal cortex | Multi-tasking; maintaining future intentions / goals whilst currently performing other tasks or sub-goals. (The medial portion has been implicated in "theory of mind" – see Chapter 15) | |
| 24 (dorsal) 32 (dorsal Pre-SMA | Anterior cingulate cortex (dorsal) Pre-SMA | Monitoring in situations of response conflict and error detection | |
| 11, 12, 13, 14 | Orbito-frontal cortex | Executive processing of emotional stimuli (e.g. evaluating rewards and risks) | |

The prefrontal cortex has three different surfaces: the lateral surface (top left), the medial surface (top right) and the orbitofrontal surface (bottom). The numbers refer to Brodmann areas that are discussed in the text.

# THE EXTRAORDINARY CASE OF PHINEAS GAGE

One of the most famous cases in the neuropsychological literature is that of Phineas Gage (Harlow, 1993; Macmillan, 1986). On September 13, 1848, Gage was working on the Rutland and Burlington railroad. He was using a large metal rod (a tamping iron) to pack explosive charges into the ground when the charge accidentally exploded, pushing the tamping iron up through the top of his skull; it landed about 30 m behind him. The contemporary account noted that Gage was momentarily knocked over but that he then walked over to an ox-cart, made an entry in his time book, and went back to his hotel to wait for a doctor. He sat and waited half an hour for the doctor and greeted him with, "Doctor, here is business enough for you!" (Macmillan, 1986).

Not only was Gage conscious after the accident, he was able to walk and talk. Although this is striking in its own right, it is the cognitive consequences of the injury that have led to Gage's notoriety. Before the injury, Gage held a position of responsibility as a foreman and was described as shrewd and smart. After the injury, he was considered unemployable by his previous company; he was "no longer Gage" (Harlow, 1993). Gage was described as

> irreverent, indulging at times in grossest profanity ... manifesting but little deference for his fellows, impatient of restraint or advice when it conflicts with his desires ... devising many plans of future operation, which are no sooner arranged than they are abandoned in turn for others.
>
> (Harlow, 1993)

After various temporary jobs, including a stint in Barnum's Museum, he died of epilepsy (a secondary consequence of his injury) in San Francisco, some 12 years after his accident.

Where was Phineas Gage's brain lesion? This question was answered by an MRI reconstruction of Gage's skull, which found damage restricted to the frontal lobes, particularly the left orbitofrontal/ventromedial region and the left anterior region (Damasio et al., 1994). Research suggests that this region is crucial for certain aspects of decision making, planning, and social regulation of behavior, all of which appeared to have been disrupted in Gage. Other areas of the lateral prefrontal cortex are likely to have been spared.

The skull of Phineas Gage, with tamping iron *in situ* and a recently discovered photograph of Gage. Modern reconstructions suggest that his brain lesion may have been specific to the medial and orbital surfaces of the prefrontal cortex, sparing the lateral surfaces

Damasio et al., 1994. From the collection of Jack and Beverly Wilgus.

# EXECUTIVE FUNCTIONS IN PRACTICE

This section considers some concrete situations in which executive functions are needed. Evidence will be presented that the prefrontal cortex (or sub-regions within it) are important for implementing this kind of behavior.

## Task-setting and problem-solving

Problem-solving is synonymous with many lay notions of what it is to exhibit intelligent behavior and it is not surprising that executive functions, and the prefrontal cortex, have been linked to intelligence both within and across species. For instance, performance on tests of executive function tends to correlate with each other and also correlates with certain standardized measures of intelligence (Duncan *et al.*, 1997). In the lab, problem-solving is often tested by giving an end point (a goal) and, optionally, a starting point (a set of objects) and participants must generate a solution of their own. This kind of open-ended solution is also referred to as task-setting.

Patients with lesions to the prefrontal cortex often show clinical symptoms of poor task-setting and problem solving. To test this formally, a number of tests have been devised. Shallice (1982) reports a test called the "Tower of London," in which patients must move beads from one stake to another to reach a specified end-point. Patients with damage to the left prefrontal cortex take significantly more moves. This implies that they perform by trial and error rather than planning their moves (see also Morris *et al.*, 1997). Functional imaging studies of healthy participants suggest that activity within the dorsolateral prefrontal cortex increases with the number of moves needed to reach the end- point (Rowe *et al.*, 2001).

A number of verbal tests also involve finding solutions to problems in which there is no readily available answer. In the Cognitive Estimates Test (Shallice & Evans, 1978), patients with damage to the prefrontal cortex are impaired at producing estimates for questions in which an exact answer is unlikely to be known ("How many camels are in Holland?") but can be inferred from other relevant knowledge (e.g. camels only likely to reside in a small number of zoos). In the **FAS Test** (Miller, 1984), participants must generate a sequence of words (not proper names) beginning with a specified letter ("F," "A" or "S") in a one-minute period. This test is not as easy as it sounds (have a try) and involves generating novel strategies, selecting between alternatives and avoiding repeating previous responses. Patients with left lateral prefrontal lesions are particularly impaired (Stuss *et al.*, 1998).

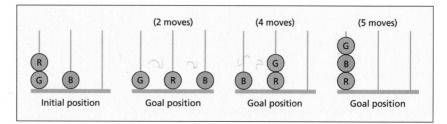

The "Tower of London" task requires beads to be moved from an initial position to a specified end-point. Performance can be measured in terms of time to complete task or number of moves taken (relative to the optimal number of moves).
From Shallice, 1982. Royal Society of London.

# Overcoming potent or habitual responses

The classic example of overcoming a habitual response is provided by the **Stroop Test** (Stroop, 1935). In this task, participants must name the color of the ink and ignore reading the word (which also happens to be a color name). The standard explanation for the response conflict generated by this task is that reading of the word occurs automatically and can generate a response that is incompatible with the one required (MacLeod & MacDonald, 2000). Performance on the Stroop test has long been linked with integrity of the prefrontal cortex (Perret, 1974).

**Go/No-Go** tests involve the participant making a set of responses to some stimuli ("go" trials) but withholding responses to a subset of stimuli ("no-go" or "stop" trials). The no-go trials are often infrequent, so the participant gets into the habit of making a response. No-go rules can be defined in terms of simple rules (e.g. "respond to all stimuli except the letter B") or more complex rules (e.g. "respond to all stimuli except the letter B when it follows another letter B"). Brain activity during successful no-go trials is normally taken as indexing response inhibition, and the proportion of errors on no-go trials is taken as a behavioral marker of **impulsivity** (Perry & Carrol, 2008).

Both the Stroop test and the Go/No-Go test are related by virtue of the fact that they are typically explained with respect to the concept of inhibition. Inhibition, in terms of neural activity, has a very specific definition (reduced spiking rate) with a relatively well characterized mechanism at the synaptic level. Behavioral or cognitive inhibition simply means reducing the likelihood of a particular thought/action and the mechanism behind it, at the neuronal level, is not clear. Some contemporary models of executive function do not rely on the concept of inhibition at all and rely solely on biasing activation signals, also termed "gain" (Stuss & Alexander, 2007). Certainly, tasks such as the Stroop and Go/No-Go are likely to involve a variety of functions such as task-setting and monitoring ongoing performance, in addition to biasing of competing responses (either via gain or inhibition).

Contemporary research has suggested that performance on these tasks is related to particular brain regions rather than the "prefrontal cortex" in general. A meta-analysis of functional imaging studies of the Go/No-Go task suggests that a region of the medial prefrontal cortex (specifically the pre-SMA, pre-supplementary motor area) was common across tasks for No-Go stimuli with right lateral prefrontal cortex also implicated in more complex No-Go rules (Simmonds *et al.*, 2008). Studies of patients with damage to the prefrontal cortex confirm that the pre-SMA region and the right lateral prefrontal cortex are important for this task (Picton *et al.*, 2007). With regards to the Stroop test, a similar picture emerges that highlights the importance of the anterior cingulate cortex and the nearby pre-SMA region (Alexander *et al.*, 2007).

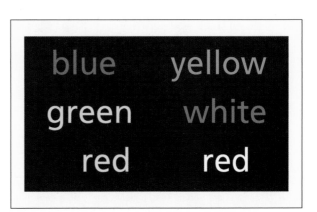

The Stroop test involves naming the color of the ink and ignoring the written color name (i.e. "red, green, yellow, blue, yellow, white").

## Task switching

In the **Wisconsin Card Sorting Test**, a series of cards must be matched against reference cards (Milner, 1963; Nelson, 1976). The cards can be matched according to one of three dimensions, namely color, number and shape. For example, in the color condition a blue card must be grouped with blue cards and red cards grouped with red cards (ignoring number and shape). After each trial, participants are told whether they are correct or not. Eventually, they are told that they are incorrect and they must then spontaneously switch task, i.e. start sorting according to number or shape. Many patients with damage to the prefrontal cortex fail to make this shift and continue to incorrectly sort according to the previous rule, a behavior termed **perseveration**.

The Wisconsin Card Sorting Test has a number of features that make it demanding: the switches are unpredictable and, moreover, the relevant dimensions (color, shape, number) are not given but need to be inferred. This also makes it hard to know why, in cognitive terms, failure on the task happens. Other **task-switching** paradigms have been developed that enable more finer-grained analysis of the underlying mechanisms. These tend to be used in studies of non-braindamaged participants using fMRI or TMS. To give an example of a task that involves switches that occur predictably, imagine that you are a participant looking at a square 2 × 2 grid. A digit and/or number pair (e.g. L9) will appear in each part of the grid, moving clockwise, and you must make a response to each stimulus. When the stimulus is in the upper half of the grid, you must decide if the letter is a consonant or vowel. When the stimulus is in the lower half, you must decide if the digit is odd or even (some participants would get the complementary set of instructions). This produces two types of trial—those in which the task switches and those in which it does not. The reaction times for the switch trials are significantly slower, and this difference remains even though the change is predictable and even if the subject is given over a second to prepare before each stimulus is presented (Rogers & Monsell, 1995). This difference in reaction time between switch and non- switch trials is called the **switch cost**.

The switch cost could either reflect suppressing the old task or reflect setting up the new task. This can be evaluated by considering switches between easy and hard tasks. Is it more difficult to switch from an easy to a hard task or from a hard to an easy task? Surprisingly, perhaps, the switch cost is greater when switching from hard to easy. For example, bilinguals are slower at switching from their second to their first language than from their first to their second language in picture naming (Meuter & Allport, 1999). With Stroop stimuli, people are faster at switching from word naming to color naming (easy to hard) than color naming to word naming (hard to easy) (Allport et al., 1994). The switch cost has more to do with inhibiting the old task than setting up the new one.

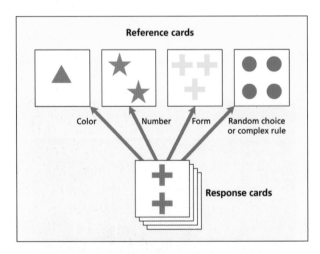

In the Wisconsin Card Sorting Test, patients are given a card that can be sorted by a number of rules (matching shape, number, or color). Sometimes the rule unexpectedly changes and the patients must adjust their responses to the new rule.

Based on Milner, 1963.

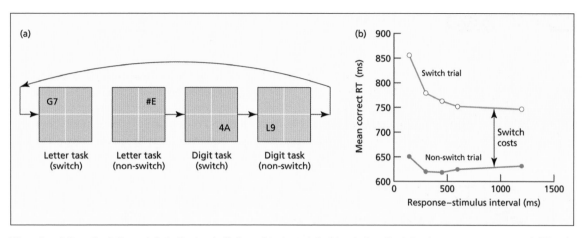

When the digit and/or letter pair is in the top half, the subject must decide whether the letter is a consonant or vowel. When it is in the bottom half, the digit must be classified as odd or even. This generates two types of trial—those in which the task switches and those in which it does not. Switch trials are significantly slower even though the switch is predictable and even if participants are given over 1 sec to prepare before the stimulus is shown.

Reprinted from Monsell, 2003. © 2003, with permission from Elsevier.

Functional imaging studies reveal a variety of prefrontal regions together with the anterior cingulate cortex/pre-SMA to be involved in task switching, by comparing switch trials with no-switch trials (Ravizza & Carter, 2008) or contrasting the switch preparation time (before the stimulus) with switch execution after the stimulus (Brass & von Cramon, 2002). However, it is not always straightforward to link specific regions with specific cognitive processes because there are often different types of switching mechanism. Most task-switching experiments involve both a switching of response rules and a switching of the stimulus selected. In the study described previously, for example, the left hand switches from responding "consonant" to responding "odd," and the stimulus selected switches from letter to digit (i.e. multiple aspects of the task are switched). Rushworth *et al.* (2002) attempted to control for these differences in a combined fMRI and TMS study. They found that the medial frontal lobes (the pre-SMA region) are important for reassignment of stimulus–response pairings (e.g. which button to press), whereas lateral frontal regions may be involved in selection of the current rule (e.g. whether to respond to color or shape).

Bilingual speakers are faster at switching from their first to their second language, than from their second to their first language. How can this apparently paradoxical result be explained?

# Multi-tasking

**Multi-tasking** experiments can be regarded as having an element of maintaining future goals while current goals are being dealt with. This is related to, but an extension of, task switching. In task-switching one goal is substituted for another. In multi-tasking several goals are maintained at the same time (but only one executed).

Patients with lesions in to the prefrontal cortex may be particularly impaired at multi-tasking, even though each task in isolation may be successfully performed and even though they perform normally on other tests of executive function, including the Wisconsin Card Sorting Test and FAS test (Burgess *et al.*, 2000; Shallice & Burgess, 1991). This suggests a possible fractionation of executive functions (assuming it isn't simply related to task difficulty)—an idea returned to later in the chapter. In the "Six Element Test" the participant is given six open- ended tasks to perform within a 15-minute period (e.g. arithmetic, writing out names of pictures). Critically, they are instructed to attempt each task. However, they will be unable to complete all of them in the time allowed, and more points are awarded for earlier items. Constraints are placed on some of the ordering of tests. Patients with prefrontal lesions would often fail to switch tasks, spend too long planning (e.g. taking notes) but never execute the plans, and so on. The patients could easily perform the isolated tasks, but their difficulties were only apparent when they had to coordinate between them (Shallice & Burgess, 1991).

How do we perform multi-tasking? Could the anterior prefrontal region hold the key?

## Evaluation

By the mid-1990s there was a generally agreed upon definition of what the essential features of executive functions were: e.g. allowing flexible or "intelligent" behavior, exerting control via a biasing influence. There was also a general consensus that the prefrontal cortex had a critical role in implementing this, and there were also a set of frequently used tasks that were assumed to be a good indicator of prefrontal functioning (e.g. the Wisconsin Card Sort, the Stroop test). There was also agreement on the kind of model that could account for this. One simple model of executive functions is the original version of the SAS (Supervisory Attentional System) model—introduced in Chapter 8. This consists of a set of tasks and behaviors (termed schemas) and a biasing mechanism that activated/ suppressed these schemas according to the individual's current goals (Norman & Shallice, 1986). The activation of schemas was conceptualized as a balance between bottom- up processes (cues in the environment, habits, etc.) and top-down processes (task instructions, long- term plans, etc.). Disruption of this balance, for example, by a prefrontal lesion would tend to result in recent or habitual responses being inappropriately elicited (e.g. in the Stroop Test, or Wisconsin Card Sort), poor planning, and so on.

Although these core ideas and empirical results are as valid today as they were in the 1990s, the contemporary intellectual landscape relating to executive functions is far more detailed and complex. In the mid-1990s there was already some evidence that was hard to accommodate by existing theories. For instance, it was found that some patients with prefrontal lesions could pass the standard tests of executive functions, but yet show significant impairments in organizing their daily life and in their social interactions (Shallice & Burgess, 1991; Eslinger & Damasio, 1985). This revealed a potential flaw in the early accounts. However, these observations could still be explained away: for instance, by pointing out that lab tests may not be fully sensitive to deficits apparent in the "real world." While difficulties on the Stroop task and making socially inappropriate jokes can both be conceptualized in terms of a weaker biasing influence of top-down control (e.g. "lack of inhibition") more recent evidence suggests they are related to rather different mechanisms involving the prefrontal cortex (Glascher et al., 2012). Brain imaging has made a very significant contribution toward moving the debate forward. This has enabled a much finer grained analysis of the functions of different regions of the prefrontal cortex (and their connectivity) both in studying healthy participants (in fMRI) but also in identifying more precise lesion locations in patients. The next section considers various ways in which executive functions might be organized in the brain.

## EGAS MONIZ AND THE PREFRONTAL LOBOTOMY

The career of Egas Moniz was an eventful one. In politics, he served as Portuguese Ambassador to Spain and was President of the Portuguese Delegation at the Paris Peace Conference in 1918, following the First World War. However, it is his contribution to neurology and neurosurgery that gained him fame and infamy. In the 1920s he developed cerebral angiography, enabling blood vessels to be visualized with radioactive tracers. In 1935, he developed the prefrontal lobotomy/leucotomy for the treatment of psychiatric illness. Between then and 1954, more than 50,000 patients would have the procedure in the USA (Swayze, 1995) and over 10,000 in the UK (Tooth & Newton, 1961). This brought Moniz mixed fortunes. He was awarded the Nobel Prize for Medicine. However, he had to attend the ceremony in a wheelchair because, some years previously, he had been shot in the spine and partially paralyzed by one of his lobotomized patients.

Moniz's operation was designed to sever the connections between the prefrontal cortex and other areas, notably the limbic system (Moniz, 1937, 1954). This procedure was adapted by others in frighteningly simple ways. For instance, an ice-pick-type implement was inserted through the thin bony plate above the eyes and waggled from side to side.

At that point, there were no pharmacological treatments for psychiatric complaints. Lobotomy was used for a variety of disorders, including obsessive-compulsive disorder, depression, and schizophrenia. The measurement of "improvement" in the patients was rather subjective, and the fact that the lobotomized patients tended to be duller and more apathetic than before was not sufficient to halt the appeal of the lobotomy. Formal assessments of cognitive function, if they had been carried out, would undoubtedly have revealed impairments in executive function.

Moniz died in 1955. By then, his surgical innovation had been phased out and its success has been left to history to judge.

# THE ORGANIZATION OF EXECUTIVE FUNCTIONS

Although there are many different approaches to explaining executive functions, it is important to emphasize from the outset that there are some things that all models of executive functions appear to have in common. First, there is broad agreement as to what kinds of things that a model of executive functions needs to explain. As already outlined, this includes the ability to override automatic behavior in order to deal with novel situations, switch flexibly between tasks, and carry out a current task while holding in mind other goals. Second, in order to account for this, the different models typically have a common set of core features. The type of processing must be inherently flexible in order to cope with changing tasks from moment to moment. It can implement a seemingly infinite range of "if-then" type mappings ("wink whenever I say bumbly-doodle" to take an example from Miller and Cohen, 2001). Furthermore, almost all models assume that executive functions have a biasing influence (they make certain behaviors more or less likely) rather than dictating to the rest of the brain. This could be achieved via inhibition (suppressing certain stimuli/responses) or gain/facilitation (activating certain stimuli/responses) or both. As for differences between models, one of the key distinctions is the extent to which different models assume that executive functions can be decomposed into several modular-like processes versus executive functions construed as a more unitary idea. This is not an all-or-nothing debate, as some models may assume relative degrees of specialization.

## "Hot" versus "cold" control processes

Perhaps the least controversial principle of organisation of executive functions is the distinction between the control of affective or reward-related stimuli (i.e. "hot") versus purely cognitive (i.e. "cold") stimuli. Reward-related stimuli includes money (in humans) and food (typically used in studies of nonhuman animals), whereas purely cognitive stimuli often involve sensory dimensions (such as color or shape). Most of the tests of executive function described thus far are of the latter kind (e.g. Stroop test, Wisconsin Card Sort). Hot cognitive control involves primarily the orbitofrontal cortex (and associated ventromedial PFC), whereas cold cognitive control involves primarily the lateral PFC. This reflects the anatomical connectivity of these frontal regions to posterior regions involved in affective versus sensory/motor processes (Öngür & Price, 2000).

Dias *et al.* (1996) designed a test of task-switching that could be learned by marmosets (a species of primate). As noted before, the seemingly simple task-switching paradigm has several processes (establishing new tasks, inhibiting old tasks) that can be configured in different ways (switching stimuli, switching responses, switching rewards). The stimuli in their study consisted of compounds of black lines superimposed on blue shapes. The animals were trained to respond to only one of these dimensions (shapes or lines) and had to remember which shapes or lines were correct. For instance, they may learn that a blue circle is rewarded (i.e. correct), but a blue star is not. They then received neurotoxic lesions, either to the lateral or orbital PFC, and subsequently undertook further training sessions that involved a task-switch. In the **reversal learning** condition, the same stimuli were presented, but such that the previously rewarded stimuli were no longer rewarded (in the example above, the blue star is now rewarded, but the blue circle is not). In the dimensional-shift condition (which resembles the

Wisconsin Card Sorting Task), new shapes and lines were presented and the animals had to learn, for instance, that lines were now rewarded and not shapes. Lesions of the orbitofrontal cortex disrupted the ability to respond to the fact that the rewards had been switched (but not that the relevant cognitive dimension had switched), whereas lesions of the lateral PFC disrupted the ability to respond to the fact that the relevant cognitive dimension had switched from shapes to lines (but these animals were able to learn that previously rewarded shapes were no longer rewarded). They interpreted this double dissociation as evidence for two separate inhibitory control processes: one reward-related and another related to stimulus dimensions.

The distinction between executive processing of affective versus nonaffective stimuli can account for one puzzle from the older literature. Namely, the fact that some brain-damaged patients with known pathology of the prefrontal cortex exhibit poor regulation of behavior in the "real world" (particularly with regards to financial management and social interactions) despite passing standard (i.e. "cold") tests of executive function (Eslinger & Damasio, 1985). Damasio and colleagues have developed the **Somatic Marker Hypothesis** to account for this (Damasio, 1994, 1996). In this theory, somatic markers form the link between previous situations stored throughout the cortex and the "feeling" of those situations stored in regions of the brain dedicated to emotion (e.g. the amygdala) and the representation of the body states (e.g. the insula). The somatic markers are assumed to be stored in the ventromedial frontal cortex (including parts of the orbital surface) and have a direct role in controlling ongoing behavior, notably in those situations in which feelings are critical (e.g. when taking risk, or interacting socially). To investigate this hypothesis, they devised the **Iowa Gambling Task** that has been shown to distinguish between different lesion sites and cognitive profiles (Bechara *et al.*, 1994; Bechara *et al.*, 1998; Bechara *et al.*, 1999). Players are given four decks of cards (A to D), a "loan" of $2,000 in fake bank notes, and are instructed to play so that they win the most and lose the least. On turning each card, the player receives either a monetary penalty or

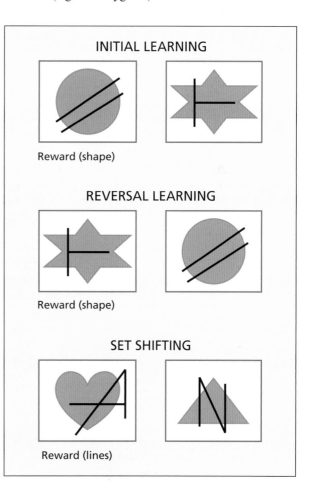

INITIAL LEARNING

Reward (shape)

REVERSAL LEARNING

Reward (shape)

SET SHIFTING

Reward (lines)

Marmosets were trained to respond using a touch screen to compound stimuli, presented in pairs, either to certain shapes or lines. After lesioning to the orbitofrontal cortex or lateral prefrontal cortex there were several kinds of task-switches. In the reversal learning condition, the same stimuli were presented, but previously rewarded shapes/lines were no longer rewarded (lesions to orbitofrontal cortex impairs responding to this task-switch). In the dimensional shift condition, different shapes and lines were presented and the animals had to shift from responding to shapes and respond to lines or vice versa (lesions to the lateral prefrontal cortex impairs responding to this task-switch). Adapted from Dias *et al.*, 1996.

gain. Playing mostly from packs A and B leads to a net loss, whereas playing mostly from packs C and D will lead to a net gain. Control participants, without a brain lesion, learn to choose from C and D and to avoid A and B. Patients with lesions to the ventromedial frontal cortex do not (Bechara *et al.*, 1994). Moreover, control participants generate an anticipatory skin conductance response (SCR) before making a selection from a risky pile (A and B), whereas these patients do not (suggesting the patients cannot use affective states to regulate behavior). Patients with lesions to the orbital/ventromedial PFC are impaired on the Iowa Gambling Task, but not on working memory tests (Bechara *et al.*, 1998) and not impaired on tests such as the Stroop or Wisconsin Card Sorting (Glascher *et al.*, 2012). Patients with lesions to the lateral PFC show the reverse profile.

When testing their patients with orbital and ventromedial prefrontal lobe lesions, Damasio and colleagues (1990) noted that many of their patients met a published American Psychiatric Association (APA) criterion for **sociopathy**

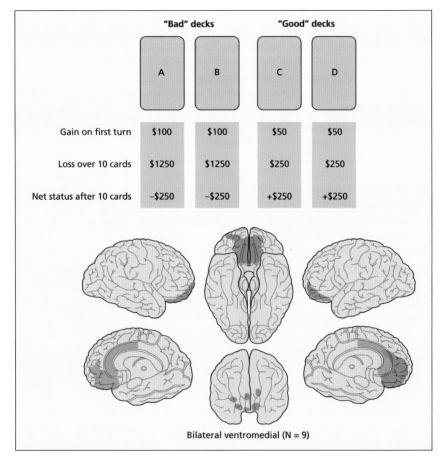

Players receive $2,000 and must choose hidden cards from one of four packs, A to D. Playing preferentially from packs A and B will result in loss, whereas playing preferentially from packs C and D will result in gain. Players are not informed of this contingency. Will they learn to avoid A and B? Patients with damage to ventromedial frontal lobes are impaired on this task.

From Bechara *et al.*, 1998. © 1998 by the Society for Neuroscience.

(or Anti-Social Personality Disorder as it is now termed). The term *acquired* sociopathy is used to refer to those individuals who did not exhibit such symptoms prior to their brain injury. It is diagnosed by behavior such as: a failure to conform to social norms; irritability and aggressiveness; impulsivity or failure to plan ahead; and having shallow or seemingly nonexistent feelings. This is linked to poor executive control of social and emotional information, rather than lack of knowledge of conventional social rules (Saver and Damasio, 1991).

A somewhat different explanation of the results from the Iowa Gambling Task is that it reflects a failure of reversal learning (Maia and McClelland, 2004). This is because cards from bad decks A and B are rewarded with $100 dollars on the first turn, and cards from the good decks C and D are rewarded with only $50. Thus, patients must have to learn to avoid the previously advantageous decks, A and B. If there is initially no larger reward on the first trial of the bad decks, then patients with ventromedial frontal lesions perform normally (Fellows & Farah, 2003). Other studies have shown a link between failure on reversal learning and poor regulation of social behavior (Hornak *et al.*, 2004).

Finally, studies of **delay discounting** (or **temporal discounting**) also point to a clear difference between the lateral and orbital PFC. Delay discounting refers to the fact that future rewards are valued less than equivalent current rewards (e.g. $100 now has a higher subjective value than $100 next year). Tasks of delay discounting require decisions to be made whether to choose reward X at time 1 or reward Y at time 2. In the real world, one is faced with decisions such as whether to go on holiday this year or invest the money for a better holiday in the future or to spend money now or invest in a pension scheme. Recall that patients with orbitofrontal lesions fail to plan ahead and exhibit impulsive behavior by opting for immediate rewards. McClure *et al.* (2004a) argued, from the results of an fMRI study of normal participants, that there are two different mechanisms for delay discounting, depending on whether an immediate reward was an option (i.e. a reward now compared with at some future time) or not (i.e. different rewards at two future points in time). Whereas the former was associated with activation in the medial orbitofrontal cortex and reward circuitry (e.g. nucleus accumbens), the latter was more associated with lateral prefrontal and parietal regions (the nonaffective/cold executive system). The same pattern is found when the rewards are food-related and the time intervals are shorter (McClure *et al.*, 2007).

## The multiple-demand network

The evidence above suggests that executive functions are organized into at least two broad divisions: those requiring control or evaluation of affectively loaded stimuli (requiring orbitofrontal and ventromedial cortex) and those requiring control or evaluation of nonaffective stimuli (requiring lateral PFC). However, are there further sub-divisions of organization within the lateral PFC itself? In this section, one theory is considered (the Multiple-Demand Network) that provides a generally negative answer to this question. In subsequent sections, alternative viewpoints are elaborated.

The **multiple-demand network** refers to a set of brain regions predominantly in the prefrontal cortex that are activated in fMRI studies by a wide set of tasks involving cognitive control and also by tasks in general relative to a resting baseline (Duncan, 2010). The network is identified by meta-analysis of large numbers of fMRI studies (Duncan & Owen, 2000). This network includes regions

## NEUROECONOMICS

The relatively new field of **neuroeconomics** uses neuroscientific methods and theories to account for economic decision making (for a review see, Loewenstein et al., 2008). The term "economic" can be construed in the broadest sense as referring not only to financial decisions (e.g. whether to spend, save or invest) but to other kinds of decisions that require allocation of a scarce resource (e.g. time) or an assignment of "value." Whereas much of theoretical economics describes how people should make decisions to achieve maximum benefits, the psychology of economics (and neuroeconomics) is concerned with how people actually do make decisions. For example, most people do not purchase clothing for purely utilitarian reasons (i.e. to keep warm) but for other reasons, including

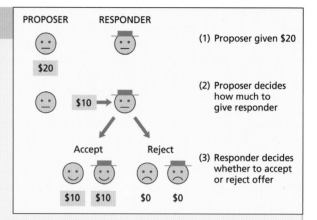

Sanfey et al. (2003) studied the Ultimatum Game using fMRI, in which participants acted as responders and received either fair or unfair offers. Activity in a part of the brain that is linked with emotional processes (the insula) reliably predicts whether a player will reject an unfair offer. However, applying TMS over the right lateral prefrontal cortex increases the probability of accepting unfair offers (Knoch et al., 2006). This is consistent with a biasing control signal (from the prefrontal cortex) and a bottom-up emotional response competing for selection.

the need to advertise one's social status or personality, or, in some cases, because one simply enjoys the act of shopping (retail therapy). That is, the concept of value may have more to do with the perceived rewards to a given individual than the actual functional reward that may ultimately be obtained.

There is also a strong social element as to how economic decisions are made. For example, consider the financial sharing game termed the **ultimatum game** (Guth et al., 1982). This involves two players: a proposer and a responder. The proposer is given a sum of money (e.g. $20) and must decide how much to give to the responder (between $1 and $20). The responder must then decide whether to accept the offer (and the offer is then split) or reject the offer (both players leave with nothing). From a purely financial point of view, in a one-trial game, the optimal decision of the proposer is to give the minimum ($1) and the optimal decision of the responder is to accept whatever is given (because something is always better than nothing). In reality, the responder typically rejects offers that are less than 20 percent of the pot, because they perceive the offer as unfair and wish to punish the proposer. Another way of thinking about it is that they are weighing up two values: a purely monetary value pitted against a social value of fairness.

Much of the emerging field of neuroeconomics is concerned with the interaction between one's gut reactions (intuition or emotion) and one's goals and beliefs. For example, one's brand loyalty (e.g. to Pepsi versus Coke) may sometimes be at odds with one's true taste preferences when they are assessed blind. Whereas the dorsolateral prefrontal cortex is associated with people's beliefs about which of two brands they are tasting (Pepsi or Coke), the orbitofrontal cortex is associated with their actual ratings of how nice each drink is (McClure et al., 2004b).

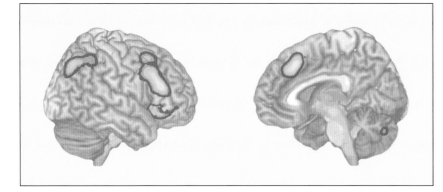

The multiple-demand network is identified, primarily, from meta-analyses of fMRI studies that show that common regions of the lateral prefrontal cortex (together with regions in parietal lobe and anterior cingulate) are activated by a wide variety of tasks requiring some form of nonautomatic behavior.

From Duncan, 2010.

of the lateral PFC (left and right) and the anterior cingulate cortex. It also includes regions of the parietal lobes, notably around the intra-parietal sulcus (IPS). However, it excludes the orbitofrontal cortex (and related ventromedial PFC) and generally excludes the anterior-most portion of the PFC (termed the frontal poles or BA10).

According to Duncan (2010), cognitive control involves several elements: focusing on the relevant features of the sub-task; as sub-tasks are completed the new elements must be focused upon and old ones discarded; and selected results must be passed from one sub-task to another. Evidence from single-cell recordings in the primate lateral PFC sheds some light as to how this is achieved. These neurons respond primarily to the rules of the task rather than the specific stimulus or response (Asaad *et al.*, 1998, 2000). For example, they may respond to a conjunction of a stimulus and response (e.g. "look left when I see object A"), but not to the same stimulus out of context ("see object A") or the same response in a different context (e.g. "look left when I see object B"). Thus, the coding of the task-relevant features is highly flexible. During performance of the task itself, the coding is also highly focused. In tasks such as these, up to 50 percent of all cells recorded in lateral prefrontal cortex discriminated targets from non-targets but, by contrast, many fewer cells made the task-irrelevant discriminations between one non-target and another (Everling *et al.*, 2002). However, when the task involves multiple sub-tasks then different sub-populations of neurons with the lateral PFC tend to separately code for different attributes of the sub-tasks (Sigala *et al.*, 2008).

One claim is that the multiple-demand network is related specifically to **fluid intelligence** (Duncan, 2010; Woolgar *et al.*, 2010). Fluid intelligence relates to problem-solving ability, and is tested using measures such as Raven's matrices (Raven, 1960). This test involves attending to multiple-features of a problem: in the example printed here, the solution involves processing orientation, size and shape as three different sub-tasks. This can be contrasted with **crystallized intelligence** (Cattell, 1971) which relies heavily on prior expertise and knowledge and is assessed by measures of IQ such as the WAIS (Wechsler Adult Intelligence

Patients with frontal lobe damage are impaired on tests of "fluid intelligence" such as this.

Reprinted from Duncan et al., 1995. © 1995, with permission from Elsevier.

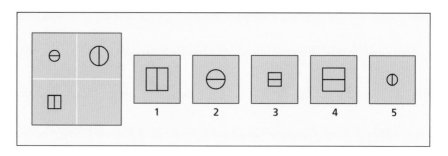

Scale; Wechsler, 1981). The latter measures mental arithmetic, factual knowledge, speed of processing, and so on. Meta-analyses of functional imaging tests of fluid intelligence produce a very similar pattern to that of the multiple-demand network (Jung & Haier, 2007).

Patients with lesions of prefrontal cortex fare no worse on tests such as the WAIS relative to other brain-damaged controls (Warrington & James, 1986). By contrast, patients with lesions to the prefrontal cortex who score well on the WAIS IQ (scores between 125–130 with a scale average of 100) score 22–38 points lower on measures of fluid intelligence (Duncan et al., 1995). Moreover, performance on standard tests of executive function by patients with PFC lesions correlates strongly with fluid intelligence measures and with each other (Roca et al., 2010).

Claims such as these (i.e. that all tests of executive function tap the same network) have lead some researchers to characterize the multiple-demand network as an undifferentiated entity. However, some relative degree of specialization of function within the network is tentatively acknowledged (Hampshire et al., 2011) but without recourse to any modularization of different executive components. Moreover, regions normally regarded as outside of the network (e.g. the frontal poles) are acknowledged to have a qualitatively different functional role (Roca et al., 2010).

## A posterior to anterior organization?

Until recently, little was known about the function of the anterior-most part of the frontal lobes (also called rostral prefrontal cortex or the frontal pole). However, a number of recent studies and reviews have suggested that the region is specifically involved when multiple tasks need to be coordinated (Burgess, 2000; Christoff et al., 2001; Koechlin et al., 1999a; Ramnani & Owen, 2004). Koechlin et al. (1999a) performed an fMRI experiment in which participants were required to hold in mind a main goal while concurrently performing sub-goals. Neither holding in mind a goal by itself (working memory) nor switching between alternate goals was associated with activity in this region. Only when these two elements were combined was activity found in this region. The fact that some patients with frontal lesions are specifically impaired on multi-tasking, but not the component tasks and not other measures of executive function (e.g. the Wisconsin Card Sort, which involves task-switching but not multi-tasking) supports the view that there is a separate neuroanatomical substrate for this (Burgess et al., 2000). This has led to the proposal that there is a hierarchical organization of executive functions such that posterior parts of the prefrontal cortex (including what Duncan refers to as the Multiple-Demand-Network) implements tasks with a single goal including those requiring switching to different sub-tasks, but that the anterior most PFC implements multiple tasks simultaneously.

Koechlin and Summerfield (2007) propose a specific model along these lines consisting of a hierarchy that runs from the premotor cortex (posteriorly) to the frontal poles (anteriorly). The premotor cortex is not anatomically part of the PFC but is known to implement simple stimulus-response mappings such as "press the left button when you see red, and right for green" (Passingham, 1988). However, adding contextual information (e.g. "perform consonant/vowel discrimination for red letters and UPPER/lower case discrimination for green letters") cannot be performed automatically, at least not without training, and does require cognitive control. Moreover, switching the instructions on a block-by-block basis (e.g. so that red becomes the UPPER/low task and green the consonant/vowel task) requires what Koechlin and Summerfield (2007) term episodic control, i.e. knowing which context to apply at a given moment in time. The highest level in their model, termed "branching control," involves holding in mind pending tasks while carrying out an ongoing task (i.e. multi-tasking). In an fMRI study, Koechlin *et al.* (2003) compared the first three types of situation (sensorimotor rules, contextual rules, episodic rules) using the letter and color stimuli described above. Implementing the sensorimotor rules (common to all tasks) invoked the premotor cortex, whereas the presence of contextual rules invoked more anterior activity, and the presence of episodic rules was more anterior still.

Badre and D'Esposito (2009) present a related view of the organization of the lateral PFC to Koechlin and Summerfield (2007). One of the key differences in their formulation is that they propose two different posterior to anterior gradients in the lateral PFC: one that is ventrally based and one that is dorsally based. This is consistent with several other prominent views that allocate different functions to dorsal and ventral regions of the lateral PFC (e.g. Fletcher & Henson, 2001; Petrides, 2000). In their model, the dorsal posterior-anterior gradient is linked specifically to action planning (perhaps by virtue of connectivity to the parietal lobes), whereas the ventral posterior-anterior gradient is linked to, among others, language and objects (perhaps by virtue of connectivity to the temporal lobes). To give a concrete example from the literature, one study found a posterior-anterior gradient in the ventral part of the lateral PFC when participants were asked to make semantic decisions about objects such as "Is the object bigger than a 13-inch box?" or "Is the object made of an organic substance?" (Race *et al.*, 2009). The clever aspect of the study design is that they measured how the BOLD signal was affected when different aspects of the experiment were repeated: either by repeating the same semantic item (irrespective of task or response), the same task (e.g. size judgment), or the same manual response. This led to a gradient of activity (anterior-most for semantic repetition, posterior-most for manual repetition) running along the ventral portion of the lateral PFC.

Finally, Burgess *et al.* (2007) have proposed a theory concerning the functions of the frontal pole region (BA 10) but without an assumption of a gradient/ hierarchy across the lateral PFC. They suggest that its specific role is to act as a "gateway" between stimulus-driven cognition (e.g. maintaining focus on a task involving sensorimotor demands) versus internal thoughts (thinking "in one's head"). Multi-tasking involves maintaining internal cognitions (i.e. future intentions) while engaging with an external task. Moreover, they propose that, whereas the lateral surface of this region is involved in orienting to external stimuli/tasks, the medial surface of this region is involved in orienting to internal

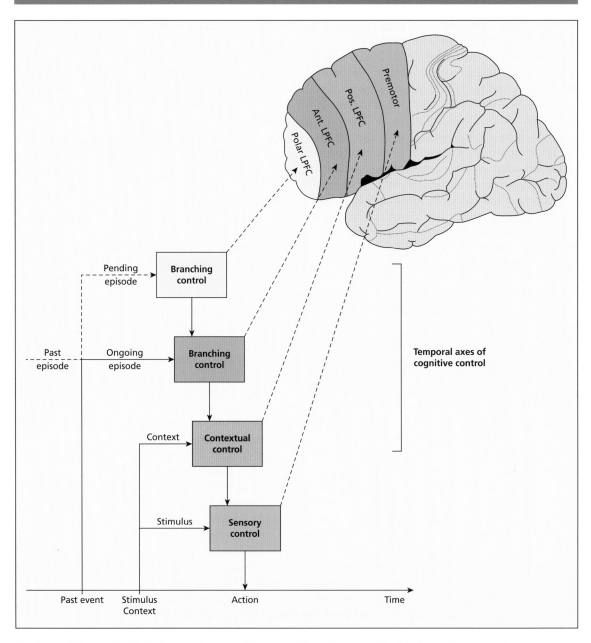

Koechlin and Summerfield (2007) argue for a posterior–anterior hierarchy of executive functions with more posterior regions involved in implementing simple stimulus–response mappings (e.g. "red stimulus → left button press"), and more anterior regions involved in more complex mappings (e.g. "red stimulus → left button press, but only if the stimulus is also a vowel").
From Koechlin & Summerfield, 2007.

cognitions. This connects their theory to a much wider literature showing that the medial anterior PFC region tends to be activated in tasks involving social cognition (e.g. thinking about thoughts; Amodio & Frith, 2006) and, unlike the lateral prefrontal cortex, the medial frontal poles tends to be more active during rest than when engaged in tasks (Buckner *et al.*, 2008). It is unclear what "rest" consists of, in cognitive terms, but it is reasonable to assume that it generally consists of some kind of "inner thought" rather than absence of cognition (Morcom & Fletcher, 2007). Patients with lesions limited to the frontal poles are impaired on tasks of multi-tasking and on tasks of social cognition (theory-of-mind, understanding *Faux pas*) but perform well on many other tests of executive function (Roca *et al.*, 2010; Roca *et al.*, 2011).

## Hemispheric differences

Functional differences between the left and right lateral PFC are more controversial than the other principles of organization discussed thus far. For instance, they tend not to be found in single-cell recordings from the monkey PFC (Miller & Cohen, 2001), but this may not be surprising since humans are known to possess far more lateralization of higher cognitive functions than other primates. It is also less apparent in the functional imaging data of humans (Duncan & Owen, 2000). Perhaps the most convincing evidence comes from neuropsychological investigations of lesions to the PFC which has revealed reliable functional differences (Stuss & Alexander, 2007). Even here, it is to be noted, that the dissociations tend to be relative rather than absolute: i.e. patients with left and right PFC lesions differ with respect to each other, but both groups are impaired relative to controls. That is, "classical" dissociations tend not to be observed (to use the terminology of Shallice, 1988). This may also explain why the functional imaging data is not so clear-cut in this regard; i.e. both hemispheres appear active, and the statistical difference in activation between hemispheres is not directly assessed. Nor is it clear whether hemispheric differences in activation relate to actual differences in behavior from fMRI studies (e.g. does activity reflect working harder or contributing more?).

One of the main models regarding hemispheric specializations of executive function originates from Stuss and colleagues (Stuss *et al.*, 1995). In their model, the *left* lateral PFC is considered relatively specialized for task-setting, whereas the *right* lateral PFC is relatively specialized for task **monitoring**. Task-setting will tend to be maximized when the task itself is open-ended (e.g. problem solving) as opposed to situations in which explicit instructions are given as to how the task is to be performed. As noted previously, these problem-solving tasks tend to be more impaired after damage to the left frontal lobe irrespective of whether the stimuli are verbal (e.g. the FAS test; Stuss *et al.*, 1998) or visuo-spatial (e.g. the Tower-of-London; Shallice, 1982). Task monitoring is linked to the notion of **sustained attention** and involves keeping "on task" and maintaining the currently relevant rules. They associate a rather different functional role ("energization") to medial regions of the frontal lobes, including both the anterior cingulated and pre-SMA region. The revised version of the SAS model contains many modular-like components of executive function but also groups these into different stages including a task-setting stage for creating new schemas (which they link to the left lateral PFC) and monitoring the outcomes after schema implementation (which is linked to the right lateral PFC) (Shallice & Burgess, 1996; Shallice, 2002).

The Wisconsin Card Sorting Test is impaired after lesions of both the left and right lateral PFC relative to controls (Stuss *et al.*, 2000). However, a left-right hemispheric dissociation is found for different versions of administering it. In the standard version, the participant is given no information about the three rules or when they will change. Patients with left lateral PFC damage perform worse than

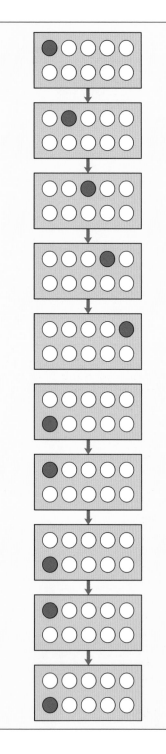

right PFC damage on this version. In a modified version, the patient is told of the rules, is given a starting rule (sort by color) and is told when the rules will change (after every 10 trials). In this version, patients with right lateral PFC lesions fare worse than their left hemispheric counterparts. In the standard/open-ended version, the performance limitations may stem primarily from task-setting (taxing the left hemisphere more), whereas in the more constrained version performance limitations may come from monitoring the current rule (taxing the right hemisphere more).

Patients with both left and right prefrontal lesions are impaired at task switching but for different reasons (Aron *et al.*, 2004a; Mayr *et al.*, 2006). In the study of Aron *et al.* (2004a) patients with left lateral PFC damage tended to show much longer switch costs (consistent with a general impairment in task-setting), but patients with right lateral PFC damage tended to be particularly error-prone, specifically in the tendency to perseverate to the previous task-set (interpreted by the authors as a failure of response inhibition but potentially explicable in terms of failed monitoring).

Reverberi *et al.* (2005) devised a test of rule induction that appears to be sensitive to the laterality of prefrontal lesions. Patients are shown a sequence of cards containing ten numbered circles. One of the circles is colored blue. Their task is to decide which of the next circles will be colored in. The rules can change unexpectedly, and the rules themselves are more abstract than in the Wisconsin Card Sorting Test. Patients with left lateral prefrontal lesions were impaired at inducing the rules, and that this difficulty was found irrespective of whether they had a working memory impairment (as assessed by their memory of successive spatial positions). They suggest that the difficulty lies in setting up task schemas. In a second phase of the experiment, the sequence of blue circles was interspersed with sequences of red circles that followed a different rule. When red circles appeared, the task was simply to press that circle. When the blue circles appeared, the task was to predict the next in the sequence. Patients with right lateral pre-frontal lesions (and those with anterior cingulate lesions) failed to revert back to the blue rule after the interfering red sequence, despite being instructed to do so. Reverberi *et al.* interpreted this as a failure to check or monitor their responses, consistent with a right frontal involvement in this function.

In a review of the literature, Frith (2000) argues that the role of the left dorso-lateral PFC is in "sculpting the response space." He suggests that the region is responsible for highlighting the range of possible responses and for suppressing inappropriate responses. This is related to the concept of task-setting. It suggests that this region will be recruited more when the task parameters are not strongly constrained (e.g. when there is a large range of stimulus-response mappings to choose from). For instance, this region is activated more when

Patients are shown a sequence of cards containing ten numbered circles. One of the circles is colored blue. Their task is to decide which of the next circles will be colored in. The rules can change unexpectedly. In this example, the rule shifts from +1 to alternation (between circles 1 and 6).

participants have to choose which finger to move relative to when they are told which finger to move, and also when they are asked to generate a word from a letter cue (e.g. "F") relative to simple repetition of a word (Frith *et al.*, 1991). The region is also active when participants are free to select *when* to make a response (Jahanshahi *et al.*, 1995). Generating random sequences (e.g. of digits) is a cognitively demanding task that involves setting up and selecting "freely" from a pool of potential responses. There is a tendency, particularly under time pressure, for randomness to break down and participants start generating familiar sequences from memory, such as consecutive runs (4, 5, 6; X, Y, Z) or stored knowledge (e.g. acronyms, "B, B, C"; telephone numbers). Repetitive TMS over the left, but not right, DLPFC results in less random and more familiar sequences (Jahanshahi *et al.*, 1998). Another study found that repetitive TMS over left DLPFC impairs "free choice" even in tasks with no working memory demands (Hadland *et al.*, 2001). The previous responses were displayed on a monitor so they need not be held in mind.

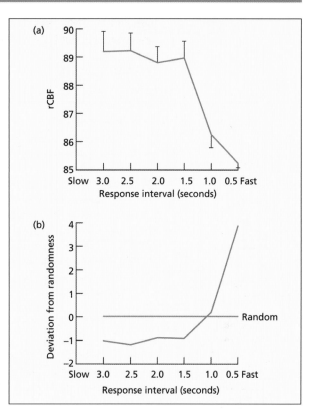

Activity in the left dorsolateral prefrontal cortex (a) is associated with ability to generate random sequences (b). When responses are required at a fast rate, the activity decreases and the responses start to deviate substantially from randomness.

Reprinted from Jahanshahi *et al.*, 2000. © 2000 with permission from Elsevier.

Monitoring is the process of relating information currently held in mind back to the task requirements. It is also a checking mechanism to ascertain whether retrieved or perceived information is valid. The region may be important both for monitoring the content of internally held information, such as monitoring the content of episodic or working memory (Habib *et al.*, 2003), as well as for monitoring the content of externally presented information, as in tasks of sustained attention (Kanwisher & Wojciulik, 2000). Cabeza *et al.* (2003) directly compared fMRI activity in a memory retrieval task (word recognition) with a non-memory task of sustained attention (did the stimulus blip once, twice or never during a 12-sec presentation). The study found common regions of right DLPFC activity between the two tasks. As such, it appears as if the region is related more to monitoring and attending than to memory or perception per se.

A study comparing brain-damage to the right and left lateral PFC is also consistent with a greater role of the right PFC in monitoring. Stuss *et al.* (2005) administered relatively simple stimulus-response paradigms (e.g. press left hand for "A" and right hand for other letters), but varied the time interval between the end of the trial (i.e. after making a response) and the start of the next one (i.e. when the next letter is shown). For healthy controls, and indeed patients with left lateral PFC lesions, having a longer interval results in a subsequently *faster* response, because participants prepare themselves for the stimulus onset. For the patients with right lateral PFC lesions, the opposite was true: a longer wait for the onset of a stimulus resulted in *slower* responding, presumably because they had become more disengaged from the task during the waiting period. In healthy participants, TMS over the right, but not left, prefrontal cortex of neurotypical people reduces this speeding-up effect relating to longer preparatory times (Vallesi et al., 2007).

An alternative view of the function of the right (inferior) lateral prefrontal cortex is that it functionally specialized for response inhibition (Aron et al., 2004a). This view emerges from studies on paradigms such as Go/No-Go which are shown to activate the right more than left in healthy participants (on No-Go trials) and be particularly disrupted by lesions to the right lateral PFC (Aron et al., 2003). The inhibition explanation is not straightforward to separate from the monitoring account as a failure to monitor adequately would tend to lead to the automatic "go" response on No-Go trials. One fMRI study investigated the functional connectivity of brain regions during the processing of No-Go signals and found that the right lateral PFC was involved in the *detection* of the No-Go signal (i.e. consistent with the monitoring account) which then influenced the pre-SMA area (Duann et al., 2009). The pre-SMA area is, according to Duann et al. (2009), directly implicated in response inhibition of the motor program via the basal ganglia circuitry.

## Evaluation

Although contemporary models of executive function retain their earlier character (i.e. flexibly implement task rules, controlling nonautomatic responses) far more is now known about how (and where) they are implemented in the prefrontal cortex. The notion of a general workspace that is essentially undifferentiated in character is not supported by the weight of evidence. Models along these lines would be the earlier versions of the SAS model (Norman & Shallice, 1986) and the models of Miller and Cohen (2001) and Goldman-Rakic (1996). The Multiple Demand Network (Duncan, 2010) is also largely an undifferentiated workspace, but it is certainly not to be considered synonymous with the entire prefrontal cortex (but rather the mid-lateral regions and certain parietal regions). Although we could conceptualize, from first principles, that a diverse range of tasks such as the Stroop, multi-tasking, and reversal learning all require the same kind of control mechanism (e.g. flexibly associating stimuli and responses) the evidence suggests that the brain treats tasks such as these rather differently. Needless to say, the most extreme alternative viewpoint—i.e. that each task has its own dedicated mechanisms—is untenable, because this is incompatible with the behavioral flexibility that needs to be explained in the first place.

In the sections above several different levels of organization are considered. The distinction between cognitive versus affective control is well-supported empirically and suggests a division according to the type of information processed. There is some evidence of a posterior-anterior difference in prefrontal functioning that depends on whether single or multiple tasks are being simultaneously performed (and possibly finer gradients within that). The evidence for hemispheric differences in the lateral PFC is rather different in character from the other principles of organization in that claims have been made about the type of operation performed (left = task-setting; right = task-monitoring) rather than the type of information processed. The next section will consider in more detail another region, not strictly part of the prefrontal cortex, but strongly connected to it and implicated in other aspects of executive function: namely the anterior cingulate cortex.

# THE ROLE OF THE ANTERIOR CINGULATE IN EXECUTIVE FUNCTIONS

KEY TERM

**Error-related negativity**
An event-related potential component in EEG that can be detected at the scalp when an error is made.

Historically, the anterior cingulate cortex has been classified as belonging to the limbic lobe rather than the frontal lobes. However, a more detailed understanding of its neural connectivity has suggested that it may function as an interface between limbic and frontal regions. In their review, Bush *et al.* (2000) distinguish between two functionally different regions of the anterior cingulate. A more dorsal region is termed the "cognitive division" and may be related to executive functions. It has strong interconnections with the DLPFC. This may explain why these regions tend to be activated together in functional imaging studies. It also has connections with parietal, premotor, and supplementary motor areas. A more rostral "affective division" is connected with limbic and orbitofrontal regions. The remainder of this section will focus on the cognitive/executive region of the anterior cingulate, and further use of the term "anterior cingulate" in this chapter will be used to refer to this region unless stated otherwise.

One postulated role of the anterior cingulate in executive functions is in the detection of errors (Carter *et al.*, 1998). In human reaction time experiments, the trial immediately after an error (error + 1) tends to be slower and more accurate than after a correct trial (correct + 1) (Rabbitt, 1966). This implies the existence of some cognitive mechanism that monitors for errors and recalibrates task performance accordingly (e.g. slowing down to ensure greater accuracy). In macaque monkeys with anterior cingulate lesions, errors are more likely on "error + 1" trials than "correct + 1" trials (Rushworth *et al.*, 2003). This suggests that no such adjustment is made following errorful behavior, and errors are more likely to follow errors. Moreover, when monkeys (Gemba *et al.*, 1986) and humans (Dehaene *et al.*, 1994) make errors an error potential can be detected at the scalp that appears to have its origins in the anterior cingulate. This response is called an **error-related negativity** and its onset is simultaneous with the error being made and peaks around 100 ms after the response (Gehring *et al.*, 1993). The studies cited above are ambiguous as to whether the anterior cingulate is important just for the detection of the error, or also for the subsequent compensatory behavior. Event-related fMRI shows anterior cingulate activity on the error trial, with greater activity on the error + 1 trial in the lateral prefrontal cortex associated with behavioral adjustment (Kerns *et al.*, 2004). This suggests that the anterior cingulate's role is limited to error detection and not compensation, and the lateral prefrontal cortex is responsible for adjusting ongoing behavior.

A related role for the anterior cingulate may be in evaluating response conflict. The classic example of response conflict is provided by the Stroop test. Patients with lesions in this region perform poorly on the task (Alexander *et al.*, 2007). In fMRI of healthy participants, a comparison of incongruent trials (with high response conflict) relative to congruent trials is linked to

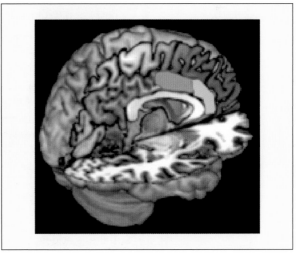

The anterior cingulate cortex lies above the corpus callosum on the medial surface of each hemisphere. It has been suggested that there are two broad divisions: a dorsal region implicated in executive functions (blue) and a ventral region implicated in emotional processing (green).

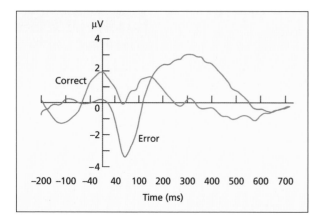

Error-related negativity is found at EEG scalp recordings following production of an incorrect response.

activity in the anterior cingulate (Carter *et al.*, 2000). This occurs in the absence of errors. As such, one more general account of anterior cingulate functioning is that it generates a conflict signal both in situations of likely error as well as after an actual error (e.g., van Veen & Carter, 2002).

An alternative way of conceptualising the role of the anterior cingulate is that it is involved in motivation (Kouneiher *et al.*, 2009) or energization (Stuss & Alexander, 2007). Errors are motivationally salient events (that people work to avoid) as are rewards and punishments. The anterior cingulate also responds to the latter (e.g. monetary rewards or losses) even when there is no conflict between a habitual and nonhabitual response (Blair *et al.*, 2006). In the fMRI study of Kouneiher *et al.* (2009), participants performed a task-switching study involving different monetary incentives: some blocks had a high incentive (more money for being correct) and others a lower incentive. Within these blocks, there were either regular trials or "bonus trials" in which an even higher payoff could be obtained. High-incentive blocks were linked to greater sustained activity of the anterior cingulate. By contrast, performance on bonus trials was linked to pre-SMA activity.

## SUMMARY AND KEY POINTS OF THE CHAPTER

- Executive functions are needed to optimize performance when: several cognitive processes need to be coordinated; a situation is novel or difficult; a situation does not require an automatic response (troubleshooting, problem solving). The role of executive functions is typically described as "supervisory" or "controlling."
- Functional imaging studies and studies of brain-damaged patients point to a key role of the prefrontal cortex in executive functions. Patients with lesions here may have difficulties in problem solving, overcoming habitual responses, multi-tasking, and so on.
- The orbitofrontal and ventromedial prefrontal cortex has strong connections with regions involved in processing emotions; whereas the lateral (and dorsal medial) surfaces have strong connections to sensory and motor regions. Damaging these regions affects the ability to behave flexibly in response to changes in emotional value (orbital PFC) or changes in the task-relevant stimulus features (lateral PFC).
- There is evidence of a posterior-to-anterior organization of executive functions with the anterior most region (frontal pole) implicated in multi-tasking.
- In humans, there is a degree of relative specialization of function between the left and right lateral prefrontal cortex: with the left more

implicated in task-setting, and the right more implicated in task-monitoring.

- The dorsal anterior cingulate appears to be important for detecting errors and detecting response conflict, although lateral prefrontal regions may be needed to act on this information and modify behavior.

Visit the companion website at www. psypress/cw/ward for:

- References to key papers and readings
- Video lectures and interviews on key topics with several leading experts and author Jamie Ward, and a documentary discussing Phineas Gage and the prefrontal cortex
- Multiple choice questions and interactive flashcards to test your knowledge
- Downloadable glossary

## EXAMPLE ESSAY QUESTIONS

- Can executive functions be fractionated?
- What are the problems faced by clinical tests aimed at detecting deficits in executive function?
- Is there an executive component to working memory? What is the evidence for it? (Refer also to Chapter 9.)
- Do the functions of the left prefrontal lobe differ from the right prefrontal lobe?
- How do we switch from one task to another?

## RECOMMENDED FURTHER READING

- Goldberg, E. (2001). *The executive brain: Frontal lobes and the civilised mind*. Oxford, UK: Oxford University Press. A good place to start for the uninitiated.
- Miller, E. K. & Cohen, J. D. (2001). An integrative theory of prefrontal cortex function. *Annual Review of Neuroscience, 24*, 167–202. A good overview of the neuroscientific evidence.
- Monsell, S. & Driver, J. (2000). *Control of cognitive processes: Attention and performance*, XVIII. Cambridge, MA: MIT Press. A useful collection of papers at a more advanced level.
- Stuss, D. T. & Knight, R. T. (2002). *Principles of frontal lobe function*. Oxford, UK: Oxford University Press. A useful collection of papers at a more advanced level.

# CHAPTER 15

# The social and emotional brain

## CONTENTS

**Emotions** act as internal signposts: they guide us how to behave, what to avoid, and what to seek out. Emotions are one way of tagging certain stimuli to ensure that they receive priority treatment and are responded to appropriately. Emotions are linked to stimuli and situations in which there is an inherent survival value: for instance, fear may be linked to threatening stimuli that require vigilance or withdrawal; disgust may be linked to stimuli relating to contamination; anger may be linked to situations that threaten territory and status; and so on. Although some stimuli may be naturally rewarding (e.g. food, sex) or punishing (e.g. pain), we can learn to assign emotional states to a wide range of novel stimuli such as pop music and fashions, giving rise to extremes from phobias to fetishes. There is an almost unlimited flexibility in the range of stimuli that can be linked to emotions even though they may ultimately tap into a narrower repertoire of emotional-related responses (fight, flight, avoidance, etc.) and states (fear, anger, etc.).

Emotions also play a crucial role for guiding social behavior in most social species, including humans and primates. Group living has obvious survival advantages. There is safety in numbers and cooperation enables the sharing of limited resources. As such, it not surprising that emotions guide social decision making. This chapter gives many examples of how the emotional brain is recruited in social situations. For instance, social rejection may share neural circuitry with physical pain, and moral disgust may have something in common

**KEY TERMS**

**Emotion**
A state associated with
stimuli that are rewarding
(i.e. that one works to
obtain) or punishing (i.e.
that one works to avoid).
These stimuli often have
inherent survival value.

**Mentalizing**
The process of inferring or
attributing mental states
to others.

**Mirroring**
The process of sharing
the emotions or mental
states of others.

**Mood**
An emotional state that is
extended over time (e.g.
anxiety is a mood and
fear is an emotion).

with contamination-related disgust. Similarly, the reward circuitry of the brain is activated more if $10 is won by cooperating with another player than if the same amount is obtained without cooperation. It is as if the act of cooperating is a reward in its own right. However, we are not a slave to our emotions. We do not always act on our "gut instincts" and can engage in nonaffective cognitive control to guide behavior. Indeed, thinking about other people's intentions, desires, and beliefs via perspective taking (or **mentalizing**) is linked to a rather different brain network to that involved in emotional evaluations.

The chapter begins by considering various theories of emotion, both historical and contemporary, and then places these theories into the context of the known neuroscientific basis of emotional processing. The chapter then considers how social information is extracted from facial expressions and eye gaze. This provides an important introduction to how *perceiving* emotions (in other people) may result in a simulation of that emotional state in the perceiver (i.e. a sharing of emotion). This idea is taken further in relation to the neural mechanisms of empathy. This discussion considers the extent to which we understand others through a process of simulation of emotional, motor or bodily states (also called **mirroring**) or inferring mental states (mentalizing, also called theory-of-mind).

## THEORIES OF EMOTION

Emotions are multi-faceted in nature, and the list below captures the key characteristics. Some theories of emotion have tended to concentrate on some aspects more than others based on the assumption that some features are more core than others. It also means that there are many different ways of measuring emotion depending on whether one concentrates on their subjective nature (e.g. using questionnaires), their bodily responses (e.g. using skin conductance, or recordings of facial expression), or their behavioral consequences (e.g. pressing a lever for a reward).

## SOME CHARACTERISTICS OF EMOTIONS

- An emotion is a state associated with stimuli that are **rewarding** (i.e. that one works to obtain) or **punishing** (i.e. that one works to avoid). These stimuli often have inherent survival value.
- Emotions are transient in nature (unlike a **mood**, which is where an emotional state becomes extended over time), although the emotional status of stimuli is stored in long-term memory.
- An emotional stimulus directs attention to itself, to enable more detailed evaluation or to prompt a response.
- Emotions have a **hedonic value**, that is, they are subjectively liked or disliked.
- Emotions have a particular "feeling state" in terms of an internal bodily response (e.g. sweating, heart rate, hormone secretion).
- Emotions elicit particular external motor outcomes in the face and body, which include emotional **expressions**. These may prepare the organism (e.g. for fighting) and send signals to others (e.g. that one intends to fight).

## Darwin and Freud

Two early views of emotion came from some well-known figures in science: Charles Darwin (1809–1882) and Sigmund Freud (1856–1939). Although their approaches are very different from each other, they share the fundamental assumption that human emotions possess continuity with their animal counterparts.

In 1872, Charles Darwin published "The Expression of the Emotions in Man and Animals" (Darwin, 1872/1965). For much of this work Darwin was concerned with documenting the outward manifestations of emotions—**expressions**—in which animals produce facial and bodily gestures that characterize a particular emotion such as fear, anger, or happiness. Darwin noted how many expressions are conserved across species; anger involves a direct gaze with mouth opened and teeth visible, and so on. He claimed that such expressions are innate "that is, have not been learnt by the individual." Moreover, such expressions enable one animal to interpret the emotional state of another animal; for example, whether an animal is likely to attack, or is likely to welcome a sexual advance. Darwin's contribution was to provide preliminary evidence as to how emotions may be conserved across species. His reliance on expressions resonates with some contemporary approaches, such as Ekman's attempts to define "basic" emotions from cross-cultural comparisons of facial expressions (Ekman *et al.*, 1972). More recent research has elucidated the functional origins of some of these expressions. For instance, a posed fear expression increases the visual field and nasal volume and leads to faster eye movements (adaptive for detecting danger), whereas a disgust expression has an opposite effective (adaptive for avoiding contaminants) (Susskind *et al.*, 2008).

For Freud, our minds could be divided into three different kinds of mechanisms: the id, the ego, and the super-ego (e.g. Freud, 1920/2010). The id was concerned with representing our "primitive" urges that connect us to nonhuman ancestry including our basic emotional needs for sex, food, warmth, and so on. The id was concerned with unconscious motivations, but these ideas would sometimes be accessible via the ego (the conscious mind), and perhaps conflict with our super-ego (our cultural norms and our aspirations). Freud's basic idea that emotions are an unconscious bias on our behavior is very much relevant to current thinking (Tamietto & De Gelder, 2010). Freud's other enduring influence is the notion that many psychiatric disorders (such as anxiety) can be understood

**KEY TERM**

**Expression**
External motor outcomes in the face and body associated with emotional states.

Darwin argued that many emotional expressions have been conserved by evolution.
From Ward, 2012, p. 73.

as emotional disturbances (Le Doux, 1996). Although some of the general approach is recognizable today, the specific details of Freud's theory no longer have contemporary currency (e.g. ideas relating to childhood sexual fantasies).

## James-Lange and Cannon-Bard

According to the **James–Lange theory** of emotion, it is the self-perception of bodily changes that produces emotional experience (James, 1884). Thus, changes in bodily state occur before the emotional experience rather than the other way around. We feel sad because we cry, rather than we cry because we feel sad. This perspective seems somewhat radical compared with the contemporary point of view. For instance, it raises the question of what type of processing leads to the change in bodily states and whether this early process could itself be construed as a part of the emotion.

Changes in the body are mediated by the autonomic nervous system (ANS), a set of nerves located in the body that controls activity of the internal organs (the soma). There is good empirical evidence to suggest that changes in bodily states, in themselves, are not sufficient to produce an emotion. Schacter and Singer (1962) injected participants with epinephrine (also termed adrenaline), a drug that induces autonomic changes such as to heart rate. They found that the presence of the drug by itself did not lead to self-reported experiences of emotion, contrary to the James–Lange theory. However, in the presence of an appropriate cognitive setting (e.g. an angry or happy man enters the room), the participants did self-report an emotion. A cognitive setting, without epinephrine, produced less intense emotional ratings. This study suggests that bodily experiences do not create emotions (contrary to James–Lange), but they can enhance conscious emotional experiences.

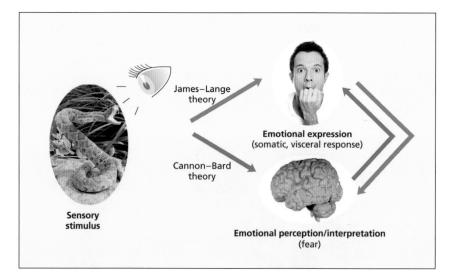

According to the James–Lange theory, bodily reactions occur first and emotional processing occurs after (as the perception/interpretation of those reactions). According to the Cannon–Bard theory, the emotional perception/interpretation occurs first and the bodily reaction occurs after.

From Ward, 2012, p. 75.

There are several contemporary theories that bear similarity to the James-Lange theory, most notably Damasio's (1994) suggestion that bodily responses linked to emotions guide decision making. This is the Somatic Marker Hypothesis discussed in more detail in Chapter 14. Although James-Lange theory states that these bodily responses must be consciously perceived, Damasio (1994) takes the different view that they are unconscious modifiers of behavior.

The **Cannon-Bard theory** of emotions that emerged in the 1920s argued that bodily feedback could not account for the differences between the emotions (Cannon, 1927). According to this view, the emotions could be accounted for solely within the brain and that bodily responses occur *after* the emotion itself. The Cannon-Bard theory was inspired by neurobiology. Earlier research had noted that animals still exhibit emotional expressions (e.g. of rage) after removal of the cortex. This was considered surprising given that it was known that cortical motor regions are needed to initiate most other movements (Fritsch & Hitzig, 1870). In a series of lesion studies, Cannon and Bard concluded that the hypothalamus is the centerpiece of emotions. They believed that the hypothalamus received and evaluated sensory inputs in terms of emotional content, and then sent signals to the autonomic system (to induce the bodily feelings discussed by James) and to the cortex (giving rise to conscious experiences of emotion).

## Papez circuit and the limbic brain

Papez (1937) drew upon the work of Cannon-Bard in arguing that the hypothalamus was a key part of emotional processing, but extended this into a circuit of other regions that included the regions of the cingulate cortex, hippocampus, hypothalamus and anterior nucleus of the thalamus. Papez argued that the feeling of emotions originated in the sub-cortical **Papez circuit** which was hypothesized to be involved in bodily regulation. A second circuit, involving the cortex, was assumed to involve a deliberative analysis that retrieved memory associations about the stimulus. The work of MacLean (1949) extended this idea to incorporate regions such as the amygdala and orbitofrontal cortex, which he termed the "Limbic Brain." The different regions were hypothesized to work together to produce an integrated "emotional brain."

There are a number of reasons why these earlier neurobiological views are no longer endorsed by contemporary cognitive neuroscience. First, some of the key regions of the Papez circuit can no longer be considered to carry out functions that relate primarily to the emotions. For example, the role of the hippocampus in memory was not appreciated until the 1950s (Scoville & Milner, 1957), and the hypothalamus is not a central nexus of emotions although it does regulate bodily homeostasis. Second, contemporary research places greater emphasis on different types of emotion (e.g. fear versus disgust) having different neural substrates.

## Contemporary views of emotion: categories, dimensions, and appraisals

The dominant alternative view to that of an undifferentiated "limbic brain" in the contemporary literature is to postulate different categories of emotion (e.g. fear, anger, disgust). However, within this broad framework there are very different views as to where such categories emerge from. In one approach, called the **basic emotions** approach (Ekman, 1992), there are postulated to be small number of distinct emotions that have been shaped by different evolutionary demands, are linked to distinct neural substrates in the brain, and have specific facial expressions that do not vary across cultures. The alternative contemporary approach is to argue that different categories of emotions are *constructed* from different kinds of core processes such as autonomic responses, approach/avoidance reactions, and other on-going cognitions (e.g. beliefs, appraisals). These theories do not dismiss the notion of qualitatively different types of emotion (such as disgust or fear). They make the claim that these categories are not "natural kinds," but rather represent different points within a broader space of emotional experience (Feldman Barrett, 2006).

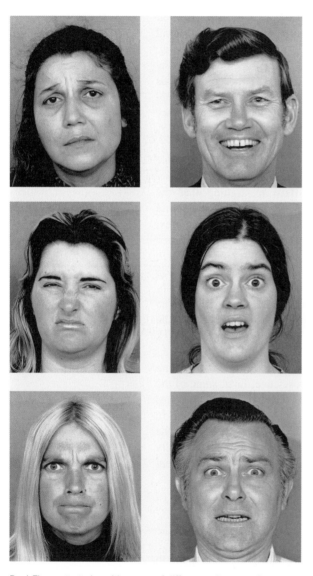

Paul Ekman tested a wide range of different cultures and concluded that there are six basic types of emotion expressed in faces: sad, happy, disgust, surprise, anger and fear.

© Paul Ekman. Reproduced with permission.

One of the most influential ethnographic studies of the emotions concluded that there are six basic emotions that are independent of culture (Ekman & Friesen, 1976; Ekman *et al.*, 1972). These are: happy, sad, disgust, anger, fear and surprise. These studies were based on comparisons of the way that facial expressions are categorized and posed across diverse cultures. Ekman (1992) considers other characteristics for classifying an emotion as "basic" aside from universal facial expressions, such as each emotion having its own specific neural basis; each emotion having evolved to deal with different survival problems; and occurring automatically. This approach to emotions has been very influential within cognitive neuroscience. However, it encounters various problems. It doesn't appear to be the case that each basic emotion has its own unique set of brain regions or networks (although some degree of specialization is found for some categories). Some emotions may also appear to "basic" in some ways but not others: for instance, the emotion of love reflects a clear evolutionary adaptation (for nurturing) and has some specialized neural circuitry, but isn't linked to a facial expression.

Not all contemporary theories endorse the idea of distinct emotional categories. Two will be considered here, namely the theories of Feldman-Barret (2006) and Rolls (2005). The theory of Feldman-Barrett and colleagues (Barrett & Wager, 2006; Feldman Barrett, 2006; Lindquist & Barrett, 2012) assumes that all emotions tap into a system termed *core affect* that is organized along two dimensions: pleasant-unpleasant and high/low arousal. The latter is also termed activation. Evidence that emotional experience can be classified along these two dimensions comes from studies employing factor analysis of current mood ratings (Yik *et al.*, 1999). In biological terms, this is linked to bodily feelings of emotion and linked to limbic structures such as medial temporal lobes, cingulate and orbitofrontal cortex (Lindquist & Barrett, 2012). This echoes the older ideas of Papez and Maclean. The novel aspect of the model is the idea that categories of emotion are constructed (and can be differentiated from each other) because they tap the core affect system in somewhat different ways and because they are linked to certain kinds of information processed outside of the core affect system, including executive control (for regulating and appraising emotions), language (for categorizing and labeling), theory-of-mind (for conceptualizing emotions in terms of other agents), and so on.

Finally, the theory of Rolls (2005) also argues for a constructionist approach to emotions, without relying on the notion of a core set of basic emotions. However, his account is different in detail to that of Feldman-Barrett (2006). Rather than the notion of "core affect" (with dimensions of arousal and pleasantness), the central part of Rolls' theory is concerned with the dimensions of reward and punishment, their presence/absence and intensity. Different types of emotion emerge by considering whether a reward or punishment is applied (e.g. pleasure compared with fear), whether a reward is taken away (e.g. anger) or a punishment is taken away (e.g. relief). These may occur in combination: for example guilt may be a combination of reward and punishment learning.

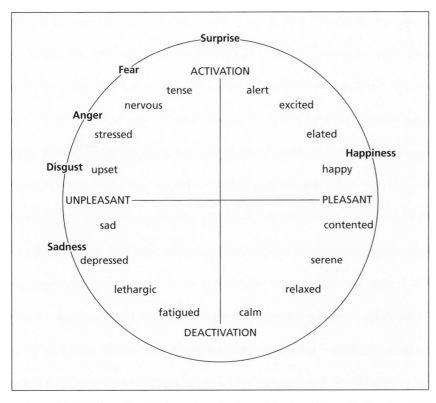

In the model of Feldman-Barrett, all emotions (and mood) involve a "core affect" system that is organized along two dimensions corresponding to pleasantness and arousal (/activation). Different categories of emotion are points in that space (and linked to associated cognitions—language, memory, perception, theory-of-mind) but are not afforded a special status.

From Russell and Feldman-Barrett, 1999. *Journal of Personality and Social Psychology*.

## KEY TERM

**Moral emotions**
Emotions that are related to the behavior of oneself (in relation to others) or the behavior of others (in relation to oneself or others.

In addition, the context in which an emotional stimulus appears is important and an integral part of the constructed emotion. For example, whether the stimulus is social or not (i.e. related to other people) may determine whether the emotion feels like love, anger, jealousy (emotions implying another agent) versus enjoyment, frustration or sadness (emotions that need not imply another agent). Indeed the eliciting stimulus is considered part of the emotional state, so love for one person may be different to love to another person just because the individual is different.

It is important to note that advocates of the "basic emotions" approach do not deny that *some* emotions are constructed, but they differ from theories such as those of Feldman-Barrett (2006) and Rolls (2005) that assume that *all* emotions are constructed. One possibility within the basic emotion approach is to consider some emotions as being comprised of two or more basic emotions: for example, joy + fear = guilt, and fear + surprise = alarm (Plutchik, 1980). Another possibility is that some emotions are constructed from a basic emotion(s) plus a nonemotional cognitive appraisal. An *appraisal* of an emotion involves an evaluation of both the content (e.g. negative feeling) and the context. So a similar feeling could be appraised as either shame or guilt depending on whether it is contextualized relative to the self (shame) or other (guilt). Haidt (2003) has used the term **moral emotions** to refer to emotions that are related to the behavior of oneself (in relation to others) or the behavior of others (in relation to oneself or others). It implies the existence of some normative benchmark with which to evaluate our actions. These norms could be a product of both innate mechanisms (e.g. an instinctive desire not to harm others) and culturally accepted norms (e.g. law and religion). In this view, the existence of moral emotions depends on an evolutionarily older set of emotional processes together with an evolutionarily newer ability to reflect on the behavior of self and others. Along these lines, Smith and Lazarus (1990) argue that pride, shame, and gratitude might be uniquely human emotions. Darwin (1872) also believed that blushing (linked to shame or embarrassment) might be a uniquely human expression.

## Evaluation

Although there are many different theories of emotion (some in vogue, some rejected), there are a core set of ideas concerning emotions that have stood the test of time. This includes the idea that emotions have an evolved adaptive value, and this is largely conserved across species. It also includes the notion that emotions are multi-faceted: they contain both conscious (at least in humans) and unconscious processes; they involve the interplay of brain and body via the autonomic system (although emotions cannot be reduced to bodily sensations); and that (at least in humans) some emotions are constructed from both affective mechanisms and cognitive ones (e.g. appraisal). A good example of the latter is the so-called moral emotions (e.g. guilt, pride). Contemporary theories emphasize categorical distinctions between emotions (such as anger, fear sadness) but differ with regards to whether these categories represent natural kinds (i.e. innately specified categorical differences, as in the basic emotion approach) or are themselves constructed from different combinations of building blocks of other kinds of core processes (e.g. reward/punishment, pleasure, arousal, appraisals). This idea will be returned to again in the next section.

## MORALITY IN THE BRAIN

Moral judgments involve an evaluation of actions and intentions (either our own or that of others) against some standard of acceptable behavior. Moral emotions occur when we compare behavior against those standards (Haidt, 2003). For instance, if our own actions exceed our standards then we may feel pride, but if they fall below those standards we may feel shame, guilt, or embarrassment. If other people's behavior falls below standard then we may feel anger or disgust. The question of where the moral standards come from is an interesting one. It is likely to derive from a core set of instincts around love for one's family, need for affiliation, empathy, and fairness (including retribution against unfairness).

What regions of the brain are activated when viewing (or thinking about) scenes involving moral transgressions, such as domestic violence? Is it the same pattern found when viewing other emotional stimuli that do not involve a transgression?

Cultural norms, including religion and the law, tend to uphold this (can you think of a successful religion that does not preach love for one's family and in-group?). But they may extend moral norms in more idiosyncratic ways (e.g. what to eat and wear).

There is evidence consistent with the view that processing of moral emotions involves brain structures involved in both emotion and in cognitive appraisal. Moll et al. (2002) presented pictures of three kinds of emotional scenes to participants undergoing fMRI: images of moral violations (e.g. images of physical assaults, abandoned children), images of aversive scenes (e.g. dangerous animal) and pleasant images. These were matched for their self-reported arousal. The moral-violation and aversive images were matched in terms of how negatively they were judged, but the moral violation images were judged as more morally unacceptable than the other affective stimuli. All affective stimuli (relative to a neutral set of images) tended to activate regions linked to emotional processing such as the amygdala and insula, but moral emotions (relative to other affective stimuli) additionally activated regions such as the orbitofrontal cortex, the medial prefrontal cortex and the right posterior superior temporal sulcus (STS). The medial prefrontal cortex and right posterior STS have been linked to theory-of-mind (Amodio & Frith, 2006; Saxe, 2006), whereas the orbitofrontal cortex is implicated in the regulation of social behavior. Similar results were obtained for the moral emotions of embarrassment (Berthoz et al., 2002) and guilt (Takahashi et al., 2004) elicited by reading verbal narratives; for example, "I left the restaurant without paying" (guilt) and "I mistook a stranger for my friend" (embarrassment).

Patients with acquired lesions to the orbitofrontal (and ventromedial prefrontal) cortex often display poor social functioning (see Chapter 14 for more discussion). These patients are judged by family members to exhibit low levels of empathy, embarrassment and guilt (Koenigs et al., 2007). That is, their impairments extend to the moral emotions. When given certain moral dilemmas they tend to perform atypically. For instance, if asked whether they would be willing to push one person under a train to save the lives of five people they are inclined to agree with this course of action (Koenigs et al., 2007). The explanation for this is that there are two conflicting answers in this dilemma. There is a numerically logical answer that killing one life is better than killing five lives. There is also a more emotionally loaded proposition, namely that it would be wrong to push someone under a train. In patients with orbitofrontal lesions, logic may win when pitted against a moral emotion.

## NEURAL SUBSTRATES OF EMOTION PROCESSING

This section introduces many of the key brain regions involved in emotional processing and considers their possible functions. The section will show how the same brain networks are used to process both social stimuli (our perceptions and interactions with others) as well as nonsocial stimuli with affective properties (such as snakes, food, electric shocks). Another aim of the current section is to use this evidence to adjudicate between various theories in the field: for instance, to determine whether there are basic emotions with distinct neural substrates.

### The amygdala: fear and other emotions

The **amygdala** (from the Latin word for almond) is a small mass of gray matter that lies buried in the tip of the left and right temporal lobes. It lies to the front of the hippocampus and, like the hippocampus, is believed to be important for memory—particularly for the emotional content of memories (Richardson *et al.*, 2004) and for learning whether a particular stimulus/response is rewarded or punished (Gaffan, 1992). In monkeys, bilateral lesions of the amygdala have been observed to produce a complex array of behaviors that have been termed the **Kluver–Bucy syndrome** (Kluver & Bucy, 1939; Weiskrantz, 1956). These behaviors include an unusual tameness and emotional blunting; a tendency to examine objects with the mouth; and dietary changes. This is explained in terms of objects losing their learned emotional value. The monkeys typically also lose their social standing (Rosvold *et al.*, 1954).

The role of the amygdala in fear conditioning is well established (Le Doux, 1996; Phelps, 2006). If a stimulus that does not normally elicit a fear response, such as an auditory tone (unconditioned stimulus, CS–), is paired with a stimulus

The amygdala is buried, bilaterally, in the anterior portion of the temporal lobes.

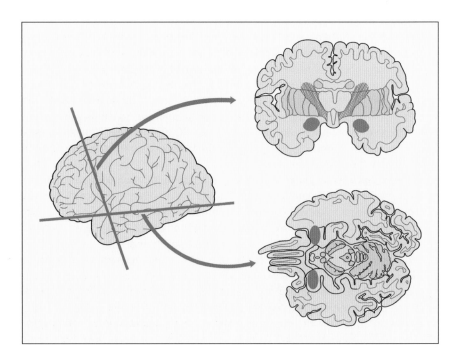

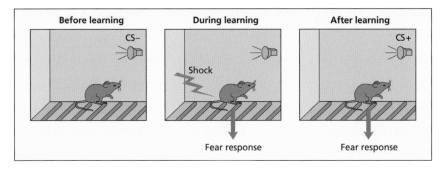

The basic procedure in fear conditioning involves presenting an initially neutral stimulus (the CS–, e.g. a tone) with a shock. After sufficient pairings, the stimulus will elicit a fear response without an accompanying shock (it has become a CS+).

From Ward, 2012, p. 83.

**KEY TERMS**

**Skin conductance response (SCR)**
Changes in electrical conductivity on a person's skin, triggered by certain stimuli (e.g. emotional or familiar stimuli).

that does normally evoke a fear response (termed conditioned response), such as an electric shock, then the tone will come to elicit a fear response by itself (it becomes a conditioned stimulus, CS+). If the amygdala is lesioned in mice (specifically the basolateral nucleus of the amygdala) then the animal does not show this learning, and if the lesion is performed after the animal has been trained then this learned association is lost (Phillips & Ledoux, 1992). That is, the amygdala is important for both learning and storing the conditioned fear response (although for a different view see Cahill *et al.*, 1999). Single cell recordings suggest that different cells within the amygdala could be involved in learning versus storage of the association (Repa *et al.*, 2001). Animals with lesions to the amygdala still show a fear response to normal fear-evoking stimuli (such as shocks) which suggests that its role is in learning and storing the emotional status of stimuli that are initially emotionally neutral.

In humans, a comparison of learned fear responses to a shock (CS+) with neutral stimuli (CS–) reveals amygdala activation during fMRI that correlated with the degree of conditioned response, in this instance a skin conductance response (LaBar *et al.*, 1998). The **skin conductance response** is a measure of autonomic arousal and, hence, a body-based measure of emotion processing (see figure opposite for further details). Bechara *et al.* (1995) report that humans with amygdala damage fail to show this conditioned response, but nevertheless are able to verbally learn the association ("when I saw the blue square I got a shock"), whereas amnesic patients with hippocampal damage show a normal conditioned response, but cannot recall the association. This suggests that the association is stored in more than one place: in the amygdala (giving rise to the conditioned fear response) plus in the hippocampus (giving rise to declarative memories of the association). fMRI studies also show that the amygdala may be important for fear-related conditioning in social settings in which participants learn fear associations by watching someone else receive a shock (Olsson & Phelps, 2004).

Amygdala lesions in humans can selectively impair the ability to *perceive* fear in others but not necessarily the other Ekman categories of emotion (Adolphs *et al.*, 1994; Calder *et al.*, 1996). For example, patient DR suffered bilateral amygdala damage and subsequently displayed a particular difficulty with recognizing fear (Calder *et al.*, 1996). She was also impaired to a lesser degree in recognizing facial anger and disgust. She could imagine the facial features of

The skin conductance response (SCR) method involves recording changes in electrical conductivity on a person's skin on the hand. Heightened arousal can lead to more sweat even without overt sweating taking place. A person's SCR can be plotted as a continuous trace throughout the experiment. A peak SCR occurs between 1 and 5 s after face presentation.

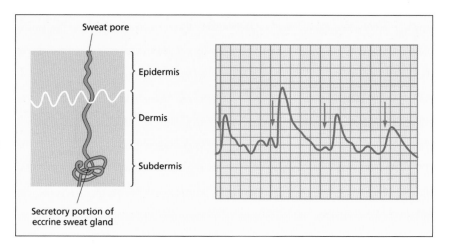

famous people, but not of emotional expressions. She could recognize famous faces and match different views of unfamiliar people, but could not match pictures of the same person when the expression differed (Young *et al.*, 1996). DR also shows comparable deficits in recognizing vocal emotional expressions, suggesting that the deficit is related to emotion processing rather than modality-specific perceptual processes (Scott *et al.*, 1997). While it has been suggested that selective impairments in fear may arise because of a failure to attend closely to the eyes (Adolphs *et al.*, 2005), this cannot account for the fact that some patients fail to recognize fear in speech (Scott *et al.*, 1997) or music (Gosselin *et al.*, 2007).

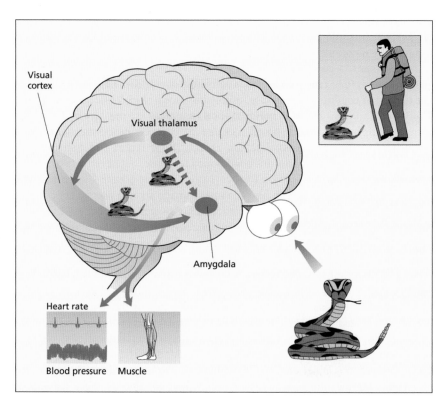

Le Doux has argued that the amygdala has a fast response to the presence of threatening stimuli such as snakes.

Functional imaging studies generally support, and extend, these conclusions. Morris *et al.* (1996) presented participants with morphed faces on a happy–neutral–fearful continuum. Participants were required to make male–female classifications (i.e. the processing of emotion was incidental). Left amygdala activation was found only in the fear condition; the happy condition activated a different neural circuit. Winston *et al.* (2003) report that amygdala activation was independent of whether participants engaged in incidental viewing or explicit emotion judgments. However, other regions, including the ventromedial frontal lobes, were activated only when making explicit judgments about the emotion. This was interpreted as reinstatement of the "feeling" of the emotion.

Some researchers have argued that the ability to detect threat is so important, evolutionarily, that it may occur rapidly and without conscious awareness (Le Doux, 1996). Ohman *et al.* (2001) report that people are faster at detecting snakes and spiders among flowers and mushrooms than the other way around, and that search times are suggestive of preattentive "pop-out" (see Chapter 7). When spiders or snakes are presented subliminally to people with spider or snake phobias, then participants do not report seeing the stimulus but show a skin conductance response indicative of emotional processing (Ohman & Soares, 1994). In these experiments, arachnophobic participants show the response to spiders, not snakes; and ophidiophobic participants show a response to snakes, but not spiders. In terms of neural pathways, it is generally believed that there is a fast subcortical route from the thalamus to the amygdala and a slow route to the amygdala via the primary visual cortex (Adolphs, 2002; Morris *et al.*, 1999). Functional imaging studies suggest that the amygdala is indeed activated by unconscious fearful expressions in both healthy participants (Morris *et al.*, 1999) and in a "blindsight" patient with damage to primary visual cortex (Tamietto *et al.*, 2012). This is consistent with a subcortical route to the amygdala, although it is to be noted that the temporal resolution of fMRI does not enable any conclusions to be drawn about whether the route is fast or slow.

While there is convincing evidence for the role of the amygdala in fear processing it should not be concluded that the amygdala is the "fear center" of the brain. First, fear may depend on a wider network (of which the amygdala is a key hub). Indeed, it affects the autonomic system (via the hypothalamus) to generate a fight or flight reaction (Le Doux *et al.*, 1988) and it increases activity

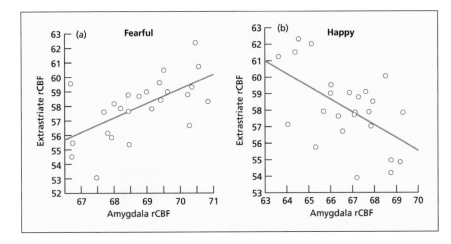

When shown fearful faces, increases in regional cerebral blood flow in the amygdala (rCBF) are associated with increases in blood flow in extrastriate visual regions involved in recognition of the potential threat. The reverse is true of happy faces.

From Morris et al., 1998. Reprinted by permission of Oxford University Press.

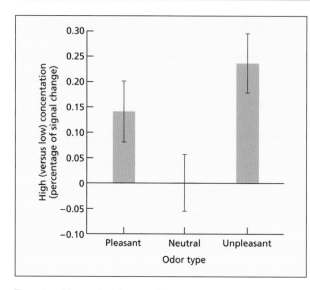

There is evidence that the amygdala responds to pleasant and unpleasant smells (but not neutral smells). This suggests a wider role of the amygdala in emotion processing, in contrast to the commonly held assumption that it is specific to fear.

From Dolan, R. J., 2007. The human amygdala and orbitofrontal cortex in behavioural regulation. *Philosophical Transactions of the Royal Society of London Series B* , 362, 787–799. Reproduced with permission.

in visual cortex to promote vigilance to threat (Morris *et al.*, 1998), among others. Second, the fact that the amygdala is a key part of the fear network doesn't preclude it from being involved in other forms of emotional processing. With regards to learning of stimulus-emotion associations there is evidence that the amygdala is involved in learning positive associations, based on food rewards, as well as fear-conditioning (Baxter & Murray, 2002). However, the amygdala system for positive associations operates somewhat differently to fear-conditioning and depends on different nuclei. For example, selective lesions of the amygdala in animals does *not* affect learning of classically conditioned light-food associations, in which the animal learns to approach the food cup when the light comes on (Hatfield *et al.*, 1996), although such lesions are known to affect learning that a light predicts a shock. However, amygdala lesions do affect other aspects of reward-based learning such as second order conditioning in which a light + tone is subsequently paired with absence of food (after learning that a light alone predicts food), or learning that the food is devalued (Hatfield *et al.*, 1996). Recent functional imaging studies that compare stimuli with learned positive and negative associations relative to emotionally neutral ones but do not rely on facial expressions have revealed amygdala activation to negative and positive affective stimuli; for instance, comparing positive, negative, and neutral tastes (Small *et al.*, 2003), smells (Winston *et al.*, 2005), pictures, and sounds (Anders *et al.*, 2008). However, most fMRI studies do not have the spatial resolution to reliably distinguish between subregions within the amygdala.

## The insula: disgust and interoception

The **insula** is a small region of cortex buried beneath the temporal lobes (it literally means "island"). It is involved in various aspects of bodily perception including important roles in pain perception and taste perception. The word *disgust* literally means "bad taste," and this category of emotion may be evolutionarily related to contamination and disease through ingestion.

Patients with Huntington's disease can show selective impairments in recognizing facial expressions of disgust (Sprengelmeyer *et al.*, 1997) and relative impairments in vocal expressions of disgust (Sprengelmeyer *et al.*, 1996). The degree of the disgust-related impairments in this group correlates with the amount of damage in the insula (Kipps *et al.*, 2007). Selective lesions resulting from brain injury the insula can affect disgust perception more than recognition of other facial expressions (Calder *et al.*, 2000). In healthy participants undergoing fMRI, facial expressions of disgust activate this region, but not the amygdala (Phillips *et al.*, 1997). Feeling disgust oneself and seeing someone else disgusted activates the same region of insula (Wicker *et al.*, 2003).

**KEY TERM**

**Insula**
A region of cortex buried beneath the temporal lobes; involved in body perception and contains the primary gustatory cortex; responds to disgust.

We use the word "disgust" in at least one other context, namely to refer to social behavior that violates moral conventions. Disgusting behavior is said, metaphorically, to "leave a bad taste in the mouth." But is there more to this than metaphor? Some have argued that moral disgust has evolved out of nonsocial, contamination-related disgust (Tybur *et al.*, 2009). Moral disgust also results in activity in the insula (Moll *et al.*, 2005) and is associated with subtle oral facial expressions characteristic of disgust more generally (Chapman *et al.*, 2009).

The insula is generally considered to have a wider role in emotional processing, in addition to a more specific involvement in disgust. Specifically, it is regarded as monitoring (probably both consciously and unconsciously) the internal state of the body—a process known as *interoception*. Bodily reactions are characteristic of emotions and may constitute the "feeling" of an emotion (Craig, 2009; Singer *et al.*, 2009). This is reminiscent of James-Lange theory, but, whereas that account argued that emotions can be reduced to bodily states (i.e. are synonymous with them), modern accounts assume that they are one aspect of an emotion.

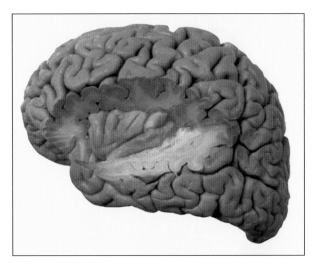

The insula is an island of cortex lying, bilaterally, underneath the temporal lobes. It is implicated in the creation of bodily feelings associated with emotions, and in the perception of disgust in particular.

From Singer *et al.*, 2009. © 2009 Elsevier. Reproduced with permission.

## Orbitofrontal cortex: contextualized emotions, and emotional feelings

One general function of the orbitofrontal cortex is in computing the *current* value of a stimulus, i.e. how rewarding the stimulus is within the current context. For example, chocolate may be a rewarding stimulus, but it may not be *currently rewarding* if one is full-up or if eating it may incur the anger of someone else. Small *et al.* (2001) asked participants to eat chocolate between several blocks of functional imaging. Initially, the chocolate was rated as pleasant and participants were motivated to eat it, but the more they ate the less pleasant it became and they were less motivated to eat it. This change in behavior was linked to changes in activity in orbitofrontal regions. Specifically, there was a shift in activity from medial regions (pleasant/wanting) to lateral regions (unpleasant/not-wanting). Other studies are consistent with different regions of orbitofrontal cortex coding rewards and punishments (e.g. for a review see Kringelbach, 2005). For instance, activation of lateral orbitofrontal cortex is found when a rewarding smile is expected, but an angry face is instead presented (Kringelbach & Rolls, 2003) and is correlated with amount of monetary loss on a trial (O'Doherty *et al.*, 2001).

The orbitofrontal cortex may enable flexible changes in behavior to stimuli that are normally rewarding (or recently rewarding) but suddenly cease to be. This can account for its role in reversal learning (in which rewarded and nonrewarded stimuli are reversed) and **extinction** (in which a rewarded stimulus is no longer rewarded). Eating chocolate until it is no longer pleasant can be regarded as a form of extinction. Lesions in these regions in humans lead to difficulties on these

**KEY TERMS**

**Extinction learning**
Learning that a previously rewarded stimulus is no longer rewarded.

The same stimulus can elicit pleasure or aversion depending on context (e.g. the person's motivational state). Chocolate is normally pleasant, but if you have just eaten two bars of it you probably do not want any more. The orbitofrontal cortex computes the current emotional status of a stimulus (i.e. whether it is *currently* desired or not), thus enabling flexible behavior. Other regions in the brain may code the long-term value of a stimulus (i.e. whether it is *normally* desired or not).

tasks, and the amount of difficulty in reversal learning correlates with the level of socially inappropriate behavior of the patients (Rolls *et al.*, 1994).

Activity in the orbitofrontal cortex has been linked to participants' subjective reports of pleasantness to stimuli such as tastes (McClure *et al.*, 2004b) and music (Blood & Zatorre, 2001). Importantly, these ratings of pleasantness are not just affected by the stimulus itself, but also the participants' beliefs about the product. Being told the price of a wine affects ratings of pleasantness upon tasting it—more expensive wines taste nicer—and perceived pleasantness was again related to activity in the medial part of the orbitofrontal cortex (Plassmann *et al.*, 2008). Of course, the experimenters administered some of the same wines twice giving the participants different prices so the stimuli were physically identical but their beliefs about the quality of the wine were not identical.

The lateral prefrontal cortex and the orbitofrontal cortex might serve somewhat different functions in regulating and contextualizing emotions. Ochsner *et al.* (2002) presented negative images (e.g. of someone in traction in a hospital) to participants in one of two conditions: either passively viewing them or a cognitive condition in which they were instructed to reappraise each image "so that it no longer elicited a negative response." Their analysis revealed a trade-off between activity in the lateral prefrontal cortex (high when reappraising) and the medial/orbital frontal cortex and amygdala (high during passive looking). When participants are asked to reappraise the stimulus negatively, i.e. making it worse than it looks, then this also engenders a similar network in the lateral prefrontal cortex but tends *not* to dampen activity in the ventromedial prefrontal cortex and amygdala (Ochsner *et al.*, 2004).

## Anterior cingulate: response evaluation, autonomic responses, and pain

In the chapter on the Executive Brain, it was noted that the anterior cingulate is involved in the detection of errors and monitoring of response conflict such as on the Stroop test. Although this theory is not normally couched in terms of emotional processing (Carter *et al.*, 1998) it can be. Rushworth *et al.* (2007) argue that the function of the anterior cingulate is to assess the value of responses, i.e. whether an *action* is likely to elicit a reward or punishment. This may differ from the function of the orbitofrontal cortex which computes whether a given *stimulus* is currently rewarded or punished. Male monkeys with anterior cingulate lesions fail to adjust their responses, when reaching for food, when simultaneously shown a dominant male or a female in estrus, whereas most control monkeys will pay close attention to these social stimuli, and hence take longer to respond to the food (Rudebeck *et al.*, 2006).

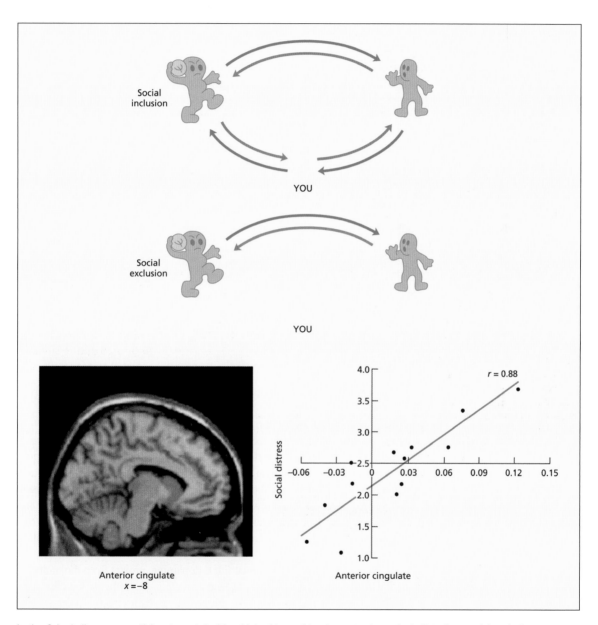

In the Cyberball game a participant must decide which of two other players to throw the ball to. In a social exclusion condition, two of the players always send the ball to each other and never to the participant. In a social inclusion condition, all players get to play. Social exclusion tends to activate the anterior cingulate and this correlates with subjective levels of distress. Bottom figures from Eisenberger *et al.*, 2003. © 2003 American Association for the Advancement of Science. Reproduced with permission.

From Ward, 2012, p. 195.

The anterior cingulate cortex, like the insula, is involved in processing bodily signals that characterize emotions but, whereas the insula is more concerned with the input (and awareness) of these signals, the anterior cingulate is more concerned with the output of bodily responses. Lesions in this area disrupt the skin conductance response (Tranel & Damasio, 1995) and changes in heart rate and blood pressure (Critchley et al., 2003) to emotional stimuli.

The anterior cingulate also receives inputs (via the thalamus) relating to pain, and may regulate feelings of pain via output connections to the periaqueductal gray (a region that is rich in endogenous opioids). As well as responding (e.g. in fMRI) to physically painful stimuli, such as mild electric shocks, watching someone else in pain activates some of the same regions (Singer et al., 2004). Thus it responds to the perception of pain in others as well as to physical pain in oneself. This idea is returned to in later discussions on empathy. It has also been claimed that being separated from a loved one or being socially excluded in general is "painful," and these more social forms of pain may indeed involve the pain circuitry of the brain. Eisenberger et al. (2003) conducted an fMRI study of a Cyberball game involving three players, including the one person being scanned. Players could opt to throw the ball to one of the two other players. However, after a while the game was fixed such that two players consistently threw to each other excluding the person in the scanner. There were two other conditions: one in which the player was included, and one in which they were excluded but given the cover story of "due to technical difficulties." Activity in the anterior cingulate correlated with self-reported distress during social exclusion. A region in the prefrontal cortex (right ventro-lateral prefrontal cortex) was linked to social exclusion, but not exclusion due to "technical difficulties" which they interpret as playing a controlling role in limiting the distress of social exclusion.

## Ventral striatum and reward

The dorsal region of the striatum has more sensorimotor properties (e.g. involved in habit formation), whereas the ventral region may be more specialized for emotions, although the distinction is relative not absolute (Voorn et al., 2004). There are several loops that connect regions within the frontal cortex to the basal ganglia and on to the thalamus before returning to the frontal cortex (Alexander & Crutcher, 1990). The loops modulate brain activity within these frontal structures and, hence, increase or decrease the probability of a particular behavior. The loop that is of particular relevance to reward-based learning (the "limbic circuit") starts and ends in the orbitofrontal cortex and limbic regions (including amygdala and anterior cingulate), passing through the basal ganglia (including the **ventral striatum**) and thalamus.

Neurons containing the neurotransmitter, dopamine, project from the midbrain to a region in the ventral striatum called the nucleus accumbens. Psychomotor stimulants such as amphetamine and cocaine may exert their effects via this system (Koob, 1992). Other rewarding stimuli activate this region. Dopamine release in the nucleus accumbens of male rats increases when a female is introduced to the cage, and increases further if they have sex (Pfaus et al., 1990). Neutral stimuli previously associated with food increase the release of dopamine in the nucleus accumbens of rats (Robbins et al., 1989). In humans, an fMRI study shows that the greater the monetary reward that could be obtained in a task the larger the activity in the ventral striatum (Knutson *et al.*, 2001). However, social stimuli are rewarding too, and activity in this region tends to be greater when a reward (e.g. monetary) is obtained via cooperation with another human, than when it is obtained from noncooperation with a human or cooperation with a nonsocial agent such as a computer (Rilling *et al.*, 2002).

One contemporary idea is that these dopaminergic neurons are not encoding reward per se, but the difference between the *predicted* reward and *actual* reward (e.g. Schultz *et al.*, 1997). After training to perform an action when presented with a light or tone cue, dopaminergic neurons in monkeys eventually respond to the conditioned cue itself rather than the subsequent reward (Schultz *et al.*, 1992). If no subsequent reward appears then their activity drops below baseline, indicating that a reward was expected. Some fMRI studies of decision making in humans also suggest that activity in the ventral striatum is greater when a reward is better than expected, rather than when a reward is high per se (Hare *et al.*, 2008). Self-reported lonely people show less activity in the ventral striatum when shown photos of social scenes (relative to non-lonely people), arguably because they predict them to be less rewarding (Cacioppo *et al.*, 2009).

## Evaluation

This section has outlined a set of regions that are critically involved in the processing of emotions. In social animals, such as humans, these emotional brain regions play a key role in evaluating and judging social stimuli. For instance, the amygdala is not only implicated in evaluating whether a tone will lead to a shock, but also in evaluating whether another person is afraid; the anterior cingulate responds not only to physical pain but also responds to social pain relating to separation and social exclusion; and the nucleus accumbens responds not only to basic rewards (food, sex) but also responds when we opt to cooperate with another person.

The different regions of the emotional brain serve different functions, and this is at odds with earlier theories of emotion (e.g. the Papez circuit and Maclean's "limbic brain"). However, there is not a simple one-to-one mapping between brain structure and emotional category (e.g. amygdala = fear, insula = disgust) as predicted by a strong version of the "basic emotion" approach. Of course, "basic emotions" could still be said to exist at the level of brain circuits connecting specialized sub-regions and the best documented examples in the literature are fear and disgust. Other contemporary theories postulate the notion of "core affect"

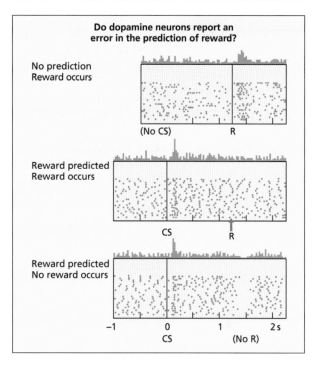

Single-cell recordings of dopamine neurons in the ventral striatum of monkeys show that the neuron responds when an unexpected reward of fruit juice is given (top), but if the reward is predicted by a cue (the conditioned stimulus) then the neuron responds to the cue and not the reward (middle). If an expected reward is omitted (bottom) the firing of the neuron falls below baseline. The results suggest that these neurons code the difference between the predicted reward and actual reward, rather than reward itself.

From Schultz *et al.*, 1997. © 1997 American Association for the Advancement of Science. Reproduced with permission.

which consists of perceived internal body states and organized around the dimensions of intensity and pleasantness (Feldman Barrett, 2006). While there are brain regions that appear to have these characteristics (e.g. the amygdala shows some evidence of tracking intensity) on closer inspection their functioning is far more complex (e.g. the evidence that the amygdala has somewhat different roles in fear versus reward conditioning).

Finally, almost all contemporary theories of emotion allow for a role of "cognition" by which is meant thoughts and beliefs, appraisals, control mechanisms and the like. This is supported by the neuroscience evidence but stands in contrast to some earlier views that emotion was somehow distinct from cognition (for a summary see Phelps, 2006). An emotion is best regarded as a complex affective state in which cognitions are intrinsically embedded rather than standing apart.

## READING FACES

The visual processing of faces has been considered previously (see Chapter 6). However, a face is far more than a visual object—it is also a social object, denoting a **conspecific**. A face conveys important information about another person's feeling states (e.g. their current emotion), their intentions (e.g. eye gaze provides some clues), their membership of social categories (e.g. race, gender), and perhaps even their dispositions (e.g. trustworthiness). This section first considers facial expressions followed by gaze detection. Evaluating race and personality in a face is covered elsewhere (Kubota *et al.*, 2012; Ward, 2012).

### Recognizing facial expressions

The two models of face processing already considered in some detail in Chapter 6 are the cognitive model of Bruce and Young (1986) and the neuroanatomical model of Haxby *et al.* (2000). Both models assume that extracting socially relevant information from faces (e.g. knowing they are happy) is largely separable from recognizing facial identity (i.e. knowing who the person is). However, the two models make different assumptions as to how this is done. In Bruce and Young's (1986) model there is a dedicated route for recognizing emotional expressions. This route is also assumed to be different from the mechanism needed for tasks such as lip-reading or gaze detection. By contrast, the model of Haxby *et al.* (2000) makes a broad division between time-invariant representations of a face (needed for facial identity and linked to the fusiform face area FFA) and time-varying representations of a face. The latter is assumed to be needed *both* for recognizing expressions and for gaze processing, and is linked to the superior temporal sulcus (STS). Both the fusiform face area and the superior temporal sulcus are assumed to be part of the "core system" of face processing (i.e. relatively specialized for faces in particular), but, for expressions, this would additionally involve the "extended system" dealing with emotions (including the amygdala, insula, and so on).

To what extent does the available evidence support these two models? According to Calder and Young (2005) the evidence does not equivocally support either of these models. Brain-damaged patients who are poor at recognizing facial expressions but who are relatively good at recognizing facial identity do exist.

However, the lesion sites of these patients tend to be in regions such as orbital and ventromedial frontal lesions (Heberlein *et al.*, 2008; Hornak *et al.*, 1996) or somatosensory regions (Adolphs *et al.*, 2000), but *not* the superior temporal sulcus as predicted by the model of Haxby *et al.* (2000). There is convincing evidence that the superior temporal sulcus plays an important role in detecting gaze direction and lip-reading (outlined in the next section), but the evidence that it is crucially involved in expression recognition is lacking. Difficulties in recognizing facial expressions appears to depend on the integrity of the extended system (to borrow the terminology of Haxby *et al.*, 2000) that is involved in the general processing of emotion and is not specific to faces. Calder and Young (2005) also argue that this is inconsistent with the assumption of a single route for recognizing expressions, as originally postulated by the Bruce and Young (1986) model. Instead they argue that the recognition of particular emotion expressions is divided up among different brain regions that are specialized for different categories of emotion (e.g. the amygdala for fear, insula for disgust) or for emotional experience in general (e.g. the orbitofrontal cortex).

Although not specifically discussed by Calder and Young (2005) or Haxby *et al.* (2000), there is one candidate mechanism that could serve as a general system for recognizing expressions, but not identity—namely in terms of sensorimotor simulation (Heberlein & Adolphs, 2007). **Simulation theory** consists of a collection of somewhat different theories based around a unifying idea—namely that we come to understand others (their emotions, actions, mental states) by vicariously producing their current state on ourselves. With regard to emotions, the claim is that when we see someone smiling then we also activate our own affective pathways for happiness. Moreover, we may activate the motor programs needed to make us smile (this may make us smile back, or it may prepare a smile response) and we may simulate what this might feel like in terms of its sensory consequences (e.g. muscle stretch and tactile sensations on the face). As such, one could possibly recognize emotions such as happiness, fear, and disgust not just in terms of their visual appearance but in terms of the way that the activate the sensorimotor programs of the perceiver.

There is evidence from electromyographic (EMG) studies that viewing a facial expression produces corresponding tiny changes in our own facial musculature,

**KEY TERM**

**Simulation theory**
The theory that we come to understand others (their emotions, actions, mental states) by vicariously producing their current state in ourselves.

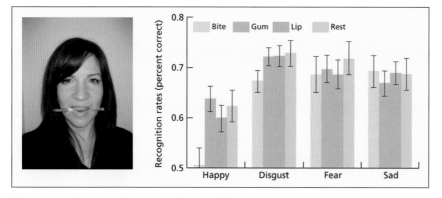

Placing a pen in the mouth horizontally and holding it with the teeth uses many of the same muscles as smiling. Performing this task can also disrupt recognition of facial expressions of happiness.

Data from Oberman *et al.*, 2007.

**Social referencing**
The emotional response of another person may lead to avoidance or interaction with a previously neutral stimulus.

**Capgras syndrome**
People report that their acquaintances (spouse, family, friends and so on) have been replaced by "body doubles."

even if the face is viewed briefly so as to be unconsciously perceived (Dimberg *et al.*, 2000). However, this does not necessarily imply that this is used to recognize expressions. To address this, Oberman *et al.* (2007) report that biting a pen length-ways uses many of the same muscles involved in smiling. They subsequently showed that the bite task selectively disrupts the recognition of happiness. Lesion studies (Adolphs *et al.*, 2000) and TMS over the somatosensory cortex (Pitcher *et al.*, 2008) also suggest a direct contribution of simulation mechanisms to recognizing emotional expressions.

Facial expressions are helpful not only for enabling us to understand what someone else is feeling (e.g. via simulation) but may also be used to modify our own behavior. If human infants are given a novel object, their behavior will be influenced by the response of their primary caregiver—a phenomenon termed **social referencing** (Klinnert *et al.*, 1983). If the caregiver displays disgust or fear, then the object will be avoided, but if the caregiver smiles, then the child will interact with the object. This is analogous to the classical conditioning scenario illustrated on p. 383 in which facial expressions trigger a conditioned response (e.g. fear, happiness) which becomes associated with the novel object.

## "YOU LOOK LIKE MY WIFE, BUT YOU ARE AN IMPOSTER!"

In the **Capgras syndrome**, people report that their acquaintances (spouse, family, friends, and so on) have been replaced by "body doubles" (Capgras & Reboul-Lachaux, 1923; Ellis & Lewis, 2001). They will acknowledge that their husband/wife looks like their husband/wife. Indeed, they are able to pick out their husband/wife from a line-up while maintaining all along that he/she is an imposter. To account for this, Ellis and Young (1990) suggest that they can consciously recognize the person, but they lack an emotional response to them. As such, the person is interpreted as an imposter. This explains why the people who are doubled are those closest to the patient, as these would be expected to produce the largest emotional reaction. This theory

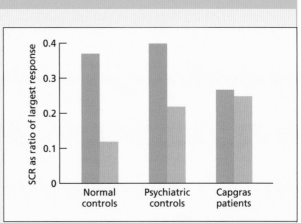

Most people produce a greater skin conductance response (SCR) to personally familiar faces, but patients with Capgras delusion do not.

Reprinted from Ellis and Lewis, 2001. © 2001 with permission from Elsevier.

"makes the clear prediction that Capgras patients will not show the normally appropriate skin conductance responses to familiar faces" (Ellis & Young, 1990, p. 244). One general finding in the neurotypical population is that familiar faces, relative to unfamiliar faces, have an emotional component that reveals itself as a skin conductance response (Tranel *et al.*, 1995). Subsequent research has confirmed that this skin conductance response response to familiar people is disrupted in Capgras syndrome (Ellis *et al.*, 1997).

## Detecting and utilizing eye gaze information

The eye region distinguishes between many emotions, such as smiling or frowning. Moreover, making eye contact can be important for establishing one-to-one communication (dyadic communication), and the direction of gaze can be important for orienting attention to critical objects in the environment. Direct eye contact, in many primates, can be sufficient to initiate emotional behaviors. Macaques are more likely to show appeasement behaviors when shown a direct gaze relative to indirect or averted gazes (Perrett & Mistlin, 1990), and dominance struggles are often initiated with a mutual gaze and terminated when one animal averts its gaze (Chance, 1967).

Baron-Cohen argues that an "eye direction detector" is an innate and distinct component of human cognition (Baron-Cohen, 1995a; Baron-Cohen & Cross, 1992). Babies are able to detect eye contact from birth, suggesting that it is not a learned response (Farroni *et al.*, 2002). This ability is likely to be important for the development of social competence, because the eyes code relational properties between objects and agents (e.g. "mummy sees daddy," "mummy sees the box"). The superior temporal sulcus contains many cells that respond to eye direction (Perrett *et al.*, 1985), and lesions in this area can impair the ability to detect gaze direction (Campbell *et al.*, 1990). Functional imaging studies show that when participants are asked to make judgments about eye gaze (deciding whether the face is looking in the same direction as the last face) then activity is increased in the superior temporal sulcus, but not the fusiform face area (Hoffman & Haxby, 2000). In contrast, when participants are asked to make judgments about face identity (deciding whether the face is the same as the last one presented) then activity is increased in the fusiform face area, but not the superior temporal sulcus.

Children with autism can detect whether the eyes of another person are directed at them and, as such, do not appear to be impaired in the perception of gaze (Baron-Cohen *et al.*, 1995). They do, however, have difficulties in using gaze information to predict behavior or infer desire. In the four sweets task, a cartoon face of Charlie directs his gaze to one of the sweets. Children with autism are unable to decide: "which chocolate will Charlie take?" or "which one does Charlie want?." The difficulty in utilizing gaze information manifests itself as an absence of joint attention in the social interactions of autistic people (Sigman *et al.*, 1986).

Children with autism are able to detect which person is looking at them (top), but are unable to infer behavior or desires from eye direction (bottom). For example, they are impaired when asked "which chocolate will Charlie take?" or "which one does Charlie want?."

Top photo from Baron-Cohen and Cross, 1992. Reprinted with permission of Blackwell Publishing. Bottom panel from Baron-Cohen *et al.*, 1995. Reproduced with permission from *British Journal of Developmental Psychology*. © British Psychological Society.

## Evaluation

Recognizing facial expressions may depend on several mechanisms in the brain. Expressions may be recognized using regions of the brain specialized for emotional processing (including the amygdala and orbitofrontal cortex). However, sensorimotor simulation may also contribute to recognizing expressions. The superior temporal sulcus is important for recognizing eye gaze and facial/bodily movements, but it is presently unclear whether it is critically involved in expression recognition. The recognition of eye gaze provides important clues about the intentions of others and may interface with other regions involved in making mentalizing inferences.

## READING MINDS

Facial expressions are only an outward manifestation of someone's unobservable mental state. The term *mental states* is used to refer to knowledge, beliefs, feelings, intentions, and desires. Being able to know the content of someone's mind is a good way of predicting their behavior. Humans, and other species, have evolved mechanisms for dealing with this. One mechanism that has already been touched upon is simulation. Simulation Theories have in common the basic idea that we understand others through a self-centered approach. This may be achieved by a mirroring of states: for instance, seeing you afraid, makes me afraid (by activating my fear-related circuits), and this enables me to infer your mental state. The most common version of simulation theory is linked to perception-action coupling and with the candidate neural mechanism being mirror neurons (Gallese, 2001, 2003; Gallese & Goldman, 1998). The other main explanation suggests that there is a mechanism for inferring and reasoning about the mental states of others that is commonly referred to as **theory-of-mind** (Dennett, 1978). One hallmark of theory-of-mind is that it enables the representation of different states of mind to one's own (e.g. "you think it is in the box, I know it is in the basket")—this is not straightforward for most simulation theories to explain. In some stronger accounts, it is assumed that there is a domain-specific module in the brain for theory-of-mind. The term *mentalizing* is used by some researchers instead of theory-of-mind to denote essentially the same thing, but without carrying the connotation that it may be a special mechanism. Although there are more nuanced theories, the debate between mirroring versus mentalizing offers the clearest way of understanding this literature.

## Empathy, mirroring, and simulation theory

**Empathy** refers, in the broadest sense, an emotional reaction to (or understanding of) another person's feelings. In experimental settings, empathy is often studied by presenting a stimulus relating to one person (e.g. an image or description of someone in distress) and measuring their response in various ways (brain activity, subjective report, bodily response). It is also possible to measure individual differences in empathy, i.e. the tendency for different people to respond empathically, and this is most frequently done via questionnaire (Davis, 1980). From first principles, empathy could be related to either mirroring or mentalizing mechanisms or both. However, research on empathy typically differs from that done with theory-of-mind in that the latter tends to directly probe knowledge of mental states (e.g. what does Sally think?"), whereas studies on empathy tend not to.

Iacoboni (2009) has argued that the mirror system for action may be co-opted by other regions of the brain to support empathy. Carr *et al.* (2003) examined a possible link between empathy and action perception/production using fMRI in humans. They showed participants emotional facial expressions under two conditions: observation versus deliberate imitation. They found increased activation for the imitation condition relative to observation in classical mirror-system areas such as the premotor cortex. In addition, they found increased activation in areas involved in emotion such as the amygdala and insula. Their claim was that imitation activates shared motor representations between self and other, but, crucially, there is a second step in which this information is relayed to limbic areas via the insula. This action-to-emotion route was hypothesized to underpin empathy.

Simulation theories extend the notion of a mirror neuron (see Chapter 8) not only to action, but also to sensation (such as pain and touch) and emotion. The term **mirror system** is used to convey the idea of neural circuits that disregard the distinction between self and other, but need not necessarily imply action-coding mirror neurons. For example, the insula region is activated both when we are disgusted and when we look at someone else scrunching up their face in an expression of disgust (Phillips *et al.*, 1997). Moreover, people who score higher on questionnaire measures of empathy show greater activation of their own disgust regions when watching other people being disgusted (Jabbi *et al.*, 2007). This suggests that we may, in some literal sense, share the emotions of the people around us.

Singer and colleagues (2004) investigated empathy for pain. The brain was scanned when anticipating and watching a loved-one suffer a mild electric shock. There was an overlap between regions activated by expectancy of another person's pain and experiencing pain oneself, including the anterior cingulate cortex and the insula. In a follow-up to this study, participants in an fMRI scanner watched electric shocks delivered to people who were considered either good or bad on the basis of whether they had played fairly or unfairly in a game (Singer *et al.*, 2006). While participants empathically activated their own pain regions when watching the "goodie" receive the electric shock, this response was attenuated when they saw the "baddie" receiving the shock. In fact, male participants often activated their ventral striatum (linked to better than expected rewards) when watching the baddie receive the shock—i.e. the exact opposite of simulation theory. This brain activity correlated with their reported desire for revenge. This suggests that, although simulation may tend to operate automatically, it is not protected from our higher order beliefs. Other research has shown that pain-related regions are activated differently when watching someone in pain depending on whether one takes a self-centered or other-centered perspective and depending on one's beliefs about whether the pain was necessary (Lamm *et al.*, 2007). This suggests a significant amount of flexibility in mirroring that some simple versions of simulation theory would not predict.

In order to capture the fact that mirroring does not always occur, some researchers have argued that empathy should be understood in terms of the coordinated operation of different kinds of processes. Some researchers argue for a division between cognitive empathy and affective empathy for which the former is effectively synonymous with theory-of-mind and the latter with simulation theory (Baron-Cohen & Wheelwright, 2004; Shamay-Tsoory *et al.*, 2009). Decety and Jackson (2004; 2006) offer a different model of empathy comprising of three

Do you empathize with someone by simulating how you would feel in their situation? An image such as this one tends to activate parts of the brain involved in the physical perception of pain.

© Image Source/Corbis.

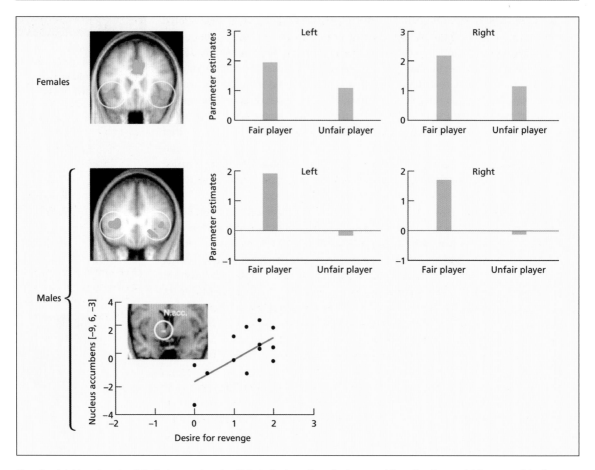

Females (pink) and males (blue) show reduced activity in brain regions that respond to pain when watching an unfair player receive a shock (shown here for the insula). In males, activity in the nucleus accumbens, measured while the unfair player received a shock, correlates with their self-reported desire for revenge.

From Singer *et al.*, 2006. © 2006 Nature Publishing Group. Reproduced with permission.

mechanisms. The first relates to simulation but is assumed to reflect a property of many brain systems (rather than converging on action-based mirror neurons). The second relates to a mechanism for recognizing self and other as distinct, and this is assumed to be related to the temporoparietal junction area (a key region for theory-of-mind, discussed later). This region responds more when participants are asked to imagine someone else's feelings and beliefs compared with their own (Ruby & Decety, 2004). A third mechanism relates specifically to deliberate efforts to shift perspectives between self and other, and is related to executive functioning (and the lateral prefrontal cortex).

## Mind-reading in autism

*He wandered about smiling, making stereotyped movements with his fingers, crossing them about in the air. He shook his head from side to side, whispering or humming the same three-note tune. He spun with great pleasure anything he could seize upon to spin … When taken into a room, he completely disregarded the people and instantly went for objects, preferably those that could be spun … He angrily shoved away the hand that was in his way or the foot that stepped on one of his blocks.*

*(This description of Donald, aged five, was given by Leo Kanner (1943), who also coined the term "autism." The disorder was independently noted by Hans Asperger (1944), whose name now denotes a variant of autism).*

**Autism** has been formally defined as "persistent deficits in social communication and social interaction across multiple contexts" and "restricted, repetitive patterns of behavior, interests, or activities" (the American Psychiatric Association, 2013, *Diagnostic and Statistical Manual*; DSM-V). It is a severe developmental condition that is evident before 3 years of age and lasts throughout life. There are a number of difficulties in diagnosing autism. First, it is defined according to behavior because no specific biological markers are known (for a review, see Hill & Frith, 2003). Second, the profile and severity may be modified during the course of development. It can be influenced by external factors (e.g. education, temperament) and may be accompanied by other disorders (e.g. attention deficit and hyperactivity disorder, psychiatric disorders). As such, autism is now viewed as a spectrum of conditions spanning all degrees of severity. It affects 1.2 percent of the childhood population, and is three times as common in males (Baird *et al.*, 2006). **Asperger syndrome** falls within this spectrum, and is often considered a special subgroup. The diagnosis of Asperger syndrome requires that there is no significant delay in early language and cognitive development. The term is more commonly used to denote people with autism who fall within the normal range of intelligence. Learning disability, defined as an IQ lower than 70, is present in around half of all cases of autism (Baird *et al.*, 2006).

Much of the behavioral data has been obtained from high-functioning individuals in an attempt to isolate a specific core of deficits. One candidate deficit is the ability to represent mental states (Baron-Cohen, 1995b; Fodor, 1992). The first empirical evidence in favor of this hypothesis came with the development of a test of **false belief,** devised by Wimmer and Perner (1983) and tested on autistic children by Baron-Cohen *et al.* (1985). In the version used with autistic children, the *Sally–Anne task*, the child is introduced to two characters, Sally and Anne. Sally puts a marble in a basket so that Anne can see. Anne then leaves the room, and Sally moves the marble to a box. When Anne enters the room, the child is asked: "Where will Anne look for the marble?" or "Where does Anne think the marble is?". Children with autism reply: "In the box"; whereas normal children (aged 4+) and learning-disabled controls reply: "In the basket." The erroneous reply is not due to a failure of memory, because the children can remember the initial location. It is as if they fail to understand that Anne has a belief that differs from physical reality—that is, a failure to represent mental states. This has also been called "mind-blindness" (Baron-Cohen, 1995b).

A number of other studies have pointed to selective difficulties in mentalizing compared with carefully controlled conditions. For example, people with autism can understand false photographs, but not false beliefs (Leekam & Perner, 1991); can sequence behavioral pictures, but not mentalistic pictures (Baron-Cohen *et al.*, 1986); are good at sabotage, but not deception (Sodian & Frith, 1992); and tend to use desire and emotion words, but not belief and idea words (Tager-

## KEY TERMS

**Autism**
The presence of markedly abnormal or impaired development in social interaction and communication, and a markedly restricted repertoire of activities and interests.

**Asperger syndrome**
Autism with no significant delay in early language and cognitive development.

**False belief**
A belief that differs from one's own belief and that differs from the true state of the world.

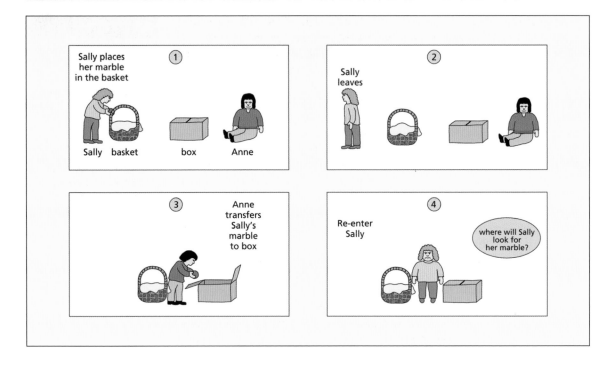

The Sally–Anne task requires an understanding of "false belief" and tends to be failed by children with autism.

Adapted from Wimmer and Perner, 1983.

Flusberg, 1992). In all instances, the performance of people with autism is compared with mental-age controls to establish that the effects are related to autism and not general level of functioning.

The mentalizing or theory-of-mind account of autism has not been without its critics. These criticisms generally take two forms: either that other explanations can account for the data without postulating a difficulty in mentalizing (Russell, 1997; Stone & Gerrans, 2006), or that a difficulty with mentalizing is necessary but insufficient to explain all of the available evidence (Frith, 1989).

One difficulty with the theory-of-mind explanation is that it fails to account for cognitive strengths as well as weaknesses. One popular notion of autistic people is that they have unusual gifts or "savant" skills, as in the film *Rain Man*. In reality, these skills are found only in around 10 percent of the autistic population (Hill & Frith, 2003). Nevertheless, some account of them is needed for a full explanation of autism. The unusual skills of some autistic people may be partly an outcome of their limited range of interests. Perhaps one reason why some individuals are good at memorizing dates is that they practice it almost all the time. However, there is also evidence for more basic differences in processing style. For example, people on the autistic spectrum are superior at detecting embedded figures (Shah & Frith, 1983). One explanation for this is in terms of "weak central coherence" (Frith, 1989; Happe, 1999). This is a cognitive style, assumed to be present in autism, in which processing of parts (or local features) takes precedent over processing of wholes (or global features). A different explanation describes *all* individuals as having a mix of two different processing styles termed "empathizing" and "systemizing" (Baron-Cohen *et al.*, 2003). Most nonautistic people would lie near the middle and possess a mix of both. People with autism would lie at the extreme systemizing end and lack empathizing (Baron-Cohen, 2002). Empathizing allows one to predict another person's behavior, and care about how others feel. Thus, a lack of empathizing would account for the mentalizing difficulties. Systemizing requires an understanding of lawful, rule-based systems and requires an attention to detail. This would account for their preserved abilities and unusual interests (e.g. in calendar systems).

There are several theories that attempt to explain the social deficits in autism without recourse to a deficit in mentalizing or without postulating the absence of a specialized theory-of-mind mechanism. An earlier suggestion is that primary deficit in autism is one of executive functioning (Hughes *et al.*, 1994; Ozonoff *et al.*, 1991; Russell, 1997). For example, on false belief tasks the incorrect answer might be chosen because of a failure to suppress the strongly activated "physical reality" alternative. The **broken-mirror theory** of autism argues that the social difficulties linked to autism are a consequence of mirror-system dysfunction (Iacoboni & Dapretto, 2006; Oberman & Ramachandran, 2007; Ramachandran & Oberman, 2006; Rizzolatti & Fabbri-Destro, 2010). Several lines of evidence have been taken to support this. Hadjikhani *et al.* (2006) found, using structural MRI, that autistic individuals had reduced gray matter in several regions linked to the mirror system, including the inferior frontal gyrus (Broca's region). Dapretto *et al.* (2006) conducted an fMRI study in which autistic children and matched controls either observed or imitated emotional expressions. The imitation condition produced less activity in the inferior frontal gyrus of the autistic children relative to controls, and this was correlated with symptom severity. Oberman *et al.* (2005) used EEG to record mu waves over the motor cortex of high-functioning autistic children and controls. **Mu oscillations** occur at a particular frequency (8–13 Hz) and are greatest when participants are doing nothing. However, when they perform an action there is a decrease in the number of mu waves, a phenomenon termed mu suppression. Importantly, in typical controls mu suppression also occurs when people *observe* actions and, as such, it has been regarded by some as a measure of mirror-system activity (Pineda, 2005). Oberman *et al.* (2005) found that the autistic children failed to show as much mu suppression as controls during action observation (watching someone else make a pincer movement) but did so in the control condition of action execution (they themselves make a pincer movement). Finally, watching someone perform an action increases ones own motor excitability, measured as a motor-evoked potential (MEP) on the body, when TMS is applied to the motor cortex. However, this effect is reduced in autistic people, even though their motor cortex behaves normally in other contexts (Theoret *et al.*, 2005).

In sum, there is convincing evidence for mirror-system dysfunction in autism. What is less clear is whether this represents the core deficit and whether it is sufficient to account for the full range of social impairments (including false belief). First, tasks involving imitation and empathy do not rely solely on these kinds of simulation mechanisms but also involve deliberate perspective taking, knowledge of social rules, and cognitive control critics (Dinstein *et al.*,

**KEY TERMS**

**Broken-mirror theory**
An account of autism in which the social difficulties are considered as a consequence of mirror-system dysfunction.

**Mu oscillations**
EEG oscillations at 8–13 Hz over sensorimotor cortex that are greatest when participants are at rest.

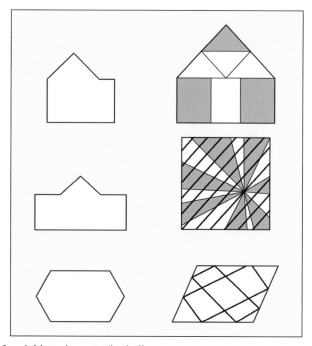

People with autism may be faster at spotting embedded figures similar to the ones shown here.

## IS AUTISM AN EXTREME FORM OF THE MALE BRAIN?

Baron-Cohen (2002) argues that the characteristics of all individuals can be classified according to two dimensions: "empathizing" and "systemizing." Empathizing allows one to predict a person's behavior and to care about how others feel. Systemizing requires an understanding of lawful, rule-based systems and requires an attention to detail. Males tend to have a brain type that is biased toward systemizing (S > E), and females tend to have a brain type that is biased toward empathizing (E > S). However, not all men and women have the "male type" and "female type," respectively. Autistic people appear to have an extreme male type (S >> E), characterized by a lack of empathizing (this would account for the mentalizing difficulties) and a high degree of systemizing (this would account for their preserved abilities and unusual interests). A questionnaire study suggests that these distinctions hold true (Baron-Cohen et al., 2003). However, it remains to be shown whether these distinctions are merely descriptive or indeed do reflect two real underlying mechanisms at the cognitive or neural level.

One observation that needs to be accounted for is the fact that autism is more common in males. The "male brain hypothesis" offers a simple explanation: males are more likely to have a male-type brain. An alternative, but potentially related, account may be in terms of genetic factors. Whereas it is likely that multiple genes confer autistic susceptibility (Maestrini et al., 2000), one of them may lie on the sex-linked X chromosome. Evidence for this comes from Turner's syndrome. Most men have one X chromosome from their mother and a Y chromosome from their father (XY). Most women have two X chromosomes (XX), one from each parent. Women with Turner's syndrome have only a single X chromosome (XO) from either their father or mother. If the X chromosome has a maternal origin, then the woman often falls on the autistic spectrum; she does not if it has a paternal origin (Creswell & Skuse, 1999). It is suggested that the paternal X chromosome may have a preventive effect on autistic tendencies. An absence of this chromosome in some Turner's women and all normal males (who get their X chromosome from their mother) may leave them susceptible to autism.

2008; Southgate & Hamilton, 2008). Second, a core deficit elsewhere (e.g. in representing mental states) could nevertheless affect the functioning of the mirror system, and perhaps even lead to structural changes within that system. Heyes (2010) argues that the properties of mirror neurons may be learned as a result of social interactions. So impoverished social interactions may cause mirror-system dysfunction, as well as vice versa.

### Neural basis of theory-of-mind

Evidence for the neural basis of theory-of-mind has come from two main sources: functional imaging studies of normal participants and behavioral studies of patients with brain lesions. Numerous tasks have been used, including directly inferring mental states from stories (e.g. Fletcher et al., 1995), from cartoons (Gallagher et al., 2000) or when interacting with another person (McCabe et al., 2001). A review and meta-analysis of the functional imaging literature was provided by Frith and Frith (2003), who identified three key regions involved in mentalizing.

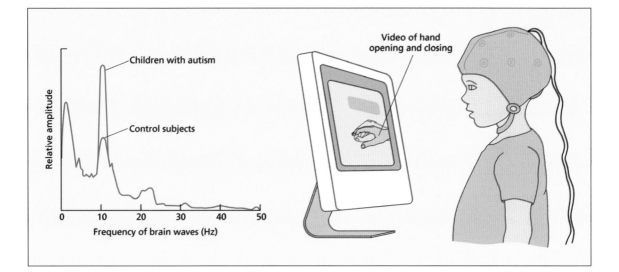

## Temporal poles

This region is normally activated in tasks of language and semantic memory. Frith and Frith (2003) suggest that this region is involved with generating schemas that specify the current social or emotional context, as well as in semantics more generally. Zahn *et al.* (2007) report an fMRI study suggesting that this region responds to comparisons between social concepts (e.g. brave–honorable) more than matched nonsocial concepts (e.g. nutritious–useful). Not all the tests of mentalizing that activated this region involved linguistic stimuli. For example, one study used triangles that appeared to interact by, say, chasing or encouraging each other (Castelli *et al.*, 2000).

## Medial prefrontal cortex

Frith and Frith (2003) reported that this region is activated in all functional imaging tasks of mentalizing to that date. Functional imaging studies reliably show that this region responds more to thinking about people than thinking about other entities such as computers or dogs (e.g. Mitchell *et al.*, 2002, 2005); and thinking about the *minds* of people than thinking about their other attributes such as their physical characteristics (Mitchell *et al.*, 2005), Some studies of patients with frontal lobe damage have suggested that the medial regions are necessary for theory-of-mind (Stuss *et al.*, 2001b; Roca *et al.*, 2011). This region also seems to be implicated in the pragmatics of language such as irony ("Peter is well read. He has even heard of Shakespeare") and metaphor ("your room is a pigsty"; Bottini *et al.*, 1994). Interestingly, people with autism have difficulties with this aspect of language (Happe, 1995). In such instances, the speaker's *intention* must be derived from the ambiguous surface properties of the words (e.g. the room is not literally a pigsty). Functional imaging suggests that this region is involved both in theory-of-mind and in establishing the pragmatic coherence between ideas/sentences, including those that do not involve mentalizing (Ferstl & von Cramon, 2002).

Krueger *et al.* (2009) argue that the function of this region is to bind together different kinds of information (actions, agents, goals, objects, beliefs) to create

Mu waves are EEG oscillations in the 8–13 Hz range that are reduced both when performing an action and when watching someone else perform an action (relative to rest). As such, they may provide a neural signature for human mirror neurons. Autistic children show less mu suppression when watching others perform a hand action, which provides evidence in support of broken mirror theory.

From Ramachandran and Oberman, 2006. Reproduced with permission from Lucy Reading-Ikkanda for *Scientific American* Magazine.

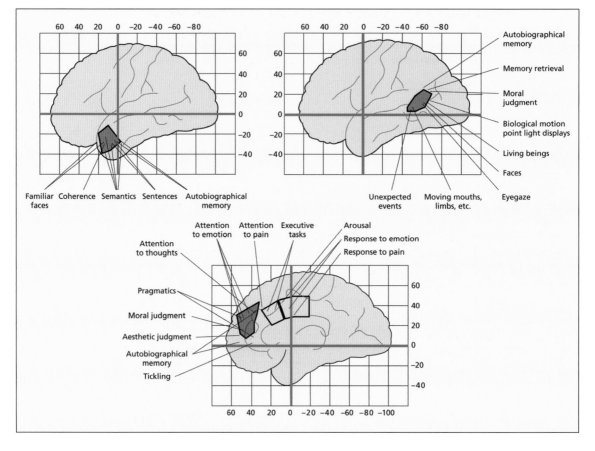

Functional imaging and lesion studies implicate three important regions in theory-of-mind (shaded): temporal poles (top left), temporal-parietal junction (top right), and the medial frontal lobes including a portion of the anterior cingulate (bottom; note the anterior cingulate is drawn as divided into functionally separate areas).

From Frith and Frith, 2003. Reprinted by permission of Royal Society of London and the author.

what they term a "social event." They note that within this region some sub-regions respond more when participants make judgments about themselves, and also judgments about others who are considered to be similar to themselves. This suggests that this region is not attributing mental states per se, but is considering the self in relation to others. The notion of creating internal social events could also explain some of the findings of the role of this region in linking ideas in story comprehension (Ferstl & von Cramon, 2002).

### Temporal-parietal junction

This region tends to be not only activated in tests of mentalizing, but also in studies of the perception of biological motion, eye gaze, moving mouths, and living things in general. These skills are clearly important for detecting other "agents" and processing their observable actions. Simulation theories argue that mentalizing need not involve anything over and above action perception. However, it is also conceivable that this region goes beyond the processing of observable actions, and is also concerned with representing mental states. Patients with lesions in this region fail theory-of-mind tasks that can't be accounted for by difficulties in body perception (Samson *et al.*, 2004). Saxe and Kanwisher (2003) found activity in this region, on the right, when comparing false belief tasks (requiring mentalizing) with false photograph tasks (not requiring mentalizing but entailing a conflict with reality). The result was also found when the false photograph involved people and actions, consistent with a role in mentalizing beyond any role in action/person perception. Saxe and Powell (2006) have shown that this region responds to attribution of contentful mental states (such as thoughts and beliefs) rather than subjective states (such as hunger or tiredness). This suggests that it may have a role over and above "thinking about others" which they claim is specific to thinking about mental states.

## Evaluation

Performance on tasks of theory-of-mind typically requires the use of several nonspecialized (i.e. domain general) processes, including language processing, executive functions and action perception. The controversy lies in whether these mechanisms are the *only* ones that are needed to account for theory-of-mind (in some forms of simulation theory) or whether there is additionally the need for a specialized (i.e. domain-specific) mechanism that is specific to representing the mental states of others. Functional imaging and brain-lesion studies highlight the importance of several key regions in theory-of-mind, but the extent to which these regions are specific to theory-of-mind is controversial. Autism still offers the most convincing evidence for a specialized mechanism.

## SUMMARY AND KEY POINTS OF THE CHAPTER

- Contemporary models of emotion differ with respect to whether there are a finite number of discrete emotions or whether there is a continuous range of emotional processes but with categories of emotion being constructed through interactions with nonaffective processes (e.g. appraisal, language).
- Different regions of the "emotional brain" have different functions; although these functions do not precisely map on to discrete categories of emotion (such as fear, happiness, etc.). The amygdala has a key role in emotional learning and memory (e.g. fear conditioning); the insula and anterior cingulate have key roles in bodily related aspects of emotion experience; the orbitofrontal cortex is crucial for the appraisal and control of social and emotional stimuli; and the ventral striatum has a key role in reward prediction.
- The functions of the emotional brain described above operate in both the social realm (e.g. when the stimuli consist of conspecifics) and the nonsocial realm.
- Recognizing facial expressions, processing eye gaze, and recognizing facial identity depend on different neural mechanisms. The superior temporal sulcus is particularly important for gaze detection, whereas recognizing expressions depends, at least in part, on simulating the affective and sensorimotor components of that expression.
- Mirroring (and simulation theory) is an important aspect of explaining empathy, but there is more to empathy than this. Empathy is

Visit the companion website at www. psypress/cw/ward for videos on key topics covered in this chapter, references to key papers and readings, multiple choice questions and interactive glossary flashcards.

modulated be social knowledge of others and may also require a mentalizing component.

- People with autism may lack a theory-of-mind mechanism, but impaired theory-of-mind alone cannot explain the full pattern of strengths and weaknesses in autism. It is unclear whether theory-of-mind is the core deficit in autism or whether a defective mirror system is the core deficit.

- Thinking about the mental states of others involves a core network of regions (including temporoparietal junction and medial prefrontal cortex) that differ from those involved in executive functions more generally, or involved in emotional evaluation or person perception. Whether it is a domain-specific module remains contested.

## EXAMPLE ESSAY QUESTIONS

- Are there discrete categories of different emotions?
- Contrast the different roles of the amygdala and orbitofrontal cortex in emotion processing?
- Can autism be explained as "mind-blindness"?
- To what extent can empathy and theory-of-mind be explained by a process of simulation?
- To what extent are recognizing facial identity, expression recognition, and gaze recognition served by different mechanisms?
- What is the role of mirror systems in social cognition?

## RECOMMENDED FURTHER READING

- Hill, E. L. & Frith, U. (2004). *Autism: Mind and brain*. Oxford, UK: Oxford University Press (also published as an issue of *Philosophical Transactions of the Royal Society of London* B (2003), *358*, 277–427).
- Lane, R. D. & Nadel, L. (2000). *Cognitive neuroscience of emotion*. Oxford, UK: Oxford University Press. A collection of papers covering many of the issues related to the first half of this chapter.
- Saxe, R. & Baron-Cohen, S. (2006). *Theory of mind*. Hove, UK: Psychology Press (also published as an issue of *Social Neuroscience*, *1*, 135–416).
- Ward, J. (2012). *The student's guide to social neuroscience*. New York: Psychology Press. An accessible introduction to all topics in the area. Start here.

# CHAPTER 16

# The developing brain

## CONTENTS

Many people are drawn into a subject like psychology because of one nagging question: What makes us who we are? Were we predestined to become the person we are today as a result of our genetic endowment? If so, could a parent of the late twenty-first century be reading their child's genetic "blueprint" to figure out their cognitive strengths and weaknesses, their personality and disposition? Or are we shaped by our experiences and circumstances during life and during our formative years of development? These questions are central to the **nature–nurture debate**, i.e. the extent to which cognition and behavior can be attributed to genes or environment. While the nature–nurture debate still has contemporary relevance and continues to excite both scientists and lay people, this chapter will consider how many of the commonly held assumptions surrounding this debate are misguided. For example, genes do not provide a predetermined blueprint,but are themselves switched on and off by the environment; and the contemporary notion of "environment" is far broader than is commonly understood. It includes biological circumstances (e.g. diet, exposure to toxins), as well as personal and social circumstances.

Historically, the pendulum has swung between opposing extremes of this debate. For example, in 1874, Francis Galton published *English Men of Science: Their Nature and Nurture*, arguing that geniuses are born and not made. As well

## KEY TERMS

**Nature–nurture debate**
The extent to which cognition and behavior can be attributed to genes or environment.

**Neuroconstructivism**
A process of interaction between environment and multiple, brain-based constraints that leads to the mature cognitive system emerging out of transformations of earlier ones.

**Near-infrared spectroscopy (NIRS)**
A hemodynamic method that measures blood oxygenation, normally in one brain region.

In Piaget's sensorimotor stage (0–2 years), a child learns about the nature of objects (e.g. that they still exist when hidden) and about the nature of cause and effect (e.g. that actions have consequences on the objects around). The child then passes through other stages (preoperational, concrete, and formal operational) with greater degrees of abstraction. Although the stages can be regarded as fixed and predetermined, Piaget stressed the role of the environment to successfully develop the cognitive processes required for the next stage.

© Brooke Fasani/Corbis.

as coining the phrase "nature or nurture," he was the first person to realize that heredity could be estimated by comparing identical and nonidentical twins. Galton's advocacy of nature over nurture would become associated with the discredited eugenics movement, which promoted selective breeding of the more cognitively able (although in practice this was often implemented by sterilization of the "feeble-minded").

In the early twentieth century, the pendulum had swung to the other extreme. Freudian theory, for example, emphasized the importance of early experiences and parenting style in development. The Russian psychologist Lev Vygotsky (1896–1934) also emphasized the role of culture and interpersonal communication in development. Behaviorist theories, such as those put forward by B. F. Skinner (1904–1990), argued that all behavior was a product of learning as a result of rewards and punishments.

Jean Piaget (1896–1980) is regarded as the founding father of modern Western developmental psychology. Piaget took a middle ground with regards to the nature–nurture debate. He regarded development as a cyclical process of interactions between the child and his or her environment. In his view, the genetic contribution consists of developing a brain that is ready to learn in certain ways, but progression through the stages involves assimilating evidence from the environment and then developing new mechanisms in light of the feedback obtained. While many of Piaget's experimental studies have not stood the test of time (e.g. children show evidence of reasoning long before Piaget suggested they should), his basic approach to development has been more enduring.

Following on from the developmental psychology tradition, developmental cognitive neuroscience has focused on brain-based explanations of developmental change (Johnson, 2005). One particular current approach is termed **neuroconstructivism** (Westermann et al., 2007). Like Piaget's approach, this assumes constant interaction between environment and genetic factors, with a mature cognitive system emerging out of transformations of earlier ones. Unlike Piaget's approach, the predetermined aspect of development is construed in terms of multiple, brain-based constraints (developmental changes in synapse formation, myelination, etc.), rather than the less well-defined notion of predetermined "stages."

This chapter will first consider the structural development of the brain, both prenatally and postnatally. It will then go on to consider the nature of developmental change, including evidence for critical/sensitive periods and innate knowledge. An overview of the origin of genetic differences and behavioral genetics will then go on to consider some specific examples of genetic influences in developmental cognitive neuroscience. Together with the advances made in

## ADAPTING THE METHODS OF COGNITIVE NEUROSCIENCE FOR INFANTS AND CHILDREN

Methods such as fMRI and EEG are generally considered suitable for infants and children. One advantage of using these methods in younger people is that they do not necessarily require a verbal or motor response to be made.

### Functional MRI

Gaillard et al. (2001) provide an overview of some of the considerations needed. If one wants to compare across different ages, then the most significant problem is that the structural properties of the brain change during development. Although the volume of the brain is stable by about 5 years of age, there are differences in white and gray matter volumes until adulthood (Reiss et al., 1996). The hemodynamic response function is relatively stable after 7 years of age but differs below this age (Marcar et al., 2004). The differences in both brain structure and blood flow make it harder to compare activity in the same region across different ages. Younger children also find it harder to keep still in the scanner, and this motion can disrupt the reliability of the MR signal.

### Near-infrared spectroscopy

One relatively new method that is now being used in developmental cognitive neuroscience is **near-infrared spectroscopy** (**NIRS**) (for a summary, see Lloyd-Fox et al., 2010). This measures the amount of oxygenated blood and is—like fMRI—a hemodynamic method. Unlike fMRI it accommodates a good degree of movement and is more portable. The infant can sit upright on their parent's lap. However, it has poorer spatial resolution and does not normally permit whole-head coverage.

### ERP/EEG

When working with young participants using ERP/EEG, a limiting factor is the child's willingness to tolerate the electrodes, the task, and the time commitment required (Thomas & Casey, 2003). Children and adults can show quite different patterns of ERP (e.g. in terms of latency, amplitude, or scalp distribution), even for tasks that both groups find easy (Thomas & Nelson, 1996). These could either reflect age-related cognitive differences (i.e. the same task can be performed in different ways at different ages) or noncognitive differences (e.g. the effects of skull thickness, cell-packing density or myelination).

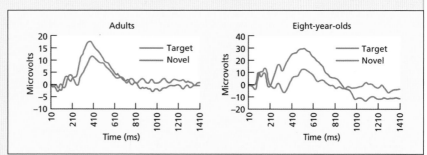

### TMS

Current ethical and safety guidelines (Wassermann, 1996) do not recommend *repetitive* TMS to children except for compelling therapeutic purposes (e.g. treatment of depression).

Adults and children show very different visual ERP waveforms, despite having equivalent behavioral performance.

Adapted from Thomas and Nelson, 1996.

molecular genetics, it is now becoming possible to understand how genetic influences and experience create changes in the structure and function of the brain. This is leading to an exciting rethink of the nature–nurture debate.

## STRUCTURAL DEVELOPMENT OF THE BRAIN

Gottlieb (1992) discusses different ideas about development. In *predetermined development*, genes dictate the structure of the brain, which enables the particular functions of the brain, which determines the kinds of experiences we have. This is a traditional view of how genes affect cognition. In contrast, Gottlieb also outlines a *probabilistic developmental* perspective in which brain structure, and even the expression of genes, can be influenced by experience as well as vice versa. This represents the dominant view in modern developmental cognitive neuroscience. Even environmental influences in the womb, such as the diet of the mother and the presence of viruses or toxic agents, could alter brain structure and, hence, function. Following birth, all of our everyday experiences result in tiny changes to the structure of our brain, in the form of altering the pattern of synaptic connections. Sometimes these changes are even visible at the macroscopic level. Adults who learn to juggle with three balls over a 3-month period show increased gray matter density, assessed with MRI, in a region, V5/MT, specialized for detecting visual motion (Draganski *et al.*, 2004). This example illustrates a central concept of this chapter—namely, *plasticity*. Plasticity refers to experience-dependent changes in neural functioning. However, even here there may be a role of genetic factors that, for instance, increase the brain's capability for plastic change at particular time points (sensitive periods) for different regions.

The structural development of the brain can be conveniently divided into the periods before and after birth (i.e. prenatal and postnatal, respectively).

---

**GOTTLIEB'S (1992) DIFFERENT VIEWS OF DEVELOPMENT**

Predetermined development:

> Genes → Brain structure → Brain function → Experience

Probabilistic development:

> Genes ←→ Brain structure ←→ Brain function ←→ Experience

---

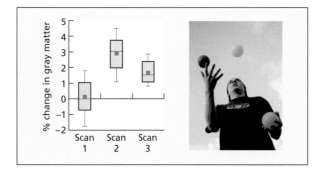

MRI scans were obtained at three time intervals: before learning to juggle; after 3 months of training; and after a further 3 months of no practice. The graph shows increases in gray matter density in an area associated with visual motion perception, area V5/MT.

Reprinted by permission from Macmillan Publishers Ltd: Draganski *et al.*, 2004. © 2004.

# Prenatal development

The human gestation period is around 38 weeks from conception. The newly formed embryo undergoes a rapid process of cell division, followed by a process of differentiation during which the different cells become increasingly specialized. The nervous system derives from a set of cells arranged in a hollow cylinder, the **neural tube**. By around 5 weeks, the neural tube has organized into a set of bulges and convolutions that will go on to form various parts of the brain (e.g. the cortex, the thalamus and hypothalamus, the midbrain). Closer to the hollow of the neural tube are several proliferative zones in which neurons and glial cells are produced by division of proliferating cells (**neuroblasts** and glioblasts). Purves (1994) estimates that the fetal brain must add 250,000 neurons per minute at certain periods in early development.

The newly formed neurons must then migrate outwards toward the region where they will be employed in the mature brain. This occurs in two ways. Passively, older cells tend to be pushed to the surface of the brain. Structures such as the hippocampus are formed this way. There is also an active mechanism by which newer cells are guided to particular destinations, pushing past the older cells. Rakic (1988) identified **radial glial cells** that act like climbing ropes, ensuring that newly formed neurons are guided to their final destination. The convoluted surface of the brain, the neocortex, is formed in this way.

# Postnatal development

At birth, the head makes up approximately a quarter of the length of the infant. Although the brain itself is small (450 g) relative to adult human size (1400 g), it is large in comparison to remote human ancestors and living primates (a newborn human brain is about 75 percent of that of an adult chimpanzee). The vast majority of neurons are formed prior to birth, so the expansion in brain volume during postnatal development is due to factors such as the growth of synapses, dendrites, and axon bundles; the proliferation of glial cells; and the myelination of nerve fibers.

Huttenlocher and Dabholkar (1997) measured the synaptic density in various regions of human cortex. This is a measure of the degree to which neurons are connected to each other and is unrelated to number of neurons per se or how active the synapses are. In all cortical areas studied to date, there is a characteristic rise and then fall in synapse formation (synaptogenesis). In primary visual and primary auditory cortex, the peak density is between 4 and 12 months, at which

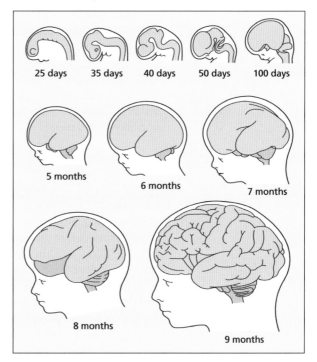

The embryonic and fetal development of the human brain. Cortical asymmetries between the left and right hemispheres, implicated in language acquisition, are present at 24 weeks.

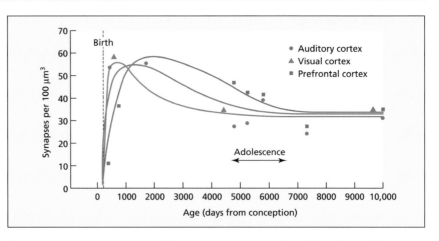

Synapse formation has a rise-and-fall pattern. It peaks soon after birth, although different cortical regions differ greatly in the time taken to fall again to adult synaptic levels.

From Huttenlocher and Dabholkar, 1997. Reprinted with permission of John Wiley & Sons Inc.

point it is 150 percent above adult levels, but falls to adult levels between 2 and 4 years. In prefrontal cortex, the peak is reached after 12 months, but does not return to adult levels until 10–20 years old. PET studies of glucose metabolism in developing brains show a similar rise and fall to studies of synaptogenesis, although peaking time tends to be somewhat later (Chugani *et al.*, 1987). Glucose metabolism may be a measure of actual neural activity rather than neural structural changes. Why does the number of synapses fall during the course of development? It is not necessarily the case that more synapses reflects more efficient functioning. During development a process of fine-tuning the brain to the needs of the environment renders some connections redundant.

**Myelination** refers to the increase in the fatty sheath that surrounds axons and increases the speed of information transmission. In structural MRI, the increase in white matter volume over the first two decades of life may reflect the time course of myelination (Giedd *et al.*, 1999). Again, the prefrontal cortex is one of the last areas to achieve adult levels of myelination, and this, together with the late fine-tuning and elimination of synapses in this region, may contribute to the development of mature social behavior during adolescence and the control of behavior in general.

## Protomap and protocortex theories of brain development

Different regions of the cortex have structural differences. This is manifest in terms of the grouping of cell types in the different layers and also in terms of the patterns of their input–output connections, which ultimately determine the type of function they are likely perform. But how does this regional organization come about, and when? Specifically, to what extent is it a product of prenatal or postnatal brain development? The protomap (Rakic, 1988) and protocortex (O'Leary, 1989) theories of brain development provide different answers to these same questions.

The protomap theory argues that the regional layout of the cortex is established at the prenatal stages of development. The early proliferating zone is assumed to specify the ultimate layout of different cortical regions. This may be achieved through the radial glial fibers that carry new neurons away from the proliferation zone (Rakic, 1988) and through regional differences in various molecular signals (called transcription factors) that affect the neurons' structure, migration, and survival (see Sur & Rubenstein, 2005). Different doses of these signals determine the dimensions of the various lobes of the brain, such that, for example, a dose above a certain threshold may instruct a new neuron to develop features characteristic of a frontal lobe neuron (e.g. in terms of its connectivity) but below that dose it may resemble a parietal neuron (Fukuchi-Shimogori & Grove, 2001). This suggests a simple mechanism for creating individual differences in brain structure and also for evolutionary development (e.g. a shifting dose could enable an evolutionary jump in frontal lobe enlargement).

The protocortex theory, on the other hand, argues that different regions of the cortex are initially equivalent but become specialized as a result of projections from the thalamus (O'Leary, 1989). This is assumed to be influenced by postnatal sensory experience. What would happen if part of the developing visual cortex were transplanted into parts of the brain normally specialized for touch or hearing? The protocortex theory predicts that regions of cortex can initially be interchanged and that the transplanted visual cortex would now respond to touch or sound because it would be innervated by somatosensory or auditory projections from the thalamus. To some extent, this is indeed what happens. Visual cortex transplanted into somatosensory cortex responds to touch on a mouse's whiskers and reconnects to the somatosensory region of the thalamus (Schlagger & O'Leary, 1991). If visual information from the eyes is rerouted to the auditory cortex of a ferret (by rewiring from the retina to auditory regions of the thalamus that then project to auditory cortex), then the auditory cortex takes on visual properties. The "auditory" neurons respond to particular visual orientations and movement directions (Sharma *et al.*, 2000; Sur Garraghty & Roe, 1988).

How can the two theories be reconciled? In their review, Sur and Rubenstein (2005) conclude that, "the protomap/protocortex controversy no longer remains" (p. 809). The protomap theory never completely excluded a role of environmental inputs. Conversely, visually rewired "auditory" cortex still retains vestiges of normal auditory cortex connections and the visual representations are poorer than those found in true visual cortex (Sharma *et al.*, 2000). This suggests that the protocortex theory should not assume complete exchangeability of different cortical regions.

## Evaluation

The section began with Gottlieb's (1992) distinction between predetermined development, in which brain structure is predetermined by genes, and probabilistic development, in which brain structure is determined by both genes and experiences. Evidence from studies of brain development supports the latter view.

## FUNCTIONAL DEVELOPMENT OF THE BRAIN: SENSITIVE PERIODS AND INNATE KNOWLEDGE?

Having considered how brain *structure* is changed during development, the present section is primarily concerned with how brain *function* (i.e. different types of ability and knowledge) changes developmentally. In particular, two broad issues will be considered: first, the role of critical/sensitive periods in development; and, second, the extent to which any kind of knowledge or ability can be said to be innate.

## Critical and sensitive periods in development

In 1909, a young Austrian boy named Konrad Lorenz and his friend (and later wife), Gretl, were given two newly hatched ducklings by a neighbor. The ducklings followed them everywhere, apparently mistaking them for their parents. This process, now termed **filial imprinting**, was studied intensively by the adult Lorenz using goslings and earned him a Nobel Prize (see Tinbergen, 1951). Lorenz observed that there was a narrow window of opportunity, between 15 hours and 3 days, for a gosling to imprint. Once imprinted, the gosling is unable to learn to follow a new foster parent. The movement of a stimulus was deemed to be crucial for determining what object the gosling will imprint to. A region of the chick forebrain known as intermediate and medial of the hyperstriatum ventrale (IMHV), which may correspond to mammalian cortex, is critical for enabling imprinting (Horn & McCabe, 1984).

The studies above suggest that there is a **critical period** for imprinting. A critical period has two defining features: first, learning can only take place within a limited time window; and, second, the learning is hard to reverse in the face of later experience. Subsequent evidence suggests that the window of opportunity can be extended by lack of suitable early experience (e.g. initial absence of a moving object), and that learning can be reversed in certain circumstances. As such, many researchers prefer the more moderate terminology of a **sensitive period**. For instance, a chick imprinted to one object will often generalize to other objects of similar appearance (e.g. color and shape). By gradually changing the features of the objects to which it is exposed, the chick's final preference can be different from its initial preference, even after the end of the "critical" period (Bolhuis, 1990).

These goslings follow the Austrian professor, Konrad Lorenz, as if he is their mother! This process is called filial imprinting.
© Science Photo Library.

The development of visual abilities also shows evidence of a sensitive period. For example, Hubel and Wiesel (1970b) took single-cell recordings from the primary visual cortex of cats in whom one eye had been deprived of visual input in early life (by sewing it shut). They found that the cells responded to input from the sighted eye only, whereas normally reared cats possess cells that respond to inputs from both eyes. During a sensitive period between 4 and 5 weeks after birth, eye closure for 3–4 days leads to a sharp decline in the number of cells that will respond to input from both eyes.

What of "higher" cognitive abilities, such as language? Lenneburg (1967) initially argued that language acquisition has a critical period that ends abruptly at puberty. However, the ability to comprehend and produce language is likely to depend on other skills such as hearing, motor ability, working memory capacity, and so on. Each of these basic skills may have its own sensitive period, which means that different components of language may have their own sensitive period rather than a fixed cut-off point at puberty. For example, the sensitive period for making phonemic discriminations such as the distinction between r and l, occurs during infancy and is resistant to subsequent exposure (McCandliss *et al.*, 2002). In contrast, accents are more fluid during childhood but become notoriously hard to change from the onset of adulthood.

Studies of feral children offer some support to Lenneburg's idea. Genie had been locked away by her mentally unstable family from the age of 20 months to 13 years when she was discovered in Los Angeles in 1970 (Curtiss, 1977). During this period she was severely maltreated and was not allowed to speak or be spoken to. On being rescued she was almost entirely mute, with a vocabulary of around 20 words. Within the first 18 months of being placed with a foster parent, her language was reported to have developed well on all fronts, including both vocabulary and grammar, and this was cited as evidence *against* a sensitive period (Fromkin *et al.*, 1974). However, subsequent studies are more consistent with a sensitive period and have revealed that her language acquisition remained very poor compared with young children; although it remains debated as to the extent to which her grammar was specifically affected or whether all aspects of language were affected (Jones, 1995).

Thankfully, research in which exposure to a first language is withheld from a child is limited to a tiny number of cases. However, second language acquisition offers a richer source of evidence to test for the existence of a sensitive period. Rather than a fixed point at which the sensitive period closes, the evidence suggests that second language attainment decreases linearly with age (Birdsong, 2006). Many adults are able to become fluent in a second language, but they may do so in different ways from children (e.g. more explicit strategy use). Brain imaging studies reveal that both age-of-acquisition and level of proficiency determine the neural substrates of second language processing in adults. One study compared syntactic and semantic language tasks in Italian-German bilinguals using fMRI (Wartenburger *et al.*, 2003). For syntactic judgments, the age-of-acquisition was critical: those who learned the second language later in life showed more activity in language-related brain regions when processing syntax irrespective of their level of proficiency. This suggests a sensitive period for grammar in terms of neural efficiency (more activity is interpreted here as less efficiency). For semantic judgments, by contrast, the pattern of activity was related to proficiency level in the second language rather than age of acquisition (i.e. little influence of sensitive periods for language semantics).

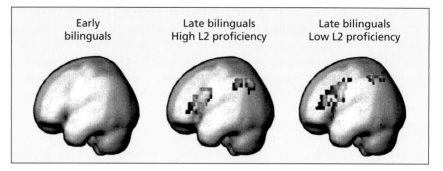

Early
bilinguals

Late bilinguals
High L2 proficiency

Late bilinguals
Low L2 proficiency

When brain activity linked to grammatical processing is contrasted for first (L1) and second (L2) languages, there are no differences for early bilinguals (L2 from birth). However, L2 (relative to L1) is linked to more activity in language-related regions when late bilinguals (L2 after 6 years) make grammatical judgments, irrespective of their proficiency in that language. This suggests a sensitive period for efficient grammatical acquisition.

From Perani & Abutalebi, 2005.

## RECOVERY OF FUNCTION AFTER EARLY BRAIN DAMAGE

Although strokes are rare in infancy and childhood, they do occur. Typically, however, the long-term effects on cognition are neither as severe nor as specific as those arising from strokes in adulthood. This is consistent with the view that plasticity is greatest earlier in life. Several studies have found that children who had strokes around the time of birth go on to develop intellectual and language skills in the normal range (Aram & Ekelman, 1986; Ballantyne et al., 2008). With regards to language, it is often found that early lesions to the left hemisphere can result in later right hemisphere language as assessed using fMRI (Liegeois et al., 2004). In this study, even lesions outside of "classical" language areas (e.g. Broca's area) were just as likely to result in right hemispheric language consistent with the view that functional specialization of regions emerges gradually and in a way that is not completely predetermined. Given that the brain has very limited scope to grow new neurons, one may wonder whether accommodating language in the right hemisphere would have a detrimental outcome on traditional right hemispheric functions (e.g. visuo-spatial skills). There is some evidence for this. Lidzba et al. (2006) report that the extent of right hemispheric language (assessed by fMRI) resulting from early stroke correlated negatively with performance on visuo-spatial tasks (i.e. greater right hemisphere language is associated with poorer visuo-spatial skills). This suggests that, while early plasticity can aid recovery, this may not be completely without a cost.

What general properties of the nervous system give rise to sensitive periods in development? Thomas and Johnson (2008) provide an overview. One possibility is that there is a strict maturational timetable in which a set of neurons are readied for learning (e.g. by synaptogenesis) and are then later "fossilized" (e.g. reducing plasticity, removing weaker connections) according to a strict timetable. A second possibility is that a set of neurons are readied for learning but that the process is self-terminating to some extent, i.e. the sensitive period will "wait" for suitable exposure. For example, in filial imprinting there is evidence that a particular gene is switched on at the start of the sensitive period but is switched off again ten hours after imprinting has occurred (Harvey *et al.*, 1998). In human infants born with dense cataracts over both eyes, there is a rapid increase in visual acuity when the cataracts are surgically removed, even as late as nine months after birth (Maurer *et al.*, 1999). This suggests that the development of visual acuity will, to some extent, "wait" for an appropriate environment. However, this is only partly true, as 9-year-old children who had cataracts removed in the first 6 months of life had some difficulties in visual processing of faces (Le Grand *et al.*, 2001).

## Innate knowledge?

Perhaps the most controversial topic in developmental cognitive neuroscience is the extent to which any form of knowledge or ability can be said to be innate (Karmiloff-Smith, 2006; Spelke, 1998). This division has a long historical and philosophical tradition between so-called **empiricists** (who believed that the mind is a blank slate) and **nativists** (who believed that at least some forms of knowledge are innate).

The word innate itself conjures up somewhat different connotations to different researchers. For some, the word is synonymous with the idea that behavior is a product of natural selection (Ridley, 2003). The word **instinct** is often used in this context and suitable examples would be filial imprinting in birds (Tinbergen, 1951) or even language in humans (Pinker, 1994). In this usage of the word "innate," there is still a role for experience to play, perhaps within a sensitive period of development. A chick will only imprint if it is exposed to a suitable stimulus in the environment, and a child will only learn sophisticated language given suitable inputs. However, in both examples the particular content of the behavior cannot be said to be innate. The chick will as happily imprint to an Austrian professor as to its mother, and a child is capable of learning a diverse

### KEY TERMS

**Empiricism**
In philosophy, the view that the newborn mind is a blank slate.

**Nativism**
In philosophy, the view that at least some forms of knowledge are innate.

**Instinct**
A behavior that is a product of natural selection.

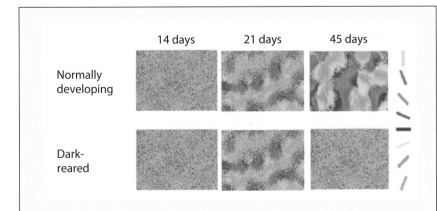

Orientation selectivity at 14, 21, and 45 days in the primary visual cortex of cats reared in a normal visual environment (top) and a dark-reared environment (bottom). The dark-reared cats show normal development up to 21 days but then show a decrease. The different colors represent the extent to which neurons respond to particular orientations.

Adapted from Crair *et al.*, 1998.

Harlow, in his famous article "The Nature of Love," argues that monkeys have an innate preference for a soft versus wire "mother" even if the wire "mother" provides the infant with milk.

From Harlow, 1958. Reproduced with kind permission of Harlow Primate Laboratory, University of Wisconsin.

range of vocabulary and syntax, and not even the manner of production (e.g. speaking versus sign language) is strongly predetermined. In this sense of the word "innate," there is a readiness for certain knowledge to be acquired, but the knowledge itself is not strictly innate.

This leads to a consideration of the second way in which the word "innate" is applied: namely, that knowledge or behavior can be said to be innate if it comes about in the absence of appropriate experience. It is this particular usage of the term that has attracted much controversy (Spelke, 1998). The very early development of the primary visual cortex of the cat can, in this sense, be said to be innate, because it make no difference whether the cat has visual experience or not (Blakemore & Vansluyters, 1975). Both normally developing cats and cats that have been visually deprived in *both* eyes have cells that respond to lines of particular orientations up to around three weeks after birth (Blakemore & Vansluyters, 1975). However, experience is needed for a mature system to form. In the presence of complex visual experience, these cells become more finely tuned and resemble those of an adult by 4 weeks, but in the absence of appropriate visual experience the blind cats lose this specificity.

Similar conclusions arise when one considers the development of phobias. Humans can easily learn to become fearful of certain stimuli such as snakes (e.g. by pairing with an electric shock), but it is hard to become fearful of stimuli such as flowers—a phenomenon that has been termed **prepared learning** (Seligman, 1971). In a series of studies, Mineka and colleagues studied fear conditioning in monkeys (for a review, see Ohman & Mineka, 2001). Whereas monkeys born in captivity to wild-born monkeys show fear of snakes, monkeys who were born from mothers raised in captivity do not. The fearless monkeys could acquire fear of snakes by watching videos of other monkeys reacting with fear to snakes, but they could not acquire fear of flowers using the same method. This suggests that fear of snakes does require suitable experience, even if that fear is transmitted vicariously via other monkeys rather than through contact with snakes. That is, this behavior can be said to be innate in the sense of being a product of natural selection, but not in the sense of developing without experience.

Some preferences could, arguably, be said to be innate in the sense that they do not appear to depend on experience. Newborn infants prefer sweet tastes over neutral and sour ones (Desor *et al.*, 1975), and they prefer some visual patterns over others. Harlow (1958) reported a series of ethically dubious experiments in which newborn monkeys were isolated from their natural mothers but "reared" by artificially created mothers such as a stuffed toy monkey or a metal wire monkey. The monkeys preferred to cling to the furry stuffed toy rather than the metal one, even if the metal one provided the monkey with milk. This went against the standard behaviorist doctrine at the time that maternal love was merely a learned reward for satisfying basic needs such as hunger (in which case the monkey should show affection to the wire mother).

Some abilities could also, arguably, be said to be innate in the sense that they do not appear to depend on experience. Newborn infants will imitate tongue protrusion (Meltzoff & Moore, 1977, 1983). That is, they demonstrate an understanding that a seen tongue being protruded corresponds to their own, unseen, motor ability to do the same. Meltzoff & Moore concluded that "the ability to use intermodal equivalences is an innate ability of humans" (1977, p. 78).

The studies above suggest that certain dispositions (e.g. to fear certain types of thing), preferences (e.g. sweet), and abilities (e.g. to detect edges, intermodal matching) can—in some sense of the word—be said to be innate. However, the issue of whether the specific content of knowledge (or so-called representations) is innate is much harder to substantiate. For example, newborn infants prefer to look at real faces relative to faces with the parts rearranged, but this could reflect a tendency to prefer certain symmetrical patterns (Johnson *et al.*, 1991). However, they will also prefer to look at a jumbled up face provided it is top-heavy (Macchi Cassia *et al.*, 2004). This makes it hard to argue that the specific *knowledge* of what a face looks like is innate, although one could still reasonably claim that a preference for particular kinds of pattern is an evolutionary adaptation.

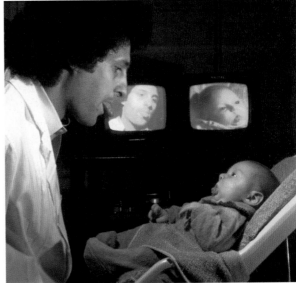

This 23-day-old infant imitates the tongue protrusion of the experimenter, suggesting an understanding of the link between seen actions of another and their own, unseen actions.

Photo by Andrew N. Meltzoff and E. Ferorelli, with permission from Andrew N. Meltzoff.

## BEHAVIORAL GENETICS

**Behavioral genetics** is concerned with studying the inheritance of behaviors and cognitive skills. The approach has traditionally been applied to psychiatric disorders such as depression and schizophrenia, but more recently it has been used to investigate specific aspects of cognition such as reading ability and memory ability (Plomin *et al.*, 2001). The classic methods of behavioral genetics are twin studies and adoption studies. These provide ways of disentangling nature and nurture.

### Twin studies and adoption studies

Most behaviors run in families, but it is hard to know to what extent this reflects shared environment or shared genes. When a child is placed into an adopted home, he or she will effectively have two sets of relatives: biological relatives with whom the child no longer shares any environment, and adopted relatives with whom the child shares an environment, but not genes. Will the child more closely resemble the biological or adoptive family, thus emphasizing a role of nature or nurture, respectively? In many cases, it is not possible to contact or test the biological relatives, but the genetic contribution can still be estimated by comparing the adopted child with non-adopted siblings in the household (i.e. both the adopted and non-adopted siblings share family environment, but not genes).

## THE ORIGINS OF GENETIC DIFFERENCES

The human genetic code is organized on to 23 pairs of **chromosomes**, making a total of 46 chromosomes. One of the chromosomes of each pair comes from the maternal line and one from the paternal line. In each individual there are two copies of each gene normally present, one on each chromosome. However, genes may exist in different forms, termed **alleles**. The different alleles represent changes (or mutations) in the sequence of the gene that is propagated over many generations, unless natural selection intervenes. Many different allelic forms are common and benign, but they account for the individual differences that are found between humans as well as differences between species. For example, two different alleles of a single gene determine whether the earlobes will be hanging or attached. In other instances single gene mutations are not benign, as in the case of Huntington's disease (see Chapter 8). A different allele may mean that the end-product encoded by the gene (such as enzymes) works less efficiently, more efficiently or not at all. Alternatively, it may mean that the gene works in an entirely novel way by, for example, altering the expression of other genes. Most behavioral traits will be an outcome of the concerted action of many genes. Even though a given gene may exist in only a small number of discrete allelic types, when many such genetic variants are combined together they may produce an outcome that is continuously distributed—such as the normal distribution found for height or IQ. Disorders such as autism, dyslexia, and schizophrenia also appear to be polygenic in nature (see Tager-Flusberg, 2003).

As well as differences in alleles, individuals differ in the spacing of genes on the chromosomes (most of the genome contains nongene segments). While it is unclear whether this contributes to observable individual differences, an analysis of the spacing of various genomic markers is central to techniques such as genetic "finger-printing" and attempts to locate candidate genes on the basis of behavioral markers (e.g. presence of schizophrenia).

During production of eggs, and sperm the genes from the maternal and paternal chromosomes are "shuffled" so that a single new chromosome is created that is a combination of the original two. This mechanism prevents the number of chromosomes doubling in each generation. This provides one mechanism leading to genetic variation through producing different combinations of a finite set of alleles. This process can also go wrong if segments of DNA get deleted or duplicated. Some relatively common genetic disorders formed in this way are summarized below.

| Genetic disorder | Origins | Cognitive developmental characteristics |
| --- | --- | --- |
| Down's syndrome | A duplicated copy of chromosome 21 | General learning difficulties (IQ < 70), poor fine motor control, delayed and impaired expressive language |
| Turner syndrome | A missing copy of the X-chromosome (or deletion of part of it) | Not associated with mental retardation, but verbal IQ tends to be higher than nonverbal; some difficulties in executive functions and social skills (Ross et al., 2000) |
| William's syndrome | A deleted segment of chromosome 7 | General intellectual impairment but with some tendency for language abilities to be better than spatial abilities; high sociability, but not necessarily high social intelligence (Karmiloff-Smith, 2007) |

Twin studies follow a similar logic. Twins are formed either when a single fertilized egg splits in two (monozygotic or **MZ twins**) or when two eggs are released at the same time and separately fertilized (dizygotic or **DZ twins**). MZ twins are genetically identical; they share 100 percent of their genes. DZ twins are nonidentical and share only 50 percent of their genes (i.e. the same as non-twin siblings). Given that both are assumed to share the same family environment, any difference between MZ and DZ twins is assumed to reveal genetic influences. Studies of twins reared apart combine the advantages of the standard twin study and adoption study.

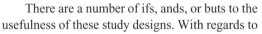
Identical twins look the same, but do they think the same?

There are a number of ifs, ands, or buts to the usefulness of these study designs. With regards to twin studies, it is assumed that MZ and DZ twins experience similar environments. However, MZ twins could be treated more similarly by others. Also, MZ twins often have more similar prenatal environments: many MZ twins share the same sac (called the chorion) within the placenta, but DZ twins never do. As such, MZ twins may be more likely to be exposed to the same viruses prenatally. With regards to adoption studies, selective placement could mean that children tend to get adopted into similar environments (e.g. with regard to race or socioeconomic status). Another issue is whether families who adopt or who give up their children for adoption are representative of the general population. Plomin *et al.* (2001) provide an assessment of this debate and argue that the main findings are relatively robust to these potential drawbacks.

## The concept of heritability

Twin studies and adoption studies are ways of establishing whether there is genetic influence. **Heritability** is an estimate of *how much* genetics contributes to a trait. In particular, heritability is the proportion of variance in a trait, in a given population, that can be accounted for by genetic differences among individuals. It can be estimated from the correlations for relatives on a given measure, such as IQ. If the correlation between IQ scores for biological parents and their adopted-away children is zero, then heritability is zero. If the correlation between biological parents and their adopted-away children is 0.50, then heritability is 100 percent, because biological parents and their children have 50 percent of their genes in common (as do all full siblings and DZ twins). Similarly, a correlation of 0.5 between two sets of adopted-away relatives who share half their genes suggests a heritability of 100 percent.

In twin studies, if MZ twins correlate with each other by 1.00 and if DZ twins correlate with each other by 0.50, then heritability is 100 percent. A rough estimate of heritability in a twin study can be made by doubling the difference between the MZ and DZ correlations (Plomin *et al.*, 2001).

The concept of heritability, although useful, is easily misunderstood. It measures how much variability is due to genetic factors within a given population, not the contribution it makes in a given individual. If the heritability of height is

**KEY TERMS**

**Chromosome**
An organized package of DNA bound up with proteins; each chromosome contains many genes.

**Allele**
Different versions of the same gene.

**MZ twins (monozygotic)**
Genetically identical twins caused when a fertilized egg splits in two.

**DZ twins (dizygotic)**
Twins who share half of their genes, caused when two eggs are fertilized by two different sperm.

**Heritability**
The proportion of variance in a trait, in a given population, that can be accounted for by genetic differences among individuals.

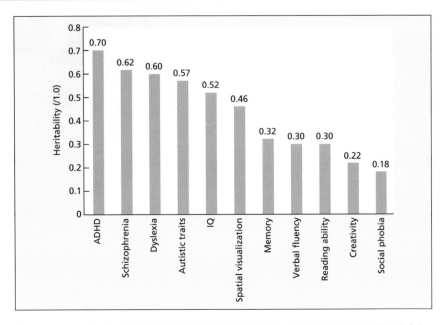

The approximate heritability of various psychological abilities and conditions: attention deficit and hyperactivity disorder, ADHD (Eaves *et al.*, 1997); schizophrenia (Gottesman, 1991); dyslexia (Hawke *et al.*, 2006); autistic traits (Hoekstra *et al.*, 2007); IQ (Bouchard & McGue, 1981); spatial visualization, memory, verbal fluency (Nichols, 1978); reading ability in elementary school (Thompson *et al.*, 1991); creativity (Nichols, 1978); and social phobia (Kendler *et al.*, 1992).

about 0.69 (Hemani *et al.*, 2013), it doesn't mean that 69 percent of a person's height has come from their genes and 31 percent from their environment. It means that 69 percent of the differences in height between different people, within that population, are due to their genes. To give another example, most people have ten fingers and this is genetically specified. However, the heritability measure for number of fingers is low, because the *variability* in the number of fingers is due primarily to environmental reasons—industrial accidents, and so on. (the example is from Ridley, 2003).

To consider a cognitive example, the fact that heritability for reading ability in elementary school pupils is 0.30 (Thompson *et al.*, 1991) does not mean that 30 percent of a child's ability is due to genes and 70 percent due to environment. Reading requires an appropriate environment (i.e. living in a literate culture), otherwise literacy will not exist at all. It also requires an appropriate brain architecture that will support reading. Both are equally essential. The measure of heritability may also vary according to the population studied. If one were to measure reading ability in a country in which education was not universal, then heritability would almost certainly be lower because reading ability would be an outcome of opportunity, i.e. an environmental factor. It is curious, but true, that the more that we become a meritocracy based upon equal opportunities the more that genetic differences will matter. To give one final example, the heritability for reading disability, or dyslexia, in Western societies is higher, at 0.60 (Hawke *et al.*, 2006), than for reading ability per se, because the diagnostic criteria for dyslexia typically assume adequate opportunity and intellect; i.e. variability in environmental factors is minimized by the selection criteria.

## Evaluation

Behavioral genetics is concerned with quantifying the heritable component of behavior and cognition. It uses methods such as the adoption study and twin study. While these methods are successful in identifying a heritable component, they do not in themselves elucidate the mechanism by which genes affect cognition. Moreover, the "heritability" of a trait depends on the environmental circumstances within the sample selected rather than being a pure measure of "nature."

## BEYOND NATURE VERSUS NURTURE: GENE–ENVIRONMENT INTERPLAY

The evidence discussed so far suggests that the development of cognition does not neatly fit into a divide between nature and nurture. In their book *Rethinking Innateness*, Elman and colleagues (1996) put it this way: "The answer is not Nature *or* Nurture; it's Nature *and* Nurture. But to say that is to trade one platitude for another; what is necessary is to understand the nature of the interaction" (p. 357). The advances made in identifying genes and in understanding genetic mechanisms at the molecular level are now being used to inform theories in developmental cognitive neuroscience. In particular, one is now in a position to investigate whether there are indeed genes for specific cognitive functions (a gene for grammar, a gene for schizophrenia, etc.). While behavioral genetics may show that there is a genetic contribution to individual differences in cognitive traits, it is now possible to explore what that contribution consists of in more mechanistic terms.

Rutter *et al.* (2006) provide an overview of mechanisms of gene–environment interplay. Their review highlights four types of mechanism:

1. Environmental influences can alter the effects of genes. Although the sequence of DNA is normally fixed in a given individual and across all cells in his or her body, the timing and the degree of functioning of genes in the DNA can be affected by the environment (so-called epigenetic events). For example, increased maternal nurturing by a rat affects expression of a stress-reducing gene in its offspring that persists throughout their lifetime (Weaver *et al.*, 2004).
2. Heritability varies according to environmental circumstances. As noted previously, the amount of variation in a population that is due to genetic factors is dependent on the environmental context. In an "equal opportunities" environment heritability tends to be maximized, but in populations with a large environmental risk (e.g. to certain pathogens) or high social control (e.g. on acceptable behavior) heritability will be minimized.
3. **Gene–environment correlations** (rGE) are genetic influences on people's exposure to different environments (Plomin *et al.*, 1977). For example, people will seek out different environments (e.g. drug taking and novelty seeking) depending on their genotype (Benjamin *et al.*, 1996; Kotler *et al.*, 1997). Also, the environment that a parent creates for raising his or her children will depend on the parent's own dispositions (intellect, personality, mental illnesses), which are partly genetic in origin.
4. **Gene X–environment interactions** (G x E) occur when susceptibility to a trait depends on a particular combination of a gene and environment. The effects of the gene and environment together exceed what would be expected from the sum of the parts.

Collectively, these four factors make it less plausible that there will be a "gene for" any given cognitive ability or behavior, as most genes do not appear to have a deterministic (all-or-nothing) role (Kendler, 2005). The sections below will provide a few illustrative examples from cognitive neuroscience. First, the evidence for the role of the gene FOXP2 in language acquisition will be presented and discussed in the context of whether this may constitute a "gene for grammar." Second, how a culturally acquired skill, reading, can have a genetic component will be discussed, and finally the question of whether cannabis use contributes to a G x E interaction in the onset of schizophrenia will be considered.

## FOXP2, speech, and grammar

In 1990, a remarkable family came to the attention of the scientific community. Around half of the members of the so-called KE family had problems in producing speech and language and, moreover, the pattern of inheritance was consistent with a single gene mutation. Affected family members would come out with sentences like "The boys eat four cookie" and "Carol is cry in the church." Indeed, early reports of the family suggested that they may have problems in specific aspects of grammar (Gopnik, 1990; Gopnik & Crago, 1991), i.e. a potential "gene for grammar." Since then, the affected mutation in the FOXP2 gene has been identified, the nature of the speech problems have been described in more detail, and the neural substrates have been explored in both humans and other species (for a review, see Vargha-Khadem *et al.*, 2005).

While the core deficit in the family remains debated, the deficits are certainly not limited to grammar. Affected KE family members, relative to unaffected ones, score poorly on tests of pronunciation, grammar, semantics, verbal IQ, and even nonverbal IQ, although the scores from the two groups overlap (Vargha-Khadem *et al.*, 1995). Tests of oral praxis and orofacial praxis (e.g. copying tongue protrusions or lip pouting) do produce nonoverlapping test scores, suggesting that **orofacial dyspraxia** is a core deficit. There is reduced volume in the basal ganglia (caudate nucleus) that correlates with their level of orofacial dyspraxia (Watkins *et al.*, 2002). The basal ganglia have a key role in the control of voluntary movement. The basal ganglia, and the caudate in particular, have also been linked to implicit rule learning in artificial grammars (Lieberman *et al.*, 2004) suggesting a possible link to the grammatical deficits. Other families with Specific Language Impairment (SLI) of developmental origin do not appear to have the FOXP2 gene affected (Newbury *et al.*, 2002), although some of them do perform poorly on grammar in the absence of orofacial dyspraxia (Falcaro *et al.*, 2008). As such, there are likely to be multiple genes that affect grammar and, at present, there are no known genes that specifically affect only grammar.

What do studies of the *normal* version of the FOXP2 gene reveal about its possible function? The product of the FOXP2 gene is what is called a **transcription factor**, i.e. its molecular function is to affect the expression of other genes (see Vargha-Khadem *et al.*, 2005). As such, its effects may be wide-ranging and it is expressed in various tissues in the body, not just the brain. Haesler *et al.* (2004) found that FOXP2 expression in birds who need to learn their vocalization (e.g. canaries) had greater expression in the avian equivalent of the basal ganglia during song learning than song production. Intriguingly, the FOXP2 proteins of chimpanzee, gorilla, and rhesus macaque are identical to each other but differ from humans" in terms of two small sequence changes, one of which is likely to be functional and has been dated to 200,000 years ago, about the time that anatomically modern humans emerged (Enard *et al.*, 2002). The final word concerning the function of this gene has yet to be written.

## Developmental dyslexia

The ability to read is a cultural invention. It is perhaps surprising to discover that a skill that is, by definition, a product of "nurture" should show an influence of "nature." However, learning to read will place demands on basic cognitive processes involved in visual recognition, phonological encoding, and so on, and it is entirely likely that there are genetically mediated differences in these abilities. Although culture is by definition environmental/nongenetic, the brain's ability to create and absorb cultural knowledge will be under genetic influence and be a product of evolution.

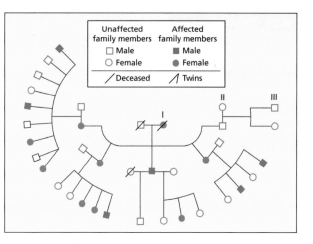

The family tree of three generations of the KE family shows that around half of the members have significant problems in speech and language. This problem has now been linked to a mutation in a single gene called FOXP2. Does this gene have a role to play in the evolution of human language?

Reprinted by permission from Macmillan Publishers Ltd: Watkins *et al.*, 2002. © 2004.

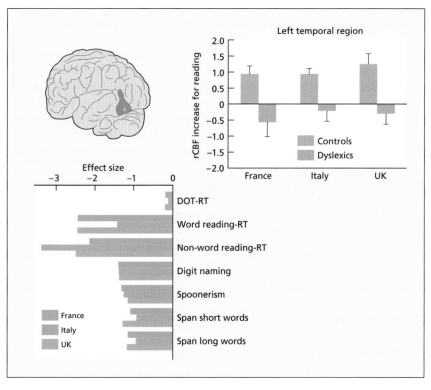

English, French, and Italian dyslexics show less activation in a left temporal region relative to controls. English, French, and Italian dyslexics show normal reaction time to a dot appearing, but have difficulties on word and nonword reading, and other nonreading tasks including digit naming, spoonerisms ("lucky duck" to "ducky luck"), and span tasks (repeating lists of short or long words).

From Paulesu *et al.*, 2001. Reprinted with permission from AAAS.

With regard to reading, different cultures have adopted different solutions for mapping between spelling and sound. For example, English and French have a high proportion of irregular mappings (e.g. compare the different pronunciations of MINT and PINT), whereas Italian has very few of these. One consequence of this is that learning to read and write in English and French is harder than in Italian, and rates of developmental dyslexia are higher in countries who speak those languages (Lindgren *et al.*, 1985). There could be several different "core" difficulties which vary from dyslexic to dyslexic (Castles *et al.*, 1999), but that nevertheless transcend cultural differences in reading systems. One candidate core deficit is in phonological processing. Paulesu *et al.* (2001) compared English, French, and Italian dyslexics and normally reading controls matched for IQ and education level. The English and French dyslexics had received a formal diagnosis. Given that it is very unusual for Italian adults to receive a diagnosis of dyslexia, a large sample was screened, and those falling in the bottom 10 percent of a number of speed-reading tasks were considered dyslexic. (Note: the Italian "dyslexics" were better readers than their English and French counterparts given the nature of their reading system, but were nevertheless poor readers with respect to their Italian controls.) All three groups of dyslexics showed evidence of poor performance in a number of verbal skills, suggesting a core deficit in this area. Brain activity when reading, measured using PET, was consistently reduced in the left posterior temporal region in dyslexics relative to controls, suggesting a common neural mechanism independent of the reading system involved.

## Schizophrenia and cannabis use

**Schizophrenia** is a severe disturbance of thought and affect characterized by a loss of contact with reality (i.e. a **psychosis**). The key symptoms include **hallucinations** (e.g. hearing voices), **delusions** (e.g. of being persecuted), disorganized thought and behavior (e.g. incoherence), and emotional disturbances (e.g. blunting of emotions, or inappropriate emotional responses). Some symptoms may be more pronounced in different individuals or in the same individual over time. In order to receive a formal diagnosis, one also needs social and/or occupational dysfunction (e.g. an inability to hold down a job or relationship), and the symptoms must be persisting for at least six months (American Psychiatric Association, 1994). The symptoms often appear in early adulthood, and it is equally common in males and females but with an earlier onset in males (Castle *et al.*, 1991). Typically, there is no known precipitating event such as a head injury or family trauma. Longitudinal studies suggest that adults with symptoms of schizophrenia are more likely to report psychotic symptoms at 11 years of age (e.g. in response to questions such as, "Have you ever had messages sent just to you through the television or radio?"), although these early differences are not diagnostic insofar as they do not uniquely predict who will and will not go on to develop it (Poulton *et al.*, 2000).

Although the causes of schizophrenia are likely to be manifold, one potential cause that has been extensively discussed in the media and is pertinent to the present discussion is the role of one particular environmental factor—namely, cannabis use. Given that most cannabis users do not become schizophrenic and most schizophrenics have not used cannabis prior to the symptoms emerging, a possible mechanism is a gene X environment interaction. That is, cannabis use may tend to lead to schizophrenia in individuals with a particular genetic susceptibility. Caspi *et al.* (2005) provide evidence for this conclusion. Over the last 30 years a remarkable experiment has been conducted in Dunedin, New Zealand, in which over 1,000 consecutive births have been systematically studied at subsequent time points (between 3 and 38 years, so far). At age 11, participants were given a childhood psychiatric assessment that included questions about psychosis. They have been asked about cannabis usage from the age of 13. At age 26, participants were formally assessed for schizophrenia. Participants who reported some symptoms but did not meet the full diagnostic criteria (schizophreniform disorder) were also considered. In addition, the presence of a particular genetic variant was assessed, namely the COMT gene. The product of this gene is involved in the metabolism of the neurotransmitter **dopamine** released into synapses. Disturbances in dopamine pathways have long been implicated in schizophrenia (see Kapur, 2003). In particular, a common mutation at one place in the gene leads to the

Is smoking cannabis linked to schizophrenia?

substitution of an amino acid (from valine, Val, to methionine, Met), such that those with two copies of the Val allele (Val/Val) are more efficiently able to break down dopamine, those with two copies of the Met allele (Met/Met) are least able to break down dopamine, and those with a copy of both (Val/Met) are intermediate.

The results of Caspi *et al.*'s study showed a significant relationship between the COMT genotype and cannabis use, such that those with a Val allele (i.e. more efficient metabolism of dopamine) were more likely to show symptoms of schizophrenia, particularly if they had used cannabis (Caspi *et al.*, 2005). Moreover, they found that there was a sensitive period during adolescence in which this gene X environment was important. The elevated risk of psychotic symptoms was not found in cannabis users who started smoking it after 21 years of age. Given the fact that the participants had been assessed throughout childhood, it was possible to exclude other factors such as childhood cognitive deficits, previous use of other drugs, and conduct disorder at school. It was also possible to rule out the possibility that those with the Val allele were more likely to develop schizophrenia because they were more inclined to try cannabis (a possible gene–environment correlation). Those with the Met allele were just as likely to use it as those with the Val allele, but only those with the Val allele showed the increased risk.

The explanation involving the COMT gene and cannabis use may explain only a small, but significant, part of schizophrenia. Genetic linkage studies have identified potential "schizophrenia genes" on almost every chromosome, often with poor replications in different samples (Levinson, 2003). As such, it is possible that different schizophrenics have entirely different causes in terms of the genetic and environmental contributions, despite having equivalent symptoms. It still remains possible that a single brain pathway is being disrupted in multiple ways. It is also possible, if not probable, that there are not strictly any "genes for"

## KEY TERM

**Dopamine**
A neurotransmitter with important roles, including in reward, motivation, attention, and learning.

The COMT gene is involved in the metabolism of the neurotransmitter dopamine and the gene exists in two main forms (termed Val and Met). Each person has two copies of the gene. If you have a Val copy of the gene *and* you smoke cannabis during adolescence, then there is an increased risk of displaying symptoms of schizophrenia at age 26—a gene X–environment interaction.

Reprinted from Caspi *et al.*, 2005. © 2005, with permission from Elsevier.

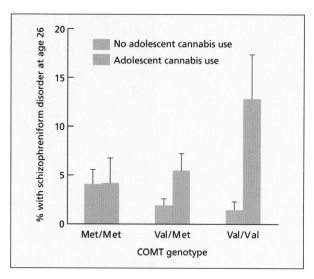

schizophrenia (i.e. in the deterministic sense that this set of genes will inevitably result in schizophrenia). The Val allele of COMT is *not* a gene for schizophrenia. But this doesn't mean that there isn't a genetic component. The Val allele of COMT is a normal gene that is present in a large proportion of the population that conveys susceptibility. The example of the COMT gene and cannabis use offers an important insight into how the tired nature–nurture debate can move forward. Instead of concluding that a given aspect of cognition is "part nature and part nurture," we can begin to understand what that could mean in terms of an underlying brain mechanism.

## SUMMARY AND KEY POINTS OF THE CHAPTER

- Structural changes in the brain occur throughout life. Genes not only influence prenatal development (e.g. the formation of large numbers of synapses around birth) but have a lifelong influence. Environmental influences can switch genes on or off and can also influence brain structure (e.g. determining whether connections are used or lost).
- There is good evidence from both animal studies and human research for sensitive periods in development in which the brain is optimally readied to acquire certain skills or knowledge. However, these periods may be more flexible than were first thought.
- The word "innate" can mean at least two different things: either referring to instincts that have been shaped by natural selection (language being one candidate); or referring to knowledge/skills/resources acquired in the absence of experience (candidates include certain preferences and dislikes, and the existence of orientation-selective cells in visual cortex).
- Twin and adoption studies provide one way of showing that there is a genetic contribution for a given trait. However, the concept of

"heritability" is not a pure measure of genetics because the amount of variance in a trait that is due to genetic factors will also depend on the amount of variance that is due to nongenetic factors.

- Genetic disorders can often affect some cognitive abilities more than others. However, genes are rarely highly specific for psychological/cognitive traits. This is because genes interact with other genes, and there is a complex interplay between genes and environment. Sometimes a gene makes certain environments more likely to be sought out (a gene–environment correlation), and sometimes a gene leads to a susceptibility that also depends crucially on environmental circumstance (a gene–environment interaction).

Visit the companion website at www. psypress/cw/ward for:

- References to key papers and readings
- Video lectures and interviews on key topics with leading psychologists Charles Nelson, Elizabeth Spelke, David Hubel, and author Jamie Ward
- Multiple choice questions and interactive flashcards to test your knowledge
- Downloadable glossary

## EXAMPLE ESSAY QUESTIONS

- Evaluate the protomap and protocortex theories of brain development.
- What is the evidence for sensitive periods in development and what kinds of neural mechanism could give rise to them?
- To what extent can any kind of behavior be said to be innate?
- What is meant by the term "heritability" and how can it be measured?
- How might gene–environment interplay contribute to developmental and psychiatric disorders?

## RECOMMENDED FURTHER READING

- Goswami, U. (2008). *Cognitive development: The learning brain*. Hove, UK: Psychology Press. An introductory textbook on all aspects of development, including evidence from developmental cognitive neuroscience.
- Johnson, M. H. (2005). *Developmental cognitive neuroscience: An introduction* (2nd edition). Oxford, UK: Blackwell. A good introductory overview.
- Nelson, C. A. & Luciana, M. (2008). *Handbook of developmental cognitive neuroscience* (3rd edition). Boston, MA: MIT Press. A comprehensive selection of advanced topics.

# References

Abell, F., Krams, M., Ashburner, J., Passingham, R., Friston, K., Frackowiak, R., Happe, F., Frith, C., & Frith, U. (1999). The neuroanatomy of autism: A voxel-based whole brain analysis of structural scans. *NeuroReport*, *10*, 1647–1651.

Accornero, N., Voti, P. L., La Riccia, M., & Gregori, B. (2007). Visual evoked potentials modulation during direct current cortical polarization. *Experimental Brain Research*, *178*(2), 261–266.

Addis, D. R., Wong, A. T., & Schacter, D. L. (2007). Remembering the past and imagining the future: Common and distinct neural substrates during event construction and elaboration. *Neuropsychologia*, *45*(7), 1363–1377.

Adolphs, R. (2002). Neural systems for recognizing emotion. *Current Opinion in Neurobiology*, *12*, 169–177.

Adolphs, R., Tranel, D., Damasio, H., & Damasio, A. (1994). Impaired recognition of emotion in facial expressions following bilateral damage to the human amygdala. *Nature*, *372*, 669–672.

Adolphs, R., Damasio, H., Tranel, D., Cooper, G., & Damasio, A. R. (2000). A role for somatosensory cortices in the visual recognition of emotion as revealed by three-dimensional lesion mapping. *Journal of Neuroscience*, *20*(7), 2683–2690.

Adolphs, R., Gosselin, F., Buchanan, T. W., Tranel, D., Schyns, P., & Damasio, A. R. (2005). A mechanism for impaired fear recognition after amygdala damage. *Nature*, *433*, 68–72.

Aggleton, J. P. & Brown, M. W. (1999). Episodic memory, amnesia, and the hippocampal-anterior thalamic axis. *Behavioral and Brain Sciences*, *22*, 425–489.

Aglioti, S., DeSouza, J. F. X., & Goodale, M. A. (1995). Size-contrast illusions deceive the eye but not the hand. *Current Biology*, *5*, 679–685.

Agranoff, B. W., David, R. E., & Brink, J. J. (1966). Chemical studies on memory fixation in goldfish. *Brain Research*, *1*, 303–309.

Agrillo, C., Piffer, L., Bisazza, A., & Butterworth, B. (2012). Evidence for two numerical systems that are similar in humans and guppies. *PLoS One*, *7*(2).

Aguirre, G. K., Zarahn, E., & D'Esposito, M. (1998). The variability of human BOLD hemodynamic response. *NeuroImage*, *8*, 360–369.

Alcock, K. J., Passingham, R. E., Watkins, K., & Vargha-Khadem, F. (2000a). Pitch and timing abilities in inherited speech and language impairment. *Brain and Language*, *75*, 34–46.

Alcock, K. J., Wade, D., Anslow, P., & Passingham, R. E. (2000b). Pitch and timing abilities in adult left-hemispheredysphasic and right-hemisphere-damaged subjects. *Brain and Language*, *75*, 47–65.

Alexander, G. E. & Crutcher, M. D. (1990). Functional architecture of basal ganglia circuits: Neural substrates of parallel processing. *Trends in Neurosciences*, *13*, 266–271.

Alexander, M. P., Stuss, D. T., Picton, T., Shallice, T., & Gillingham, S. (2007). Regional frontal injuries cause distinct impairments in cognitive control. *Neurology*, *68*(18), 1515–1523.

Alho, K. (1995). Cerebral generators of mismatch negativity (MMN) and its magnetic counterpart (mMMN) elicited by sound changes. *Ear and Hearing*, *16*, 38–51.

Alho, K., Woods, D. L., & Algazi, A. (1994). Processing of auditory-stimuli during auditory and visual attention as revealed by event-related potentials. *Psychophysiology*, *31*, 469–479.

Allport, D. A. (1985). Distributed memory, modular systems and dysphasia. In S. K. Newman, & R. Epstein (Eds.), *Current perspectives in dysphasia*. Edinburgh: Churchill Livingstone.

Allport, D. A., Styles, E. A., & Hsieh, S. (1994). Shifting intentional set: Exploring the dynamic control of tasks. In C. Umiltà & M. Moscovitch (Eds.), *Attention and performance XV: Conscious and nonconscious information processing*. Cambridge, MA: MIT Press.

Altmann, C. F., Bulthoff, H. H., & Kourtzi, Z. (2003). Perceptual organization of local elements into global shapes in the human visual cortex. *Current Biology*, *13*, 342–349.

Altmann, G. T., Garnham, A., & Henstra, J. A. (1994). Effects of syntax in human sentence parsing: Evidence against a structure-based parsing mechanism. *Journal of Experimental Psychology: Learning, Memory, and Cognition*, *20*, 209–216.

Amedi, A., Floel, A., Knecht, S., Zohary, E., & Cohen, L. G. (2004). Transcranial magnetic stimulation of the occipital pole interferes with verbal processing in blind subjects. *Nature Neuroscience*, *7*, 1266–1270.

American Psychiatric Association (2013). *Diagnostic and statistical manual of mental disorders*, 4th edition. (*DSM-IV*). American Psychiatric Association: Washington, DC.

Amodio, D. M. & Frith, C. D. (2006). Meeting of minds: the medial frontal cortex and social cognition. *Nature Reviews Neuroscience*, *7*(4), 268–277.

Anders, S., Eippert, F., Weiskopf, N., & Veit, R. (2008). The human amygdala is sensitive to the valence of pictures and sounds irrespective of arousal: an fMRI study. *Social Cognitive and Affective Neuroscience*, *3*(3), 233–243.

Anderson, M. C., Bjork, R. A., & Bjork, E. L. (1994). Remembering can cause forgetting: Retrieval dynamics in long-term memory. *Journal of Experimental Psychology: Learning, Memory and Cognition*, *20*, 1063–1087.

Anderson, M. C., Ochsner, K. N., Kuhl, B., Cooper, J., Robertson, E., Gabrieli, S. W., Glover, G. H., & Gabrieli, J. D. E. (2004). Neural systems underlying the suppression of unwanted memories. *Science*, *303*, 232–235.

Anderson, M. I. & Jeffery, K. J. (2003). Heterogeneous modulation of place cell firing by changes in context. *Journal of Neuroscience*, *23*, 8827–8835.

Anderson, S. W., Damasio, A. R., & Damasio, H. (1990). Troubled letters but not numbers. *Brain*, *113*, 749–766.

Ansari, D., Garcia, N., Lucas, E., Hamon, K., & Dhital, B. (2005). Neural correlates of symbolic number processing in children and adults. *NeuroReport*, *16*(16), 1769–1773.

Antal, A., Nitsche, M. A., & Paulus, W. (2001). External modulation of visual perception in humans. *NeuroReport*, *12*(16), 3553–3555.

Antell, S. E. & Keating, D. P. (1983). Perception of numerical invariance in neonates. *Child Development*, *54*, 695–701.

Aram, D. & Ekelman, B. L. (1986). Cognitive profiles of children with unilateral brain lesions. *Developmental Neuropsychology*, *2*, 155–172.

Aron, A. R., Fletcher, P. C., Bullmore, E. T., Sahakian, B. J., & Robbins, T. W. (2003). Stop-signal inhibition disrupted by damage to right inferior frontal gyrus in humans. *Nature Neuroscience*, *6*, 115–116.

Aron, A. R., Monsell, S., Sahakian, B. J., & Robbins, T. W. (2004a). A componential analysis of task-switching deficits associated with lesions of left and right frontal cortex. *Brain*, *127*, 1561–1573.

Aron, A. R., Robbins, T. W., & Poldrack, R. A. (2004b). Inhibition and the right inferior frontal cortex. *Trends in Cognitive Sciences*, *8*, 170–177.

Arrington, C. M., Carr, T. H., Mayer, A. R., & Rao, S. M. (2000). Neural mechanisms of visual attention: Object-based selection of a region in space. *Journal of Cognitive Neuroscience*, *12*, 106–117.

Asaad, W. F., Rainer, G., & Miller, E. K. (1998). Neural activity in the primate prefrontal cortex during associative learning. *Neuron*, *21*, 1399–3407.

Asaad, W. F., Rainer, G., & Miller, E. K. (2000). Task-specific neural activity in the primate prefrontal cortex. *Journal of Neurophysiology*, *84*, 451–459.

Ashbridge, E., Walsh, V., & Cowey, A. (1997). Temporal aspects of visual search studied by transcranial magnetic stimulation. *Neuropsychologia*, *35*, 1121–1131.

Ashbridge, E., Cowey, A., & Wade, D. (1999). Does parietal cortex contribute to feature binding? *Neuropsychologia*, *37*, 999–1004.

Ashburner, J. & Friston, K. J. (2000). Voxel-based morphometry: The methods. *NeuroImage*, *11*, 805–821.

Asperger, H. (1944). "Autistic psychopathy" in childhood. In U. Frith (Ed.), *Autism and Asperger syndrome*. Cambridge, UK: Cambridge University Press.

Assal, F., Schwartz, S., & Vuilleumier, P. (2007). Moving with or without will: Functional neural correlates of alien hand syndrome. *Annals of Neurology*, *62*(3), 301–306.

Astafiev, S. V., Shulman, G. L., Stanley, C. M., Snyder, A. Z., Van Essen, D. C., & Corbetta, M. (2003). Functional organization of human intraparietal and frontal cortex for attending, looking, and pointing. *Journal of Neuroscience*, *23*(11), 4689–4699.

Atkinson, R. C. & Shiffrin, R. M. (1968). Human memory: A proposed system and its control processes. In K. W. Spence & J. T. Spence (Eds.), *The psychology of learning and motivation: Advances in research and theory* (Vol. 2). New York: Academic Press.

Attwell, D. & Iadecola, C. (2002). The neural basis of functional brain imaging signals. *Trends in Neurosciences*, *25*, 621–625.

Awh, E. & Pashler, H. (2000). Evidence for split attentional foci. *Journal of Experimental Psychology-Human Perception and Performance*, *26*(2), 834–846.

Ayotte, J., Peretz, I., & Hyde, K. (2002). Congenital amusia: A group study of adults afflicted with a music-specific disorder. *Brain*, *125*, 238–251.

Azevedo, F.A.C., Carvalho, L.R.B., Grinberg, L.T., Farfel, J.M., Ferretti, R.E.L., Leite, R.E.P., Jacob Filho, W., Lent, R. & Herculano-Houzel, S. (2009) Equal numbers of neuronal and nonneuronal cells make the human brain an isometrically scaled-up primate brain. *Journal of Comparative Neurology*, *513*, 532–541.

Bachevalier, J. & Nemanic, S. (2008). Memory for spatial location and object-place associations are differently processed by the hippocampal formation, parahippocampal areas TH/TF and perirhinal cortex. *Hippocampus*, *18*, 64–80.

Bachtold, D., Baumuller, M., & Brugger, P. (1998). Stimulus-response compatibility in representational space. *Neuropsychologia*, *36*, 731–735.

Baddeley, A. D. (1966). Short-term memory for word sequences as a function of acoustic, semantic and formal similarity. *Quarterly Journal of Experimental Psychology*, *18*, 334–365.

Baddeley, A. D. (1986). *Working memory*. Oxford, UK: Oxford University Press.

Baddeley, A. D. (1990). *Human memory: Theory and practice*. Hove, UK: Psychology Press.

Baddeley, A. D. (1993). Short-term phonological memory and long-term learning: A single case study. *European Journal of Cognitive Psychology*, *5*, 129–148.

Baddeley, A. D. (1996). Exploring the central executive. *Quarterly Journal of Experimental Psychology*, *49A*, 5–28.

Baddeley, A. D. (2000). The episodic buffer: a new component of working memory? *Trends in Cognitive Sciences*, *4*(11), 417–423.

Baddeley, A. D. (2012). Working memory: theories, models, and controversies. In S. T. Fiske, D. L. Schacter, & S. E. Taylor (Eds.), *Annual Review of Psychology* (Vol. 63, pp. 1–29).

Baddeley, A. D. & Hitch, G. J. (1974). Working memory. In G. A. Bower (Ed.), *Recent advances in learning and motivation* (Vol. 8). New York: Academic Press.

Baddeley, A. D. & Warrington, E. K. (1970). Amnesia and the distinction between long-and short-term memory. *Journal of Verbal Learning and Verbal Behavior, 9,* 176–189.

Baddeley, A. D., Thomson, N., & Buchanan, M. (1975). Word length and the structure of short-term memory. *Journal of Verbal Learning and Verbal Behavior, 9,* 176–189.

Baddeley, A. D., Lewis, V., & Vallar, G. (1984). Exploring the articulatory loop. *Quarterly Journal of Experimental Psychology, 36,* 233–252.

Baddeley, A. D., Papagno, C., & Vallar, G. (1988). When long-term learning depends on short-term storage. *Journal of Memory and Language, 27,* 586–595.

Badecker, W. & Caramazza, A. (1985). On considerations of method and theory governing the use of clinical categories in neurolinguistics and cognitive neuropsychology. *Cognition, 20,* 97–125.

Badre, D. & D'Esposito, M. (2009). Is the rostro-caudal axis of the frontal lobe hierarchical? *Nature Reviews Neuroscience, 10*(9), 659–669.

Bahlmann, J., Schubotz, R. I., & Friederici, A. D. (2008). Hierarchical artificial grammar processing engages Broca's area. *NeuroImage, 42*(2), 525–534.

Baird, G., Simonoff, E., Pickles, A., Chandler, S., Loucas, T., Meldrum, D., & Charman, T. (2006). Prevalence of disorders of the autism spectrum in a population cohort of children in South Thames: The Special Needs and Autism Project (SNAP). *Lancet, 368*(9531), 210–215.

Bakker, A., Kirwan, C. B., Miller, M., & Stark, C. E. L. (2008). Pattern separation in the human hippocampal CA3 and dentate gyrus. *Science, 319*(5870), 1640–1642.

Balan, P. F. & Gottlieb, J. P. (2009). Functional significance of nonspatial information in monkey lateral intraparietal area. *Journal of Neuroscience, 29,* 8166–8176.

Baldo, J. V., Katseff, S., & Dronkers, N. F. (2012). Brain regions underlying repetition and auditory-verbal short-term memory deficits in aphasia: Evidence from voxel-based lesion symptom mapping. *Aphasiology, 26*(3–4), 338–354.

Balint, R. (1909, trans., 1995). *Cognitive Neuropsychology, 12,* 265–281.

Ballantyne, A. O., Spilkin, A. M., Hesselink, J., & Trauner, D. A. (2008). Plasticity in the developing brain: Intellectual, language and academic functions in children with ischaemic perinatal stroke. *Brain, 131,* 2975–2985.

Barker, A. T., Jalinous, R., & Freeston, I. L. (1985). Noninvasive magnetic stimulation of human motor cortex. *Lancet, 1,* 1106–1107.

Barlow, H. B. (1953). Summation and inhibition in the frog's retina. *Journal of Physiology, 119,* 69–88.

Barlow, H. B., Kohn, H. I., & Walsh, E. G. (1947). Visual sensations aroused by magnetic fields. *American Journal of Physiology, 148,* 372–375.

Baron-Cohen, S. (1995a). The Eye-Direction Detector (EDD) and the Shared Attention Mechanism (SAM): Two cases for evolutionary psychology. In C. Moore & P. Dunham (Eds.), *The role of joint attention in development.* Hillsdale, NJ: Lawrence Erlbaum.

Baron-Cohen, S. (1995b). *Mindblindness: An essay on autism and theory of mind.* Cambridge, MA: MIT Press.

Baron-Cohen, S. (2002). The extreme male brain theory of autism. *Trends in Cognitive Sciences, 6,* 248–254.

Baron-Cohen, S. & Cross, P. (1992). Reading the eyes: Evidence for the role of perception in the development of theory of mind. *Mind and Language, 6,* 166–180.

Baron-Cohen, S. & Wheelwright, S. (2004). The empathy quotient: An investigation of adults with Asperger syndrome or high functioning autism and normal sex differences. *Journal of Autism and Developmental Disorders, 34,* 163–175.

Baron-Cohen, S., Leslie, A., & Frith, U. (1985). Does the autistic child have a "theory of mind"? *Cognition, 21,* 37–46.

Baron-Cohen, S., Leslie, A. M., & Frith, U. (1986). Mechanical, behavioral and intentional understanding of picture stories in autistic children. *British Journal of Developmental Psychology*, *4*, 113–125.

Baron-Cohen, S., Campbell, R., Karmiloff-Smith, A., Grant, J., & Walker, J. (1995). Are children with autism blind to the mentalistic significance of eyes? *British Journal of Developmental Psychology*, *13*, 379–398.

Baron-Cohen, S., Richler, J., Bisarya, D., Gurunathan, N., & Wheelwright, S. (2003). The systemizing quotient: An investigation of adults with Asperger syndrome or high-functioning autism, and normal sex differences. *Philosophical Transactions of the Royal Society of London B*, *358*, 361–374.

Barraclough, N. E., Xiao, D., Baker, C. I., Oram, M. W., & Perrett, D. I. (2005). Integration of visual and auditory information by superior temporal sulcus neurons responsive to the sight of actions. *Journal of Cognitive Neuroscience*, *17*, 377–391.

Barrett, D. J. & Hall, D. A. (2006). Response preferences for "what" and "where" in human non-primary auditory cortex. *Neuroimage*, *32*, 968–977.

Barrett, L. F. & Wager, T. D. (2006). The structure of emotion—Evidence from neuroimaging studies. *Current Directions in Psychological Science*, *15*(2), 79–83.

Barry, C., Morrison, C. M., & Ellis, A. W. (1997). Naming the Snodgrass and Vanderwart pictures: Effects of age of acquisition, frequency and name agreement. *Quarterly Journal of Experimental Psychology*, *50A*, 560–585.

Barsalou, L. W. (2008). Grounded cognition. *Annual Review of Psychology* (Vol. 59, pp. 617–645).

Bartley, A. J., Jones, D. W., & Weinberger, D. R. (1997). Genetic variability of human brain size and cortical gyral patterns. *Brain*, *120*, 257–269.

Bartolomeo, P. (2002). The relationship between visual perception and visual mental imagery: A reappraisal of the neuropsychological evidence. *Cortex*, *38*, 357–378.

Bastin, C., Van der Linden, M., Charnallet, A., Denby, C., Montaldi, D., Roberts, N., & Mayes, A. R. (2004). Dissociation between recall and recognition memory performance in an amnesic patient with hippocampal damage following carbon monoxide poisoning. *Neurocase*, *10*, 330–344.

Batteau, D. W. (1967). The role of the pinna in human localization. *Proceedings of the Royal Society of London B*, *168*, 158–180.

Baxendale, S. (2004). Memories are not made of this: Amnesia at the movies. *British Medical Journal*, *329*, 1480–1483.

Baxter, M. G., & Murray, E. A. (2002). The amygdala and reward. *Nature Reviews Neuroscience*, *3*(7), 563–573.

Baxter, D. M. & Warrington, E. K. (1986). Ideational agraphia: A single case study. *Journal of Neurology, Neurosurgery and Psychiatry*, *49*, 369–374.

Bayliss, G. C., Rolls, E. T., & Leonard, C. M. (1985). Selectivity between faces in the responses of neurons in the superior temporal sulcus of the monkey. *Brain Research*, *342*, 91–102.

Baym, C. L., Corbett, B. A., Wright, S. B., & Bunge, S. A. (2008). Neural correlates of tic severity and cognitive control in children with Tourette syndrome. *Brain*, *131*, 165–179.

Bays, P. M. & Husain, M. (2008). Dynamic shifts of limited working memory resources in human vision. *Science*, *321*(5890), 851–854.

Beauchamp, M. S., Lee, K. E., Haxby, J. V., & Martin, A. (2002). Parallel visual motion processing streams for manipulable objects and human movements. *Neuron*, *34*, 149–159.

Beauchamp, M. S., Nath, A. R., & Pasalar, S. (2010). fMRi-guided transcranial magnetic stimulation reveals that the superior temporal sulcus is a cortical locus of the McGurk effect. *Journal of Neuroscience*, *30*(7), 2414–2417.

Beauvois, M.-F. (1982). Optic aphasia: A process of interaction between vision and language. *Philosophical Transactions of the Royal Society of London*, *298*, 35–47.

Beauvois, M.-F. & Derouesne, L. (1979). Phonological alexia: Three dissociations. *Journal of Neurology, Neurosurgery and Psychiatry, 42,* 1115–1124.

Beauvois, M.-F. & Derouesne, J. (1981). Lexical or orthographic agraphia. *Brain, 104,* 21–49.

Beauvois, M.-F., & Saillant, B. (1985). Optic aphasia for colours and colour agnosia: A distinction between visual and visuo-verbal impairments in the processing of colours. *Cognitive Neuropsychology, 2,* 1–48.

Bechara, A., Damasio, A. R., Damasio, H., & Anderson, S. W. (1994). Insensitivity to future consequences following damage to human prefrontal cortex. *Cognition, 50,* 7–15.

Bechara, A., Tranel, D., Damasio, H., Adolphs, R., Rockland, C., & Damasio, A. R. (1995). Double dissociation of conditioning and declarative knowledge relative to the amygdala and hippocampus in humans. *Science, 269*(5227), 1115–1118.

Bechara, A., Damasio, H., Tranel, D., & Anderson, S. W. (1998). Dissociation of working memory from decision making within the human prefrontal cortex. *Journal of Neuroscience, 18,* 428–437.

Bechara, A., Damasio, H., Damasio, A. R., & Lee, G. P. (1999). Different contributions to the human amygdala and ventromedial prefrontal cortex to decision making. *Journal of Neuroscience, 19,* 5437–5481.

Beck, D. M. & Kastner, S. (2009). Top-down and bottom-up mechanisms in biasing competition in the human brain. *Vision Research, 49*(10), 1154–1165.

Beck, D. M., Rees, G., Frith, C. D., & Lavie, N. (2001). Neural correlates of change detection and change blindness. *Nature Neuroscience, 4,* 645–650.

Beeson, P. M., Rapcsak, S. Z., Plante, E., Chargualaf, J., Chung, A., Johnson, S. C., & Trouard, T. P. (2003). The neural substrates of writing: A functional magnetic resonance imaging study. *Aphasiology, 17,* 647–666.

Behrmann, M. & Bub, D. (1992). Surface dyslexia and dysgraphia: Dual routes, single lexicon. *Cognitive Neuropsychology, 9,* 209–251.

Behrmann, M., Moscovitch, M., & Winocur, G. (1994). Intact visual imagery and impaired visual perception in a patient with visual agnosia. *Journal of Experimental Psychology: Human Perception and Performance, 20,* 1068–1087.

Behrmann, M., Plaut, D. C., & Nelson, J. (1998). A literature review and new data supporting an interactive activation account of letter-by-letter reading. *Cognitive Neuropsychology, 15,* 7–51.

Bekesy, G. von (1960). *Experiments in hearing.* New York: McGraw-Hill.

Belin, P. & Zatorre, R. J. (2003). Adaptation to speaker's voice in right anterior temporal lobe. *NeuroReport, 14,* 2105–2109.

Belin, P., Zatorre, R. J., Lafaille, P., Ahad, P., & Pike, B. (2000). Voice-selective areas in human auditory cortex. *Nature, 403,* 309–312.

Belin, P., Bestelmeyer, P. E. G., Latinus, M., & Watson, R. (2011). Understanding Voice Perception. *British Journal of Psychology, 102,* 711–725.

Bendor, D. & Wang, X. Q. (2005). The neuronal representation of pitch in primate auditory cortex. *Nature, 436,* 1161–1165.

Bengtsson, S. L., Nagy, Z., Skare, S., Forsman, L., Forssberg, H., & Ullen, F. (2005). Extensive piano practicing has regionally specific effects on white matter development. *Nature Neuroscience, 8,* 1148–1150.

Bengtsson, S. L., Ullen, F., Ehrsson, H. H., Hashimoto, T., Kito, T., Naito, E., Forssberg, H., & Sadato, N. (2009). Listening to rhythms activates motor and premotor cortices. *Cortex, 45*(1), 62–71.

Benjamin, J., Li, L., Patterson, C., Greenberg, B. D., Murphy, D. L., & Hamer, D. H. (1996). Population and familial association between the D4 dopamine receptor gene and measures of novelty seeking. *Nature Genetics, 12,* 81–84.

Bentin, S. & Deouell, L. Y. (2000). Structural encoding and identification in face processing: ERP evidence for separate mechanisms. *Cognitive Neuropsychology, 17,* 35–54.

Bentin, S., Allison, T., Puce, A., Perez, E., & McCarthy, G. (1996). Electrophysiological studies of face perception in humans. *Journal of Cognitive Neuroscience, 8,* 551–565.

Bentin, S., Mouchetant-Rostaing, Y., Giard, M. H., Echallier, J. F., & Pernier, J. (1999). ERP manifestations of processing printed words at different psycholinguistic levels. *Journal of Cognitive Neuroscience, 11,* 235–260.

Bentin, S., Sagiv, N., Mecklinger, A., Friederici, A. D., & von Cramon, Y. D. (2002). Priming visual face-processing mechanisms: Electrophysiological evidence. *Psychological Science, 13,* 190–193.

Benton, A. L. (1977). Reflections on the Gerstmann syndrome. *Brain and Language, 4,* 45–62.

Beradelli, A., Rothwell, J. C., Thompson, P. D., & Hallett, M. (2001). Pathophysiology of bradykinesia in Parkinson's disease. *Brain, 124,* 2131–2146.

Berger, H. (1929). Über das elektroenkephalogramm des menschen. *Archiv für Psychiatrie und Nervenkrankheiten, 87,* 527–570.

Bertelson, P. & Aschersleben, G. (1998). Automatic visual bias of perceived auditory location. *Psychonomic Bulletin and Review, 5,* 482–489.

Berthoz, S., Armony, J. L., Blair, R. J. R., & Dolan, R. J. (2002). An fMRI study of intentional and unintentional (embarrassing) violations of social norms. *Brain, 125,* 1696–1708.

Berti, A. & Frassinetti, F. (2000). When far becomes near: Remapping of space by tool use. *Journal of Cognitive Neuroscience, 12,* 415–420.

Best, C. T. & Avery, R. A. (1999). Left-hemisphere advantage for click consonants is determined by linguistic significance and experience. *Psychological Science, 10,* 65–70.

Bestelmeyer, P. E. G., Belin, P., & Grosbras, M.-H. (2011). Right temporal TMS impairs voice detection. *Current Biology, 21*(20), R838–R839.

Bestmann, S. & Feredoes, E. (2013). Combined neurostimulation and neuroimaging in cognitive neuroscience: past, present, and future. *Year in Cognitive Neuroscience, 1296,* 11–30.

Bever, T. G. (1970). The cognitive basis for linguistic structures. In J. R. Hayes (Ed.), *Cognition and the development of language.* New York: Wiley.

Beyerstein, B. L. (1999). Whence cometh the myth that we only use 10% of our brains? In S. D. Salla (ed.), *Mind myths.* Chichester: Wiley.

Bichot, N. P., Rossi, A. F., & Desimone, R. (2005). Parallel and serial neural mechanisms for visual search in macaque area V4. *Science, 308*(5721), 529–534.

Biederman, I. (1987). Recognition by components: A theory of human image understanding. *Psychological Review, 94,* 115–145.

Binder, J. R. & Desai, R. H. (2011). The neurobiology of semantic memory. *Trends in Cognitive Sciences, 15*(11), 527–536.

Binder, J. R., Frost, J. A., Hammeke, T. A., Bellgowan, P. S., Springer, J. A., Kaufman, J. N., & Possing, E. T. (2000). Human temporal lobe activation by speech and non-speech sounds. *Cerebral Cortex, 10,* 512–528.

Bird, H., Howard, D., & Franklin, S. (2000). Why is a verb like an inanimate object? Grammatical category and semantic category deficits. *Brain and Language, 72,* 246–309.

Birdsong, D. (2006). Age and second language acquisition and processing: A selective overview. *Language Learning, 56,* 9–49.

Bisiach, E. & Luzzatti, C. (1978). Unilateral neglect of representational space. *Cortex, 14,* 129–133.

Bisley, J. W. & Goldberg, M. E. (2010). Attention, intention, and priority in the parietal lobe. In S. E. Hyman (Ed.), *Annual Review of Neuroscience* (Vol. 33, pp. 1–21). Palo Alto, CA: Annual Reviews.

Bjork, E. L. (1998). Intentional forgetting perspective: Comments, conjectures and some directed remembering. In J. M. Golding & C. M. MacLoed (Eds.), *Intentional forgetting: Interdisciplinary approaches*. Mahwah, NJ: Lawrence Erlbaum.

Blair, K., Marsh, A. A., Morton, J., Vythilingam, M., Jones, M., Mondillo, K., Pine, D. C., Drevels, W. C., & Blair, J. R. (2006). Choosing the lesser of two evils, the better of two goods: Specifying the roles of ventromedial prefrontal cortex and dorsal anterior cingulate in object choice. *Journal of Neuroscience, 26*(44), 11379–11386.

Blakemore, C. (1977). *Mechanics of the mind*. Cambridge, UK: Cambridge University Press.

Blakemore, C. & Vansluyters, R. C. (1975). Innate and environmental factors in development of kittens' visual-cortex. *Journal of Physiology, 248*, 663–716.

Blakemore, S.-J., Rees, G., & Frith, C. D. (1998). How do we predict the consequences of our actions? A functional imaging study. *Neuropsychologia, 36*, 521–529.

Block, N. (2005). Two neural correlates of consciousness. *Trends in Cognitive Sciences, 9*, 46–52.

Blood, A. J. & Zatorre, R. J. (2001). Intensely pleasurable responses to music correlate with activity in brain regions implicated in reward and emotion. *Proceedings of the National Academy of Science, USA, 98*, 11818–11823.

Blumenfeld, R. S. & Ranganath, C. (2006). Dorsolateral prefrontal cortex promotes long-term memory formation through its role in working memory organization. *Journal of Neuroscience, 26*(3), 916–925.

Bodamer, J. (1947). Die prosopagnosie. *Archiv für Psychiatrie und Zeitschrift für Neurologie, 179*, 6–54.

Boggio, P. S., Ferrucci, R., Rigonatti, S. P., Covre, P., Nitsche, M., Pascual-Leone, A., & Fregni, F. (2006). Effects of transcranial direct current stimulation on working memory in patients with Parkinson's disease. *Journal of the Neurological Sciences, 249*(1), 31–38.

Bolger, D. J., Perfetti, C. A., & Schneider, W. (2005). Cross-cultural effect on the brain revisited: Universal structures plus writing system variation. *Human Brain Mapping, 25*, 92–104.

Bolhuis, J. J. (1990). Mechanisms of avian imprinting: A review. *Biological Reviews, 66*, 303–345.

Bonini, L., Rozzi, S., Serventi, F. U., Simone, L., Ferrari, P. F., & Fogassi, L. (2010). Ventral premotor and inferior parietal cortices make distinct contribution to action organization and intention understanding. *Cerebral Cortex, 20*(6), 1372–1385.

Bonnici, H. M., Chadwick, M. J., & Maguire, E. A. (2013). Representations of recent and remote autobiographical memories in hippocampal subfields. *Hippocampus, 23*(10), 849–854.

Bor, D., Cumming, N., Scott, C. E. L., & Owen, A. M. (2004). Prefrontal cortical involvement in verbal encoding strategies. *European Journal of Neuroscience, 19*(12), 3365–3370.

Borra, E., Belmalih, A., Calzavara, R., Gerbella, M., Murata, A., Rozzi, S., & Luppino, G. (2008). Cortical connections of the macaque anterior intraparietal (AIP) area. *Cerebral Cortex, 18*(5), 1094–1111.

Bottini, G., Corcoran, R., Sterzi, R., Paulesu, E., Schenone, P., Scarpa, P., Frackowiak, R. S. J., & Frith, C. D. (1994). The role of the right hemisphere in the interpretation of figurative aspects of language: A positron emission tomography activation study. *Brain, 117*, 1241–1253.

Botvinick, M. & Cohen, J. (1998). Rubber hands "feel" touch that eyes see. *Nature, 391*, 756.

Boucart, M. & Humphreys, G. W. (1992). The computation of perceptual structure and closure: Normality and pathology. *Neuropsychologia, 30*, 527–546.

Bouchard, T. J. J. & McGue, M. (1981). Familial studies of intelligence: A review. *Science, 212*, 1055–1059.

Bowers, D. & Heilman, K. M. (1980). Pseudoneglect: Effects of hemispace on a tactile line bisection task. *Neuropsychologia*, *18*, 491–498.

Bowers, J. S. (2009). On the biological plausibility of grandmother cells: Implications for neural network theories in psychology and neuroscience. *Psychological Review*, *116*(1), 220–251.

Bowers, J. S., Bub, D., & Arguin, M. (1996). A characterisation of the word superiority effect in pure alexia. *Cognitive Neuropsychology*, *13*, 415–441.

Bowles, B., Crupi, C., Mirsattari, S. M., Pigott, S. E., Parrent, A. G., Pruessner, J. C., Yonelinas, A. P., & Kohler, S. (2007). Impaired familiarity with preserved recollection after anterior temporal-lobe resection that spares the hippocampus. *Proceedings of the National Academy of Sciences, USA*, *104*, 16382–16387.

Bowling, D. L., Sundararajan, J., Han, S. e., & Purves, D. (2012). Expression of Emotion in Eastern and Western Music Mirrors Vocalization. *PLoS One*, *7*(3).

Brambati, S. M., Ogar, J., Neuhaus, J., Miller, B. L., & Gorno-Tempini, M. L. (2009). Reading disorders in primary progressive aphasia: A behavioral and neuroimaging study. *Neuropsychologia*, *47*(8–9), 1893–1900.

Brammer, M. J. (2001). Head motion and its correction. In P. Jezzard, P. M. Matthews, & S. M. Smith (Eds.), *Functional MRI*. Oxford, UK: Oxford University Press.

Brannon, E. M. & Terrace, H. S. (1998). Ordering of the numerosities 1 to 9 by monkeys. *Science*, *282*, 746–749.

Brass, M. & von Cramon, D. Y. (2002). The role of the frontal cortex in task preparation. *Cerebral Cortex*, *12*, 908–914.

Brass, M. & Haggard, P. (2007). To do or not to do: The neural signature of self-control. *Journal of Neuroscience*, *27*, 9141–9145.

Bredart, S., Brennen, T., & Valentine, T. (1997). Dissociations between the processing of proper and common names. *Cognitive Neuropsychology*, *14*, 209–217.

Bremmer, F., Schlack, A., Shah, N. J., Zafiris, O., Kubischik, M., Hoffmann, K. P., Zilles, K., & Fink, G. R. (2001). Polymodal motion processing in posterior parietal and premotor cortex: A human fMRI study strongly implies equivalencies between humans and monkeys. *Neuron*, *29*, 287–296.

Bressler, S. L., Tang, W., Sylvester, C. M., Shulman, G. L., & Corbetta, M. (2008). Top-down control of human visual cortex by frontal and parietal cortex in anticipatory visual spatial attention. *Journal of Neuroscience*, *28*(40), 10056–10061.

Broadbent, D. E. (1958). *Perception and communication*. London: Pergamon Press.

Broca, P. (1861). Remarques sur le siège de la faculté du langagé articule, suivies d'une observation d'aphémie. *Bulletin et Mémoires de la Société Anatomique de Paris*, *2*, 330–357.

Brooks, D. J., Ibanez, V., Sawles, G. V., Quinn, N., Lees, A. J., Mathias, C. J., Banniseter, R., Marsden, C. D. & Frackowiak, R. S. J. (1990). Differing patterns of striatal 18F-dopa uptake in Parkinson's disease, multiple system atrophy, and progressive supranuclear palsy. *Annals of Neurology*, *28*, 547–555.

Brouwer, G. J. & Heeger, D. J. (2009). Decoding and reconstructing color from responses in human visual cortex. *Journal of Neuroscience*, *29*(44), 13992–14003.

Brown, A. S. (1991). A review of the tip-of-the-tongue experience. *Psychological Bulletin*, *109*, 204–223.

Brown, R. & McNeill, D. (1966). The "tip of the tongue" phenomenon. *Journal of Verbal Learning and Verbal Behavior*, *5*, 325–337.

Brown, R. G. & Marsden, C. D. (1988). Internal versus external cues and the control of attention in Parkinson's disease. *Brain*, *111*, 323–345.

Brown, S., Ngan, E., & Liotti, M. (2008). A larynx area in the human motor cortex. *Cerebral Cortex*, *18*(4), 837–845.

Bruandet, M., Molko, N., Cohen, L., & Dehaene, S. (2003). A cognitive characterisation of dyscalculia in Turner syndrome. *Neuropsychologia*, *42*, 288–298.

Bruce, C. J., Goldberg, M. E., Bushnell, M. C., & Stanton, G. B. (1985). Primate frontal eye fields: II. Physiological and anatomical correlates of electrically evoked eye movements. *Journal of Neurophysiology*, *54*, 714–734.

Bruce, V. & Valentine, T. (1986). Semantic priming of familiar faces. *Quarterly Journal of Experimental Psychology*, *38A*, 125–150.

Bruce, V. & Young, A. W. (1986). Understanding face recognition. *British Journal of Psychology*, *77*, 305–327.

Brugge, J. F. & Merzenich, M. M. (1973). Responses of neurons in auditory cortex of the macaque monkey to monaural and binaural stimulation. *Journal of Neurophysiology*, *36*, 1138–1158.

Brysbaert, M. (1995). Arabic number reading: On the nature of the numerical scale and the origin of phonological recoding. *Journal of Experimental Psychology: General*, *124*, 434–452.

Bub, D. & Kertesz, A. (1982). Deep agraphia. *Brain and Language*, *17*, 146–165.

Buccino, G., Lui, F., Canessa, N., Patteri, I., Lagravinese, G., Benuzzi, F., Porro, C. A., & Rizzolatti, G. (2004). Neural circuits involved in the recognition of actions performed by nonconspecifics: An fMRI study. *Journal of Cognitive Neuroscience*, *16*, 114–126.

Buchsbaum, B. R. & D'Esposito, M. (2008). The search for the phonological store: From loop to convolution. *Journal of Cognitive Neuroscience*, *20*, 762–778.

Buchsbaum, B. R., Baldo, J., Okada, K., Berman, K. F., Dronkers, N., D'Esposito, M., & Hickok, G. (2011). Conduction aphasia, sensory-motor integration, and phonological short-term memory—An aggregate analysis of lesion and fMRI data. *Brain and Language*, *119*(3), 119–128.

Buckner, R. L., Kelley, W. M., & Petersen, S. E. (1999). Frontal cortex contributes to human memory formation. *Nature Neuroscience*, *2*, 311–314.

Buckner, R. L., Andrews-Hanna, J. R., & Schacter, D. L. (2008). The brain's default network: Anatomy, function, and relevance to disease. *Annals of the New York Academy of Sciences*, *1124*, 1–38.

Bueti, D. & Walsh, V. (2009). The parietal cortex and the representation of time, space, number and other magnitudes. *Philosophical Transactions of the Royal Society B-Biological Sciences*, *364*(1525), 1831–1840.

Burani, C., Barca, L., & Ellis, A. W. (2006). Orthographic complexity and word naming in Italian: Some words are more transparent than others. *Psychonomic Bulletin & Review*, *13*, 346–352.

Burbaud, P., Camus, O., Guehl, D., Biolac, B., Caille, J. M., & Allard, M. (1999). A functional magnetic resonance imaging study of mental subtraction in human subjects. *Neuroscience Letters*, *273*, 195–199.

Burgess, N. (2002). The hippocampus, space, and viewpoints in episodic memory. *Quarterly Journal of Experimental Psychology*, *55A*, 1057–1080.

Burgess, N., Maguire, E. A., & O'Keefe, J. (2002). The human hippocampus and spatial and episodic memory. *Neuron*, *35*(4), 625–641.

Burgess, P. W. (2000). Strategy application disorder: The role of the frontal lobes in human multitasking. *Psychological Research*, *63*, 279–288.

Burgess, P. W., Veitch, E., Costello, A., & Shallice, T. (2000). The cognitive and neuroanatomical correlates of multitasking. *Neuropsychologia*, *38*, 848–863.

Burgess, P. W., Dumontheil, I., & Gilbert, S. J. (2007). The gateway hypothesis of rostral prefrontal cortex (area 10) function. *Trends in Cognitive Sciences*, *11*(7), 290–298.

Bush, G., Luu, P., & Posner, M. I. (2000). Cognitive and emotional influences in anterior cingulate cortex. *Trends in Cognitive Sciences*, *4*, 215–222.

Buttelmann, D., Carpenter, M., Call, J., & Tomasello, M. (2007). Enculturated chimpanzees imitate rationally. *Developmental Science*, *10*, F31–F38.

Butters, N. & Cermak, L. S. (1986). A case study of the forgetting of autobiographical knowledge: Implications for the study of retrograde amnesia. In D. C. Rubin (Ed.), *Autobiographical memory*. Cambridge, UK: Cambridge University Press.

Butters, N. & Pandya, D. N. (1969). Retention of delayed-alternation: Effect of selective lesion of sulcus principalis. *Science*, *165*, 1271–1273.

Butterworth, B. (1999). *The mathematical brain*. London: Macmillan.

Butterworth, B. & Warrington, E. K. (1995). Two routes to repetition: Evidence from a case of "deep dysphasia." *Neurocase*, *1*, 55–66.

Butterworth, B., Cipolotti, L., & Warrington, E. K. (1996). Short-term memory impairments and arithmetical ability. *Quarterly Journal of Experimental Psychology*, *49A*, 251–262.

Cabeza, R., Rao, S. M., Wagner, A. D., Mayer, A. R., & Schacter, D. L. (2001). Can medial temporal lobe regions distinguish true from false? An event-related functional fMRI study of veridical and illusory recognition memory. *Proceedings of the National Academy of Science, USA*, *98*, 4805–4810.

Cabeza, R., Dolcos, F., Prince, S. E., Rice, H. J., Weissman, D. H., & Nyberg, L. (2003). Attention-related activity during episodic memory retrieval: A cross-function fMRI study. *Neuropsychologia*, *41*, 390–399.

Cacioppo, J. T., Norris, C. J., Decety, J., Monteleone, G., & Nusbaum, H. (2009). In the eye of the beholder: Individual differences in perceived social isolation predict regional brain activation to social stimuli. *Journal of Cognitive Neuroscience*, *21*(1), 83–92.

Cahill, L., Weinberger, N. M., Roozendaal, B., & McGaugh, J. L. (1999). Is the amygdala a locus of "conditioned fear"? Some questions and caveats. *Neuron*, *23*, 227–228.

Calder, A. J. & Young, A. W. (2005). Understanding the recognition of facial identity and facial expression. *Nature Reviews Neuroscience*, *6*(8), 641–651.

Calder, A. J., Young, A. W., Rowland, D., Perrett, D. I., Hodges, J. R., & Etcoff, N. L. (1996). Facial emotion recognition after bilateral amygdala damage: Differentially severe impairment of fear. *Cognitive Neuropsychology*, *13*, 699–745.

Calder, A. J., Keane, J., Manes, F., Antoun, N., & Young, A. W. (2000). Impaired recognition and experience of disgust following brain injury. *Nature Neuroscience*, *3*(11), 1077–1078.

Callan, D., Callan, A., Gamez, M., Sato, M., & Kawato, M. (2010). Premotor cortex mediates perceptual performance. *NeuroImage*, *51*(2), 844–858.

Calvanio, R., Petrone, P. N., & Levine, D. N. (1987). Left visual spatial neglect is both environment-centred and body-centred. *Neurology*, *37*, 1179–1183.

Calvert, G. A. (2001). Crossmodal processing in the human brain: Insights from functional neuroimaging studies. *Cerebral Cortex*, *11*, 1110–1123.

Calvert, G. A., Campbell, R., & Brammer, M. J. (2000). Evidence from functional magnetic resonance imaging of crossmodal binding in the human heteromodal cortex. *Current Biology*, *10*, 649–657.

Calvert, G. A., Hansen, P. C., Iversen, S. D., & Brammer, M. J. (2001). Detection of audio-visual integration sites in humans by application of electrophysiological criteria to the BOLD effect. *NeuroImage*, *14*, 427–438.

Campbell, J. I. (1994). Architectures for numerical cognition. *Cognition*, *53*, 1–44.

Campbell, R., Landis, T., & Regard, M. (1986). Face recognition and lip reading: A neurological dissociation. *Brain*, *109*, 509–521.

Campbell, R., Heywood, C., Cowey, A., Regard, M., & Landis, T. (1990). Sensitivity to eye gaze in prosopagnosic patients and monkeys with superior temporal sulcus ablation. *Neuropsychologia*, *28*, 1123–1142.

Campion, J., Latto, R., & Smith, Y. M. (1983). Is blindsight an effect of scattered light, spared cortex, and near-threshold vision? *Behavioral and Brain Sciences*, *6*, 423–486.

Cannon, W. B. (1927). The James-Lange theory of emotions: a critical examination and an alternative theory. *American Journal of Pschology*, *39*, 106–124.

Cantlon, J. F. & Brannon, E. M. (2007). Basic math in monkey and college students. *PLoS Biology*, *5*, 2912–2919.

Capgras, J. & Reboul-Lachaux, J. (1923). L'illusion des sosies dans un delire systematisé chronique. *Bulletin de la Société Clinique de Médecine Mentale*, *2*, 6–16.

Capitani, E., Laiacona, M., Mahon, B., & Caramazza, A. (2003). What are the facts of semantic category-specific deficits? A critical review of the clinical evidence. *Cognitive Neuropsychology, 20,* 213–261.

Caplan, D. (1988). On the role of group studies in neuropsychological and patho-psychological research. *Cognitive Neuropsychology, 5,* 535–548.

Caplan, D. & Waters, G. S. (1990). Short-term memory and language comprehension: A critical review of the neuropsychology literature. In G. Vallar, & T. Shallice (Eds.), *Neuropsychological impairments of short-term memory.* Cambridge, UK: Cambridge University Press.

Cappelletti, M., Kopelman, M. D., & Butterworth, B. (2002). Why semantic dementia drives you to the dogs (but not to the horses): A theoretical account. *Cognitive Neuropsychology, 19,* 483–503.

Caramazza, A. (1986). On drawing inferences about the structure of normal cognitive systems from the analysis of patterns of impaired performance: The case for single-patient studies. *Brain and Cognition, 5,* 41–66.

Caramazza, A. (1992). Is cognitive neuropsychology possible? *Journal of Cognitive Neuroscience, 4,* 80–95.

Caramazza, A. (1997). How many levels of processing are there in lexical access? *Cognitive Neuropsychology, 14,* 177–208.

Caramazza, A. & Badecker, W. (1989). Patient classification in neuropsychological research. *Brain and Cognition, 10,* 256–295.

Caramazza, A. & Badecker, W. (1991). Clinical syndromes are not God's gift to cognitive neuropsychology: A reply to a rebuttal to an answer to a response to the case against syndrome-based research. *Brain and Cognition, 16,* 211–227.

Caramazza, A. & Hillis, A. E. (1990a). Levels of representation, co-ordinate frames, and unilateral neglect. *Cognitive Neuropsychology, 7,* 391–445.

Caramazza, A. & Hillis, A. E. (1990b). Where do semantic errors come from? *Cortex, 26,* 95–122.

Caramazza, A. & Hillis, A. E. (1991). Lexical organization of nouns and verbs in the brain. *Nature, 349,* 788–790.

Caramazza, A. & McCloskey, M. (1988). The case for single-patient studies. *Cognitive Neuropsychology, 5,* 517–528.

Caramazza, A. & Miceli, G. (1990). The structure of graphemic representations. *Cognition, 37,* 243–297.

Caramazza, A. & Miozzo, M. (1997). The relation between syntactic and phonological knowledge in lexical access: Evidence from the "tip-of-the-tongue" phenomenon. *Cognition, 64,* 309–343.

Caramazza, A. & Shelton, R. S. (1998). Domain-specific knowledge systems in the brain: The animate–inanimate distinction. *Journal of Cognitive Neuroscience, 10,* 1–34.

Caramazza, A. & Zurif, E. B. (1976). Dissociation of algorithmic and heuristic processes in language comprehension. *Brain and Language, 3,* 572–582.

Caramazza, A., Hillis, A. E., Villa, G., & Romani, C. (1987). The role of the graphemic buffer in spelling: Evidence from a case of acquired dysgraphia. *Cognition, 26,* 59–85.

Caramazza, A., Hillis, A. E., Rapp, B. C., & Romani, C. (1990). Multiple semantics or multiple confusions? *Cognitive Neuropsychology, 7,* 161–168.

Caramazza, A., Capasso, R., & Miceli, G. (1996). The role of the graphemic buffer in reading. *Cognitive Neuropsychology, 13,* 673–698.

Carmel, D. & Bentin, S. (2002). Domain specificity versus expertise: Factors influencing distinct processing of faces. *Cognition, 83,* 1–29.

Carr, L., Iacoboni, M., Dubeau, M. C., Mazziotta, J. C., & Lenzi, G. L. (2003). Neural mechanisms of empathy in humans: A relay from neural systems for imitation to limbic areas. *Proceedings of the National Academy of Sciences of the United States of America, 100*(9), 5497–5502.

Carr, T. H., Posner, M. I., Pollatsek, A., & Snyder, C. R. (1979). Orthography and familiarity effects in word processing. *Journal of Experimental Psychology: General*, *108*, 389–414.

Carter, C. S., Braver, T. S., Barch, D. M., Botvinick, M. M., Noll, D., & Cohen, J. D. (1998). Anterior cingulate cortex, error detection, and the online monitoring of performance. *Science*, *280*, 747–749.

Carter, C. S., MacDonald, A. M., Botvinick, M., Ross, L. L., Stenger, V. A., Noll, D., & Cohen, J. D. (2000). Parsing executive processes: Strategic vs. evaluative functions of the anterior cingulate cortex. *Proceedings of the National Academy of Science, USA*, *97*, 1944–1948.

Caspi, A., Moffitt, T. E., Cannon, M., McClay, J., Murray, R. M., Harrington, H. L., Taylor, A., Arseneault, L., Williams, B., Braithwaite, A., Poulton, R., & Craig, I. W. (2005). Moderation of the effect of adolescent-onset cannabis use on adult psychosis by a functional polymorphism in the catechol-o-methyltransferase gene: Longitudinal evidence for a gene X–environment interaction. *Biological Psychiatry*, *57*, 1117–1127.

Castelli, F., Glaser, D. E., & Butterworth, B. (2006). Discrete and analogue quantity processing in the parietal lobe: A functional MRI study. *Proceedings of the National Academy of Sciences of the United States of America*, *103*(12), 4693–4698.

Castelli, F., Happé, F., Frith, U., & Frith, C. D. (2000). Movement and mind: A functional imaging study of perception and interpretation of complex intentional movements. *NeuroImage*, *12*, 314–325.

Castle, D., Wesseley, S., Der, G., & Murray, R. M. (1991). The incidence of operationally defined schizophrenia in Camberwell 1965–84. *British Journal of Psychiatry*, *159*, 790–794.

Castles, A., Datta, H., Gayan, J., & Olson, R. K. (1999). Varieties of developmental reading disorder: Genetic and environmental influences. *Journal of Experimental Child Psychology*, *72*, 73–94.

Cattell, J. M. (1886). The inertia of the eye and brain. *Brain*, *8*, 295–312.

Cattell, R. B. (1971). *Abilities: Their structure, growth and action*. Boston, MA: Houghton Mifflin.

Cattinelli, I., Borghese, N. A., Gallucci, M., & Paulesu, E. (2013). Reading the reading brain: A new meta-analysis of functional imaging data on reading. *Journal of Neurolinguistics*, *26*(1), 214–238.

Cermak, L. S. & O'Connor, M. (1983). The anterograde and retrograde retrieval ability of a patient with amnesia due to encephalitis. *Neuropsychologia*, *21*, 213–234.

Chakraborty, S., Anderson, M. I., Chaudhry, A. M., Mumford, J. C., & Jeffery, K. J. (2004). Context-independent directional cue learning by hippocampal place cells. *European Journal of Neuroscience*, *20*, 281–292.

Chamberlain, S. R., Menzies, L., Hampshire, A., Suckling, J., Fineberg, N. A., del Campo, N., Aitken, M., Craig, K., Owen, A. M., Bullmore, E. T., Robbins, T. W., & Sahakian, B. J. (2008). Orbitofrontal dysfunction in patients with obsessive-compulsive disorder and their unaffected relatives. *Science*, *321*(5887), 421–422.

Chance, M. (1967). The interpretation of some agonistic postures: The role of "cut-off" acts and postures. *Symposium of the Zoological Society of London*, *8*, 71–89.

Chao, L. L. & Martin, A. (1999). Cortical regions associated with perceiving, naming and knowing about colours. *Journal of Cognitive Neuroscience*, *11*, 25–35.

Chao, L. L. & Martin, A. (2000). Representation of manipulable man-made objects in the dorsal stream. *NeuroImage*, *12*, 478–484.

Chapin, J. K. (2004). Using multi-neuron population recordings for neural prosthetics. *Nature Neuroscience*, 7, 452–455.

Chapman, H. A., Kim, D. A., Susskind, J. M., & Anderson, A. K. (2009). In bad taste: Evidence for the oral origins of moral disgust. *Science*, *323*(5918), 1222–1226.

Chechlacz, M., Rotshtein, P., & Humphreys, G. W. (2012). Neuroanatomical dissections of unilateral visual neglect symptoms: ALE meta-analysis of lesion-symptom mapping. *Frontiers in Human Neuroscience*, *6*.

Chee, M. W. L., Weekes, B., Lee, K. M., Soon, C. S., Schreiber, A., Hoon, J. J., & Chee, M. (2000). Overlap and dissociation of semantic processing of Chinese characters, English words, and pictures: Evidence from fMRI. *NeuroImage, 12*, 392–403.

Chen, J. L., Zatorre, R. J., & Penhune, V. B. (2006). Interactions between auditory and dorsal premotor cortex during synchronization to musical rhythms. *NeuroImage, 32*(4), 1771–1781.

Chen, Y. P., Fu, S. M., Iversen, S. D., Smith, S. M., & Matthews, P. M. (2002). Testing for dual brain processing routes in reading: A direct contrast of Chinese character and pinyin reading using fMRI. *Journal of Cognitive Neuroscience, 14*, 1088–1098.

Chevillet, M. A., Jiang, X., Rauschecker, J. P., & Riesenhuber, M. (2013). Automatic phoneme category selectivity in the dorsal auditory stream. *Journal of Neuroscience, 33*(12), 5208–5215.

Christoff, K., Prabhakaran, V., Dorfman, J., Zhao, Z., Kroger, J. K., Holyoak, K. J., & Gabrieli, J. D. E. (2001). Rostrolateral prefrontal cortex involvement in relational integration during reasoning. *NeuroImage, 14*, 1136–1149.

Chugani, H. T., Phelps, M. E., & Mazziotta, J. C. (1987). Positron emission tomography study of human brain functional development. *Annals of Neurology, 22*, 487–497.

Chumbley, J. I. & Balota, D. A. (1984). A word's meaning affects the decision in lexical decision. *Memory and Cognition, 12*, 590–606.

Church, J. A., Balota, D. A., Petersen, S. E., & Schlaggar, B. L. (2011). Manipulation of length and lexicality localizes the functional neuroanatomy of phonological processing in adult readers. *Journal of Cognitive Neuroscience, 23*(6), 1475–1493.

Churchland, P. M. (1995). *The engine of reason, the seat of the soul*. Cambridge, MA: MIT Press.

Churchland, P. S. & Sejnowski, T. J. (1988). Perspectives on cognitive neuroscience. *Science, 242*(4879), 741–745.

Ciaghi, M., Pancheri, E., & Miceli, G. (2010). Semantic paralexias: A group-case study on the underlying functional mechanisms, incidence and clinical features in a consecutive series of 340 Italian aphasics. *Brain and Language, 115*(2), 121–132.

Cipolotti, L. (1995). Multiple routes for reading words, why not numbers? Evidence from a case of Arabic numeral dyslexia. *Cognitive Neuropsychology, 12*, 313–342.

Cipolotti, L. & Butterworth, B. (1995). Toward a multi-route model of number processing: Impaired number transcoding with preserved calculation skills. *Journal of Experimental Psychology: General, 124*, 375–390.

Cipolotti, L. & Denes, G. (1989). When a patient can write but not copy: Report of a single case. *Cortex, 25*, 331–337.

Cipolotti, L. & Warrington, E. K. (1995a). Neuropsychological assessment. *Journal of Neurology, Neurosurgery and Psychiatry, 58*, 655–664.

Cipolotti, L. & Warrington, E. K. (1995b). Semantic memory and reading abilities: A case report. *Journal of the International Neuropsychological Society, 1*, 104–110.

Cipolotti, L. & Warrington, E. K. (1996). Does recognizing orally spelled words depend on reading? An investigation into a case of better written than oral spelling. *Neuropsychologia, 34*, 427–440.

Cipolotti, L., Butterworth, B., & Denes, G. (1991). A specific deficit for numbers in a case of dense acalculia. *Brain, 114*, 2619–2637.

Cipolotti, L., Butterworth, B., & Warrington, E. K. (1994). From "one thousand nine hundred and forty-five" to 1000,945. *Neuropsychologia, 32*, 503–509.

Cipolotti, L., Warrington, E. K., & Butterworth, B. (1995). Selective impairment in manipulating Arabic numerals. *Cortex, 31*, 73–86.

Cipolotti, L., Shallice, T., Chan, D., Fox, N., Scahill, R., Harrison, G., Stevens, J., & Rudge, P. (2001). Long-term retrograde amnesia: The crucial role of the hippocampus. *Neuropsychologia, 39*, 151–172.

Clarey, J. C., Barone, P., & Imig, T. J. (1994). Functional organization of sound direction and sound pressure level in primary auditory cortex of the cat. *Journal of Neurophysiology, 72*, 2383–2405.

Cloutman, L., Gingis, L., Newhart, M., Davis, C., Heidler-Gary, J., Crinion, J., & Hillis, A. E. (2009). A neural network critical for spelling. *Annals of Neurology*, *66*(2), 249–253.

Cocchini, G., Beschin, N., & Jehkonen, M. (2001). The fluff test: A simple task to assess body representational neglect. *Neuropsychological Rehabilitation*, *11*, 17–31.

Cochon, F., Cohen, L., van de Moortele, P. F., & Dehaene, S. (1999). Differential contributions of the left and right inferior parietal lobules to number processing. *Journal of Cognitive Neuroscience*, *11*, 617–630.

Cohen, J. D., Peristein, W. M., Braver, T. S., Nystrom, L. E., Noll, D. C., Jonides, J., & Smith, E. E. (1997). Temporal dynamics of brain activation during a working memory task. *Nature*, *386*, 604–607.

Cohen, L. & Dehaene, S. (1996). Cerebral networks for number processing: Evidence from a case of posterior callosal lesion. *Neurocase*, *2*, 155–174.

Cohen, L. & Dehaene, S. (2000). Calculating without reading: Unsuspected residual abilities in pure alexia. *Cognitive Neuropsychology*, *17*, 563–583.

Cohen, L. & Dehaene, S. (2004). Specialization within the ventral stream: The case for the visual word form area. *NeuroImage*, *22*, 466–476.

Cohen, L. G., Bandinelli, S., Findley, T. W., & Hallett, M. (1991). Motor reorganization after upper limb amputation in man: A study with focal magnetic stimulation. *Brain*, *114*, 615–627.

Cohen, L. G., Celnik, P., Pascual-Leone, A., Corwell, B., Faiz, L., Dambrosia, J., Honda, M., Sadato, N., Gerloff, C., Catala, M. D., & Hallett, M. (1997b). Functional relevance of cross-modal plasticity in blind humans. *Nature*, *389*, 180–183.

Cohen, L., Lehericy, S., Chochon, F., Lemer, C., Rivaud, S., & Dehaene, S. (2002). Language-specific tuning of visual cortex functional properties of the Visual Word Form Area. *Brain*, *125*, 1054–1069.

Cohen Kadosh, R. & Henik, A. (2006). A common representation for semantic and physical properties. *Experimental Psychology*, *53*, 87–94.

Cohen Kadosh, R., Kadosh, K., Schuhmann, T., Kaas, A., Goebel, R., Henik, A., & Sack, A. T. (2007). Virtual dyscalculia induced by parietal-lobe TMS impairs automatic magnitude processing. *Current Biology*, *17*(8), 689–693.

Cohen Kadosh, R., Kadosh, K., & Henik, A. (2008). When brightness counts: The neuronal correlate of numerical-luminance interference. *Cerebral Cortex*, *18*(2), 337–343.

Cohen Kadosh, R., Bien, N., & Sack, A. T. (2012). Automatic and intentional number processing both rely on intact right parietal cortex: A combined fMRI and neuro-navigated TMS study. *Frontiers in Human Neuroscience*, *6*.

Collins, A. M. & Quinlan, M. R. (1969). Retrieval time from semantic memory. *Journal of Verbal Learning and Verbal Behavior*, *8*, 240–247.

Collins, D., Neelin, P., Peters, T., & Evans, A. (1994). Automatic 3D intersubject registration of MR volumetric data in standardized Talairach space. *Journal of Computer Assisted Tomography*, *18*, 192–205.

Coltheart, M. (2004a). Are there lexicons? *Quarterly Journal of Experimental Psychology*, *57A*, 1153–1171.

Coltheart, M. (2004b). Brain imaging, connectionism and cognitive neuropsychology. *Cognitive Neuropsychology*, *21*, 21–26.

Coltheart, M. & Funnell, E. (1987). Reading and writing: One lexicon or two? In D. A. Allport, D. Mackay, W. Prinz & E. Scheerer (Eds.), *Language perception and production: Relationships between listening, speaking, reading and writing*. London: Academic Press.

Coltheart, M., Curtis, B., Atkins, P., & Haller, M. (1993). Models of reading aloud. Dual-route and parallel distributed approaches. *Psychological Review*, *4*, 589–608.

Coltheart, M., Davelaar, E., Jonasson, J. T., & Besner, D. (1977). Access to the internal lexicon. In S. Dornic (Ed.), *Attention and performance VI*. Hillsdale, NJ: Lawrence Erlbaum.

Coltheart, M., Patterson, K. E., & Marshall, J. C. (1980). *Deep dyslexia*. London: Routledge.

Coltheart, M., Inglis, L., Cupples, L., Michie, P., Bates, A., & Budd, B. (1998). A semantic subsystem specific to the storage of information about visual attributes of animate and inanimate objects. *Neurocase, 4*, 353–370.

Conway, M. A. & Fthenaki, A. (2003). Disruption of inhibitory control of memory following lesions to the frontal and temporal lobes. *Cortex, 39*, 667–686.

Cooper, N. R., Croft, R. J., Dominey, S. J. J., Burgess, A. P., & Gruzelier, J. H. (2003). Paradox lost? Exploring the role of alpha oscillations during externally vs. internally directed attention and the implications for idling and inhibition hypotheses. *International Journal of Psychophysiology, 47*(1), 65–74.

Cooper, R. & Shallice, T. (2000). Contention scheduling and the control of routine activities. *Cognitive Neuropsychology, 17*, 297–338.

Corballis, M. C. (2002). From mouth to hand: Gesture, speech, and the evolution of right-handedness. *Behavioral and Brain Sciences*. 26, 199–208.

Corbetta, M. & Shulman, G. L. (2002). Control of goal-directed and stimulus-driven attention in the brain. *Nature Reviews Neuroscience, 3*(3), 201–215.

Corbetta, M. & Shulman, G. L. (2011). Spatial neglect and attention networks. *Annual Review of Neuroscience, 34*, 569–599.

Corbetta, M., Schulman, G., Miezin, F., & Petersen, S. (1995). Superior parietal cortex activation during spatial attention shifts and visual feature conjunctions. *Science, 270*, 802–805.

Corbetta, M., Kincade, J. M., Ollinger, J. M., McAvoy, M. P., & Shulman, G. L. (2000). Voluntary orienting is dissociated from target detection in human posterior parietal cortex. *Nature Neuroscience, 3*(3), 292–297.

Corkin, S. (1984). Lasting consequences of bilateral medial temporal lobectomy: Clinical course and experimental findings in HM. *Seminars in Neurology, 4*, 249–259.

Corkin, S. (2002). What's new with the amnesic patient HM? *Nature Reviews Neuroscience, 3*, 153–160.

Corthout, E., Uttle, B., Ziemann, U., Cowey, A., & Hallett, M. (1999). Two periods of processing in the (circum)striate visual cortex as revealed by transcranial magnetic stimulation. *Neuropsychologia, 37*, 137–145.

Coslett, H. B. (1991). Read but not write "Idea": Evidence for a third reading mechanism. *Brain and Language, 40*, 425–443.

Costanzo, F., Menghini, D., Caltagirone, C., Oliveri, M., & Vicari, S. (2012). High frequency rTMS over the left parietal lobule increases non-word reading accuracy. *Neuropsychologia, 50*(11), 2645–2651.

Cowan, N. (2001). The magical number 4 in short-term memory: A reconsideration of mental storage capacity. *Behavioral and Brain Sciences, 24*, 87–185.

Cowan, W. M. (1979). The development of the brain. *Scientific American, September*, 56–69.

Cowey, A. (2004). Fact, artefact and myth about blindsight. *Quarterly Journal of Experimental Psychology, 57A*, 577–609.

Craig, A. D. (2009). How do you feel—now? The anterior insula and human awareness. *Nature Reviews Neuroscience, 10*(1), 59–70.

Craik, F. I. M. & Lockhart, R. S. (1972). Levels of processing: A framework for memory research. *Journal of Verbal Learning and Verbal Behavior, 11*, 671–684.

Crair, M. C., Gillespie, D. C., & Stryker, M. P. (1998). The role of visual experience in the development of columns in cat visual cortex. *Science, 279*, 566–570.

Creswell, C. S. & Skuse, D. H. (1999). Autism in association with Turner syndrome: Genetic implications for male vulnerability to pervasive developmental disorders. *Neurocase, 5*, 511–518.

Crick, F. (1994). *The astonishing hypothesis: The scientific search for the soul*. New York: Charles Scribner's Sons.

Critchley, H. D., Mathias, C. J., Josephs, O., O'Doherty, J., Zanini, S., Dewar, B. K., Cipolotti, L., Shallice, T., & Dolan, R. J. (2003). Human cingulate cortex and autonomic control: Converging neuroimaging and clinical evidence. *Brain, 126*, 2139–2152.

Cubelli, R. (1991). A selective deficit for writing vowels in acquired dysgraphia. *Nature, 353*, 258–260.

Cubelli, R. & Lupi, G. (1999). Afferent dysgraphia and the role of vision in handwriting. *Visual Cognition, 6*, 113–128.

Culham, J. (2004). Human brain imaging reveals a parietal area specialized for grasping. In N. Kanwisher & J. Duncan (Eds.), *Functional neuroimaging of visual cognition*. Oxford, UK: Oxford University Press.

Curtiss, S. (1977). *Genie: A psycholinguistic study of a modern-day "wild child."* New York: Academic Press.

Cusack, R. (2005). The intraparietal sulcus and perceptual organization. *Journal of Cognitive Neuroscience, 17*, 641–651.

Cusack, R., Carlyon, R. P., & Robertson, I. H. (2000). Neglect between but not within auditory objects. *Journal of Cognitive Neuroscience, 12*, 1056–1065.

Custance, D. M., Whiten, A., & Bard, K. A. (1995). Can young chimpanzees (Pan troglodytes) imitate arbitrary actions? Hayes and Hayes (1952) revisited. *Behaviour, 132*, 837–859.

Cutler, A. & Butterfield, S. (1992). Rhythmic cues to speech segmentation: Evidence from juncture misperception. *Journal of Memory and Language, 25*, 385–400.

D'Ausilio, A., Bufalari, I., Salmas, P., & Fadiga, L. (2012). The role of the motor system in discriminating normal and degraded speech sounds. *Cortex, 48*(7), 882–887.

D'Esposito, M. (2007). From cognitive to neural models of working memory. *Philosophical Transactions of the Royal Society B-Biological Sciences, 362*(1481), 761–772.

Dagenbach, D. & McCloskey, M. (1992). The organization of arithmetic facts in memory: Evidence from a brain-damaged patient. *Brain and Cognition, 20*, 345–366.

Dale, A. M. & Buckner, R. L. (1997). Selective averaging of rapidly presented individual trials using fMRI. *Human Brain Mapping, 5*(5), 329–340.

Damasio, A. R. (1994). *Descartes' error: Emotion, reason and the human brain*. New York: G. P. Putnam & Sons.

Damasio, A. R. (1996). The somatic marker hypothesis and the possible functions of the prefrontal cortex. *Philosophical Transactions of the Royal Society of London B, 351*, 1413–1420.

Damasio, A. R., Graff-Radford, N. R., Eslinger, P. J., Damasio, H. & Kassell, N. (1985). Amnesia following basal forebrain lesions. *Archives of Neurology, 42*, 263–271.

Damasio, A. R., Tranel, D. & Damasio, H. (1990). Individuals with sociopathic behavior caused by frontal damage fail to respond autonomically to social stimuli. *Behavioral Brain Research, 41*, 81–94.

Damasio, H. & Damasio, A. (1989). *Lesion analysis in neuropsychology*. New York: Oxford University Press.

Damasio, H., Grabowski, T., Frank, R., Galaburda, A. M., & Damasio, A. R. (1994). The return of Phineas Gage: Clues about the brain from the skull of a famous patient. *Science, 264*, 1102–1105.

Damoiseaux, J. S., Rombouts, S. A. R. B., Barkhof, F., Scheltens, P., Stam, C. J., Smith, S. M., & Beckmann, C. F. (2006). Consistent resting-state networks across healthy subjects. *Proceedings of the National Academy of Sciences of the United States of America, 103*(37), 13848–13853.

Dapretto, M., Davies, M. S., Pfeifer, J. H., Scott, A. A., Sigman, M., Bookheimer, S. Y., & Iacoboni, M. (2006). Understanding emotions in others: Mirror neuron dysfunction in children with autism spectrum disorders. *Nature Neuroscience, 9*, 28–30.

Darwin, C. J. (1871). *The descent of man and selection in relation to sex*. London: John Murray.

Darwin, C. J. (1872/1965). *The expression of the emotions in man and animals.* Chicago, IL: University of Chicago Press.

Davachi, L., Mitchell, J. P., & Wagner, A. D. (2003). Multiple routes to memory: Distinct medial temporal lobe processes build item and source memories. *Proceedings of the National Academy of Sciences of the United States of America, 100*(4), 2157–2162.

Davies, R. R., Graham, K. S., Xuereb, J. H., Williams, G. B., & Hodges, J. R. (2004). The human perirhinal cortex and semantic memory. *European Journal of Neuroscience, 20*(9), 2441–2446.

Davis, M. H. (1980). A multi-dimensional approach to individual differences in empathy. *JCAS Catalog of Selected Documents in Psychology, 75,* 989–1015.

De Bastiani, P., Barry, C., & Carreras, M. (1988). Mechanisms for reading non-words: Evidence from a case of phonological dyslexia in an Italian reader. In C. Semenza & G. Denes (Eds.), *Perspectives on cognitive neuropsychology.* Hillsdale, NJ: Lawrence Erlbaum.

De Renzi, E. (1986). Prosopagnosia in two patients with CT scan evidence of damage confined to the right hemisphere. *Neuropsychologia, 24,* 385–389.

De Renzi, E. & di Pellegrino, G. (1998). Prosopagnosia and alexia without object agnosia. *Cortex, 34,* 403–415.

Dean, A. (1946). *Fundamentals of play directing.* New York: Rhinehart & Company.

Decety, J. & Jackson, P. J. (2004). The functional architecture of human empathy. *Behavioral and Cognitive Neuroscience Reviews, 3,* 71–100.

Decety, J. & Jackson, P. L. (2006). A social-neuroscience perspective on empathy. *Current Directions in Psychological Science, 15*(2), 54–58.

Dehaene, S. (1992). Varieties of numerical abilities. *Cognition, 44,* 1–42.

Dehaene, S. (1997). *The number sense.* New York: Oxford University Press.

Dehaene, S. (2010). *Reading in the brain: The new science of how we read.* London: Penguin Books.

Dehaene, S., Changeux, J.-P., Naccache, L., Sackur, J., & Sergent, C. (2006). Conscious, preconscious, and subliminal processing: A testable taxonomy. *Trends in Cognitive Sciences, 10*(204–211).

Dehaene, S. & Cohen, L. (1991). Two mental calculation systems: A case study of severe acalculia with preserved approximation. *Neuropsychologia, 29,* 1045–1074.

Dehaene, S. & Cohen, L. (1995). Towards an anatomical and functional model of number processing. *Mathematical Cognition, 1,* 83–120.

Dehaene, S. & Cohen, L. (1997). Cerebral pathways for calculation: Double dissociation between rote and quantitative knowledge of arithmetic. *Cortex, 33,* 219–250.

Dehaene, S. & Cohen, L. (2011). The unique role of the visual word form area in reading. *Trends in Cognitive Sciences, 15*(6), 254–262.

Dehaene, S., Bossini, S., & Giraux, P. (1993). The mental representation of parity and numerical magnitude. *Journal of Experimental Psychology: General, 122,* 371–396.

Dehaene, S., Dupoux, E., & Mehler, J. (1990). Is numerical comparison digital? Analogical and symbolic effects in two-digit number comparison. *Journal of Experimental Psychology: Human Perception and Performance, 16,* 626–641.

Dehaene, S., Posner, M. I., & Tucker, D. M. (1994). Localisation of a neural system for error detection and compensation. *Psychological Science, 5,* 303–305.

Dehaene, S., Dehaene-Lambertz, G., & Cohen, L. (1998a). Abstract representations of numbers in the animal and human brain. *Trends in Neurosciences, 21,* 355–361.

Dehaene, S., Cohen, L., Sigman, M., & Vinckier, F. (2005). The neural code for written words: A proposal. *Trends in Cognitive Sciences, 9*(7), 335–341.

Dehaene, S., Naccache, L., Le Clec'H, G., Koechlin, E., Mueller, M., Dehaene-Lambertz, G., Van de Moortele, P. F., & Le Bihan, D. (1998b). Imaging unconscious semantic priming. *Nature, 395,* 597–600.

Dehaene, S., Naccache, L., Cohen, L., Le Bihan, D., Mangin, J. F., Poline, J.-B., & Riviere, D. (2001). Cerebral mechanisms of word masking and unconscious repetition priming. *Nature Neuroscience, 4,* 752–758.

Dehaene, S., Le Clec'H, G., Poline, J.-B., Le Bihan, D., & Cohen, L. (2002). The visual word form area: A prelexical representation of visual words in the fusiform gyrus. *NeuroReport*, *13*, 321–325.

Dehaene, S., Piazza, M., Pinel, P., & Cohen, L. (2003). Three parietal circuits for number processing. *Cognitive Neuropsychology*, *20*, 487–506.

Dehaene, S., Izard, V., Spelke, E., & Pica, P. (2008). Log or linear? Distinct intuitions of the number scale in western and amazonian indigene cultures. *Science, 320*(5880), 1217–1220.

Dehaene, S., Pegado, F., Braga, L. W., Ventura, P., Nunes, G., Jobert, A., Dehaene-Lambertz, G., Kolinsky, R., Morais, J., & Cohen, L. (2010). How learning to read changes the cortical networks for vision and language. *Science, 330*(6009), 1359–1364.

Dejerine, J. (1892). Contribution a l'étude anatomoclinique et clinique des différentes variétés de cécité verbale. *Mémoires de la Société de Biologie, 4*, 61–90.

Del Grosso Destreri, N., Farina, E., Alberoni, M., Pomati, S., Nichelli, P., & Mariani, C. (2000). Selective uppercase dysgraphia with loss of visual imagery of letter forms: A window on the organization of graphomotor patterns. *Brain and Language, 71*, 353–372.

Delazer, M. & Benke, T. (1997). The arithmetic facts without meaning. *Cortex, 33*, 697–710.

Dell, G. S. (1986). A spreading activation theory of retrieval in sentence production. *Psychological Review, 93*, 283–321.

Dell, G. S. & O'Seaghdha, P. G. (1991). Mediated and convergent lexical priming in language production: A comment on Levelt *et al.* (1991). *Psychological Review, 98*, 604–614.

Dell, G. S. & Reich, P. A. (1981). Stages in sentence production: An analysis of speech error data. *Journal of Verbal Learning and Verbal Behavior, 20*, 611–629.

Dell, G. S., Burger, L. K., & Svec, W. R. (1997). Language production and serial order: A functional analysis and a model. *Psychological Review, 104*, 123–147.

Della Sala, S., Gray, C., Baddeley, A. D., Allamano, N., & Wilson, L. (1999). Pattern span: A tool for unwelding visuo-spatial memory. *Neuropsychologia, 37*(10), 1189–1199.

Della Sala, S., Marchetti, C., & Spinnler, H. (1991). Right-sided anarchic (alien) hand: A longitudinal study. *Neuropsychologia, 29*, 1113–1127.

DeLong, M. R. (1990). Primate models of movement disorders of basal ganglia origin. *Trends in Neurosciences, 13*, 281–285.

Denis, M., Beschin, N., Logie, R. H., & Della Sala, S. (2002). Visual perception and verbal descriptions as sources for generating mental representations: Evidence from representational neglect. *Cognitive Neuropsychology, 19*, 97–112.

Dennett, D. C. (1978). Beliefs about beliefs. *Behavioral and Brain Sciences, 1*, 568–570.

Desimone, R. & Duncan, J. (1995). Neural mechanisms of selective visual-attention. *Annual Review of Neuroscience, 18*, 193–222.

Desor, J. A., Maller, O., & Andrews, K. (1975). Ingestive responses of human newborns to salty, sour and bitter stimuli. *Journal of Comparative Physiological Psychology, 89*, 966–970.

Devlin, J. T., Gonnerman, L. M., Andersen, S. E., & Seidenberg, M. S. (1998). Category-specific semantic deficits in focal and widespread brain damage: A computational account. *Journal of Cognitive Neuroscience, 10*, 77–94.

DeWitt, I. & Rauschecker, J. P. (2012). Phoneme and word recognition in the auditory ventral stream. *Proceedings of the National Academy of Sciences of the United States of America, 109*(8), E505–E514.

Di Pietro, M., Laganaro, M., Leeman, B., & Schinder, A. (2004). Receptive amusia: Temporal auditory processing deficit in a professional musician following a left tempero-parietal lesion. *Neuropsychologia, 42*, 868–877.

Diamond, M. C., Scheibel, A. B., & Elson, L. M. (1986). *The human brain coloring book*. New York: HarperCollins.

Diamond, R. & Carey, S. (1986). Why faces are and are not special: An effect of expertise. *Journal of Experimental Psychology: General, 115*, 107–117.

Dias, R., Robbins, T. W., & Roberts, A. C. (1996). Dissociation in prefrontal cortex of affective and attentional shifts. *Nature, 380*(6569), 69–72.

Diester, I. & Nieder, A. (2007). Semantic associations between signs and numerical categories in the prefrontal cortex. *PLoS Biology, 5*(11), 2684–2695.

Dimberg, U., Thunberg, M., & Elmehed, K. (2000). Unconscious facial reactions to emotional facial expressions. *Psychological Science, 11*(1), 86–89.

Dinstein, I., Thomas, C., Behrmann, M., & Heeger, D. J. (2008). A mirror up to nature. *Current Biology, 18*(1), R13–R18.

Dodd, M. D., Van der Stigchel, S., Leghari, M. A., Fung, G., & Kingstone, A. (2008). Attentional SNARC: There's something special about numbers (let us count the ways). *Cognition, 108*(3), 810–818.

Dolan, R. J. (2007). The human amygdala and orbitofrontal cortex in behavioural regulation. *Philosophical Transactions of the Royal Society of London Series B, 362*, 787–799.

Donchin, E. (1981). Surprise! Surprise? *Psychophysiology, 18*, 493–513.

Doricchi, F., Guariglia, P., Gasparini, M., & Tomaiuolo, F. (2005). Dissociation between physical and mental number line bisection in right hemisphere brain damage. *Nature Neuroscience, 8*, 1663–1665.

Dormal, V., Dormal, G., Joassin, F., & Pesenti, M. (2012). A common right frontoparietal network for numerosity and duration processing: An fMRI study. *Human Brain Mapping, 33*(6), 1490–1501.

Dowling, W. J. & Harwood, D. L. (1986). *Music cognition*. Orlando, FL: Academic Press.

Downing, P. E., Jiang, Y. H., Shuman, M., & Kanwisher, N. (2001). A cortical area selective for visual processing of the human body. *Science, 293*, 2470–2473.

Downar, J., Crawley, A. P., Mikulis, D. J., & Davis, K. D. (2000). A multimodal cortical network for the detection of changes in the sensory environment. *Nature Neuroscience, 3*(3), 277–283.

Draganski, B., Gaser, C., Busch, V., Schurierer, G., Bogdahn, U., & May, A. (2004). Neuroplasticity: Changes in gray matter induced by training. *Nature, 427*, 311–312.

Driver, J. & Halligan, P. W. (1991). Can visual neglect operate in object centred co-ordinates? An affirmative case study. *Cognitive Neuropsychology, 8*, 475–496.

Driver, J. & Spence, C. J. (1994). Spatial synergies between auditory and visual attention. In C. Umiltà & M. Moscovitch (Eds.), *Attention and performance XV: Conscious and nonconscious information processing*, 311–331, Cambridge, MA: MIT Press.

Dronkers, N. F. (1996). A new brain region for coordinating speech articulation. *Nature, 384*, 159–161.

Dronkers, N. F., Wilkins, D. P., Van Valin, R. D., Redfern, B. B., & Jaeger, J. J. (2004). Lesion analysis of the brain areas involved in language comprehension. *Cognition, 92*, 145–177.

Druks, J. (2002). Verbs and nouns: A review of the literature. *Journal of Neurolinguistics, 15*, 289–315.

Druks, J. & Masterson, J. (2000). *An object and action naming battery*. Hove, UK: Psychology Press.

Duann, J. R., Ide, J. S., Luo, X., & Li, C. R. (2009). Functional connectivity delineates distinct roles of the inferior frontal cortex and presupplementary motor area in stop signal inhibition. *Journal of Neuroscience, 29*(32), 10171–10179.

Duarte, A., Henson, R. N. A., Knight, R. T., Emery, T., & Graham, K. S. (2010). Orbitofrontal cortex is necessary for temporal context memory. *Journal of Cognitive Neuroscience, 22*(8), 1819–1831.

Duarte, A., Ranganath, C., & Knight, R. T. (2005). Effects of unilateral prefrontal lesions on familiarity, recollection, and source memory. *Journal of Neuroscience, 25*(36), 8333–8337.

Dudai, Y. (2004). The neurobiology of consolidations, or, how stable is the engram? *Annual Review of Psychology, 55*, 51–86.

Duncan, J. (2010). The multiple-demand (MD) system of the primate brain: Mental programs for intelligent behaviour. *Trends in Cognitive Sciences, 14*(4), 172–179.

Duncan, J. & Humphreys, G. W. (1989). Visual search and visual similarity. *Psychological Review, 96*, 433–458.

Duncan, J. & Owen, A. M. (2000). Common regions of the human frontal lobe recruited by diverse cognitive demands. *Trends in Neurosciences, 23*, 475–483.

Duncan, J., Burgess, P. W., & Emslie, H. (1995). Fluid intelligence after frontal lobe damage. *Neuropsychologia, 33*, 261–268.

Duncan, J., Johnson, R., Swales, M., & Freer, C. (1997). Frontal lobe deficits after head injury: Unity and diversity of function. *Cognitive Neuropsychology, 14*, 713–741.

Dunn, J. C. & Kirsner, K. (2003). What can we infer from double dissociations? *Cortex, 39*, 1–7.

Dushanova, J. & Donoghue, J. (2010). Neurons in primary motor cortex engaged during action observation. *European Journal of Neuroscience, 31*, 386–398.

Dusoir, H., Kapur, N., Byrnes, D. P., McKinstry, S., & Hoare, R. D. (1990). The role of diencephalic pathology in human-memory disorder—evidence from a penetrating paranasal brain injury. *Brain, 113*, 1695–1706.

Dux, P. E. & Marois, R. (2009). The attentional blink: A review of data and theory. *Attention Perception & Psychophysics, 71*(8), 1683–1700.

Eaves, L. J., Silberg, J. L., Meyer, J. M., Maes, H. H., Simonoff, E., Pickles, A., Rutter, M., Neale, M. C., Reynolds, C. A., Erikson, M. T., Heath, A. C., Loeber, R., Truett, K. R., & Hewitt, J. K. (1997). Genetic and developmental psychopathology: 2. The main effects of genes and environment on behavioral problems in the Virginia twin study of adolescent development. *Journal of Child Psychology and Psychiatry, 38*, 965–980.

Edelman, D. B. & Seth, A. K. (2009). Animal consciousness: A synthetic approach. *Trends in Neurosciences, 32*(9), 476-484.

Eger, E., Schyns, P. G., & Kleinschmidt, A. (2004). Scale invariant adaptation in fusiform face-responsive regions. *NeuroImage, 22*, 232–242.

Egner, T., Monti, J. M. P., Trittschuh, E. H., Wieneke, C. A., Hirsch, J., & Mesulam, M. M. (2008). Neural integration of top-down spatial and feature-based information in visual search. *Journal of Neuroscience, 28*(24), 6141–6151.

Eichenbaum H., Yonelinas A. P., Ranganath C., 2007. The medial temporal lobe and recognition memory. *Annual Review of Neuroscience 30*,123–152.

Eimas, P. D. (1963). The relation between identification and discrimination along speech and nonspeech continua. *Language and Speech, 6*, 206–217.

Eisenberger, N. I., Lieberman, M. D., & Williams, K. D. (2003). Does rejection hurt? An fMRI study of social exclusion. *Science, 302*(5643), 290–292.

Eisner, F., McGettigan, C., Faulkner, A., Rosen, S., & Scott, S. K. (2010). Inferior frontal gyrus activation predicts individual differences in perceptual learning of cochlear-implant simulations. *Journal of Neuroscience, 30*(21), 7179–7186.

Ekman, P. (1992). An argument for basic emotions. *Conition and Emotion, 6*, 169–200.

Ekman, P. & Friesen, W. V. (1976). *Pictures of facial affect*. Palo Alto, CA: Consulting Psychologists Press.

Ekman, P., Friesen, W. V., & Ellsworth, P. (1972). *Emotion in the human face: Guidelines for research and an integration of findings*. New York: Pergamon.

Ekstrom, A. D., Kahana, M. J., Caplan, J. B., Fields, T. A., Isham, E. A., Newman, E. L., & Fried, I. (2003). Cellular networks underlying human spatial navigation. *Nature, 425*, 184–187.

Ekstrom, L. B., Roelfsema, P. R., Arsenault, J. T., Bonmassar, G., & Vanduffel, W. (2008). Bottom-up dependent gating of frontal signals in early visual cortex. *Science, 321*(5887), 414–417.

Ellis, A. W. (1979). Slips of the pen. *Visible Language, 13*, 265–282.

Ellis, A. W. (1980). On the Freudian theory of speech errors. In V. A. Fromkin (Ed.), *Errors in linguistic performance*. New York: Academic Press.

Ellis, A. W. (1982). Spelling and writing (and reading and speaking). In A. W. Ellis (Ed.), *Normality and pathology in cognitive functions*. London: Academic Press.

Ellis, A. W. (1993). *Reading, writing and dyslexia: A cognitive analysis*. Hillsdale, NJ: Lawrence Erlbaum.

Ellis, A. W. & Lambon Ralph, M. A. (2000). Age of acquisition effects in adult lexical processing reflect loss of plasticity in maturing systems: Insights from connectionist networks. *Journal of Experimental Psychology: Learning, Memory and Cognition, 26*, 1103–1123.

Ellis, A. W., Miller, D., & Sin, G. (1983). Wernicke's aphasia and normal language processing: A case study in cognitive neuropsychology. *Cognition, 15*, 111–144.

Ellis, A. W., Young, A. W., & Critchley, E. M. R. (1989). Loss of memory for people following temporal lobe damage. *Brain, 112*, 1469–1483.

Ellis, A. W., Young, A. W., & Flude, B. M. (1987). "Afferent dysgraphia" in a patient and in normal subjects. *Cognitive Neuropsychology, 4*, 465–486.

Ellis, H. D. & Lewis, M. B. (2001). Capgras delusion: A window on face recognition. *Trends in Cognitive Sciences, 5*, 149–156.

Ellis, H. D. & Young, A. W. (1990). Accounting for delusional misidentifications. *British Journal of Psychiatry, 157*, 239–248.

Ellis, H. D., Young, A. W., Quayle, A. H., & DePauw, K. W. (1997). Reduced autonomic responses to faces in Capgras delusion. *Proceedings of the Royal Society of London B, 264*, 1085–1092.

Ellis, R. & Humphreys, G. W. (1999). *Connectionist psychology: A text with readings*. Hove, UK: Psychology Press.

Elman, J., Bates, E., Johnson, M. H., Karmiloff-Smith, A., Parisi, D., & Plunkett, K. (1996). *Rethinking innateness: A connectionist perspective on development*. Cambridge, MA: MIT Press.

Enard, W., Przeworski, M., Fisher, S. E., Lai, C. S. L., Wiebe, V., Kitano, T., Monaco, A. P., & Paabo, S. (2002). Molecular evolution of FOXP2, a gene involved in speech and language. *Nature, 418*, 869–872.

Engel, A. K., Konig, P., & Singer, W. (1991). Direct physiological evidence for scene segmentation by temporal encoding. *Proceedings of the National Academy of Science, USA, 88*, 9136–9140.

Engel, A. K., Moll, C. K. E., Fried, I., & Ojemann, G. A. (2005). Invasive recordings from the human brain: Clinical insights and beyond. *Nature Reviews Neuroscience, 6*, 35–47.

Epstein, R. & Kanwisher, N. (1998). A cortical representation of the local visual environment. *Nature, 392*, 598–601.

Erikson, C. W., Pollack, M. D., & Montague, W. E. (1970). Implicit speech: Mechanisms in perceptual encoding? *Journal of Experimental Psychology, 84*, 502–507.

Eslinger, P. J. & Damasio, A. R. (1985). Severe disturbance of higher cognition after bilateral frontal ablation: Patient EVR. *Neurology, 35*, 1731–1741.

Evarts, E. V., Teravainen, H., & Calne, D. B. (1981). Reaction time in Parkinson's disease. *Brain, 104*, 167–186.

Everling, S., Tinsley, C. J., Gaffan, D., & Duncan, J. (2002). Filtering of neural signals by focused attention in the monkey prefrontal cortex. *Nature Neuroscience, 5*(7), 671–676.

Eysenck, M. W. (1974). Age differences in incidental learning. *Developmental Psychology, 10*, 936–941.

Fabiani, M., Stadler, M. A., & Wessels, P. M. (2000). True but not false memories produce a sensory signature in human lateralised brain potentials. *Journal of Cognitive Neuroscience, 12*, 941–949.

Falcaro, M., Pickles, A., Newbury, D. F., Addis, L., Banfield, E., Fisher, S. E., Monaco, A. P., Simkin, Z., & Conti-Ramsden, G. (2008). Genetic and phenotypic effects of phonological short-term memory and grammatical morphology in specific language impairment. *Genes, Brain and Behavior, 7*, 393–402.

Farah, M. J. (1990). *Visual agnosia.* Cambridge, MA: MIT Press.

Farah, M. J. (1994). Neuropsychological inference with an interactive brain: A critique of the "locality" assumption. *Behavioral and Brain Sciences, 17*, 43–104.

Farah, M. J. (1997). Distinguishing perceptual and semantic impairments affecting visual object recognition. *Visual Cognition, 4*, 199–206.

Farah, M. J. & McClelland, J. L. (1991). A computational model of semantic memory impairment: Modality specificity and emergent category specificity. *Journal of Experimental Psychology: General, 120*, 339–357.

Farah, M. J. & Wallace, M. (1991). Pure alexia as a visual impairment: A reconsideration. *Cognitive Neuropsychology, 8*, 313–334.

Farah, M. J., Levinson, K. L., & Klein, K. L. (1995a). Face perception and within-category discrimination in prosopagnosia. *Neuropsychologia, 33*, 661–674.

Farah, M. J., Wilson, K. D., Drain, H. M., & Tanaka, L. W. (1995b). The inverted inversion effect in prosopagnosia: Evidence for mandatory, face-specific perceptual mechanisms. *Vision Research, 35*, 2089–2093.

Farah, M. J., Stowe, R. M., & Levinson, K. L. (1996). Phonological dyslexia: Loss of a reading-specific component of the cognitive architecture? *Cognitive Neuropsychology, 13*, 849–868.

Farah, M. J., Wilson, K. D., Drain, H. M., & Tanaka, J. W. (1998). What is special about face perception? *Psychological Review, 105*, 482–498.

Farroni, T., Csibra, G., Simion, G., & Johnson, M. H. (2002). Eye contact detection in humans from birth. *Proceedings of the National Academy of Science, USA, 99*, 9602–9605.

Fay, D. & Cutler, A. (1977). Malapropisms and the structure of the mental lexicon. *Linguistic Inquiry, 8*, 505–520.

Fedorenko, E., Duncan, J., & Kanwisher, N. (2013). Broad domain generality in focal regions of frontal and parietal cortex. *Proceedings of the National Academy of Sciences of the United States of America, 110*(41), 16616–16621.

Feldman Barrett, L. (2006). Are emotions natural kinds? *Perspectives on Psychological Science, 1*, 28–58.

Fell, J., Klaver, P., Lehnertz, G., T., Schaller, C., Elger, C. E., & Fernandez, G. (2001). Human memory formation is accompanied by rhinal-hippocampal coupling and decoupling. *Nature Neuroscience, 4*, 1259–1264.

Fellows, L. K. & Farah, M. J. (2003). Ventromedial frontal cortex mediates affective shifting in humans: Evidence from a reversal learning paradigm. *Brain, 126*, 1830–1837.

Fera, P. & Besner, D. (1992). The process of lexical decision: More words about a parallel distributed processing model. *Journal of Experimental Psychology: Learning, Memory and Cognition, 18*, 749–764.

Ferro, J. M. & Botelho, M. A. S. (1980). Alexia for arithmetical signs: A case of disturbed calculation. *Cortex, 16*, 175–180.

Ferstl, E. C. & von Cramon, D. Y. (2002). What does the frontomedian cortex contribute to language processing: Coherence or theory of mind? *NeuroImage, 17*, 1599–1612.

Ffytche, D. H., Howard, R. J., Brammer, M. J., David, A., Woodruff, P., & Williams, S. (1998). The anatomy of conscious vision: An fMRI study of visual hallucinations. *Nature Neuroscience, 1*, 738–742.

Fias, W., Lammertyn, J., Reynvoet, B., Dupont, P., & Orban, G. A. (2003). Parietal representation of symbolic and nonsymbolic magnitude. *Journal of Cognitive Neuroscience, 15*, 47–56.

Fiebach, C. J., Friederici, A. D., Muller, K., & von Cramon, D. Y. (2002). fMRI evidence for dual routes to the mental lexicon in visual word recognition. *Journal of Cognitive Neuroscience, 14*, 11–23.

Fierro, B., Brighina, F., Oliveri, M., Piazza, A., La Bua, V., Buffa, D., & Bisiach, E. (2000). Contralateral neglect induced by right posterior parietal rTMS in healthy subjects. *NeuroReport, 11*, 1519–1521.

Fiez, J. A. & Petersen, S. E. (1998). Neuroimaging studies of word reading. *Proceedings of the National Academy of Science, USA, 95*, 914–921.

Fiez, J. A., Balota, D. A., Raichle, M. E., & Petersen, S. E. (1999). Effects of lexicality, frequency, and spelling-to-sound consistency on the functional anatomy of reading. *Neuron, 24*, 205–218.

Fiez, J. A., Tranel, D., Seager-frerichs, D., & Damasio, H. (2006). Specific reading and phonological processing deficits are associated with damage to the left frontal operculum. *Cortex, 42*, 624–643.

Fink, G. R., Marshall, J. C., Shah, N. J., Weiss, P. H., Halligan, P. W., Grosse-Ruyken, M., Ziemons, K., Zilles, K., & Freund, H. J. (2000). Line bisection judgments implicate right parietal cortex and cerebellum as assessed by fMRI. *Neurology, 54*, 1324–1331.

Fischer, M. H., Castel, A. D., Dodd, M. D., & Pratt, J. (2003). Perceiving numbers causes spatial shifts of attention. *Nature Neuroscience, 6*, 555–556.

Fletcher, P. C. & Henson, R. N. A. (2001). Frontal lobes and human memory: Insights from functional neuroimaging. *Brain, 124*, 849–881.

Fletcher, P. C., Happé, F., Frith, U., Baker, S. C., Dolan, R. J., Frackowiak, R. S. J., & Frith, C. D. (1995). Other minds in the brain: A functional imaging study of "theory of mind" in story comprehension. *Cognition, 57*, 109–128.

Fletcher, P. C., Shallice, T., Frith, C. D., Frackowiak, R. S. J., & Dolan, R. J. (1998). The functional roles of prefrontal cortex in episodic memory: II. Retrieval. *Brain, 121*, 1249–1256.

Flourens, M. J. P. (1824). *Recherches expérimentales sur les propriétés et les fonctions du systéme nerveux dans les animaux vertébrés*. Paris: J. B. Ballière.

Fodor, J. A. (1983). *The modularity of mind*. Cambridge, MA: MIT Press.

Fodor, J. A. (1992). A theory of the child's theory of mind. *Cognition, 44*, 283–296.

Fodor, J. A. (1998). *In critical condition: Polemical essays on cognitive science and the philosophy of mind*. Cambridge, MA: Bradford Books.

Formisano, E., Kim, D. S., Di Salle, F., van de Moortele, P. F., Ugurbil, K., & Goebel, R. (2003). Mirror-symmetric tonotopic maps in human primary auditory cortex. *Neuron, 40*, 859–869.

Forster, K. I. (1976). Accessing the mental lexicon. In R. J. Wales & C. T. Walker (Eds.), *New approaches to language mechanisms*. Amsterdam: North Holland.

Frankland, P. W. & Bontempi, B. (2005). The organization of recent and remote memories. *Nature Reviews Neuroscience, 6*, 119–130.

Frazier, L. & Rayner, K. (1982). Making and correcting errors in the analysis of structurally ambiguous sentences. *Cognitive Psychology, 14*, 178–210.

Freiwald, W. A., Tsao, D. Y., & Livingstone, M. S. (2009). A face feature space in the macaque temporal lobe. *Nature Neuroscience, 12*(9), 1187-U1128.

Freud, S. (1920/2010). *Beyond the Pleasure Principle*. New York: Bartelby.

Friederici, A. D. (2002). Towards a neural basis of auditory sentence processing. *Trends in Cognitive Sciences, 6*, 78–84.

Friederici, A. D. (2011). The brain basis of language processing: from structure to function. *Physiological Reviews, 91*(4), 1357–1392.

Friederici, A. D. (2012). The cortical language circuit: from auditory perception to sentence comprehension. *Trends in Cognitive Sciences, 16*(5), 262–268.

Friederici, A. D. & Meyer, M. (2004). The brain knows the difference: Two types of grammatical violations. *Brain Research, 1000*, 72–77.

Friederici, A. D., Opitz, B., & von Cramon, D. Y. (2000). Segregating semantic and syntactic aspects of processing in the human brain: An fMRI investigation of different word types. *Cerebral Cortex, 10*(7), 698–705.

Friederici, A. D., Bahlmann, J., Heim, S., Schubotz, R. I., & Anwander, A. (2006a). The brain differentiates human and non-human grammars: Functional localization and structural connectivity. *Proceedings of the National Academy of Sciences of the United States of America, 103*(7), 2458–2463.

Friederici, A. D., Fiebach, C. J., Schlesewsky, M., Bornkessel, I. D., & von Cramon, D. Y. (2006b). Processing linguistic complexity and grammaticality in the left frontal cortex. *Cerebral Cortex, 16*(12), 1709–1717.

Friedman-Hill, S., Robertson, L. C., & Treisman, A. (1995). Parietal contributions to visual feature binding: Evidence from a patient with bilateral lesions. *Science, 269*, 853–855.

Friston, K. J. (1997). Imaging cognitive anatomy. *Trends in Cognitive Sciences, 1*, 21–27.

Friston, K. J. (2002). Beyond phrenology: What can neuroimaging tell us about distributed circuitry? *Annual Review of Neuroscience, 25*, 221–250.

Friston, K. J. & Frith, C. D. (1995). Schizophrenia: A disconnection syndrome? *Clinical Neuroscience, 3*, 89–97.

Friston, K. J., Price, C. J., Fletcher, P., Moore, C., Frackowiak, R. S. J., & Dolan, R. J. (1996). The trouble with cognitive subtraction. *NeuroImage, 4*, 97–104.

Frith, C. D. (2000). The role of dorsolateral prefrontal cortex in the selection of action, as revealed by functional imaging. In S. Monsell & J. Driver (Eds.), *Attention and performance XVIII: Control of cognitive performance*, Cambridge, MA: MIT Press.

Frith, C. D., Friston, K., Liddle, P. F., & Frackowiak, R. S. J. (1991). Willed action and the prefrontal cortex in man: A study with PET. *Proceedings of the Royal Society of London, 244*, 241–246.

Frith, U. (1985). Beneath the surface of developmental dyslexia. In K. E. Patterson & J. Marshall (Eds.), *Surface dyslexia: Neuropsychological and cognitive studies of phonological reading*. Hillsdale, NJ: Lawrence Erlbaum.

Frith, U. (1989). *Autism: Explaining the enigma*. Oxford, UK: Blackwell.

Frith, U. & Frith, C. D. (2003). Development and neurophysiology of mentalizing. *Philosophical Transactions of the Royal Society of London B, 358*, 459–472.

Fritsch, G. T. & Hitzig, E. (1870). On the electrical excitability of the cerebrum. In: G. Von Bonin (1960) (trans.), *Some papers on the cerebral cortex*. Springfield, IL: Charles C. Thomas.

Fritz, T., Jentschke, S., Gosselin, N., Sammler, D., Peretz, I., Turner, R., Friederici, A. D., & Koelsch, S. (2009). Universal recognition of three basic emotions in music. *Current Biology, 19*(7), 573–576.

Fromkin, V. A. (1971). The non-anomalous nature of anomalous utterances. *Language, 51*, 696–719.

Fromkin, V., Krashen, S., Curtiss, S., Rigler, D., & Rigler, M. (1974). The development of language in Genie: A case of language acquisition beyond the "critical period." *Brain and Language, 1*, 81–107.

Fukuchi-Shimogori, T. & Grove, E. A. (2001). Neocortex patterning by the secreted signaling molecule FGF8. *Science, 294*, 1071–1074.

Funahashi, S., Bruce, C. J., & Goldman-Rakic, P. S. (1989). Mnemonic coding of visual space in the monkey's dorsolateral prefrontal cortex. *Journal of Neurophysiology, 61*, 1–19.

Funnell, E. (1983). Phonological processes in reading: New evidence from acquired dyslexia. *British Journal of Psychology, 74*, 159–180.

Funnell, E. & DeMornay Davies, P. (1996). JBR: A reassessment of concept familiarity and a category-specific disorder for living things. *Neurocase, 2*, 461–474.

Furst, A. J. & Hitch, G. J. (2000). Separate roles for executive and phonological components of working memory in mental arithmetic. *Memory and Cognition, 28*, 774–782.

Fushimi, T., Komori, K., Patterson, K. E., Ijuin, M., & Tanabe, H. (2003). Surface dyslexia in a Japanese patient with semantic dementia: Evidence for similarity-based orthography-to-phonology translation. *Neuropsychologia, 41*, 1644–1658.

Fuster, J. M. (1989). *The prefrontal cortex: Anatomy, physiology, and neuropsychology of the frontal lobe* (2nd edition). New York: Raven Press.

Gabrieli, J. D. E., Cohen, N. J., & Corkin, S. (1988). The impaired learning of semantic knowledge following bilateral medial temporal-lobe resection. *Brain, 7,* 157–177.

Gabrieli, J. D. E., Fleischman, D., Keane, M., Reminger, S., & Morell, F. (1995). Double dissociation between memory systems underlying explicit and implicit memory in the human brain. *Psychological Science, 6,* 76–82.

Gaffan, D. (1992). Amygdala and the memory of reward. In J. P. Aggleton (Ed.), *The amygdala: Neurobiological aspects of emotion, memory and mental dysfunction.* New York: Wiley-Liss.

Gaillard, W. D., Grandon, C. B., & Xu, B. (2001). Developmental aspects of pediatric fMRI: Considerations for image acquisition, analysis and interpretation. *NeuroImage, 13,* 239–249.

Gall, F. J. & Spurzheim, J. C. (1810). *Anatomie et physiologie du système nerveux.* Paris: Schoell.

Gallagher, H. L., Happé, F., Brunswick, N., Fletcher, P. C., Frith, U., & Frith, C. D. (2000). Reading the mind in cartoons and stories: An fMRI study of "theory of mind" in verbal and nonverbal tasks. *Neuropsychologia, 38,* 11–21.

Gallese, V. (2001). The "shared manifold" hypothesis: From mirror neurons to empathy. *Journal of Consciousness Studies, 8,* 33–50.

Gallese, V. (2003). The manifold nature of interpersonal relations: The quest for a common mechanism. *Philosophical Transactions of the Royal Society of London B, 358,* 517–528.

Gallese, V. & Goldman, A. (1998). Mirror neurons and the simulation theory of mind-reading. *Trends in Cognitive Sciences, 2,* 493–501.

Ganis, G., Kosslyn, S. M., Stose, S., Thompson, W. L., & Yurgelun-Todd, D. A. (2003). Neural correlates of different types of deception: An fMRI investigation. *Cerebral Cortex, 13,* 830–836.

Gardiner, J. M. (2000). On the objectivity of subjective experiences and autonoetic and noetic consciousness. In E. Tulving (Ed.), *Memory, consciousness and the brain: The Tallinn conference* (pp. 159–172). Philadelphia, PA: Psychology Press.

Gardner, M. (1990). *Mathematical carnival.* London: Penguin.

Gardner, R. A., Gardner, B. T., & van Cantford, T. E. (1989). *Teaching sign language to chimpanzees.* Albany, NY: SUNY Press.

Garrard, P., Maloney, L. M., Hodges, J. R., & Patterson, K. E. (2005). The effects of very early Alzheimer's disease on the characteristics of writing by a renowned author. *Brain, 128,* 250–260.

Garrett, M. F. (1992). Disorders of lexical selection. *Cognition, 42,* 143–180.

Garrido, L., Eisner, F., McGettigan, C., Stewart, L., Sauter, D., Hanley, R., Schweinberger, S. R., Warren, J., & Duchaine, B. (2009). Developmental phonagnosia: A selective deficit of vocal identity recognition. *Neuropsychologia, 47,* 123–131.

Gathercole, S. E. & Baddeley, A. D. (1990). The role of phonological memory in vocabulary acquisition: A study of young children learning arbitrary names of toys. *British Journal of Psychology, 81,* 439–454.

Gaur, A. (1987). *A history of writing.* London: British Library.

Gauthier, I. & Logothetis, N. K. (2000). Is face recognition not so unique after all? *Cognitive Neuropsychology, 17,* 125–142.

Gauthier, I. & Tarr, M. J. (1997). Becoming a "Greeble" expert: Exploring mechanisms for face recognition. *Vision Research, 37,* 1673–1682.

Gauthier, I., Tarr, M. J., Anderson, A. W., Skudlarski, P., & Gore, J. C. (1999). Activation of middle fusiform "face area" increases with expertise in recognizing novel objects. *Nature Neuroscience, 2,* 568–573.

Gauthier, I., Skudlarski, P., Gore, J. C., & Anderson, A. W. (2000). Expertise for cars and birds recruits brain areas involved in face recognition. *Nature Neuroscience, 3,* 191–197.

Gazzaley, A., Rissman, J., & D'Esposito, M. (2004). Functional connectivity during working memory maintenance. *Cognitive Affective & Behavioral Neuroscience, 4*(4), 580–599.

Gazzaniga, M. S. (2000). Cerebral specialization and interhemispheric communication: Does the corpus callosum enable the human condition? *Brain, 123,* 1293–1326.

Gazzaniga, M. S., Mangun, G., & Ivry, R. (2002). Cognitive Neuroscience: The new biology of the mind. New York: W. W. Norton.

Gehring, W. J., Goss, B., Coles, M. G. H., Meyer, D. E., & Donchin, E. (1993). A neural system for error detection and compensation. *Psychological Science, 4,* 385–390.

Gelman, R. & Butterworth, B. (2005). Number and language: how are they related? *Trends in Cognitive Sciences, 9*(1), 6–10.

Gelman, R. & Gallistel, C. R. (1978). *The child's understanding of number.* Cambridge, MA: Harvard University Press.

Gemba, H., Sasaki, H., & Brooks, V. B. (1986). "Error" potentials in limbic cortex (anterior cingulate area 24) of monkeys during motor learning. *Neuroscience Letters, 70,* 223–227.

George, M. S., Wassermann, E. M., Williams, W. A., Callahan, A., Ketter, T. A., Basse, P., Hallett, M., & Post, R. M. (1995). Daily repetitive transcranial magnetic stimulation improves mood in depression. *NeuroReport, 6,* 1853–1856.

Georgopoulos, A. P. (1997). Voluntary movement: Computational principles and neural mechanisms. In M. D. Rugg (Ed.), *Cognitive neuroscience.* Hove, UK: Psychology Press.

Georgopoulos, A. P., Caminiti, R., Kalaska, J. F., & Massey, J. T. (1983). Spatial coding of movement: A hypothesis concerning the coding of movement direction by motor cortical populations. *Experimental Brain Research, Supplement, 7,* 327–336.

Georgopoulos, A. P., Kalaska, J. F., & Caminiti, R. (1985). Relations between two-dimensional arm movements and single cell discharge in motor cortex and area 5: Movement direction versus movement endpoint. *Experimental Brain Research Supplement, 10,* 176–183.

Georgopoulos, A. P., Schwartz, A. B., & Kettner, R. E. (1986). Neuronal population coding of movement direction. *Science, 233,* 1416–1419.

Gergely, G., Bekkering, H., & Kiraly, I. (2002). Rational imitation in preverbal infants. *Nature, 415,* 755–755.

Gerloff, C., Corwell, B., Chen, R., Hallett, M., & Cohen, L. G. (1997). Stimulation over the human supplementary motor area interferes with the organization of future elements in complex motor sequences. *Brain, 120,* 1587–1602.

Gerstmann, J. (1940). Syndrome of finger agnosia, disorientation for right and left, agraphia and acalculia. *Archives of Neurology and Psychiatry, 44,* 398–408.

Gevers, W., Reynvoet, B., & Fias, W. (2003). The mental representation of ordinal sequences is spatially organized. *Cognition, 87,* B87–B95.

Gevers, W., Santens, S., Dhooge, E., Chen, Q., Van den Bossche, L., Fias, W., & Verguts, T. (2010). Verbal-spatial and visuospatial coding of number-space interactions. *Journal of Experimental Psychology-General, 139*(1), 180–190.

Gibson, J. J. (1979). *The ecological approach to visual perception.* London: Houghton Mifflin.

Giedd, J. N., Blumenthal, J., Jeffries, N. O., Castellanos, F. X., Liu, H., Zijdenbos, A., Paus, T., Evans, A. C., & Rapoport, J. L. (1999). Brain development during childhood and adolescence: A longitudinal MRI study. *Nature Neuroscience, 2,* 861–863.

Giersch, A., Humphreys, G. W., Boucart, M., & Kovacs, I. (2000). The computation of occluded contours in visual agnosia: Evidence for early computation prior to shape binding and figure-ground coding. *Cognitive Neuropsychology, 17,* 731–759.

Gilboa, A. & Moscovitch, M. (2002). The cognitive neuroscience of confabulation: A review and a model. In A. D. Baddeley, M. D. Kopelman & B. A. Wilson (Eds.), *Handbook of memory disorders.* London: Wiley.

Gilboa, A., Winocur, G., Grady, C. L., Hevenor, S. J., & Moscovitch, M. (2004). Remembering our past: Functional neuroanatomy of recollection of recent and very remote personal events. *Cerebral Cortex, 14*, 1214–1225.

Girelli, L., Lucangeli, D., & Butterworth, B. (2000). The development of automaticity in accessing number magnitude. *Journal of Experimental Child Psychology, 76*, 104–122.

Glascher, J., Adolphs, R., Damasio, H., Bechara, A., Rudrauf, D., Calamia, M., Paul, L. K., & Tranel, D. (2012). Lesion mapping of cognitive control and value-based decision making in the prefrontal cortex. *Proceedings of the National Academy of Sciences of the United States of America, 109*(36), 14681–14686.

Godden, D. & Baddeley, A. D. (1975). Context-dependent memory in two natural environments: On land and under water. *British Journal of Psychology, 66*, 325–331.

Goldberg, E. (2001). *The executive brain: Frontal lobes and the civilized mind.* Oxford, UK: Oxford University Press.

Goldberg, G. (1985). Supplementary motor area structure and function: Review and hypotheses. *Behavioral and Brain Sciences, 8*, 567–616.

Goldenberg, G. & Hagmann, S. (1998). Tool use and mechanical problem solving in apraxia. *Neuropsychologia, 36*, 581–589.

Goldman-Rakic, P. S. (1992). Working memory and mind. *Scientific American, 267*, 73–79.

Goldman-Rakic., P. S. (1996). The prefrontal landscape: Implications of functional architecture for understanding human mentation and the central executive. *Philosophical Transactions of the Royal Society of London B, 351*, 1445–1453.

Goldstein, E. B. (2012) *Sensation and perception.* Boston, MA: Cengage Learning.

Gonzalez Rothi, L. J., Ochipa, C., & Heilman, K. M. (1991). A cognitive neuropsychological model of limb apraxia. *Cognitive Neuropsychology, 8*, 443–458.

Goodale, M. A. & Milner, A. D. (1992). Separate visual pathways for perception and action. *Trends in Neurosciences, 15*, 20–25.

Goodale, M. A., Meenan, J. P., Bulthoff, H. H., Nicolle, D. A., Murphy, K. J., & Racicot, C. I. (1994). Separate neural pathways for the visual analysis of object shape in perception and prehension. *Current Biology, 4*, 604–610.

Goodglass, H. & Kaplan, E. (1972). *The assessment of aphasia and related disorders.* Philadelphia, PA: Lea and Febiger.

Goodglass, H. & Kaplan, E. (1983). *The Boston diagnostic aphasia examination.* Philadelphia, PA: Lea and Febiger.

Goodman, R. A. & Caramazza, A. (1986a). Aspects of the spelling process: Evidence from a case of acquired dysgraphia. *Language and Cognitive Processes, 1*, 263–296.

Goodman, R. A. & Caramazza, A. (1986b). Dissociation of spelling errors in written and oral spelling: The role of allographic conversion in writing. *Cognitive Neuropsychology, 3*, 179–206.

Goodwin, D. W., Powell, B., Bremer, D., Hoine, H., & Stern, J. (1969). Alcohol and recall: State dependent effects in man. *Science, 163*, 1358.

Gopnik, M. (1990). Genetic basis of grammar defect. *Nature, 347*, 25.

Gopnik, M. & Crago, M. (1991). Familial aggregation of developmental language disorder. *Cognition, 39*, 1–50.

Gosselin, N., Peretz, I., Johnsen, E., & Adolphs, R. (2007). Amygdala damage impairs emotion recognition from music. *Neuropsychologia, 45*, 236–244.

Gottesman, I. I. (1991). *Schizophrenia genes: The origins of madness.* New York: Freeman.

Gottlieb, G. (1992). *Individual development and evolution.* New York: Oxford University Press.

Gottlieb, J. P., Kusunoki, M., & Goldberg, M. E. (1998). The representation of visual salience in monkey parietal cortex. *Nature, 391*, 481–484.

Gough, P. M., Nobre, A. C., & Devlin, J. T. (2005). Dissociating linguistic processes in the left inferior frontal cortex with transcranial magnetic stimulation. *Journal of Neuroscience, 25*(35), 8010–8016.

Gouvea, A. C., Phillips, C., Kazanina, N., & Poeppel, D. (2010). The linguistic processes underlying the P600. *Language and Cognitive Processes*, *25*(2), 149–188.

Graf, P., Squire, L. R., & Mandler, G. (1984). The information that amnesic patients do not forget. *Journal of Experimental Psychology: Learning, Memory and Cognition*, *10*, 164–178.

Grafman, J., Passafiume, D., Faglioni, P., & Boller, F. (1982). Calculation disturbances in adults with focal hemispheric damage. *Cortex*, *18*, 37–50.

Graham, K. S., Hodges, J. R., & Patterson, K. E. (1994). The relationship between comprehension and oral reading in progressive fluent aphasia. *Neuropsychologia*, *32*, 299–316.

Graham, N. L., Patterson, K. E., & Hodges, J. R. (2000). The impact of semantic memory impairment on spelling: Evidence from semantic dementia. *Neuropsychologia*, *38*, 143–163.

Grahn, J. A. & Rowe, J. B. (2013). Finding and feeling the musical beat: Striatal dissociations between detection and prediction of regularity. *Cerebral Cortex*, *23*(4), 913–921.

Graziano, M. S. A. (1999). Where is my arm? The relative role of vision and proprioception in the neuronal representation of limb position. *Proceedings of the National Academy of Sciences of the United States of America*, *96*, 10418–10421.

Graziano, M. S., Cooke, D. F., & Taylor, C. S. R. (2000). Coding the location of the arm by sight. *Science*, *290*, 1782–1786.

Griffiths, T. D. & Warren, J. D. (2002). The planum temporale as a computational hub. *Trends in Cognitive Sciences*, *25*, 348–353.

Gross, C. G. (1992). Representation of visual stimuli in inferior temporal cortex. *Philosophical Transactions of the Royal Society of London B*, *335*, 3–10.

Gross, C. G. (2000). Neurogenesis in the adult brain: death of a dogma. *Nature Reviews Neuroscience*, *1*, 67–73.

Gross, C. G., Rocha-Miranda, C. E., & Bender, D. B. (1972). Visual properties of neurons in the inferotemporal cortex of the macaque. *Journal of Neurophysiology*, *35*, 96–111.

Grossman, E., Donnelly, M., Price, R., Pickens, D., Morgan, V., Neighbor, G., & Blake, R. (2000). Brain areas involved in perception of biological motion. *Journal of Cognitive Neuroscience*, *12*(5), 711–720.

Guariglia, C. & Antonucci, G. (1992). Personal and extrapersonal space: A case of neglect dissociation. *Neuropsychologia*, *30*, 1001–1009.

Guth, W., Schmittberger, R., & Schwarze, B. (1982). An experimental analysis of ultimatum bargaining. *Journal of Economics, Behavior, & Organizations*, *3*, 367–388.

Habib, R., Nyberg, L., & Tulving, E. (2003). Hemispheric asymmetries of memory: The HERA model revisited. *Trends in Cognitive Sciences*, *7*, 241–245.

Hadjikhani, N., Joseph, R. M., Snyder, J., & Tager-Flusberg, H. (2006). Anatomical differences in the mirror neuron system and social cognition network in autism. *Cerebral Cortex*, *16*(9), 1276–1282.

Hadland, K. A., Rushworth, M. F. S., Passingham, R. E., Jahanshahi, M., & Rothwell, J. (2001). Interference with performance of a response selection task has no working memory component: An rTMS comparison of the dorsolateral prefrontal and medial frontal cortex. *Journal of Cognitive Neuroscience*, *13*, 1097–1108.

Haesler, S., Wada, K., Nshdejan, A., Morrisey, E. E., Lints, T., Jarvis, E. D., & Scharff, C. (2004). FoxP2 expression in avian vocal learners and non-learners. *Journal of Neuroscience*, *24*, 3164–3175.

Hafting, T., Fyhn, M., Molden, S., Moser, M. B., & Moser, E. I. (2005). Microstructure of a spatial map in the entorhinal cortex. *Nature*, *436*(7052), 801–806.

Haggard, P. (2001). The psychology of action. *British Journal of Psychology*, *92*, 113–128.

Haggard, P. (2008). Human volition: Towards a neuroscience of will. *Nature Reviews Neuroscience*, *9*, 934–946.

Haggard, P. & Eimer, M. (1999). On the relation between brain potentials and conscious awareness. *Experimental Brain Research*, *126*, 128–133.

Haggard, P., Miall, R. C., Wade, D., Fowler, S., Richardson, A., Anslow, P., & Stein, J. (1995). Damage to cerebellocortical pathways after closed head injury: A behavioural and magnetic resonance imaging study. *Journal of Neurology, Neurosurgery and Psychiatry*, *58*, 433–438.

Hagoort, P. (2008). The fractionation of spoken language understanding by measuring electrical and magnetic brain signals. *Philosophical Transactions of the Royal Society B-Biological Sciences*, *363*(1493), 1055–1069.

Hagoort, P. & Brown, C. (1994). Brain responses to lexical ambiguity resolution and parsing *Perspectives on Sentence Processing* (pp. 45–80).

Hagoort, P., Hald, L., Bastiaansen, M., & Petersson, K. M. (2004). Integration of word meaning and world knowledge in language comprehension. *Science*, *304*, 438–441.

Hahne, A. & Friederici, A. D. (1999). Electrophysiological evidence for two steps in syntactic analysis: Early automatic and late controlled processes. *Journal of Cognitive Neuroscience*, *11*(2), 194–205.

Haidt, J. (2003). The moral emotions. In R. J. Davidson, K. R. Scherer, & H. H. Goldsmith (Eds.), *Handbook of Affective Sciences*. Oxford, UK: Oxford University Press.

Haist, F., Bowden Gore, J., & Mao, H. (2001). Consolidation of human memory over decades revealed by functional magnetic resonance imaging. *Nature Neuroscience*, *4*, 1139–1145.

Halberda, J., Mazzocco, M. M. M., & Feigenson, L. (2008). Individual differences in non-verbal number acuity correlate with maths achievement. *Nature*, *455*(7213), 665–U662.

Halit, H., de Haan, M., & Johnson, M. H. (2003). Cortical specialization for face processing: Face-sensitive event-related potential components in 3- and 12-month old infants. *NeuroImage*, *19*, 1180–1193.

Hall, D. A. & Riddoch, M. J. (1997). Word meaning deafness: Spelling words that are not understood. *Cognitive Neuropsychology*, *14*, 1131–1164.

Hall, D. A., Haggard, M. P., Akeroyd, M. A., Palmer, A. R., Summerfield, A. Q., Elliott, M. R., Gurney, E. M. & Bowtell, R. W. (1999). "Sparse" temporal sampling in auditory fMRI. *Human Brain Mapping*, *7*, 213–223.

Halligan, P. W. & Marshall, J. C. (1991). Left neglect for near but not far space. *Nature*, *350*, 498–500.

Halligan, P. W. & Marshall, J. C. (1992). Left unilateral neglect: A meaningless entity. *Cortex*, *28*, 525–535.

Halsband, U., Matsuzaka, Y., & Tanji, J. (1994). Neuronal activity in the primate supplementary, pre-supplementary and premotor cortex during externally and internally instructed movement sequences. *Neuroscience Research*, *20*, 149–155.

Hamilton, R., Keenan, J. P., Catala, M., & Pascual-Leone, A. (2000). Alexia for Braille following bilateral occipital stroke in an early blind woman. *NeuroReport*, *11*, 237–240.

Hampshire, A., Thompson, R., Duncan, J., & Owen, A. M. (2011). Lateral prefrontal cortex subregions make dissociable contributions during fluid reasoning. *Cerebral Cortex*, *21*(1), 1–10.

Hanley, J. R. & McDonnell, V. (1997). Are reading and spelling phonologically mediated? Evidence from a patient with a speech production impairment. *Cognitive Neuro-psychology*, *14*, 3–33.

Hanley, J. R., Young, A. W., & Pearson, N. A. (1991). Impairment of visuo-spatial sketch-pad. *Quarterly Journal of Experimental Psychology*, *43A*, 101–125.

Hanley, J. R., Smith, S. T., & Hadfield, J. (1998). I recognise you but I can't place you: An investigation of familiar-only experiences during tests of voice and face recognition. *Quarterly Journal of Experimental Psychology*, *51*, 179–195.

Hannula, D. E. & Ranganath, C. (2009). The eyes have it: Hippocampal activity predicts expression of memory in eye movements. *Neuron, 63*(5), 592–599.

Happé, F. G. E. (1995). Understanding minds and metaphors: Insights from the study of figurative language in autism. *Metaphor and Symbolic Activity, 10,* 275–295.

Happé, F. G. E. (1999). Autism: Cognitive deficit or cognitive style? *Trends in Cognitive Sciences, 3,* 216–222.

Hare, T. A., O'Doherty, J., Camerer, C. F., Schultz, W., & Rangel, A. (2008). Dissociating the role of the orbitofrontal cortex and the striatum in the computation of goal values and prediction errors. *Journal of Neuroscience, 28*(22), 5623–5630.

Harley, T. A. (2004). Does cognitive neuropsychology have a future? *Cognitive Neuropsychology, 21,* 3–16.

Harlow, H. F. (1958). The nature of love. *American Psychologist, 13,* 673–685.

Harlow, J. M. (1993). Recovery from the passage of an iron bar through the head. *History of Psychiatry, 4,* 271–281 (original work published in 1848 in *Publications of the Massachusetts Medical Society*).

Harris, A. & Aguirre, G. K. (2008). The representation of parts and wholes in face-selective cortex. *Journal of Cognitive Neuroscience, 20*(5), 863–878.

Harris, I. M., Harris, J. A., & Caine, D. (2001). Object orientation agnosia: A failure to find the axis? *Journal of Cognitive Neuroscience, 13,* 800–812.

Harrison, B. J., Soriano-Mas, C., Pujol, J., Ortiz, H., Lopez-Sola, M., Hernandez-Ribas, R., Deus, J., Alonso, P., Yucel, M., Pantelis, C., Menchon, J. M., & Cardoner, N. (2009). Altered corticostriatal functional connectivity in obsessive-compulsive disorder. *Archives of General Psychiatry, 66*(11), 1189–1200.

Hart, J., Berndt, R. S., & Caramazza, A. (1985). Category-specific naming deficit following cerebral infarction. *Nature, 316,* 439–440.

Hartley, T., Maguire, E. A., Spiers, H. J., & Burgess, N. (2003). The well-worn route and the path less travelled: Distinct neural bases of route following and wayfinding in humans. *Neuron, 37,* 877–888.

Hartley, T., Bird, C. M., Chan, D., Cipolotti, L., Husain, M., Vargha-Khadem, F., & Burgess, N. (2007). The hippocampus is required for short-term topographical memory in humans. *Hippocampus, 17,* 34–48.

Harvey, R. J., McCabe, B. J., Solomonia, R. O., Horn, G., & Darlison, M. G. (1998). Expression of the GABA(A) receptor gamma 4-subunit gene: Anatomical distribution of the corresponding mRNA in the domestic chick forebrain and the effect of imprinting training. *European Journal of Neuroscience, 10,* 3024–3028.

Hassabis, D., Kumaran, D., Vann, S. D., & Maguire, E. A. (2007). Patients with hippocampal amnesia cannot imagine new experiences. *Proceedings of the National Academy of Sciences of the United States of America, 104*(5), 1726–1731.

Hasselmo, M. E., Rolls, E. T., & Bayliss, G. C. (1989). The role of expression and identity in the face-selective responses of neurons in the temporal visual cortex of the monkey. *Experimental Brain Research, 75,* 417–429.

Hatfield, T., Han, J. S., Conley, M., Gallagher, M., & Holland, P. (1996). Neurotoxic lesions of basolateral, but not central, amygdala interfere with pavlovian second-order conditioning and reinforcer devaluation effects. *Journal of Neuroscience, 16*(16), 5256–5265.

Hauk, O., Johnsrude, I., & Pulvermuller, F. (2004). Somatotopic representation of action words in human motor and premotor cortex. *Neuron, 41,* 301–307.

Hauk, O., Patterson, K. E., Woollams, A., Watling, L., Pulvermuller, F., & Rogers, T. T. (2006). Q: When would you prefer a SOSSAGE to a SAUSAGE? A: At about 100 ms. ERP correlates of orthographic typicality and lexicality in written word recognition. *Journal of Cognitive Neuroscience, 18*(5), 818–832.

Hauser, M. D., MacNeilage, P., & Ware, M. (1996). Numerical representations in primates. *Proceedings of the National Academy of Science, USA, 93,* 1514–1517.

Hauser, M. D., Chomsky, N., & Fitch, W. T. (2002). The faculty of language: What is it, who has it, and how did it evolve? *Science, 298,* 1569–1579.

Hawke, J. L., Wadsworth, S. J., & DeFries, J. C. (2006). Genetic influences on reading difficulties in boys and girls: The Colorado twin study. *Dyslexia, 12,* 21–29.

Haxby, J. V., Hoffman, E. A., & Gobbini, M. I. (2000). The distributed human neural system for face perception. *Trends in Cognitive Sciences, 4*(6), 223–233.

Haxby, J. V., Gobbini, M. I., Furey, M. L., Ishai, A., Schouten, J. L., & Pietrini, P. (2001). Distributed and overlapping representations of faces and objects in ventral temporal cortex. *Science, 293,* 2425–2430.

Haynes, J. D. & Rees, G. (2006). Decoding mental states from brain activity in humans. *Nature Reviews Neuroscience, 7,* 523–534.

Haynes, J. D., Sakai, K., Rees, G., Gilbert, S., Frith, C., & Passingham, R. E. (2007). Reading hidden intentions in the human brain. *Current Biology, 17*(4), 323–328.

Heberlein, A. S. & Adolphs, R. (2007). Neurobiology of emotion recognition: Current evidence for shared substrates. In E. Harmon-Jones & P. Winkielman (Eds.), *Social Neuroscience.* New York: Guilford Press.

Heberlein, A. S., Padon, A. A., Gillihan, S. J., Farah, M. J., & Fellows, L. K. (2008). Ventromedial frontal lobe plays a critical role in facial emotion recognition. *Journal of Cognitive Neuroscience, 20*(4), 721–733.

Heim, S., Alter, K., Ischebeck, A. K., Amunts, K., Eickhoff, S. B., Mohlberg, H., Zilles, K., von Cramon, D. Y., & Friederici, A. D. (2005). The role of the left Brodmann's areas 44 and 45 in reading words and pseudowords. *Cognitive Brain Research, 25*(3), 982–993.

Heimer, L. & Robards, M. J. (1981). *Neuroanatomical tract tracing methods.* New York: Plenum Press.

Hemani, G., Yang, J., Vinkhuyzen, A., Powell, J. E., Willemsen, G., Hottenga, J. J., & Visscher, P. M. (2013). Inference of the genetic architecture underlying BMI and height with the use of 20,240 sibling pairs. *American Journal of Human Genetics, 93*(5), 865–875.

Henderson, L. (1985). On the use of the term "grapheme." *Language and Cognitive Processes, 1,* 135–148.

Hendry, S. H. C. & Reid, R. C. (2000). The koniocellular pathway in primate vision. *Annual Review of Neuroscience, 23,* 127–153.

Henik, A. & Tzelgov, J. (1982). Is 3 greater than 5: The relation between physical and semantic size in comparison tasks. *Memory & Cognition, 10,* 389–395.

Henik, A., Leibovich, T., Naparstek, S., Diesendruck, L., & Rubinsten, O. (2012). Quantities, amounts, and the numerical core system. *Frontiers in Human Neuroscience, 5.*

Henson, R. N. A. (2005). What can functional neuroimaging tell the experimental psychologist? *Quarterly Journal of Experimental Psychology, 58A,* 193–233.

Henson, R. N. A., Rugg, M. D., Shallice, T., Josephs, O., & Dolan, R. J. (1999a). Recollection and familiarity in recognition memory: An event-related functional magnetic resonance imaging study. *Journal of Neuroscience, 19,* 3962–3972.

Henson, R. N. A., Shallice, T., & Rugg, M. D. (1999b). Right prefrontal cortex and episodic memory retrieval: A functional MRI test of the monitoring hypothesis. *Brain, 122,* 1367–1381.

Henson, R. N. A., Rugg, M. D., Shallice, T., & Dolan, R. J. (2000). Confidence in recognition memory for words: Dissociating right prefrontal roles in episodic retrieval. *Journal of Cognitive Neuroscience, 12,* 913–923.

Hermelin, B. & O'Connor, N. (1986). Idiot savant calendrical calculators: Rules and regularites. *Psychological Medicine, 16,* 1–9.

Herrnstein, R., Lovelend, D., & Cable, C. (1977). Natural concepts in pigeons. *Journal of Experimental Psychology: Animal Learning and Memory, 2,* 285–302.

Herzmann, G., Schweinberger, S. R., Sommer, W., & Jentzsch, I. (2004). What's special about personally familiar faces? A multimodal approach. *Psychophysiology, 41,* 688–701.

Hesselmann, G., Sadaghiani, S., Friston, K. J., & Kleinschmidt, A. (2010). Predictive coding or evidence accumulation? False inference and neuronal fluctuations. *PLoS One*, *5*(3), 5.

Heyes, C. (2010). Where do mirror neurons come from? *Neuroscience and Biobehavioral Reviews*, *34*(4), 575–583.

Heywood, C. A., Cowey, A., & Newcombe, F. (1991). Chromatic discrimination in a cortically color-blind observer. *European Journal of Neuroscience*, *3*, 802–812.

Heywood, C. A., Kentridge, R. W., & Cowey, A. (1998). Cortical color blindness is not "blindsight for color." *Consciousness and Cognition*, *7*, 410–423.

Hickok, G. (2012). Computational neuroanatomy of speech production. *Nature Reviews Neuroscience*, *13*(2), 135–145.

Hickok, G. & Poeppel, D. (2004). Dorsal and ventral streams: A framework for understanding aspects of the functional anatomy of language. *Cognition*, *92*, 67–99.

Hickok, G., Costanzo, M., Capasso, R., & Miceli, G. (2011). The role of Broca's area in speech perception: Evidence from aphasia revisited. *Brain and Language*, *119*(3), 214–220.

Hill, E. L. & Frith, U. (2003). Understanding autism: Insights from mind and brain. *Philosophical Transactions of the Royal Society of London B*, *358*, 281–289.

Hill, K. T. & Miller, L. M. (2010). Auditory attentional control and selection during cocktail party listening. *Cerebral Cortex*, *20*(3), 583–590.

Hillis, A. E. & Caramazza, A. (1991). Mechanisms for accessing lexical representations for output: Evidence from a category-specific semantic deficit. *Brain and Language*, *40*, 106–144.

Hillis, A. E., Work, M., Barker, P. B., Jacobs, M. A., Breese, E. L., & Maurer, K. (2004). Re-examining the brain regions crucial for orchestrating speech articulation. *Brain*, *127*, 1479–1487.

Hillis, A. E., Newhart, M., Heidler, J., Barker, P. B., & Degaonkar M. (2005). Anatomy of spatial attention: Insights from perfusion imaging and hemispatial neglect in acute stroke. *Journal of Neuroscience*, *25*, 3161–3167.

Hirst, W., Phelps, E. A., Johnson, M. K., & Volpe, B. T. (1988). Amnesia and second language learning. *Brain and Cognition*, *8*, 105–116.

Hochberg, L. R., Bacher, D., Jarosiewicz, B., Masse, N. Y., Simeral, J. D., Vogel, J., Haddadin, S., Liu, J., Cash, S. S., & Donoghue, J. P. (2012). Reach and grasp by people with tetraplegia using a neurally controlled robotic arm. *Nature*, *485*(7398), 372-U121. doi: 10.1038/nature11076.

Hodges, J. R. & Graham, K. S. (1998). A reversal of the temporal gradient for famous person knowledge in semantic dementia: Implications for the neural organization of long-term memory. *Neuropsychologia*, *36*, 803–825.

Hodges, J. R., Patterson, K. E., Oxbury, S., & Funnell, E. (1992). Semantic dementia. *Brain*, *115*, 1783–1806.

Hodges, J. R., Patterson, K. E., & Tyler, L. K. (1994). Loss of semantic memory: Implications for the modularity of mind. *Cognitive Neuropsychology*, *11*, 505–542.

Hodges, J. R., Bozeat, S., Lambon Ralph, M. A., Patterson, K. E., & Spatt, J. (2000). The role of conceptual knowledge in object use: Evidence from semantic dementia. *Brain*, *123*, 1913–1925.

Hoekstra, R. A., Bartels, M., Verweij, C. J. H., & Boosma, D. I. (2007). Heritability of autistic traits in the general population. *Archives of Pediatrics and Adolescent Medicine*, *161*, 372–377.

Hoffman, E. & Haxby, J. V. (2000). Distinct representations of eye gaze and identity in the distributed human neural system for face perception. *Nature Neuroscience*, *3*, 80–84.

Hoge, R. D. & Pike, G. B. (2001). Quantitative measurement using fMRI. In P. Jezzard, P. M. Matthews & S. M. Smith (Eds.), *Functional MRI*. Oxford, UK: Oxford University Press.

Holcomb, P. J. & Neville, H. J. (1990). Auditory and visual semantic priming in lexical decision—a comparison using event-related brain potentials. *Language and Cognitive Processes*, *5*(4), 281–312.

Holdstock, J. S., Mayes, A. R., Isaac, C. L., Gong, Q., & Roberts, N. (2002). Differential involvement of the hippocampus and temporal lobe cortices in rapid and slow learning of new semantic information. *Neuropsychologia*, *40*, 748–768.

Horn, G. & McCabe, B. J. (1984). Predispositions and preferences: Effects on imprinting of lesions to the chick brain. *Brain Research*, *168*, 361–373.

Hornak, J., Rolls, E. T., & Wade, D. (1996). Face and voice expression identification inpatients with emotional and behavioural changes following ventral frontal lobe damage. *Neuropsychologia*, *34*(4), 247–261.

Hornak, J., O'Doherty, J., Bramham, J., Rolls, E. T., Morris, R. G., Bullock, P. R., & Polkey, C. E. (2004). Reward-related reversal learning after surgical excisions in orbito-frontal or dorsolateral prefrontal cortex in humans. *Journal of Cognitive Neuroscience*, *16*(3), 463–478.

Horwitz, B., Tagamets, M.-A., & McIntosh, A. R. (1999). Neural modelling, functional brain imaging, and cognition. *Trends in Cognitive Sciences*, *3*, 91–98.

Houghton, G. & Zorzi, M. (2003). Normal and impaired spelling in a connectionist dual-route architecture. *Cognitive Neuropsychology*, *20*(2), 115–162.

Howard, D. & Patterson, K. E. (1992). *The pyramids and palm trees test*. Bury St Edmunds, UK: Thames Valley Test Corporation.

Hsieh, S., Hornberger, M., Piguet, O., & Hodges, J. R. (2011). Neural basis of music knowledge: Evidence from the dementias. *Brain*, *134*, 2523–2534.

Hubbard, E. M., Piazza, M., Pinel, P., & Dehaene, S. (2005). Interactions between numbers and space in parietal cortex. *Nature Reviews Neuroscience*, *6*, 435–448.

Hubel, D.H. (1963). The visual cortex of the brain. *Scientific American*, 209, 54–62.

Hubel, D. H. & Wiesel, T. N. (1959). Receptive fields of single neurones in the cat's striate cortex. *Journal of Physiology*, *148*, 574–591.

Hubel, D. H. & Wiesel, T. N. (1962). Receptive fields, binocular interaction and functional architecture in the cat's visual cortex. *Journal of Physiology*, *160*, 106–154.

Hubel, D. H. & Wiesel, T. N. (1965). Receptive fields and functional architecture of monkey striate cortex. *Journal of Neurophysiology*, *28*, 289–299.

Hubel, D. H. & Wiesel, T. N. (1968). Receptive fields and functional architecture of monkey striate cortex. *Journal of Physiology*, *195*, 215–243.

Hubel, D. H. & Wiesel, T. N. (1970a). Cells sensitive to binocular depth in area 18 of the macaque monkey cortex. *Nature*, *225*, 41–42.

Hubel, D. H. & Wiesel, T. N. (1970b). The period of susceptibility to the physiological effects of unilateral eye closure in kittens. *Journal of Physiology*, *206*, 419–436.

Hughes, C., Russell, J., & Robbins, T. W. (1994). Evidence for executive dysfunction in autism. *Psychological Medicine*, *27*, 209–220.

Hummel, F., Celnik, P., Giraux, P., Floel, A., Wu, W. H., Gerloff, C., & Cohen, L. G. (2005). Effects of non-invasive cortical stimulation on skilled motor function in chronic stroke. *Brain*, *128*, 490–499.

Humphreys, G. W. & Forde, E. M. E. (1998). Disorder action schema and action dysorganisation syndrome. *Cognitive Neuropsychology*, *15*, 771–811.

Humphreys, G. W. & Forde, E. M. E. (2001). Hierarchies, similarity, and interactivity in object recognition: "Category-specific" neuropsychological deficits. *Behavioral and Brain Sciences*, *24*, 453–509.

Humphreys, G. W. & Riddoch, M. J. (1984). Routes to object constancy: Implications from neurological impairments of object constancy. *Quarterly Journal of Experimental Psychology*, *36A*, 385–415.

Humphreys, G. W. & Riddoch, M. J. (1987). *To see but not to see: A case of visual agnosia*. Hove, UK: Psychology Press.

Humphreys, G. W. & Rumiati, R. I. (1998). Agnosia without prosopagnosia or alexia: Evidence for stored visual memories specific to objects. *Cognitive Neuropsychology*, *15*, 243–277.

Humphreys, G. W., Cinel, C., Wolfe, J., Olson, A., & Klempen, N. (2000). Fractionating the binding process: Neuropsychological evidence distinguishing binding of form from binding of surface features. *Vision Research*, *40*, 1569–1596.

Hunter, M. D., Griffiths, T. D., Farrow, T. F. D., Zheng, Y., Wilkinson, I. D., Hegde, N., Woods, W., Spence, S. A., & Woodruff, P. W. R. (2003). A neural basis for the perception of voices in external auditory space. *Brain*, *126*, 161–169.

Huron, D. (2001). Is music an evolutionary adaptation? In R. J. Zatorre, & I. Peretz (Eds.), *The biological foundations of music*. New York: New York Academy of Sciences.

Husain, M., Shapiro, K., Martin, J., & Kennard, C. (1997). Abnormal temporal dynamics of visual attention in spatial neglect patients. *Nature*, *385*(6612), 154–156.

Hutchins, S. & Peretz, I. (2012). Amusics can imitate what they cannot discriminate. *Brain and Language*, *123*(3), 234–239.

Huttenlocher, P. R. & Dabholkar, A. S. (1997). Regional differences in synaptogenesis in human cerebral cortex. *Journal of Comparative Neurology*, *387*, 167–178.

Hyde, K. L. & Peretz, I. (2004). Brains that are out of tune but in time. *Psychological Science*, *15*, 356–360.

Hyde, K. L., Lerch, J. P., Zatorre, R. J., Griffiths, T. D., Evans, A. C., & Peretz, I. (2007). Cortical thickness in congenital amusia: When less is better than more. *Journal of Neuroscience*, *27*, 13028–13032.

Iacoboni, M. (2009). Imitation, empathy, and mirror neurons. *Annual Review of Psychology*, *60*, 653–670.

Iacoboni, M. & Dapretto, M. (2006). The mirror neuron system and the consequences of its dysfunction. *Nature Reviews Neuroscience*, *7*(12), 942–951.

Iacoboni, M., Woods, R., Brass, M., Bekkering, H., Mazziotta, J. C., & Rizzolatti, G. (1999). Cortical mechanisms of human imitation. *Science*, *286*, 2526–2528.

Ifrah, G. (1985). *From one to zero: A universal history of numbers* (L. Blair trans.). New York: Viking (original work published 1981).

Indefrey, P. & Levelt, W. J. M. (2004). The spatial and temporal signatures of word production components. *Cognition*, *92*, 101–144.

Iriki, A., Tanaka, M. & Iwamura, Y. (1996). Coding of modified body schema during tool use by macaque post-central neurons. *NeuroReport*, *7*, 2325–2330.

Isaacs, E. B., Edmonds, C. J., Lucas, A., & Gadian, D. G. (2001). Calculation difficulties in children of very low birth weight. *Brain*, *124*, 1701–1707.

Ischebeck, A., Zamarian, L., Siedentopf, C., Koppelstatter, F., Benke, T., Felber, S., & Delazer, M. (2006). How specifically do we learn? Imaging the learning of multiplication and subtraction. *NeuroImage*, *30*(4), 1365–1375. doi: 10.1016/j.neuroimage.2005.11.016.

Isenberg, A. L., Vaden, K. I., Jr., Saberi, K., Muftuler, L. T., & Hickok, G. (2012). Functionally distinct regions for spatial processing and sensory motor integration in the planum temporale. *Human Brain Mapping*, *33*(10), 2453–2463.

Ishibashi, R., Ralph, M. A. L., Saito, S., & Pobric, G. (2011). Different roles of lateral anterior temporal lobe and inferior parietal lobule in coding function and manipulation tool knowledge: Evidence from an rTMS study. *Neuropsychologia*, *49*(5), 1128–1135.

Itti, L. & Koch, C. (2001). Computational modelling of visual attention. *Nature Reviews Neuroscience*, *2*(3), 194–203.

Jabbi, M., Swart, M., & Keysers, C. (2007). Empathy for positive and negative emotions in gustatory cortex. *NeuroImage*, *34*, 1744–1753.

Jackson, S. R. & Shaw, A. (2000). The Ponzo illusion affects grip-force but not grip-aperture scaling during prehension movements. *Journal of Experimental Psychology: Human Perception and Performance*, *26*, 418–423.

Jackson, S. R., Parkinson, A., Jung, J., Ryan, S. E., Morgan, P. S., Hollis, C., & Jackson, G. M. (2011). Compensatory neural reorganization in Tourette syndrome. *Current Biology*, *21*(7), 580–585.

Jacobs, S., Danielmeier, C., & Frey, S. H. (2010). Human anterior intraparietal and ventral premotor cortices support representations of grasping with the hand or a novel tool. *Journal of Cognitive Neuroscience*, *22*(11), 2594–2608.

Jahanshahi, M., Jenkins, I. H., Brown, R. G., Marsden, C. D., Passingham, R. E., & Brooks, D. J. (1995). Self-initiated versus externally triggered movements: An investigation using measurement of regional cerebral blood flow with PET and movement-related potentials in normal and Parkinson's disease subjects. *Brain*, *118*, 913–933.

Jahanshahi, M. & Frith, C. D. (1998). Willed action and its impairments. *Cognitive Neuropsychology*, *15*, 483–533.

Jahanshahi, M., Profice, P., Brown, R. G., Ridding, M. C., Dirnberger, G., & Rothwell, J. C. (1998). The effects of transcranial magnetic stimulation over dorsolateral prefrontal cortex on suppression of habitual counting during random number generation. *Brain*, *112*, 1533–1544.

Jahanshahi, M., Dirnberger, G., Fuller, R., & Frith, C. D. (2000). The role of dorsolateral prefrontal cortex in random number generation: A study with positron emission tomography. *NeuroImage*, *12*, 713–725.

James, W. (1884). What is an emotion? *Mind*, *9*, 188–205.

Janowsky, J. S., Shimamura, A. P., & Squire, L. R. (1989). Source memory impairment in patients with frontal lobe lesions. *Neuropsychologia*, *27*, 1043–1056.

Jasper, H. A. (1958). The ten-twenty system of the international federation. *Electro-encephalography and Clinical Neurophysiology*, *10*, 371–375.

Jeannerod, M. (1997). *The cognitive neuroscience of action*. Oxford, UK: Blackwell.

Jescheniak, J. D. & Levelt, W. J. M. (1994). Word frequency effects in speech production: Retrieval of syntactic information and of phonological form. *Journal of Experimental Psychology: Learning, Memory and Cognition*, *20*, 824–843.

Ji, D. & Wilson, M. A. (2007). Coordinated memory replay in the visual cortex and hippocampus during sleep. *Nature Neuroscience*, *10*(1), 100–107.

Job, R., Sartori, G., Masterson, J., & Coltheart, M. (1983). Developmental surface dyslexia in Italian. In R. N. Malatesha, & M. Coltheart (Eds.), *Dyslexia: A global issue*. The Hague, The Netherlands: Martinus Njihoff Publishers.

Jobard, G., Crivello, F., & Tzourio-Mazoyer, N. (2003). Evaluation of the dual route theory of reading: A metanalysis of 35 neuroimaging studies. *NeuroImage*, *20*, 693–712.

Johansson, G. (1973). Visual perception of biological motion and a model for its analysis. *Perception and Psychophysics*, *14*, 201–211.

Johnson, M. H. (2005). *Developmental cognitive neuroscience: An introduction* (2nd edition). Oxford, UK: Blackwell.

Johnson, M. H., Dziurawiec, S., Ellis, H. D., & Morton, J. (1991). Newborns' preferential tracking of face-like stimuli and its subsequent decline. *Cognition*, *40*, 1–19.

Johnson, M. K. (1988). Reality monitoring: An experimental phenomenological approach. *Journal of Experimental Psychology: General*, *117*, 390–394.

Johnson, M. K., Foley, M. A., & Leach, K. (1988). The consequences for memory of imagining in another person's voice. *Memory and Cognition*, *16*, 337–342.

Johnson, M. K., Hashtroudi, S., & Lindsay, D. S. (1993). Source monitoring. *Psychological Bulletin*, *114*, 3–28.

Jones, D. M., Macken, W. J., & Nicholls, A. P. (2004). The phonological store of working memory: Is it phonological and is it a store? *Journal of Experimental Psychology: Learning, Memory and Cognition*, *30*, 656–674.

Jones, G. V. (2002). Predictability (ease of predication) as semantic substrate of imageability in reading and retrieval. *Brain and Language*, *82*, 159–166.

Jones, P. E. (1995). Contradictions and unanswered questions in the Genie case: A fresh look at the linguistic evidence. *Language and Communication*, *15*, 261–280.

Josephs, O. & Henson, R. N. A. (1999). Event-related functional magnetic resonance imaging: Modelling, inference and optimization. *Philosophical Transactions of the Royal Society B*, *354*, 1215–1228.

Jueptner, M. & Weiller, C. (1995). Does measurement of regional cerebral blood flow reflect synaptic activity? Implications for PET and fMRI. *NeuroImage*, *2*, 148–156.

Jung, R. E. & Haier, R. J. (2007). The Parieto-Frontal Integration Theory (P-FIT) of intelligence: Converging neuroimaging evidence. *Behavioral and Brain Sciences*, *30*, 135.

Juphard, A., Vidal, J. R., Perrone-Bertolotti, M., Minotti, L., Kahane, P., Lachaux, J. P., & Baciu, M. (2011). Direct evidence for two different neural mechanisms for reading familiar and unfamiliar words: an intra-cerebral EEG study. *Frontiers in Human Neuroscience*, *5*.

Kaan, E., Harris, A., Gibson, E., & Holcomb, P. (2000). The P600 as an index of syntactic integration difficulty. *Language and Cognitive Processes*, *15*(2), 159–201.

Kaas, J. H. & Hackett, T. A. (1999). "What" and "where" processing in auditory cortex. *Nature Neuroscience*, *2*, 1045–1047.

Kaas, J. H., Hackett, T. A., & Tramo, M. J. (1999). Auditory processing in primate cerebral cortex. *Current Opinion in Neurobiology*, *9*, 164–170.

Kajikawa, Y., de la Mothe, L. A., Blumell, S., Sterbing-D'Angelo, S. J., D'Angelo, W., Camalier, C. R., & Hackett, T. A. (2008). Coding of FM sweep trains and twitter calls in area CM of marmoset auditory cortex. *Hearing Research*, *239*, 107–125.

Kanai, R. & Rees, G. (2011). The structural basis of inter-individual differences in human behaviour and cognition. *Nature Reviews Neuroscience*, *12*, 231–242.

Kanai, R., Carmel, D., Bahrami, B., & Rees, G. (2011). Structural and functional fractionation of right superior parietal cortex in bistable perception. *Current Biology*, *21*(3), R106–R107.

Kane, N. M., Curry, S. H., Butler, S. R., & Cummins, B. H. (1993). Electrophysiological indicator of awakening from coma. *Lancet*, *341*, 688–688.

Kanner, L. (1943). Autistic disturbances of affective contact. *Nervous Child*, *2*, 217–250.

Kanwisher, N. & Wojciulik, E. (2000). Visual attention: Insights from brain imaging. *Nature Reviews Neuroscience*, *1*, 91–100.

Kanwisher, N. & Yovel, G. (2006). The fusiform face area: A cortical region specialized for the perception of faces. *Philosophical Transactions of the Royal Society of London*, Series B, 361(1476), 2109–2128.

Kanwisher, N., McDermott, J., & Chun, M. M. (1997). The fusiform face area: A module in human extrastriate cortex specialized for face perception. *Journal of Neuroscience*, *17*, 4302–4311.

Kapur, N. (1999). Syndromes of retrograde amnesia: A conceptual and empirical synthesis. *Psychological Bulletin*, *125*, 800–825.

Kapur, S. (2003). Psychosis as a state of abnormal salience: A framework linking biology, phenomenology, and pharmacology in schizophrenia. *American Journal of Psychiatry*, *160*, 13–23.

Kapur, S., Craik, F. I. M., Tulving, E., Wilson, A. A., Houle, S., & Brown, G. M. (1994). Neuroanatomical correlates of encoding in episodic memory: Levels of processing effect. *Proceedings of the National Academy of Science, USA*, *91*, 2008–2011.

Karmiloff-Smith, A. (1992). *Beyond modularity: A developmental perspective on cognitive science*. Cambridge, MA: MIT Press.

Karmiloff-Smith, A. (2006). Modules, genes, and evolution: What have we learned from atypical development? *Attention and Performance XXI*, 563–583.

Karmiloff-Smith, A. (2007). Williams syndrome. *Current Biology*, *17*, R1035–R1036.

Karnath, H.-O. & Perenin, M.-T. (2005). Cortical control of visually guided reaching: Evidence from patients with optic ataxia. *Cerebral Cortex*, *15*, 1561–1569.

Karnath, H.-O., Ferber, S., & Bulthoff, H. (2000). Neuronal representation of object orientation. *Neuropsychologia*, *38*, 1235–1241.

Kastner, S., Pinsk, M. A., De Weerd, P., Desimone, R., & Ungerleider, L. G. (1999). Increased activity in human visual cortex during directed attention in the absence of visual stimulation. *Neuron, 22*(4), 751–761.

Kastner, S., De Weerd, P., Pinsk, M. A., Elizondo, M. I., Desimone, R., & Ungerleider, L. G. (2001). Modulation of sensory suppression: Implications for receptive field sizes in the human visual cortex. *Journal of Neurophysiology, 86*(3), 1398–1411.

Kaufmann, J. M. & Schweinberger, S. R. (2008). Distortions in the brain? ERP effects of caricaturing familiar and unfamiliar faces. *Brain Research, 1228,* 177–188.

Kay, J. & Ellis, A. W. (1987). A cognitive neuropsychological case study of anomia. *Brain, 110,* 613–629.

Kay, J. & Hanley, R. (1991). Simultaneous form perception and serial letter recognition in a case of letter-by-letter reading. *Cognitive Neuropsychology, 8,* 249–273.

Kay, J. & Hanley, R. (1994). Peripheral disorders of spelling: The role of the graphemic buffer. In G. D. A. Brown & N. C. Ellis (Eds.), *Handbook of spelling: Theory, process and intervention.* London: Wiley.

Kay, J., Lesser, R., & Coltheart, M. (1992). *Psycholinguistic assessments of language processing in aphasia.* Hove, UK: Psychology Press.

Keil, J., Muller, N., Ihssen, N., & Weisz, N. (2012). On the variability of the McGurk effect: Audiovisual integration depends on prestimulus brain states. *Cerebral Cortex, 22*(1), 221–231.

Kellenbach, M. L., Wijers, A. A., Hovius, M., Mulder, J., & Mulder, G. (2002). Neural differentiation of lexico-syntactic categories or semantic features? Event-related potential evidence for both. *Journal of Cognitive Neuroscience, 14,* 561–577.

Kelley, W. M., Miezin, F. M., McDermott, K. B., Buckner, R. L., Raichle, M. E., Cohen, N. J., Ollinger, J. M., Akbudak, E., Conturo, T. E., Snyder, A. V., & Petersen, S. E. (1998). Hemispheric specialization in human dorsal frontal cortex and medial temporal lobe for verbal and nonverbal memory encoding. *Neuron, 20,* 927–936.

Kendler, K. S. (2005). "A gene for. . . ." The nature of gene action in psychiatric disorders. *American Journal of Psychiatry, 162,* 433–440.

Kendler, K. S., Neale, M. C., Kessler, R. C., Heath, A. C., & Eaves, L. J. (1992). The genetic epidemiology of phobias in women: The interrelationship of agoraphobia, social phobia, situational phobia and simple phobia. *Archives of General Psychiatry, 49,* 273–281.

Kent, R. D., Duffy, J. R., Slama, A., Kent, J. F., & Clift, A. (2001). Clinicoanatomic studies in dysarthria: Review, critique, and directions for research. *Journal of Speech, Language and Hearing Research, 44,* 535–551.

Kerlin, J. R., Shahin, A. J., & Miller, L. M. (2010). Attentional gain control of ongoing cortical speech representations in a "cocktail party." *Journal of Neuroscience, 30*(2), 620–628.

Kerns, J. G., Cohen, J. D., MacDonald, A. W., Cho, R. Y., Stenger, V. A., & Carter, C. S. (2004). Anterior cingulate conflict monitoring and adjustments in control. *Science, 303,* 1023–1026.

Kiang, N. Y.-S., Watanabe, T., Thomas, E. C., & Clark, L. F. (1965). *Discharge patterns of single fibres in the cat's auditory nerve.* Cambridge, MA: MIT Press.

Kim, J. J. & Fanselow, M. S. (1992). Modality-specific retrograde amnesia for fear. *Science, 256,* 675–677.

Kim, S. P., Simeral, J. D., Hochberg, L. R., Donoghue, J. P., & Black, M. J. (2008). Neural control of computer cursor velocity by decoding motor cortical spiking activity in humans with tetraplegia. *Journal of neural engineering, 5*(4), 455–476.

Kinsbourne, M. & Warrington, E. K. (1962a). A disorder of simultaneous form perception. *Brain, 85,* 461–486.

Kinsbourne, M. & Warrington, E. K. (1962b). A study of finger agnosia. *Brain, 85,* 47–66.

Kinsbourne, M. & Warrington, E. K. (1965). A case showing selectively impaired oral spelling. *Journal of Neurology, Neurosurgery and Psychiatry, 28,* 563–566.

Kipps, C. M., Duggins, A. J., McCusker, E. A., & Calder, A. J. (2007). Disgust and happiness recognition correlate with anteroventral insula and amygdala volume respectively in preclinical Huntington's disease. *Journal of Cognitive Neuroscience*, *19*, 1206–1217.

Kitchener, E. G., Hodges, J. R., & McCarthy, R. (1998). Acquisition of post-morbid vocabulary and semantic facts in the absence of episodic memory. *Brain*, *121*, 1313–1327.

Klein, D. C., Moore, R. Y., & Reppert, S. M. (1991). *Suprachiasmatic nucleus: The mind's clock*. Oxford, UK: Oxford University Press.

Klein, S. B., Rozendal, K., & Cosmides, L. (2002). A social-cognitive neuroscience analysis of the self. *Social Cognition*, *20*, 105–135.

Kleinschmidt, A., Buchel, C., & Zeki, S. (1998). Human brain activity during spontaneously reversing perception of ambiguous figures. *Proceedings of the National Academy of Science, USA*, *265*, 2427–2433.

Klinnert, M. D., Campos, J. J., & Source, J. (1983). Emotions as behavior regulators: Social referencing in infancy. In R. Plutchik, & H. Kellerman (Eds.), *Emotions in early development*. New York: Academic Press.

Kluver, H., & Bucy, P. C. (1939). Preliminary analysis of functions of the temporal lobes in monkeys. *Archives of Neurology and Psychiatry*, *42*, 979–1000.

Knoch, D., Pascual-Leone, A., Meyer, K., Treyer, V., & Fehr, E. (2006). Diminishing reciprocal fairness by disrupting the right prefrontal cortex. *Science*, *314*(5800), 829–832.

Knowlton, B. J., Squire, L. R., & Gluck, M. A. (1994). Probabilistic category learning in amnesia. *Learning and Memory*, *1*, 106–120.

Knowlton, B. J., Mangels, J. A., & Squire, L. R. (1996). A neostriatal habit learning system in humans. *Science*, *273*, 1399–1402.

Knudsen, E. I. (2007). Fundamental components of attention. *Annual Review of Neuro-science* (Vol. 30, pp. 57–78).

Knutson, B., Adams, C. M., Fong, G. W., & Hommer, D. (2001). Anticipation of increasing monetary reward selectively recruits nucleus accumbens. *Journal of Neuroscience*, *21*(16), art. no.-RC159.

Knutson, B., Rick, S., Wirnmer, G. E., Prelec, D., & Loewenstein, G. (2007). Neural predictors of purchases. *Neuron*, *53*(1), 147–156.

Koch, C. & Tsuchiya, N. (2007). Attention and consciousness: two distinct brain processes. *Trends in Cognitive Sciences*, *11*(1), 16–22.

Koechlin, E., Basso, G., Pietrini, P., Panzer, S., & Grafman, J. (1999a). The role of the anterior prefrontal cortex in human cognition. *Nature*, *399*, 148–151.

Koechlin, E., Naccache, L., Block, E., & Dehaene, S. (1999b). Primed numbers: Exploring the modularity of numerical representations with masked and unmasked semantic priming. *Journal of Experimental Psychology: Human Perception and Performance*, *25*, 1882–1905.

Koechlin, E. & Summerfield, C. (2007). An information theoretical approach to prefrontal executive function. *Trends in Cognitive Sciences*, *11*(6), 229–235.

Koechlin, E., Ody, C., & Kouneiher, F. (2003). The architecture of cognitive control in the human prefrontal cortex. *Science*, *302*(5648), 1181–1185.

Koelsch, S. & Siebel, W. A. (2005). Towards a neural basis of music perception. *Trends in Cognitive Sciences*, *9*, 578–584.

Koelsch, S., Fritz, T. V., von Cramon, D. Y., Muller, K., & Friederici, A. D. (2006). Investigating emotion with music: An fMRI study. *Human Brain Mapping*, *27*, 236–250.

Koenigs, M., Young, L., Adolphs, R., Tranel, D., Cushman, F., Hauser, M., & Damasio, A. (2007). Damage to the prefrontal cortex increases utilitarian moral judgements. *Nature*, *446*(7138), 908–911.

Kogo, N. & Wagemans, J. (2013). The "side" matters: How configurality is reflected in completion. *Cognitive Neuroscience*, *4*(1), 3–45.

Kohler, E., Keysers, C., Umilta, M. A., Fogassi, L., Gallese, V., & Rizzolatti, G. (2002). Hearing sounds, understanding actions: Action representation in mirror neurons. *Science, 297*, 846–848.

Kolb, B. & Whishaw, I. Q. (2002). *Fundamentals of Human Neuropsychology* (5th edition). New York: Worth/Freeman.

Koob, G. F. (1992). Dopamine, addiction and reward. *Seminars in the Neurosciences, 4,* 139–148.

Kopelman, M. D. (2000). Focal retrograde amnesia: An exceptionally critical review. *Cognitive Neuropsychology, 17,* 585–621.

Kopelman, M. D. & Stanhope, N. (1998). Recall and recognition memory in patients with focal frontal, temporal lobe and diencephalic lesions. *Neuropsychologia, 36,* 785–795.

Kopelman, M. D., Wilson, B. A., & Baddeley, A. D. (1990). *The autobiographical memory interview.* Bury St. Edmunds, UK: Thames Valley Test Company.

Kosaki, H., Hashikawa, T., He, J., & Jones, E. G. (1997). Tonotopic organization of auditory cortical fields delineated by parvalbumin immunoreactivity in macaque monkeys. *Journal of Comparative Neurology, 386,* 304–316.

Kosslyn, S. M. (1999). If neuroimaging is the answer, what is the question? *Philosophical Transactions of the Royal Society of London B, 354,* 1283–1294.

Kosslyn, S. M. & Van Kleek, M. H. (1990). Broken brains and normal minds: Why Humpty-Dumpty needs a skeleton. In E. L. Schwartz (Ed.), *Computational neuroscience.* Cambridge, MA: MIT Press.

Kosslyn, S. M., Thompson, W. L., Kim, I. J., & Alpert, N. M. (1995). Topographical representations of mental images in primary visual cortex. *Nature, 478,* 496–498.

Kosslyn, S. M., Pascual-Leone, A., Felician, O., Camposano, S., Keenan, J. P., Thompson, W. L., Ganis, G., Sukel, K. E., & Alpert, N. M. (1999). The role of area 17 in visual imagery: Convergent evidence from PET and rTMS. *Science, 284,* 167–170.

Kosslyn, S. M., Ganis, G., & Thompson, W. L. (2001). Neural foundations of imagery. *Nature Reviews Neuroscience, 2,* 635–642.

Kotler, M., Cohen, H., Segman, R., Gritsenko, I., Nemanov, L., Lerer, B., Kramer, I., ZerZion, M., Kletz, I., & Ebstein, R. P. (1997). Excess dopamine D4 receptor (D4DR) exon III seven repeat allele in opioid-dependent subjects. *Molecular Psychiatry, 2,* 251–254.

Kouneiher, F., Charron, S., & Koechlin, E. (2009). Motivation and cognitive control in the human prefrontal cortex. *Nature Neuroscience, 12*(7), 939–U167.

Koutstaal, W., Schacter, D. L., Verfaellie, M., Brenner, C., & Jackson, E. M. (1999). Perceptually based false recognition of novel objects in amnesia: Effects of category size and similarity to category prototypes. *Cognitive Neuropsychology, 16,* 317–341.

Kraemer, D. J. M., Macrae, C. N., Green, A. E., & Kelley, W. M. (2005). Musical imagery: Sound of silence activates auditory cortex. *Nature, 434,* 158–158.

Krams, M., Rushworth, M. F. S., Deiber, M. P., Frackowiak, R. S. J., & Passingham, R. E. (1998). The preparation, execution and suppression of copied movements. *Experimental Brain Research, 120,* 386–398.

Kranczioch, C., Debener, S., Schwarzbach, J., Goebel, R., & Engel, A. K. (2005). Neural correlates of conscious perception in the attentional blink. *NeuroImage, 24*(3), 704–714.

Kriegstein, K. von, Kleinschmidt, A., Sterzer, P., & Giraud, A. L. (2005). Interaction of face and voice areas during speaker recognition. *Journal of Cognitive Neuroscience, 17,* 367–376.

Kringelbach, M. L. (2005). The human orbitofrontal cortex: linking reward to hedonic experience. *Nature Reviews Neuroscience, 6,* 691–702.

Kringelbach, M. L. & Rolls, E. T. (2003). Neural correlates of rapid context-dependent reversal learning in a simple model of human social interaction. *NeuroImage, 20,* 1371–1383.

Kritchevsky, M., Chang, J., & Squire, L. R. (2004). Functional amnesia: Clinical description and neuropsychological profile of 10 cases. *Learning and Memory, 11,* 213–226.

Kroliczak, G., Piper, B. J., & Frey, S. H. (2011). Atypical lateralization of language predicts cerebral asymmetries in parietal gesture representations. *Neuropsychologia*, *49*(7), 1698–1702.

Kronbichler, M., Bergmann, J., Hutzler, F., Staffen, W., Mair, A., Ladurner, G., & Wimmer, H. (2007). Taxi vs. Taksi: On orthographic word recognition in the left ventral occipitotemporal cortex. *Journal of Cognitive Neuroscience*, *19*(10), 1584–1594.

Krueger, F., Barbey, A. K., & Grafman, J. (2009). The medial prefrontal cortex mediates social event knowledge. *Trends in Cognitive Sciences*, *13*(3), 103–109.

Kubota, J.T., Banaji. M.R. & Phelps, E.A. (2012).The neuroscience of race. *Nature Reviews Neuroscience*, *15*, 940–948

Kuemmerer, D., Hartwigsen, G., Kellmeyer, P., Glauche, V., Mader, I., Kloeppel, S., Suchan, J., Karnath, H. O., Weiller, C., & Saur, D. (2013). Damage to ventral and dorsal language pathways in acute aphasia. *Brain*, *136*, 619–629.

Kuffler, S. W. & Barlow, H. B. (1953). Discharge patterns and functional organization of mammalian retina. *Journal of Neurophysiology*, *16*, 37–63.

Kutas, M. & Federmeier, K. D. (2011). Thirty years and counting: Finding meaning in the n400 component of the event-related brain potential (ERP). In S. T. Fiske, D. L. Schacter & S. E. Taylor (Eds.), *Annual Review of Psychology* (Vol. 62, pp. 621–647). Palo Alto, CA: Annual Reviews.

Kutas, M. & Hillyard, S. (1980). Reading senseless sentences: Brain potentials reflect semantic incongruity. *Science*, *207*, 203–205.

LaBar, K. S., Gatenby, J. C., Gore, J. C., LeDoux, J. E., & Phelps, E. A. (1998). Human amygdala activation during conditioned fear acquisition and extinction: A mixed-trial fMRI study. *Neuron*, *20*(5), 937–945.

La Berge, D. (1983). Spatial extent of attention to letters and words. *Journal of Experimental Psychology: Human Perception and Performance*, *9*, 371–379.

Lambon Ralph, M. A., Ellis, A. W., & Franklin, S. (1995). Semantic loss without surface dyslexia. *Neurocase*, *1*, 363–369.

Lambon Ralph, M. A., Howard, D., Nightingale, G., & Ellis, A. W. (1998). Are living and non-living category-specific deficits causally linked to impaired perceptual or associative knowledge? Evidence from a category-specific double dissociation. *Neurocase*, *4*, 311–338.

Lamm, C., Batson, C.D., & Decety, J. (2007). The neural substrate of human empathy: Effects of perspective taking and cognitive appraisal. *Journal of Cognitive Neuroscience*, 19 (1), 42–58.

Lamme, V. A. F. (1995). The neurophysiology of figure ground segregation in primary visual cortex. *Journal of Neuroscience*, *15*(2), 1605–1615.

Lamme, V. A. F. (2010). How neuroscience will change our view on consciousness. *Cognitive Neuroscience*, *1*, 204–210.

Lamme, V. A. F. & Roelfsema, P. R. (2000). The distinct modes of vision offered by feedforward and recurrent processing. *Trends in Neurosciences*, *23*(11), 571–579.

Lancy, D. F. (1983). *Cross-cultural studies in cognition and mathematics*. New York: Academic Press.

Land, E. H. (1964). The retinex. *Scientific American*, *52*, 247–264.

Land, E. H. (1983). Recent advances in retinex theory and some implications for cortical computations. *Proceedings of the National Academy of Science, USA*, *80*, 5163–5169.

Langleben, D. D., Schroeder, L., Maldjian, J. A., Gur, R. C., McDonald, S., Ragland, J. D., O'Brien, C. P., & Childress, A. R. (2002). Brain activity during simulated deception: An event-related functional magnetic resonance study. *NeuroImage*, *15*, 727–732.

Langner, R., Kellermann, T., Boers, F., Sturm, W., Willmes, K., & Eickhoff, S. B. (2011). Modality-specific perceptual expectations selectively modulate baseline activity in auditory, somatosensory, and visual cortices. *Cerebral Cortex*, *21*(12), 2850–2862.

Lashley, K. S. (1929). *Brain mechanisms and intelligence*. Chicago, IL: Chicago University Press.

Lauro-Grotto, R., Piccini, C., & Shallice, T. (1997). Modality-specific operations in semantic dementia. *Cortex, 33*, 593–622.

Lavie, N. (1995). Perceptual load as a necessary condition for selective attention. *Journal of Experimental Psychology: Human Perception and Performance, 21*, 451–468.

Le Bihan, D., Mangin, J. F., Poupon, C., Clark, C. A., Pappata, S., Molko, N., & Chabriat, H. (2001). Diffusion tensor imaging: Concepts and applications. *Journal of Magnetic Resonance Imaging, 13*, 534–546.

Le Doux, J. E. (1996). *The emotional brain.* New York: Simon and Schuster.

Le Doux, J. E., Iwata, J., Cicchetti, P., & Reis, D. (1988). Differential projections of the central amygdaloid nucleus mediate autonomic and behavioral correlates of conditioned fear. *Journal of Neuroscience, 8*, 2517–2529.

Le Grand, R., Mondloch, C., Maurer, D., & Brent, H. P. (2001). Neuroperception: Early visual experience and face processing. *Nature, 410*, 890.

Lee, K. M. & Kang, S.-Y. (2002). Arithmetic operation and working memory: Differential suppression in dual tasks. *Cognition, 83*, B63–B68.

Lee, Y.-S., Turkeltaub, P., Granger, R., & Raizada, R. D. S. (2012). Categorical speech processing in Broca's area: An fMRI study using multivariate pattern-based analysis. *Journal of Neuroscience, 32*(11), 3942–3948.

Leekam, S. R. & Perner, J. (1991). Does the autistic child have a metarepresentational deficit? *Cognition, 40*, 203–218.

Lenneberg, E. (1967). *Biological foundations of language.* New York: Wiley.

Levelt, W. J. M. (1989). *Speaking: From intention to articulation.* Cambridge, MA: MIT Press.

Levelt, W. J. M. (1999). Models of word production. *Trends in Cognitive Sciences, 3*, 223–232.

Levelt, W. J. M. (2001). Spoken word production: A theory of lexical access. *Proceedings of the National Academy of Science, USA, 98*, 13464–13471.

Levelt, W. J. M. & Wheeldon, L. R. (1994). Do speakers have access to a mental syllabary? *Cognition, 50*, 239–269.

Levelt, W. J. M., Schriefers, H., Vorberg, D., Meyer, A. S., Pechmann, T., & Havinga, J. (1991). The time course of lexical access in speech production: A study of picture naming. *Psychological Review, 98*, 122–142.

Levine, D. N., Warach, J., & Farah, M. (1985). Two visual systems in mental imagery: Dissociation of "what" and "where" in imagery disorders due to bilateral posterior cerebral lesions. *Neurology, 35*, 1010–1018.

Levinson, D. F. (2003). Molecular genetics of schizophrenia: A review of the recent literature. *Current Opinion in Psychiatry, 16*, 157–170.

Liberman, A. M. & Mattingly, I. G. (1985). The motor theory of speech perception revised. *Cognition, 21*, 1–36.

Liberman, A. M. & Whalen, D. H. (2000). On the relation of speech to language. *Trends in Cognitive Sciences, 4*, 187–196.

Libet, B., Gleason, C. A., Wright, E. W., & Pearl, D. K. (1983). Time of conscious intention to act in relation to onset of cerebral activity (readiness potential): The unconscious initiation of a freely voluntary act. *Brain, 102*, 623–642.

Lichtheim, L. (1885). On aphasia. *Brain, 7*, 433–484.

Lidzba, K., Staudt, M., Wilke, M., & Krageloh-Mann, I. (2006). Visuospatial deficits in patients with early left-hemispheric lesions and functional reorganization of language: Consequence of lesion or reorganization? *Neuropsychologia, 44*, 1088–1094.

Lieberman, M. D., Chang, G. Y., Chiao, J., Bookheimer, S. Y., & Knowlton, B. J. (2004). An event-related fMRI study of artificial grammar learning in a balanced chunk strength design. *Journal of Cognitive Neuroscience, 16*, 427–438.

Liegeois, F., Connelly, A., Cross, J. H., Boyd, S. G., Gadian, D. G., Vargha-Khadem, F., & Baldeweg, T. (2004). Language reorganization in children with early onset lesions of the left hemisphere: An fMRI study. *Brain, 127*, 1229–1236.

Liepmann, H. (1905). Die linke hemisphere und das handeln. *Munchner Medizinische Wochenschrift, 49,* 2322–2326.

Lindgren, S. D., De Renzi, E., & Richman, L. C. (1985). Cross-national comparisons of developmental dyslexia in Italy and the United States. *Child Development, 56,* 1404–1417.

Lindquist, K. A. & Barrett, L. F. (2012). A functional architecture of the human brain: Emerging insights from the science of emotion. *Trends in Cognitive Sciences, 16*(11), 533–540.

Lissauer, H. (1890). A case of visual agnosia with a contribution to theory. *Archiv für Psychiatrie und Nervenrankheiten, 21,* 222–270.

Lloyd-Fox, S., Blasi, A., & Elwell, C. E. (2010). Illuminating the developing brain: The past, present and future of functional near-infrared spectroscopy. *Neuroscience and Biobehavioral Review, 34,* 269–284.

Loetscher, T., Schwarz, U., Schubiger, M., & Brugger, P. (2008). Head turns bias the brain's random number generator. *Current Biology, 18,* R60–R62.

Loewenstein, G., Rick, S., & Cohen, J. D. (2008). Neuroeconomics. *Annual Review of Psychology, 59,* 647–672.

Logie, R. H. (1995). *Visuospatial working memory.* Hove, UK: Psychology Press.

Logie, R. H., Gilhooly, K. J., & Wynn, V. (1994). Counting on working memory in arithmetic problem solving. *Memory and Cognition, 22,* 395–410.

Logothetis, N. K., Pauls, J., Augath, M., Trinath, T., & Oeltermann, A. (2001). Neurophysiological investigation of the basis of the fMRI signal. *Nature, 412,* 150–157.

Lømo, T. (1966). Frequency potentiation of excitatory synaptic activity in the dentate area of the hippocampal formation. *Acta Physiologica Scandinavica* 68 (Suppl 277): 128.

Long, N. M., Oztekin, I., & Badre, D. (2010). Separable prefrontal cortex contributions to free recall. *Journal of Neuroscience, 30*(33), 10967–10976.

Lotto, A. J., Hickok, G. S., & Holt, L. L. (2009). Reflections on mirror neurons and speech perception. *Trends in Cognitive Sciences, 13*(3), 110–114.

Luck, S. J. & Girelli, M. (1998). Electrophysiological approaches to the study of selective attention in the human brain. In R. Parasuraman (Ed.), *The Attentive Brain* (pp. 71–94). Cambridge, MA: MIT Press.

Luck, S. J. (2005). Ten simple rules for designing ERP experiments. In T. C. Handy (Ed.), *Event-related potentials: A methods handbook.* Cambridge, MA: MIT Press.

Luck, S. J. & Vogel, E. K. (1997). The capacity of visual working memory for features and conjunctions. *Nature, 390*(6657), 279–281.

Luck, S. J., Chelazzi, L., Hillyard, S. A., & Desimone, R. (1997). Neural mechanisms of spatial selective attention in areas V1, V2, and V4 of macaque visual cortex. *Journal of Neurophysiology, 77*(1), 24–42.

Luders, E., Narr, K. L., Thompson, P. M., Rex, D. E., Jancke, L., Steinmetz, H., & Toga, A. W. (2004). Gender differences in cortical complexity. *Nature Neuroscience, 7,* 799–800.

Luo, H. & Poeppel, D. (2012). Cortical oscillations in auditory perception and speech: Evidence for two temporal windows in human auditory cortex. *Frontiers in psychology, 3,* 170–170.

Luzzatti, C. & Davidoff, J. (1994). Impaired retrieval of object-colour knowledge with preserved colour naming. *Neuropsychologia, 32,* 933–950.

Lyons, F., Hanley, J. R., & Kay, J. (2002). Anomia for common names and geographical names with preserved retrieval of people: A semantic memory disorder. *Cortex, 38,* 23–35.

Macaluso, E., George, N., Dolan, R., Spence, C., & Driver, J. (2004). Spatial and temporal factors during processing of audiovisual speech: A PET study. *NeuroImage, 21,* 725–732.

McCabe, K., Houser, D., Ryan, L., Smith, V., & Trouard, T. (2001). A functional imaging study of cooperation in two-person reciprocal exchange. *Proceedings of the National Academy of Sciences, USA, 98,* 11832–11835.

McCandliss, B. D., Fiez, J. A., Protopapas, A., Conway, M., & McClelland, J. L. (2002). Success and failure in teaching the [r]–[l] contrast to Japanese adults: Tests of a Hebbian model of plasticity and stabilization in spoken language perception. *Cognitive, Affective, & Behavioural Neuroscience, 2*, 89–108.

McCandliss, B. D., Cohen, L. & Dehaene, S. (2003). The visual word form area: Expertise for reading in the fusiform gyrus. *Trends in Cognitive Sciences, 7*, 293–299.

McCarthy, R. A. & Warrington, E. K. (1990). *Cognitive neuropsychology: A clinical introduction.* London: Academic Press.

Macchi Cassia, V., Turati, C., & Simion, F. (2004). Can a nonspecific bias toward top-heavy patterns explain new-borns face preference? *Psychological Science, 15*, 379–383.

McClelland, J. L. & Rumelhart, D. E. (1981). An interactive activation model of context effects in letter perception: Part 1. An account of the basic findings. *Psychological Review, 88*, 375–407.

McClelland, J. L., Rumelhart, D. E., & Group, T. P. R. (1986). *Parallel distributed processing: Volume 2. Psychological and biological models.* Cambridge, MA: MIT Press.

McClelland, J. L., St John, M., & Taraban, R. (1989). Sentence comprehension: A parallel distributed processing approach. *Language and Cognitive Processes, 4*, 287–335.

McClelland, J. L., McNaughton, B. L., & O'Reilly, R. C. (1995). Why there are complementary learning systems in the hippocampus and neocortex: Insights from the successes and failures of connectionist models of learning and memory. *Psychological Review, 102*, 419–457.

McCloskey, M. (1992). Cognitive mechanisms in numerical processing: Evidence from acquired dyscalculia. *Cognition, 44*, 107–157.

McCloskey, M. & Caramazza, A. (1988). Theory and methodology in cognitive neuropsychology: A response to our critics. *Cognitive Neuropsychology, 5*, 583–623.

McCloskey, M., Caramazza, A., & Basili, A. (1985). Cognitive mechanisms in number processing and calculation: Evidence from dyscalculia. *Brain and Cognition, 4*, 171–196.

McCloskey, M., Sokol, S. M., & Goodman, R. A. (1986). Cognitive processes in verbal-number production: Inferences from the performance of brain-damaged subjects. *Journal of Experimental Psychology: General, 115*, 307–330.

McClure, S., Laibson, D., Lowenstein, G., & Cohen, J. D. (2004a). Separate neural systems value immediate and delayed rewards. *Science, 306*, 503–507.

McClure, S., Lee, J., Tomlin, D., Cypert, K., Montague, L., & Montague, P. R. (2004b). Neural correlates of behavioural preferences for culturally familiar drinks. *Neuron, 44*, 379–387.

McClure, S. M., Ericson, K. M., Laibson, D. I., Loewenstein, G., & Cohen, J. D. (2007). Time discounting for primary rewards. *Journal of Neuroscience, 27*(21), 5796–5804.

McCormick, D. A. & Bal, T. (1997). Sleep and arousal: Thalamocortical mechanisms. *Annual Review of Neuroscience, 20*, 185–215.

McCrink, K., Spelke, E. S., Dehaene, S., & Pica, P. (2013). Non-symbolic halving in an Amazonian indigene group. *Developmental Science, 16*(3), 451–462.

McDermott, J. & Hauser, M. D. (2007). Nonhuman primates prefer slow tempos but dislike music overall. *Cognition, 104*, 654–668.

MacDonald, M. C., Pearlmutter, N. J., & Seidenberg, M. S. (1994). Lexical nature of syntactic ambiguity resolution. *Psychological Review, 101*, 676–703.

MacDonald, M. E., Gines, S., Gusella, J. F., & Wheeler, V. C. (2003). Huntington's disease. *Neuromolecular Medicine, 4*, 7–20.

McGettigan, C., Warren, J. E., Eisner, F., Marshall, C. R., Shanmugalingam, P., & Scott, S. K. (2011). Neural correlates of sublexical processing in phonological working memory. *Journal of Cognitive Neuroscience, 23*(4), 961–977.

McGugin, R. W., Gatenby, J. C., Gore, J. C., & Gauthier, I. (2012). High-resolution imaging of expertise reveals reliable object selectivity in the fusiform face area related to perceptual performance. *Proceedings of the National Academy of Sciences of the United States of America, 109*(42), 17063–17068.

McGurk, H. & MacDonald, J. (1976). Hearing lips and seeing voices. *Nature, 264*, 746–748.

MacLean, P. D. (1949). Psychosomatic disease and the "visceral brain": Recent developments bearing on the Papez theory of emotion. *Psychosomatic Medicine, 11*, 338–353.

McLennan, J. E., Nakano, K., Tyler, H. R., & Schwab, R. S. (1972). Micrographia in Parkinson's disease. *Journal of Neurological Science, 15*, 141–152.

MacLeod, C. M. & MacDonald, P. A. (2000).Interdimensional interference in the Stroop effect: Uncovering the cognitive and neural anatomy of attention. *Trends in Cognitive Sciences, 4*, 383–391.

McLeod, P., Heywood, C. A., Driver, J., & Zihl, J. (1989). Selective deficits of visual search in moving displays after extrastriate damage. *Nature, 339*, 466–467.

McLeod, P., Dittrich, W., Driver, J., Perrett, D., & Zihl, J. (1996). Preserved and impaired detection of structure from motion by a "motion-blind" patient. *Visual Cognition, 3*, 363–391.

McMains, S. A., Fehd, H. M., Emmanouil, T.-A., & Kastner, S. (2007). Mechanisms of feature- and space-based attention: Response modulation and baseline increases. *Journal of Neurophysiology, 98*(4), 2110–2121.

McManus, I. C. (2002). *Right hand, left hand*. London: Weidenfield & Nicolson.

Macmillan, M. B. (1986). A wonderful journey through skull and brains: The travels of Mr. Gage's tamping iron. *Brain and Cognition, 5*, 67–107.

McNeil, J. E. & Warrington, E. K. (1993). Prosopagnosia: A face-specific disorder. *Quarterly Journal of Experimental Psychology, 46A*, 1–10.

McQueen, J. M. & Cutler, A. (2001). Spoken word access processes: An introduction. *Language and Cognitive Processes, 16*, 469–490.

Maess, B., Koelsch, S., Gunter, T. C., & Friederici, A. D. (2001). Musical syntax is processed in Broca's area: An MEG study. *Nature Neuroscience, 4*, 540–545.

Maestrini, E., Paul, A., Monaco, A. P., & Bailey, A. (2000). Identifying autism susceptibility genes. *Neuron, 28*, 19–24.

Magnussen, C. E. & Stevens, H. C. (1914). Visual sensation caused by a magnetic field. *Philosophical Magazine, 28*, 188–207.

Maguire, E. A., Gadian, D. G., Johnsrude, I. S., Good, C. D., Ashburner, J., Frackowiak, R. S. J., & Frith, C. D. (2000). Navigation-related structural change in the hippocampi of taxi drivers. *Proceedings of the National Academy of Science, USA, 97*, 4398–4403.

Maguire, E. A., Nannery, R., & Spiers, H. J. (2006). Navigation around London by a taxi driver with bilateral hippocampal lesions. *Brain, 129*, 2894–2907.

Mahon, B. Z. & Caramazza, A. (2008). A critical look at the embodied cognition hypothesis and a new proposal for grounding conceptual content. *Journal of Physiology-Paris, 102*(1–3), 59–70.

Maia, T. V. & McClelland, J. L. (2004). A re-examination of the evidence for the somatic marker hypothesis: What participants really know in the Iowa gambling task. *Proceedings of the National Academy of Science, USA, 101*, 16075–16080.

Mainy, N., Jung, J., Baciu, M., Kahane, P., Schoendorff, B., Minotti, L., Hoffman, D., Bertrand, O., & Lachaux, J. P. (2008). Cortical dynamics of word recognition. *Human Brain Mapping, 29*(11), 1215–1230.

Makuuchi, M., Bahlmann, J., Anwander, A., & Friederici, A. D. (2009). Segregating the core computational faculty of human language from working memory. *Proceedings of the National Academy of Sciences of the United States of America, 106*(20), 8362–8367.

Mandler, G. (1980). Recognising: The judgement of a previous occurrence. *Psychological Review, 27*, 252–271.

Mandler, G. & Shebo, B. J. (1982). Subitizing: An analysis of its component processes. *Journal of Experimental Psychology: General, 11*, 1–22.

Manns, J. R., Hopkins, R. O., Reed, J. M., Kitchener, E. G., & Squire, L. R. (2003a). Recognition memory and the human hippocampus. *Neuron, 37*, 171–180.

Manns, J. R., Hopkins, R. O., & Squire, L. R. (2003b). Semantic memory and the human hippocampus. *Neuron, 38*, 127–133.

Marcar, V. L., Strassle, A. E., Loenneker, T., Schwarz, U., & Martin, E. (2004). The influence of cortical maturation on the BOLD response: An fMRI study of visual cortex in children. *Pediatric Research, 56*, 967–974.

Marcel, A. J. (1998). Blindsight and shape perception: Deficit of visual consciousness or of visual function? *Brain, 121*, 1565–1588.

Marchetti, C. & Della Sala, S. (1998). Disentangling alien and anarchic hand. *Cognitive Neuropsychiatry, 3*, 191–207.

Marie, P. (1906). Révision de la question sur l'aphasie: La troisième convolution frontale gauche ne joue aucun role spéciale dans la fonction du langage. *Semaine Medicale, 21*, 241–247.

Maril, A., Wagner, A. D., & Schacter, D. L. (2001). On the tip of the tongue: An event-related fMRI study of semantic retrieval failure and cognitive control. *Neuron, 31*, 653–660.

Marr, D. (1976). Early processing of visual information. *Philosophical Transactions of the Royal Society of London B, 275*, 483–524.

Marr, D. & Nishihara, H. K. (1978). Representation and recognition of the spatial organization of three-dimensional shapes. *Proceedings of the Royal Society of London B, 200*, 269–294.

Marshack, A. (1970). *Notation dans les gravures du paléolithique supérieur.* Bordeaux, France: Delmas.

Marshack, A. (1991). *The roots of civilization* (2nd edition). London: Moyer Bell.

Marshall, J. C. & Halligan, P. W. (1990). Line bisection in a case of visual neglect: Psychophysical studies with implications for theory. *Cognitive Neuropsychology, 7*, 107–130.

Marshall, J. C. & Newcombe, F. (1973). Patterns of paralexia: A psycholinguistic approach. *Journal of Psycholinguistic Research, 2*, 175–199.

Marslen-Wilson, W. D. & Warren, P. (1994). Levels of perceptual representation and process in lexical access: Words, phonemes and features. *Psychological Review, 101*, 653–675.

Marslen-Wilson, W. D. (1987). Functional parallelism in spoken word recognition. *Cognition, 25*, 71–102.

Marslen-Wilson, W. D. & Tyler, L. K. (1980). The temporal structure of spoken language understanding. *Cognition, 8*, 1–71.

Martin, A. (2007). The representation of object concepts in the brain *Annual Review of Psychology* (Vol. 58, pp. 25–45).

Martin, A. & Chao, L. L. (2001). Semantic memory and the brain: Structure and processes. *Current Opinion in Neurobiology, 11*, 194–201.

Martin, J. P. (1967). *The basal ganglia and posture.* London: Pitman.

Martin, K., Jacobs, S., & Frey, S. H. (2011). Handedness-dependent and -independent cerebral asymmetries in the anterior intraparietal sulcus and ventral premotor cortex during grasp planning. *NeuroImage, 57*(2), 502–512.

Mattingley, J. B., Driver, J., Beschin, N., & Robertson, I. H. (1997). Attentional competition between modalities: Extinction between touch and vision after right hemisphere damage. *Neuropsychologia, 35*, 867–880.

Maunsell, J. H. R. (1987). Physiological evidence for two visual subsystems. In L. M. Vaina (Ed.), *Matters of intelligence.* Dordrecht, The Netherlands: Reidel.

Maurer, D. Lewis, T. L., Brent, H. P., & Levin, A. V (1999). Rapid improvement in the acuity of infants after visual input. *Science*, *286*, 108–110.

Mayall, K. & Humphreys, G. W. (2002). Presentation and task effects on migration errors in attentional dyslexia. *Neuropsychologia*, *40*, 1506–1515.

Mayall, K., Humphreys, G. W., & Olson, A. (1997). Disruption to word or letter processing? The origins of case-mixing effects. *Journal of Experimental Psychology: Learning, Memory and Cognition*, *23*, 1275–1286.

Mayes, A. R. (1988). *Human organic memory disorders*. Cambridge, UK: Cambridge University Press.

Mayes, A. R., Isaac, C. L., Holdstock, J. S., Hunkin, N. M., Montaldi, D., Downes, J. J., MacDonald, C., Cezayirli, E. & Roberts, J. N. (2001). Memory for single items, word pairs, and temporal order of different kinds in a patient with selective hippocampal lesions. *Cognitive Neuropsychology*, *18*, 97–123.

Mayes, A. R., Holdstock, J. S., Isaac, C. L., Hunkin, N. M., & Roberts, N. (2002). Relative sparing of item recognition memory in a patient with adult-onset damage limited to the hippocampus. *Hippocampus*, *12*, 325–340.

Mayes, A. R., Holdstock, J. S., Isaac, C. L., Montaldi, D., Grigor, J., Gummer, A., Cariga, P., Downes, J. J., Tsivilis, D., Gaffan, D., Gong, Q. Y., & Norman, K. A. (2004). Associative recognition in a patient with selective hippocampal lesions and relatively normal item recognition. *Hippocampus*, *14*, 763–784.

Mayes, A., Montaldi, D., & Migo, E. (2007). Associative memory and the medial temporal lobes. *Trends in Cognitive Sciences*, *11*(3), 126–135.

Mayr, U., Diedrichsen, J., Ivry, R., & Keele, S. W. (2006). Dissociating task-set selection from task-set inhibition in the prefrontal cortex. *Journal of Cognitive Neuroscience*, *18*, 14–21.

Meadows, J. C. (1974). Disturbed perception of colours associated with localized cerebral lesions. *Brain*, *97*, 615–632.

Mechelli, A., Gorno-Tempini, M. L., & Price, C. J. (2003). Neuroimaging studies of word and pseudoword reading: Consistencies, inconsistencies, and limitations. *Journal of Cognitive Neuroscience*, *15*, 260–271.

Mechelli, A., Josephs, O., Ralph, M. A. L., McClelland, J. L., & Price, C. J. (2007). Dissociating stimulus-driven semantic and phonological effect during reading and naming. *Human Brain Mapping*, *28*(3), 205–217.

Mehler, J., Dommergues, J. Y., Frauenfelder, U. H., & Segui, J. (1981). The syllable's role in speech segmentation. *Journal of Verbal Learning and Verbal Behavior*, *20*, 298–305.

Meltzoff, A. N. & Moore, M. K. (1977). Imitation of facial and manual gestures by human neonates. *Science*, *198*, 75–78.

Meltzoff, A. N. & Moore, M. K. (1983). Newborn infants imitate adult facial gestures. *Child Development*, *54*, 702–709.

Mendez, M. (2001). Generalized auditory agnosia with spared music recognition in a left-hander: Analysis of a case with right temporal stroke. *Cortex*, *37*, 139–150.

Merzenich, M. M., Knight, P. L., & Roth, G. L. (1973). Cochleotopic organization of primary auditory cortex in the cat. *Brain Research*, *63*, 343–346.

Mesulam, M. M. (1999). Spatial attention and neglect: Parietal, frontal and cingulate contributions to the mental representation and attentional targeting of salient extrapersonal events. *Philosophical Transactions of the Royal Society of London B*, *354*, 1325–1346.

Meuter, R. F. I. & Allport, D. A. (1999). Bilingual language-switching in naming: Asymmetrical costs of language selection. *Journal of Memory and Language*, *40*, 25–40.

Mevorach, C., Humphreys, G. W., & Shalev, L. (2006). Opposite biases in salience-based selection for the left and right posterior parietal cortex *Nature Neuroscience*, *9*(6), 740–742.

Mevorach, C., Hodsoll, J., Allen, H., Shalev, L., & Humphreys, G. (2010). Ignoring the elephant in the room: A neural circuit to downregulate salience. *Journal of Neuroscience*, *30*(17), 6072–6079.

Meyer, D. E. & Schvaneveldt, R. W. (1971). Facilitation in recognizing pairs of words: Evidence of a dependence between retrieval operations. *Journal of Experimental Psychology*, *90*, 227–234.

Miceli, G., Gainotti, G., Caltagirone, C., & Masullo, C. (1980). Some aspects of phonological impairment in aphasia. *Brain and Language*, *11*, 159–169.

Miceli, G., Mazzucchi, A., Menn, L., & Goodglass, H. (1983). Contrasting cases of Italian agrammatic aphasia without comprehension disorder. *Brain and Language*, *19*, 65–97.

Miceli, G., Capasso, R., Daniele, A., Esposito, T., Magarelli, M., & Tomaiuolo, F. (2000). Selective deficit for people's names following left temporal damage: An impairment of domain-specific conceptual knowledge. *Cognitive Neuropsychology*, *17*, 489–516.

Miceli, G., Fouch, E., Capasso, R., Shelton, J. R., Tomaiuolo, F., & Caramazza, A. (2001). The dissociation of color from form and function knowledge. *Nature Neuroscience*, *4*, 662–667.

Miller, E. (1984). Verbal fluency as a function of a measure of verbal intelligence and in relation to different types of pathology. *British Journal of Clinical Psychology*, *23*, 359–369.

Miller, E. K. & Cohen, J. D. (2001). An integrative theory of prefrontal cortex function. *Annual Review of Neuroscience*, *24*, 167–202.

Miller, G. A. (1956). The magical number seven, plus or minus two: Some limits on our capacity for processing information. *Psychological Review*, *63*, 81–97.

Miller, K. F. & Stigler, J. W. (1987). Counting in Chinese: Cultural variation in a basic skill. *Cognitive Development*, *2*, 279–305.

Milner, A. D. & Goodale, M. A. (1995). *The visual brain in action*. Oxford, UK: Oxford University Press.

Milner, A. D., Perrett, D. I., Johnston, R. S., Benson, P. J., Jordan, T. R., Heeley, D. W., Bettucci, D., Mortara, F., Mutani, R., Terazzi, E., & Davidson, D. L. W. (1991a). Perception and action in visual form agnosia. *Brain*, *114*, 405–428.

Milner, B., Corsi, P., & Leonard, G. (1991b). Frontal lobe contribution to recency judgements. *Neuropsychologia*, *29*, 601–618.

Milner, B. (1963). Effects of brain lesions on card sorting. *Archives of Neurology*, *9*, 90–100.

Milner, B. (1966). Amnesia following operation on the medial temporal lobes. In C. W. Whitty & O. L. Zangwill (Eds.), *Amnesia*. London: Butterworth.

Milner, B. (1971). Interhemispheric differences in the location of psychological processes in man. *British Medical Bulletin*, *27*, 272–277.

Miozzo, M. & Caramazza, A. (1998). Varieties of pure alexia: The case of failure to access graphemic representations. *Cognitive Neuropsychology*, *15*, 203–238.

Mitchell, J. P., Heatherton, T. F., & Macrae, C. N. (2002). Distinct neural systems subserve person and object knowledge. *Proceedings of the National Academy of Sciences of the United States of America*, *99*(23), 15238–15243.

Mitchell, J. P., Banaji, M. R., & Macrae, C. N. (2005). General and specific contributions of the medial prefrontal cortex to knowledge about mental states. *NeuroImage*, *28*(4), 757–762.

Mitchell, R. W. & Anderson, J. R. (1993). Discrimination learning of scratching, but failure to obtain imitation and self-recognition in a long-tailed macaque. *Primates*, *34*, 301–309.

Mitchell, T. M., Shinkareva, S. V., Carlson, A., Chang, K.-M., Malave, V. L., Mason, R. A., & Just, M. A. (2008). Predicting human brain activity associated with the meanings of nouns. *Science*, *320*(5880), 1191–1195.

Mithen, S. (2005). *The singing Neanderthal: The origins of music, language, and body*. London: Weidenfield and Nicolson.

Miyawaki, Y., Uchida, H., Yamashita, O., Sato, M.-a., Morito, Y., Tanabe, H. C., Sadato, N., & Kamitani, Y. (2008). Visual image reconstruction from human brain activity using a combination of multiscale local image decoders. *Neuron*, *60*(5), 915–929.

Moen, I. (2000). Foreign accent syndrome: A review of contemporary explanations. *Aphasiology*, *14*, 5–15.

Moll, J., Oliveira-Souza, R., Bramati, I. E., & Grafman, J. (2002). Functional networks in emotional, moral and nonmoral social judgments. *NeuroImage*, *16*, 696–703.

Moll, J., de Oliveira-Souza, R., Moll, F. T., Ignacio, F. A., Bramati, I. E., Caparelli-Daquer, E. M., & Eslinger, P. J. (2005). The moral affiliations of disgust—a functional MRI study. *Cognitive and Behavioral Neurology*, *18*(1), 68–78.

Moniz, E. (1937). Prefrontal leucotomy in the treatment of mental disorders. *American Journal of Psychiatry*, *93*, 1379–1385.

Moniz, E. (1954). How I succeeded in performing the prefrontal leucotomy. *Journal of Clinical and Experimental Psychopathology*, *15*, 373–379.

Monsell, S. (2003). Task switching. *Trends in Cognitive Sciences*, *7*, 134–140.

Monti, A., Cogiamanian, F., Marceglia, S., Ferrucci, R., Mameli, F., Mrakic-Sposta, S., Vergari., M., Zafo, S., & Priori, A. (2008). Improved naming after transcranial direct current stimulation in aphasia. *Journal of Neurology Neurosurgery and Psychiatry*, *79*(4), 451–453.

Monti, M. M., Vanhaudenhuyse, A., Coleman, M. R., Boly, M., Pickard, J. D., Tshibanda, L., Owen, A. M., & Laureys, S. (2010). Willful modulation of brain activity in disorders of consciousness. *New England Journal of Medicine*, *362*(7), 579–589.

Moore, T. & Fallah, M. (2001). Control of eye movements and spatial attention. *Proceedings of the National Academy of Sciences of the United States of America*, *98*(3), 1273–1276.

Moran, J. & Desimone, R. (1985). Selective attention gates visual processing in the extrastriate cortex. *Science*, *229*(4715), 782–784.

Morcom, A. M. & Fletcher, P. C. (2007). Does the brain have a baseline? Why we should be resisting a rest. *NeuroImage*, *37*(4), 1073–1082.

Morris, J. S., Frith, C. D., Perrett, D., Rowland, D., Young, A. W., Calder, A. J., & Dolan, R. J. (1996). A differential neural response in the human amygdala to fearful and happy facial expressions. *Nature*, *383*, 812–815.

Morris, R. G., Miotto, E. C., Feigenbaum, J. D., Bullock, P., & Polkey, C. E. (1997). The effect of goal-subgoal conflict on planning ability after frontal-and temporal-lobe lesions in humans. *Neuropsychologia*, *35*, 1147–1157.

Morris, J. S., Friston, K. J., Buechel, C., Frith, C. D., Young, A. W., Calder, A. J., & Dolan, R. J. (1998). A neuromodulatory role for the human amygdala in processing emotional facial expressions. *Brain*, *121*, 47–57.

Morris, J. S., Ohman, A., & Dolan, R. (1999). A sub-cortical pathway to the right amygdala mediating "unseen" fear. *Proceedings of the National Academy of Science, USA*, *96*, 1680–1685.

Morris, R. G. M., Garrud, P., Rawlins, J. N. P., & O'Keefe, J. (1982). Place navigation impaired in rats with hippocampal lesions. *Nature*, *297*, 681–683.

Mort, D. J., Malhotra, P., Mannan, S. K., Rorden, C., Pambajian, A., Kennard, C., & Husain, M. (2003). The anatomy of visual neglect. *Brain*, *126*, 1986–1997.

Morton, J. (1969). Interaction of information in word recognition. *Psychological Review*, *76*, 165–178.

Morton, J. (1980). The logogen model and orthographic structure. In U. Frith (Ed.), *Cognitive processes in spelling*. London: Academic Press.

Moscovitch, M., Winocur, G., & Behrmann, M. (1997). What is special about face recognition? Nineteen experiments on a person with visual object agnosia and dyslexia but normal face recognition. *Journal of Cognitive Neuroscience*, *9*, 555–604.

Moyer, R. S. & Landauer, T. K. (1967). Time required for judgements of numerical inequality. *Nature*, *215*, 1519–1520.

Mullally, S. L., Intraub, H., & Maguire, E. A. (2012). Attenuated Boundary Extension Produces a Paradoxical Memory Advantage in Amnesic Patients. *Current Biology*, *22*(4), 261–268.

Mummery, C. J., Patterson, K. E., Price, C. J., Ashburner, J., Frackowiak, R. S. J., & Hodges, J. R. (2000). A voxel-based morphometry study of semantic dementia: Relationship between temporal lobe atrophy and semantic memory. *Annals of Neurology*, *47*, 36–45.

Murata, A., Gallese, V., Luppino, G., Kaseda, M., & Sakata, H. (2000). Selectivity for the size, shape and orientation of objects for grasping in neurons of monkey parietal area AIP. *Journal of Neurophysiology*, *83*, 2580–2601.

Murray, E. A. & Baxter, M. G. (2006). Cognitive neuroscience and nonhuman primates: Lesion studies. In C. Senior, T. Russell, & M. S. Gazzaniga (Eds.), *Methods in mind*. Cambridge, MA: MIT Press.

Murray, E. A., & Bussey, T. J. (1999). Perceptual-mnemonic functions of the perirhinal cortex. *Trends in Cognitive Sciences*, *3*, 142–151.

Mushiake, H., Saito, N., Sakamoto, K., Itoyama, Y., & Tanji, J. (2006). Activity in the lateral prefrontal cortex reflects multiple steps of future events in action plans. *Neuron*, *50*(4), 631–641.

Musiek, F. E., Baran, J. A., Shinn, J. B., Guenette, L., & Zaidan, E. (2007). Central deafness: An audiological case study. *International Journal of Audiology*, *46*, 433–441.

Näätänen, R., Gaillard, A. W. K., & Mantysalo, S. (1978). Early selective-attention effect on evoked-potential reinterpreted. *Acta Psychologica*, *42*, 313–329.

Näätänen, R., Tervaniemi, M., Sussman, E., Paavilainen, P., & Winkler, I. (2001). "Primitive intelligence" in the auditory cortex. *Trends in Neurosciences*, *24*, 283–288.

Nadel, L. & Moscovitch, M. (1997). Memory consolidation, retrograde amnesia and the hippocampal complex. *Current Opinion in Neurobiology*, *7*, 217–222.

Nakamura, K., Honda, M., Okada, T., Hankawa, T., Toma, K., Fukuyama, H., Konishi, J., & Shibasaki, H. (2000). Participation of the left posterior inferior temporal cortex in writing and mental recall of Kanji orthography: A functional MRI study. *Brain*, *123*, 954–967.

Nan, Y., Sun, Y., & Peretz, I. (2010). Congenital amusia in speakers of a tone language: Association with lexical tone agnosia. *Brain*, *133*, 2635–2642.

Naselaris, T., Prenger, R. J., Kay, K. N., Oliver, M., & Gallant, J. L. (2009). Bayesian Reconstruction of Natural Images from Human Brain Activity. *Neuron*, *63*(6), 902–915.

Nath, A. R. & Beauchamp, M. S. (2012). A neural basis for interindividual differences in the McGurk effect, a multisensory speech illusion. *NeuroImage*, *59*(1), 781–787.

Nelson, H. E. (1976). A modified card sorting test sensitive to frontal lobe deficits. *Cortex*, *12*, 313–324.

Nelson, M. E. & Bower, J. M. (1990). Brain maps and parallel computers. *Trends in Neurosciences*, *13*, 403–408.

Nelson, T. M. & MacDonald, G. A. (1971). Lateral organization, perceived depth and title preference in pictures. *Perceptual and Motor Skills*, *33*, 983–986.

Nestor, P. J., Graham, K. S., Bozeat, S., Simons, J. S., & Hodges, J. R. (2002). Memory consolidation and the hippocampus: Further evidence from studies of autobiographical memory in semantic dementia and frontal variant frontotemporal dementia. *Neuropsychologia*, *40*, 633–654.

Newbury, D. F., Bonora, M., Lamb, J. A., Fisher, S. E., Lai, C. S. L., Baird, G., Jannoun, L., Slonims, V., Stott, C. M., Merricks, M. J., Bolton, P. F., Bailey, A. J., & Monaco, A. P. (2002). FOXP2 is not a major susceptibility gene for autism or specific language impairment. *American Journal of Human Genetics*, *70*, 1318–1327.

Newman, S. D., Just, M. A., Keller, T. A., Roth, J., & Carpenter, P. A. (2003). Differential effects of syntactic and semantic processing on the subregions of Broca's area. *Cognitive Brain Research*, *16*, 297–307.

Nicholls, M.E.R., Loftus, A., Mayer, K. & Mattingley, J.B. (2007). Things that go bump in the right: The effect of unimanual activity on rightward collisions. *Neuropsychologia*, *45*(5), 1122–1126.

Nichols, R. C. (1978). Twin studies of ability, personality and interests. *Homo*, *29*, 158–173.

Nieder, A. (2012). Supramodal numerosity selectivity of neurons in primate prefrontal and posterior parietal cortices. *Proceedings of the National Academy of Sciences of the United States of America*, *109*(29), 11860–11865.

Nieder, A. (2013). Coding of abstract quantity by "number neurons" of the primate brain. *Journal of Comparative Physiology a-Neuroethology Sensory Neural and Behavioral Physiology*, *199*(1), 1–16.

Nieder, A. & Dehaene, S. (2009). Representation of number in the brain *Annual Review of Neuroscience* (Vol. 32, pp. 185–208).

Nieder, A. & Miller, E. K. (2004). A parietofronto network for visual numerical information in the monkey. *Proceedings of the National Academy of Science, USA*, *101*, 7457–7462.

Nieder, A., Diester, I., & Tudusciuc, O. (2006). Temporal and spatial enumeration processes in the primate parietal cortex. *Science*, *313*(5792), 1431–1435.

Niswander, E., Pollatsek, A., & Rayner, K. (2000). The processing of derived and inflected suffixed words during reading. *Language and Cognitive Processes*, *15*, 389–420.

Nitsche, M. A., Cohen, L. G., Wassermann, E. M., Priori, A., Lang, N., Antal, A., & Pascual-Leone, A. (2008). Transcranial direct current stimulation: State of the art 2008. *Brain Stimulation, 1*, 206–223.

Nitsche, M. A., Liebetanz, D., Lang, N., Antal, A., Tergau, F., & Paulus, W. (2003). Safety criteria for transcranial direct current stimulation (tDCS) in humans. *Clinical Neurophysiology*, *114*(11), 2220–2222.

Nobre, A. C., Gitelman, D. R., Dias, E. C., & Mesulam, M. M. (2000). Covert visual spatial orienting and saccades: Overlapping neural systems. *NeuroImage*, *11*(3), 210–216.

Nolan, K. A. & Caramazza, A. (1982). Modality-independent impairments in word processing in a deep dyslexia patient. *Brain and Language*, *16*, 237–264.

Noppeney, U. & Price, C. J. (2004). An fMRI study of syntactic adaptation. *Journal of Cognitive Neuroscience*, *16*, 702–713.

Norman, D. A. & Shallice, T. (1986). Attention to action. In R. J. Davidson, G. E. Schwartz, & D. Shapiro (Eds.), *Consciousness and self regulation*. New York: Plenum Press.

Norman, K. A., Polyn, S. M., Detre, G. J., & Haxby, J. V. (2006). Beyond mind-reading: Multi-voxel pattern analysis of fMRI data. *Trends in Cognitive Sciences*, *10*, 424–430.

Norris, D. (1986). Word recognition: Context effects without priming. *Cognition*, *22*, 93–136.

Nuerk, H.-C., Weger, U., & Willmes, K. (2001). Decade breaks in the mental number line? Putting the tens and units back in different bins. *Cognition*, *82*, B25–B33.

Nunes, T., Schliemann, A. D., & Carraher, D. W. (1993). *Street mathematics and school mathematics*. Cambridge, UK: Cambridge University Press.

Nunez, P. L. (1981). *Electric fields of the brain: The neurophysics of EEG*. London: Oxford University Press.

Nyberg, L. & Tulving, E. (1996). Classifying human long-term memory: Evidence from converging dissociations. *European Journal of Cognitive Psychology*, *8*, 163–183.

O'Craven, K. M., Downing, P. E., & Kanwisher, N. (1999). fMRI evidence for objects as the units of attentional selection. *Nature*, *401*(6753), 584–587.

O'Craven, K. M. & Kanwisher, N. (2000). Mental imagery of faces and places activates corresponding stimulus-specific brain regions. *Journal of Cognitive Neuroscience*, *12*, 1013–1023.

O'Doherty, J., Kringelbach, M. L., Rolls, E. T., Hornak, J., & Andrews, C. (2001). Abstract reward and punishment representations in the human orbitofrontal cortex. *Nature Neuroscience*, *4*, 95–102.

O'Keefe, J. (1976). Place units in the hippocampus of the freely moving rat. *Experimental Neurology, 51*, 78–109.

O'Keefe, J. & Nadel, L. (1978). *The hippocampus as a cognitive map.* Oxford, UK: Oxford University Press.

O'Leary, D. D. M. (1989). Do cortical areas emerge from a protocortex? *Trends in Neurosciences, 12*, 400–406.

Oberman, L. M., Hubbard, E. M., McCleery, J. P., Altschuler, E. L., Ramachandran, V. S., & Pineda, J. A. (2005). EEG evidence for mirror neuron dysfunction in autism spectrum disorders. *Cognitive Brain Research, 24*, 190–198.

Oberman, L. M. & Ramachandran, V. S. (2007). The simulating social mind: The role of the mirror neuron system and simulation in the social and communicative deficits of autism spectrum disorders. *Psychological Bulletin, 133*(2), 310–327.

Oberman, L. M., Winklelman, P., & Ramachandran, V. S. (2007). Face to face: Blocking facial mimicry can selectively impair recognition of emotional expressions. *Social Neuroscience, 2*(3–4), 167–178.

Ochsner, K. N., Bunge, S. A., Gross, J. J., & Gabrieli, J. D. E. (2002). Rethinking feelings: An fMRI study of the cognitive regulation of emotion. *Journal of Cognitive Neuroscience, 14*(8), 1215–1229.

Ochsner, K. N., Ray, R. D., Cooper, J. C., Robertson, E. R., Chopra, S., Gabrieli, J. D. E., & Gross, J. J. (2004). For better or for worse: Neural systems supporting the cognitive down- and up-regulation of negative emotion. *NeuroImage, 23*(2), 483–499.

Ogawa, S., Lee, T. M., Kay, A. R., & Tank, D. W. (1990). Brain magnetic resonance imaging with contrast dependent on blood oxygenation. *Proceedings of the National Academy of Science, USA, 87*, 9862–9872.

Ohman, A. & Mineka, S. (2001). Fears, phobias, and preparedness: Toward an evolved module of fear and fear learning. *Psychological Review, 108*, 483–522.

Ohman, A. & Soares, J. J. F. (1994). Unconscious anxiety: Phobic responses to masked stimuli. *Journal of Abnormal Psychology, 102*, 121–132.

Ohman, A., Flykt, A., & Esteves, F. (2001). Emotion drives attention: Detecting the snake in the grass. *Journal of Experimental Psychology: General, 130*, 466–478.

Ohyama, T., Nores, W. L., Murphy, M., & Mauk, M. D. (2003). What the cerebellum computes. *Trends in Neurosciences, 26*, 222–227.

Oliveri, M., Finocchiar, C., Shapiro, K., Gangitano, M., Caramazza, A., & Pascual-Leone, A. (2004). All talk and no action: A transcranial magnetic stimulation study of motor cortex activation during action word production. *Journal of Cognitive Neuroscience, 16*, 374–381.

Olsson, A. & Phelps, E. A. (2004). Learned fear of "unseen" faces after Pavlovian, observational, and instructed fear. *Psychological Science, 15*(12), 822–828.

Öngür, D. & Price, J. L. (2000). The organization of networks within the orbital and medial prefrontal cortex of rats, monkeys and humans. *Cerebral Cortex, 10*, 206–219.

Oppenheim, G. M. & Dell, G. S. (2008). Inner speech slips exhibit lexical bias, but not the phonemic similarity effect. *Cognition, 106*(1), 528–537.

Owen, A. M., Evans, A. C., & Petrides, M. P. (1996). Evidence of a two-stage model of spatial working memory processing within lateral prefrontal cortex: A positron emission tomography study. *Cerebral Cortex, 6*, 31–38.

Owen, A. M., Coleman, M. R., Boly, M., Davis, M. H., Laureys, S., & Pickard, J. D. (2006). Detecting awareness in the vegetative state. *Science, 313*(5792), 1402–1402.

Ozonoff, S., Pennington, B. F., & Rogers, S. J. (1991). Executive function deficits in high-functioning autistic individuals: Relationship to theory of mind. *Journal of Child Psychology and Psychiatry, 32*, 1081–1105.

Packard, M. G. & Knowlton, B. J. (2002). Learning and memory functions of the basal ganglia. *Annual Review of Neuroscience, 25*, 563–593.

Pakkenberg, B. & Gundersen, H. J. G. (1997). Neocortical neuron number in humans: effect of sex and age. *Journal of Comparative Neurology, 384*, 312–320.

Pallier, C., Devauchelle, A.-D., & Dehaene, S. (2011). Cortical representation of the constituent structure of sentences. *Proceedings of the National Academy of Sciences of the United States of America*, *108*(6), 2522–2527.

Palmer, S. E., Rosch, E., & Chase, P. (1981). Canonical perspective and the perception of objects. In J. Long, & A. D. Baddeley (Eds.), *Attention and performance IX*. Hillsdale, NJ: Lawrence Erlbaum.

Papanicolaou, A. C. (1995). An introduction to magnetoencephalography with some applications. *Brain and Cognition*, *27*, 331–352.

Papez, J. W. (1937). A proposed mechanism of emotion. *Archives of Neurology and Psychiatry*, *38*(4), 725–743.

Parkin, A. J. (1982). Residual learning capacity in organic amnesia. *Cortex*, *18*, 417–440.

Parkin, A. J. (1996). *Explorations in Cognitive Neuropsychology*. Oxford, UK: Blackwell.

Parkin, A. J. (1999) *Memory and amnesia*. Hove, UK: Psychology Press.

Parkin, A. J. (2001). The structure and mechanisms of memory. In B. Rapp (Ed.), *The handbook of cognitive neuropsychology: What deficits reveal about the human mind*. New York: Psychology Press.

Parkin, A. J. & Leng, N. R. C. (1993). *Neuropsychology of the amnesic syndrome*. Hove, UK: Psychology Press.

Parkin, A. J., Montaldi, D., Leng, N. R. C., & Hunkin, N. M. (1990). Contextual cueing effects in the remote memory of alcoholic Korsakoff patients and normal subjects. *Quarterly Journal of Experimental Psychology*, *42A*, 585–596.

Parkman, J. M. & Groen, G. (1971). Temporal aspects of simple additions and comparison. *Journal of Experimental Psychology*, *92*, 437–438.

Pascual-Leone, A. & Torres, F. (1993). Plasticity of sensorimotor cortex representation of the reading finger in Braille readers. *Brain*, *116*, 39–52.

Pascual-Leone, A., Bartres-Faz, D., & Keenan, J. P. (1999). Transcranial magnetic stimulation: Studying the brain-behavior relationship by induction of "virtual lesions." *Philosophical Transactions of the Royal Society of London B*, *354*, 1229–1238.

Passingham, R. E. (1988). Premotor cortex and preparation for movement. *Experimental Brain Research*, *70*, 590–596.

Patel, A. D., Peretz, I., Tramo, M., & Labrecque, R. (1998). Processing prosodic and musical patterns: A neuropsychological investigation. *Brain and Language*, *61*, 123–144.

Patriot, A., Grafman, J., Sadato, N., Flitman, S., & Wild, K. (1996). Brain activation during script event processing. *Journal of Cognitive Neuroscience*, *7*, 761–766.

Patterson, K. E. (1981). Neuropsychological approaches to the study of reading. *British Journal of Psychology*, *72*, 151–174.

Patterson, K. E. (2007). The reign of typicality in semantic memory. *Philosophical Transactions of the Royal Society B-Biological Sciences*, *362*(1481), 813–821.

Patterson, K. E. & Kay, J. (1982). Letter-by-letter reading: Psychological descriptions of a neurological syndrome. *Quarterly Journal of Experimental Psychology*, *34A*, 411–441.

Patterson, K. E. & Marcel, A. J. (1992). Phonological ALEXIA or PHONOLOGICAL alexia? In J. Alegria, D. Holender, J. J. de Morais, & M. Radeus (Eds.), *Analytic approaches to human cognition*. Amsterdam: Elsevier.

Patterson, K. E., & Wing, A. M. (1989). Processes in handwriting: A case for case. *Cognitive Neuropsychology*, *6*, 1–23.

Patterson, K. E., Nestor, P. J., & Rogers, T. T. (2007). Where do you know what you know? The representation of semantic knowledge in the human brain. *Nature Reviews Neuroscience*, *8*(12), 976–987.

Patterson, K. E., Marshall, J. C., & Coltheart, M. (1985). *Surface dyslexia: Neuropsychological and cognitive studies of phonological reading*. Hove, UK: Psychology Press.

Patterson, K. E., Suzuki, T., & Wydell, T. N. (1996). Interpreting a case of Japanese phonological alexia: The key is in phonology. *Cognitive Neuropsychology*, *13*, 803–822.

Patterson, R. D., Uppenkamp, S., Johnsrude, I. S., & Griffiths, T. D. (2002). The processing of temporal pitch and melody information in auditory cortex. *Neuron, 36,* 767–776.

Paulesu, E., Frith, C. D., & Frackowiak, R. S. J. (1993). The neural correlates of the verbal component of working memory. *Nature, 362,* 342–345.

Paulesu, E., McCrory, E., Fazio, F., Menoncello, L., Brunswick, N., Cappa, S. F., Cotelli, M., Cossu, G., Corte, F., Lorusso, M., Pesenti, S., Gallagher, A., Perani, D., Price, C., Frith, C. D., & Frith, U. (2000). A cultural effect on brain function. *Nature Neuroscience, 3,* 91–96.

Paulesu, E., Demonet, J. F., Fazio, F., McCrory, E., Chanoine, V., Brunswick, N., Cappa, S. F., Cossu, G., Habib, M., Frith, C. D., & Frith, U. (2001). Dyslexia: Cultural diversity and biological unity. *Science, 5511,* 2165–2167.

Paus, T. (1999). Imaging the brain before, during and after transcranial magnetic stimulation. *Neuropsychologia, 37,* 207–217.

Pavani, F., Ladavas, E., & Driver, J. (2002). Selective deficit of auditory localisation in patients with visuospatial neglect. *Neuropsychologia, 40,* 291–301.

Payne, D. G., Elie, C. J., Blackwell, J. M., & Neuschatz, J. S. (1996). Memory illusions: Recalling, recognizing and recollecting events that never occurred. *Journal of Memory and Language, 35,* 261–285.

Pearce, A. J., Thickbroom, G. W., Byrnes, M. L., & Mastaglia, F. L. (2000). Functional reorganisation of the corticomotor projection to the hand in skilled racquet players. *Experimental Brain Research, 130,* 238–243.

Pell, M. D. (1999). The temporal organization of affective and non-affective speech in patients with right-hemisphere infarcts. *Cortex, 35,* 455–477.

Pellegrino, G. di, Fadiga, L., Fogassi, L., Gallese, V., & Rizzolatti, G. (1992). Understanding motor events: A neurophysiological study. *Experimental Brain Research, 91,* 176–180.

Penfield, W. & Rasmussen, T. L. (1950). *The cerebral cortex of man: A clinical study of localisation of function.* New York: Macmillan.

Perani, D. & Abutalebi, J. (2005). The neural basis of first and second language processing. *Current Opinion in Neurobiology, 15*(2), 202–206.

Perenin, M.-T. & Vighetto, A. (1988). Optic ataxia: A specific disruption in visuomotor mechanisms. I. Different aspects of the deficit in reaching for objects. *Brain, 111,* 643–674.

Peretz, I. (1996). Can we lose memories for music? The case of music agnosia in a nonmusician. *Journal of Cognitive Neuroscience, 8,* 481–496.

Peretz, I. (2006). The nature of music from a biological perspective. *Cognition, 100,* 1–32.

Peretz, I. & Coltheart, M. (2003). Modularity of music processing. *Nature Neuroscience, 6,* 688–691.

Perret, E. (1974). The left frontal lobe in man and the suppression of habitual responses in verbal categorical behavior. *Neuropsychologia, 12,* 323–330.

Perrett, D. I. & Mistlin, A. (1990). Perception of facial characteristics by monkeys. In W. Stebbins, & M. Berkley (Eds.), *Comparative perception. Volume 2: Complex signals.* New York: Wiley.

Perrett, D. I., Smith, P., Potter, D., Mistlin, A., Head, A., Milner, A. D., & Jeeves, M. (1985). Visual cells in the temporal cortex sensitive to face view and gaze direction. *Proceedings of the Royal Society of London B, 223,* 293–317.

Perrett, D. I., Harries, M. H., Bevan, R., Thomas, S., Benson, P. J., Mistlin, A. J., Chitty, A. J., Hietanen, J. K., & Ortega, J. E. (1989). Frameworks of analysis for the neural representation of animate objects and actions. *Journal of Experimental Biology, 146,* 87–113.

Perrett, D. I., Hietanen, J. K., Oram, M. W., & Benson, P. J. (1992). Organization and functions of cells responsive to faces in the temporal cortex. *Philosophical Transactions of the Royal Society London B, 335,* 23–30.

Perrett, D. I., Oram, M. W., & Wachsmuth, E. (1998). Evidence accumulation in cell populations responsive to faces: An account of generalisation of recognition without mental transformations. *Cognition, 67,* 111–145.

Perry, J. L. & Carrol, M. E. (2008). The role of impulsive behavior in drug abuse. *Psychopharmacology*, *200*(1), 1–26.

Pesenti, M., Zago, L., Crivello, F., Mellet, E., Samson, D., Duroux, B., Seron, X., Mazoyer, B., & Tzourio-Mazoyer, N. (2001). Mental calculation in a prodigy is sustained by right prefrontal and medial temporal areas. *Nature Neuroscience*, *4*, 103–107.

Petersen, S. E., Fox, P. T., Posner, M. I., Mintun, M., & Raichle, M. E. (1988). Positron emission tomographic studies of the cortical anatomy of single-word processing. *Nature*, *331*, 585–589.

Petersen, S. E., Fox, P. T., Snyder, A. Z., & Raichle, M. E. (1990). Activation of extrastriate and frontal cortical areas by visual words and word-like stimuli. *Science*, *249*, 1041–1044.

Petersson, K. M., Nichols, T. E., Poline, J.-B., & Holmes, A. P. (1999a). Statistical limitations in functional neuroimaging I: Non-inferential methods and statistical models. *Philosophical Transactions of the Royal Society of London B*, *354*, 1239–1260.

Petersson, K. M., Nichols, T. E., Poline, J.-B., & Holmes, A. P. (1999b). Statistical limitations in functional neuroimaging II: Signal detection and statistical inference. *Philosophical Transactions of the Royal Society of London B*, *354*, 1261–1281.

Petersson, K. M., Reis, A., Askelof, S., Castro-Caldas, A., & Ingvar, M. (2000). Language processing modulated by literacy: A network analysis of verbal repetition in literate and illiterate subjects. *Journal of Cognitive Neuroscience*, *12*, 364–382.

Petkov, C. I., Kayser, C., Steudel, T., Whittingstall, K., Augath, M., & Logothetis, N. K. (2008). A voice region in the monkey brain. *Nature Neuroscience*, *11*, 367–374.

Petrides, M. (1995). Impairments on nonspatial self-ordered and externally ordered working memory tasks after lesions of the mid-dorsal part of the lateral frontal cortex in monkey. *Journal of Neuroscience*, *15*, 359–375.

Petrides, M. (1996). Specialised systems for the processing of mnemonic information within the primate frontal cortex. *Philosophical Transactions of the Royal Society of London B*, *351*, 1455–1462.

Petrides, M. (2000). Middorsolateral and midventrolateral prefrontal cortex: Two levels of executive control for the processing of mnemonic information. In S. Monsell & J. Driver (Eds.), *Attention and performance XVIII: Control of cognitive performance*. Cambridge, MA: MIT Press.

Petrides, M. (2005). Lateral prefrontal cortex: Architectonic and functional organization. *Philosophical Transactions of the Royal Society B*, *360*, 781–795.

Petrides, M. & Milner, B. (1982). Deficits on subject-ordered tasks after frontal and temporal lesions in man. *Neuropsychologia*, *20*, 249–262.

Pfaus, J. G., Damsma, G., Nomikos, G. G., Wenkstern, D. G., Blaha, C. D., Phillips, A. G., & Fibiger, H. C. (1990). Sexual-behavior enhances central dopamine transmission in the male-rat. *Brain Research*, *530*(2), 345–348.

Pflugshaupt, T., Gutbrod, K., Wurtz, P., von Wartburg, R., Nyffeler, T., de Haan, B., & Mueri, R. M. (2009). About the role of visual field defects in pure alexia. *Brain*, *132*, 1907–1917.

Phelps, E. A. (2006). Emotion and cognition: Insights from studies of the human amygdala. *Annual Review of Psychology*, *57*, 27–53.

Philipose, L. E., Gottesman, R. F., Newhart, M., Kleinman, J. T., Herskovits, E. H., Pawlak, M. A., Marsh, E. B., Davis, C., Heidler-Gary, J., & Hillis, A. E. (2007). Neural regions essential for reading and spelling of words and pseudo words. *Annals of Neurology*, *62*, 481–492.

Phillips, M. L., Young, A. W., Senior, C., Brammer, M., Andrews, C., Calder, A. J., Bullmore, E. T., Perrett, D. I., Rowland, D., Williams, S. C. R., Gray, J. A., & David, A. S. (1997). A specific neural substrate for perceiving facial expressions of disgust. *Nature*, *389*, 495–498.

Phillips, R. G. & Ledoux, J. E. (1992). Differential contribution of amygdala and hippocampus to cued and contextual fear conditioning. *Behavioral Neuroscience*, *106*(2), 274–285.

Phillips, W. A., Zeki, S., & Barlow, H. B. (1984). Localisation of function in the cerebral cortex: past, present and future. *Brain*, *107*, 327–361.

Piazza, M., Facoetti, A., Trussardi, A. N., Berteletti, I., Conte, S., Lucangeli, D., Dehaene, S. & Zorzi, M. (2010). Developmental trajectory of number acuity reveals a severe impairment in developmental dyscalculia. *Cognition*, *116*(1), 33–41.

Piazza, M., Izard, V., Pinel, P., Le Bihan, D., & Dehaene, S. (2004). Tuning curves for approximate numerosity in the human intraparietal sulcus. *Neuron*, *44*, 547–555.

Piazza, M., Pinel, P., Le Bihan, D., & Dehaene, S. (2007). A magnitude code common to numerosities and number symbols in human intraparietal cortex. *Neuron*, *53*(2), 293–305.

Pica, P., Lemer, C., Izard, V., & Dehaene, S. (2004). Exact and approximate arithmetic in an Amazonion indigene group with a reduced number lexicon. *Science*, *306*, 499–503.

Picton, T. W., Bentin, S., Berg, P., Donchin, E., Hillyard, S. A., Johnson, R., Miller, G. A., Ritter, W., Ruchkin, D. S., Rugg, M. D., & Taylor, M. J. (2000). Guidelines for using human event-related potentials to study cognition: Recording standards and publication criteria. *Psychophysiology*, *37*, 127–152.

Picton, T. W., Stuss, D. T., Alexander, M. P., Shallice, T., Binns, M. A., & Gillingham, S. (2007). Effects of focal frontal lesions on response inhibition. *Cerebral Cortex*, *17*(4), 826–838.

Pineda, J. A. (2005). The functional significance of mu rhythms: Translating "seeing" and "hearing" into "doing." *Brain Research Reviews*, *50*(1), 57–68.

Pinel, P. & Dehaene, S. (2010). Beyond hemispheric dominance: Brain regions underlying the joint lateralization of language and arithmetic to the left hemisphere. *Journal of Cognitive Neuroscience*, *22*(1), 48–66.

Pinel, P., Dehaene, S., Riviere, D., & Le Bihan, D. (2001). Modulation of parietal activation by semantic distance in a number comparison task. *NeuroImage*, *14*, 1013–1026.

Pinker, S. (1994). *The language instinct*. London: Penguin.

Pinker, S. (1997). *How the mind works*. New York: Norton.

Pinker, S. & Prince, A. (1988). On language and connectionism: Analysis of a parallel distributed processing model of language acquisition. *Cognition*, *28*, 73–193.

Pitcher, D., Garrido, L., Walsh, V., & Duchaine, B. C. (2008). Transcranial magnetic stimulation disrupts the perception and embodiment of facial expressions. *Journal of Neuroscience*, *28*(36), 8929–8933.

Pittenger, C. & Kandel, E. R. (2003). In search of general mechanisms for long-lasting plasticity: Aplysia and the hippocampus *Philosophical Transactions of the Royal Society of London Series B*, *1432*, 757–763.

Plassmann, H., O'Doherty, J., Shiv, B., & Rangel, A. (2008). Marketing actions can modulate neural representations of experienced pleasantness. *Proceedings of the National Academy of Sciences of the United States of America*, *105*(3), 1050–1054.

Plaut, D. C. (1995). Double dissociation without modularity: Evidence from connectionist neuropsychology. *Journal of Clinical and Experimental Neuropsychology*, *17*, 291–321.

Plomin, R., DeFries, J. C., & Loehlin, J. C. (1977). Genotype-environment interaction and correlation in the analysis of human behavior. *Psychological Bulletin*, *84*, 309–322.

Plomin, R., DeFries, J. C., McClearn, G. E., & McGuffin, P. (2001). *Behavioral genetics* (4th edition). New York: Worth Publishers.

Plutchik, R. (1980). *Emotion: A psychoevolutionary synthesis*. New York: Harper & Row.

Pollatsek, A., Bolozky, S., Well, A. D., & Rayner, K. (1981). Asymmetries in the perceptual span for Israeli readers. *Brain and Language*, *14*, 174–180.

Pollatsek, A., Reichle, E. D., & Rayner, K. (2006). Tests of the E-Z Reader model: Exploring the interface between cognition and eye-movement control. *Cognitive Psychology*, *52*(1), 1–56.

Polyn, S. M., Natu, V. S., Cohen, J. D., & Norman, K. A. (2005). Category-specific cortical activity precedes retrieval during memory search. *Science*, *310*(5756), 1963–1966.

Posner, M. I. (1978). *Chronometric explorations of mind*. Hillsdale, NJ: Lawrence Erlbaum.

Posner, M. I. (1980). Orienting of attention: The VIIth Sir Frederic Bartlett Lecture. *Quarterly Journal of Experimental Psychology*, *32*, 3–25.

Posner, M. I. (2012). Attentional networks and consciousness. *Frontiers in psychology*, *3*.

Posner, M. I. & Cohen, Y. (1984). Components of visual orienting. In H. Bouma & D. G. Bouwhuis (Eds.), *Attention and performance X: Control of language processes*. Philadelphia: Lawrence Erlbaum.

Posner, M. I. & Petersen, S. E. (1990). The attentional system of the human brain. *Annual Review of Neuroscience*, *13*, 25–42.

Pouget, A. & Driver, J. (2000). Relating unilateral neglect to the neural coding of space. *Current Opinion in Neurobiology*, *10*, 242–249.

Poulton, R., Caspi, A., Moffitt, T. E., Cannon, M., Murray, R. M., & Harrington, H. L. (2000). Children's self-reported psychiatric symptoms predict adult schizophreniform disorders: A 15-year longitudinal study. *Archives of General Psychiatry*, *57*, 1053–1058.

Power, R. & Dal Martello, M. F. (1997). From 834 to eighty thirty four: The reading of Arabic numerals by seven-year-old children. *Mathematical Cognition*, *3*, 63–85.

Price, C. J. & Devlin, J. T. (2003). The myth of the visual word form area. *NeuroImage*, *19*, 473–481.

Price, C. J. & Devlin, J. T. (2011). The interactive account of ventral occipitotemporal contributions to reading. *Trends in Cognitive Sciences*, *15*(6), 246–253.

Price, C. J., Wise, R., Ramsay, S., Friston, K., Howard, D., Patterson, K. E., & Frackowiak, R. (1992). Regional response differences within the human auditory-cortex when listening to words. *Neuroscience Letters*, *146*, 179–182.

Price, C. J., Moore, C. J., Humphreys, G. W., Frackowiak, R. S. J., & Friston, K. J. (1996a). The neural regions sustaining object recognition and naming. *Proceedings of the Royal Society of London B*, *263*, 1501–1507.

Price, C. J., Wise, R. J. S., & Frackowiak, R. S. J. (1996b). Demonstrating the implicit processing of words and pseudowords. *Cerebral Cortex*, *6*, 62–70.

Price, C. J., Warburton, E. A., Moore, C. J., Frackowiak, R. S. J., & Friston, K. J. (2001). Dynamic diaschisis: Anatomically remote and context-sensitive human brain lesions. *Journal of Cognitive Neuroscience*, *13*, 419–429.

Purves, D. (1994). *Neural activity and the growth of the brain*. Cambridge, UK: Cambridge University Press.

Quiroga, R. G., Reddy, L., Kreiman, G., Koch, C., & Fried, I. (2005). Invariant visual representation by single neurons in the human brain. *Nature*, *435*, 1102–1107.

Rabbitt, P. M. A. (1966). Errors and error-correction in choice-response tasks. *Journal of Experimental Psychology*, *71*, 264–272.

Race, E. A., Shanker, S., & Wagner, A. D. (2009). Neural priming in human frontal cortex: Multiple forms of learning reduce demands on the prefrontal executive system. *Journal of Cognitive Neuroscience*, *21*(9), 1766–1781.

Radach, R., Inhoff, A., & Heller, D. (2004). Orthographic regularity gradually modulates saccade amplitudes in reading. *European Journal of Cognitive Psychology*, *16*, 27–51.

Raichle, M. E. (1987). Circulatory and metabolic correlates of brain function in normal humans. In F. Plum & V. Mountcastle (Eds.), *Handbook of physiology: The nervous system*. Baltimore, MD: Williams & Wilkins.

Raichle, M. E. (1998). Behind the scenes of functional brain imaging: A historical and physiological perspective. *Proceedings of the National Academy of Science, USA*, *95*, 765–772.

Raichle, M. E., MacLoed, A. M., Snyder, A. Z., Powers, W. J., Gusnard, D. A., & Shulman, G. L. (2001). A default mode of brain function. *Proceedings of the National Academy of Science, USA*, *98*, 676–682.

Rakic, P. (1988). Specification of cerebral cortical areas. *Science*, *241*, 170–176.

Ramachandran, V. S. & Hirstein, W. (1998). The perception of phantom limbs. *Brain, 121,* 1603–1630.

Ramachandran, V. S. & Oberman, L. M. (2006). Broken mirrors—a theory of autism. *Scientific American, 295*(5), 62–69.

Ramachandran, V. S. & Rogers-Ramachandran, D. (1996). Synaesthesia in phantom limbs induced with mirrors. *Proceedings of the Royal Society of London B, 263,* 377–386.

Ramnani, N. & Owen, A. M. (2004). Anterior prefrontal cortex: Insights into function from anatomy and neuroimaging. *Nature Reviews Neuroscience, 5,* 184–194.

Ramnani, N., Toni, I., Passingham, R. E., & Haggard, P. (2001). The cerebellum and parietal cortex play a specific role in coordination: A PET study. *NeuroImage, 14,* 899–911.

Ranganath, C., Cohen, M. X., Dam, C., & D'Esposito, M. (2004). Inferior temporal, prefrontal, and hippocampal contributions to visual working memory maintenance and associative memory retrieval. *Journal of Neuroscience, 24*(16), 3917–3925.

Rao, S. C., Rainer, G., & Miller, E. K. (1997). Integration of what and where in the primate prefrontal cortex. *Science, 276,* 821–824.

Rapp, B. & Caramazza, A. (1997). From graphemes to abstract letter shapes: Levels of representation in written spelling. *Journal of Experimental Psychology: Human Perception and Performance, 25,* 1130–1152.

Rasmussen, G. L. (1953). Further observations of the efferent cochlear bundle. *Journal of Comparative Neurology, 99,* 61–74.

Rasmussen, T. & Milner, B. (1977). The role of early left-brain injury in determining lateralization of cerebral speech functions. *Annals of the New York Academy of Sciences, 299.*

Rauschecker, A. M., Pringle, A., & Watkins, K. E. (2008). Changes in neural activity associated with learning to articulate novel auditory pseudowords by covert repetition. *Human Brain Mapping, 29*(11), 1231–1242.

Rauschecker, J. P. & Tian, B. (2000). Mechanisms and streams for processing "what" and "where" in auditory cortex. *Proceedings of the National Academy of Science, USA, 97,* 11800–11806.

Rauschecker, J. P. & Scott, S. K. (2009). Maps and streams in the auditory cortex: nonhuman primates illuminate human speech processing. *Nature Neuroscience, 12*(6), 718–724.

Rauschecker, J. P., Tian, B., & Hauser, M. D. (1995). Processing of complex sounds in the macaque nonprimary auditory cortex. *Science, 268,* 111–114.

Raven, J. C. (1960). *Guide to the Standard Progressive Matrices.* London: H. K. Lewis.

Ravizza, S. M. & Carter, C. S. (2008). Shifting set about task switching: Behavioral and neural evidence for distinct forms of cognitive flexibility. *Neuropsychologia, 46,* 2924–2935.

Raymond, J. E., Shapiro, K. L., & Arnell, K. M. (1992). Temporary suppression of visual processing in an rsvp task—an attentional blink. *Journal of Experimental Psychology-Human Perception and Performance, 18*(3), 849–860.

Rayner, K. (1979). Eye guidance in reading: Fixation locations within words. *Perception, 8,* 21–30.

Rayner, K. (2009). Eye movements and attention in reading, scene perception, and visual search. *Quarterly Journal of Experimental Psychology, 62*(8), 1457–1506.

Rayner, K. & Duffy, S. A. (1986). Lexical complexity and fixation times in reading: Effects of word frequency, verb complexity, and lexical ambiguity. *Memory and Cognition, 14,* 191–201.

Rayner, K. & Juhasz, B. J. (2004). Eye movements in reading: Old questions and new directions. *European Journal of Cognitive Psychology, 16,* 340–352.

Rayner, K. & McConkie, G. W. (1976). What guides a reader's eye movements? *Vision Research, 16,* 829–837.

Rayner, K., Well, A. D., & Pollatsek, A. (1980). Asymmetry of the effective visual field in reading. *Perception and Psychophysics, 27,* 537–544.

Rayner, K., Binder, K. S., Ashby, J., & Pollatsek, A. (2001). Eye movement control in reading: Word predictability has little influence on initial landing positions in words. *Vision Research*, *41*, 943–954.

Reason, J. T. (1984). Lapses of attention in everyday life. In R. Parasuraman & D. R. Davies (Eds.), *Varieties of attention*. Orlando, FL: Academic Press.

Rees, G., Frith, C., & Lavie, N. (1997). Modulating irrelevant motion perception by varying attentional load in an unrelated task. *Science*, *278*, 1616–1619.

Rees, G. & Lavie, N. (2001). What can functional imaging reveal about the role of attention in visual awareness? *Neuropsychologia*, *39*, 1343–1353.

Rees, G., Wojciulik, E., Clarke, K., Husain, M., Frith, C., & Driver, J. (2000). Unconscious activation of visual cortex in the damaged right hemisphere of a parietal patient with extinction. *Brain*, *123*, 1624–1633.

Reich, L., Szwed, M., Cohen, L., & Amedi, A. (2011). A ventral visual stream reading center independent of visual experience. *Current Biology*, *21*(5), 363–368.

Reicher, G. M. (1969). Perceptual recognition as a function of meaningfulness of stimulus materials. *Journal of Experimental Psychology*, *81*, 274–280.

Reilly, R. G. & Radach, R. (2006). Some empirical tests of an interactive activation model of eye movement control in reading. *Cognitive Systems Research*, *7*(1), 34–55.

Reiss, A. L., Abrams, M. T., Singer, H. S., Ross, J. L., & Denckla, M. B. (1996). Brain development, gender and IQ in children: A volumetric imaging study. *Brain*, *119*, 1763–1774.

Reivich, M., Kuhl, D., Wolf, A., Greenberg, J., Phelps, M., Ido, T., Casella, V., Fowler, J., Hoffman, E., Alavi, A., Som, P., & Sokoloff, L. (1979). The [18F]fluorodeoxyglucose method for the measurement of local cerebral glucose utilization in man. *Circulation Research*, *44*(1), 127–137.

Rensink, R. A., O'Regan, J. K., & Clark, J. J. (1997). To see or not to see: The need for attention to perceive changes in scenes. *Psychological Science*, *8*, 368–373.

Repa, J. C., Muller, J., Apergis, J., Desrochers, T. M., Zhou, Y., & LeDoux, J. E. (2001). Two different lateral amygdala cell populations contribute to the initiation and storage of memory. *Nature Neuroscience*, *4*(7), 724–731.

Restle, J., Murakami, T., & Ziemann, U. (2012). Facilitation of speech repetition accuracy by theta burst stimulation of the left posterior inferior frontal gyms. *Neuropsychologia*, *50*(8), 2026–2031.

Reverberi, C., Lavaroni, A., Gigli, G. L., Skrap, M., & Shallice, T. (2005). Specific impairments of rule induction in different frontal subgroups. *Neuropsychologia*, *43*, 460–472.

Revkin, S. K., Piazza, M., Izard, V., Cohen, L., & Dehaene, S. (2008). Does subitizing reflect numerical estimation? *Psychological Science*, *19*(6), 607–614.

Rey, A. (1964). *L'examen clinique en psychologie*. Paris: Presses Universitaires de France.

Rhodes, G. (1996). *Superportraits: Caricatures and recognition*. Hove, UK: Psychology Press.

Rhodes, G. & Tremewan, T. (1993). The Simon then Garfunkel effect: Semantic priming, sensitivity, and the modularity of face recognition. *Cognitive Psychology*, *25*, 147–187.

Rhodes, G., Brennan, S., & Carey, S. (1987). Identification and ratings of caricatures: Implications for mental representation of faces. *Cognitive Psychology*, *19*, 473–497.

Ribot, T. (1882). *Diseases of memory*. New York: Appleton.

Richardson, M. P., Strange, B. A., & Dolan, R. J. (2004). Encoding of emotional memories depends on amygdala and hippocampus and their interactions. *Nature Neuroscience*, *7*, 278–285.

Riddoch, M. J., Chechlacz, M., Mevorach, C., Mavritsaki, E., Allen, H., & Humphreys, G. W. (2010). The neural mechanisms of visual selection: the view from neuropsychology. In A. Kingstone & M. B. Miller (Eds.), *Year in Cognitive Neuroscience 2010* (Vol. 1191, pp. 156–181). Malden, MA: Wiley-Blackwell.

Riddoch, M. J. & Humphreys, G. W. (1983). The effect of cueing on unilateral neglect. *Neuropsychology*, *21*, 589–599.

Riddoch, M. J. & Humphreys, G. W. (1995). *Birmingham object recognition battery*. Hove, UK: Psychology Press.

Riddoch, M. J. & Humphreys, G. W. (2001). Object recognition. In B. Rapp (Ed.), *Handbook of cognitive neuropsychology*. Hove, UK: Psychology Press.

Riddoch, M. J., Humphreys, G. W., & Price, C. J. (1989). Routes to action: Evidence from apraxia. *Cognitive Neuropsychology*, *6*, 437–454.

Riddoch, M. J., Humphreys, G. W., Gannon, T., Blott, W., & Jones, V. (1999). Memories are made of this: The effects of time on stored visual knowledge in a case of visual agnosia. *Brain*, *122*, 537–559.

Ridley, M. (2003). *Nature via nurture*. London: Fourth Estate.

Rilling, J. K., Gutman, D. A., Zeh, T. R., Pagnoni, G., Berns, G. S., & Kilts, C. D. (2002). A neural basis for social cooperation. *Neuron*, *35*(2), 395–405.

Rizzolatti, G. & Arbib, M. A. (1998). Language within our grasp. *Trends in Neuroscience*, *21*, 188–194.

Rizzolatti, G. & Craighero, L. (2004). The mirror-neuron system. *Annual Review of Neuroscience*, *27*, 169–192.

Rizzolatti, G. & Fabbri-Destro, M. (2010). Mirror neurons: From discovery to autism. *Experimental Brain Research*, *200*(3–4), 223–237.

Rizzolatti, G. & Luppino, G. (2001). The cortical motor system. *Neuron*, *31*, 889–901.

Rizzolatti, G. & Matelli, M. (2003). Two different streams form the dorsal visual system: Anatomy and functions. *Experimental Brain Research*, *153*(2), 146–157.

Rizzolatti, G., Riggio, L., Dascola, I., & Umilta, C. (1987). Reorienting attention across the horizontal and vertical meridians—evidence in favor of a premotor theory of attention. *Neuropsychologia*, *25*(1A), 31–40.

Rizzolatti, G., Riggio, L., & Sheliga, B. M. (1994). Space and selective attention. In C. Umilta & M. Moscovitch (Eds.), *Attention and Performance: Conscious and Nonconscious Information Processing* (Vol. 15, pp. 231–265).

Rizzolatti, G., Fadiga, L., Fogassi, L., & Gallese, V. (1996). Premotor cortex and the recognition of motor actions. *Cognitive Brain Research*, *3*, 131–141.

Rizzolatti, G., Fogassi, L., & Gallese, V. (2002). Motor and cognitive functions of the ventral premotor cortex. *Current Opinion in Neurobiology*, *12*, 149–154.

Robbins, T. W., Cador, M., Taylor, J. R., & Everitt, B. J. (1989). Limbic-striatal interactions in reward-related processes. *Neuroscience and Biobehavioral Reviews*, *13*(2–3), 155–162.

Roberts, D. J., Ralph, M. A. L., & Woollams, A. M. (2010). When does less yield more? The impact of severity upon implicit recognition in pure alexia. *Neuropsychologia*, *48*(9), 2437–2446.

Robertson, E. M., Theoret, H., & Pascual-Leone, A. (2003). Studies in cognition: The problems solved and created by transcranial magnetic stimulation. *Journal of Cognitive Neuroscience*, *15*, 948–960.

Robertson, I. H., Nico, D., & Hood, B. (1995). The intention to act improves unilateral neglect: Two demonstrations. *Neuroreport*, *7*, 246–248.

Robertson, L. C. (2004). *Space, objects, minds and brains*. New York: Psychology Press.

Robertson, L. C., Knight, R. T., Rafal, R., & Shimamura, A. P. (1993). Cognitive neuropsychology is more than single-case studies. *Journal of Experimental Psychology: Learning, Memory and Cognition*, *19*, 710–717.

Robertson, L. C., Treisman, A., Friedman-Hill, S., & Grabowecky, M. (1997). The interaction of spatial and object pathways: Implications from a patient with Balint's syndrome. *Journal of Cognitive Neuroscience*, *9*, 295–317.

Robson, H., Sage, K., & Ralph, M. A. L. (2012). Wernicke's aphasia reflects a combination of acoustic-phonological and semantic control deficits: A case-series comparison of Wernicke's aphasia, semantic dementia and semantic aphasia. *Neuropsychologia*, *50*(2), 266–275.

Roca, M., Parr, A., Thompson, R., Woolgar, A., Torralva, T., Antoun, N., & Duncan, J. (2010). Executive function and fluid intelligence after frontal lobe lesions. *Brain, 133*, 234–247.

Roca, M., Torralva, T., Gleichgerrcht, E., Woolgar, A., Thompson, R., Duncan, J., & Manes, F. (2011). The role of Area 10 (BA10) in human multitasking and in social cognition: A lesion study. *Neuropsychologia, 49*(13), 3525–3531.

Rochon, E., Kave, G., Cupit, J., Jokel, R., & Winocur, G. (2004). Sentence comprehension in semantic dementia: A longtitudinal case study. *Cognitive Neuropsychology, 21*, 317–330.

Rodriguez, E., George, N., Lachaux, J. P., Martinerie, J., Renault, B., & Varela, F. J. (1999). Perception's shadow: Long-distance synchronization of human brain activity. *Nature, 397*(6718), 430–433.

Rogalsky, C., & Hickok, G. (2011). The role of Broca's area in sentence comprehension. *Journal of Cognitive Neuroscience, 23*(7), 1664–1680.

Roediger, H. L. (1980). Memory metaphors in cognitive psychology. *Memory and Cognition, 8*, 231–246.

Roediger, H. L., & McDermott, K. B. (1995). Creating false memories: Remembering words not presented in lists. *Journal of Experimental Psychology: Learning, Memory and Cognition, 21*, 803–814.

Rogalsky, C. & Hickok, G. (2011). The role of Broca's area in sentence comprehension. *Journal of Cognitive Neuroscience, 23*(7), 1664–1680.

Rogers, R. D. & Monsell, S. (1995). Costs of a predictable switch between simple cognitive tasks. *Journal of Experimental Psychology: General, 124*, 207–231.

Rogers, T. T. & Patterson, K. E. (2007). Object categorization: Reversals and explanations of the basic-level advantage. *Journal of Experimental Psychology-General, 136*(3), 451–469.

Rogers, T. T., Patterson, K. E., & Graham, K. (2007). Colour knowledge in semantic dementia: It is not all black and white. *Neuropsychologia, 45*(14), 3285–3298.

Rogers, T. T., Hocking, J., Noppeney, U., Mechelli, A., Gorno-Tempini, M. L., Patterson, K. E., & Price, C. J. (2006). Anterior temporal cortex and semantic memory: Reconciling findings from neuropsychology and functional imaging. *Cognitive Affective & Behavioral Neuroscience, 6*, 201–213.

Roitman, J. D., Brannon, E. M., & Platt, M. L. (2007). Monotonic coding of numerosity in macaque lateral intraparietal area. *PLoS Biology, 5*(8), 1672–1682.

Rolls, E. T. (2005). *Emotion Explained*. Oxford, UK: Oxford University Press.

Rolls, E. T. & Deco, G. (2002). *Computational neuroscience of vision*. Oxford, UK: Oxford University Press.

Rolls, E. T. & Tovee, M. J. (1995). Sparseness of the neuronal representation of stimuli in the primate temporal visual cortex. *Journal of Neurophysiology, 73*, 713–726.

Rolls, E. T., Hornak, J., Wade, D., & McGrath, J. (1994). Emotion-related learning in patients with social and emotional changes associated with frontal damage. *Journal of Neurology, Neurosurgery and Psychiatry, 57*, 1518–1524.

Rolls, E. T., Robertson, R. G., & Georges-Francois, P. (1997). Spatial view cells in the primate hippocampus. *European Journal of Neuroscience, 9*, 1789–1794.

Romani, C. (1994). The role of phonological short-term memory in syntactic parsing: A case study. *Language and Cognitive Processes, 9*, 29–67.

Rorden, C. & Karnath, H. O. (2004). Using human brain lesions to infer function: A relic from a past era in the fMRI age? *Nature Reviews Neuroscience, 5*, 813–819.

Rosenbaum, R. S., Priselac, S., Kohler, S., Black, S. E., Gao, F. Q., Nadel, L., & Moscovitch, M. (2000). Remote spatial memory in an amnesic person with extensive bilateral hippocampal lesions. *Nature Neuroscience, 3*(10), 1044–1048.

Ross, J., Zinn, A., & McCauley, E. (2000). Neurodevelopmental and psychosocial aspects of Turner syndrome. *Mental Retardation and Developmental Disabilities Research Reviews, 6*, 135–141.

Rosser, M. N., Warrington, E. K., & Cipolotti, L. (1995). The isolation of calculation skills. *Journal of Neurology, 242*, 78–81.

Rossi, S., Hallett, M., Rossini, P. M., Pascual-Leone, A., & Safety TMS Consensus Group (2009). Safety, ethical considerations, and application guidelines for the use of transcranial magnetic stimulation in clinical practice and research. *Clinical Neurophysiology, 120*(12), 2008–2039.

Rossion, B., Gauthier, I., Goffaux, V., Tarr, M. J., & Crommelinck, M. (2002). Expertise training with novel objects leads to left-lateralized facelike electrophysiological responses. *Psychological Science, 13*, 250–257.

Rosvold, H. E., Mirsky, A. F., & Pribram, K. H. (1954). Influence of amygdalactomy on social behaviour in monkeys. *Journal of Comparative Physiological Psychology, 47*, 173–178.

Rothwell, J. C., Traub, M. M., Day, B. L., Obeso, J. A., Thomas, P. K., & Marsden, C. D. (1982). Manual motor performance in a deafferented man. *Brain, 105*, 515–542.

Rotshtein, P., Henson, R. N. A., Treves, A., Driver, J., & Dolan, R. J. (2005). Morphing Marilyn into Maggie dissociates physical and identity face representations in the brain. *Nature Neuroscience, 8*, 107–113.

Rotzer, S., Kucian, K., Martin, E., von Aster, M., Klaver, P., & Loenneker, T. (2008). Optimized voxel-based morphometry in children with developmental dyscalculia. *NeuroImage, 39*(1), 417–422.

Rousselet, G. A., Mace, M. J.-M., & Thorpe, M. F. (2004). Animal and human faces in natural scenes: How specific to human faces is the N170 ERP component? *Journal of Vision, 4*, 13–21.

Rowe, J. B., Owen, A. M., Johnsrude, I. S., & Passingham, R. E. (2001). Imaging the mental components of a planning task. *Neuropsychologia, 39*, 315–327.

Ruby, P. & Decety, J. (2004). How would you feel versus how do you think she would feel? A neuroimaging study of perspective-taking with social emotions. *Journal of Cognitive Neuroscience, 16*(6), 988–999.

Rudebeck, P. H., Buckley, M. J., Walton, M. E., & Rushworth, M. F. S. (2006). A role for the macaque anterior cingulate gyrus in social valuation. *Science, 313*(5791), 1310–1312.

Rumelhart, D. E. & McClelland, J. L. (1982). An interactive activation model of context effects in letter perception: Part 2. The contextual enhancement effect and some tests and extensions of the model. *Psychological Review, 89*, 60–94.

Rumiati, R. I., Humphreys, G. W., Riddoch, M. J., & Bateman, A. (1994). Visual object agnosia without prosopagnosia or alexia: Evidence for hierarchical theories of visual recognition. *Visual Cognition, 1*, 181–225.

Rumiati, R. I., Weiss, P. H., Shallice, T., Ottoboni, G., Noth, J., Zilles, K., & Fink, G. R. (2004). Neural basis of pantomiming the use of visually presented objects. *NeuroImage, 21*, 1224–1231.

Rusconi, E., Bueti, D., Walsh, V., & Butterworth, B. (2011). Contribution of frontal cortex to the spatial representation of number. *Cortex, 47*(1), 2–13.

Rusconi, E., Walsh, V., & Butterworth, B. (2005). Dexterity with numbers: rTMS over left angular gyrus disrupts finger gnosis and number processing. *Neuropsychologia, 43*, 1609–1624.

Rusconi, E., Turatto, M., & Umilta, C. (2007). Two orienting mechanisms in posterior parietal lobule: An rTMS study of the Simon and SNARC effects. *Cognitive Neuropsychology, 24*(4), 373–392.

Rushworth, M. F. S., Hadland, K. A., Gaffan, D., & Passingham, R. E. (2003). The effect of cingulate cortex lesions on task switching and working memory. *Journal of Cognitive Neuroscience, 15*, 338–353.

Rushworth, M. F. S., Hadland, K. A., Paus, T., & Sipila, P. K. (2002). Role of the human medial frontal cortex in task switching: A combined fMRI and TMS study. *Journal of Neurophysiology, 87*, 2577–2592.

Rushworth, M. F. S., Behrens, T. E. J., Rudebeck, P. H., & Walton, M. E. (2007). Contrasting roles for cingulate and orbitofrontal cortex in decisions and social behaviour. *Trends in Cognitive Sciences*, *11*(4), 168–176.

Russell, J. (1997). *Autism as an executive disorder*. Oxford, UK: Oxford University Press.

Russell, J. A., & Barrett, L. F. (1999). Core affect, prototypical emotional episodes, and other things called emotion: Dissecting the elephant. *Journal of Personality and Social Psychology*, *76*, 805–819.

Rutter, M., Moffitt, T. E., & Caspi, A. (2006). Gene–environment interplay and psychopathology: Multiple varieties but real effects. *Journal of Child Psychology and Psychiatry*, *47*, 226–261.

Saarinen, J., Paavilainen, P., Schoger, E., Tervaniemi, M., & Näätänen, R. (1992). Representation of abstract stimulus attributes in human brain. *NeuroReport*, *3*, 1149–1151.

Sadato, N., Pascual-Leone, A., Grafman, J., Ibanez, V., Deiber, M.-P., Dold, G., & Hallett, M. (1996). Activation of primary visual cortex by Braille reading in blind subjects. *Nature*, *380*, 526–528.

Saenz, M. & Koch, C. (2008). The sound of change: Visually induced auditory synesthesia. *Current Biology*, *18*, R650–R651.

Sagar, J. H., Cohen, N. J., Corkin, S., & Growden, J. H. (1985). Dissociations among processes in remote memory. *Annals of the New York Academy of Science*, *444*, 533–535.

Sagiv, N. & Bentin, S. (2001). Structural encoding of human and schematic faces: Holistic and part based processes. *Journal of Cognitive Neuroscience*, *13*, 1–15.

Salinas, E. & Abbott, L. F. (1994). Vector reconstruction from firing rates. *Journal of Computational Neuroscience*, *1*, 89–107.

Sammler, D., Koelsch, S., Ball, T., Brandt, A., Grigutsch, M., Huppertz, H.-J., & Schulze-Bonhage, A. (2013). Co-localizing linguistic and musical syntax with intracranial EEG. *NeuroImage*, *64*, 134–146.

Sammler, D., Koelsch, S., & Friederici, A. D. (2011). Are left frontotemporal brain areas a prerequisite for normal music-syntactic processing? *Cortex*, *47*(6), 659–673.

Samson, D. & Pillon, A. (2003). A case of impaired knowledge for fruit and vegetables. *Cognitive Neuropsychology*, *20*, 373–400.

Samson, D., Apperly, I. A., Chiavarino, C., & Humphreys, G. W. (2004). Left temporoparietal junction is necessary for representing someone else's belief. *Nature Neuroscience*, *7*, 499–500.

Samson, S. & Zatorre, R. J. (1994). Contribution of the right temporal lobe to musical timbre discrimination. *Neuropsychologia*, *32*, 231–240.

Sanders, H. I. & Warrington, E. K. (1971). Memory for remote events in amnesic patients. *Brain*, *94*, 661–668.

Sanfey, A., Rilling, J., Aaronson, J., Nystron, L., & Cohen, J. (2003). Probing the neural basis of economic decision-making: An fMRI investigation of the ultimatum game. *Science*, *300*, 1755–1758.

Sartori, G. (1987). Leonardo da Vinci, omo sanza lettere: A case of surface dysgraphia? *Cognitive Neuropsychology*, *4*, 1–10.

Savage-Rumbaugh, E. S., & Lewin, R. (1994). *Kanzi: At the brink of the human mind*. New York: Wiley.

Savage-Rumbaugh, E. S., McDonald, K., Sevcik, R. A., Hopkins, W. D., & Rupert, E. (1986). Spontaneous symbol acquisition and communicative use by pygmy chimpanzee (*Pan paniscus*). *Journal of Experimental Psychology: General*, *115*, 211–235.

Savage-Rumbaugh, E. S., Pate, J. L., Lawson, J., Smith, S. T., & Rosenbaum, S. (1983). Can a chimpanzee make a statement? *Journal of Experimental Psychology: General*, *112*, 457–492.

Saver, J. L. & Damasio, A. R. (1991). Preserved access and processing of social knowledge in a patient with acquired sociopathy due to ventromedial frontal damage. *Neuropsychologia*, *29*, 1241–1249.

Savoy, R. L. (2002). Functional magnetic resonance imaging fMRI. In V. Ramachandran (Ed.), *Encyclopedia of the brain*. San Diego: Academic Press.

Saxe, R. (2006). Uniquely human social cognition. *Current Opinion in Neurobiology, 16*(2), 235–239.

Saxe, R. & Kanwisher, N. (2003). People thinking about thinking people: The role of the temporoparietal junction in "theory of mind." *NeuroImage, 19*, 1835–1842.

Saxe, R. & Powell, L. J. (2006). It's the thought that counts: specific brain regions for one component of theory of mind. *Psychological Science, 17*, 692–699.

Schacter, D. L. (1986). Amnesia and crime: How much do we really know? *American Psychologist, 41*, 286–295.

Schacter, D. L. (1987). Implicit memory: History and current status. *Journal of Experimental Psychology: Learning, Memory and Cognition, 113*, 501–518.

Schacter, D. L. & Badgaiyan, R. D. (2001). Neuroimaging of priming: New perspectives on implicit and explicit memory. *Current Directions in Psychological Science, 10*, 1–4.

Schacter, D. L. & Slotnick, S. D. (2004). The cognitive neuroscience of memory distortion. *Neuron, 44*, 149–160.

Schacter, D. L., Cooper, L., & Delaney, S. (1990). Implicit memory for unfamiliar objects depends on access to structural descriptions. *Journal of Experimental Psychology: General, 119*, 5–24.

Schacter, D. L., Norman, K. A., & Koutstaal, W. (1998). The cognitive neuroscience of constructive memory. *Annual Review of Psychology, 49*, 289–318.

Schacter, S. & Singer, J. E. (1962). Cognitive, social, and physiological determinants of emotional state. *Psychology Review, 69*, 379–399.

Schadwinkel, S. & Gutschalk, A. (2010). Activity associated with stream segregation in human auditory cortex is similar for spatial and pitch cues. *Cerebral Cortex, 20*(12), 2863–2873.

Schechtman, E., Shrem, T., & Deouell, L. Y. (2012). Spatial localization of auditory stimuli in human auditory cortex is based on both head-independent and head-centered coordinate systems. *Journal of Neuroscience, 32*(39), 13501–13509.

Scherer, K. R., Banse, R., & Wallbott, H. G. (2001). Emotion inferences from vocal expression correlate across languages and cultures. *Journal of Cross-Cultural Psychology, 32*, 76–92.

Schlagger, B. L. & O'Leary, D. D. M. (1991). Potential of visual cortex to develop an array of functional units unique to somatosensory cortex. *Science, 252*, 1556–1560.

Schmidt, R. A. (1975). A schema theory of discrete motor skill learning. *Psychological Review, 82*, 225–232.

Schneider, W. & Shiffrin, R. M. (1977). Controlled and automatic human information processing: I. Detection, search and attention. *Psychological Review, 84*, 1–66.

Schnider, A. (2003). Spontaneous confabulation and the adaptation of thought to ongoing reality. *Nature Reviews Neuroscience, 4*, 662–671.

Schnider, A. & Ptak, R. (1999). Spontaneous confabulators fail to suppress currently irrelevant memory traces. *Nature Neuroscience, 2*, 677–681.

Schnider, A., Treyer, V., & Buck, A. (2000). Selection of currently relevant memories by the human posterior medial orbitofrontal cortex. *The Journal of Neuroscience, 20*, 5880–5884.

Schultz, W., Apicella, P., Scarnati, E., & Ljungberg, T. (1992). Neuronal-activity in monkey ventral striatum related to the expectation of reward. *Journal of Neuroscience, 12*(12), 4595–4610.

Schultz, W., Dayan, P., & Montague, P. R. (1997). A neural substrate of prediction and reward. *Science, 275*(5306), 1593–1599.

Schurger, A., Sitt, J. D., & Dehaene, S. (2012). An accumulator model for spontaneous neural activity prior to self-initiated movement. *Proceedings of the National Academy of Sciences of the United States of America, 109*(42), E2904–E2913.

Schurz, M., Sturm, D., Richlan, F., Kronbichler, M., Ladurner, G., & Wimmer, H. (2010). A dual-route perspective on brain activation in response to visual words: Evidence for a length by lexicality interaction in the visual word form area (VWFA). *NeuroImage, 49*(3), 2649–2661.

Schwartz, D. A., Howe, C. Q., & Purves, D. (2003). The statistical structure of human speech sounds predicts musical universals. *Journal of Neuroscience, 23*(18), 7160–7168.

Schwartz, M. F., Montgomery, M. W., Fitzpatrick-DeSalme, E. J., Ochipa, C., Coslett, H. B., & Mayer, N. H. (1995). Analysis of a disorder of everyday action. *Cognitive Neuropsychology, 12*, 863–892.

Schweinberger, S. R. (1996). How Gorbachev primed Yeltsin: Analyses of associative priming in person recognition by means of reaction times and event-related brain potentials. *Journal of Experimental Psychology: Learning, Memory and Cognition, 22*, 1383–1407.

Schweinberger, S. R., Pickering, E. C., Burton, A. M., & Kaufmann, J. M. (2002a). Human brain potential correlates of repetition priming in face and name recognition. *Neuropsychologia, 40*, 2057–2073.

Schweinberger, S. R., Pickering, E. C., Jentzsch, I., Burton, A. M., & Kaufmann, J. M. (2002b). Event-related brain potential evidence for a response of inferior temporal cortex to familiar face repetitions. *Cognitive Brain Research, 14*, 398–409.

Schwoebel, J., Buxbaum, L. J., & Coslett, H. B. (2004). Representations of the human body in the production and imitation of complex movements. *Cognitive Neuropsychology, 21*, 285–298.

Scott, S. K. (2008). Voice processing in human and monkey brain. *Trends in Cognitive Sciences, 12*, 323–325.

Scott, S. K., Blank, S. C., Rosen, S., & Wise, R. J. S. (2000). Identification of a pathway for intelligible speech in the left temporal lobe. *Brain, 123*, 2400–2406.

Scott, S. K., McGettigan, C., & Eisner, F. (2009). A little more conversation, a little less action—candidate roles for the motor cortex in speech perception. *Nature Reviews Neuroscience, 10*(4), 295–302.

Scott, S. K. & Wise, R. J. S. (2004). The functional neuroanatomy of prelexical processing in speech perception. *Cognition, 92*, 13–45.

Scott, S. K., Young, A. W., Calder, A. J., Hellawell, D. J., Aggleton, J. P., & Johnson, M. (1997). Impaired auditory recognition of fear and anger following bilateral amygdala lesions. *Nature, 385*, 254–257.

Scoville, W. B., & Milner, B. (1957). Loss of recent memory after bilateral hippocampal lesions. *Journal of Neurology, Neurosurgery and Psychiatry, 20*, 11–21.

Scragg, D. G. (1974). *A history of English spelling*. Manchester, UK: Manchester University Press.

Searle, J. (1980). Minds, brains and programs. *Behavioral and Brain Sciences, 3*, 417–458.

Searle, J. (1990). Is the brain's mind a computer program? *Scientific American, 13*, 585–642.

Sebanz, N., Bekkering, H., & Knoblich, G. (2006). Joint action: Bodies and minds moving together. *Trends in Cognitive Sciences, 10*, 70–76.

Seidenberg, M. S. & Petitto, L. A. (1987). Communication, symbolic communication, and language: Comment on Savage-Rumbaugh, McDonald, Sevcik, Hopkins and Rupert (1986). *Journal of Experimental Psychology: General, 116*, 279–287.

Seidenberg, M. S., Waters, G. S., Barnes, M. A., & Tanenhaus, M. K. (1984). When does irregular spelling or pronunciation influence word recognition? *Journal of Verbal Learning and Verbal Behaviour, 23*, 383–404.

Seligman, M. E. (1971). Phobias and preparedness. *Behavior Therapy, 2*, 307–320.

Semenza, C. (1988). Impairment in localization of body parts following brain damage. *Cortex, 24*, 443–449.

Semenza, C. & Goodglass, H. (1985). Localization of body parts in brain injured subjects. *Neuropsychologia, 23*, 161–175.

Semenza, C. & Zettin, M. (1988). Generating proper names: A case of selective inability. *Cognitive Neuropsychology, 5*, 711–721.

Serences, J. T., Schwarzbach, J., Courtney, S. M., Golay, X., & Yantis, S. (2004). Control of object-based attention in human cortex. *Cerebral Cortex, 14*(12), 1346–1357.

Sergent, J. & Signoret, J.-L. (1992). Varieties of functional deficits in prosopagnosia. *Cerebral Cortex, 2*, 375–388.

Seron, X. & Noel, M. P. (1995). Transcoding numbers from the Arabic code to the verbal one or vice versa: How many routes? *Mathematical Cognition, 1*, 215–243.

Shah, A. & Frith, U. (1983). Islet of ability in autistic-children: A research note. *Journal of Child Psychology and Psychiatry and Allied Disciplines, 24*, 613–620.

Shaki, S., Fischer, M. H., & Gobel, S. M. (2012). Direction counts: A comparative study of spatially directional counting biases in cultures with different reading directions. *Journal of Experimental Child Psychology, 112*(2), 275–281.

Shalev, L. & Humphreys, G. W. (2002). Implicit location encoding via stored representations of familiar objects: Neuropsychological evidence. *Cognitive Neuropsychology, 19*, 721–744.

Shallice, T. (1979). Case study approach in neuropsychological research. *Journal of Clinical Neuropsychology, 1*, 183–211.

Shallice, T. (1981). Phonological agraphia and the lexical route in writing. *Brain, 104*, 413–429.

Shallice, T. (1982). Specific impairment of planning. *Philosophical Transactions of the Royal Society of London B, 298*, 199–209.

Shallice, T. (1988). *From neuropsychology to mental structure*. Cambridge, UK: Cambridge University Press.

Shallice, T. (2002). Fractionation of the supervisory system. In D. T. Stuss & R. T. Knight (Eds.), *Principles of frontal lobe function*. New York: Oxford University Press.

Shallice, T. & Burgess, P. (1996). The domain of supervisory process and temporal organization of behaviour. *Philosophical Transactions of the Royal Society of London B, 351*, 1405–1412.

Shallice, T. & Burgess, P. W. (1991). Deficits in strategy application following frontal lobe damage in man. *Brain, 114*, 727–741.

Shallice, T. & Evans, M. E. (1978). The involvement of the frontal lobes in cognitive estimation. *Cortex, 14*, 294–303.

Shallice, T. & Saffran, E. (1986). Lexical processing in the absence of explicit word identification: Evidence from a letter-by-letter reader. *Cognitive Neuropsychology, 3*, 429–458.

Shallice, T., Warrington, E. K., & McCarthy, R. (1983). Reading without semantics. *Quarterly Journal of Experimental Psychology, 35A*, 111–138.

Shallice, T., Burgess, P. W., Schon, F., & Baxter, D. M. (1989). The origins of utilization behaviour. *Brain, 112*, 1587–1598.

Shallice, T., Glasspool, D. W., & Houghton, G. (1995). Can neuropsychological evidence inform connectionist modelling? *Language and Cognitive Processes, 10*, 195–225.

Shamay-Tsoory, S. G., Aharon-Peretz, J., & Perry, D. (2009). Two systems for empathy: a double dissociation between emotional and cognitive empathy in inferior frontal gyrus versus ventromedial prefrontal lesions. *Brain, 132*, 617–627.

Shammi, P. & Stuss, D. T. (1999). Humour appreciation: A role of the right frontal lobe. *Brain, 122*, 657–666.

Shapiro, K. & Caramazza, A. (2003). The representation of grammatical categories in the brain. *Trends in Cognitive Sciences, 7*, 201–206.

Sharma, J., Angelucci, A., & Sur, M. (2000). Induction of visual orientation modules in auditory cortex. *Nature, 404*, 841–847.

Shellock, F. G. (2014). *Reference manual for magnetic resonance safety, implants and devices*. Los Angeles, CA: Biomedical Research Publishing Company.

Shelton, J. R. & Martin, R. C. (1992). How semantic is automatic semantic priming? *Journal of Experimental Psychology: Learning, Memory and Cognition*, *18*, 1191–1209.

Shelton, J. R., Fouch, E., & Caramazza, A. (1998). The relative sparing of body part knowledge: A case study. *Neurocase*, *4*, 339–351.

Sheppard, D. M., Bradshaw, J. L., Purcell, R., & Pantelis, C. (1999). Tourette's and Comorbid syndromes: Obsessive compulsive and attention deficit hyperactivity disorder. A common etiology? *Clinical Psychology Review*, *19*(5), 531–552.

Shibahara, N., Zorzi, M., Hill, M. P., Wydell, T., & Butterworth, B. (2003). Semantic effects in word naming: Evidence from English and Japanese Kanji. *Quarterly Journal of Experimental Psychology*, *56A*, 263–286.

Shimazu, H., Maier, M. A., Cerri, G., Kirkwood, P. A., & Lemon, R. N. (2004). Macaque ventral premotor cortex exerts powerful facilitation of motor cortex outputs to upper limb motoneurons. *Journal of Neuroscience*, *24*(5), 1200–1211.

Shuman, M. & Kanwisher, N. (2004). Numerical magnitude in the human parietal lobe: Tests of representational generality and domain specificity. *Neuron*, *44*, 557–589.

Sigala, N., Kusunoki, M., Nimmo-Smith, I., Gaffan, D., & Duncan, J. (2008). Hierarchical coding for sequential task events in the monkey prefrontal cortex. *Proceedings of the National Academy of Sciences of the United States of America*, *105*(33), 11969–11974.

Sigman, M., Mundy, P., Ungerer, J., & Sherman, T. (1986). Social Interactions of autistic, learning-disabled, and normal children and their caregivers. *Journal of Child Psychology and Psychiatry*, *27*, 647–656.

Simmonds, D. J., Pekar, J. J., & Mostofsky, S. H. (2008). Meta-analysis of Go/No-go tasks, demonstrating that fMRI activation associated with response inhibition is task-dependent. *Neuropsychologia*, *46*(1), 224–232.

Simons, D. J. & Chabris, C. F. (1999). Gorillas in our midst: Sustained inattentional blindness for dynamic events. *Perception*, *28*, 1059–1074.

Simons, D. J. & Levin, D. T. (1998). Failure to detect changes to people during a real-world interaction. *Psychonomic Bulletin and Review*, *5*, 644–649.

Simons, J. S., Peers, P. V., Mazuz, Y. S., Berryhill, M. E., & Olson, I. R. (2010). Dissociation Between Memory Accuracy and Memory Confidence Following Bilateral Parietal Lesions. *Cerebral Cortex*, *20*(2), 479–485.

Sincich, L. C., Park, K. F., Wohlgemuth, M. J., & Horton, J. C. (2004). Bypassing V1: A direct geniculate input to area MT. *Nature Neuroscience*, *7*(10), 1123–1128.

Singer, T., Critchley, H. D., & Preuschoff, K. (2009). A common role of insula in feelings, empathy and uncertainty. *Trends in Cognitive Sciences*, *13*(8), 334–340.

Singer, T., Seymour, B., O'Doherty, J., Kaube, H., Dolan, R. J., & Frith, C. D. (2004). Empathy for pain involves the affective but not the sensory components of pain. *Science*, *303*, 1157–1162.

Singer, T., Seymour, B., O'Doherty, J. P., Stephan, K. E., Dolan, R. J., & Frith, C. D. (2006). Empathic neural responses are modulated by the perceived fairness of others. *Nature*, *439*, 466–469.

Singh, K. D. (2006). Magnetoencephalography. In C. Senior, T. Russell, & M. S. Gazzaniga (Eds.), *Methods in mind*. Cambridge, MA: MIT Press.

Sip, K., Roepstorff, A., McGregor, W., & Frith, C. D. (2007). Detecting deception: The scope and limits. *Trends in Cognitive Sciences*, *12*, 48–53.

Sirigu, A., Zalla, T., Pillon, B., Grafman, J., Agid, Y., & Dubois, B. (1995). Selective impairments in managerial knowledge following pre-frontal cortex damage. *Cortex*, *31*, 301–316.

Skipper, J. I., van Wassenhove, V., Nusbaum, H. C., & Small, S. L. (2007). Hearing lips and seeing voices: How cortical areas supporting speech production mediate audiovisual perception. *Cerebral Cortex*, *17*, 2387–2399.

Sliwinska, M. W., Khadilkar, M., Campbell-Ratcliffe, J., Quevenco, F., & Devlin, J. T. (2012). Early and sustained supramarginal gyrus contributions to phonological processing. *Frontiers in psychology*, *3*.

Slotnick, S. D. & Schacter, D. L. (2004). A sensory signature that distinguishes true from false memories. *Nature Neuroscience*, *7*, 664–672.

Small, D. M., Gregory, M. D., Mak, Y. E., Gitelman, D., Mesulam, M. M., & Parrish, T. (2003). Dissociation of neural representation of intensity and affective valuation in human gustation. *Neuron*, *39*(4), 701–711.

Small, D. M., Zatorre, R. J., Dagher, A., Evans, A. C., & Jones-Gotman, M. (2001). Changes in brain activity related to eating chocolate: from pleasure to aversion. *Brain*, *124*, 1720–1733.

Smith, C. A. & Lazarus, R. S. (1990). Emotion and adaptation. In L. A. Pervin (Ed.), *Handbook of Personality: Theory and Research*. New York: Guilford.

Smith, D. T., & Schenk, T. (2012). The Premotor theory of attention: Time to move on? *Neuropsychologia*, *50*(6), 1104–1114.

Smith, D. T., Rorden, C., & Jackson, S. R. (2004). Exogenous orienting of attention depends upon the ability to execute eye movements. *Current Biology*, *14*(9), 792–795.

Smith, S. B. (1983). *The great mental calculators*. New York: Columbia University Press.

Snowdon, C. T. & Teie, D. (2010). Affective responses in tamarins elicited by species-specific music. *Biology Letters*, *6*(1), 30–32.

Sodian, B. & Frith, U. (1992). Deception and sabotage in autistic, retarded and normal children. *Journal of Child Psychology and Psychiatry*, *33*, 591–605.

Southgate, V. & Hamilton, A. F. C. (2008). Unbroken mirrors: Challenging a theory of autism. *Trends in Cognitive Sciences*, *12*, 225–229.

Sparks, D. L. (1999). Conceptual issues related to the role of the superior colliculus in the control of gaze. *Current Opinion in Neurobiology*, *9*, 698–707.

Spelke, E. S. (1998). Nativism, empiricism, and the origins of knowledge. *Infant Behavior and Development*, *21*, 181–200.

Spiers, H. J., Burgess, N., Maguire, E. A., Baxendale, S. A., Hartley, T., Thompson, P. J., & O'Keefe, J. (2001a). Unilateral temporal lobectomy patients show lateralised topographical and episodic memory deficits in a virtual town. *Brain*, *124*, 2476–2489.

Spiers, H. J., Maguire, E. A., & Burgess, N. (2001b). Hippocampal amnesia. *Neurocase*, *7*, 357–382.

Sporns, O., Chialvo, D. R., Kaiser, M., & Hilgetag, C. C. (2004). Organization, development and function of complex brain networks. *Trends in Cognitive Sciences*, *8*, 418–425.

Sprengelmeyer, R., Young, A. W., Calder, A. J., Karnat, A., Lange, H., Homberg, V., Perrett, D., & Rowland, D. (1996). Loss of disgust: Perception of faces and emotions in Huntington's disease. *Brain*, *119*, 1647–1665.

Sprengelmeyer, R., Young, A. W., Sprengelmeyer, A., Calder, A. J., Rowland, D., Perrett, D., Homberg, V., & Lange, H. (1997). Recognition of facial expression: Selective impairment of specific emotions in Huntington's disease. *Cognitive Neuropsychology*, *14*, 839–879.

Squire, L. R. (1992). Memory and the hippocampus: A synthesis from findings with rats, monkeys and humans. *Psychological Review*, *99*, 195–231.

Squire, L. R. & Bayey, P. J. (2007). The neuroscience of remote memory. *Current Opinion in Neurobiology*, *17*(2), 185–196.

Squire, L. R., Knowlton, B., & Musen, G. (1993). The structure and organisation of memory. *Annual Review of Psychology*, *44*, 453–495.

Squire, L. R., Stark, C. E. L., & Clark, R. E. (2004). The medial temporal lobe. *Annual Review of Neuroscience*, *27*, 279–306.

Stagg, C. J. & Nitsche, M. A. (2011). Physiological basis of transcranial direct current stimulation. *Neuroscientist*, *17*(1), 37–53.

Stanescu-Cosson, R., Pinel, P., Van de Moortele, P.-F., Le Bihan, D., Cohen, L., & Dehaene, S. (2000). Cerebral basis of calculation processes: Impact of number size on the cerebral circuits for exact and approximate calculation. *Brain, 123*, 2240–2255.

Stein, B. E. & Stanford, T. R. (2008). Multisensory integration: Current issues from the perspective of the single neuron. *Nature Reviews Neuroscience, 9*, 255–266.

Sternberg, S. (1969). The discovery of processing stages: Extensions of Donders' method. *Acta Psychologica, 30*, 276–315.

Stevens, S. S. (1935). The relation of pitch to intensity. *Journal of the Acoustical Society of America, 6*, 150–154.

Stewart, L., Battelli, L., Walsh, V., & Cowey, A. (1999). Motion perception and perceptual learning studied by magnetic stimulation. *Electroencephalography and Clinical Neurophysiology, 3*, 334–350.

Stoerig, P. & Cowey, A. (1997). Blindsight in man and monkey. *Brain, 120*, 535–559.

Stone, V. E. & Gerrans, P. (2006). What's domain-specific about theory of mind? *Social Neuroscience, 1*, 309–319.

Strafella, A. P. & Paus, T. (2000). Modulation of cortical excitability during action observation: A transcranial magnetic stimulation study. *Experimental Brain Research, 11*, 2289–2292.

Strauss, M. S. & Curtis, L. E. (1981). Infant perception of numerosity. *Child Development, 52*, 97–127.

Stricanne, B., Andersen, R. A., & Mazzoni, P. (1996). Eye-centered, head-centered, and intermediate coding of remembered sound locations in area LIP. *Journal of Neurophysiology, 76*(3), 2071–2076.

Stroop, J. R. (1935). Studies of interference in serial verbal reactions. *Journal of Experimental Psychology: General, 106*, 404–426.

Stuss, D. T. & Alexander, M. P. (2007). Is there a dysexecutive syndrome? *Philosophical Transactions of the Royal Society B-Biological Sciences, 362*(1481), 901–915.

Stuss, D. T., Shallice, T., Alexander, M. P., & Picton, T. W. (1995). A multidisciplinary approach to anterior attentional functions. *Structure and Functions of the Human Prefrontal Cortex* (Vol. 769, pp., 191–211).

Stuss, D. T., Alexander, M. P., Hamer, L., Palumbo, C., Dempster, R., Binns, M., Levine, B., & Izukawa, D. (1998). The effects of focal anterior and posterior brain lesions on verbal fluency. *Journal of the International Neuropsychological Society, 4*, 265–278.

Stuss, D. T., Levine, B., Alexander, M. P., Hong, J., Palumbo, C., Hamer, L., Murphy, K. J., & Izukawa, D. (2000). Wisconsin Card Sorting Test performance in patients with focal frontal and posterior brain damage: effects of lesion location and test structure on separable cognitive processes. *Neuropsychologia, 38*(4), 388–402.

Stuss, D. T., Floden, D., Alexander, M. P., Levine, B., & Katz, D. (2001a). Stroop performance in focal lesion patients: Dissociation of processes and frontal lobe lesion location. *Neuropsychologia, 39*, 771–786.

Stuss, D. T., Gallup, G. G., & Alexander, M. P. (2001b). The frontal lobes are necessary for 'theory of mind." *Brain, 124*, 279–286.

Stuss, D. T., Alexander, M. P., Floden, D., Binns, M. A., Levine, B., McIntosh, A. R., Rajah, N., & Hevenor, S. J. (2002). Fractionation and localization of distinct frontal lobe processes: Evidence from focal lesions in humans. In D. T. Stuss & R. T. Knight (Eds.), *Principles of frontal lobe function*. Oxford, UK: Oxford University Press.

Stuss, D. T., Alexander, M. P., Shallice, T., Picton, T. W., Binns, M. A., Macdonald, R., Borowiec, A., & Katz, D. I. (2005). Multiple frontal systems controlling response speed. *Neuropsychologia, 43*(3), 396–417.

Sumby, W. H. & Pollack, I. (1954). Visual contribution to speech intelligibility in noise. *Journal of the Acoustical Society of America, 26*, 212–215.

Sun, J. & Perona, P. (1998). Where is the sun? *Nature Neuroscience, 1*, 183–184.

Sur, M. & Leamey, C. A. (2001). Development and plasticity of cortical areas and networks. *Nature Reviews Neuroscience, 2*, 251–262.

Sur, M. & Rubenstein, J. L. R. (2005). Patterning and plasticity of the cerebral cortex. *Science, 310*, 805–810.

Sur, M., Garraghty, P. E., & Roe, A. W. (1988). Experimentally induced visual projections into auditory thalamus and cortex. *Science, 242*, 1437–1441.

Susskind, J. M., Lee, D. H., Cusi, A., Feiman, R., Grabski, W., & Anderson, A. K. (2008). Expressing fear enhances sensory acquisition. *Nature Neuroscience, 11*(7), 843–850.

Sutton, S., Tueting, P., Zubin, J., & John, E. R. (1967). Information delivery and the sensory evoked potential. *Science, 155*, 1436–1439.

Swayze, V. W. (1995). Frontal leukotomy and related psychosurgical procedures in the era before antipsychotics (1935–1954): A historical overview. *American Journal of Psychiatry, 152*, 505–515.

Tager-Flusberg, H. (1992). Autistic children's talk about psychological states: Deficits in the early acquisition of a theory of mind. *Child Development, 63*, 161–172.

Tager-Flusberg, H. (2003). Developmental disorders of genetic origin. In M. De Haan, & M. H. Johnson (Eds.), *The cognitive neuroscience of development*. New York: Psychology Press.

Tainturier, M.-J. & Caramazza, A. (1996). The status of double letters in graphemic representations. *Journal of Memory and Language, 35*, 53–75.

Tainturier, M.-J. & Rapp, B. (2003). Is a single graphemic buffer used in reading and spelling? *Aphasiology, 17*, 537–562.

Takahashi, H., Yahata, N., Koeda, M., Matsuda, T., Asai, K., & Okubo, Y. (2004). Brain activation associated with evaluative processes of guilt and embarrassment: An fMRI study. *NeuroImage, 23*(3), 967–974.

Takahashi, N., Kawamura, M., Shinotou, H., Hirayama, K., Kaga, K., & Shindo, M. (1992). Pure word deafness due to left-hemisphere damage. *Cortex, 28*, 295–303.

Talairach, J. & Tournoux, P. (1988). *A co-planar stereotactic atlas of the human brain*. Stuttgart, Germany: Thieme Verlag.

Tamietto, M. & De Gelder, B. (2010). Neural bases of the non-conscious perception of emotional signals. *Nature Reviews Neuroscience, 11*, 697–709.

Tamietto, M., Pullens, P., de Gelder, B., Weiskrantz, L., & Goebel, R. (2012). Subcortical connections to human amygdala and changes following destruction of the visual cortex. *Current Biology, 22*(15), 1449–1455.

Tang, J., Ward, J. & Butterworth, B. (2008). Number forms in the brain. *Journal of Cognitive Neuroscience, 20*, 1547–1556.

Tang, Y., Zhang, W., Chen, K., Feng, S., Ji, Y., Shen, J., Reiman, E. M., & Liu, Y. (2006). Arithmetic processing in the brain shaped by cultures. *Proceedings of the National Academy of Science, USA, 103*, 10775–10780.

Tanji, J., Okano, K. & Sato, K. C. (1998). Neuronal activity in cortical motor areas related to ipsilateral, contralateral and bilateral digit movements in the monkey. *Journal of Neurophysiology, 60*, 325–343.

Tartter, V.C. (1986). *Language processes*. New York: Holt, Rinehart & Winston.

Taylor, A. E., Saint-Cyr, J. A., & Lang, A. E. (1986). Frontal lobe dysfunction in Parkinson's disease. *Brain, 109*, 845–883.

Tervaniemi, M., Maury, S., & Näätänen, R. (1994). Neural representations of abstract stimulus features in the human brain as reflected by the mismatch negativity. *NeuroReport, 9*, 4167–4170.

Theoret, H., Halligan, E., Kobayashi, M., Fregni, F., Tager-Flusberg, H., & Pascual-Leone, A. (2005). Impaired motor facilitation during action observation in individuals with autism spectrum disorder. *Current Biology, 15*(3), R84–R85.

Thomas, K. M. & Casey, B. J. (2003). Methods for imaging the developing brain. In M. De Haan & M. H. Johnson (Eds.), *The cognitive neuroscience of development*. New York: Psychology Press.

Thomas, K. M. & Nelson, C. A. (1996). Age-related changes in the electrophysiological response to visual stimulus novelty: A topographical approach. *Electroencephalography and Clinical Neurophysiology, 98*, 294–308.

Thomas, M. S. C. & Karmiloff-Smith, A. (2002). Are developmental disorders like cases of adult brain damage? Implications of connectionist modelling. *Behavioral and Brain Sciences, 25*, 727–788.

Thomas, M. S. C. & Johnson, M. H. (2008). New advances in understanding sensitive periods in brain development. *Current Directions in Psychological Science, 17*, 1–5.

Thompson, L. A., Detterman, D. K., & Plomin, R. (1991). Associations between cognitive abilities and scholastic achievement: Genetic overlap but environmental differences. *Psychological Science, 2*, 158–165.

Thompson, P. (1980). Margaret Thatcher: A new illusion. *Perception, 9*, 483–484.

Thompson, P. M., Schwartz, C., Lin, R. T., Khan, A. A., & Toga, A. W. (1996). Three-dimensional statistical analysis of sulcal variability in the human brain. *Journal of Neuroscience, 16*, 4261–4274.

Thompson-Schill, S. L. (2003). Neuroimaging studies of semantic memory: Inferring "how" from "where." *Neuropsychologia, 41*(3), 280–292.

Thompson-Schill, S. L., D'Esposito, M. D., Aguirre, G. K., & Farah, M. J. (1997). Role of inferior prefrontal cortex in retrieval of semantic knowledge: A reevaluation. *Proceedings of the National Academy of Science, USA, 94*, 14792–14797.

Thompson-Schill, S. L., Swick, D., Farah, M. J., D'Esposito, M., Kan, I. P., & Knight, R. T. (1998). Verb generation in patients with focal frontal lesions: A neuropsychological test of neuroimaging findings. *Proceedings of the National Academy of Science, USA, 95*, 15855–15860.

Thompson-Schill, S. L., D'Esposito, M. D., & Kan, I. P. (1999). Effects of repetition and competition on activity in left prefrontal cortex during word generation. *Neuron, 23*, 513–522.

Tian, B., Kusmierek, P., & Rauschecker, J. P. (2013). Analogues of simple and complex cells in rhesus monkey auditory cortex. *Proceedings of the National Academy of Sciences of the United States of America, 110*(19), 7892–7897.

Tillmann, B., Rusconi, E., Traube, C., Butterworth, B., Umilta, C., & Peretz, I. (2011). Fine-grained pitch processing of music and speech in congenital amusia. *Journal of the Acoustical Society of America, 130*(6), 4089–4096.

Tinbergen, N. (1951). *The study of instinct*. Oxford, UK: Oxford University Press.

Tipper, S. P. (1985). The negative priming effect: Inhibitory priming by ignored objects. *Quarterly Journal of Experimental Psychology, 37A*, 571–590.

Tipper, S. P., Driver, J., & Weaver, B. (1991). Object-centred inhibition of return of visual attention. *Quarterly Journal of Experimental Psychology, 43A*, 289–298.

Titone, D. A. & Salisbury, D. F. (2004). Contextual modulation of N400 amplitude to lexically ambiguous words. *Brain and Cognition, 55*, 470–478.

Todd, J. J. & Marois, R. (2004). Capacity limit of visual short-term memory in human posterior parietal cortex. *Nature, 428*(6984), 751–754.

Todd, J. J. & Marois, R. (2005). Posterior parietal cortex activity predicts individual differences in visual short-term memory capacity. *Cognitive Affective & Behavioral Neuroscience, 5*(2), 144–155.

Tong, F. & Pratte, M. S. (2012). Decoding patterns of human brain activity. In S. T. Fiske, D. L. Schacter & S. E. Taylor (Eds.), *Annual Review of Psychology, Vol 63* (Vol. 63, pp. 483–509). Palo Alto, CA: Annual Reviews.

Tooth, G. C. & Newton, M. P. (1961). *Leukotomy in England and Wales 1942–1954*. London: Her Majesty's Stationery Office.

Torjussen, T. (1976). Visual processing in cortically blind hemifields. *Neuropsychologia, 16*, 15–21.

Tranel, D. & Damasio, H. (1995). Neuroanatomical correlates of electrodermal skin conductance responses. *Psychophysiology, 31*, 427–438.

Tranel, D., Damasio, A. R., & Damasio, H. (1988). Intact recognition of facial expression, gender and age in patients with impaired recognition of face identity. *Neurology, 38*, 690–696.

Tranel, D., Damasio, H., & Damasio, A. R. (1995). Double dissociation between overt and covert face recognition. *Journal of Cognitive Neuroscience, 7,* 425–432.

Tranel, D., Kemmerer, D., Adolphs, R., Damasio, H., & Damasio, A. R. (2003). Neural correlates of conceptual knowledge for actions. *Cognitive Neuropsychology, 20,* 409–432.

Treisman, A. (1988). Features and objects: The fourteenth Bartlett memorial lecture. *Quarterly Journal of Experimental Psychology, 40A,* 201–237.

Treisman, A. & Schmidt, H. (1982). Illusory conjunctions in the perception of objects. *Cognitive Psychology, 14,* 107–141.

Treisman, A. M. & Gelade, G. (1980). A feature-integration theory of attention. *Cognitive Psychology, 12,* 97–136.

Troncoso, X. G., Macknik, S. L., Otero-Millan, J., & Martinez-Conde, S. (2008). Microsaccades drive illusory motion in the Enigma illusion. *Proceedings of the National Academy of Sciences, USA, 41,* 16033–16038.

Tse, C. Y. & Penney, T. B. (2008). On the functional role of temporal and frontal cortex activation in passive detection of auditory deviance. *NeuroImage, 41*(4), 1462–1470.

Tse, P. U., Martinez-Conde, S., Schlegel, A. A., & Macknik, S. L. (2005). Visibility, visual awareness, and visual masking of simple unattended targets are confined to areas in the occipital cortex beyond human V1/V2. *Proceedings of the National Academy of Sciences of the United States of America, 102*(47), 17178–17183.

Tudusciuc, O. & Nieder, A. (2007). Neuronal population coding of continuous and discrete quantity in the primate posterior parietal cortex. *Proceedings of the National Academy of Sciences of the USA, 104,* 14513–14518.

Tulving, E. (1972). Episodic and semantic memory. In E. Tulving, & W. Donaldson (Eds.), *Organisation of memory* (pp. 381–403). New York: Academic Press.

Tulving, E. (1983). *Elements of episodic memory.* Oxford, UK: Oxford University Press.

Tulving, E. (1985). Memory and consciousness. *Canadian Psychologist, 26,* 1–12.

Tulving, E. & Schacter, D. L. (1990). Priming and human memory systems. *Science, 247,* 301–306.

Tulving, E., Schacter, D. L., McLachlan, D. R., & Moscovitch, M. (1988). Priming of semantic autobiographical knowledge: A case study of retrograde amnesia. *Brain and Cognition, 8,* 3–20.

Turnbull, O. H., Della Sala, S., & Beschin, N. (2002). Agnosia for object orientation: Naming and mental rotation evidence. *Neurocase, 8,* 296–305.

Tybur, J. M., Lieberman, D., & Griskevicius, V. (2009). Microbes, mating, and morality: Individual differences in three functional domains of disgust. *Journal of Personality and Social Psychology, 97*(1), 103–122.

Tyler, L. K., Voice, J. K., & Moss, H. E. (2000). The interaction of meaning and sound in spoken word recognition. *Psychonomic Bulletin & Review, 7*(2), 320–326.

Tyler, L. K. & Moss, H. E. (2001). Towards a distributed account of conceptual knowledge. *Trends in Cognitive Sciences, 5,* 244–252.

Tyler, L. K., Marslen-Wilson, W. D., Randall, B., Wright, P., Devereux, B. J., Zhuang, J., & Stamatakis, E. A. (2011). Left inferior frontal cortex and syntax: function, structure and behaviour in patients with left hemisphere damage. *Brain, 134,* 415–431.

Umiltà, M. A., Kohler, E., Gallese, V., Fogassi, L., Fadiga, L., Keysers, C., & Rizzolatti, G. (2001). I know what you are doing: A neurophysiological study. *Neuron, 25,* 287–295.

Underwood, B. J. (1965). False recognition produced by implicit verbal responses. *Journal of Experimental Psychology, 70,* 122–129.

Ungerleider, L. G. & Mishkin, M. (1982). Two cortical systems. In D. J. Ingle, M. A. Goodale, & R. J. W. Mansfield (Eds.), *Analysis of visual behaviour.* Cambridge, MA: MIT Press.

Uttal, W. R. (2001). *The new phrenology: The limits of localising cognitive processes in the brain.* Cambridge, MA: MIT Press.

Vaina, L. M., Solomon, J., Chowdhury, S., Sinha, P., & Belliveau, J. W. (2001). Functional neuroanatomy of biological motion perception in humans. *Proceedings of the National Academy of Sciences USA*, *98*, 11656–11661.

Valentine, T. (1991). A unified account of the effects of distinctiveness, inversion and race in face recognition. *Quarterly Journal of Experimental Psychology*, *43A*, 161–204.

Vallar, G. & Baddeley, A. D. (1984). Phonological short-term store and phonological processing, and sentence comprehension. *Cognitive Neuropsychology*, *1*, 121–141.

Vallentin, D. & Nieder, A. (2010). Representations of visual proportions in the primate posterior parietal and prefrontal cortices. *European Journal of Neuroscience*, *32*(8), 1380–1387.

Vallesi, A., Shallice, T., & Walsh, V. (2007). Role of the prefrontal cortex in the foreperiod effect: TMS evidence for dual mechanisms in temporal preparation. *Cerebral Cortex*, *17*(2), 466–474.

Valyear, K. F., Culham, J. C., Sharif, N., Westwood, D., & Goodale, M. A. (2006). A double dissociation between sensitivity to changes in object identity and object orientation in the ventral and dorsal visual streams: A human fMRI study. *Neuropsychologia*, *44*(2), 218–228.

van den Brink, D., Brown, C. M., & Hagoort, P. (2001). Electrophysiological evidence for early contextual influences during spoken-word recognition: N200 versus N400 effects. *Journal of Cognitive Neuroscience*, *13*(7), 967–985.

van den Brink, D., Brown, C. M., & Hagoort, P. (2006). The cascaded nature of lexical selection and integration in auditory sentence processing. *Journal of Experimental Psychology-Learning Memory and Cognition*, *32*(2), 364–372.

Van der Haegen, L., Cai, Q., & Brysbaert, M. (2012). Colateralization of Broca's area and the visual word form area in left-handers: fMRI evidence. *Brain and Language*, *122*(3), 171–178.

Van Harskamp, N. J. & Cipolotti, L. (2001). Selective impairments for addition, subtraction and multiplication: Implications for the organisation of arithmetical facts. *Cortex*, *37*, 363–388.

Van Harskamp, N. J., Rudge, P., & Cipolotti, L. (2002). Are multiplication facts implemented by the left supramarginal and angular gyri? *Neuropsychologia*, *40*, 1786–1793.

Van Lancker, D. & Klein, K. (1990). Preserved recognition of familiar personal names in global aphasia. *Brain and Language*, *39*, 511–529.

Van Orden, G. C. (1987). A rows is a rose: Spelling, sound, and reading. *Memory and Cognition*, *14*, 371–386.

Van Orden, G. C., Johnston, J. C., & Hele, B. L. (1988). Word identification in reading proceeds. from spelling to sound to meaning. *Journal of Experimental Psychology: Learning, Memory and Cognition*, *14*, 371–386.

Vargha-Khadem, F., Isaacs, E., & Mishkin, M. (1994). Agnosia, alexia and a remarkable form of amnesia in an adolescent boy. *Brain*, *117*, 683–703.

Vargha-Khadem, F., Watkins, K., Alcock, K., Fletcher, P., & Passingham, R. (1995). Cognitive and praxic deficits in a large family with a genetically transmitted speech and language disorder. *Proceedings of the National Academy of Science, USA*, *92*, 930–933.

Vargha-Khadem, F., Carr, L. J., Isaacs, E., Brett, E., Adams, C., & Mishkin, M. (1997a). Onset of speech after left hemispherectomy in a nine-year-old boy. *Brain*, *120*, 159–182.

Vargha-Khadem, F., Gadian, D. G., Watkins, K. E., Connelly, A., Van Paesschen, W., & Mishkin, M. (1997b). Differential effects of early hippocampal pathology on episodic and semantic memory. *Science*, *277*, 376–380.

Vargha-Khadem, F., Gadian, D. G., Copp, A., & Mishkin, M. (2005). FOXP2 and the neuroanatomy of speech and language. *Nature Reviews Neuroscience*, *6*, 131–138.

Veen, V. van & Carter, C. S. (2002). The anterior cingulate as a conflict monitor: fMRI and ERP studies. *Physiology and Behavior*, *77*, 477–482.

Velmans, M. (2000). *Understanding consciousness*. London: Routledge.

Verfaellie, M., Reiss, L., & Roth, H. L. (1995). Knowledge of new English vocabulary in amnesia: An examination of premorbidly acquired semantic memory. *Journal of International Neuropsychological Society*, *1*, 443–453.

Verfaellie, M., Koseff, P., & Alexander, M. P. (2000). Acquisition of novel semantic information in amnesia: Effects of lesion location. *Neuropsychologia*, *38*, 484–492.

Vesalius, A. (1543). *De humani corporis fabrica*. Basel, Switzerland: Oporinus.

Viessens, R. de (1685). *Neurographia universalis*. Lyons, France: Certe.

Vigliocco, G., Antonini, T., & Garrett, M. F. (1997). Grammatical gender is on the tip of Italian tongues. *Psychological Science*, *8*, 314–317.

Volkow, N. D., Wang, G.-J., Fowler, J. S., Logan, J., Gatley, S. J., Hitzemann, R., Chen, A. D., Dewey, S. L., & Pappas, N. (1997). Decreased striatal dopamine responsiveness in detoxified cocaine-dependent subjects. *Nature*, *386*, 830–835.

Von der Heydt, R., Peterhans, E., & Baumgartner, G. (1984). Illusory contours and neuron cortical responses. *Science*, *224*(4654), 1260–1262.

Voorn, P., Vanderschuren, L., Groenewegen, H. J., Robbins, T. W., & Pennartz, C. M. A. (2004). Putting a spin on the dorsal-ventral divide of the striatum. *Trends in Neurosciences*, *27*(8), 468–474.

Vuilleumier, P., Valenza, N., Mayer, E., Reverdin, A., & Landis, T. (1998). Near and far visual space in unilateral neglect. *Annals of Neurology*, *43*, 406–410.

Vuilleumier, P., Henson, R. N. A., Driver, J., & Dolan, R. J. (2002a). Multiple levels of visual object constancy revealed by event-related fMRI of repetition priming. *Nature Neuroscience*, *5*, 491–499.

Vuilleumier, P., Schwartz, S., Clarke, K., Husain, M., & Driver, J. (2002b). Testing memory for unseen visual stimuli in patients with extinction and spatial neglect. *Journal of Cognitive Neuroscience*, *14*, 875–886.

Vul, E., Hanus, D., & Kanwisher, N. (2009). Attention as inference: Selection is probabilistic; responses are all-or-none samples. *Journal of Experimental Psychology-General*, *138*(4), 546–560.

Vuokko, E., Niemivirta, M., & Helenius, P. (2013). Cortical activation patterns during subitizing and counting. *Brain Research*, *1497*, 40–52.

Wagner, A. D., Poldrack, R. A., Eldridge, L. L., Desmond, J. E., Glover, G. H., & Gabrieli, G. D. E. (1998a). Material-specific lateralization of prefrontal activation during episodic encoding and retrieval. *Neuroreport*, *9*, 3711–3717.

Wagner, A. D., Schacter, D. L., Rotte, M., Koutstaal, W., Maril, A., Dale, A. M., Rosen, B. R., & Buckner, R. I. (1998b). Building memories: Remembering and forgetting of verbal experiences as predicted by brain activity. *Science*, *281*, 1188–1191.

Walsh, V. (2003). A theory of magnitude: Common cortical metrics of time, space and quantity. *Trends in Cognitive Sciences*, *7*, 483–488.

Walsh, V. & Cowey, A. (1998). Magnetic stimulation studies of visual cognition. *Trends in Cognitive Sciences*, *2*, 103–110.

Walsh, V. & Rushworth, M. F. S. (1999). A primer of magnetic stimulation as a tool for neuropsychology. *Neuropsychologia*, *37*, 125–135.

Walsh, V., Ashbridge, E., & Cowey, A. (1998a). Cortical plasticity in perceptual learning demonstrated by transcranial magnetic stimulation. *Neuropsychologia*, *36*, 363–367.

Walsh, V., Ellison, A., Battelli, L., & Cowey, A. (1998b). Task-induced impairments and enhancements induced by magnetic stimulation of human area V5. *Proceedings of the Royal Society of London B*, *265*, 537–543.

Ward, J. (2003). Understanding oral spelling: A review and synthesis. *Neurocase*, *9*, 1–14.

Ward, J. (2012). *The student's guide to social neuroscience*. New York: Psychology Press.

Ward, J., Stott, R., & Parkin, A. J. (2000). The role of semantics in reading and spelling: Evidence for the 'Summation Hypothesis'. *Neuropsychologia*, *38*, 1643–1653.

Ward, L. M. (2003). Synchronous neural oscillations and cognitive processes. *Trends in Cognitive Sciences, 7*(12), 553–559.

Wardak, C., Olivier, E., & Duhamel, J. R. (2004). A deficit in covert attention after parietal cortex inactivation in the monkey. *Neuron, 42*(3), 501–508.

Warren, J. D., Scott, S. K., Price, C. J., & Griffiths, T. D. (2006). Human brain mechanisms for the early analysis of voices. *NeuroImage, 31,* 1389–1397.

Warrington, E. K. (1982). The fractionation of arithmetical skills: A single case study. *Quarterly Journal of Experimental Psychology, 34A,* 31–51.

Warrington, E. K. & James, M. (1986). Visual object recognition in patients with right hemisphere lesions: Axes or features? *Perception, 15,* 355–356.

Warrington, E. K. & Langdon, D. (1994). Spelling dyslexia: A deficit of the visual word-form. *Journal of Neurology, Neurosurgery and Psychiatry, 57,* 211–216.

Warrington, E. K. & McCarthy, R. (1983). Category specific access dysphasia. *Brain, 106,* 859–878.

Warrington, E. K. & McCarthy, R. A. (1987). Categories of knowledge. *Brain, 110,* 1273–1296.

Warrington, E. K. & McCarthy, R. A. (1988). The fractionation of retrograde amnesia. *Brain and Cognition, 7,* 184–200.

Warrington, E. K. & Shallice, T. (1969). The selective impairment of auditory verbal short-term memory. *Brain, 92,* 885–896.

Warrington, E. K. & Shallice, T. (1980). Word-form dyslexia. *Brain, 103,* 99–112.

Warrington, E. K. & Shallice, T. (1984). Category specific semantic impairments. *Brain, 107,* 829–854.

Warrington, E. K. & Taylor, A. M. (1973). The contribution of the right parietal lobe to object recognition. *Cortex, 9,* 152–164.

Wartenburger, I., Heekeren, H. R., Abutalebi, J., Cappa, S. F., Villringer, A., & Perani, D. (2003). Early setting of grammatical processing in the bilingual brain. *Neuron, 37*(1), 159–170.

Washburn, D. A. & Rumbaugh, D. M. (1991). Ordinal judgments of numerical symbols by macaques (Macaca mulatta). *Psychological Science, 2,* 190–193.

Wassermann, E. M., Cohen, L. G., Flitman, S. S., Chen, R., & Hallett, M. (1996). Seizures in healthy people with repeated "safe" trains of transcranial magnetic stimulation. *Lancet, 347,* 825–826.

Watkins, K. E., Vargha-Khadem, F., Ashburner, J., Passingham, R. E., Connelly, A., Friston, K. J., Frackowiak, R. S. J., Mishkin, M., & Gadian, D. G. (2002). MRI analysis of an inherited speech and language disorder: Structural brain abnormalities. *Brain, 125,* 465–478.

Weaver, I. C. G., Cervoni, N., Champagne, F. A., D'Alessio, A. C., Charma, S., Seckl, J., Dymov, S., Szyf, M., & Meaney, M. J. (2004). Epigenetic programming by maternal behavior. *Nature Neuroscience, 7,* 847–854.

Wechsler, D. (1981). *Wechsler Adult Intelligence Scale—Revised.* New York: Psychological Corporation.

Wechsler, D. (1984). *Wechsler Memory Scale—Revised.* New York: Psychological Corporation.

Weekes, B. & Chen, H. Q. (1999). Surface dyslexia in Chinese. *Neurocase, 5,* 161–172.

Weiskrantz, L. (1956). Behavioral changes associated with ablations of the amygdaloid complex in monkeys. *Journal of Comparative Physiological Psychology, 49,* 381–391.

Weiskrantz, L. (1986). *Blindsight: A case study and implications.* Oxford, UK: Oxford University Press.

Weiskrantz, L., Warrington, E. K., Sanders, M. D., & Marshall, J. (1974). Visual capacity in the hemianopic field following a restricted occipital ablation. *Brain, 97,* 709–728.

Wenzel, E. M., Arruda, M., Kistler, D. J., & Wightman, F. L. (1993). Localization using non-individualized head-related transfer functions. *Journal of the Acoustical Society of America*, *94*, 111–123.

Wernicke, C. (1874). *Der aphasiche symptomenkomplex*. Breslau, Poland: Cohen and Weigart.

Westermann, G., Mareschal, D., Johnson, M. H., Sirois, S., Spratling, M. W., & Thomas, M. S. C. (2007). Neuroconstructivism. *Developmental Science*, *10*, 75–83.

Westmacott, R. & Moscovitch, M. (2002). Temporally graded semantic memory loss in amnesia and semantic dementia: Further evidence for opposite gradients. *Cognitive Neuropsychology*, *19*, 135–163.

Wheeldon, L. R. & Monsell, S. (1992). The locus of repetition priming of spoken word production. *Quarterly Journal of Experimental Psychology*, *44A*, 723–761.

Wheeler, M. A., Stuss, D. T., & Tulving, E. (1997). Toward a theory of episodic memory: The frontal lobes and autonoetic consciousness. *Psychological Bulletin*, *121*, 331–354.

White, I. M. & Wise, S. P. (1999). Rule-dependent neuronal activity in the prefrontal cortex. *Experimental Brain Research*, *126*(3), 315–335.

Whitfield, I. C. & Evans, E. F. (1965). Responses of auditory cortical neurons to stimuli of changing frequency. *Journal of Neurophysiology*, *28*, 655–672.

Wichmann, T. & DeLong, M. R. (1996). Functional and pathophysiological models of the basal ganglia. *Current Opinion in Neurobiology*, *6*, 751–758.

Wickens, A.P. (2015). *A history of the brain: How we have come to understand the most complex object in the universe*. New York: Psychology Press.

Wicker, B., Keysers, C., Plailly, J., Royet, J. P., Gallese, V., & Rizzolatti, G. (2003). Both of us disgusted in my insula: The common neural basis of seeing and feeling disgust. *Neuron*, *40*, 655–664.

Wilkins, A. J. (1971). Conjoint frequency, category size, and categorization time. *Journal of Verbal Learning and Verbal Behaviour*, *10*, 382–385.

Wilson, M. (2002). Six views of embodied cognition. *Psychonomic Bulletin & Review*, *9*(4), 625–636.

Wilson, M. A., Joubert, S., Ferre, P., Belleville, S., Ansaldo, A. I., Joanette, Y., Rouleau, I., & Brambati, S. M. (2012). The role of the left anterior temporal lobe in exception word reading: Reconciling patient and neuroimaging findings. *NeuroImage*, *60*(4), 2000–2007.

Wilson, S. M., Brambati, S. M., Henry, R. G., Handwerker, D. A., Agosta, F., Miller, B. L., & Gorno-Tempini, M. L. (2009). The neural basis of surface dyslexia in semantic dementia. *Brain*, *132*, 71–86.

Wimmer, H. & Perner, J. (1983). Beliefs about beliefs: Representation and the constraining function of wrong beliefs in young children's understanding of deception. *Cognition*, *13*, 103–128.

Wing, A. M. & Baddeley, A. D. (1980). Spelling errors in handwriting: A corpus and a distributional analysis. In U. Frith (Ed.), *Cognitive processes in spelling*. London: Academic Press.

Winocur, G., Moscovitch, M., & Bontempi, B. (2010). Memory formation and long-term retention in humans and animals: Convergence towards a transformation account of hippocampal-neocortical interactions. *Neuropsychologia*, *48*(8), 2339–2356.

Winocur, G., Moscovitch, M., & Sekeres, M. (2007). Memory consolidation or transformation: context manipulation and hippocampal representations of memory. *Nature Neuroscience*, *10*(5), 555–557.

Winston, J. S., Gottfried, J. A., Kilner, J. M., & Dolan, R. J. (2005). Integrated neural representations of odor intensity and affective valence in human amygdala. *Journal of Neuroscience*, *25*(39), 8903–8907.

Winston, J. S., O'Doherty, J., & Dolan, R. J. (2003). Common and distinct neural responses during direct and incidental processing of multiple facial emotions. *NeuroImage*, *20*, 84–97.

Wise, R. J. S., Greene, J., Buchel, C., & Scott, S. K. (1999). Brain regions involved in articulation. *Lancet, 353*, 1057–1061.

Wise, R. J. S., Scott, S. K., Blank, S. C., Mummery, C. J., & Warbuton, E. (2001). Identifying separate neural subsystems within Wernicke's area. *Brain, 124*, 83–95.

Witelson, S. F., Kigar, D. L., & Harvey, T. (1999). The exceptional brain of Albert Einstein. *Lancet, 353*, 2149–2153.

Witkin, H. A., Wapner, S., & Leventhal, T. (1952). Sound localization with conflicting visual and auditory cues. *Journal of Experimental Psychology, 43*, 58–67.

Wixted, J. T. (2004). The psychology and neuroscience of forgetting. *Annual Review of Psychology, 55*, 235–269.

Wixted, J. T. & Stretch, V. (2004). In defence of the signal detection interpretation of remember/know judgments. *Psychonomic Bulletin and Review, 11*, 616–641.

Wohlschlager, A., Gattis, M., & Bekkering, H. (2003). Action generation and action perception in imitation: An instance of the ideomotor principle. *Philosophical Transactions of the Royal Society of London B, 358*, 501–515.

Wojciulik, E., Husain, M., Clarke, K., & Driver, J. (2001). Spatial working memory deficit in unilateral neglect. *Neuropsychologia, 39*, 390–396.

Wolfe, J. M. (2003). Moving towards solutions to some enduring controversies in visual search. *Trends in Cognitive Sciences, 7*(2), 70–76.

Wolf, S. M., Lawrenz, F. P., Nelson, C. A., Kahn, J. P., Cho, M. K., Clayton, E. W., Fletcher, J. G., Georgieff, M. K., Hammerschmidt, D., Hudson, K., Illes, J., Kapur, V., Keane, M. A., Koenig, B. A., LeRoy, B. S., McFarland, E. G., Paradise, J., Parker, L. S., Terry, S. F., Van Ness, B., & Wilfond, B. S. (2008). Managing incidental findings in human subjects research: Analysis and recommendations. *Journal of Law, Medicine and Ethics, 36*, 219–248.

Wolpert, D. M. & Ghahramani, Z. (2000). Computational principles of movement neuroscience. *Nature Neuroscience, 3*, 1212–1217.

Wolpert, D. M., Ghahramani, Z., & Jordan, M. I. (1995). An internal model for sensorimotor integration. *Science, 269*, 1880–1882.

Wolpert, D. M., Miall, R. C., & Kawato, M. (1998). Internal models in the cerebellum. *Trends in Cognitive Sciences, 2*(9), 338–347.

Woolgar, A., Parr, A., Cusack, R., Thompson, R., Nimmo-Smith, I., Torralva, T., & Duncan, J. (2010). Fluid intelligence loss linked to restricted regions of damage within frontal and parietal cortex. *Proceedings of the National Academy of Sciences of the United States of America, 107*(33), 14899–14902.

Woollams, A. M., Ralph, M. A. L., Plaut, D. C., & Patterson, K. E. (2007). SD-squared: On the association between semantic dementia and surface dyslexia. *Psychological Review, 114*(2), 316–339.

Woollett, K. & Maguire, E. A. (2011). Acquiring "the Knowledge" of London's layout drives structural brain changes. *Current Biology, 21*(24), 2109–2114.

Worden, F. G. (1971). Hearing and the neural detection of acoustic patterns. *Behavioral Science, 16*, 20–30.

Worden, M. S., Foxe, J. J., Wang, N., & Simpson, G. V. (2000). Anticipatory biasing of visuospatial attention indexed by retinotopically specific alpha-band electroencephalography increases over occipital cortex. *Journal of Neuroscience, 20*(6), RC63.

Wurtz, R. H. (2008). Neuronal mechanisms of visual stability. *Vision Research, 48*(20), 2070–2089.

Wurtz, R. H., Goldberg, M. E., & Robinson, D. L. (1982). Brain mechanisms of visual attention. *Scientific American, 246*, 124–135.

Wynn, K. (1992). Addition and subtraction by human infants. *Nature, 358*, 749–750.

Xu, F. & Spelke, E. S. (2000). Large number discrimination in 6-month old infants. *Cognition, 74*, B1–B11.

Yik, M. S. M., Russell, J. A., & Barrett, L. F. (1999). Structure of self-reported current affect: Integration and beyond. *Journal of Personality and Social Psychology*, *77*(3), 600–619.

Yin, R. K. (1969). Looking at upside-down faces. *Journal of Experimental Psychology*, *81*, 141–145.

Yin, W. G., & Weekes, B. S. (2003). Dyslexia in Chinese: Clues from cognitive neuropsychology. *Annals of Dyslexia*, *53*, 255–279.

Yoneda, Y., Mori, E., Yamashita, H., & Yamadori, A. (1994). MRI volumetry of medial temporal lobe structures in amnesia following herpes simplex encephalitis. *European Neurology*, *34*, 243–252.

Yoon, J. H., Curtis, C. E., & D'Esposito, M. (2006). Differential effects of distraction during working memory on delay-period activity in the prefrontal cortex and the visual association cortex. *NeuroImage*, *29*(4), 1117–1126.

Young, A. W., Hellawell, D., & De Haan, E. H. F. (1988). Cross-domain semantic priming in normal subjects and a prosopagnosic patient. *Quarterly Journal of Experimental Psychology*, *40A*, 561–580.

Young, A. W., Hellawell, D. J., Van de Wal, C., & Johnson, M. (1996). Facial expression processing after amygdalectomy. *Neuropsychologia*, *34*, 31–39.

Zahn, R., Moll, J., Krueger, F., Huey, E. D., Garrido, G., & Grafman, J. (2007). Social concepts are represented in the superior anterior temporal cortex. *Proceedings of the National Academy of Sciences, USA*, *104*, 6430–6435.

Zanini, S., Rumiati, R. I., & Shallice, T. (2002). Action sequencing deficit following frontal lobe lesion. *Neurocase*, *8*, 88–99.

Zatorre, R. J., Belin, P., & Penhune, V. B. (2002). Structure and function of auditory cortex: Music and speech. *Trends in Cognitive Sciences*, *6*, 37–46.

Zatorre, R. J. & Baum, S. R. (2012). Musical melody and speech intonation: Singing a different tune? *PLoS Biology*, *10*(7).

Zeki, S. M. (1969). Representation of central visual fields in prestriate cortex of monkeys. *Brain Research*, *14*, 733–747.

Zeki, S. M. (1974). Functional organisation of a visual area in the posterior bank of the superior temporal sulcus of the rhesus monkey. *Journal of Physiology*, *236*, 549–573.

Zeki, S. M. (1983). Colour coding in the cerebral cortex: The reaction of cells in monkey visual cortex to wavelengths and colours. *Neuroscience*, *9*, 741–756.

Zeki, S. M. (1990). A century of cerebral achomatopsia. *Brain*, *113*, 1721–1777.

Zeki, S. M. (1991). Cerebral akinetopsia (visual motion blindness): A review. *Brain*, *114*, 811–824.

Zeki, S. M. (1993). *A vision of the brain*. Oxford, UK: Blackwell.

Zeki, S. M. & Marini, L. (1998). Three cortical stages of colour processing in the human brain. *Brain*, *121*, 1669–1685.

Zeki, S. M., Watson, J. D. G., Lueck, C. J., Friston, K. J., Kennard, C., & Frackowiak, R. S. J. (1991). A direct demonstration of functional specialization in human visual cortex. *Journal of Neuroscience*, *11*, 641–649.

Zeki, S. M., Watson, D. G., & Frackowiak, R. S. J. (1993). Going beyond the information given: The relation of illusory visual motion to brain activity. *Proceedings of the Royal Society of London B*, *252*, 212–222.

Zettin, M., Cubelli, R., Perino, C., & Rago, R. (1995). Impairment of letter formation: The case of "ideomotor" apraxic agraphia. *Aphasiology*, *9*, 283–294.

Zhuang, J., Randall, B., Stamatakis, E. A., Marslen-Wilson, W. D., & Tyler, L. K. (2011). The interaction of lexical semantics and cohort competition in spoken word recognition: An fMRI study. *Journal of Cognitive Neuroscience*, *23*(12), 3778–3790.

Zihl, J., von Cramon, D., & Mai, N. (1983). Selective disturbance of movement vision after bilateral brain damage. *Brain*, *106*, 313–340.

Zorzi, M., Priftis, K., & Umiltà, C. (2002). Brain damage—neglect disrupts the mental number line. *Nature*, *417*, 138–139.

Zorzi, M., Priftis, K., Meneghello, F., Marenzi, R., & Umilta, C. (2006). The spatial representation of numerical and non-numerical sequences: Evidence from neglect. *Neuropsychologia*, *44*(7), 1061–1067.

Zurif, E. B., Gardner, H., & Brownell, H. H. (1989). The case against the case against group studies. *Brain and Cognition*, *10*, 237–255.

Zwaan, R. A., Stanfield, R. A., & Yaxley, R. H. (2002). Language comprehenders mentally represent the shapes of objects. *Psychological Science*, *13*(2), 168–171.

Zwitserlood, P. (1989). The locus of the effects of sentential-semantic context in spoken word processing. *Cognition*, *32*, 25–64.

# Author index

# Subject index

Page numbers in **bold** indicate key terms, when used in main entries.